Contents

The Scottish Football League,
Hampden Park, Glasgow G42 9EB.
Secretary: Peter Donald
Telephone Number: (0141) 620 4160
Telefax Number: (0141) 620 4161
e–mail: info@scottishfootballleague.com
website: www.scottishfootballleague.com

SPL SCOTTISH PREMIER LEAGUE

The Scottish Premier League,
Hampden Park, Glasgow, G42 9DE.
Secretary: Iain J. Blair
Telephone Number: (0141) 620 4140
Telefax Number: (0141) 620 4141
Website: www.scotprem.com

CRE8

Published and Produced on behalf of
The Scottish Football League by:
CRE8, The Kiln, The Old Brewery.
Priory Lane, Burford, Oxfordshire, OX18 4SG.
Telephone Number: (01993) 822811
Telefax Number: (01993) 822887
ISDN: (01993) 822899
e–mail: studio@cre8ing.com
website: www.cre8ing.com

ACKNOWLEDGEMENTS

Editorial contributions by: Stephen Halliday (The Scotsman),
Kevin McCarra (The Guardian), John Litster (Programme Monthly &
Football Collectable Magazine), Donald Walker (The Scotsman),
Darryl Broadfoot (The Herald), Rodger Baillie (The Scottish Sun)
Willie Young & Tony Higgins

Photographs by: SNS Group, Brian Stewart & Action Images.

The Scottish Football League would like to express appreciation to
the following individuals and organisations:–

David C. Thomson; all of the staff at The Scottish Football League and
in particular, Jan Murdoch, Anton Fagan, Brian Jamieson, Maureen
Cooper and Geraldine Walsh; Greig Mailer and Gavin McCann of The
Scottish Premier League; all SFL and SPL clubs; Jim Jeffrey; our
contributors; the various sectors of the media for their co–operation
and everyone at CRE8 and in particular, Danny Lake, Roisin Mclory,
Bob Magill, Wes Strange, Mark Rogers, Jordan Crouch, Ben Goddard.

Sincere thanks to Alan and Heather Elliott for their time and effort in
providing statistical information for this publication.

ISBN 0-9548556-0-4

Welcome

A very warm welcome to the 2004/05 edition of The Scottish Football Review. As you will have already noted from the front and back covers, this season's Review celebrates its silver anniversary, having been first published back in season 1980/81.

Looking back at that very first edition, I note that the then Secretary of The Scottish Football League, Jim Farry, wrote that he hoped the publication would be the forerunner of even more exciting things to come. There is certainly no doubt that during the past 24 editions, the Review has established itself as Scottish football's most authoritative and respected reference book with supporters, officials, players and the various sectors of the media constantly referring to the back editions on a regular basis.

The 2003/04 season was again exciting and dramatic, with the First and Third Divisions of the Bell's Scottish Football League Championships not being decided until the final day of the season, with the outcome of the Second Division only being settled the previous Saturday with nearly all of the other promotion and relegation issues only being decided during the final two or three weeks of the season. Certainly, the First, Second and Third Divisions have proved to be extremely competitive in recent years and this, together with the uncertainty of outcome at our matches, has resulted in attendances at Scottish Football League matches having increased steadily for the past four seasons.

I would like to place on record my congratulations to Inverness Caledonian Thistle for winning the Bell's First Division and also gaining promotion to The Scottish Premier League, to Airdrie United for winning the Bell's Second Division and promotion to the First Division along with Hamilton Academical, and Stranraer for securing the Bell's Third Division Championship by narrowly edging out Stirling Albion, who also gained promotion as runners-up. The CIS Insurance Cup was won by Livingston, who defeated Hibernian 2-0 at Hampden Park, while a similar scoreline was recorded by Inverness Caledonian Thistle in The Bell's Cup Final at McDiarmid Park against Airdrie United, resulting in Caley Thistle enjoying a League and Cup double.

I write this article at a time when it would be fair to say that we are entering an extremely crucial chapter in what has been a long and eventful history for our national game with many memorable and glorious moments to savour and look back on with great pleasure and pride. As I have previously mentioned, the photographs on the front and back covers of this special 25th edition remind us all of the great players and managers that have been involved in Scottish football over the past quarter of a century and, with the exception of Martin O'Neill, Henrik Larsson and Brian Laudrup, are all Scottish who were involved with the Scotland International set-up either in a playing or management capacity.

For a number of years, some of my predecessors in this column have stated that we must address several very important issues, most importantly the skill factor and how we must encourage youngsters firstly, to actively participate in the game, and secondly, develop their technique and harness their skill level on a par with players in other countries. Sadly, we have failed in these objectives and this has resulted in our national team having failed to qualify for any major Finals since 1998. Our very disappointing start to the 2006 World Cup qualifying campaign only adds to the shortcomings of our game at the present time.

Certainly, the Scottish game at all levels, has not been helped by the political bickering that has manifested itself for far too long and whilst I do not have all of the answers to the current problems facing our game it is my view that now is the time to consider some form of rationalisation of the structure of Scottish football.

Enjoy the 25th edition of The Scottish Football Review. There is no harm whatsoever in indulging in some form of nostalgia and looking back with great pride to celebrate all of the many great moments enjoyed by Scottish football during the past two and a half decades. However, the present and future are now our priorities and, providing that we are all bold enough to take some very important decisions in the next year or so, our game can prosper once again. For the sake of Scottish football, let us all hope so!

JOHN SMITH
President,
The Scottish Football League

On behalf of everyone involved in the SPL, I would like to welcome you to the 25th Edition of The Scottish Football Review.

Last season, Celtic were runaway and worthy winners of our title. They also had another exciting season of European football without quite matching their UEFA Cup Final place in season 2002/2003.

Our clubs again scooped the pool of the other domestic Scottish honours. Celtic completed the double by beating Dunfermline Athletic in the Tennent's Scottish Cup Final and Livingston beat Hibernian in The CIS Insurance Cup Final.

Last season was also a challenging one off the field. Money remains tight and our clubs have had to continue to work hard to make ends meet. On a more positive note, we have been able to put in place a range of new broadcasting and commercial deals that will provide an income of around £60 million over the next four years. Bank of Scotland has been an excellent sponsor since the inception of the SPL and we are delighted that they have renewed their sponsorship for the next three years.

One measure of a nation's football standing is determined by how its clubs fair in European competitions. When the SPL was set up, the top League in Scotland was 26th in Europe. We currently have the prospect of being able to achieve 8th place and with it, an opportunity for 6 of our clubs to qualify for European competition.

This season, jointly with the SFL, and the support of the SFA, it was agreed to introduce a change to the stadia criteria for entry to our competition. From the start of season 2005/2006, the stadia requirement is for 6,000 covered seats compared with the previous level of 10,000.

From the SPL's inception there has been a continual focus on youth development and Scottish football as a whole is now reaping the rewards for that co-ordinated effort. For example, Chris Burke, Zander Diamond, David Clarkson and Derek Riordan have become regulars in their respective first teams. Their rapid rise to the top may in part be due to the financial restrictions that the current climate places on our clubs but it is testament to our Youth Initiative that such talented youngsters are available to make the step up.

The path the next generation of graduates take to the first team in the SPL will be slightly different. The Under–21 League was one of the fresh ideas that the SPL brought to Scottish football and the time is right to make the Under–19 League the senior development league for our youth players with more and more of them leapfrogging the Under–21 League completely on their road to the first team.

The detail of the events of last season will be covered thoroughly throughout this edition of The Scottish Football Review, but I would like to take this opportunity to congratulate Celtic on their tremendous Championship–winning campaign and welcome newly promoted Inverness Caledonian Thistle.

Hopefully this publication will capture some of the drama, passion and achievement of last season and there will be many more memorable moments to savour on the field in the months that lie ahead.

**LEX GOLD
Chairman,
The Scottish Premier League**

Welcome

Looking back over

25 years

of the SFL Review

Editorial by Kevin McCarra
The Guardian

This 25th edition of The Scottish Football League Review will join the complete set of its predecessors on the bookshelves of my home in London. There are all sorts of reference works on the game but this is the one I would most hate to lose. The devotion and painstaking work of the editor David Thomson makes it wonderfully accurate, but that is not the only reason I find myself thumbing through old copies.

These volumes are the family albums of the Scottish game. The Review was first published in 1980, in a large format of 84 pages. Plenty of the faces are instantly identifiable. Alex McLeish, for example, is on the top corner of the front cover. He was then part of the Aberdeen team that had just won the League title for the first time in 25 years. The centre spread of the annual is a squad picture that includes Alex Ferguson, a manager with further glories and a knighthood still to come.

The Review is beguiling to me, though, because of the tale it tells of Scottish football quietly sustaining itself, with each generation making its own contribution.

JIM McLEAN

PAUL GASCOIGNE

WILLIE MILLER & EUROPEAN CUP WINNER'S CUP

BRIAN LAUDRUP

What other publication would tell you, as the 1980 edition did, that Brechin City, despite drawing for supporters on the smallest population of any senior club in Britain, was still building a new 250–seater stand?

There is a variety of other ways, too, in which clubs can punch above their weight. The 1981/82 volume signals the rise, under Jim McLean, of Dundee United, who had just won the League Cup for the second year in a row.

The fringe benefits of a healthy domestic scene saw most of us worrying over how Scotland would do in the major tournaments instead of fretting that we might not make the Finals at all. That year's Review has an article by the then manager of the national team Jock Stein, who gives thanks for players like Willie Miller, McLeish, David Narey and Paul Sturrock, who were all with Scottish clubs.

A year later, the Review opens not just with comments on the performances at the 1982 World Cup, but also by extending congratulations to the Scotland squad that had just won the European Youth Championship by beating Czechoslovakia in Helsinki. Pat Nevin, Paul McStay and the others triumphed in a tournament that had included the likes of Holland, West Germany, Portugal and Spain. It remains the only major competition our national team has ever won at any level.

The side was coached by Andy Roxburgh. That same year, Craig Brown, another future manager of Scotland, had taken Clyde into the First Division. The impression that Scottish football was on the rise is overwhelmingly confirmed in the following year's Review. With lucky timing, 1983 was also the year in which I organised an exhibition on the history of Scottish football.

Although there was a modern alarm system at the Third Eye Centre, I used to fear that thieves could break in and make off with trophies into the Glasgow night before the police got there. For that reason, I used to stash the silverware beside the pots of paint in a storeroom at closing time. One of them, amazingly, was the European Cup Winners' Cup that Aberdeen had seized so magnificently by beating Real Madrid in Gothenburg in 1983.

The late Alex Cameron, writing in the 1983/84 Review, salutes that mighty feat, but within the pages there is also acclaim for Dundee United, who had won the League title for the first time in their history. Jim McLean's team would go on to a European Cup Semi-Final and the 1987 UEFA Cup Final. The Review would later chronicle championships for Aberdeen in seasons 1983/84 and 1984/85, as the nickname of the New Firm that was applied to them and Dundee United took on substance.

On the European scene at least, the Old Firm were overshadowed then. Celtic were the better of the two powerful Glasgow clubs in the early part of the 1980's and the 1988/89 edition of the Review also testifies to Billy McNeill's work in leading the club to the Double in its Centenary year.

Nonetheless, the nature of Old Firm rivalry was altering and the whole condition of Scottish football was to change radically as well. In his introduction to the 1986/87 edition of the Review, the then President of The Scottish Football League, Ian Gellatly, compliments prize winners, who included the new members of the Premier Division Hamilton Academical.

Rangers go unmentioned since they had lifted no honours in the 1985/86 season but they had acquired a manager in Graeme Souness and supplied him with the means to ensure that he could operate at a financial level never before attained by any club in Scottish football. The ramifications of that will be debated for decades to come.

Marvellous signings were made. It was astonishing to find Terry Butcher, who would captain England in the 1990 World Cup Semi-Final. We were privileged, too, to see the skills of Brian Laudrup and Paul Gascoigne. Without spending quite as much, Celtic were able to bring the extraordinary Henrik Larsson to these shores.

All countries were to become more cosmopolitan and that, in an expanded European Union, can never change. The trouble, of course, was that the trend of spending heavily contributed to the financial crises that affected virtually every full-time club. It may, too, have distracted us for a while from producing our own talent.

Flicking through that 1980 copy of the Review again, I see not only the names of McLeish, Miller, Sturrock and Narey but also those, amongst others, of Gordon Strachan, Charlie Nicholas, Andy

JOCK STEIN AND ALEX FERGUSON

THE UEFA CUP FINAL 2003

Ritchie and Davie Cooper. We need to get back to raising footballers of that calibre.

There are always individual achievements to be applauded and the Review certainly recognised the great period of Rangers' command, largely under Walter Smith's control, that peaked in season 1996/97 when they equalled the record of Jock Stein's Celtic by winning a ninth championship in a row.

Football at large, though, should also celebrate its success in remaining at the front of the mind and deep in the heart of so many people. The Scottish Football League deserved congratulation on reaching its Centenary in 1990. The edition of the Review that was published that year rightly puts the accent on the heritage of the game. There is a piece on the history of every club, reminding us, for example, that Morton were simply named after the terrace where its founders lived.

Turn a page, though, and there is a lesson in the game's knack of evolving. One hundred years after Morton came into being, Meadowbank Thistle were admitted to the League. No one can forget that there would later be heartache, anger and financial trouble. As you can see elsewhere in this copy of the Review, the controversial move to another town did see them develop and, as Livingston, they are the holders of the League Cup.

It would be deceitful to pretend that survival is always guaranteed. Airdrieonians, for example, became the first club since Third Lanark, in 1967, to go out of business.

Against that, a new team was soon taking the field in the town and The Scottish Football League was extending its frontiers. With its Highland clubs and an addition to the Borders, in the shape of Gretna, the competition is more representative of the nation as a whole than it has ever been.

The endurance of football is not always harmonious. In the edition of the Review for 1998/99, I find an article by myself explaining the partitioning of Scottish football, when ten clubs broke away from the SFL to form The Scottish Premier League. It is a subject over which feelings are raw even now, but there must be hope that all clubs will remember how much they have in common.

More than ever, they surely ought to know that they are all, at different levels, straining to make ends meet. In addition to that, they are starting to concentrate on developing the homegrown players who delight supporters and put a smile on the accountants' faces.

The durability of the sport can never be forgotten. Celtic, near bankruptcy ten years ago, reached the 2003 UEFA Cup Final. It seems that every club gets its own particular taste of joy. The League Challenge Cup, for instance, has established itself. Stenhousemuir, Stranraer, Alloa and Queen of the South, to name but a few, will not forget the afternoons when they were trophy winners.

It is the hardiness that keeps coming to mind when I browse through these Reviews. Clubs surmount financial crises. They fight back from relegation. In virtually every case, they defy the odds by building entirely new grounds or radically reconstructing the familiar ones.

Down the years, too, there are sponsors upon sponsors to lend a hand. The marketing experts realise how football can get a brand into every community, but I also suspect that businessman, like the rest of us, just can't stay away from the game.

Each Review brings me another engrossing episode in a story than can never have a final chapter. Maybe I should get that bookshelf reinforced.

UEFA CHAMPIONS LEAGUE

TENNENT'S SCOTTISH CUP

INTERNATIONALS

TENNENT'S SCOTTISH CUP 2004/05

First Round	Saturday, 20th November, 2004
Second Round	Saturday, 11th December, 2004
Third Round	Saturday, 8th January, 2005
Fourth Round	Saturday, 5th February, 2005
Fifth Round	Saturday, 26th February, 2005
Semi-Finals	Sat 9th & Sun 10th April, 2005
Final	Saturday, 28th May, 2005

TENNENT'S SCOTTISH QUALIFYING CUPS 2004/05 – NORTH & SOUTH

Preliminary Round (South)	Saturday, 14th August, 2004
First Round	Saturday, 28th August, 2004
Second Round	Saturday, 11th September, 2004
Semi-Finals	Saturday, 2nd October, 2004
Final (North)	Saturday, 6th November, 2004
Final (South)	Saturday, 7th May, 2005

FIFA WORLD CUP 2006 - QUALIFYING COMPETITION - GROUP 5

Scotland –v– Slovenia	Wednesday, 8th September, 2004
Scotland –v– Norway	Saturday, 9th October, 2004
Moldova –v– Scotland	Wednesday, 13th October, 2004
Italy –v– Scotland	Saturday, 26th March, 2005
Scotland –v– Moldova	Saturday, 4th June, 2005
Belarus –v– Scotland	Wednesday, 8th June, 2005

INTERNATIONAL CHALLENGE MATCHES

Scotland –v– Hungary	Wednesday, 18th August, 2004
Spain –v– Scotland	Friday, 3rd September, 2004
Scotland –v– Sweden	Wednesday, 17th November, 2004

SCOTLAND FUTURE TEAM

Germany –v– Scotland	Tuesday, 7th December, 2004
Scotland –v– Poland	Tuesday, 22nd February, 2005
Austria –v– Scotland	Tuesday, 19th April, 2005
Scotland –v– Turkey	Tuesday, 31st May, 2005

EUROPEAN "UNDER-21" CHAMPIONSHIP - 2004/06 QUALIFYING MATCHES

Scotland –v– Slovenia	Tuesday, 7th September, 2004
Scotland –v– Norway	Friday, 8th October, 2004
Moldova –v– Scotland	Tuesday, 12th October, 2004
Italy –v– Scotland	Friday, 25th March, 2005
Scotland –v– Moldova	Friday, 3rd June, 2005
Belarus –v– Scotland	Tuesday, 7th June, 2005

"UNDER-21" INTERNATIONAL CHALLENGE MATCHES

Hungary –v– Scotland	Tuesday, 17th August, 2004
Spain –v– Scotland	Thursday, 2nd September, 2004
Scotland –v– Sweden	Tuesday, 16th November, 2004

UEFA "UNDER-19" CHAMPIONSHIP 2004/05

Belgium, San Marino, Turkey and Scotland.
First Round, Qualifying Group, Hosted by Belgium, 6th, 8th & 10th October, 2004. The winners and runners–up of the First Qualifying Round groups, as well as the best third place team, will qualify for the Second Qualifying Round.

"UNDER-18" INTERNATIONAL CHALLENGE MATCHES

Germany –v– Scotland   Wednesday, 24th November, 2004

"UNDER-18" INTERNATIONALS

Scotland, Belguim, Northern Ireland
Three Nations Tournament, Scotland.
20th, 22nd & 24th September, 2004.

UEFA "UNDER-17" CHAMPIONSHIP 2004/05

Scotland, Faroe Islands, Israel and Norway.
First Round, Qualifying Group, Hosted by Scotland 18th, 20th & 22nd October, 2004. The winners and runners–up of the First Qualifying Round groups, as well as the best third place team, will qualify for the Second Qualifying Round.

"UNDER-17" NORDIC CUP

Scotland, Finland, Iceland, Norway, England, Sweden, Faroe Islands & Denmark.
Hosted by Finland, Group Matches – 3rd, 4th & 6th August, 2004, Final or Place Match – 8th August, 2004

"UNDER-17" INTERNATIONAL CHALLENGE MATCHES

Sweden –v– Scotland	Tuesday, 21st September, 2004
Sweden –v– Scotland	Thursday, 23rd September, 2004

WOMEN'S EUROPEAN CHAMPIONSHIP 2003/05

Scotland –v–Czech Republic Sunday, 5th September, 2004

WOMEN'S "A" INTERNATIONAL CHALLENGE MATCHES

Scotland –v–Switzerland Thursday, 19th August, 2004

UEFA WOMEN'S "UNDER-19" CHAMPIONSHIP 2004/05

First Round, Qualifying Group, Hosted by Moldova, 27th September to 3rd October, 2004
Scotland, Belarus, Moldova & Ukraine
The winners and runners–up of the First Qualifying Round groups will qualify for the Second Qualifying Round.

WOMEN'S "UNDER-19" INTERNATIONAL CHALLENGE MATCH

Northern Ireland –v– Scotland   Saturday, 28th August, 2004

UEFA CHAMPIONS LEAGUE

Qualifying Round 1
First-Leg matches	Wednesday, 14th July, 2004
Second-Leg matches	Wednesday, 21st July, 2004

Qualifying Round 2
First-Leg matches	Wednesday, 28th July, 2004
Second-Leg matches	Wednesday, 4th August, 2004

Qualifying Round 3
First-Leg matches	Tuesday 10th & Wednesday 11th August, 2004
Second-Leg matches	Tuesday 24th & Wednesday 25th August, 2004

Group Stage:
1st Match Days:	Tuesday, 14th September & Wednesday, 15th September, 2004
2nd Match Days:	Tuesday, 28th September & Wednesday, 29th September, 2004
3rd Match Days:	Tuesday, 19th October & Wednesday, 20th October, 2004
4th Match Days:	Tuesday, 2nd November & Wednesday, 3rd November, 2004
5th Match Days:	Tuesday, 23rd November & Wednesday, 24th November, 2004
6th Match Days:	Tuesday, 7th December & Wednesday, 8th December, 2004

First Knock-Out Round:
First-Leg:	Tuesday, 22nd February & Wednesday, 23rd February, 2005
Second-Leg:	Tuesday, 8th March & Wednesday, 9th March, 2005

Quarter Finals:
First-Leg:	Tuesday, 5th April & Wednesday, 6th April, 2005
Second-Leg:	Tuesday, 12th April & Wednesday, 13th April, 2005

Semi Finals:
First-Leg:	Tuesday, 26th April & Wednesday, 27th April, 2005
Second-Leg:	Tuesday, 3rd May & Wednesday, 4th May, 2005
Final:	Wednesday, 25th May, 2005

U.E.F.A. CUP

First Qualifying Round:
First-Leg matches:	Thursday, 15th July, 2004
Second-Leg matches:	Thursday, 29th July, 2004

Second Qualifying Round:
First-Leg matches:	Thursday, 12th August, 2004
Second-Leg matches:	Thursday, 26th August, 2004

First Round:
First-Leg matches:	Thursday, 16th September, 2004
Second-Leg matches:	Thursday, 30th September, 2004

Group Stage:
1st Match Day:	Thursday, 21st October, 2004
2nd Match Day:	Thursday, 4th November, 2004
3rd Match Day:	Thursday, 25th November, 2004
4th Match Days:	Wednesday, 1st December & Thursday, 2nd December, 2004
5th Match Days:	Wednesday, 15th December & Thursday, 16th December, 2004

First Knock-Out Round:
First-Leg matches:	Wednesday, 16th & Thursday, 17th February, 2005
Second-Leg matches:	Thursday, 24th February, 2005

Second Knock-Out Round:
First-Leg matches:	Thursday, 10th March, 2005
Second-Leg matches:	Wednesday, 16th & Thursday, 17th March, 2005

Quarter Finals:
First-Leg matches:	Thursday, 7th April, 2005
Second-Leg matches:	Thursday, 14th April, 2005

Semi-Finals:
First-Leg matches:	Thursday, 28th April, 2005
Second-Leg matches:	Thursday, 5th May, 2005
Final:	Wednesday, 18th May, 2005

Bank of Scotland Premierleague Fixtures 2004/05

SATURDAY 7TH AUGUST 2004
Aberdeen V Rangers 12.30pm
Dundee V Hearts
Dunfermline V Dundee United
Hibernian V Kilmarnock
Livingston V Inverness CT
SUNDAY 8TH AUGUST 2004
Celtic V Motherwell 2.00pm
SATURDAY 14TH AUGUST 2004
Hearts V Aberdeen
Kilmarnock V Celtic
Motherwell V Hibernian
Rangers V Livingston
SUNDAY 15TH AUGUST 2004
Dundee United V Dundee 2.00pm
Inverness CT V Dunfermline
SATURDAY 21ST AUGUST 2004
Dundee V Motherwell
Dunfermline V Aberdeen
Hearts V Kilmarnock
Livingston V Dundee United
Rangers V Hibernian
SUNDAY 22ND AUGUST 2004
Inverness CT V Celtic 2.00pm
SATURDAY 28TH AUGUST 2004
Aberdeen V Livingston
Dundee United V Inverness CT
Hibernian V Dundee
Motherwell V Hearts
SUNDAY 29TH AUGUST 2004
Celtic V Rangers 1.00pm
Kilmarnock V Dunfermline
SATURDAY 11TH SEPTEMBER 2004
Celtic V Dundee
Dundee United V Aberdeen
Dunfermline V Motherwell
Inverness CT V Hibernian
Livingston V Kilmarnock
SUNDAY 12TH SEPTEMBER 2004
Hearts V Rangers
SATURDAY 18TH SEPTEMBER 2004
Dundee V Livingston
Kilmarnock V Aberdeen
Motherwell V Dundee United
SUNDAY 19TH SEPTEMBER 2004
Dunfermline V Hearts
Hibernian V Celtic
Rangers V Inverness CT
SATURDAY 25TH SEPTEMBER 2004
Aberdeen V Hibernian
Celtic V Dunfermline
Hearts V Inverness CT
Kilmarnock V Dundee United
Livingston V Motherwell
SUNDAY 26TH SEPTEMBER 2004
Dundee V Rangers
SATURDAY 2ND OCTOBER 2004
Aberdeen V Dundee
Dunfermline V Hibernian
SUNDAY 3RD OCTOBER 2004
Dundee United V Celtic
Hearts V Livingston
Inverness CT V Motherwell
Rangers V Kilmarnock
SATURDAY 16TH OCTOBER 2004
Celtic V Hearts
Dundee V Kilmarnock
Hibernian V Dundee United

Inverness CT V Aberdeen
Livingston V Dunfermline
SUNDAY 17TH OCTOBER 2004
Motherwell V Rangers
SATURDAY 23RD OCTOBER 2004
Aberdeen V Motherwell
Dundee V Dunfermline
Hearts V Hibernian
Kilmarnock V Inverness CT
Rangers V Dundee United
SUNDAY 24TH OCTOBER 2004
Livingston V Celtic
TUESDAY 26TH OCTOBER 2004
Dundee United V Hearts 7.45pm
WEDNESDAY 27TH OCTOBER 2004
Celtic V Aberdeen 7.45pm
Dunfermline V Rangers 7.45pm
Hibernian V Livingston 7.45pm
Inverness CT V Dundee 7.45pm
Motherwell V Kilmarnock 7.45pm
SATURDAY 30TH OCTOBER 2004
Dundee United V Dunfermline
Hearts V Dundee
Inverness CT V Livingston
Kilmarnock V Hibernian
Motherwell V Celtic
SUNDAY 31ST OCTOBER 2004
Rangers V Aberdeen
SATURDAY 6TH NOVEMBER 2004
Aberdeen V Hearts
Celtic V Kilmarnock
Dundee V Dundee United
Dunfermline V Inverness CT
Hibernian V Motherwell
SUNDAY 7TH NOVEMBER 2004
Livingston V Rangers
SATURDAY 13TH NOVEMBER 2004
Aberdeen V Dunfermline
Celtic V Inverness CT
Dundee United V Livingston
Kilmarnock V Hearts
Motherwell V Dundee
SUNDAY 14TH NOVEMBER 2004
Hibernian V Rangers
SATURDAY 20TH NOVEMBER 2004
Dundee V Hibernian
Dunfermline V Kilmarnock
Hearts V Motherwell
Inverness CT V Dundee United
Livingston V Aberdeen
Rangers V Celtic
SATURDAY 27TH NOVEMBER 2004
Aberdeen V Dundee United
Hibernian V Inverness CT
Kilmarnock V Livingston
Motherwell V Dunfermline
Rangers V Hearts
SUNDAY 28TH NOVEMBER 2004
Dundee V Celtic
SATURDAY 4TH DECEMBER 2004
Aberdeen V Kilmarnock
Celtic V Hibernian
Dundee United V Motherwell
Hearts V Dunfermline
Livingston V Dundee
SUNDAY 5TH DECEMBER 2004
Inverness CT V Rangers

SATURDAY 11TH DECEMBER 2004
Dundee United V Kilmarnock
Hibernian V Aberdeen
Inverness CT V Hearts
Motherwell V Livingston
Rangers V Dundee
SUNDAY 12TH DECEMBER 2004
Dunfermline V Celtic
SATURDAY 18TH DECEMBER 2004
Celtic V Dundee United
Dundee V Aberdeen
Hibernian V Dunfermline
Livingston V Hearts
Motherwell V Inverness CT
SUNDAY 19TH DECEMBER 2004
Kilmarnock V Rangers
SUNDAY 26TH DECEMBER 2004
Hearts V Celtic
MONDAY 27TH DECEMBER 2004
Aberdeen V Inverness CT
Dundee United V Hibernian
Dunfermline V Livingston
Kilmarnock V Dundee
Rangers V Motherwell
SATURDAY 1ST JANUARY 2005
Celtic V Livingston
Dundee United V Rangers
Dunfermline V Dundee
Inverness CT V Kilmarnock
Motherwell V Aberdeen
SUNDAY 2ND JANUARY 2005
Hibernian V Hearts
SATURDAY 15TH JANUARY 2005
Aberdeen V Celtic
Dundee V Inverness CT
Hearts V Dundee United
Kilmarnock V Motherwell
Livingston V Hibernian
Rangers V Dunfermline
SATURDAY 22ND JANUARY 2005
Aberdeen V Rangers
Celtic V Motherwell
Dundee V Hearts
Dunfermline V Dundee United
Hibernian V Kilmarnock
Livingston V Inverness CT
SATURDAY 29TH JANUARY 2005
Dundee United V Dundee
Hearts V Aberdeen
Inverness CT V Dunfermline
Kilmarnock V Celtic
Motherwell V Hibernian
Rangers V Livingston
SATURDAY 12TH FEBRUARY 2005
Dundee V Motherwell
Dunfermline V Aberdeen
Hearts V Kilmarnock
Inverness CT V Celtic
Livingston V Dundee United
Rangers V Hibernian
SATURDAY 19TH FEBRUARY 2005
Aberdeen V Livingston
Celtic V Rangers
Dundee United V Inverness CT
Hibernian V Dundee
Kilmarnock V Dunfermline
Motherwell V Hearts

TUESDAY 1ST MARCH 2005
Dundee United V Aberdeen 7.45pm
WEDNESDAY 2ND MARCH 2005
Celtic V Dundee 7.45pm
Dunfermline V Motherwell 7.45pm
Hearts V Rangers 7.45pm
Inverness CT V Hibernian 7.45pm
Livingston V Kilmarnock 7.45pm
SATURDAY 5TH MARCH 2005
Dundee V Livingston
Dunfermline V Hearts
Hibernian V Celtic
Kilmarnock V Aberdeen
Motherwell V Dundee United
Rangers V Inverness CT
SATURDAY 12TH MARCH 2005
Aberdeen V Hibernian
Celtic V Dunfermline
Dundee V Rangers
Hearts V Inverness CT
Kilmarnock V Dundee United
Livingston V Motherwell
SATURDAY 19TH MARCH 2005
Aberdeen V Dundee
Dundee United V Celtic
Dunfermline V Hibernian
Hearts V Livingston
Inverness CT V Motherwell
Rangers V Kilmarnock
SATURDAY 2ND APRIL 2005
Celtic V Hearts
Dundee V Kilmarnock
Hibernian V Dundee United
Inverness CT V Aberdeen
Livingston V Dunfermline
Motherwell V Rangers
SATURDAY 9TH APRIL 2005
Aberdeen V Motherwell
Dundee V Dunfermline
Hearts V Hibernian
Kilmarnock V Inverness CT
Livingston V Celtic
Rangers V Dundee United
SATURDAY 16TH APRIL 2005
Celtic V Aberdeen
Dundee United V Hearts
Dunfermline V Rangers
Hibernian V Livingston
Inverness CT V Dundee
Motherwell V Kilmarnock

Copyright © and Database Right
2004. The Scottish Premier
League Limited. All fixtures subject
to change. Matches kick-off at
3.00pm except where stated.
Fixtures 33 to 38 to be
announced in due course.

Bell's Scottish Football League Fixtures 2004/05

INVERNESS CALEDONIAN THISTLE

AIRDRIE UNITED

STRANRAER

SATURDAY 7TH AUGUST 2004
FIRST DIVISION
Airdrie United v. St. Johnstone
Clyde v. Partick Thistle
Hamilton Academical v. Raith Rovers
Queen of the South v. Ross County
St. Mirren v. Falkirk
SECOND DIVISION
Berwick Rangers v. Morton
Dumbarton v. Ayr United
Forfar Athletic v. Brechin City
Stirling Albion v. Arbroath
Stranraer v. Alloa Athletic
THIRD DIVISION
East Fife v. Montrose
Gretna v. Albion Rovers
Peterhead v. East Stirlingshire
Queen's Park v. Cowdenbeath
Stenhousemuir v. Elgin City
SATURDAY 14TH AUGUST 2004
FIRST DIVISION
Falkirk v. Hamilton Academical
Partick Thistle v. Airdrie United
Raith Rovers v. Clyde
Ross County v. St. Mirren
St. Johnstone v. Queen of the South
SECOND DIVISION
Alloa Athletic v. Forfar Athletic
Arbroath v. Dumbarton
Ayr United v. Berwick Rangers
Brechin City v. Stirling Albion
Morton v. Stranraer
THIRD DIVISION
Albion Rovers v. East Fife
Cowdenbeath v. Stenhousemuir
East Stirlingshire v. Gretna
Elgin City v. Queen's Park
Montrose v. Peterhead
SATURDAY 21ST AUGUST 2004
FIRST DIVISION
Airdrie United v. Raith Rovers
Clyde v. Ross County
Hamilton Academical v. Partick Thistle
Queen of the South v. Falkirk
St. Mirren v. St. Johnstone
SECOND DIVISION
Berwick Rangers v. Brechin City
Dumbarton v. Morton
Forfar Athletic v. Arbroath
Stirling Albion v. Alloa Athletic
Stranraer v. Ayr United
THIRD DIVISION
East Fife v. Cowdenbeath
Gretna v. Montrose
Peterhead v. Elgin City
Queen's Park v. Albion Rovers
Stenhousemuir v. East Stirlingshire
SATURDAY 28TH AUGUST 2004
FIRST DIVISION
Falkirk v. Airdrie United
Queen of the South v. Clyde
Ross County v. Partick Thistle
St. Johnstone v. Raith Rovers

St. Mirren v. Hamilton Academical
SECOND DIVISION
Arbroath v. Stranraer
Ayr United v. Morton
Brechin City v. Alloa Athletic
Dumbarton v. Forfar Athletic
Stirling Albion v. Berwick Rangers
THIRD DIVISION
Albion Rovers v. Peterhead
Cowdenbeath v. East Stirlingshire
East Fife v. Stenhousemuir
Elgin City v. Montrose
Queen's Park v. Gretna
SATURDAY 4TH SEPTEMBER 2004
FIRST DIVISION
Airdrie United v. Queen of the South
Clyde v. St. Mirren
Hamilton Academical v. St. Johnstone
Partick Thistle v. Falkirk
Raith Rovers v. Ross County
SECOND DIVISION
Alloa Athletic v. Ayr United
Berwick Rangers v. Dumbarton
Forfar Athletic v. Stirling Albion
Morton v. Arbroath
Stranraer v. Brechin City
THIRD DIVISION
East Stirlingshire v. Elgin City
Gretna v. Cowdenbeath
Montrose v. Albion Rovers
Peterhead v. East Fife
Stenhousemuir v. Queen's Park
SATURDAY 11TH SEPTEMBER 2004
FIRST DIVISION
Clyde v. Airdrie United
Falkirk v. Raith Rovers
Queen of the South v. Hamilton Academical
Ross County v. St. Johnstone
St. Mirren v. Partick Thistle
SECOND DIVISION
Ayr United v. Forfar Athletic
Berwick Rangers v. Alloa Athletic
Brechin City v. Arbroath
Dumbarton v. Stranraer
Stirling Albion v. Morton
THIRD DIVISION
Albion Rovers v. Stenhousemuir
Cowdenbeath v. Elgin City
East Fife v. East Stirlingshire
Peterhead v. Gretna
Queen's Park v. Montrose
SATURDAY 18TH SEPTEMBER 2004
FIRST DIVISION
Airdrie United v. Ross County
Hamilton Academical v. Clyde
Partick Thistle v. Queen of the South
Raith Rovers v. St. Mirren
St. Johnstone v. Falkirk
SECOND DIVISION
Alloa Athletic v. Dumbarton
Arbroath v. Ayr United
Forfar Athletic v. Berwick Rangers
Morton v. Brechin City

Stranraer v. Stirling Albion
THIRD DIVISION
East Stirlingshire v. Queen's Park
Elgin City v. Albion Rovers
Gretna v. East Fife
Montrose v. Cowdenbeath
Stenhousemuir v. Peterhead
SATURDAY 25TH SEPTEMBER 20
FIRST DIVISION
Falkirk v. Clyde
Hamilton Academical v. Ross County
Raith Rovers v. Queen of the South
St. Johnstone v. Partick Thistle
St. Mirren v. Airdrie United
SECOND DIVISION
Alloa Athletic v. Morton
Ayr United v. Brechin City
Berwick Rangers v. Arbroath
Dumbarton v. Stirling Albion
Forfar Athletic v. Stranraer
THIRD DIVISION
Albion Rovers v. East Stirlingshire
East Fife v. Queen's Park
Gretna v. Elgin City
Montrose v. Stenhousemuir
Peterhead v. Cowdenbeath
SATURDAY 2ND OCTOBER 20
FIRST DIVISION
Airdrie United v. Hamilton Academic
Clyde v. St. Johnstone
Partick Thistle v. Raith Rovers
Queen of the South v. St. Mirren
Ross County v. Falkirk
SECOND DIVISION
Arbroath v. Alloa Athletic
Brechin City v. Dumbarton
Morton v. Forfar Athletic
Stirling Albion v. Ayr United
Stranraer v. Berwick Rangers
THIRD DIVISION
Cowdenbeath v. Albion Rovers
East Stirlingshire v. Montrose
Elgin City v. East Fife
Queen's Park v. Peterhead
Stenhousemuir v. Gretna
SATURDAY 16TH OCTOBER 20
FIRST DIVISION
Airdrie United v. Partick Thistle
Clyde v. Raith Rovers
Hamilton Academical v. Falkirk
Queen of the South v. St. Johnston
St. Mirren v. Ross County
SECOND DIVISION
Berwick Rangers v. Ayr United
Dumbarton v. Arbroath
Forfar Athletic v. Alloa Athletic
Stirling Albion v. Brechin City
Stranraer v. Morton
THIRD DIVISION
East Fife v. Albion Rovers
Gretna v. East Stirlingshire
Peterhead v. Montrose
Queen's Park v. Elgin City

Stenhousemuir v. Cowdenbeath

SATURDAY 23RD OCTOBER 2004
FIRST DIVISION
Falkirk v. St. Mirren
Partick Thistle v. Clyde
Raith Rovers v. Hamilton Academical
Ross County v. Queen of the South
St. Johnstone v. Airdrie United
SECOND DIVISION
Alloa Athletic v. Stranraer
Arbroath v. Stirling Albion
Ayr United v. Dumbarton
Brechin City v. Forfar Athletic
Morton v. Berwick Rangers
THIRD DIVISION
Albion Rovers v. Gretna
Cowdenbeath v. Queen's Park
East Stirlingshire v. Peterhead
Elgin City v. Stenhousemuir
Montrose v. East Fife

SATURDAY 30TH OCTOBER 2004
FIRST DIVISION
Airdrie United v. Falkirk
Clyde v. Queen of the South
Hamilton Academical v. St. Mirren
Partick Thistle v. Ross County
Raith Rovers v. St. Johnstone
SECOND DIVISION
Alloa Athletic v. Brechin City
Berwick Rangers v. Stirling Albion
Forfar Athletic v. Dumbarton
Morton v. Ayr United
Stranraer v. Arbroath
THIRD DIVISION
East Stirlingshire v. Cowdenbeath
Gretna v. Queen's Park
Montrose v. Elgin City
Peterhead v. Albion Rovers
Stenhousemuir v. East Fife

SATURDAY 6TH NOVEMBER 2004
FIRST DIVISION
Falkirk v. Partick Thistle
Queen of the South v. Airdrie United
Ross County v. Raith Rovers
St. Johnstone v. Hamilton Academical
St. Mirren v. Clyde
SECOND DIVISION
Arbroath v. Morton
Ayr United v. Alloa Athletic
Brechin City v. Stranraer
Dumbarton v. Berwick Rangers
Stirling Albion v. Forfar Athletic
THIRD DIVISION
Albion Rovers v. Montrose
Cowdenbeath v. Gretna
East Fife v. Peterhead
Elgin City v. East Stirlingshire
Queen's Park v. Stenhousemuir

SATURDAY 13TH NOVEMBER 2004
FIRST DIVISION
Airdrie United v. Clyde
Hamilton Academical v. Queen of the South
Partick Thistle v. St. Mirren
Raith Rovers v. Falkirk
St. Johnstone v. Ross County
SECOND DIVISION
Alloa Athletic v. Berwick Rangers
Arbroath v. Brechin City
Forfar Athletic v. Ayr United
Morton v. Stirling Albion
Stranraer v. Dumbarton
THIRD DIVISION
East Stirlingshire v. East Fife
Elgin City v. Cowdenbeath

Gretna v. Peterhead
Montrose v. Queen's Park
Stenhousemuir v. Albion Rovers

SATURDAY 20TH NOVEMBER 2004
FIRST DIVISION
Clyde v. Hamilton Academical
Falkirk v. St. Johnstone
Queen of the South v. Partick Thistle
Ross County v. Airdrie United
St. Mirren v. Raith Rovers

SATURDAY 27TH NOVEMBER 2004
FIRST DIVISION
Falkirk v. Ross County
Hamilton Academical v. Airdrie United
Raith Rovers v. Partick Thistle
St. Johnstone v. Clyde
St. Mirren v. Queen of the South
SECOND DIVISION
Ayr United v. Arbroath
Berwick Rangers v. Forfar Athletic
Brechin City v. Morton
Dumbarton v. Alloa Athletic
Stirling Albion v. Stranraer
THIRD DIVISION
Albion Rovers v. Elgin City
Cowdenbeath v. Montrose
East Fife v. Gretna
Peterhead v. Stenhousemuir
Queen's Park v. East Stirlingshire

SATURDAY 4TH DECEMBER 2004
FIRST DIVISION
Airdrie United v. St. Mirren
Clyde v. Falkirk
Partick Thistle v. St. Johnstone
Queen of the South v. Raith Rovers
Ross County v. Hamilton Academical
SECOND DIVISION
Arbroath v. Berwick Rangers
Brechin City v. Ayr United
Morton v. Alloa Athletic
Stirling Albion v. Dumbarton
Stranraer v. Forfar Athletic
THIRD DIVISION
Cowdenbeath v. Peterhead
East Stirlingshire v. Albion Rovers
Elgin City v. Gretna
Queen's Park v. East Fife
Stenhousemuir v. Montrose

SATURDAY 11TH DECEMBER 2004
FIRST DIVISION
Airdrie United v. St. Johnstone
Clyde v. Partick Thistle
Hamilton Academical v. Raith Rovers
Queen of the South v. Ross County
St. Mirren v. Falkirk

SATURDAY 18TH DECEMBER 2004
FIRST DIVISION
Falkirk v. Queen of the South
Partick Thistle v. Hamilton Academical
Raith Rovers v. Airdrie United
Ross County v. Clyde
St. Johnstone v. St. Mirren
SECOND DIVISION
Alloa Athletic v. Arbroath
Ayr United v. Stirling Albion
Berwick Rangers v. Stranraer
Dumbarton v. Brechin City
Forfar Athletic v. Morton
THIRD DIVISION
Albion Rovers v. Cowdenbeath
East Fife v. Elgin City
Gretna v. Stenhousemuir
Montrose v. East Stirlingshire
Peterhead v. Queen's Park

SUNDAY 26TH DECEMBER 2004
FIRST DIVISION
Falkirk v. Airdrie United
Queen of the South v. Clyde
St. Johnstone v. Raith Rovers
St. Mirren v. Hamilton Academical

MONDAY 27TH DECEMBER 2004
FIRST DIVISION
Ross County v. Partick Thistle
SECOND DIVISION
Berwick Rangers v. Morton
Dumbarton v. Ayr United
Forfar Athletic v. Brechin City
Stirling Albion v. Arbroath
Stranraer v. Alloa Athletic
THIRD DIVISION
East Fife v. Montrose
Gretna v. Albion Rovers
Peterhead v. East Stirlingshire
Queen's Park v. Cowdenbeath
Stenhousemuir v. Elgin City

WEDNESDAY 29TH DECEMBER 2004
FIRST DIVISION
Airdrie United v. Queen of the South
Clyde v. St. Mirren
Hamilton Academical v. St. Johnstone
Partick Thistle v. Falkirk
Raith Rovers v. Ross County

SATURDAY 1ST JANUARY 2005
FIRST DIVISION
Clyde v. Airdrie United
Falkirk v. Raith Rovers
Queen of the South v. Hamilton Academical
St. Mirren v. Partick Thistle
SECOND DIVISION
Alloa Athletic v. Stirling Albion
Arbroath v. Forfar Athletic
Ayr United v. Stranraer
Brechin City v. Berwick Rangers
Morton v. Dumbarton
THIRD DIVISION
Albion Rovers v. Queen's Park
Cowdenbeath v. East Fife
East Stirlingshire v. Stenhousemuir
Elgin City v. Peterhead
Montrose v. Gretna

MONDAY 3RD JANUARY 2005
FIRST DIVISION
Ross County v. St. Johnstone
SECOND DIVISION
Arbroath v. Stranraer
Ayr United v. Morton
Brechin City v. Alloa Athletic
Dumbarton v. Forfar Athletic
Stirling Albion v. Berwick Rangers
THIRD DIVISION
Albion Rovers v. Peterhead
Cowdenbeath v. East Stirlingshire
East Fife v. Stenhousemuir
Elgin City v. Montrose
Queen's Park v. Gretna

SATURDAY 15TH JANUARY 2005
FIRST DIVISION
Airdrie United v. Ross County
Hamilton Academical v. Clyde
Partick Thistle v. Queen of the South
Raith Rovers v. St. Mirren
St. Johnstone v. Falkirk
SECOND DIVISION
Alloa Athletic v. Ayr United
Berwick Rangers v. Dumbarton
Forfar Athletic v. Stirling Albion
Morton v. Arbroath
Stranraer v. Brechin City

THIRD DIVISION
East Stirlingshire v. Elgin City
Gretna v. Cowdenbeath
Montrose v. Albion Rovers
Peterhead v. East Fife
Stenhousemuir v. Queen's Park

SATURDAY 22ND JANUARY 2005
FIRST DIVISION
Falkirk v. Clyde
Hamilton Academical v. Ross County
Raith Rovers v. Queen of the South
St. Johnstone v. Partick Thistle
St. Mirren v. Airdrie United
SECOND DIVISION
Ayr United v. Forfar Athletic
Berwick Rangers v. Alloa Athletic
Brechin City v. Arbroath
Dumbarton v. Stranraer
Stirling Albion v. Morton
THIRD DIVISION
Albion Rovers v. Stenhousemuir
Cowdenbeath v. Elgin City
East Fife v. East Stirlingshire
Peterhead v. Gretna
Queen's Park v. Montrose

SATURDAY 29TH JANUARY 2005
FIRST DIVISION
Airdrie United v. Hamilton Academical
Clyde v. St. Johnstone
Partick Thistle v. Raith Rovers
Queen of the South v. St. Mirren
Ross County v. Falkirk
SECOND DIVISION
Alloa Athletic v. Dumbarton
Arbroath v. Ayr United
Forfar Athletic v. Berwick Rangers
Morton v. Brechin City
Stranraer v. Stirling Albion
THIRD DIVISION
East Stirlingshire v. Queen's Park
Elgin City v. Albion Rovers
Gretna v. East Fife
Montrose v. Cowdenbeath
Stenhousemuir v. Peterhead

SATURDAY 5TH FEBRUARY 2005
SECOND DIVISION
Alloa Athletic v. Morton
Ayr United v. Brechin City
Berwick Rangers v. Stranraer
Dumbarton v. Stirling Albion
Forfar Athletic v. Stranraer
THIRD DIVISION
Albion Rovers v. East Stirlingshire
East Fife v. Queen's Park
Gretna v. Elgin City
Montrose v. Stenhousemuir
Peterhead v. Cowdenbeath

SATURDAY 12TH FEBRUARY 2005
FIRST DIVISION
Falkirk v. Hamilton Academical
Partick Thistle v. Airdrie United
Raith Rovers v. Clyde
Ross County v. St. Mirren
St. Johnstone v. Queen of the South
SECOND DIVISION
Arbroath v. Alloa Athletic
Brechin City v. Dumbarton
Morton v. Forfar Athletic
Stirling Albion v. Ayr United
Stranraer v. Berwick Rangers
THIRD DIVISION
Cowdenbeath v. Albion Rovers
East Stirlingshire v. Montrose
Elgin City v. East Fife

INVERNESS CALEDONIAN THISTLE

Queen's Park v. Peterhead
Stenhousemuir v. Gretna
SATURDAY 19TH FEBRUARY 2005
FIRST DIVISION
Airdrie United v. Raith Rovers
Clyde v. Ross County
Hamilton Academical v. Partick Thistle
Queen of the South v. Falkirk
St. Mirren v. St. Johnstone
SECOND DIVISION
Berwick Rangers v. Brechin City
Dumbarton v. Morton
Forfar Athletic v. Arbroath
Stirling Albion v. Alloa Athletic
Stranraer v. Ayr United
THIRD DIVISION
East Fife v. Cowdenbeath
Gretna v. Montrose
Peterhead v. Elgin City
Queen's Park v. Albion Rovers
Stenhousemuir v. East Stirlingshire
SATURDAY 26TH FEBRUARY 2005
SECOND DIVISION
Alloa Athletic v. Forfar Athletic
Arbroath v. Dumbarton
Ayr United v. Berwick Rangers
Brechin City v. Stirling Albion
Morton v. Stranraer
THIRD DIVISION
Albion Rovers v. East Fife
Cowdenbeath v. Stenhousemuir
East Stirlingshire v. Gretna
Elgin City v. Queen's Park
Montrose v. Peterhead
SATURDAY 5TH MARCH 2005
FIRST DIVISION
Falkirk v. Partick Thistle
Queen of the South v. Airdrie United
Ross County v. Raith Rovers
St. Johnstone v. Hamilton Academical
St. Mirren v. Clyde
SECOND DIVISION
Arbroath v. Morton
Ayr United v. Alloa Athletic
Brechin City v. Stranraer
Dumbarton v. Berwick Rangers
Stirling Albion v. Forfar Athletic
THIRD DIVISION
Albion Rovers v. Montrose
Cowdenbeath v. Gretna
East Fife v. Peterhead
Elgin City v. East Stirlingshire

Queen's Park v. Stenhousemuir
SATURDAY 12TH MARCH 2005
FIRST DIVISION
Airdrie United v. Falkirk
Clyde v. Queen of the South
Hamilton Academical v. St. Mirren
Partick Thistle v. Ross County
Raith Rovers v. St. Johnstone
SECOND DIVISION
Alloa Athletic v. Brechin City
Berwick Rangers v. Stirling Albion
Forfar Athletic v. Dumbarton
Morton v. Ayr United
Stranraer v. Arbroath
THIRD DIVISION
East Stirlingshire v. Cowdenbeath
Gretna v. Queen's Park
Montrose v. Elgin City
Peterhead v. Albion Rovers
Stenhousemuir v. East Fife
SATURDAY 19TH MARCH 2005
FIRST DIVISION
Airdrie United v. Clyde
Hamilton Academical v. Queen of the South
Partick Thistle v. St. Mirren
Raith Rovers v. Falkirk
St. Johnstone v. Ross County
SECOND DIVISION
Alloa Athletic v. Berwick Rangers
Arbroath v. Brechin City
Forfar Athletic v. Ayr United
Morton v. Stirling Albion
Stranraer v. Dumbarton
THIRD DIVISION
East Stirlingshire v. East Fife
Elgin City v. Cowdenbeath
Gretna v. Peterhead
Montrose v. Queen's Park
Stenhousemuir v. Albion Rovers
SATURDAY 2ND APRIL 2005
FIRST DIVISION
Clyde v. Hamilton Academical
Falkirk v. St. Johnstone
Queen of the South v. Partick Thistle
Ross County v. Airdrie United
St. Mirren v. Raith Rovers
SECOND DIVISION
Ayr United v. Arbroath
Berwick Rangers v. Forfar Athletic
Brechin City v. Morton
Dumbarton v. Alloa Athletic
Stirling Albion v. Stranraer

THIRD DIVISION
Albion Rovers v. Elgin City
Cowdenbeath v. Montrose
East Fife v. Gretna
Peterhead v. Stenhousemuir
Queen's Park v. East Stirlingshire
SATURDAY 9TH APRIL 2005
FIRST DIVISION
Falkirk v. Ross County
Hamilton Academical v. Airdrie United
Raith Rovers v. Partick Thistle
St. Johnstone v. Clyde
St. Mirren v. Queen of the South
SECOND DIVISION
Alloa Athletic v. Arbroath
Ayr United v. Stirling Albion
Berwick Rangers v. Stranraer
Dumbarton v. Brechin City
Forfar Athletic v. Morton
THIRD DIVISION
Albion Rovers v. Cowdenbeath
East Fife v. Elgin City
Gretna v. Stenhousemuir
Montrose v. East Stirlingshire
Peterhead v. Queen's Park
SATURDAY 16TH APRIL 2005
FIRST DIVISION
Airdrie United v. St. Mirren
Clyde v. Falkirk
Partick Thistle v. St. Johnstone
Queen of the South v. Raith Rovers
Ross County v. Hamilton Academical
SECOND DIVISION
Arbroath v. Berwick Rangers
Brechin City v. Ayr United
Morton v. Alloa Athletic
Stirling Albion v. Dumbarton
Stranraer v. Forfar Athletic
THIRD DIVISION
Cowdenbeath v. Peterhead
East Stirlingshire v. Albion Rovers
Elgin City v. Gretna
Queen's Park v. East Fife
Stenhousemuir v. Montrose
SATURDAY 23RD APRIL 2005
FIRST DIVISION
Falkirk v. St. Mirren
Partick Thistle v. Clyde
Raith Rovers v. Hamilton Academical
Ross County v. Queen of the South
St. Johnstone v. Airdrie United

SECOND DIVISION
Alloa Athletic v. Stirling Albion
Arbroath v. Forfar Athletic
Ayr United v. Stranraer
Brechin City v. Berwick Rangers
Morton v. Dumbarton
THIRD DIVISION
Albion Rovers v. Queen's Park
Cowdenbeath v. East Fife
East Stirlingshire v. Stenhousemuir
Elgin City v. Peterhead
Montrose v. Gretna
SATURDAY 30TH APRIL 2005
FIRST DIVISION
Airdrie United v. Partick Thistle
Clyde v. Raith Rovers
Hamilton Academical v. Falkirk
Queen of the South v. St. Johnstone
St. Mirren v. Ross County
SECOND DIVISION
Berwick Rangers v. Ayr United
Dumbarton v. Arbroath
Forfar Athletic v. Alloa Athletic
Stirling Albion v. Brechin City
Stranraer v. Morton
THIRD DIVISION
East Fife v. Albion Rovers
Gretna v. East Stirlingshire
Peterhead v. Montrose
Queen's Park v. Elgin City
Stenhousemuir v. Cowdenbeath
SATURDAY 7TH MAY 2005
FIRST DIVISION
Falkirk v. Queen of the South
Partick Thistle v. Hamilton Academical
Raith Rovers v. Airdrie United
Ross County v. Clyde
St. Johnstone v. St. Mirren
SECOND DIVISION
Alloa Athletic v. Stranraer
Arbroath v. Stirling Albion
Ayr United v. Dumbarton
Brechin City v. Forfar Athletic
Morton v. Berwick Rangers
THIRD DIVISION
Albion Rovers v. Gretna
Cowdenbeath v. Queen's Park
East Stirlingshire v. Peterhead
Elgin City v. Stenhousemuir
Montrose v. East Fife

1ST ROUND

Airdrie United	v	East Fife
Berwick Rangers	v	Elgin City
Brechin City	v	Cowdenbeath
Dumbarton	v	Ross County
Falkirk	v	Montrose
Peterhead	v	East Stirlingshire
St. Johnstone	v	Alloa Athletic
St. Mirren	v	Forfar Athletic
Stenhousemuir	v	Arbroath
Stranraer	v	Raith Rovers

Above Ties to be played on Tuesday, 10th August, 2004.

Stirling Albion	v	Queen's Park

Above Tie to be played on Wednesday 11th August, 2004.

Hamilton Academical	v	Ayr United
Morton	v	Gretna
Queen of the South	v	Albion Rovers

Above Ties to be played on Tuesday, 17th August, 2004.

2ND ROUND

....	v	....
....	v	....
....	v	....
....	v	....
....	v	....
....	v	....
....	v	....
....	v	....
....	v	....
....	v	....

Ties to be played on Tuesday, 24th or Wednesday, 25th August, 2004.

3RD ROUND

....	v	....
....	v	....
....	v	....
....	v	....
....	v	....
....	v	....
....	v	....
....	v	....

Ties to be played on Tuesday, 21st or Wednesday, 22nd September, 2004.

4TH ROUND

....	v	....
....	v	....
....	v	....
....	v	....

Ties to be played on Tuesday, 9th or Wednesday, 10th November, 2004.

SEMI-FINALS

....	v	....
....	v	....

Ties to be played on Tuesday, 1st and Wednesday, 2nd February, 2005.

THE CIS INSURANCE CUP FINAL

....	v	....

To be played on Sunday, 20th March, 2005.

In the event of a draw after normal time in all rounds, extra time of 30 minutes (i.e. 15 minutes each way) will take place and thereafter, if necessary, Kicks from the Penalty Mark in accordance with the Rules laid down by The International Football Association Board will be taken.

The Bell's Cup draw season 2004/05

1ST ROUND

Alloa Athletic	v	Elgin City
Partick Thistle	v	Brechin City
East Fife	v	Cowdenbeath
Airdrie United	v	Queen of the South
St. Johnstone	v	Hamilton Academical
Ross County	v	St. Mirren
East Stirlingshire	v	Berwick Rangers
Gretna	v	Montrose
Ayr United	v	Falkirk
Forfar Athletic	v	Morton
Dumbarton	v	Stirling Albion
Raith Rovers	v	Albion Rovers
Queen's Park	v	Stenhousemuir
Arbroath	v	Peterhead

Byes: Clyde and Stranraer

Above ties to be played on Saturday, 31st July, 2004.

2ND ROUND

....	v	....
....	v	....
....	v	....
....	v	....
....	v	....
....	v	....
....	v	....
....	v	....

Above ties to be played on Tuesday, 31st August or Wednesday, 1st September, 2004.

3RD ROUND

....	v	....
....	v	....
....	v	....
....	v	....

Above ties to be played on Tuesday, 14th or Wednesday, 15th September, 2004.

SEMI-FINALS

....	v	....
....	v	....

Above ties to be played on Tuesday, 28th or Wednesday, 29th September, 2004.

THE BELL'S CUP FINAL

....	v	....

To be played on Sunday, 7th November, 2004.

In the event of a draw after normal time in all rounds, extra time of 30 minutes (i.e. 15 minutes each way) will take place and thereafter, if necessary, kicks from the penalty mark in accordance with the rules laid down by the International Football Association Board will be taken.

ABERDEEN FC

Pittodrie Stadium, Pittodrie Street,
Aberdeen, AB24 5QH
CHAIRMAN Stewart Milne
PRESIDENT Ian R. Donald
DIRECTORS Gordon A. Buchan,
Martin J. Gilbert, Hugh Little,
Christopher Gavin, William F. Miller,
Duncan Fraser & Ken Matheson
GENERAL MANAGER David Johnston
SECRETARY Duncan Fraser (01224) 650424
MANAGER Jimmy Calderwood
ASSISTANT MANAGER Jimmy Nicholl
GOALKEEPING COACH Jim Leighton
DIRECTOR OF YOUTH DEVELOPMENT
Chic McLelland
SENIOR COMMUNITY COACH Neil Simpson
COMMUNITY CO-ORDINATOR Sandy Finnie
COMMUNITY COACHES Jim Crawford,
Stuart Glennie & Scott Anderson
U19 YOUTH COACH Neil Cooper
CHIEF SCOUT John Kelman
**FOOTBALL SAFETY OFFICERS'
ASSOCIATION REPRESENTATIVE /
STADIUM MANAGER**
John Morgan (01224) 650405
**COMMERCIAL, SALES &
MARKETING MANAGER**
Ian Riddoch (01224) 650443
HOSPITALITY MANAGER
Paul Quick (01224) 650430
CORPORATE SALES MANAGER
Harvey Smith (01224) 650426
CUSTOMER SERVICES MANAGER
Peter Roy (01224) 650428
CLUB DOCTORS
Dr. Derek Gray & Dr. Stephen Wedderburn
PHYSIOTHERAPISTS
David Wylie & John Sharp
GROUNDSMAN Paul Fiske
KIT MANAGER Jim Warrender
MEDIA LIAISON PERSON Dave Macdermid
MATCHDAY PROGRAMME EDITOR
Malcolm Panton (01224) 650402
TELEPHONES
Ground/General Enquiries (01224) 650400
Football Dept (01224) 650479
Commercial Dept (01224) 650426
Marketing & PR Dept (01224) 650406
Community Dept (01224) 650432
Ticket Enquiries 087 1983 1903
Fax (01224) 644173
Operations Dept (01224) 650405
E-Mail & Internet Address
davidj@afc.co.uk & feedback@afc.co.uk
www.afc.co.uk
CLUB SHOPS
Pittodrie Club Shop, Pittodrie Stadium,
Aberdeen. Tel (087) 1983 1903
Buy on-line at www.afc.co.uk/shop
OFFICIAL SUPPORTERS CLUB
Association Secretary: Mrs. Susan Scott,
'Aldon', Wellington Road, Aberdeen, AB12 4BJ
Tel (01224) 898260/450378
susan.scott1@virgin.net
TEAM CAPTAIN Russell Anderson
SHIRT SPONSOR ADT FIRE & SECURITY
KIT SUPPLIER NIKE

LIST OF PLAYERS 2004/05

SQUAD NO.	PLAYERS SURNAME	FIRST NAME	MIDDLE NAME	DATE OF BIRTH	PLACE OF BIRTH	DATE SIGNED	HEIGHT FT INS	WEIGHT ST LBS	POSITION ON PITCH	PREVIOUS CLUB
10	ADAMS	DEREK	WATT	25/06/75	ABERDEEN	5/7/04	5' 10"	12ST 7LB	MID	MOTHERWELL
4	ANDERSON	RUSSELL		25/10/78	ABERDEEN	19/7/96	6' 1"	12ST 6LB	DEF	DYCE JUNIORS
-	BAGSHAW	ANDREW	GEORGE	04/07/88	ABERDEEN	1/7/04	5' 8"	11ST 0LB	FWD	ABERDEEN YOUTHS
-	BLANCHARD	JAMES	FINDLAY	03/07/86	BANFF	16/7/02	6' 2"	11ST 4LB	GK	DEVERONVALE
-	BRUCE	JOHN		16/01/88	DUNDEE	1/7/04	5' 9"	11ST 0LB	FWD	ABERDEEN YOUTHS
22	BUCKLEY	RICHARD		25/01/85	RUTHERGLEN	10/7/03	5' 10"	11ST 6LB	DEF	ABERDEEN YOUTHS
11	CLARK	CHRISTOPHER		15/09/80	ABERDEEN	16/8/97	5' 9"	11ST 3LB	MID	HERMES
-	CONSIDINE	ANDREW		01/04/87	TORPHINS	28/8/03	6' 0.5"	11ST 12LB	DEF	ABERDEEN YOUTHS
9	CRAIG	STEVEN		05/02/81	BLACKBURN	2/6/04	5' 11"	12ST 4LB	FWD	MOTHERWELL
5	DIAMOND	ALEXANDER		12/03/85	ALEXANDRIA	12/7/02	6' 2"	11ST 7LB	DEF	ABERDEEN 'S' FORM
-	DONALD	DAVID		09/11/87	ABERDEEN	6/1/04	5' 7"	10ST 13LB	DEF	GLENDALE
-	DONNELLY	CIARAN	ANTHONY	30/04/86	RUTHERGLEN	22/7/04	5' 11"	13ST 1LB	MID	HAMILTON ACADEMICAL
20	ESSON	RYAN	JOHN	19/03/80	ABERDEEN	23/10/96	6' 1.5"	13ST 3LB	GK	ROTHERHAM UNITED
21	FOSTER	RICHARD	MARTYN	31/07/85	ABERDEEN	2/9/98	5' 9.5"	11ST 8LB	MID	ABERDEEN YOUTHS
-	FRASER	GRANT	CALLUM	22/03/86	ABERDEEN	9/7/03	6' 0"	11ST 2LB	DEF	ABERDEEN 'S' FORM
15	HART	MICHAEL		10/02/80	BELLSHILL	24/1/03	5' 11.5"	12ST 2LB	MID	LIVINGSTON
8	HEIKKINEN	MARKUS		13/10/78	KATRINEHOLM	4/8/03	6' 0"	13ST 1LB	MID	PORTSMOUTH
-	KEILY	WILLIE	JOHN	25/06/88	WATERFORD	14/7/04	5' 7"	11ST 8LB	FWD	CHERRY ORCHARD
-	KELLY	GREG		28/04/87	BELLSHILL	7/7/04	6' 2"	12ST 0LB	GK	ABERDEEN YOUTHS
-	McAULAY	KYLE	DONALD	13/05/86	ELGIN	25/5/04	5' 10"	11ST 12LB	MID	ABERDEEN B.C.
14	MACKIE	DARREN	GRAHAM	05/01/82	INVERURIE	13/7/98	5' 9"	10ST 10LB	FWD	ABERDEEN 'S' FORM
2	McGUIRE	PHILIP		04/03/80	GLASGOW	19/9/97	6' 0"	12ST 5LB	DEF	DYCE JUNIORS
-	McINNES	ASHLEY		22/04/87	ABERDEEN	9/7/03	5' 7"	9ST 8LB	MID	ABERDEEN YOUTHS
3	McNAUGHTON	KEVIN	PAUL	28/08/82	DUNDEE	20/7/99	5' 10"	11ST 6LB	DEF	ABERDEEN 'S' FORM
16	MORRISON	SCOTT	ALEXANDER	23/05/84	ABERDEEN	26/5/99	5' 9"	11ST 11LB	DEF	COLONY PARK
18	MUIRHEAD	SCOTT		08/05/84	PAISLEY	27/9/01	6' 1"	11ST 13LB	MID	NEILSTON THISTLE
-	NEILL	BRIAN		11/01/88	ABERDEEN	1/7/04	5' 7"	10ST 2LB	MID	ABERDEEN YOUTHS
-	O'LEARY	RYAN		24/08/87	GLASGOW	9/7/03	6' 0"	11ST 11LB	DEF	ABERDEEN YOUTHS
24	PASQUINELLI	FERNANDO	ADRIAN	13/03/80	BUENOS AIRES	18/8/04	6' 0"	13ST 2LB	FWD	LIVINGSTON
1	PREECE	DAVID	DOUGLAS	26/08/76	SUNDERLAND	30/7/99	6' 2"	13ST 2LB	GK	DARLINGTON
6	SEVERIN	SCOTT	DEREK	15/02/79	STIRLING	5/7/04	5' 11"	12ST 12LB	MID	HEARTS
-	SHIELDS	GARY		28/04/88	GLASGOW	1/7/04	5' 7"	10ST 2LB	FWD	ABERDEEN YOUTHS
19	STEWART	JOHN		08/03/85	BELLSHILL	13/1/03	5' 10"	9ST 9LB	FWD	AIRDRIE UNITED
-	THOMAS	MARK		03/01/88	GLASGOW	7/7/04	5' 8.5"	12ST 0LB	DEF	ABERDEEN YOUTHS
-	THOMSON	ROBERT		24/05/87	BELLSHILL	9/7/03	5' 8"	10ST 3LB	DEF	ABERDEEN YOUTHS
17	TIERNAN	FERGUS	ALEXANDER	03/01/82	ABEOKUTA	13/7/98	6' 2"	11ST 12LB	MID	ABERDEEN 'S' FORM
7	TOSH	STEVEN	WILLIAM	27/04/73	KIRKCALDY	8/1/03	5' 10"	11ST 12LB	MID	FALKIRK
23	WHELAN	NOEL	DAVID	30/12/74	LEEDS	6/8/04	6' 2"	13ST 6LB	FWD	MILLWALL

TICKET INFORMATION

SEASON TICKET INFORMATION

	ADULT	CONC	U12	1 ADULT /2CONC	2 ADULT 2 CONC	1 ADULT 2 U12	2 ADULT 2 U12
MAIN STAND	350	198	125	647	898	538	825
MERKLAND	220	98	45	367	538	288	485
RDSTAND	260	135	80	463	655	380	600
RDS CENTRE PADDED	350	198	125	647	898	538	825
SOUTH STAND	260	135	80	463	655	380	600

MATCH TICKET INFORMATION

	ADULT	CONC.	UNDER 12
MAIN STAND	25	18	10
MERKLAND	15	8	5
RDSTAND	20	15	8
RDS CENTRE PADDED	25	18	10
SOUTH STAND	20	15	8

THE DONS' 10 YEAR LEAGUE RECORD

SEASON	DIV	P	W	D	L	F	A	PTS.
1994-95	P	36	10	11	15	43	46	41
1995-96	P	36	16	7	13	52	45	55
1996-97	P	36	10	14	12	45	54	44
1997-98	P	36	9	12	15	39	53	39
1998-99	SPL	36	10	7	19	43	71	37
1999-00	SPL	36	9	6	21	44	83	33
2000-01	SPL	38	11	12	15	45	52	45
2001-02	SPL	38	16	7	15	51	49	55
2002-03	SPL	38	13	10	15	41	54	49
2003-04	SPL	38	9	7	22	39	63	34

The dons stats 2003/04

SEASON STATS 2003/04

Player columns (left to right): PREECE D., McGUIRE P., McNAUGHTON K., ANDERSON R., McQUILKEN J., HART M., TOSH S., HEIKKINEN M., SHEERIN P., HINDS L., ZDRILIC D., MACKIE D., BOOTH S., CLARK C., DELOUMEAUX E., MUIRHEAD S., BIRD M., TIERNAN F., DIAMOND A., FOSTER R., RUTKIEWICZ K., MORRISON S., PRUNTY B., STEWART J., SOUTAR K., BUCKLEY R., HIGGINS C., ESSON R., O'LEARY R., LOMBARDI M., McCULLOCH M., CONSODINE A., DONALD D., TARDITI S.

DATE	VENUE	OPPONENTS	ATT	RES
-AUG	A	HEARTS	14,260	0-2
6-AUG	H	RANGERS	16,348	2-3
8-AUG	H	DUNFERMLINE ATH	10,810	1-2
0-AUG	A	HIBERNIAN	10,682	1-1
3-SEP	H	PARTICK THISTLE	10,597	2-1
0-SEP	A	DUNDEE	7,887	0-2
7-SEP	H	LIVINGSTON	10,307	0-3
-OCT	A	KILMARNOCK	6,023	3-1
3-OCT	H	DUNDEE UNITED	11,234	2-1
5-OCT	A	CELTIC	59,574	0-4
-NOV	H	MOTHERWELL	9,895	0-3
-NOV	H	HEARTS	9,687	0-1
2-NOV	A	RANGERS	49,962	0-3
9-NOV	A	DUNFERMLINE ATH	5,254	2-2
-DEC	H	HIBERNIAN	7,863	3-1
3-DEC	A	PARTICK THISTLE	5,189	3-0
0-DEC	H	DUNDEE	10,354	2-2
7-DEC	A	LIVINGSTON	6,020	1-1
-JAN	H	KILMARNOCK	11,699	3-1
7-JAN	A	DUNDEE UNITED	8,888	†2-3
4-JAN	H	CELTIC	16,452	1-3
1-FEB	A	HEARTS	11,236	0-1
4-FEB	H	RANGERS	15,815	1-1
1-FEB	H	DUNFERMLINE ATH	11,035	2-0
4-FEB	A	MOTHERWELL	5,220	0-1
8-FEB	A	HIBERNIAN	10,416	1-1
-MAR	H	PARTICK THISTLE	7,395	0-0
3-MAR	A	DUNDEE	6,839	1-1
1-MAR	H	LIVINGSTON	7,477	1-2
7-MAR	A	KILMARNOCK	7,251	1-3
8-APR	H	DUNDEE UNITED	8,449	3-0
8-APR	H	MOTHERWELL	7,246	0-2
1-APR	A	CELTIC	57,385	2-1
24-APR	A	LIVINGSTON	3,133	0-2
-MAY	A	PARTICK THISTLE	2,839	0-2
3-MAY	H	HIBERNIAN	6,781	0-1
2-MAY	A	KILMARNOCK	4,987	0-4
5-MAY	H	DUNDEE	7,878	1-2

TOTAL FULL APPEARANCES: 36 16 15 25 7 10 24 38 27 23 23 4 20 18 8 24 3 17 12 16 26 6 3 1 6 4 2 2 1 1

TOTAL SUB APPEARANCES: 1 2 1 2 6 7 8 12 1 5 3 8 2 3 2 6 1 12 5 2 2 1 2 1 1

TOTAL GOALS SCORED: 2 5 3 1 6 4 8 1 2 2 1 1 2

Bold figures denote goalscorers. † denotes opponent's own goal.

LEADING GOALSCORERS:

SEASON	DIV	GOALS	PLAYER
94-95	P	15	W. Dodds
95-96	P	9	S. Booth, J. Miller
96-97	P	15	W. Dodds
97-98	P	10	W. Dodds
98-99	SPL	14	E. Jess
99-00	SPL	9	A. Stavrum
00-01	SPL	17	A. Stavrum
01-02	SPL	13	R. Winters
02-03	SPL	8	P. Sheerin
03-04	SPL	8	S. Booth

MILESTONES:

YEAR OF FORMATION: 1903
MOST CAPPED PLAYER: Alex McLeish
NO. OF CAPS: 77
MOST LEAGUE POINTS IN A SEASON:
64 (Premier Division – Season 1992/93) (44 games) (2 Points for a Win)
MOST LEAGUE GOALS SCORED BY A PLAYER IN A SEASON:
Benny Yorston (Season 1929/30)
NO. OF GOALS SCORED: 38
RECORD ATTENDANCE: 45,061
(-v- Heart of Midlothian – 13.3.1954)
RECORD VICTORY: 13-0 (-v- Peterhead – Scottish Cup, 9.2.1923)
RECORD DEFEAT: 0-8 (-v- Celtic - Division 1, 30.1.1965)

ABERDEEN PLAYING KITS SEASON 2004/05

FIRST KIT   SECOND KIT   THIRD KIT

Celtic

CELTIC FC
Celtic Park, Glasgow, G40 3RE
CHAIRMAN
Brian Quinn, C.B.E.
CELTIC PLC DIRECTORS
Brian Quinn, C.B.E., Dermot F. Desmond,
Eric J. Riley, Tom Allison,
Eric Hagman C.B.E. & Peter T. Lawwell
**CELTIC FOOTBALL & ATHLETIC
COMPANY DIRECTORS**
Kevin Sweeney, John S. Keane, Michael A.
McDonald, Eric J. Riley & Peter T. Lawwell
CHIEF EXECUTIVE
Peter T. Lawwell
COMPANY SECRETARY
Robert M. Howat
FOOTBALL MANAGER
Martin O'Neill
FOOTBALL ASSISTANT MANAGER
John Robertson
FIRST TEAM COACH
Steve Walford
RESERVE COACH
Kenny McDowall
DIRECTOR OF YOUTH DEVELOPMENT
Tommy Burns
YOUTH DEVELOPMENT MANAGER
John Stephenson
HEAD YOUTH COACH
Willie McStay
CLUB DOCTOR
Roddy McDonald
PHYSIOTHERAPIST
Tim Wilkinson
**FOOTBALL SAFETY OFFICERS'
ASSOCIATION REPRESENTATIVE**
Ronnie Hawthorn (0141) 551 4256
COMMERCIAL MANAGER
David McNally (0141) 551 4246
LOTTERY MANAGER
John Maguire (0141) 551 4006
GROUNDSMAN
John Hayes
KIT CONTROLLER
John Clark
PUBLIC RELATIONS/MEDIA LIASON MANAGER
Iain Jamieson (0141) 551 4235
MATCHDAY PROGRAMME EDITOR
Paul Cuddihy
TELEPHONES
Ground/General Enquiries 0845 671 1888
Celtic Home Ticketline 0870 060 1888
All other Ticket Enquiries 0870 161 1888
International Enquiries +44 141 627 1888
Celtic View (0141) 551 4218
Stadium (Matchday) Catering (0141) 551 9955
Mail Order Enquiries 0845 077 1888
Museum (0141) 551 4308
Ticket Hotline Fax (0141) 551 4223
Fax (0141) 551 8106
EMAIL & INTERNET ADDRESS
atraynor@celticfc.co.uk
www.celticfc.net
CLUB SHOPS
SUPERSTORE, Celtic Park, Glasgow, G40 3RE
Tel (0141) 551 4231
21 HIGH STREET, Glasgow, G1 1LX
Tel (0141) 552 7630
STORES ALSO AT: Argyle St, Sauchiehall St
and 40 Dundas St, Glasgow.
Frederick St, Edinburgh & Glasgow Airport
OFFICIAL SUPPORTERS CLUB
Celtic Supporters Association,
1524 London Road, Glasgow G40 3RJ
Tel (0141) 556 1882/554 6250/554 6342
CAPTAIN
Team Captain: Jackie McNamara
Club Captain: Paul Lambert
SHIRT SPONSOR
Carling
KIT SUPPLIER
Umbro

LIST OF PLAYERS 2004/05

SQUAD NO.	PLAYERS SURNAME	FIRST NAME	MIDDLE NAME	DATE OF BIRTH	PLACE OF BIRTH	DATE SIGNED	HEIGHT FT INS	WEIGHT ST LBS	POSITION ON PITCH	PREVIOUS CLUB
17	AGATHE	DIDIER		16/08/75	ST. PIERRE LA REUNION	1/9/00	5' 11"	12ST 0LB	FWD	HIBERNIAN
6	BALDE	DIANBOBO		05/10/75	MARSEILLE	25/7/01	6' 3"	14ST 9LB	DEF	TOULOUSE
37	BEATTIE	CRAIG		16/01/84	GLASGOW	4/7/03	6' 1"	12ST 12LB	FWD	CELTIC YOUTHS
-	CADDIS	PAUL		19/04/88	IRVINE	26/7/04	5' 7"	11ST 1LB	DEF	CELTIC YOUTHS
27	CAMARA	HENRI		10/05/77	DAKAR	2/8/04	5' 8"	11ST 0LB	FWD	WOLVERHAMPTON WANDERERS
-	CHRISTIE	GARETH		08/01/87	DUBLIN	16/7/03	6' 0"	13ST 5LB	DEF	HOME FARM B.C.
-	CONROY	RYAN		28/04/87	VALE OF LEVEN	3/7/03	5' 10"	10ST 8LB	FWD	CELTIC YOUTHS
49	CUTHBERT	SCOTT		15/06/87	ALEXANDRIA	16/7/03	6' 2"	14ST 0LB	DEF	CELTIC YOUTHS
20	DOUGLAS	ROBERT	JAMES	24/04/72	LANARK	18/10/00	6' 3"	14ST 12LB	GK	DUNDEE
-	DUNPHY	GARY		13/01/88	WATERFORD	27/7/04	5' 10"	10ST 10LB	MID	FERRYBANK AFC
-	ELLIOT	JAMES	CHARLES	22/12/86	GLASGOW	3/7/03	5' 7"	12ST 11LB	MID	CELTIC YOUTHS
12	FERNANDEZ	DAVID		20/01/76	CORUNA	31/5/02	5' 9"	11ST 2LB	MID	LIVINGSTON
-	FERRY	SIMON		11/01/88	DUNDEE	19/11/04	5' 8"	11ST 0LB	MID	CELTIC 'S' FORM
-	FOX	SCOTT		28/06/87	BELLSHILL	24/7/03	6' 0"	12ST 0LB	GK	DUNDEE UNITED
-	GARDYNE	MICHAEL		23/01/86	DUNDEE	10/1/02	5' 7"	10ST 0LB	MID/FWD	CELTIC YOUTHS
7	GIROLDO JUNIOR	(JUNINHO)	OSWALDO	22/02/73	SAO PAULO	27/8/04	5' 5"	9ST 10LB	FWD	MIDDLESBROUGH
-	GRANT	CHARLES	JOSEPH	27/01/87	BELLSHILL	14/1/03	5' 6"	10ST 3LB	MID	CELTIC YOUTHS
-	HARRIS	ROSS		16/04/85	GLASGOW	16/1/02	5' 11"	11ST 11LB	FWD	CELTIC YOUTHS
10	HARTSON	JOHN		05/04/75	SWANSEA	2/8/01	6' 1"	15ST 0LB	FWD	COVENTRY CITY
21	HEDMAN	MAGNUS	CARL	19/03/73	STOCKHOLM	16/7/04	6' 4"	14ST 10LB	GK	ANCONA
-	HUDSON	KIRK		12/12/86	ROCHFORD	16/7/03	6' 0"	9ST 11LB	FWD	IPSWICH TOWN
-	HUTCHISON	PAUL		19/05/87	WALLSEND	16/7/03	6' 0"	12ST 6LB	DEF	SUNDERLAND
-	IRVINE	GARY		17/03/85	BELLSHILL	6/7/01	5' 11"	12ST 0LB	DEF	CELTIC YOUTHS
41	KENNEDY	JOHN		18/08/83	BELLSHILL	20/8/99	6' 2"	13ST 7LB	DEF	CELTIC 'S' FORM
14	LAMBERT	PAUL		07/08/69	PAISLEY	7/11/97	5' 11"	11ST 8LB	MID	BV09 BORUSSIA DORTMUND
16	LAURSEN	ULRIK	ROSENLOEV	28/02/76	ODENSE	1/8/02	6' 3"	14ST 0LB	DEF	HIBERNIAN
-	LAWSON	PAUL	WILLIAM	15/05/84	ABERDEEN	10/7/00	5' 9"	11ST 10LB	MID	CELTIC 'S' FORM
18	LENNON	NEIL	FRANCIS	25/06/71	LURGAN	8/12/00	5' 9"	13ST 2LB	MID	LEICESTER CITY
29	MALONEY	SHAUN	RICHARD	24/01/83	MIRRI	7/7/99	5' 6"	11ST 0LB	FWD	CELTIC YOUTH INITIATIVE
22	MARSHALL	DAVID	JAMES	05/03/85	GLASGOW	6/7/01	6' 2"	14ST 3LB	GK	CELTIC YOUTHS
-	McBRIDE	KEVIN		14/06/81	BELLSHILL	10/7/98	5' 6"	9ST 7LB	MID	CELTIC B.C.
-	McCAFFERTY	RYAN		22/04/87	FALKIRK	13/1/04	5' 11"	10ST 10LB	DEF	CELTIC YOUTHS
46	McGEADY	AIDEN		04/04/86	GLASGOW	9/7/02	5' 10"	11ST 4LB	MID	CELTIC 'S' FORM
-	McGEOUGH	JOHN	CHRISTOPHER	24/05/88	GLASGOW	26/7/04	5' 9"	11ST 0LB	FWD	CELTIC YOUTHS
-	McGLINCHEY	MICHAEL	RYAN	07/01/87	NEW ZEALAND	3/7/03	5' 8"	9ST 6LB	FWD	CELTIC YOUTHS
47	McGOVERN	MICHAEL		12/07/84	ENNISKILLEN	24/7/01	6' 2"	14ST 0LB	GK	CELTIC YOUTHS
-	McGOWAN	PAUL		07/10/87	BELLSHILL	28/1/04	5' 6"	10ST 8LB	FWD	CELTIC YOUTHS
44	McMANUS	STEPHEN		10/09/82	LANARK	9/7/03	6' 2"	13ST 0LB	DEF	CELTIC 'S' FORM
4	McNAMARA	JACKIE		24/10/73	GLASGOW	4/10/95	5' 8"	9ST 7LB	MID	DUNFERMLINE ATHLETIC
25	McPARLAND	ANTHONY	PATRICK	20/09/82	RUTHERGLEN	20/7/99	5' 7"	10ST 4LB	MID	CELTIC 'S' FORM
-	MILLAR	MARK	JOHN	23/02/88	GREENOCK	26/7/04	5' 8"	9ST 12LB	MID	CELTIC YOUTHS
-	MULGREW	CHARLES	PATRICK	06/03/86	GLASGOW	2/7/02	6' 2"	13ST 1LB	MID	CELTIC YOUTHS
-	O'BRIEN	JAMES	JOHN	28/09/87	GLASGOW	3/7/03	6' 0"	11ST 11LB	FWD	CELTIC YOUTHS
-	O'CARROLL	DIARMUID		16/03/87	KILLARNEY	16/7/03	5' 11"	11ST 11LB	FWD	HOME FARM B.C.
48	O'DEA	DARREN		04/02/87	DUBLIN	16/7/03	6' 1"	13ST 0LB	DEF	HOME FARM B.C.
11	PEARSON	STEPHEN	PAUL	02/10/82	LANARK	9/1/04	6' 1"	11ST 6LB	MID	MOTHERWELL
19	PETROV	STILIAN		05/07/79	BULGARIA	6/8/99	5' 10"	12ST 1LB	MID	CSKA SOFIA
15	PETTA	BOBBY	ALFRED	06/08/74	ROTTERDAM	14/7/99	5' 7"	11ST 3LB	MID	IPSWICH TOWN
-	QUINN	ROCCO		07/09/86	GLASGOW	11/7/02	5' 11"	12ST 0LB	MID	CELTIC YOUTHS
-	REID	CRAIG	ROBERT	26/02/86	IRVINE	2/7/02	6' 0"	11ST 7LB	DEF	CELTIC YOUTHS
-	RICHARDSON	DEAN		02/03/87	BELLSHILL	3/7/03	5' 8"	10ST 8LB	DEF	CELTIC B.C.
-	RILEY	NICHOLAS		10/05/86	EDINBURGH	11/7/02	5' 10"	9ST 11LB	GK	CELTIC YOUTHS
9	SUTTON	CHRISTOPHER	ROY	10/03/73	NOTTINGHAM	11/7/00	6' 3"	14ST 0LB	FWD	CHELSEA
3	SYLLA	MOHAMMED		13/03/77	CONAKRY	2/8/01	6' 0"	11ST 9LB	MID	ST. JOHNSTONE
-	THOMPSON	ALAN		22/12/73	NEWCASTLE	1/9/00	6' 0"	13ST 0LB	MID	ASTON VILLA
5	VALGAEREN	JOOS		03/03/76	LOUVAIN	28/7/00	6' 1"	14ST 0LB	DEF	RODA J.C.
23	VARGA	STANISLAV		08/10/72	SLOVAKIA	16/7/03	6' 4"	14ST 3LB	DEF	SUNDERLAND
33	WALLACE	ROSS		23/05/85	DUNDEE	13/7/01	5' 7"	10ST 2LB	FWD	CELTIC 'S' FORM
-	WALSH	GARY		01/07/87	DUBLIN	16/7/03	5' 7"	11ST 3LB	MID	HOME FARM B.C.
-	WOOD	SANDY		02/04/86	ABERDEEN	10/7/03	6' 1"	13ST 7LB	GK	ABERDEEN

TICKET INFORMATION

SEASON TICKET INFORMATION

	ADULT	U16/65+	ADULT & U16/65+
SOUTH STAND REAR	530	305	N/A
SOUTH STAND FRONT	475	200	505
SOUTH WEST CORNER STAND	475	200	505
NORTH STAND UPPER	400/435/510	285/315/370*	N/A
NORTH STAND LOWER	400/435/485/530	200/270/305	N/A
JOCK STEIN STAND UPPER	435/510	315/370*	N/A
JOCK STEIN STAND LOWER	400/435/615	285/315/405*	N/A
LISBON LIONS STAND UPPER	370/440/435/510	235/315/370*	N/A
LISBON LIONS STAND LOWER	370/400/410/435	155	430

*65+ CONCESSION ONLY

LEAGUE ADMISSION PRICES

	ADULT	U16/65+
SOUTH STAND REAR	25	14
SOUTH STAND FRONT	25	14
SOUTH WEST CORNER STAND	25	14
NORTH STAND UPPER	25	
NORTH STAND LOWER	25	14
JOCK STEIN STAND UPPER	25	
JOCK STEIN STAND LOWER	25/30	
LISBON LIONS STAND UPPER	25	
LISBON LIONS STAND LOWER	25	14
RESTRICTED VIEW	22	12

* Please Note: Above prices exclude matches versus Rangers

THE BHOYS' 10 YEAR LEAGUE RECORD

SEASON	DIV	P	W	D	L	F	A	PTS
1994-95	P	36	11	18	7	39	33	51
1995-96	P	36	24	11	1	74	25	83
1996-97	P	36	23	6	7	78	32	75
1997-98	P	36	22	8	6	64	24	74
1998-99	SPL	36	21	8	7	84	35	71
1999-00	SPL	36	21	6	9	90	38	69
2000-01	SPL	38	31	4	3	90	29	97
2001-02	SPL	38	33	4	1	94	18	103
2002-03	SPL	38	31	4	3	98	26	97
2003-04	SPL	38	31	5	2	105	25	98

SEASON STATS 2003/04

DATE	VENUE	OPPONENTS	ATT	RES	DOUGLAS R.	MJALLBY J.	VALGAEREN J.	BALDE D.	THOMPSON A.	PETROV S.	LENNON N.	LAMBERT P.	AGATHE D.	LARSSON H.	MALONEY S.	SMITH J.	MILLER L.	HEDMAN M.	VARGA S.	McNAMARA J.	SYLLA M.	BEATTIE C.	HARTSON J.	CRAINEY S.	SUTTON C.	GRAY M.	KENNEDY J.	WALLACE R.	PEARSON S.	MARSHALL D.	McMANUS S.	McGEADY A.
AUG	A	DUNFERMLINE ATH	10,082	0 - 0	1	2	3	4	5	6	7	8	9	10	11	12	13															
6-AUG	H	DUNDEE UNITED	57,004	5 - 0			3	4	8^1	6				9^1	10^1	11^1	14	7	1	2	5^1	12	13									
3-AUG	A	PARTICK THISTLE	9,045	2 - 1	1		3	4	9^1	6	7	8^1		10	11		12			2	5		13									
0-AUG	H	LIVINGSTON	57,062	5 - 1				4	8^1	6	5			9	10^3	11^1		7	1	2	3	13	12	14								
3-SEP	A	DUNDEE	10,647	1 - 0				4^1	8	6	7			9	10	14		12	1	2	5	13	11	3								
0-SEP	H	MOTHERWELL	57,492	3 - 0				4	5	6	7			10^1	12^1		14	1	2	3	8		11		9^1	13						
7-SEP	A	HIBERNIAN	12,032	2 - 1				4	5^1	6	7			8	10^1	11		12	1	2	3		9									
OCT	A	RANGERS	49,825	1 - 0					5	6	7			8	10			4	1	2	3		11^1		9	12						
3-OCT	H	HEARTS	59,511	5 - 0				4	5	6	7			8	10^1	12		9^2	1	2^1	3		11			13	14					
5-OCT	A	ABERDEEN	59,574	4 - 0				3	4	5		7		8	10^3	13		6	1	2		14	11		9^1	12						
NOV	A	KILMARNOCK	12,460	5 - 0					4		6	7		10	13^1			8	1	2	3	12	11^1		9^3	5		14				
NOV	H	DUNFERMLINE ATH	58,258	5 - 0	1	14		4		6	7			5	10^1	8			2^1	3	13	11^2	9				12					
2-NOV	A	DUNDEE UNITED	10,802	5 - 1	15	3		4	5	6	7			8	10^2	14		9	1	2	12				11^3							
9-NOV	H	PARTICK THISTLE	58,194	3 - 1		3				13	7			10^1			6	1	2		4		11		9^2	12	5	8				
DEC	A	LIVINGSTON	8,065	2 - 0		12		4	8^1	6	7			10			9	1	2	3			11^1	5								
3-DEC	H	DUNDEE	57,539	3 - 2	1	3		4^1	5	6	7			10^1	11	12	8	2					9		13^1							
1-DEC	A	MOTHERWELL	10,513	2 - 0	1	3		4^1	5	6	7			10		12	8	2				11^1	9									
7-DEC	H	HIBERNIAN	59,542	6 - 0	1	3		4	8	6^1	7			10^1			12	2	5		14	11^2	9^2		13							
JAN	H	RANGERS	59,042	3 - 0	1			4	5^1	6^1	7			8	10		12	2^1	3			11	9									
3-JAN	A	HEARTS	13,753	1 - 0	1			4		6^1	7			8	10			2	3	12	11		9		5							
4-JAN	A	ABERDEEN	16,452	3 - 1	1					6^1	7			8	10^1			2	3		11		9	4		5^1						
1-JAN	H	KILMARNOCK	59,046	5 - 1	1	14			6	7	13	8^1	10^1	12				2	3		11^2	9	4		5^1							
1-FEB	A	DUNFERMLINE ATH	9,718	4 - 1	1	12		5^1	6	7	14	8	10^2	13				2^1	3		11	4	9									
4-FEB	H	DUNDEE UNITED	58,671	2 - 1	1			4	5	6	7	13	8	10	12^1			2	3		11^1		9									
2-FEB	A	PARTICK THISTLE	8,131	4 - 1	1			4	8	6	7	13		10	12			2^2	5	14	11^2	3	9									
9-FEB	H	LIVINGSTON	57,949	5 - 1	1	14		4	5^2	6	7			8	10			2			11^1	3	9^1									
4-MAR	A	MOTHERWELL	57,580	1 - 1				4		6		8	13	12^1		7		2		5	10		3	11	9	1						
7-MAR	A	DUNDEE	8,593	2 - 1				4	8	6^1	7			10	11^1		13	2	3	5	14		12		9	1						
1-MAR	A	HIBERNIAN	9,456	4 - 0		12		4		6	7	8		11^2	10^2		14		2		13		3		9	1	5					
8-MAR	A	RANGERS	49,909	2 - 1				4	5^1	6	7			8	10^1			12	2				11		3	9	1					
-APR	H	HEARTS	59,295	2 - 2				4	5	13		8	7^1	10			12	3	2		11^1				9	1	6					
8-APR	A	KILMARNOCK	14,516	1 - 0	1	5		4		6^1	7	8	11	10			12	3	2						9							
1-APR	H	ABERDEEN	57,385	1 - 2				13		6	7	8	9	10^1		12	14	3	2	4			11			1	5				
5-APR	A	HEARTS	52,112	1 - 1	2			4		6	7		11	10		5	9	3		12						1						8^1
-MAY	A	DUNFERMLINE ATH	59,719	1 - 2	2			5			7	8		10^1		4	13	3			11				12	1	6	9				
-MAY	H	RANGERS	59,180	1 - 0	2			4	5	6	7		8	10			3	2			11^1				9	1		12				
2-MAY	A	MOTHERWELL	7,749	1 - 1	2					7	8			5	6						11^1				10	9	1	4	3			
6-MAY	H	DUNDEE UNITED	58,364	2 - 1				4	5	6	7		8	10^2			3	2			11				12	9	1					
TOTAL FULL APPEARANCES					15	10	4	30	26	33	35	9	26	36	7	4	13	12	35	26	5	2	14	1	25	2	9	4	16	11	5	3
TOTAL SUB APPEARANCES					1	3	3	1		2		4	1	1	10	7	12			1	9	8	1	1		5	3	4	1			1
TOTAL GOALS SCORED								3	10	6		1	5	30	5		2			6	1		1	9		19		1	1	3		1

Bold figures denote goalscorers. † denotes opponent's own goal.

LEADING GOALSCORERS:

SEASON	DIV	GOALS	PLAYER
94-95	P	8	J. Collins
95-96	P	26	P. Van Hooijdonk
96-97	P	25	J. Cadete
97-98	P	16	H. Larsson
98-99	SPL	29	H. Larsson
99-00	SPL	25	M. Viduka
00-01	SPL	35	H. Larsson
01-02	SPL	29	H. Larsson
02-03	SPL	28	H. Larsson
03-04	SPL	30	H. Larsson

MILESTONES:

YEAR OF FORMATION: 1888
MOST CAPPED PLAYER: Paul McStay
NO. OF CAPS: 76
MOST LEAGUE POINTS IN A SEASON:
72 (Premier Division – Season 1987/88) (2 Points for a Win),
103 (SPL – Season 2001/02) (3 Points for a Win)
MOST LEAGUE GOALS SCORED BY A PLAYER IN A SEASON:
Jimmy McGrory (Season 1935/36)
NO. OF GOALS SCORED: 50
RECORD ATTENDANCE: 92,000 (-v- Rangers – 1.1.1938)
RECORD VICTORY: 11-0 (-v- Dundee – Division 1, 26.10.1895)
RECORD DEFEAT: 0-8 (-v- Motherwell - Division 1, 30.4.1937)

CELTIC PLAYING KITS SEASON 2004/05

FIRST KIT   SECOND KIT   THIRD KIT

DUNDEE
Dens Park Stadium,
Sandeman Street, Dundee, DD3 7JY

CHAIRMAN
James M. Marr

DIRECTORS
Peter Marr

ASSOCIATE DIRECTORS
Dave Forbes, Bob Hynd & James L. Thomson

CHIEF EXECUTIVE
Peter Marr

COMPANY SECRETARY
A. Ritchie Robertson

OFFICE ADMINISTRATOR
Laura Hayes

MANAGER
Jim Duffy

RESERVE COACH
Ray Farningham

GOALKEEPING COACH
Paul Mathers

YOUTH CO/ORDINATOR / U17 COACH
Kenny Cameron

**COMMUNITY COACH /
SCHOOLS DEVELOPMENT**
Kevin Lee

YOUTH DEVELOPMENT & U19 COACH
Stevie Campbell

CLUB DOCTORS
Dr. Phyllis Windsor, M.D., FRCR. &
Dr. John Vernon

PHYSIOTHERAPIST
Jim Law

MASSEUR
Jack Cashley

**FOOTBALL SAFETY OFFICERS'
ASSOCIATION REPRESENTATIVES**
John Malone & Jim Thomson

STADIUM & OPERATIONS MANAGER
Jim Thomson (01382) 815250

TICKET OFFICE MANAGER
Neil Cosgrove

GROUNDSMAN
Brian Robertson

KIT MANAGER
Brian Duncan

COMMERCIAL SECRETARY
Kirsty Cameron

MEDIA LIAISON OFFICER
Niall Scott

TELEPHONES
Football/Manager (01382) 826104
Administration/Accounts/
Youth Development (01382) 889966
Commercial/Marketing (01382) 884450
Ticket Office (01382) 889966 (option 1)
Operations Manager (01382) 815250
Fax (01382) 832284
Commercial Fax (01382) 858963

E-MAIL & INTERNET ADDRESS
laura@dundeefc.co.uk
www.dundeefc.co.uk

CLUB SHOP
DFC XARA Shop, situated between Main
Stand and Bobby Cox Stand

OFFICIAL SUPPORTERS CLUB
Contact: Norrie Price (01224) 639967

TEAM CAPTAIN
Barry Smith

SHIRT SPONSOR
Magners Original

KIT SUPPLIER
XARA

Dundee

LIST OF PLAYERS 2004/05

SQUAD NO.	PLAYERS SURNAME	FIRST NAME	MIDDLE NAME	DATE OF BIRTH	PLACE OF BIRTH	DATE SIGNED	HEIGHT FT INS	WEIGHT ST LBS	POSITION ON PITCH	PREVIOUS CLUB
-	ALLISON	MARK		22/02/87	PERTH	29/8/03	6'0"	11ST 13LB	DEF	DUNDEE YOUTHS
11	ANDERSON	IAIN	WILLIAM	23/07/77	GLASGOW	20/7/04	5'8"	9ST 7LB	FWD	GRIMSBY TOWN
14	BARRETT	NEIL	WILLIAM	24/12/81	LONDON	9/8/04	5'10"	11ST 0LB	MID	PORTSMOUTH
-	BELL	MARK	ALEXANDER	09/03/87	DUNDEE	7/6/04	5'7"	11ST 9LB	DEF	DUNDEE YOUTHS
-	BLACK	DAVID	HUGH	10/04/87	DUNDEE	7/6/04	5'8"	11ST 0LB	DEF	DUNDEE YOUTHS
12	BRADY	GARRY		07/09/76	GLASGOW	30/8/02	5'8"	10ST 10LB	MID	PORTSMOUTH
25	CAMERON	DOUGLAS		08/02/83	DUNDEE	8/9/00		12ST 0LB	MID	DUNDEE 'S' FORM
23	CLARK	NEIL		12/04/84	DUNDEE	13/7/02	5'11"	11ST 10LB	MID	DUNDEE 'S' FORM
-	CUMMING	KEVIN	NEIL	04/04/86	DUNDEE	20/1/03	6'0.5"	11ST 8LB	FWD	DUNDEE YOUTHS
-	DEASLEY	BRYAN		29/06/88	DUNDEE	1/6/04	5'7"	10ST 5LB	FWD	DUNDEE YOUTHS
-	DIXON	PAUL	ANDREW	22/11/86	ABERDEEN	10/7/03	5'9"	11ST 3LB	DEF	DUNDEE YOUTHS
30	FOTHERINGHAM	MARK	M'KAY	22/10/83	DUNDEE	28/8/03	5'11"	12ST 10LB	MID	CELTIC
-	GATES	SCOTT		14/04/88	WERBERG	7/6/04	5'7"	10ST 3LB	FWD	DUNDEE YOUTHS
-	HAY	GRAHAM		11/06/87	DUNDEE	10/7/03	6'0"	11ST 12LB	DEF	DUNDEE 'S' FORM
24	HEGARTY	CHRISTOPHER		24/07/84	DUNDEE	5/10/01	5'8"	10ST 6LB	MID	DUNDEE YOUTHS
-	HENDRY	ROBERT	DAVID	19/01/87	DUNDEE	10/7/03	5'9"	11ST 2LB	MID	DUNDEE YOUTHS
16	HERNANDEZ	JONAY	MIGUEL	15/02/79	VENEZUELA	26/7/02	5'11"	11ST 1LB	DEF/MID	REAL MADRID
4	HUTCHINSON	THOMAS	PETER	23/02/82	KINGSTON	30/8/02	6'0"	12ST 6LB	DEF	FULHAM
15	JABLONSKI	NEIL		09/03/83	KIRKCALDY	8/9/00	5'9"	11ST 0LB	MID	DUNDEE 'S' FORM
13	JACK	KELVIN	KYRON	29/04/76	TRINIDAD & TOBAGO	5/8/04	6'3"	16ST 0LB	GK	READING
7	LARSEN	GLEN	ATLE	24/08/82	NORWAY	20/7/04	5'8"	10ST 7LB	MID	VALERENGA
9	LOVELL	STEVE		06/12/80	AMERSHAM	23/8/02	6'0"	12ST 11LB	FWD	PORTSMOUTH
17	M'DONALD	CALLUM		31/05/83	PERTH	8/9/00	6'1"	11ST 7LB	DEF	DUNDEE 'S' FORM
5	MANN	ROBERT	ALEXANDER	11/01/74	DUNDEE	7/6/04	6'3"	14ST 7LB	DEF	INVERNESS C.T.
-	M'DONALD	ANDREW	JAMES	06/02/87	DUNDEE	10/7/03	5'8"	9ST 4LB	MID	DUNDEE YOUTHS
-	M'GOWAN	MICHAEL	VALENTINE	22/02/85	GLASGOW	12/8/04	5'7"	10ST 7LB	MID	STENHOUSEMUIR
-	M'LAUGHLIN	GARRY		08/02/86	DUNDEE	13/7/02	5'6"	9ST 1LB	MID	DUNDEE YOUTHS
20	M'NALLY	STEPHEN		15/03/84	DUNDEE	29/3/02	5'8.5"	11ST 10LB	DEF	DOWNFIELD JUNIORS
30	MURRAY	SCOTT	ROBERT	03/03/88	GLASGOW	6/8/04	6'2"	12ST 0LB	GK	KILMARNOCK
-	REILLY	ANDREW		25/05/86	DUNDEE	13/7/02	5'7"	10ST 8LB	MID	DUNDEE 'S' FORM
18	ROBB	STEVEN		08/03/82	PERTH	25/8/99	5'6"	9ST 4LB	MID	DUNDEE 'S' FORM
-	ROBERTSON	EUAN		25/01/87	DUNDEE	31/1/03	5'10"	11ST 7LB	MID	DUNDEE 'S' FORM
22	ROBERTSON	SCOTT		07/04/85	DUNDEE	13/7/02	6'0"	11ST 4LB	MID	DUNDEE 'S' FORM
3	SANCHO	BRENT		13/03/77	TRINIDAD & TOBAGO	31/7/03	5'11"	12ST 2LB	DEF	PORTLAND TIMBERS
2	SMITH	BARRY	MARTIN	19/02/74	PAISLEY	8/12/95	5'10"	12ST 0LB	DEF	CELTIC
1	SOUTAR	DEREK	ROBERT	04/06/81	DUNDEE	25/5/99	6'1.5"	12ST 0LB	GK	DUNDEE 'S' FORM
10	SUTTON	JOHN	WILLIAM	26/12/83	NORWICH	14/7/04	6'2"	13ST 4LB	FWD	MILLWALL
-	VOIGT	JON	WERNER	06/10/86	ARBROATH	20/1/03	5'11"	10ST 10LB	FWD	ABERDEEN
6	WILKIE	LEE		20/04/80	DUNDEE	8/9/98	6'4"	13ST 0LB	DEF	DUNDEE YOUTHS

TICKET INFORMATION

SEASON TICKET INFORMATION | **GATE PRICES**

		SEASON	CAT A	CAT B
CENTRE STAND	ADULT	350	22	20
	JUV/SEN (Over 60)	190	13	12
BOBBY COX FAMILY STAND	ADULT	300	20	18
	SENIOR (Over 60)	170	12	11
	U18	140	11	10
	U12	90	8	7
WING STAND FAMILY SECTION	ADULT	300	20	18
	SENIOR (Over 60)	170	12	11
	U18	140	11	10
	U12	90	8	7
SOUTH ENCLOSURE	ADULT	300	20	18
	SENIOR/JUV	140	11	10
	STUDENT	99	11	9

THE DARK BLUES' 10 YEAR LEAGUE RECORD

SEASON	DIV	P	W	D	L	F	A	PTS
1994-95	F	36	20	8	8	65	36	68
1995-96	F	36	15	12	9	53	40	57
1996-97	F	36	15	13	8	47	33	58
1997-98	F	36	20	10	6	52	24	70
1998-99	SPL	36	13	7	16	36	56	46
1999-00	SPL	36	12	5	19	45	64	41
2000-01	SPL	38	13	8	17	51	49	47
2001-02	SPL	38	12	8	18	41	55	44
2002-03	SPL	38	10	14	14	50	60	44
2003-04	SPL	38	12	10	16	48	57	46

The dark blues' stats 2003/04

SEASON STATS 2003/04

DATE	VENUE	OPPONENTS	ATT	RES	SPERONI J.	MACKAY D.	HERNANDEZ J.	MAIR L.	WILKIE L.	SMITH B.	NEMSADZE G.	RAE G.	BRADY G.	LOVELL S.	NOVO I.	CARRANZA L.A.	JABLONSKI N.	CABALLERO F.	SANCHO B.	SARA J.	COWAN T.	HUTCHINSON T.	FOTHERINGHAM M.	RAVANELLI F.	LINN R.	BURLEY C.	McDONALD C.	CAMERON D.	McCAFFERTY J.	McLEAN D.	ROBB S.	MILNE S.	BARRATT N.	KNEISSL S.	HEGARTY C.	CLARK N.	McNALLY S.	YOUNGSON A.	SOUTAR D.
AUG	A	MOTHERWELL	6,812	3-0	1	2	3	4	5^1	6^1	7	8^1	9	10	11	12	13	14																						
AUG	H	DUNFERMLINE ATH	7,750	0-2	1		3	4	5	6	7	8	9	10	11		13			12	2																			
AUG	H	LIVINGSTON	5,815	2-1	1	2	3	4	5	6	7	13	8	10	11^2					9		12																		
AUG	A	KILMARNOCK	5,935	1-1	1		3		5	6	7	8	9	14	11^1					10	4	13	2	12																
SEP	H	CELTIC	10,647	0-1	1	2	3	4	5	6	7	8	14	10	11					9		12		13																
SEP	H	ABERDEEN	7,887	2-0	1	2		4	5	12	7	8	6	13	11^1					9		10	3^1																	
SEP	A	RANGERS	49,548	1-3	1	2		4	5		6	7	8		11^1					10	9	12	3	13																
OCT	H	HEARTS	11,348	2-2	1	2	12	4	5	6	7	8^1	9		11^1					10		3	13																	
OCT	H	PARTICK THISTLE	6,497	1-0	1	2	3		4	6	7	8	5		11^1					10		12	14				9	13												
OCT	A	DUNDEE UNITED	12,767	1-1	1	2	3	4	5	6		8	7		11^1					10		14		13	9		12													
NOV	H	HIBERNIAN	7,392	1-1	1	2		4	5	6			7		11^1		13			12			9	10	8	3														
NOV	H	MOTHERWELL	6,674	0-1	1	2		4	5	6			3		11		12			10			9	8		7														
NOV	A	DUNFERMLINE ATH	5,458	0-2	1	2	3	4	5	6			7		11		10			8			9	13		12														
NOV	A	LIVINGSTON	3,878	1-1	1	2	3	4	5	6		13	8	10	11					7		9^1	12																	
DEC	H	KILMARNOCK	6,954	1-2	1	14	3	4	5	6		8	7		11^1					2		9					13	12	10											
DEC	A	CELTIC	57,539	2-3	1	2	3	4^1	5	6		8	10		11					7		13	9^1		12															
DEC	A	ABERDEEN	10,354	2-2	1	2	3	4	5	6			10		11^1					7		8^1	9		12															
DEC	H	RANGERS	10,948	0-2	1	2	3	4	5	6			8		11					7			9		10			12												
JAN	H	HEARTS	6,387	1-2	1	2	3		5	6			8		11	7		4					9					10^1	12	13										
JAN	A	PARTICK THISTLE	4,690	2-1	1	2	3	4	5	6^1			8		11^1	13							9					10	7	12										
JAN	H	DUNDEE UNITED	10,747	2-1	1	2	3	4	5	6			8	13^1	11^1		12						9					14	10	7										
JAN	A	HIBERNIAN	8,023	1-1	1	2	3	4					8	13	11	14	5						9^1					12	10	7										
FEB	A	MOTHERWELL	4,247	3-5	1	2	3^1	4		13			8	12	11^2								5	9				14	10	7	6									
FEB	H	DUNFERMLINE ATH	5,643	0-1	1	2	3	4		6			8	10	11								5	12				14	13	7	9									
FEB	H	LIVINGSTON	6,108	1-0	1	2		4		6			8	10	11		14						3	9			5		7	11^1	13	12								
FEB	A	KILMARNOCK	5,454	2-4	1	2	13	4		6			8	9	11^1	12							3	7			5			10^1		14								
MAR	H	ABERDEEN	6,839	1-1	1	2	3	4					8		11			5					7^1	12			13		9	10	6									
MAR	H	CELTIC	8,593	1-2	1	2	3	4					8		11			5					7	12			14		9	10	6	13^1								
MAR	A	RANGERS	49,364	0-4	1	2	3	4					13	12	11			5					6	7					9	14	8	10								
MAR	A	HEARTS	10,491	1-3	1	2		4					8	9	11		13	3					7				5		6	10^1		12	14							
APR	H	PARTICK THISTLE	5,084	2-1	1	2		4					8	9	11^1			3					7				5		12	10^1	6	13								
APR	A	DUNDEE UNITED	9,571	2-2	1	2	3	4					8	11^1				5					7						9	10^1	6		12							
APR	H	HIBERNIAN	5,508	2-2	1	2	3	4					8	11^1	12			5					7						6	10^1	13^1	9								
APR	A	PARTICK THISTLE	2,727	1-0	1	2	3	4					8	9^1	11		13	5					12				7			10	6				14					
MAY	A	HIBERNIAN	6,180	0-1	1	2	3	4					8		11		9	5						6	7				10			13	12		14					
MAY	H	KILMARNOCK	4,942	2-0	1	2	3	4		6			8		11^1	12		5		13			14	7	9				10^1											
MAY	H	LIVINGSTON	4,954	2-0	1			4		6			8	9	11^2			5					12	2					14			10	13		3					
MAY	A	ABERDEEN	7,878	2-1		2	3	4					8		11^1		14	5						13					9	10^1		12	7							1
		TOTAL FULL APPEARANCES			37	34	27	36	21	27	9	11	35	15	34			3	9	20	3	4	8	19	5	3	1	6	6		3	9	15	10	5	1		1	1
		TOTAL SUB APPEARANCES				1	2			2				2		2	6	1	2	9	4	1	7	1	4	5		9	1		5	1	1	6	5	2	6	3	2	1	1
		TOTAL GOALS SCORED					1	1	1	2			2	5	20							1	1	4								1		8	1				

bold figures denote goalscorers. † denotes opponent's own goal.

LEADING GOALSCORERS:

SEASON	DIV	GOALS	PLAYER
94-95	F	16	G. Shaw
95-96	F	14	J. Hamilton
96-97	F	10	J. O'Driscoll
97-98	F	15	J. Grady
98-99	SPL	9	E. Annand
99-00	SPL	13	W. Falconer
00-01	SPL	14	J. Sara
01-02	SPL	11	J. Sara
02-03	SPL	13	S. Lovell
03-04	SPL	20	I. Novo

MILESTONES:

YEAR OF FORMATION: 1893
MOST CAPPED PLAYER: Alex Hamilton
NO. OF CAPS: 24
MOST LEAGUE POINTS IN A SEASON:
58 (First Division – Season 1991/92) (2 Points for a Win),
70 (First Division – Season 1997/98) (3 Points for a Win)
MOST LEAGUE GOALS SCORED BY A PLAYER IN A SEASON:
Alan Gilzean (Season 1963/64) **NO. OF GOALS SCORED:** 32
RECORD ATTENDANCE: 43,024 (-v- Rangers – 1953)
RECORD VICTORY: 10-0 (-v- Fraserburgh, 1931; -v- Alloa, 1947;
-v- Dunfermline Athletic, 1947; -v- Queen of the South, 1962)
RECORD DEFEAT: 0-11 (-v- Celtic – Division 1, 26.10.1895)

DUNDEE PLAYING KITS SEASON 2004/05 — FIRST KIT — SECOND KIT — THIRD KIT

Dundee United

DUNDEE UNITED
Tannadice Park, Tannadice Street, Dundee,
DD3 7JW
CHAIRMAN
Eddie H. Thompson
DIRECTORS
Gilbert B. Haggart, J.D. Scott Carnegie, John
M. Bennett, Derek W. Robertson,
Stephen E. Thompson
& Lord Watson of Invergowrie
ASSOCIATE DIRECTORS
Mike Barile & Peter Cabrelli
SECRETARY
Spence Anderson
MANAGER
Ian McCall
ASSISTANT MANAGER
Gordon Chisholm
FIRST TEAM / RESERVE COACH
Tony Docherty
GOALKEEPING COACH
Bobby Geddes
**DIRECTOR OF YOUTH DEVELOPMENT /
YOUTH CO/ORDINATOR**
Graeme Liveston
COMMUNITY MANAGER
Gordon Grady
YOUTH TEAM COACHES
U19/Tony Docherty
U17/Graeme Liveston
U15/Dougie Robertson
U14/David Bowman
U13/Paddy Connolly
CLUB DOCTOR
Dr. Derek J. McCormack
PHYSIOTHERAPIST
Jeff Clarke
CHIEF SCOUT
Graeme Liveston
GROUNDSMAN
Albert Dawson
**FOOTBALL SAFETY OFFICERS'
ASSOCIATION REPRESENTATIVE/
OPERATIONS MANAGER**
David Anderson (01382) 833166
STADIUM MANAGER
Ron West
GENERAL/COMMERCIAL MANAGER
Bill Campbell (01382) 832202
LOTTERY MANAGER
Mike Barile (01382) 833166
SALES MANAGER
Ronnie Dare
COMMERCIAL ASSISTANTS
Paul Reid & Billy Guthrie
TELEPHONES
Ground/Ticket Office (01382) 833166
Commercial Dept (01382) 832202
Fax (01382) 889398
E-MAIL & INTERNET ADDRESS
admin@dundeeunitedfc.co.uk
www.dundeeunitedfc.co.uk
CLUB SHOP
The United Shop, Tannadice Street, Dundee
Tel: 01382 833166 Fax: 01382 889398
Open 9.00am to 5.30pm Mon-Fri,
9.00am to 5.00pm Sat
OFFICIAL SUPPORTERS CLUB
Chairman – Angus Falconer
(01224) 249858
email: federationdufc@hotmail.com
TEAM CAPTAIN
Derek McInnes
SHIRT SPONSOR
Morning Noon & Night
KIT SUPPLIER
TFG

LIST OF PLAYERS 2004/05

SQUAD NO.	PLAYERS SURNAME	FIRST NAME	MIDDLE NAME	DATE OF BIRTH	PLACE OF BIRTH	DATE SIGNED	HEIGHT FT INS	WEIGHT ST LBS	POSITION ON PITCH	PREVIOUS CLUB
32	ABBOT	STUART		21/06/86	DUNDEE	7/7/03	5' 7"	10ST 0LB	DEF	DUNDEE UNITED YOUTHS
40	ANDREONI	MARCO		12/08/88	BELLSHILL	18/8/04	5' 10"	9ST 8LB	MID	DUNDEE UNITED YOUTHS
31	ANDREW	JOSEPH		02/01/86	GLASGOW	28/6/02	5' 8"	11ST 13LB	FWD	DUNDEE UNITED YOUTHS
5	ARCHIBALD	ALAN	MAXWELL	13/12/77	GLASGOW	4/6/03	6' 0"	11ST 7LB	DEF	PARTICK THISTLE
26	BELL	STEVEN		24/02/85	GLASGOW	31/7/01	6' 0"	10ST 13LB	DEF/MID	CLYDE
8	BREBNER	GRANT	IAN	06/12/77	EDINBURGH	27/8/04	5' 10"	11ST 13LB	MID	HIBERNIAN
1	BULLOCK	ANTHONY	BRIAN	18/02/73	WARRINGTON	2/7/03	6' 1"	14ST 10LB	GK	ROSS COUNTY
38	BURNETT	GREGG		24/05/87	BANGOUR	29/6/04	5' 8"	9ST 12LB	MID	DUNDEE UNITED YOUTHS
29	CALLAGHAN	BARRY		30/11/86	GLASGOW	7/7/03	5' 8"	9ST 7LB	FWD	DUNDEE UNITED YOUTHS
36	CAMERON	GREG		10/04/88	DUNDEE	29/6/04	5' 9"	10ST 9LB	MID	DUNDEE UNITED YOUTHS
27	CONWAY	AARON		29/03/85	DUNDEE	13/3/01	5' 11"	11ST 7LB	FWD	DUNDEE UNITED B.C.
14	DODDS	WILLIAM		05/02/69	NEW CUMNOCK	1/1/03	5' 8"	12ST 2LB	FWD	RANGERS
12	DUFF	STUART		23/01/82	ABERDEEN	5/7/99	5' 11"	10ST 3LB	MID	DUNDEE UNITED B.C.
30	EASTON	WILLIAM		17/07/86	RUTHERGLEN	7/7/03	5' 7"	9ST 5LB	FWD	DUNDEE UNITED YOUTHS
34	GARDINER	ROSS	JOHN	30/12/86	BELLSHILL	7/7/03	5' 11"	9ST 10LB	FWD	ABERDEEN
16	GRADY	JAMES		14/03/71	PAISLEY	3/6/04	5' 7"	10ST 4LB	FWD	PARTICK THISTLE
17	HIRSCHFELD	LARS		17/10/78	EDMONTON	19/8/04	6' 4"	13ST 8LB	GK	TOTTENHAM HOTSPUR
22	HOLMES	GRAEME		26/03/84	MOTHERWELL	2/7/01	5' 9"	10ST 4LB	MID	DUNDEE UNITED YOUTHS
25	INNES	CHRISTOPHER		13/07/76	BROXBURN	29/8/03	6' 1"	13ST 3LB	DEF	KILMARNOCK
24	JARVIE	PAUL		14/06/82	ABERDEEN	16/5/00	6' 0"	12ST 3LB	GK	STONEYWOOD B.C.
39	KENNETH	GARY		21/06/87	DUNDEE	25/2/04	6' 4"	13ST 2LB	DEF	DUNDEE UNITED YOUTHS
21	KERKAR	KARIM		03/01/77	GIVORS	31/8/04	5' 7"	11ST 2LB	MID	CLYDE
7	KERR	MARK		02/03/82	BELLSHILL	2/7/03	5' 11.5"	10ST 11LB	MID	FALKIRK
37	McALEENAN	KIERAN		28/10/87	BELLSHILL	30/6/04	5' 7"	9ST 12LB	DEF	DUNDEE UNITED YOUTHS
3	McCRACKEN	DAVID		16/10/81	GLASGOW	30/6/98	6' 2"	11ST 6LB	DEF	DUNDEE UNITED B.C.
35	McDONALD	NICKY		22/01/86	RUTHERGLEN	28/6/02	5' 5"	8ST 6LB	MID	DUNDEE UNITED YOUTHS
4	McINNES	DEREK		05/07/71	PAISLEY	17/7/03	5' 7"	11ST 5LB	MID	WEST BROMWICH ALBION
10	McINTYRE	JAMES		24/05/72	ALEXANDRIA	6/7/01	5' 11"	11ST 5LB	FWD	READING
18	McLAREN	ANDREW		05/06/73	GLASGOW	28/8/03	5' 10.5"	11ST 7LB	FWD	KILMARNOCK
28	O'DONNELL	STEPHEN		10/07/83	BELLSHILL	4/7/00	5' 11.5"	11ST 2LB	MID	DUNDEE UNITED YOUTHS
6	PATERSON	SCOTT	THOMAS	13/05/72	ABERDEEN	4/6/03	6' 2"	13ST 0LB	DEF	PARTICK THISTLE
23	RITCHIE	PAUL	SIMON	21/08/75	KIRKCALDY	9/8/04	5' 11"	12ST 0LB	DEF	WALSALL
33	ROBERTSON	DAVID		23/09/86	BANGOUR	7/7/03	5' 10"	10ST 0LB	MID	DUNDEE UNITED YOUTHS
11	ROBSON	BARRY		07/11/78	ABERDEEN	3/6/03	5' 11"	12ST 0LB	MID/FWD	INVERNESS CAL. TH.
9	SAMUEL	COLLIN		27/08/81	MANZINILLA	25/7/03	5' 9"	12ST 7LB	MID	FALKIRK
20	SCOTLAND	JASON		18/02/79	TRINIDAD & TOBAGO	1/8/03	5' 9"	11ST 10LB	FWD	DEFENCE FORCE
2	WILSON	MARK		05/06/84	GLASGOW	2/6/00	5' 11"	11ST 13LB	MID	DUNDEE UNITED 'S FORM

TICKET INFORMATION

SEASON TICKET INFORMATION
GEORGE FOX STAND
	TOP TIER	ADULT 280/305	JUV/OAP 130/180
	MIDDLE TIER	ADULT 330/355	JUV/OAP 140/195
	LOWER TIER	ADULT 220/270	JUV/OAP 120/165
EAST STAND	TOP TIER	ADULT 270/290	JUV/OAP 120/160
	LOWER TIER	ADULT 190/210	JUV/OAP 60/140

LEAGUE ADMISSION PRICES
GEORGE FOX STAND
	TOP TIER	ADULT 20/18	JUV/OAP 12/11
	MIDDLE TIER	ADULT 22/20	JUV/OAP 12/11
	LOWER TIER	ADULT 20/18	JUV/OAP 10/9
EAST STAND	TOP TIER	ADULT 20/18	JUV/OAP 11/10
	LOWER TIER	ADULT 18/16	JUV/OAP 10/9
JERRY KERR STAND (AWAY SUPPORTERS)		ADULT 20/18	JUV/OAP 10/11
WEST STAND		ADULT 18/16	JUV/OAP 10/9

THE TERRORS' 10 YEAR LEAGUE RECORD

SEASON	DIV	P	W	D	L	F	A	PTS
1994-95	P	36	9	9	18	40	56	36
1995-96	F	36	19	10	7	73	37	67
1996-97	P	36	17	9	10	46	33	60
1997-98	P	36	8	13	15	43	51	37
1998-99	SPL	36	8	10	18	37	48	34
1999-00	SPL	36	11	6	19	34	57	39
2000-01	SPL	38	9	8	21	38	63	35
2001-02	SPL	38	12	10	16	38	59	46
2002-03	SPL	38	7	11	20	35	68	32
2003-04	SPL	38	13	10	15	47	60	49

SEASON STATS 2003/04

DATE	VENUE	OPPONENTS	ATT	RES	GALLACHER P.	ARCHIBALD A.	PATERSON S.	GRIFFIN D.	McINNES D.	KERR M.	PATERSON J.	MILLER C.	SAMUEL C.	DODDS W.	ROBSON B.	DUFF S.	McINTYRE J.	BOLLAN G.	McCRACKEN D.	EASTON C.	WILSON M.	BULLOCK A.	INNES C.	SCOTLAND J.	McLAREN A.	COYLE O.	HOLMES G.	CONWAY A.
-AUG	H	HIBERNIAN	9,809	1-2	1	2	3	4	5	6	7	8	9^1	10	11	12	13	14										
6-AUG	A	CELTIC	57,004	0-5	1	2	3	4	9	6	7	8		11	10		13		5	12	14							
8-AUG	A	HEARTS	11,395	0-3	1	2		4	7	6	14		9	10	11	12	13	3	5	8								
-AUG	H	RANGERS	11,111	1-3		2		4	7	6	14	8	9	13^1	11				5	10			1	3	12			
3-SEP	A	LIVINGSTON	4,226	0-0		2		4	7	12		6		8	10	14			5	11			1	3	13	9		
0-SEP	A	PARTICK THISTLE	4,711	2-0		2		4	7	13	6	8^2	12	14					5	11			1	3	10	9		
7-SEP	H	KILMARNOCK	6,529	1-1		2		4	7	6		8	12	13				14	5	11			1	3	10	9^1		
-OCT	A	MOTHERWELL	6,194	0-2		2		4	7	6			12					8	5	11			1	3	10	9	13	
3-OCT	A	ABERDEEN	11,234	1-0	1	2	13	7		6			10	12				11	4	8	5			3		9^1	14	
6-OCT	H	DUNDEE	12,767	1-1	1	2		7		6			10				11^1		4	8	5			3		9	12	
-NOV	A	DUNFERMLINE ATH	5,078	0-2	1	2		7	14	6		12		13	8	11			4	9	5			3		10		
-NOV	A	HIBERNIAN	8,756	2-2	1	2	12	7					10	8^1	13	11			4	6	5			3		9^1		
2-NOV	H	CELTIC	10,802	1-5	1	2		7				12	10	8		11^1			4	6	5			3		9		
0-NOV	H	HEARTS	6,343	2-1	1	2^1		7^1	8	6		13	10		12	11			4		5			3		9		
-DEC	A	RANGERS	49,307	1-2	1	2		7	6			13	14	10^1	8				4	12	5			3		9		
3-DEC	H	LIVINGSTON	5,421	2-0	1	2	13	7	6				10	10^2	8	11			4		5			3		9		
3-DEC	H	PARTICK THISTLE	6,440	0-0	1	2	3	7	6	12	8	13	10			11			4		5			3		9		
7-DEC	A	KILMARNOCK	6,062	2-0	1	2	14	7	5	6			10^1	8	13	11^1			4		3					12	9	
-JAN	A	MOTHERWELL	5,549	1-3	1	2		7	8	6		13	10		12	11			4		5^1			3		9	14	
7-JAN	H	ABERDEEN	8,888	3-2	1	2		7	6		12^1	8	10^1	11^1	3				4		5					9		
5-JAN	A	DUNDEE	10,747	1-2	1	2		7	5	6	8	12	10^1						4	13	3					9		
1-JAN	H	DUNFERMLINE ATH	5,564	1-0	1	2		12	6		8		10	7		11^1			4	13	5			3		9		
0-FEB	H	HIBERNIAN	6,389	0-0	1	2		7	6		8		10	9		11			4		5			3				
4-FEB	A	CELTIC	58,671	1-2	1	2^1		7	6		8	13	10	9	3	11			4	12	5					14		
1-FEB	A	HEARTS	10,265	1-3	1	2		7	6	12	8	10		9	3	11^1			4	13	5					14		
9-FEB	H	RANGERS	10,497	2-0	1	2		7	6^1		8			10		11^1			4		5			3		9		
3-MAR	A	PARTICK THISTLE	3,510	1-1	1	2		7	6			12	10^1		11				4	13	5			3		14	9	
0-MAR	H	KILMARNOCK	5,757	4-1	1	2		7	6		8^1		12	10		11^3			4	14	5			3		13	9	
4-MAR	A	LIVINGSTON	3,082	3-2	1	2		7	6		8	12^1				11^1			4		5			3		10^1	9	
7-MAR	H	MOTHERWELL	7,585	1-0	1	2		7	6		8		12	10		11			4	14	5			3		13^1	9	
-APR	A	ABERDEEN	8,449	0-3	1	2		7	6		8	14	13	10		11			4		5			3		12	9	
1-APR	H	DUNDEE	9,571	2-2	1	2			6	13		14	10^2	8		11			4	7	5			3		12	9	
7-APR	A	DUNFERMLINE ATH	4,405	1-1	1	2		7				13	10	8	14				4^1	6	5			3		11	9	12
4-APR	H	RANGERS	8,339	3-3	1	2		7	6		8	13	10^1	11					4		5			3		12^2	9	
-MAY	H	HEARTS	6,620	0-2	1	2			6	12		9	10	11					4	7	5			3		8		13
3-MAY	A	MOTHERWELL	5,722	1-0	1	2		7	6		8	11	12		9				4	14	5^1			3		10		13
1-MAY	H	DUNFERMLINE ATH	5,998	3-2	1	2		7	6		8^1	11^1	13	9	14				4	12	5			3^1		10		
6-MAY	A	CELTIC	58,364	1-2	1	2	13		6		12	8	11		9				4	7	5^1			3		10	14	
TOTAL FULL APPEARANCES					33	38	2	9	34	30	10	22	11	23	25		10	27	1	32	10	31	5	29	10	26		
TOTAL SUB APPEARANCES							1	4	1	3	6	4	15	10	3	8	3	1		12	1				11	1	3	3	1
TOTAL GOALS SCORED						2			1	1		5	3	10	3			10		1				3		1	4	3

Bold figures denote goalscorers. † denotes opponent's own goals.

LEADING GOALSCORERS:

SEASON	DIV	GOALS	PLAYER
94-95	P	7	C. Brewster
95-96	F	17	C. Brewster, G. McSwegan
96-97	P	12	K. Olofsson
97-98	P	18	K. Olofsson
98-99	SPL	17	W. Dodds
99-00	SPL	9	W. Dodds
00-01	SPL	6	D. Lilley
01-02	SPL	6	D. Lilley, J. McIntyre, S. Thompson
02-03	SPL	9	J. McIntyre
03-04	SPL	10	J. McIntyre, W. Dodds

MILESTONES:

YEAR OF FORMATION: 1923 (1909 as Dundee Hibs)
MOST CAPPED PLAYER: Maurice Malpas
NO. OF CAPS: 55
MOST LEAGUE POINTS IN A SEASON:
60 (Premier Division – Season 1986/87) (2 Points for a Win)
67 (First Division – Season 1995/96) (3 Points for a Win)
MOST LEAGUE GOALS SCORED BY A PLAYER IN A SEASON:
John Coyle (Season 1955/56) **NO. OF GOALS SCORED:** 41
RECORD ATTENDANCE: 28,000 (-v- Barcelona – 16.11.1966)
RECORD VICTORY: 14-0
(-v- Nithsdale Wanderers – Scottish Cup, 17.1.1931)
RECORD DEFEAT: 1-12 (-v- Motherwell – Division 2, 23.1.1954)

DUNDEE UNITED PLAYING KITS SEASON 2004/05 — FIRST KIT, SECOND KIT, THIRD KIT

Dunfermline Athletic

DUNFERMLINE ATHLETIC
East End Park, Halbeath Road,
Dunfermline, Fife, KY12 7RB
CHAIRMAN John W. Yorkston
DIRECTORS
Gavin G. Masterton, C.B.E., F.I.B. (Scot), John
Meiklem, W. Brian Robertson, W.S., Francis M.
McConnell, SSC. Edward Smyth & Rodney Shearer
CHIEF EXECUTIVE David McPherson
CLUB SECRETARY Jim Johnston
GENERAL MANAGER Robin Ozog
MANAGER David Hay
ASSISTANT MANAGER Billy Kirkwood
FIRST TEAM COACH Paul Hegarty
DIRECTOR OF FOOTBALL Jim Leishman
RESERVE COACH Craig Robertson
FITNESS COACH Tom Toward
COMMUNITY COACH Hamish French
GOALKEEPING COACH Scott Y. Thomson
YOUTH CO/ORDINATOR Hamish French/
Craig Robertson
YOUTH COACHES
U/19 David Hunter, U/17 John Darroch/Billy
Bennett, U/16 Alex Rae/George Anderson, U/15
John Young, U/14 Kenny Black, U/13 Frank McFadyen
OFFICE ADMINISTRATOR
Claire Simpson (01383) 724295
**FOOTBALL SAFETY OFFICERS'
ASSOCIATION REPRESENTATIVE**
David Dickson (01383) 724295
COMMERCIAL MANAGER
Karen McNeill
LOTTERY MANAGER Rose Robertson
MEDIA LIAISON OFFICER Stuart Arnott
CLUB DOCTOR Dr. Gerry D. Gillespie
PHYSIOTHERAPIST
Paul Atkinson (First Team)
STADIUM MANAGER
Brian Gallagher (01383) 724295
GROUNDSMAN John Wilson
KIT PERSON Andrew Hutton
CONFERENCE & BANQUETING
Robin Ozog
MARKETING & PR Tracey Martin
MATCHDAY PROGRAMME EDITOR
Duncan Simpson
CLUB SHOP
Club Shop situated at
Kingsgate Shopping Centre.
Ground only on matchdays.
Open 9.00 a.m. – 5.00 p.m.
Mon to Sat. Tel: (01383) 626737
TELEPHONES
Ground/Secretary (01383) 724295
Fax (01383) 723468
Ticket Office 0870 300 1201
Ticket Office Fax (01383) 626452
Conference & Banqueting (01383) 741147
Conference & Banqueting Fax
(01383) 741411
Pars Superstore (01383) 626737
Pars Personal Health (01383) 623655
Sports Bar (01383) 745514
E/MAIL & INTERNET ADDRESS
pars@dafc.co.uk & www.dafc.co.uk
OFFICIAL SUPPORTERS CLUB
c/o Mrs. Joan Malcolm, Secretary,
Dunfermline Athletic Supporters Club,
13 South Knowe, Crossgates, KY4 8AW
Fod Arms Travel Club – Linda Cummings
(01383) 729909
Lothian68 – John 07719 564920
Millers Bar – John (01383) 723695
TEAM CAPTAIN Scott M. Thomson
SHIRT SPONSOR
RAC Auto Windscreens
KIT SUPPLIER
TFG

LIST OF PLAYERS 2004/05

SQUAD NO.	PLAYERS SURNAME	FIRST NAME	MIDDLE NAME	DATE OF BIRTH	PLACE OF BIRTH	DATE SIGNED	HEIGHT FT INS	WEIGHT ST LBS	POSITION ON PITCH	PREVIOUS CLUB
43	ANDERSON	CHRISTOPHER	NICOL	03/08/87	BROXBURN	5/7/04	5' 10"	11ST 5LB	FWD	DUNFERMLINE ATH. YOUTHS
35	ARMOUR	DAVID		28/08/87	PAISLEY	20/5/04	5' 9"	9ST 3LB	FWD	DUNFERMLINE ATH. YOUTHS
10	BREWSTER	CRAIG		13/12/66	DUNDEE	4/7/02	6' 1"	12ST 9LB	FWD	HIBERNIAN
15	BYRNE	RICHARD		24/09/81	DUBLIN	30/8/03	6' 1"	12ST 5LB	DEF	SHAMROCK ROVERS
25	CAMPBELL	IAIN		28/06/85	KIRKCALDY	14/8/02	5' 9"	10ST 12LB	DEF	DUNFERMLINE ATH. YOUTHS
24	CLARKE	PATRICK		18/05/85	EDINBURGH	23/6/03	5' 11.5"	9ST 9LB	FWD	HIBERNIAN
12	DEMPSEY	GARY		15/01/81	WEXFORD	19/6/02	5' 9"	11ST 8LB	MID	WATERFORD UNITED
14	DONNELLY	SIMON	THOMAS	01/12/74	GLASGOW	23/7/04	5' 9"	11ST 6LB	MID/FWD	ST. JOHNSTONE
37	DUNN	JOHN		19/04/87	EDINBURGH	20/5/04	5' 10"	11ST 4LB	FWD	DUNFERMLINE ATH. YOUTHS
22	GREENHILL	GARY		16/06/85	KIRKCALDY	13/7/02	5' 10"	10ST 12LB	MID	DUNFERMLINE ATH. YOUTHS
9	HUNT	NOEL		26/12/82	WATERFORD	28/1/03	5' 8"	11ST 5LB	FWD	SHAMROCK ROVERS
34	HUNTER	DEREK		21/01/87	STIRLING	29/1/04	5' 9"	10ST 2LB	DEF	DUNFERMLINE ATH. YOUTHS
33	KAY	CLARK	LEWIS	06/08/88	DUNFERMLINE	5/7/04	5' 11"	10ST 1LB	DEF	DUNFERMLINE ATH. YOUTHS
19	LABONTE	AARON		27/11/83	MIDDLESBROUGH	14/7/03	5' 10.5"	10ST 10LB	DEF	NEWCASTLE UNITED
20	LANGFIELD	JAMES		22/12/79	PAISLEY	7/7/04	6' 4"	13ST 0LB	GK	PARTICK THISTLE
17	LYLE	DEREK		13/02/81	GLASGOW	21/7/04	5' 9"	11ST 2LB	FWD	QUEEN OF THE SOUTH
8	MASON	GARY		15/10/79	EDINBURGH	22/12/00	5' 8.5"	10ST 12LB	MID	MANCHESTER CITY
32	M'GLINCHEY	STEVEN		04/02/86	GLASGOW	19/8/03	5' 8"	10ST 8LB	FWD	BOSCO JUNIORS
27	M'GUIRE	KIERAN		29/03/86	KIRKCALDY	6/8/03	5' 10"	11ST 8LB	FWD	DUNFERMLINE ATH. YOUTHS
23	M'KEOWN	CRAIG	ALLAN	16/03/85	ABERDEEN	6/8/03	6' 0"	12ST 12LB	DEF	FORTMARTINE UNITED
21	MEHMET	BILLY		03/01/84	LONDON	10/7/03	6' 1"	12ST 13LB	FWD	WEST HAM UNITED
40	MURDOCH	SEAN		31/07/86	EDINBURGH	12/8/03	6' 2"	11ST 10LB	GK	HEARTS YOUTHS
7	NICHOLSON	BARRY		24/08/78	DUMFRIES	4/8/00	5' 7.5"	10ST 12LB	MID	RANGERS
36	OGG	DEAN		07/09/87	DUNFERMLINE	20/5/04	5' 8"	10ST 2LB	FWD	DUNFERMLINE ATH. YOUTHS
-	ROBERTSON	MICHAEL		10/03/86	FALKIRK	9/8/04	5' 11"	12ST 5LB	GK	CELTIC
42	ROSS	GREG		02/05/87	EDINBURGH	20/5/04	6' 1"	11ST 0LB	DEF	DUNFERMLINE ATH. YOUTHS
-	SCULLION	PATRICK	JAMES	02/03/86	DUNFERMLINE	16/7/04	6' 1"	12ST 2LB	DEF	CELTIC
2	SHIELDS	GREG		21/08/76	FALKIRK	23/1/04	5' 9"	10ST 10LB	DEF	KILMARNOCK
5	SKERLA	ANDRIUS		29/04/77	LITHUANIA	28/7/00	6' 1"	12ST 9LB	DEF	PSV EINDHOVEN
31	SMITH	DANIEL		11/09/86	GLASGOW	6/8/03	5' 5"	9ST 5LB	MID/FWD	BOSCO JUNIORS
1	STILLIE	DEREK		03/12/73	IRVINE	4/7/02	6' 0"	12ST 6LB	GK	WIGAN ATHLETIC
6	THOMSON	SCOTT	MUNRO	29/01/72	ABERDEEN	6/7/98	5' 10"	11ST 4LB	DEF/MID	RAITH ROVERS
30	THOMSON	SCOTT	YUILL	08/11/66	EDINBURGH	23/7/03	6' 0.5"	12ST 0LB	GK	AIRDRIEONIANS
18	TOD	ANDREW		04/11/71	DUNFERMLINE	8/8/03	6' 3"	12ST 6LB	DEF	BRADFORD CITY
41	VINTER	STEVEN		05/02/87	EDINBURGH	20/5/04	6' 2"	10ST 6LB	DEF	DUNFERMLINE ATH. YOUTHS
26	WILSON	CRAIG		28/05/86	DUNFERMLINE	6/8/03	5' 8"	10ST 2LB	FWD	DUNFERMLINE ATH. YOUTHS
3	WILSON	SCOTT		19/03/77	EDINBURGH	9/8/02	6' 2"	12ST 8LB	DEF	RANGERS
4	YOUNG	DARREN		13/10/78	GLASGOW	10/7/03	5' 9"	11ST 11LB	MID	ABERDEEN
11	YOUNG	DEREK		27/05/80	GLASGOW	10/7/03	5' 8.5"	10ST 10LB	MID	ABERDEEN

TICKET INFORMATION

SEASON TICKET INFORMATION

MAIN STAND	ADULT 320	CONCS 170	U18 90	U12 55
ALL OTHER AREAS	ADULT 265	CONCS 135	U18 75	U12 40
FAMILY TICKET	ADULT 255	1 CHILD 35	2 CHILD 30	3 CHILD 25	4 CHILD 10

MATCH TICKET INFORMATION (WALK UP PRICES)
CATEGORY A – RANGERS & CELTIC

MAIN STAND	ADULT 22	OAP/U16 15	U12 10
ALL OTHER AREAS	ADULT 20	OAP/U16 15	U12 10

CATEGORY B – ALL OTHER SPL CLUBS

MAIN STAND	ADULT 20	OAP/U16 14	U12 10
ALL OTHER AREAS	ADULT 16	OAP/U16 12	U12 8

CATEGORY A - AWAY STANDS

	ADULT 22	OAP/U16 15	U12 15

CATEGORY B - AWAY STANDS

	ADULT 19	OAP/U16 12	U12 12

THE PARS' 10 YEAR LEAGUE RECORD

SEASON	DIV	P	W	D	L	F	A	PTS
1994-95	F	36	18	14	4	63	32	68
1995-96	F	36	21	8	7	73	41	71
1996-97	P	36	12	9	15	52	65	45
1997-98	P	36	8	13	15	43	68	37
1998-99	SPL	36	4	16	16	28	59	28
1999-00	F	36	20	11	5	66	33	71
2000-01	SPL	38	11	9	18	34	54	42
2001-02	SPL	38	12	9	17	41	64	45
2002-03	SPL	38	13	7	18	54	71	46
2003-04	SPL	38	14	11	13	45	52	53

SEASON STATS 2003/04

DATE	VEN	OPPONENTS	ATT	RES	STILLIE D.	M'GROARTY C.	TOD A.	SKERLA A.	WILSON S.	YOUNG DARREN	NICHOLSON B.	MASON G.	YOUNG DEREK	CRAWFORD S.	BREWSTER C.	GRONDIN D.	BULLEN L.	DAIR J.	DEMPSEY G.	MEHMET W.	KILGANNON S.	LABONTE A.	THOMSON S.M.	BYRNE R.	M'DERMOTT A.	M'GARTY M.	HUNT N.	SHIELDS G.	CLARK P.	WILSON C.	RUITENBEEK M.	GREENHILL G.	McGUIRE K.
9-AUG	H	CELTIC	10,082	0-0	1	2	3	4	5	6	7	8	9	10	11	12																	
17-AUG	A	DUNDEE	7,750	†2-0	1	2	3	4	5		7	8	9	10^1	11			6	12	13	14												
23-AUG	A	ABERDEEN	10,810	2-1	1		3	4	5	6	7^1	8		10	11^1	2	9		13	12													
31-AUG	A	HEARTS	11,934	0-1	1		3	4	5	6	7	8		10	11	2	9		13				12										
13-SEP	A	RANGERS	49,072	0-4	1		3	4	5	6	7	8		10		2	9		11	12	13	14											
20-SEP	H	HIBERNIAN	8,715	0-0	1		3	4	5	6	7	8		10	11	2	9		13				12										
27-SEP	H	PARTICK THISTLE	4,684	2-1	1		3	4		6	7	8		10^2	11	2	5				14	9	13	12									
4-OCT	A	LIVINGSTON	3,993	0-0	1			4	5	6	7	8		10	11	2			12			9		3	13								
18-OCT	H	KILMARNOCK	4,495	2-3	1			4	5	6	7	8		10^2	11	2	12					9		3									
1-NOV	H	DUNDEE UNITED	5,078	2-0	1			4	5	6	7	8		10	11				9	13^1			12	3^1	2								
8-NOV	A	CELTIC	58,258	0-5	1			4	5	6		8		10	13				9	12	11		7	3	2		14						
22-NOV	H	DUNDEE	5,458	2-0	1				5	6	7	8	13	10^2	11	2	12		9					3	4								
25-NOV	A	MOTHERWELL	4,220	2-2	1	2			5	6	7	8	9	10^1	11^1				13	12		14		3	4								
29-NOV	H	ABERDEEN	5,254	2-2	1	2		4	5	6	7	8	9^1	10	11	12^1			13				3				14						
6-DEC	H	HEARTS	6,147	2-1	1		3	4	5^1	6	7	8	9^1	10	11	2	12					14					13						
14-DEC	H	RANGERS	8,592	†2-0	1		3	4	5	6	7^1	8	9	10^1	11		2		12								13						
21-DEC	A	HIBERNIAN	9,085	2-1	1		3	4	5	6	7	8	9	10	11^2	2			12								12	13					
27-DEC	A	PARTICK THISTLE	4,377	1-4	1	13		4	5	6	7	8	9	10	11^2	2			12					3			14						
3-JAN	H	LIVINGSTON	5,154	2-2	1		3	4		6	7^1	8	11	10^1			13	2	9								12		5				
17-JAN	A	KILMARNOCK	5,715	1-1	1	2		4	5	6	7	8	12	10^1	11				13								9	3					
24-JAN	H	MOTHERWELL	5,270	1-0	1	14		4	5	6	7	8	9^1	10	11				2				13	3				12					
31-JAN	A	DUNDEE UNITED	5,564	0-1	1	12		4	5	6	7	8	11	10					14				9	3			13	2					
11-FEB	H	CELTIC	9,718	1-4	1	8		4	5	6	7		9	10					12	13			3				11^1	2					
14-FEB	A	DUNDEE	5,643	1-0	1	14		4	5	6	7		13	10					9				12	3	8		11^1	2					
21-FEB	A	ABERDEEN	11,035	0-1	1			4	5		7		9	10	13	12							8	11	14		3	6		2			
28-FEB	H	HEARTS	8,422	0-0	1	8		4	5	6				10			12		14	13				3	9		11	2					
20-MAR	H	PARTICK THISTLE	4,351	1-0	1	14		4	5	6^1	7		9	10	11				12				8	13			3	2					
23-MAR	A	RANGERS	47,487	1-4	1	3^1		4	5	6	7		9	10	11				12				8	13	14		2						
27-MAR	A	LIVINGSTON	3,558	0-0	1	14		4	5	6	7	8	9	10	11				12	13				3			2						
3-APR	H	KILMARNOCK	3,914	2-1	1		5	4		6	7^1	8	9	10^1	11				12	13	14			3			2						
13-APR	H	HIBERNIAN	5,041	1-1	1	14		4	5	6	7		9	10	11		3		8^1	13							12	2					
15-APR	A	MOTHERWELL	3,920	0-1	1		3	4			7	8		10	14	13	5		9	11	6						12	2					
17-APR	H	DUNDEE UNITED	4,405	1-1	1		3			6		8				4			13	11	7	5					2^1	9	10	1	12		14
24-APR	H	MOTHERWELL	4,250	3-0	1			4		6	7^1	8	11^1	10			14	5	9^1	11	14		12	3			2						
2-MAY	A	CELTIC	59,719	2-1	1			4		6	7^1	8		10			5		9^1	11	14	13		3			12	2					
8-MAY	A	HEARTS	10,846	1-2	1	3^1		4			7	8		10			6		9	13	12		5				11	2					
11-MAY	A	DUNDEE UNITED	5,998	2-3	1		3	4			7	8	9	10^1		13	2^1		6				14	5			11	12					
16-MAY	H	RANGERS	6,719	2-3	1	13		4			7	8	9	10	11		2		6^2	12		5		3								14	
TOTAL FULL APPEARANCES					37	2	22	35	28	32	36	32	25	33	23	9	19		15	5	4	8	15	10	5		5	15	1	1	1		
TOTAL SUB APPEARANCES						8							3	1	3	5	8	1	17	13	7	13	1	3	1		8	2	1			1	1
TOTAL GOALS SCORED							2		1	1	5		4	13	5	2			5	1			1				2	1					

bold figures denote goalscorers. † denotes opponent's own goal.

LEADING GOALSCORERS:

SEASON	DIV	GOALS	PLAYER
1994-95	F	14	S. Petrie
1995-96	F	13	S. Petrie
1996-97	P	13	G. Britton
1997-98	P	16	A. Smith
1998-99	SPL	8	A. Smith
1999-00	F	16	S. Crawford
2000-01	SPL	9	S. Crawford
2001-02	SPL	7	B. Nicholson
2002-03	SPL	19	S. Crawford
2003-04	SPL	13	S. Crawford

MILESTONES:

YEAR OF FORMATION: 1885
MOST CAPPED PLAYER: Istvan Kozma
NO. OF CAPS: Hungary 29 (13 whilst with Dunfermline Athletic)
MOST LEAGUE POINTS IN A SEASON:
65 (First Division – Season 1993/94) (2 Points for a Win)
71 (First Division – Seasons 1995/96 and 1999/2000) (3 Points for a Win)
MOST LEAGUE GOALS SCORED BY A PLAYER IN A SEASON:
Bobby Skinner (Season 1925/26) **NO. OF GOALS SCORED:** 53
RECORD ATTENDANCE: 27,816 (-v- Celtic – 30.4.1968)
RECORD VICTORY: 11-2
(-v- Stenhousemuir – Division 2, 27.9.1930)
RECORD DEFEAT: 0-10 (-v- Dundee – Division 2, 22.3.1947)

DUNFERMLINE ATHLETIC PLAYING KITS SEASON 2004/05

FIRST KIT — SECOND KIT — THIRD KIT

HEART OF MIDLOTHIAN FOOTBALL CLUB
Tynecastle Stadium, Gorgie Road,
Edinburgh, EH11 2NL
CHAIRMAN
George Foulkes, M.P
DIRECTORS
Christopher P. Robinson, Stewart Fraser,
Brian J. Duffin & David Archer
CHIEF EXECUTIVE
Christopher P. Robinson
P.A. TO CHIEF EXECUTIVE
Irene McPhee (0131) 200 7245
FINANCE DIRECTOR/COMPANY SECRETARY
Stewart Fraser (0131) 200 7270
HEAD COACH
Craig Levein
ASSISTANT HEAD COACH
Peter Houston
FITNESS COACH
Tom Ritchie
RESERVE/U19 COACH
John McGlynn
ASSISTANT RESERVE COACH
Gary Kirk
COACHING STAFF
Stephen Frail
DIRECTOR OF YOUTH DEVELOPMENT
John Murray
CHIEF SCOUT
John Harvey
CLUB DOCTOR
Dr. Dewar Melvin
PHYSIOTHERAPIST
Alan Rae
KIT PERSON
Gordon Paterson
RETAIL MANAGER
Clare Sargent (0131) 200 7206
CORPORATE HOSPITALITY/BANQUETING
Louise Wallace (Sodexho) (0131) 200 7240
**SALES & MARKETING MANAGER
& COMMERCIAL MANAGER**
Kenny Wittmann (0131) 200 7205
**FOOTBALL SAFETY OFFICERS'
ASSOCIATION REPRESENTATIVE**
Tom Purdie (0131) 200 7254
STADIUM MANAGER
John Boag (0131) 200 7258
**MEDIA LIAISON OFFICER/
MATCHDAY PROGRAMME EDITOR**
Shelley Kay (0131) 200 7206
Clare Cowan (0131) 200 7206
TELEPHONES
Ground (0131) 200 7200
Fax (0131) 200 7222
Football Dept (0131) 451 8470
Ticket Office (0131) 200 7201
Sales & Marketing (0131) 200 7205
Credit Card Bookings (0131) 200 7209
Superstore (0131) 200 7211
E-MAIL & INTERNET ADDRESS
hearts@homplc.co.uk
www.heartsfc.co.uk
CLUB SHOP
Heart of Midlothian Superstore,
Tynecastle Stadium, Gorgie Road, Edinburgh.
Tel (0131) 200 7211
OFFICIAL SUPPORTERS CLUB
Heart of Midlothian Federation, John N. Borthwick,
21/9 Festival Gardens, Edinburgh, EH11 1RB
TEAM CAPTAIN
Steven Pressley
SHIRT SPONSOR
all:sports
KIT SUPPLIER
Reebok

LIST OF PLAYERS 2004/05

SQUAD NO.	PLAYERS SURNAME	FIRST NAME	MIDDLE NAME	DATE OF BIRTH	PLACE OF BIRTH	DATE SIGNED	HEIGHT FT INS	WEIGHT ST LBS	POSITION ON PITCH	PREVIOUS CLUB
33	ARMSTRONG	DAVID	TREVOR	23/01/87	LISBURN	4/7/03	5' 11"	11ST 2LB	FWD	LISBURN YOUTHS
37	ARMSTRONG	JOHN	WILLIAM	25/06/87	EDINBURGH	8/7/04	5' 11"	11ST 10LB	DEF	HEART OF MIDLOTHIAN YOUTHS
36	BARJAKTAREVIC	MILAN		12/06/87	STOCKHOLM	2/3/04	6' 3"	13ST 3LB	GK	HAMMARBY
21	BERRA	CHRISTOPHE		31/01/85	EDINBURGH	26/4/02	6' 1"	12ST 10LB	DEF	HEART OF MIDLOTHIAN YOUTHS
9	DE VRIES	MARK		24/08/75	SURINAM	8/7/02	6' 3"	12ST 1LB	FWD	DORDRECHT 90
44	DOHERTY	MATTHEW		29/04/87	LONDONDERRY	28/7/04	5' 11"	11ST 7LB	MID	CARLISLE UNITED
41	DRIVER	ANDREW	DAVID	12/11/87	OLDHAM	4/7/03	5' 8.5"	10ST 10LB	MID	HEART OF MIDLOTHIAN YOUTHS
35	ELLIOT	CALLUM		30/03/87	EDINBURGH	1/10/03	5' 11.5"	12ST 6LB	FWD	HEART OF MIDLOTHIAN YOUTHS
26	GARDINER	CHRISTOPHER		05/01/86	BELLSHILL	1/7/02	6' 0"	11ST 10LB	FWD	HEART OF MIDLOTHIAN YOUTHS
32	GAY	RYAN		03/07/86	EDINBURGH	1/7/02	5' 10"	10ST 9LB	MID	LEITH ATHLETIC
1	GORDON	CRAIG	SINCLAIR	31/12/82	EDINBURGH	26/10/99	6' 4"	12ST 2LB	GK	HEART OF MIDLOTHIAN YOUTHS
19	HAMILL	JOSEPH	PATRICK	25/02/84	BELLSHILL	22/8/00	5' 9"	10ST 10LB	MID	HEART OF MIDLOTHIAN YOUTHS
10	HARTLEY	PAUL	JAMES	19/10/76	GLASGOW	3/6/03	5' 8"	10ST 7LB	FWD	ST. JOHNSTONE
18	JANCZYK	NEIL		07/04/83	EDINBURGH	16/7/99	5' 10"	11ST 0LB	DEF	HEART OF MIDLOTHIAN YOUTHS
31	KENNEDY	RYAN		22/05/86	BELLSHILL	1/7/02	5' 10"	10ST 7LB	MID	RANGERS YOUTHS
3	KISNORBO	PATRICK		24/03/81	MELBOURNE	3/7/03	6' 0"	12ST 0LB	DEF	SOUTH MELBOURNE
29	McDONALD	JAMIE		17/04/86	BROXBURN	15/8/03	6' 1"	11ST 2LB	GK	MUSSELBURGH ATHLETIC JNRS
11	McFARLANE	NEIL		10/10/77	DUNOON	8/7/02	6' 1"	13ST 1LB	MID	AIRDRIEONIANS
42	MACKLE	SEAN	JAMES	10/04/88	BELFAST	8/7/04	5' 8.5"	10ST 7LB	MID	PORTADOWN
2	MAYBURY	ALAN	PAUL	08/08/78	DUBLIN	12/10/01	5' 10"	11ST 10LB	DEF	LEEDS UNITED
14	McALLISTER	JAMES	REYNOLDS	26/04/78	GLASGOW	4/6/04	5' 10"	11ST 0LB	DEF	LIVINGSTON
24	McGEOWN	DAVID	PETER	06/01/84	GLASGOW	21/7/00	5' 11"	11ST 4LB	MID	HEART OF MIDLOTHIAN YOUTHS
5	McKENNA	KEVIN		20/01/80	CALGARY	17/7/01	6' 2"	12ST 6LB	DEF	ENERGIE COTTBUS
34	McLAUGHLIN	DENIS		05/02/87	LETTERKENNY	8/7/04	5' 11"	11ST 13LB	FWD	HEART OF MIDLOTHIAN YOUTHS
13	MOILANEN	TEUVO		12/12/73	OULU	18/7/03	6' 4"	13ST 7LB	GK	PRESTON NORTH END
43	MOLE	JAMIE		01/06/88	NEWCASTLE	8/7/04	5' 9.5"	11ST 13LB	FWD	NEWBURN B.C.
25	MURTAGH	CONALL	FRANCIS	29/06/85	BELFAST	10/7/03	6' 0"	11ST 12LB	MID	CRUSADERS
40	NEILL	JOHN		17/08/87	BELLSHILL	6/8/03	5' 11"	11ST 4LB	MID	HIBERNIAN
12	NEILSON	ROBBIE		19/06/80	PAISLEY	25/10/96	5' 8"	11ST 0LB	MID	RANGERS B.C.
30	PELOSI	MARCO	GIANCARLO	22/04/86	EDINBURGH	30/8/02	5' 10"	12ST 12LB	DEF	HEART OF MIDLOTHIAN YOUTHS
15	PEREIRA	RAMON		12/09/78	BADAJUZ	2/7/04	6' 1"	11ST 6LB	FWD	RAITH ROVERS
4	PRESSLEY	STEVEN	JOHN	11/10/73	ELGIN	10/7/98	6' 0"	12ST 6LB	DEF	DUNDEE UNITED
16	SIMMONS	STEPHEN	CHRISTOPHER	27/02/82	GLASGOW	10/9/97	6' 0.5"	11ST 10LB	MID	CELTIC B.C.
28	SIVES	CRAIG	STUART	09/04/86	EDINBURGH	1/7/02	6' 3"	12ST 2LB	DEF	HEART OF MIDLOTHIAN YOUTHS
20	SLOAN	ROBERT		14/07/83	PAISLEY	14/7/99	5' 8"	9ST 12LB	MID	HEART OF MIDLOTHIAN YOUTHS
8	STAMP	PHILIP		12/12/75	MIDDLESBROUGH	29/8/02	5' 11"	12ST 0LB	MID	MIDDLESBROUGH
22	STEWART	MICHAEL		26/02/81	EDINBURGH	30/7/04	5' 11"	11ST 11LB	MID	MANCHESTER UNITED
38	THOMSON	JASON		26/07/87	EDINBURGH	10/7/03	5' 11"	11ST 7LB	DEF	HEART OF MIDLOTHIAN YOUTHS
27	TIERNEY	GARRY		19/03/86	BELLSHILL	26/1/04	5' 11"	11ST 5LB	DEF	MUSSELBURGH ATHLETIC JNRS
39	WALLACE	LEE		01/08/87	EDINBURGH	8/7/04	5' 11"	11ST 12LB	MID	HEART OF MIDLOTHIAN YOUTHS
6	WEBSTER	ANDREW	NEIL	23/04/82	DUNDEE	30/3/01	6' 0"	12ST 0LB	DEF	ARBROATH
17	WEIR	GRAHAM		10/07/84	HARTHILL	22/8/00	5' 7"	10ST 9LB	FWD	HEART OF MIDLOTHIAN YOUTHS
7	WYNESS	DENNIS		22/03/77	ABERDEEN	3/6/03	5' 10.5"	12ST 7LB	FWD	INVERNESS CAL. TH.

TICKET INFORMATION

SEASON TICKET INFORMATION

MAIN STAND
ALL SECTIONS	ADULT	330 or 285
T&N UPPER &	ADULT	230
LOWER		

WHEATFIELD STAND
UPPER	ADULT	375 or 320
LOWER	ADULT	350 or 290

GORGIE STAND
ADULT & 1 JUV	350/150/120 or 300/120/110
ADULT & 2 JUV	350/150/120 or 300/120/110
ADULT & 3 JUV	350/150/120 or 300/120/110
JUVS/SENIOR	200 or 180
DISABLED/CARER	200 or 180

LEAGUE TICKET INFORMATION

HOME SUPPORT
	ADULT/U18/U12
CATEGORY A	24/12/8
CATEGORY B	18/10/5
CAT C	16/10/5

**AWAY SUPPORT –
ROSEBURN STAND**
CATEGORY A	24/12/8
CATEGORY B	18/10/5
CAT C	16/10/5

CATEGORY A INCLUDES
RANGERS, CELTIC, HIBERNIAN

THE JAM TARTS' 10 YEAR LEAGUE RECORD

SEASON	DIV	P	W	D	L	F	A	PTS	P
1994-95	P	36	12	7	17	44	51	43	
1995-96	P	36	16	7	13	55	53	55	
1996-97	P	36	14	10	12	46	43	52	
1997-98	P	36	19	10	7	70	46	67	
1998-99	SPL	36	11	9	16	44	50	42	
1999-00	SPL	36	15	9	12	47	40	54	
2000-01	SPL	38	14	10	14	56	50	52	
2001-02	SPL	38	14	6	18	52	57	48	
2002-03	SPL	38	18	9	11	57	51	63	
2003-04	SPL	38	19	11	8	56	40	68	

SEASON STATS 2003/04

DATE	VENUE	OPPONENTS	ATT	RES	MOILANEN T.	MAYBURY A.	McCANN H.A.	PRESSLEY S.	WEBSTER A.	SLOAN R.	SEVERIN S.	STAMP P.	HARTLEY P.	DE VRIES M.	WYNESS D.	McKENNA K.	KIRK A.	McFARLANE N.	BOYACK S.	McMULLAN P.	HAMILL J.	NEILSON R.	KISNORBO P.	WEIR G.	VALOIS J-L.	SIMMONS S.	GORDON C.	BERRA C.	WALES G.	JANCZYK N.	TIERNEY G.
AUG	H	ABERDEEN	14,260	2 - 0	1	2	3	4	5	6	7	8	9	10¹	11	12	13¹	14													
AUG	A	HIBERNIAN	14,803	0 - 1	1	2	3	4	5	6	7	8	9	10	11		13	14	12												
AUG	H	DUNDEE UNITED	11,395	†3 - 0	1	2		4	5		7	8¹		10¹	11			14	9	12	3	6	13								
AUG	H	DUNFERMLINE ATH	11,934	1 - 0	1	2		4	5		7	8		10	11¹			14	9	12	3	6	13								
SEP	A	KILMARNOCK	6,925	2 - 0	1	2		4	5		7	8		10²	11		13		9	12	3	6									
SEP	H	RANGERS	14,732	0 - 4	1	2		4	5		7	8		10	11	14	12	9			6		3				13				
SEP	A	MOTHERWELL	5,888	1 - 1	1	2		4	5		7	8	9¹	10	11			6			12		3	14							
OCT	H	DUNDEE	11,348	2 - 2	1	2		4¹	5		7	8	9	10	11			6			3	13¹	12	14							
OCT	A	CELTIC	59,511	0 - 5	1	2		4	5		7	8	13	10		12		9			3	11	6	14							
OCT	A	PARTICK THISTLE	4,814	4 - 1	14		4		7		9	10¹	13	2	11²	8			5		3		6	12¹	1						
NOV	H	LIVINGSTON	11,233	3 - 1			4¹		7	8	9	10	14	2	11²		12		5		3		6	13	1						
NOV	A	ABERDEEN	9,687	1 - 0	2	3	4	5		7	12	8	10	9		6	11¹	13					14			1					
NOV	H	HIBERNIAN	16,632	††2 - 0	2			4	12			9	10	13	5	11	8		14	7	3		6		1						
NOV	A	DUNDEE UNITED	6,343	1 - 2	2			4			7¹		10	12	5	11	8		6	3			13	9	1	14					
DEC	A	DUNFERMLINE ATH	6,147	1 - 2	2¹	6		5			7		10			4	9		8	3	11	12		1		13					
DEC	H	KILMARNOCK	10,154	2 - 1	2	6	4	5			7	8¹	9	10		12	11¹	14		13	3				1						
DEC	A	RANGERS	49,592	1 - 2	2						6	7	8	10	13		4	11¹	9		5	3	12		1						
DEC	H	MOTHERWELL	10,046	0 - 0				2	6	7	8		10	13		4	11	9		5	3		12		1	14					
JAN	A	DUNDEE	6,387	2 - 1	2¹		4	5	12		8		9	10¹	14		11	7		13	3		6		1						
JAN	H	CELTIC	13,753	0 - 1	2		4	5	6	7	8		9	10	11	13				3	12				1						
JAN	H	PARTICK THISTLE	10,264	2 - 0	2		4	5	6		8		9	10	11²	12		14	7	3		13	1								
FEB	H	ABERDEEN	11,236	1 - 0	2		4¹	5	6		8		9	10	11		13	14	7	12	3				1						
FEB	A	HIBERNIAN	15,016	1 - 0	2		4¹	5			9	10	11	6		8		7	3	12		1									
FEB	H	DUNDEE UNITED	10,265	†3 - 1	2		4	5	12		8	9¹	10	11	6¹	13			7	3			1					14			
FEB	A	LIVINGSTON	4,630	3 - 2	2		4	5	13		12	9	10¹	14	6¹	11¹	8		7	3			1								
FEB	A	DUNFERMLINE ATH	8,422	0 - 0	2		4	5	9		8			11	6	10	13		7	3	12		1								
MAR	A	KILMARNOCK	5,297	1 - 1	2			5¹	9		8			4	11	10		6	7		13			1	3	12					
MAR	H	RANGERS	14,598	1 - 1	2		4	5			8	10		12¹	6	14		9	7	3	11			1			13				
MAR	H	DUNDEE	10,491	3 - 1	2		4¹				8	10¹	13	11	5		9		6¹	7	3	14		1			12				
APR	A	CELTIC	59,295	2 - 2	2		4			7		10	12¹		6¹		9		8	3	11			1	13	5					
APR	A	MOTHERWELL	5,500	1 - 1	2		4			12		9	10	11¹		13	7		6	3	8			1	5	14					
APR	A	PARTICK THISTLE	4,043	0 - 1	2		4	5			9	10	11	3	13	8		6								14	1	7			
APR	H	LIVINGSTON	10,352	1 - 1	2		4	5	13			12	6¹	11	10	9	14	8	3				1	7							
APR	H	CELTIC	12,112	1 - 1	2		4	5		7	8	10	13¹	6	11	12	9	3	14				1								
MAY	A	DUNDEE UNITED	6,620	2 - 0	2		4	5¹	7		9	10¹	14	3	13	8	6	11			1					12					
MAY	H	DUNFERMLINE ATH	10,846	2 - 1	2		4	5	7		11	10²	3		14	9	8	13	12		1				6						
MAY	A	RANGERS	47,467	1 - 0			4	13	7		10		12	9	8	5¹	6	3	11		1				2						
MAY	H	MOTHERWELL	11,619	3 - 2			4		7		10		11²	3¹	14	9	8	5	6	12	1				13	2					
		TOTAL FULL APPEARANCES			9	32	6	31	31	9	24	23	29	26	19	22	14	24	3	1	12	25	28	7	5	1	29	3	4		1
		TOTAL SUB APPEARANCES			1			1	4	2	2	1	5	9	10	10	6	5	1	6	4	3	11	6	6		3	1	7		
		TOTAL GOALS SCORED			2		5	2		1	2	3	12	7	5	9		2			1		1								

Bold figures denote goalscorers. † denotes opponent's own goal.

LEADING GOALSCORERS:

SEASON	DIV	GOALS	PLAYER
94-95	P	10	J. Robertson
95-96	P	11	J. Robertson
96-97	P	14	J. Robertson
97-98	P	14	J. Hamilton
98-99	SPL	10	S. Adam
99-00	SPL	13	G. McSwegan
00-01	SPL	12	C. Cameron
01-02	SPL	9	K. McKenna
02-03	SPL	15	M. De Vries
03-04	SPL	12	M. De Vries

MILESTONES:

YEAR OF FORMATION: 1874
MOST CAPPED PLAYER: Bobby Walker
NO. OF CAPS: 29
MOST LEAGUE POINTS IN A SEASON:
63 (Premier Division – Season 1991/92) (2 Points for a Win)
67 (Premier Division – Season 1997/98) (3 Points for a Win)
MOST LEAGUE GOALS SCORED BY A PLAYER IN A SEASON:
Barney Battles (Season 1930/31)
NO. OF GOALS SCORED: 44
RECORD ATTENDANCE: 53,396 (-v- Rangers – 13.2.1932)
RECORD VICTORY: 21-0 (-v- Anchor – EFA Cup, 1880)
RECORD DEFEAT: 1-8 (-v- Vale of Leven – Scottish Cup, 1883)

HEARTS PLAYING KITS SEASON 2004/05

FIRST KIT   SECOND KIT   THIRD KIT

HIBERNIAN
Easter Road Stadium,
12 Albion Place,
Edinburgh, EH7 5QG
CHAIRMAN
Kenneth Lewandowski
MANAGING DIRECTOR/CHIEF EXECUTIVE
Rod M. Petrie
DIRECTORS
Stephen W. Dunn (Non Executive),
Scott Lindsay (Non-Executive),
Colin McNeill (Marketing Communications),
Tim Gardiner (Financial),
Garry O'Hagan & Martin J. O'Neill, M.P
SECRETARY
Garry O'Hagan (0131) 656 7077
MANAGER
Tony Mowbray
FIRST TEAM COACH
Mark Venus
FITNESS COACH
Dougie Fowler
GOALKEEPING COACH
Ian Westwater
ACADEMY DIRECTOR/U17 COACH
John Park
YOUTH DEVELOPMENT/U19 & U15 COACH
Alistair Stevenson
FOOTBALL SAFETY OFFICERS' ASSOCIATION REPRESENTATIVE
James S.Pryde QPM (0131) 656 7081
COMMERCIAL EXECUTIVE
Russell Smith (0131) 656 7072
COMMERCIAL MANAGER
Colin McNeill
Contact (0131) 656 7095
Fax (0131) 652 2202
CLUB DOCTORS
Dr. Tom Schofield & Dr. Duncan Reid
PHYSIOTHERAPISTS
Malcolm Colquhoun & Colin McLelland
GROUNDSMAN/KIT PERSON
Tam McCourt
P.A.TO MANAGING DIRECTOR
Catherine Green (0131) 656 7071
CONFERENCE & BANQUETING
Azure Catering (0131) 656 7075
CORPORATE HOSPITALITY MANAGER
Amanda Vitesse (0131) 656 7073
MEDIA LIAISON OFFICER
David Forsyth/Benchmark Media
Tel (0131) 473 2347
Fax (0131) 473 2348
MATCHDAY PROGRAMME EDITOR
Jim Jeffrey
TELEPHONES
Ground (0131) 661 2159
Fax Ground (0131) 659 6488
Fax Commercial (0131) 652 2202
Ticket Office (0131) 661 1875
24 Hour Ticket Hotline
(0870) 840 1875
E-MAIL & INTERNET ADDRESS
club@hibernianfc.co.uk
www.hibernianfc.co.uk or www.hibs.org.uk
CLUB SHOP
12 Albion Place, Edinburgh
Open Mon.-Sat.: 9.00a.m. – 5.00p.m.,
Home matchdays:
9.30a.m. – 3.00p.m (& after match).
Tel (0131) 656 7078
e-mail: shopcounter@hibernianfc.co.uk
24 Hour Credit Card Hotline
(0870) 848 1400
OFFICIAL SUPPORTERS CLUB
11 Sunnyside Lane, Off Easter Road,
Edinburgh, EH7
TEAM CAPTAIN
Ian Murray
SHIRT SPONSOR
Whyte & Mackay
KIT SUPPLIER
Le Coq Sportif

28

LIST OF PLAYERS 2004/05

SQUAD NO.	PLAYERS SURNAME	FIRST NAME	MIDDLE NAME	DATE OF BIRTH	PLACE OF BIRTH	DATE SIGNED	HEIGHT FT INS	WEIGHT ST LBS	POSITION ON PITCH	PREVIOUS CLUB
21	BAILLIE	JONATHAN		02/09/85	IRVINE	25/7/02	6' 2"	12ST 9LB	DEF	HIBERNIAN YOUTHS
14	BEUZELIN	GUILLAUME		14/04/79	STE ADRESSE	23/7/04	5' 9"	12ST 11LB	MID	LE HAVRE
30	BROWN	ALISTAIR	HUGH	12/12/85	IRVINE	3/7/02	6' 1"	12ST 4LB	GK	HIBERNIAN YOUTHS
18	BROWN	SCOTT		25/06/85	DUNFERMLINE	25/7/02	5' 9"	12ST 4LB	FWD	HIBERNIAN 'S' FORM
1	BROWN	SIMON		03/12/76	CHELMSFORD	23/6/04	6' 2"	15ST 0LB	GK	COLCHESTER UNITED
-	BRYSON	KYLE	SCOTT	24/07/87	IRVINE	21/7/04	6' 1"	11ST 9LB	DEF	KILMARNOCK YOUTHS
4	CALDWELL	GARY		12/04/82	STIRLING	30/1/04	5' 11"	11ST 10LB	DEF	NEWCASTLE UNITED
-	CAMPBELL	ROSS	ALEXANDER	03/07/87	GALASHIELS	21/7/04	5' 10"	9ST 3LB	FWD	HIBERNIAN YOUTHS
-	CHISHOLM	ROSS	STEPHEN	14/01/88	IRVINE	30/1/04	5' 9"	10ST 4LB	DEF	HIBERNIAN YOUTHS
-	CROOKS	GARY	ALISTAIR	15/02/87	FALKIRK	11/9/03	5' 8"	11ST 0LB	MID	ST. JOHNSTONE
17	DOBBIE	STEPHEN		05/12/82	GLASGOW	4/7/03	5' 8.5"	10ST 4LB	FWD	RANGERS
-	FENWICK	PAUL	JOSEPH	25/08/69	LONDON	2/6/00	6' 2"	12ST 7LB	DEF	RAITH ROVERS
-	FLETCHER	STEVEN		26/03/87	SHREWSBURY	4/7/03	6' 1"	12ST 0LB	FWD	HIBERNIAN YOUTHS
11	GLASS	STEPHEN		23/05/76	DUNDEE	10/7/03	5' 9.5"	10ST 13LB	MID/FWD	WATFORD
-	HALPIN	PATRICK		31/01/88	DUNFERMLINE	21/7/04	5' 9"	11ST 1LB	MID	HIBERNIAN YOUTHS
-	KANE	JOHN		08/06/87	GLASGOW	22/9/03	6' 1"	10ST 8LB	MID	HIBERNIAN YOUTHS
-	LYNCH	SEAN		31/01/87	DECHMONT	26/7/04	5' 10"	10ST 10LB	MID	LIVINGSTON YOUTHS
-	MACKISON	SCOTT		24/07/86	STIRLING	4/7/03	5' 11"	11ST 0LB	DEF	RANGERS
-	M'CAFFREY	DERMOTT		29/03/86	OMAGH	30/1/04	5' 11"	10ST 12LB	DEF	HIBERNIAN YOUTHS
-	M'CANN	KEVIN		11/09/87	GLASGOW	21/7/04	5' 10"	11ST 2LB	DEF	HIBERNIAN YOUTHS
-	M'CLUSKEY	JAMIE		06/11/87	BELLSHILL	16/1/04	5' 7"	8ST 8LB	MID	HIBERNIAN YOUTHS
25	M'DONALD	KEVIN	ALAN	26/06/85	NEWCASTLE	25/7/01	5' 10"	10ST 9LB	MID	SUNDERLAND
-	M'KENZIE	JAMIE		08/05/86	KIRKCALDY	4/7/03	6' 1"	12ST 10LB	DEF	HIBERNIAN YOUTHS
7	M'MANUS	THOMAS	KELLY	28/02/81	GLASGOW	10/7/97	5' 10"	10ST 2LB	FWD	HIBERNIAN 'S' FORM
20	MORROW	SAMUEL		03/03/85	DERRY	1/7/04	6' 0"	12ST 10LB	FWD	IPSWICH TOWN
5	MURDOCK	COLIN	JAMES	02/07/75	BALLYMENA	17/7/03	6' 3"	13ST 7LB	DEF	PRESTON NORTH END
3	MURPHY	DAVID		01/03/84	HARTLEPOOL	28/7/04	6' 1"	13ST 8LB	DEF	MIDDLESBROUGH
6	MURRAY	IAN	WILLIAM	20/03/81	EDINBURGH	13/7/99	6' 0"	11ST 5LB	MID	DUNDEE UNITED
-	NELSON	KYLE		05/03/87	CO. DERRY	27/8/04	6' 2"	14ST 14LB	GK	GLENAVON YOUTHS
12	NICOL	KEVIN		19/01/82	KIRKCALDY	17/1/02	5' 10"	11ST 7LB	MID	RAITH ROVERS
-	NOBLE	STEVEN	JOHN	21/08/86	EDINBURGH	19/8/03	5' 9"	10ST 6LB	MID	RANGERS
-	NOTMAN	STEVEN		29/09/86	EDINBURGH	4/7/03	5' 11"	10ST 11LB	MID	HIBERNIAN YOUTHS
9	O'CONNOR	GARRY	LAWRENCE	07/05/83	EDINBURGH	14/5/99	6' 1"	12ST 7LB	FWD	SALVESEN B.C.
-	O'NEILL	KEVIN		16/05/86	EDINBURGH	9/7/02	6' 2"	12ST 6LB	DEF	HIBERNIAN YOUTHS
23	ORMAN	ALEN		31/05/78	BUGOJNO	28/6/01	6' 0"	12ST 12LB	DEF/MID	ROYAL ANTWERP
-	POW	RYAN		30/06/87	EDINBURGH	4/7/03	5' 8"	10ST 2LB	MID	AIRDRIEONIANS
13	REID	ANDREW	WILLIAM	06/03/85	ABERDEEN	30/6/04	6' 1"	14ST 0LB	GK	MOTHERWELL
10	RIORDAN	DEREK	GEORGE	16/01/83	EDINBURGH	14/5/99	5' 11"	10ST 8LB	FWD	HUTCHISON VALE B.C.
24	SHIELDS	JAY		06/01/85	EDINBURGH	4/7/03	5' 7"	11ST 4LB	MID	HIBERNIAN YOUTHS
22	SHIELS	DEAN		01/02/85	MAGHERFELT	9/7/04	5' 11"	9ST 10LB	FWD	ARSENAL
-	SMITH	DARREN	JAMES	06/12/86	EDINBURGH	4/7/03	5' 10"	11ST 6LB	MID	HIBERNIAN YOUTHS
2	SMITH	GARY		25/03/71	GLASGOW	13/7/00	6' 0"	12ST 3LB	DEF	ABERDEEN
19	THOMSON	KEVIN		14/10/84	EDINBURGH	10/8/01	5' 11"	11ST 4LB	MID	HIBERNIAN YOUTHS
-	VENUS	MARK		06/04/67	HARTLEPOOL	23/6/04	6' 6"	12ST 12LB	DEF	HORNCHURCH
-	WEIGHTMAN	NICHOLAS	JOHN	06/04/87	LANARK	4/7/03	5' 10"	10ST 11LB	MID	HIBERNIAN YOUTHS
15	WHITTAKER	STEVEN	GORDON	16/06/84	EDINBURGH	1/8/00	6' 1"	13ST 9LB	MID	STAR A B.C.

TICKET INFORMATION

SEASON TICKET PRICING 2004-2005

	ADULT	SENIOR	15-18/STUDENT	14 & UNDER
WEST STAND	300-325	125-175	100-150	45*-65
FAMOUS FIVE UPPER	300	125	100	45*-65
FAMOUS FIVE LOWER	275	100	75	35*-55
EAST STAND	275	175	150	105*-125

*HIBS KIDS MEMBERS

TICKET PRICING 2004-2005

STAND	CAT A ADULT	CAT A CHILD/SENIOR	CAT B ADULT	CAT B CHILD/SENIOR
WEST STAND	24	10	20	10
FAMOUS FIVE UPPER	24	10	20	10
FAMOUS FIVE LOWER (FAMILY SECTION)	20	10	20	10
EAST STAND	20	10	17	10
WHYTE & MACKAY (SOUTH) STAND	24	10	20	10

THE HIBEES' 10 YEAR LEAGUE RECORD

SEASON	DIV	P	W	D	L	F	A	PTS
1994-95	P	36	12	17	7	49	37	53
1995-96	P	36	11	10	15	43	57	43
1996-97	P	36	9	11	16	38	55	38
1997-98	P	36	6	12	18	38	59	30
1998-99	F	36	28	5	3	84	33	89
1999-00	SPL	36	10	11	15	49	61	41
2000-01	SPL	38	18	12	8	57	35	66
2001-02	SPL	38	10	11	17	51	56	41
2002-03	SPL	38	15	6	17	56	64	51
2003-04	SPL	38	11	11	16	41	60	44

SCOTTISH PREMIER LEAGUE

The hibees' stats 2003/04

SEASON STATS 2003/04

DATE	VENUE	OPPONENTS	ATT	RES	ANDERSSON D.	ORMAN A.	SMITH G.	ZAMBERNARDI Y.	KOUO-DOUMBE M.	MURRAY I.	WISS J.	BRESNER G.	GLASS S.	RIORDAN D.	BROWN S.	McMANUS T.	DOBBIE S.	O'CONNOR G.	WHITTAKER S.	MURDOCK C.	EDGE R.	REID A.	THOMSON K.	NICOL K.	McCLUSKEY J.	CALDWELL G.	BAILLIE J.	KANE J.	FLETCHER S.	SHIELDS J.	McDONALD K.
-AUG	A	DUNDEE UNITED	9,809	2-1	1	2	3	4	5	6	7	8	9	10[1]	11	12[1]	13														
-AUG	H	HEARTS	14,803	1-0	1	2	3	4	5	6	7	8	14	9	11	10	13	12[1]													
-AUG	A	RANGERS	49,642	2-5	1	2	3	4	5	6[1]	7		13	9	8	10[1]	12	11	14												
-AUG	H	ABERDEEN	10,682	1-1	1		3	4	5	6	7	8	12	13	9[1]	10	14	11		2											
-SEP	H	MOTHERWELL	8,387	0-2	1		3	4	5	6		8	7	9	11	13	14	10	12	2											
-SEP	A	DUNFERMLINE ATH	8,715	0-0	1	4		5	6	7	8		9	12	11	13		10		2	3											
-SEP	H	CELTIC	12,032	1-2	1	4		5[1]	6	7	8		9	13	12	14	11	10		2	3											
-OCT	A	PARTICK THISTLE	4,125	1-0	1	4		5	6	7	8[1]		12	9	13	11		10		2	3											
-OCT	H	LIVINGSTON	8,562	0-2	1	4		5	6	7	8		11	14	13	10				2	3											
-OCT	H	KILMARNOCK	7,191	3-1	1	4		5	6	8	7		9[1]	11[1]	14	10	13	2[1]	3	12											
-NOV	A	DUNDEE	7,392	1-1	1	4	3	5	6			7	9[1]	12	11	13	10	14	2				8								
-NOV	H	DUNDEE UNITED	8,756	†2-2	1	4	3	5	6	8			9	11[1]	14	12	10	13	2				7								
-NOV	A	HEARTS	16,632	0-2	1	4	3	5	6	8			9	11	14	13	10	12	2				7								
-NOV	H	RANGERS	11,116	0-1	1	4	3	5	6	8			9		12	10		2					7	13							
-DEC	A	ABERDEEN	7,863	1-3	1	12	3	5				8	11	13		7[1]	10		2	4			6								
-DEC	H	MOTHERWELL	4,533	1-0	1		3	4		8	7		9[1]	11		10	5	2					6								
-DEC	A	DUNFERMLINE ATH	9,085	1-2	1		3	4				9[1]	11	7	12	10	5	2					6								
-DEC	A	CELTIC	59,542	0-6	1		3	4			8		9[1]	11	7	12	10	5	2				13	6	14						
-JAN	H	PARTICK THISTLE	8,875	3-2	1	13	3			8	7		11		9[1]	10[1]	5[1]	2					12	6							
-JAN	A	LIVINGSTON	4,948	0-1	1		3	7				9	11	13	14	10	5	2					12	6	8						
-JAN	A	KILMARNOCK	5,571	2-0	1		3	7				9	11[1]	12	14	10[1]	5	2					8	6	13						
-JAN	H	DUNDEE	8,023	1-1	1		3	4		7		9[1]	11		14	10	5	2					8	6	13		12				
-FEB	A	DUNDEE UNITED	6,389	0-0	1			4		7		9		11		10	8	2	3				6			5					
-FEB	H	HEARTS	15,016	1-1	1			4		7		9[1]	11	12	14	10	13	2	3				8	6		5					
-FEB	A	RANGERS	49,698	0-3	1	2		4		7		13	11	14	12	10	8	3	9				6			5					
-FEB	H	ABERDEEN	10,416	1-1	1		3	4				9	11	8	12	10		2	6				7			5					
-MAR	H	CELTIC	9,456	0-4	1		3	13				12	11	10	9			6		4	8		7			5	2				
-MAR	H	MOTHERWELL	5,568	3-3	1			4				9[1]	11	10			12	2	3	8[1]	6	7[1]				5					
-MAR	A	PARTICK THISTLE	3,155	1-1	1			4				9	11	10		13	12	2[1]	3	8	6	7				5					
-APR	H	LIVINGSTON	6,223	3-1	1	13						9[2]	11	10[1]		12	7	2	3	8	6					5	4	14			
-APR	H	KILMARNOCK	7,287	3-0	1			4				9[1]	11			10	7	2	3	8	6[1]	12				5[1]			13		
-APR	A	DUNFERMLINE ATH	5,041	1-1	1			4				9[1]	11	10		12	13	2	3	8	6	7				5					
-APR	H	DUNDEE	5,508	2-2	1	12						9[2]	11	10		13	6	2	3	8						5					
-APR	A	KILMARNOCK	4,886	0-2	1							9	11	10		12	7	2	3	8									13		
-MAY	H	DUNDEE	6,180	1-0	1					8		9[1]	11	10	13		12	2	3	7	6	4							14		
-MAY	H	PARTICK THISTLE	5,380	1-2	1	12				8			11	10	9		13	2[1]	3	7	6	4							14		
-MAY	A	ABERDEEN	6,781	1-0	1		3	4		8			11	12			10[1]	6	2	9		7				5					
-MAY	A	LIVINGSTON	4,409	1-4	1		3	4[1]		6			11	9			10	13		7						5			8	2	12
TOTAL FULL APPEARANCES					38	13	19	7	33	14	13	22	9	27	34	18	7	27	15	32	20	16	23	11		16	2			1	1
TOTAL SUB APPEARANCES						5		1					3	7	2	14	20	6	13				4		4	1	1	1	4	1
TOTAL GOALS SCORED								2	1		1			15	3	4	2	4	1	3					1	1	1		1

Bold figures denote goalscorers. † denotes opponent's own goal.

LEADING GOALSCORERS:

SEASON	DIV	GOALS	PLAYER
94-95	P	10	D. Jackson, M. O'Neill, K. Wright
95-96	P	9	D. Jackson, K. Wright
96-97	P	11	D. Jackson
97-98	P	9	S. Crawford
98-99	F	14	S. Crawford
99-00	SPL	11	K. Miller
00-01	SPL	11	M-M. Paatelainen
01-02	SPL	10	G. O'Connor
02-03	SPL	12	T. McManus
03-04	SPL	15	D. Riordan

MILESTONES:

YEAR OF FORMATION: 1875
MOST CAPPED PLAYER: Lawrie Reilly
NO. OF CAPS: 38
MOST LEAGUE POINTS IN A SEASON:
57 (First Division – Season 1980/81) (2 Points for a Win)
89 (First Division – Season 1998/99) (3 Points for a Win)
MOST LEAGUE GOALS SCORED BY A PLAYER IN A SEASON:
Joe Baker (Season 1959/60)
NO. OF GOALS SCORED: 42
RECORD ATTENDANCE: 65,840 (-v- Heart of Midlothian – 2.1.1950)
RECORD VICTORY: 22-1 (-v- 42nd Highlanders 3.9.1881)
RECORD DEFEAT: 0-10 (-v- Rangers – 24.12.1898)

HIBERNIAN PLAYING KITS SEASON 2004/05

FIRST KIT — SECOND KIT — THIRD KIT

LIST OF PLAYERS 2004/05

SQUAD NO.	PLAYERS SURNAME	FIRST NAME	MIDDLE NAME	DATE OF BIRTH	PLACE OF BIRTH	DATE SIGNED	HEIGHT FT INS	WEIGHT ST LBS	POSITION ON PITCH	PREVIOUS CLUB
9	BAYNE	GRAHAM	PATRICK	22/08/79	KIRKCALDY	2/6/04	6' 1"	12ST 9LB	FWD	ROSS COUNTY
24	BLACK	IAN	GEORGE	14/03/85	EDINBURGH	30/7/04	5' 7.5"	9ST 12LB	MID	BLACKBURN ROVERS
1	BROWN	MARK		28/02/81	MOTHERWELL	2/8/02	6' 1.5"	13ST 2LB	GK	MOTHERWELL
11	CARRICONDO	JUANJO		04/05/77	BARCELONA	29/7/04	5' 7"	10ST 7LB	FWD	REAL JEAN
-	CHRISTIE	ARRON	IAN	29/06/86	KIRKCALDY	11/6/03	5' 8"	9ST 10LB	MID/FWD	INVERNESS CAL TH FORM D
4	DODS	DARREN		07/06/75	EDINBURGH	30/7/04	6' 1"	13ST 2LB	DEF	ST. JOHNSTONE
12	DUNCAN	RUSSELL	ALLAN	15/09/80	ABERDEEN	3/8/01	5' 10"	10ST 10LB	DEF/MID	FORFAR ATHLETIC
-	FINNIGAN	CHRISTOPHER	JAMES	05/04/86	GLASGOW	11/1/03	5' 10"	11ST 0LB	MID/FWD	INVERNESS CAL TH FORM D
23	FOX	LIAM		02/02/84	EDINBURGH	30/7/04	5' 11"	11ST 0LB	MID	CRUSADERS
21	FRASER	MICHAEL	ALAN	08/10/83	INVERNESS	9/1/03	6' 3"	12ST 7LB	GK	BRORA RANGERS
3	GOLABEK	STUART	WILLIAM	05/11/74	INVERNESS	27/5/99	5' 10"	11ST 0LB	DEF	ROSS COUNTY
10	HART	RICHARD		30/03/78	INVERNESS	1/8/02	5' 10"	12ST 5LB	DEF/MID	BRORA RANGERS
-	HASTINGS	RICHARD	COREY	18/05/77	PRINCE GEORGE B.C.	23/8/04	5' 10"	11ST 6LB	DEF	MVV MAASTRICHT
8	HISLOP	STEVEN	JAMES	14/06/78	EDINBURGH	31/1/03	6' 2"	12ST 0LB	FWD	ROSS COUNTY
-	JARVIE	DARREN	JAMES	29/08/87	INVERNESS	2/6/04	5' 11"	12ST 8LB	DEF	INVERNESS CAL TH FORM II
15	KEOGH	LIAM	MICHAEL	06/09/81	ABERDEEN	2/8/02	5' 9"	12ST 3LB	FWD	ST. MIRREN
-	KERR	GUY	DUNCAN	03/04/88	EDINBURGH	24/5/04	6' 2"	12ST 0LB	DEF	DUNFERMLINE ATHLET
-	McKINNON	LEWIS	CRAIG	21/03/85	INVERNESS	11/7/03	6' 0"	11ST 7LB	FWD	DUFFTOWN JUNIORS
-	McLAREN	PAUL	ALAN	14/04/86	INVERNESS	11/6/03	5' 10"	10ST 6LB	MID	INVERNESS CAL TH FORM D
20	McMILLAN	CRAIG	ALEXANDER	25/06/84	INVERNESS	21/5/03	6' 0"	11ST 0LB	MID	CLACHNACUDDIN
-	McRAE	DAVID	ALEXANDER	25/10/84	DRUMNADROCHIT	21/5/03	5' 11"	11ST 0LB	MID	CLACHNACUDDIN
-	McALLISTER	RORY		13/05/87	ABERDEEN	25/8/04	6' 1"	12ST 7LB	FWD	ABERDEEN
6	McBAIN	ROY	ADAM	07/11/74	ABERDEEN	4/8/00	5' 11"	11ST 5LB	DEF/MID	ROSS COUNTY
5	McCAFFREY	STUART	MUIR	30/05/79	GLASGOW	1/12/00	5' 11.5"	12ST 0LB	DEF	ABERDEEN
22	McMULLAN	PAUL	ALEXANDER	13/03/84	BELLSHILL	21/5/03	5' 8"	11ST 12LB	DEF	HEART OF MIDLOTHIAN
14	MUNRO	GRANT	JOHN	15/09/80	INVERNESS	21/2/00	6' 0"	12ST 7LB	DEF	INVERNESS CAL TH FORM S
-	MUNRO	PAUL	ALEXANDER	04/09/87	BANFF	16/8/04	5' 9"	11ST 12LB	MID	HUNTLY
18	PROCTOR	DAVID	WILLIAM	04/05/84	BELLSHILL	7/7/03	6' 0"	11ST 2LB	MID	HIBERNIAN
19	PRUNTY	BRYAN		12/01/83	COATBRIDGE	6/8/04	5' 8"	10ST 7LB	FWD	ABERDEEN
-	ROBERTSON	DEAN	FREDERICK	04/03/87	EDINBURGH	9/8/04	5' 8"	10ST 12LB	MID	HEART OF MIDLOTHIAN
-	RUTHERFORD	MARTYN		15/04/87	EDINBURGH	4/6/04	5' 10.5"	11ST 0LB	DEF/MID	HEART OF MIDLOTHIAN
-	SMITH	JONATHAN		26/11/87	INVERNESS	3/8/04	5' 10"	11ST 5LB	GK	INVERNESS CAL TH FORM D
-	SOANE	STUART		05/11/87	DUNFERMLINE	12/8/04	5' 10"	9ST 4LB	MID	INVERNESS CAL TH FORM D
-	SUTHERLAND	ALEXANDER	GEORGE	07/09/87	WICK	5/8/04	5' 6"	10ST 0LB	MID	INVERNESS CAL TH FORM D
-	SUTHERLAND	JAMES	JOHN	01/12/86	INVERNESS	29/1/03	5' 10"	10ST 7LB	MID	INVERNESS CAL TH FORM D
17	THOMSON	DARRAN	HUNTER	31/01/84	EDINBURGH	9/7/03	5' 10"	10ST 7LB	MID	HIBERNIAN
2	TOKELY	ROSS	NORMAN	08/03/79	ABERDEEN	3/6/96	6' 3"	13ST 6LB	DEF/MID	HUNTLY
-	WATSON	PHILIP		17/05/87	ABERDEEN	9/8/04	6' 0"	10ST 10LB	DEF	ABERDEEN
7	WILSON	BARRY	JOHN	16/02/72	KIRKCALDY	31/8/03	5' 11"	13ST 0LB	MID/FWD	LIVINGSTON

CALEY THISTLE'S 10 YEAR LEAGUE RECORD

SEASON	DIV	P	W	D	L	F	A	PTS
1994-95	T	36	12	9	15	48	61	45
1995-96	T	36	15	12	9	64	38	57
1996-97	T	36	23	7	6	70	37	76
1997-98	S	36	13	10	13	65	51	49
1998-99	S	36	21	9	6	80	48	72
1999-00	F	36	13	10	13	60	55	49
2000-01	F	36	14	12	10	71	54	54
2001-02	F	36	13	9	14	60	51	48
2002-03	F	36	20	5	11	74	45	65
2003-04	F	36	21	7	8	67	33	70

SEASON STATS 2003/04

DATE	VENUE	OPPONENTS	ATT	RES	BROWN M.	TOKELY R.	GOLABEK S.	MANN R.	McCAFFERY S.	DUNCAN R.	HART R.	HISLOP S.	RITCHIE P.	McBAIN R.	BINGHAM D.	PROCTOR D.	CHRISTIE C.	THOMSON D.	LOW A.	WILSON B.	KEOGH L.	McMILLAN C.	MUNRO G.	MACKIE D.	MACRAE D.	McKINNON L.
AUG	A	FALKIRK	2,619	1-2	1	2	3	4	5¹	6	7	8	9	10	11	12	15									
AUG	H	CLYDE	1,839	0-0	1	2	3	4	5	6	7	8	15	11	9				10	14						
AUG	A	ST. JOHNSTONE	3,031	2-1	1	2	3	4	5	6	7	8¹	15	11	9¹	12			10							
AUG	A	ROSS COUNTY	5,020	1-1	1	2	3	4¹	5	6	7	8	9	10	11					16						
SEP	H	AYR UNITED	1,476	1-0	1	2	3	4	5	8	10	16	9¹	6	11	12			14		7					
SEP	A	BRECHIN CITY	652	2-0	1		3	4	5	6	10		9¹	8¹	11	2			14		7					
SEP	H	ST. MIRREN	1,896	2-0	1	2	3	4	5¹	6		15	9¹	8	11	10					7					
OCT	H	RAITH ROVERS	1,707	2-1	1	2¹	3	4	5¹	6		15	9	8	11	10					7	12				
OCT	A	QUEEN OF THE SOUTH	3,547	2-3	1	2	3	4	5	6		8	9¹	10	11¹				14		7	12	16			
NOV	H	FALKIRK	2,223	†1-2	1	2	3	4	5	6	10	9	15	8	11						7	12				
NOV	H	CLYDE	734	0-1	1	2	3		5	6	10	9		8	11				14		7	12	15	4		
NOV	A	AYR UNITED	1,464	3-0	1	2	3¹		5	6	10¹	9¹		8	11				14		7	12	15	4		
NOV	H	ROSS COUNTY	3,523	3-3	1	2	3		5	6	10	9¹	16	8	11¹				7¹		12		4			
NOV	A	ST. MIRREN	2,204	4-0	1	2	3	4		6	9	16	8²	11²				14		7	10			12		
NOV	H	BRECHIN CITY	1,393	5-0	1	2²	3	4	5	6	9¹	16	8	11				14		7¹	10¹	15				
DEC	H	QUEEN OF THE SOUTH	1,745	4-1	1	2	3	4	5¹	6	9²	16	8	11				14		7¹	10	15				
DEC	A	RAITH ROVERS	1,432	3-1	1	2	3	4	5	6	9	16¹	8	11¹						7	10	15	12¹			
DEC	H	ST. JOHNSTONE	2,949	1-0	1	2	3	4	5	6	9	16	8	11						7¹	10					
JAN	A	ROSS COUNTY	6,020	0-1	1	2	3	4	5	6		9	8	11				14		7	11	15	12			
JAN	H	AYR UNITED	1,443	2-1	1	2	3	4	5	6		9¹		11¹				8		14	10		12	7		
JAN	A	BRECHIN CITY	669	4-2	1	2	3	4	5	6¹	14	9¹		11¹				8¹			10		7	16		
JAN	H	ST. MIRREN	1,913	1-1	1	2	3	4	5	6	15	9	8	11¹				14			10		12	7		
FEB	H	RAITH ROVERS	1,879	3-0	1	2	3	4		6	9	8	11¹					7		14¹	10¹		5		16	15
FEB	A	QUEEN OF THE SOUTH	2,021	1-2	1	2	3	4		6	9¹	8						11		7	10	15	5			
MAR	A	FALKIRK	2,268	1-2	1	2	3	4	5	6	15	9¹	8	11				14		7	10	16			
MAR	A	ST. JOHNSTONE	2,913	2-3	1	2	3	4	5	6		9²	8	12	16			11		7	10					
MAR	H	CLYDE	2,645	3-1	1	2	3	4	5	6	15	9¹	8	11¹	16					7¹	10		14			
MAR	A	AYR UNITED	1,207	1-0	1	2	3	4	5	6	9			11				12		7¹	10	14	8			
MAR	H	ROSS COUNTY	4,019	1-0	1	2	3	4	5	6	15	9	8					11		7¹	10		14			
APR	A	ST. MIRREN	2,272	0-0	1	2		4	5	6	14	8	9					11		7	10	3			
APR	H	BRECHIN CITY	1,198	1-0	1	2		4	5	6	10	9	16	8	11			15¹		14		3	7			
APR	H	QUEEN OF THE SOUTH	2,126	4-1	1	2	3	4	5	6	10	9²	15	8	11¹			7¹		14		16				
APR	A	RAITH ROVERS	1,748	1-0	1	2	3	4	5		6	11	9¹	8	16	15		10			7					
MAY	H	FALKIRK	2,631	0-0	1	2	3	4	5		6	16	9	8	11	15		14		7	10					
MAY	A	CLYDE	4,722	2-1	1		2	3	4	5		6	16¹	9	8	11	2			7	10¹		12			
MAY	H	ST. JOHNSTONE	6,092	3-1	1	2	3	4	5		6	16	9¹	8	11¹					7¹	10					
TOTAL FULL APPEARANCES					36	34	34	33	34	32	16	18	23	32	31	4	2	7	26	21		8	5			
TOTAL SUB APPEARANCES											5	8	11			2		7	1	14	1	3	8	10	7	1	2	1
TOTAL GOALS SCORED						3	1	1	4	1	1	9	14	3	13			1		11	3		1			

Bold figures denote goalscorers. † denotes opponent's own goal.

LEADING GOALSCORERS:

SEASON	DIV	GOALS	PLAYER
-95	T	6	C. Christie, A. Hercher
-96	T	23	I. Stewart
-97	T	27	I. Stewart
-98	S	16	I. Stewart
-99	S	20	S. McLean
-00	F	13	B. Wilson
-01	F	24	D. Wyness
-02	F	18	D. Wyness
-03	F	19	D. Wyness
-04	F	14	P. Ritchie

MILESTONES:

YEAR OF FORMATION: 1994
MOST LEAGUE POINTS IN A SEASON:
76 (Third Division – Season 1996/97) (3 Points for a Win)
MOST LEAGUE GOALS SCORED BY A PLAYER IN A SEASON:
Iain Stewart (Season 1996/97)
NO. OF GOALS SCORED: 27
RECORD ATTENDANCE: 4,931 (-v- Ross County – 23.1.1996 - at Telford Street Park) 6,290 (-v- Aberdeen – 20.2.2000 (Scottish Cup) at Caledonian Stadium)
RECORD VICTORY: 8-1 (-v- Annan Athletic – Scottish Cup, 24.1.1998)
RECORD DEFEAT: 1-5 (-v- Morton – First Division, 12.11.1999) (-v- Airdrieonians – First Division, 15.4.2000)

INVERNESS CT PLAYING KITS SEASON 2004/05

FIRST KIT   SECOND KIT   THIRD KIT

KILMARNOCK
Rugby Park, Rugby Road, Kilmarnock, KA1 2DP
CHAIRMAN
James.T. Moffat
VICE CHAIRMAN
Michael Johnston
DIRECTORS
James H. Clark, Robert Wyper,
& Gordon Jackson, M.S.P
HONORARY PRESIDENT
Sir John Orr, O.B.E
GENERAL MANAGER
David MacKinnon
**SECRETARY, OFFICE ADMINISTRATOR
& MEDIA LIAISON OFFICER**
Mrs Angela Burnett
MANAGER
Jim Jefferies
ASSISTANT MANAGER
Billy Brown
FIRST TEAM COACH
Ian Durrant
RESERVE COACH
Alan Robertson
FITNESS COACH & PHYSIOTHERAPIST
Alex MacQueen
GOALKEEPING COACH
Jim Stewart
CHIEF SCOUT
Walter Kidd
COMMUNITY COACH
Paul McDonald
YOUTH DEVELOPMENT COACH
Alan Robertson
YOUTH COACHES
Paul Clarke & Stuart McLean
CLUB DOCTOR
Dr Ivan Brenkel
GROUNDSMAN
Mark Gallacher
KIT PERSON
Manson Fowler
COMMERCIAL MANAGER Colin Fraser
**LOTTERY MANAGER
& MEDIA LIAISON OFFICER**
David MacKinnon
**COMMERCIAL ASSISTANT/
MATCHDAY HOSPITALITY**
Anne Clark & Ray Montgomerie (01563) 545312
PARK HOTEL
On site hotel situated at ground (01563) 545999
**FOOTBALL SAFETY OFFICERS'
ASSOCIATION REPRESENTATIVE**
Bob Pitt
MATCHDAY PROGRAMME EDITOR
Richard Cairns
TELEPHONES
Ground & Matchday/Ticket Information
(01563) 545300
Sec Bus (01563) 545302
Fax (01563) 545303
E/MAIL & INTERNET ADDRESS
aburnett@kilmarnockfc.co.uk
www.kilmarnockfc.co.uk
CLUB SHOP
Situated in the Commercial Centre at the
ground. Tel (01563) 545310.
Open Mon to Fri 9.00 a.m.–5.00 p.m.
Saturday home matchdays 10.00 a.m.–5.30 p.m.
Saturday away matchdays 10.00 a.m.–2.00 p.m.
buy on-line www.kilmarnockfc.co.uk/shop
OFFICIAL SUPPORTERS CLUB
c/o Rugby Park, Kilmarnock, KA1 2DP
TEAM CAPTAIN
Gary Locke
SHIRT SPONSOR
Seriously Strong Cheddar
KIT SUPPLIER
TFG

Kilmarnoc

LIST OF PLAYERS 2004/05

SQUAD NO.	PLAYERS SURNAME	FIRST NAME	MIDDLE NAME	DATE OF BIRTH	PLACE OF BIRTH	DATE SIGNED	HEIGHT FT INS	WEIGHT ST LBS	POSITION ON PITCH	PREVIOUS CLUB
36	ADAMS	JAMES	STEWART	26/08/87	STRANRAER	06/30/04	6' 1"	11ST 5LB	MID	KILMARNOCK YOUTH
32	BELL	CAMERON		18/09/86	DUMFRIES	30/8/02	5' 11"	12ST 4LB	GK	QUEEN OF THE SOUT
9	BOYD	KRIS		18/08/83	IRVINE	25/8/99	6' 0"	12ST 12LB	FWD	KILMARNOCK 'S' FOR
34	CAMPBELL	ROBERT	LINDSAY	22/07/86	GLASGOW	15/1/03	6' 2"	12ST 8LB	FWD	KILMARNOCK YOUTH
23	CANNING	MARK		12/09/83	BELLSHILL	27/10/99	5' 11"	12ST 2LB	DEF/MID	KILMARNOCK YOUTH
30	COCHRANE	ROBBIE		20/05/86	IRVINE	22/5/02	6' 2"	11ST 3LB	DEF	KILMARNOCK YOUTH
1	COMBE	ALAN		03/04/74	EDINBURGH	2/7/04	6' 2"	13ST 2LB	GK	BRADFORD CITY
37	COYNE	THOMAS		30/05/87	DUNDEE	3/9/03	6' 0"	11ST 8LB	FWD	PAISLEY UNITED
10	DARGO	CRAIG		03/01/78	EDINBURGH	6/6/00	5' 6"	10ST 1LB	FWD	RAITH ROVERS
20	DI GIACOMO	PAUL		30/06/82	GLASGOW	8/7/98	5' 11"	11ST 12LB	FWD	KILMARNOCK YOUTH
17	DILLON	SHAUN		24/08/84	GREENOCK	18/9/00	5' 9.5"	11ST 1LB	DEF	KILMARNOCK YOUTH
6	DINDELEUX	FREDERIC		16/01/74	LILLE	24/7/99	5' 11"	11ST 10LB	DEF	LILLE OLYMPIC SPORTIN
21	DODDS	RHIAN		10/03/79	IRVINE	29/8/03	5' 9"	11ST 3LB	MID	ROBERT MORRIS UNI
2	FOWLER	JAMES		26/10/80	STIRLING	18/10/97	5' 9"	10ST 11LB	DEF/MID	GAIRDOCH B.C.
5	GREER	GORDON		14/12/80	GLASGOW	31/8/03	6' 2"	12ST 5LB	DEF	BLACKBURN ROVERS
38	GRIFFIN	ANDREW	FRANCIS	20/03/88	GLASGOW	30/6/04	5' 8"	10ST 11LB	DEF	KILMARNOCK YOUTH
31	HAMILL	JAMIE		29/07/86	IRVINE	16/1/03	5' 8"	12ST 2LB	DEF	KILMARNOCK 'S' FOR
3	HAY	GARRY		07/09/77	IRVINE	18/8/95	5' 7.5"	10ST 4LB	DEF/MID	KILMARNOCK B.C.
11	INVINCIBLE	DANIELE	ANTHONY	31/03/79	BRISBANE	30/7/03	5' 11"	12ST 3LB	MID	SWINDON TOWN
12	JOHNSTON	ALLAN		14/12/73	GLASGOW	10/8/04	5' 10"	11ST 4LB	MID	MIDDLESBROUGH
29	JOHNSTONE	SCOTT		13/01/85	PAISLEY	23/5/02	5' 8"	10ST 3LB	MID	KILMARNOCK YOUTH
16	JOLY	ERIC	ANDRE	06/10/72	VALENCIENNES	5/8/04	5' 11"	12ST 8LB	MID	SA ROYAL ALBERT - ELISABETH Q.
22	LEVEN	PETER		27/09/83	GLASGOW	15/7/04	5' 11"	12ST 13LB	MID	RANGERS
4	LILLEY	DAVID	WILLIAM	31/10/77	BELLSHILL	30/1/04	6' 1"	12ST 3LB	DEF	PARTICK THISTLE
8	LOCKE	GARY		16/06/75	EDINBURGH	6/8/02	5' 10"	11ST 8LB	MID	BRADFORD CITY
39	LOY	RORY	JAMES	19/03/88	DUMFRIES	30/6/04	5' 10"	10ST 7LB	MID/FWD	KILMARNOCK YOUTH
24	MASTERTON	STEVEN	ALLAN	02/01/85	IRVINE	22/5/02	6' 0"	12ST 12LB	DEF	RANGERS
7	McDONALD	GARY	MATTHEW	10/04/82	IRVINE	4/6/99	6' 0"	11ST 6LB	FWD	KILMARNOCK YOUTH
27	McGREGOR	NEIL		17/07/85	IRVINE	26/7/01	5' 11"	11ST 9LB	DEF	KILMARNOCK 'S' FOR
40	MORT	GRAHAM		17/01/88	GLASGOW	30/6/04	5' 10"	11ST 6LB	DEF	KILMARNOCK YOUTH
19	MURRAY	STEPHEN		18/04/83	BELLSHILL	20/12/00	5' 3.5"	9ST 12LB	MID/FWD	KILMARNOCK 'S' FOR
33	NAISMITH	STEVEN	JOHN	14/09/86	IRVINE	30/8/02	5' 9"	10ST 3LB	FWD	KILMARNOCK YOUTH
15	NISH	COLIN	JOHN	07/03/81	EDINBURGH	8/7/03	6' 3"	11ST 8LB	MID	DUNFERMLINE ATHLE
41	NOBLE	STEVEN		16/04/88	PAISLEY	30/6/04	5' 10"	11ST 1LB	MID	KILMARNOCK YOUTH
26	SAMSON	CRAIG	IAN	01/04/84	IRVINE	8/7/00	6' 2"	12ST 7LB	GK	KILMARNOCK YOUTH
35	SLOAN	LEWIS		22/06/87	DUMFRIES	1/7/03	5' 7"	9ST 11LB	MID	KILMARNOCK YOUTH
13	SMITH	GRAHAM		03/10/82	BELLSHILL	9/6/99	6' 2"	12ST 8LB	GK	KILMARNOCK YOUTH
14	WALES	GARY		04/01/79	EAST CALDER	14/7/04	5' 10"	11ST 2LB	FWD	GILLINGHAM
42	WILD	GARY		12/08/88	GLASGOW	30/6/04	6' 1"	11ST 12LB	DEF	KILMARNOCK YOUTH

TICKET INFORMATION

SEASON TICKET INFORMATION
THERE IS A SEASON TICKET INITIATIVE – PLEASE CONTACT CLUB FOR DETAILS

CATEGORY	EAST & WEST STAND	MOFFAT STAND
ADULT	280	220
MOFFAT FAMILY	-	250 2 ADULTS + 2 CHILDREN (U16)
STUDENT	185	145
SENIOR CITIZEN	145	105
YOUTH 16/17	120	80
CHILD U16	75	45

LEAGUE ADMISSION INFORMATION

STANDS		CAT A	CAT B
WEST/EAST/	ADULT	22	18
MOFFAT & NORTH	OAP/U16	22	12

CATEGORY A – RANGERS & CELTIC
CATEGORY B – ALL OTHER SPL CLUBS

KILLIE'S 10 YEAR LEAGUE RECORD

SEASON	DIV	P	W	D	L	F	A	PTS
1994-95	P	36	11	10	15	40	48	43
1995-96	P	36	11	8	17	39	54	41
1996-97	P	36	11	6	19	41	61	39
1997-98	P	36	13	11	12	40	52	50
1998-99	SPL	36	14	14	8	47	29	56
1999-00	SPL	36	8	13	15	38	52	37
2000-01	SPL	38	15	9	14	44	53	54
2001-02	SPL	38	13	10	15	44	54	49
2002-03	SPL	38	16	9	13	47	56	57
2003-04	SPL	38	12	6	20	51	74	42

The Killie's stats 2003/04

SEASON STATS 2003/04

DATE	VENUE	OPPONENTS	ATT	RES	MELDRUM C.	SHIELDS G.	DINDELEUX F.	HESSEY S.	INNES C.	HAY G.	LOCKE G.	FULTON S.	INVINCIBLE D.	BOYD K.	DI GIACOMO P.	McSWEGAN G.	NISH C.	FOWLER J.	HARDIE M.	McLAUGHLIN B.	McDONALD G.	MAHOOD A.	MURRAY S.	CANERO P.	DUBOURDEAU F.	DILLON S.	DODDS R.	GREER G.	DARGO C.	SAMSON C.	SKORA E.	LILLEY D.	SMITH G.	NAISMITH S.	CANNING M.
AUG	A	RANGERS	49,108	0 - 4	1	2	3	4	5	6	7	8	9	10	11	12	13																			
AUG	H	PARTICK THISTLE	6,778	2 - 1	1	2	3	4			5	7	8	9	10¹	12	11	6		13¹	14															
AUG	A	MOTHERWELL	5,087	1 - 2	1		3¹		5			8		10	9	11	13	2		6	4	7	12	14											
AUG	H	DUNDEE	5,935	1 - 1	1	2	3		5			8		10¹	9	13	12				4	11	6	7											
SEP	H	HEARTS	6,925	0 - 2	1	2	3		5			8		10		11	13	7	12	4		6	14	9											
SEP	A	LIVINGSTON	4,846	2 - 1		2	3	5¹				8		10¹	12		7	6		11			13	9	1										
SEP	A	DUNDEE UNITED	6,529	1 - 1		2	3					8	7	13	10¹			6	5			12		9	1										
OCT	H	ABERDEEN	6,023	1 - 3		2	3	4			8	7	9	10		14	12¹	5	11			13	6	1											
OCT	A	DUNFERMLINE ATH	4,495	3 - 2	2¹		4				8	9	10		11²		6		3	13		12		1	5	7									
OCT	A	HIBERNIAN	7,191	1 - 3	2		3				8	9	10		11	13¹	6			12		14		1	5	7	4								
NOV	H	CELTIC	12,460	0 - 5	2		3	5			8	9		11	14	13	6		4	10			12	1			7								
NOV	H	RANGERS	12,204	2 - 3	2		3	5			8			12	6	10	6²			13	11²		7	9¹	1			4	14						
NOV	A	PARTICK THISTLE	4,445	4 - 2	2		3	5			8			10	6²			11					7	9¹	1			4								
NOV	H	MOTHERWELL	6,320	2 - 0	2		3	5			8			10¹		13	6	14	12			11	7	9¹	1			4								
DEC	A	DUNDEE	6,954	2 - 1	2		3	5			8			10¹	13	12	6¹	14	11				7	9	1			4								
DEC	H	HEARTS	10,154	1 - 2	2		3	5			8			10		13¹	6		12			11	7	9	1			4								
DEC	H	LIVINGSTON	5,035	0 - 3	2		3	5			8			10	12	6						11	7	9	1			4								
DEC	H	DUNDEE UNITED	6,062	0 - 2	2		3	5			8			13	10	6	12	14				11	7	9	1			4								
JAN	A	ABERDEEN	11,699	1 - 3	2		3	5	8	7			10			6¹	12	13			11	14	9					4		1					
JAN	H	DUNFERMLINE ATH	5,715	1 - 1	2		3			8	7	13	12		10¹	6	5			11				1				9	4						
JAN	H	HIBERNIAN	5,571	1 - 1			3			8	7	14	13		10	6	5		2	11				1				9	4		12				
JAN	A	CELTIC	59,046	1 - 5	13			5	8		7			10¹		12	9	2	11					1				4			6	3			
FEB	A	RANGERS	46,900	0 - 2				5			7	10		12	9	6		2	14		13		1				11	4			8	3			
FEB	H	PARTICK THISTLE	5,818	2 - 1			3			5	8			12¹	10		14	9	2			7		1				11	4	13		6	3¹		
FEB	A	MOTHERWELL	5,163	0 - 1			3			5	8			10	11	13	14	9	2			7		1				4	12			6	3		
FEB	H	DUNDEE	5,454	4 - 2	1		3			5	8			11²	10¹	13	14	6				2	12	7					9¹	4					
MAR	H	HEARTS	5,297	1 - 1	1		3			5	8			11¹	10		14	6				2		7				13		9	4	15			
MAR	A	DUNDEE UNITED	5,757	1 - 4	1		3			5	8			9¹	10			6			2	11						12	13	7	4				
MAR	H	ABERDEEN	7,251	3 - 1	1		3			5	8			10²	13	14	6						7				12	2	11¹	9	4				
APR	A	DUNFERMLINE ATH	3,914	1 - 1	1		3			5	8			11¹	10	13	14	6					7				2	12	9	4					
APR	A	LIVINGSTON	2,677	1 - 1	1		3			5	8			11	10	13	14	6					7				2	12¹	9	4					
APR	A	HIBERNIAN	7,287	0 - 3	1		3			5	8			10		12	6			14			7				2	11	9	4		13			
APR	H	CELTIC	14,516	0 - 1	1		3			5	8			11	10	13	6						7				2	12	9	4					
APR	H	HIBERNIAN	4,886	2 - 0	1		3			5			9	10²	12		4			14			7				6	2	11	8					13
MAY	H	LIVINGSTON	5,023	4 - 2	1		3			5			11	10	14¹	12²	4			13			7				6	2		8					9¹
MAY	A	DUNDEE	4,942	0 - 2	1		3			2	12			11		4			13			7				5			8					6
MAY	H	ABERDEEN	4,987	4 - 0			3			5			11	10²	13	9¹	4						7				12	14	8¹	2	1			6
MAY	A	PARTICK THISTLE	4,124	2 - 2			3			5	12			9	10¹		8	4				11	7					13¹		2	1			6
TOTAL FULL APPEARANCES					16	19	33	7	1	30	18	21	19	31	4	13	15	25	8	14	15	2	22	12	19	2	9	23	3	1	16	14	2		4
TOTAL SUB APPEARANCES					1					2		3	5	3	18	15	7	8	2	8	3	7	1			2	2	9			1		1	1	1
TOTAL GOALS SCORED						1	1	1				5	15		6	9		1		3			2					3	2	1				1

Bold figures denote goalscorers. † denotes opponent's own goal.

LEADING GOALSCORERS:

SEASON	DIV	GOALS	PLAYER
..95	P	6	C. McKee
..96	P	13	P. Wright
..97	P	15	P. Wright
..98	P	10	P. Wright
..99	SPL	7	A. McCoist
..00	SPL	8	C. Cocard
..01	SPL	8	P. Wright
..02	SPL	7	T. Johnson
..03	SPL	12	K. Boyd
..04	SPL	15	K. Boyd

MILESTONES:

YEAR OF FORMATION: 1869
MOST CAPPED PLAYER: Joe Nibloe
NO. OF CAPS: 11
MOST LEAGUE POINTS IN A SEASON:
58 (Division 2 – Season 1973/74)
MOST LEAGUE GOALS SCORED BY A PLAYER IN A SEASON:
Harry "Peerie" Cunningham (Season 1927/28)
and Andy Kerr (Season 1960/61)
NO. OF GOALS SCORED: 34
RECORD ATTENDANCE: 34,246 (-v- Rangers – August, 1963)
RECORD VICTORY: 13-2 (-v- Saltcoats – Scottish Cup, 12.9.1896)
RECORD DEFEAT: 0-8 (-v- Rangers and Hibernian – Division 1)

KILMARNOCK PLAYING KITS SEASON 2004/05

FIRST KIT SECOND KIT THIRD KIT

LIVINGSTON
Almondvale Stadium,
Alderstone Road, Livingston,
West Lothian, EH54 7DN

CHAIRMAN
Tony Kinder

HON VICE-PRESIDENTS
William L. Mill &
John L. Bain, B.E.M.

SECRETARY
Tony Kinder

ASSISTANT SECRETARY
Duncan Bennett

GENERAL MANAGER
Vivien Kyles (Lionheart Management Limited)

PA TO GENERAL MANAGER
Dianne Blair

HEAD COACH
Allan Preston

ASSISTANT MANAGER
Alan Kernaghan

DIRECTOR OF FOOTBALL
Alistair Hood

RESERVE COACH
Alan Kernaghan

GOALKEEPING COACH
Roy Baines

YOUTH DEVELOPMENT COACH
Alex Cleland

CHIEF SCOUT
James McArthur

CLUB DOCTOR
Dr. Gerard Canning

PHYSIOTHERAPIST
Mairi McPhail

PART-TIME PHYSIOTHERAPIST
Arthur Duncan

COMMERCIAL MANAGER
Charles Burnett (01506) 417000

LOTTERY MANAGER
Ray Ballantyne

CATERING MANAGER
Allison Ross

GROUNDSMAN
Colin Fraser

KIT PERSON
Danny Cunning

**FOOTBALL SAFETY OFFICERS'
ASSOCIATION REPRESENTATIVE**
John O'Lone (01506) 432142

MEDIA LIAISON OFFICER
Duncan Bennett (01506) 417000

SALES & MARKETING MANAGER
Penny Dunn

MATCHDAY PROGRAMME EDITOR
David Stoker (07778 675746)
david@livingstonfc.co.uk

TELEPHONES
Ground (01506) 417000
Fax (01506) 418888

E-MAIL & INTERNET ADDRESS
dblair@livingstonfc.co.uk
www.livingstonfc.co.uk

CLUB SHOP
Situated at the ground and the local ASDA
Store. The Club Shop is also open on home
matchdays 10.30am - 3.00pm and after the
match. (01506) 461909

SUPPORTERS LIAISON MANAGER
Kay Robertson (01506) 403431

TEAM CAPTAIN
Stuart Lovell

SHIRT SPONSOR
Intelligent Finance

KIT SUPPLIER
XARA

LIST OF PLAYERS 2004/05

SQUAD NO.	PLAYERS SURNAME	FIRST NAME	MIDDLE NAME	DATE OF BIRTH	PLACE OF BIRTH	DATE SIGNED	HEIGHT FT INS	WEIGHT ST LBS	POSITION ON PITCH	PREVIOUS CLUB
-	ADAM	STEPHEN		10/11/86	PAISLEY	9/7/03	5' 10"	11ST 6LB	MID	LIVINGSTON YOUTHS
33	ARTHUR	ROBBIE		12/08/86	EDINBURGH	9/7/03	5' 6"	10ST 9LB	MID	LIVINGSTON YOUTHS
20	BAHOKEN	GUSTAVE		13/05/79	A'DOUALA	15/7/04	5' 10"	12ST 8LB	DEF	FC ANGERS
7	BOYACK	STEVEN		04/09/76	EDINBURGH	3/8/04	5' 10"	10ST 7LB	MID	HEART OF MIDLOTHIAN
29	BOYD	SCOTT	ROBERT	04/06/86	BANGOUR	21/10/02	6' 1.5"	11ST 11LB	DEF	LIVINGSTON YOUTHS
15	BRITTAIN	RICHARD		24/09/83	BANGOUR	3/8/00	5' 9"	10ST 7LB	MID	LIVINGSTON 'S' FORM
28	CAULFIELD	RUAIRIDH	ALEXANDER	25/11/86	GLASGOW	9/7/03	5' 6"	10ST 10LB	DEF	LIVINGSTON YOUTHS
38	CREER	ALLAN	WILLIAM	12/11/86	RUTHERGLEN	3/1/03	6' 1"	13ST 5LB	GK	LIVINGSTON YOUTHS
11	DAIR	JASON		15/06/74	DUNFERMLINE	20/7/04	5' 11"	12ST 5LB	MID/FWD	MOTHERWELL
-	DAVIDSON	MURRAY		07/03/88	EDINBURGH	17/5/04	5' 11"	9ST 5LB	MID	LIVINGSTON YOUTHS
6	DORADO-RODRIGUEZ	EMMANUEL		28/03/73	BROU-SUR-CHANTERENE	27/6/02	6' 2"	13ST 0LB	DEF	MALAGA
-	DORRANS	GRAHAM		05/05/87	GLASGOW	8/7/03	5' 9"	10ST 0LB	MID	LIVINGSTON YOUTHS
12	EASTON	CRAIG		26/02/79	BELLSHILL	15/7/04	5' 10"	11ST 3LB	MID	DUNDEE UNITED
30	FLEMING	GREG	WILLIAM	27/09/86	DUNFERMLINE	9/7/03	6' 2"	10ST 7LB	GK	LIVINGSTON YOUTHS
27	FULLERTON	EAMON	JOHN	19/03/85	FALKIRK	7/7/01	5' 10.5"	11ST 8LB	DEF	LIVINGSTON YOUTHS
-	GALLOWAY	CRAIG	THOMAS	22/05/88	LANARK	4/6/04	5' 7.5"	10ST 7LB	MID	LIVINGSTON YOUTHS
-	GEGGAN	ANDREW		08/05/87	GLASGOW	21/8/03	5' 8"	9ST 4LB	DEF	ST. JOHNSTONE
-	HAMILTON	CHRISTOPHER		21/11/87	GERMANY	13/8/03	5' 7.5"	9ST 2LB	MID	QUEEN'S PARK
9	HAMILTON	JAMES		09/02/76	ABERDEEN	21/7/04	6' 0"	12ST 12LB	FWD	ROSS COUNTY
21	HARDING	RYAN		27/04/84	EDINBURGH	1/8/03	6' 1"	13ST 0LB	DEF	HIBERNIAN
5	KERNAGHAN	ALAN	NIGEL	25/04/67	OTLEY	5/8/04	6' 2"	14ST 0LB	DEF	CLYDE
24	LIBBRA	MARC		05/08/72	TOULON	15/7/04	6' 3"	12ST 8LB	FWD	AJACCIO
16	LILLEY	DEREK		09/02/74	PAISLEY	21/7/04	5' 10.5"	12ST 7LB	FWD	BOSTON UNITED
17	LOVELL	STUART		09/01/72	SYDNEY	6/7/01	5' 10"	11ST 10LB	MID	HIBERNIAN
-	M'ARTHUR	ROBERT		11/06/88	DUNFERMLINE	1/6/04	5' 8.5"	12ST 1LB	FWD	LIVINGSTON YOUTHS
1	M'KENZIE	RODERICK		08/08/75	BELLSHILL	4/8/03	6' 0"	12ST 0LB	GK	HEART OF MIDLOTHIAN
-	M'LAREN	FRASER		26/09/88	EDINBURGH	4/6/04	5' 10"	10ST 6LB	MID	LIVINGSTON YOUTHS
14	M'LAUGHLIN	SCOTT		20/01/84	GLASGOW	23/7/02	5' 9"	10ST 7LB	MID	HAMILTON ACADEMICAL
8	M'MENAMIN	COLIN		12/02/81	GLASGOW	2/8/02	5' 10"	11ST 0LB	FWD	NEWCASTLE UNITED
2	M'NAMEE	DAVID		10/10/80	GLASGOW	31/8/02	5' 11"	10ST 7LB	DEF	BLACKBURN ROVERS
22	M'PAKE	JAMES		24/06/84	BELLSHILL	1/8/00	6' 2.5"	12ST 4LB	FWD	LIVINGSTON YOUTHS
18	MELDRUM	COLIN	GEORGE	26/11/75	KILMARNOCK	15/7/04	5' 10.5"	14ST 3LB	GK	KILMARNOCK
-	MELROSE	GARY		18/01/88	UPHALL	29/1/04	5' 8"	9ST 2LB	DEF	LIVINGSTON YOUTHS
-	MILLER	GARY		15/04/87	GLASGOW	29/8/03	5' 11.5"	10ST 9LB	FWD	ST. MIRREN
-	MITCHELL	CHRISTOPHER		21/07/88	STIRLING	22/7/04	5' 9"	10ST 10LB	DEF	ST. JOHNSTONE
10	O'BRIEN	BURTON		10/06/81	SOUTH AFRICA	31/8/02	5' 11"	10ST 7LB	MID	BLACKBURN ROVERS
4	RAMOS (RUBIO)	OSCAR	MONTALBAN	17/05/76	MADRID	23/7/02	6' 0"	12ST 5LB	DEF	FARENSE
32	SCOTT	MARTIN		15/02/86	LIVINGSTON	12/2/00	5' 11"	10ST 0LB	MID	LIVINGSTON YOUTHS
25	SNODDGRASS	ROBERT		07/09/87	GLASGOW	9/7/03	5' 11.5"	12ST 2LB	MID	LIVINGSTON 'S' FORM
19	SNOWDON	WILLIAM	ROBERT	07/01/83	COLCHESTER	9/8/02	5' 11.5"	11ST 10LB	DEF	LIVINGSTON YOUTHS
3	STANIC	GORAN		08/09/72	SKOPJE	20/7/04	5' 9"	11ST 0LB	DEF	RAITH ROVERS
31	WALKER	ALLAN		03/01/86	EDINBURGH	26/7/02	5' 10"	10ST 12LB	MID	HIBERNIAN

TICKET INFORMATION

SEASON TICKET INFORMATION

ADULT	£305/220
PARENT & JUVENILE	£340/240
PARENT & 2 JUVENILES	£370/260
2 PARENTS & 1 JUVENILE	£635/440
2 PARENTS & 2 JUVENILES	£660/460
OAP & JUVENILE	£100/150/95

LEAGUE ADMISSION PRICES

	CAT A	CAT B	CAT C
ADULT	£23/£21	£20	£18
CONCESSIONS	-	£10	£10

CATEGORY A - CELTIC, HEARTS, HIBERNIAN & RANGERS
(PLEASE NOTE CONCESSIONS NOT ALWAYS APPLICABLE)

CATEGORY B - ALL OTHER MATCHES

LIVI LIONS' 10 YEAR LEAGUE RECORD

SEASON	DIV	P	W	D	L	F	A	PTS
1994-95	S	36	11	5	20	32	54	35*
1995-96	T	36	21	9	6	51	24	72
1996-97	S	36	18	10	8	56	38	64
1997-98	S	36	16	11	9	56	40	59
1998-99	S	36	22	11	3	66	35	77
1999-00	F	36	19	7	10	60	45	64
2000-01	F	36	23	7	6	72	31	76
2001-02	SPL	38	16	10	12	50	47	58
2002-03	SPL	38	9	8	21	48	62	35
2003-04	SPL	38	10	13	15	48	57	43

* 3 Points Deducted for Fielding an Ineligible Player

SEASON STATS 2003/04

	VENUE	OPPONENTS	ATT	RES	McKenzie R.	McNamee D.	McFallister J.	Rubio O.	Andrews M.	Whitmore T.	Makel L.	Wilson B.	O'Brien B.	McGovern J.P.	Pasquinelli F.	Kerr B.	Xausa D.	Main A.	Lilley D.	McLaughlin S.	Toure Maman C.	Camacho J.J.	Capin S.	Quino S.	Fernandez D.	Ipoua G.	Dorado E.	Lovell S.	Brittain R.	McMenamin C.	McPake J.	Snowdon W.
AUG	A	PARTICK THISTLE	4,220	1-1	1	2	3	4	5	6	7	8	9	10	11¹	12	13															
AUG	H	**MOTHERWELL**	4,497	**1-0**		2	3	4	5	6	7	8	9	10	11	12		1	13¹													
AUG	A	DUNDEE	5,815	1-2		2	3	4	5	14	7	8	9¹	10	11	6		1	12	13												
AUG	A	CELTIC	57,062	1-5		2	3	4	5		7	8		10	11	6		1	12¹	14	9	13										
SEP	H	**DUNDEE UNITED**	4,226	**0-0**	1		2	4	5		7			10	11	6			12				3	8	9							
SEP	H	**KILMARNOCK**	4,846	**1-2**	1		2	4	5		7¹			14	11	6			9	12			3	8	10	13						
SEP	A	ABERDEEN	10,307	1-2	1	2	3	4¹	5		7		14		11¹	9			13	12				8¹	10		6					
OCT	H	**DUNFERMLINE ATH**	3,993	**0-0**	1		2	4	5		7			10	11	6			13	12				8	9		3					
OCT	A	HIBERNIAN	8,562	2-0	1	2	3	4	5		7		12	13	8				11²						10			6	9			
OCT	H	**RANGERS**	7,689	**0-0**	1	2	3	4	5		7		12	13	8				11						10			6	9			
NOV	A	HEARTS	11,233	1-3	1	2		4	5		7		8	13	6				11¹		12				10			3	9			
NOV	H	**PARTICK THISTLE**	4,397	**2-0**	1			4	5		7¹		6	10	3				11¹		12				9			2	8			
NOV	A	MOTHERWELL	6,357	1-1	1			4	5		7		6	10	3				11¹						12	9		2	8			
NOV	H	**DUNDEE**	3,878	**1-1**	1	2	3	4	5		7		8		12				11¹						13	10		6	9			
DEC	H	**CELTIC**	8,065	**0-2**	1	2	3	4	5				8	12	10				11		13			7				6	9			
DEC	A	DUNDEE UNITED	5,421	0-2	1						7		12	13	10				11					8				6	9			
DEC	A	KILMARNOCK	5,035	3-0	1	2	3	4	5		7		8¹		10¹				11		12¹			13				6	9			
DEC	H	**ABERDEEN**	6,020	**1-1**	1	2	3	4	5		7		8¹		10				11		12			13				6	9			
JAN	A	DUNFERMLINE ATH	5,154	2-2	1	2¹	3	4	5		7¹		8						11					13	12			6	9	14		
JAN	H	**HIBERNIAN**	4,948	**1-0**	1	2	3	4	5		7¹		8		13				11					12	10			6	9			
JAN	A	RANGERS	48,638	0-1	1	2	3	4	5		7		8		13				11						10			6	9	13		
FEB	A	PARTICK THISTLE	3,011	2-5	1	2	3	4	5		7¹		8	12	10				11						9			6		13¹		
FEB	H	**MOTHERWELL**	3,624	**3-1**	1	2	3¹	4	5		7		8	13					11¹	12					10¹			6	9	14		
FEB	A	DUNDEE	6,108	0-1	1	2	3	4	5		7		8		12				11						10			6	9	13	14	
FEB	H	**HEARTS**	4,630	**2-3**	1	2		4	5		7¹		8		12				11						10			3	6		9¹	
FEB	A	CELTIC	57,949	1-5	1	2		4	5		7		8	13	10				11¹									6	9		12	
MAR	A	ABERDEEN	7,477	2-1	1	2	3	4	5				12	10¹	11				13	7					14			6		8	9¹	
MAR	H	**DUNDEE UNITED**	3,082	**2-3**	1	2¹	3	4	5		7		8						11	13¹					10			6	9		14	
MAR	H	**DUNFERMLINE ATH**	3,558	**0-0**	1	2	3	4	5		7		8	12					11	9					10				6	13		
APR	A	HIBERNIAN	6,223	1-3	1		3	4	5		7		8						11¹	6					10				9	2	12	13
APR	H	**KILMARNOCK**	2,677	**1-1**	1	14	3	4	5		13		8	9	12					7					10¹				6	11		2
APR	H	**RANGERS**	6,092	**1-1**	1	2	3	4	5		7		8	13					11	9					10			6		14	12¹	
APR	H	**HEARTS**	10,352	**1-1**	1	2	3						8						6						10		4	9	12	11¹		13
APR	H	**ABERDEEN**	3,133	**2-0**	1	2¹	3	4	5		7		8						10	13					6			9	14	11¹	12	
MAY	A	KILMARNOCK	5,023	2-4	1		3	4	5		7¹		8¹	13					11	6					10			2	9	12		
MAY	H	**PARTICK THISTLE**	2,706	**2-2**	1		3	13	4		7		8¹	12					11	6					10			2	14	5	9¹	
MAY	H	DUNDEE	4,954	0-2	1	2	3	4	5		7		8	12					11						10			6	9	10		
MAY	H	**HIBERNIAN**	4,409	**4-1**	1	2	3	4	5		7¹		6	9					11¹	12					10¹			8¹				
		TOTAL FULL APPEARANCES			35	29	34	36	38	2	35	4	28	12	16	11		3	28	8	1		2	6	25		28	24	5	7		1
		TOTAL SUB APPEARANCES				1		1		1	1		5	15	6	2	1			7	9		6		6	2	1		1	7	8	1	2
		TOTAL GOALS SCORED				3	1	1			8		5	1	3				12	1				1	3				1		7	

Bold figures denote goalscorers. † denotes opponent's own goal.

LEADING GOALSCORERS:

MILESTONES:

YEAR OF FORMATION: 1974 (From Seasons 1974/75 to 1994/95 known as Meadowbank Thistle F.C.)

MOST LEAGUE POINTS IN A SEASON:
55 (Second Division – Season 1986/87) (2 Points for a Win)
77 (Second Division – Season 1998/99) (3 Points for a Win)

MOST LEAGUE GOALS SCORED BY A PLAYER IN A SEASON:
John McGachie (Season 1986/87)

NO. OF GOALS SCORED: 21

RECORD ATTENDANCE: 2,818 (-v- Albion Rovers, 10.8.1974 at Meadowbank Stadium) & 10,024 (-v- Celtic, 18.8.2001 at West Lothian Courier Stadium)

RECORD VICTORY: 6-0 (-v- Raith Rovers – Second Division, 9.11.1985; -v- Alloa Athletic – First Division, 26.8.2000)

RECORD DEFEAT: 0-8 (-v- Hamilton Academical – Division 2, 14.12.1974)

LIVINGSTON PLAYING KITS SEASON 2004/05

FIRST KIT   SECOND KIT   THIRD KIT

MOTHERWELL
Fir Park, Firpark Street,
Motherwell, ML1 2QN
HON. LIFE PRESIDENT
James C. Chapman, O.B.E.
CHAIRMAN
William H. Dickie, R.I.B.A., A.R.I.A.S
DIRECTORS
John Boyle, Alisdair F. Barron,
Mrs. Fiona Boyle, Andrew Lapping, John
Swinburne, James McMahon, Ian Stillie,
Martin Rose & Stewart Robertson
SECRETARY
Stewart Robertson
OFFICE ADMINISTRATOR
Betty Pryde
MANAGER & FIRST TEAM COACH
Terry Butcher
**ASSISTANT MANAGER, FIRST
TEAM COACH & RESERVE COACH**
Maurice Malpas
**YOUTH DEVELOPMENT MANAGER
& U19 YOUTH TEAM COACH**
Chris McCart
COMMUNITY COACH
Graham Diamond
YOUTH TEAM COACHES
Graham Ogg & Andy Brown (U17)
Willie Pettigrew, Bill Raeside & Bobby Barr (U15)
Gordon Young & Willie Falconer (U14)
Tom McCafferty (U13)
Willie Devine & Brian Reynolds (U12)
Ian Horne & Tom McCafferty (U11)
CHIEF SCOUT
Robert Clark
CLUB DOCTOR
Dr. Robert Liddle
PHYSIOTHERAPISTS
John Porteous & Peter Salila
**FOOTBALL SAFETY OFFICERS'
ASSOCIATION REPRESENTATIVE**
Ken Davies
07762 871049 (Mobile)
GROUNDSMAN
Gus Hollas
KIT PERSON
Alan MacDonald
HOSPITALITY CO-ORDINATOR
Wendy McFarlane (01698) 338008
FACILITIES MANAGER
Ken Davies
MATCHDAY PROGRAMME EDITOR
Graham Barnstaple
TELEPHONES
Ground (01698) 333333
Ticket Information (01698) 338009
Fax (01698) 338001
Hospitality Hotline (01698) 338008/330062
E-MAIL & INTERNET ADDRESS
mfc@motherwellfc.co.uk
www.motherwellfc.co.uk
CLUB SHOP
Provan Sports, The Well Shop, Fir Park,
Motherwell. Tel (01698) 338025
Open Tues, Thurs, Fri from 9.30a.m. to 4.00p.m.
and home matchdays 10.00a.m. to 3.00p.m.
and away matchdays 10.00a.m. to 1.00p.m.
SUPPORTERS CLUB
Motherwell Central, 21 Barclay Road
Motherwell. (01698) 254307
For all other supporters clubs,
contact club for details.
TEAM CAPTAIN
Scott Leitch
SHIRT SPONSOR
Zoom Airlines
KIT SUPPLIER
XARA

36

LIST OF PLAYERS 2004/05

SQUAD NO.	PLAYERS SURNAME	FIRST NAME	MIDDLE NAME	DATE OF BIRTH	PLACE OF BIRTH	DATE SIGNED	HEIGHT FT INS	WEIGHT ST LBS	POSITION ON PITCH	PREVIOUS CLUB
41	ALEXIOU	PETER	HARRY	07/07/87	BROXBURN	9/7/04	6' 0"	12ST 12LB	GK	FALKIRK
11	BURNS	ALEXANDER		04/08/73	BELLSHILL	6/6/03	5' 7"	12ST 4LB	MID/FWD	PARTICK THISTLE
35	CALDER	DOUGLAS		01/02/86	GLASGOW	22/8/03	5.11.5"	11ST 11LB	GK	HAMILTON ACADEMI
26	CAMERON	MARK		07/02/87	RUTHERGLEN	21/1/03	5' 7.5"	9ST 6LB	DEF	MOTHERWELL 'S' C
12	CLARKSON	DAVID		10/09/85	BELLSHILL	2/6/01	5' 10.5"	10ST 2LB	FWD	MOTHERWELL YOUTH
33	COAKLEY	ADAM	THOMAS	19/10/87	GLASGOW	9/1/04	5' 9"	9ST 9LB	FWD	MOTHERWELL YOUT
28	CONNOLLY	KENNETH		08/04/87	GLASGOW	9/6/03	5' 10"	10ST 7LB	MID	MOTHERWELL YOUT
15	CORR	BARRY JOHN		13/04/81	GLASGOW	5/8/03	6' 2"	13ST 2LB	GK	CELTIC
2	CORRIGAN	MARTYN	ALEXANDER	14/08/77	GLASGOW	21/1/00	5' 11"	12ST 0LB	DEF	FALKIRK
16	COWAN	DAVID	ROBERT	05/03/82	WHITEHAVEN	20/6/03	5' 11.5"	11ST 2LB	DEF/MID	NEWCASTLE UNITED
5	CRAIGAN	STEPHEN	JAMES	29/10/76	NEWTONARDS	9/6/03	6' 1"	13ST 1LB	DEF	PARTICK THISTLE
39	DONNELLY	ALEXANDER	STEVENSON	22/03/88	GLASGOW	18/5/04	6' 1"	11ST 2LB	MID	MOTHERWELL YOUTH
27	DONNELLY	ROBERT	STEVENSON	19/01/87	GLASGOW	21/1/03	6' 1"	13ST 0LB	MID	MOTHERWELL YOUTH
25	EWINGS	JAMIE		04/08/84	BELLSHILL	27/8/04	5' 11.5"	11ST 6LB	GK	CUMBERNAULD UNITED JU
21	FAGAN	SHAUN	MICHAEL	22/03/84	BELLSHILL	14/6/00	5' 10"	10ST 7LB	MID	MOTHERWELL YOUTH
24	FITZPATRICK	MARC		11/05/86	LANARK	30/8/02	5' 10.5"	10ST 9LB	DEF	MOTHERWELL YOUTH
9	FORAN	RICHARD		16/06/80	DUBLIN	5/7/04	6' 0"	12ST 12LB	FWD	CARLISLE UNITED
38	GRANT	JOHN	PAUL	25/08/87	BELLSHILL	18/5/04	5' 8"	10ST 5LB	DEF	MOTHERWELL YOUTH
3	HAMMELL	STEVEN		18/02/82	RUTHERGLEN	31/8/99	5' 9.5"	11ST 11LB	DEF	MOTHERWELL 'X' FO
23	HIGGINS	CHRISTOPHER	JAMES	04/07/85	BROXBURN	2/6/01	5' 11"	10ST 11LB	DEF	MOTHERWELL YOUTH
32	KEOGH	DAVID	JOHN	29/08/86	EDINBURGH	9/6/03	6' 1.5"	12ST 5LB	DEF	MOTHERWELL YOUTH
4	KERR	BRIAN		12/10/81	BELLSHILL	5/7/04	5' 10.5"	11ST 5LB	MID	NEWCASTLE UNITED
22	KINNIBURGH	WILLIAM	DANIEL	08/09/84	GLASGOW	14/6/00	6' 1.5"	11ST 7LB	DEF	MOTHERWELL YOUTH
8	LEITCH	DONALD	SCOTT	06/10/69	MOTHERWELL	25/6/03	5' 10"	11ST 10LB	MID	SWINDON TOWN
29	MAGUIRE	STEPHEN		14/02/87	BELLSHILL	9/6/03	5' 7"	9ST 8LB	DEF/MID	MOTHERWELL YOUTH
1	MARSHALL	GORDON	GEORGE	19/04/64	EDINBURGH	4/7/03	6' 3"	14ST 1LB	GK	KILMARNOCK
17	M'BRIDE	KEVIN		14/06/81	BELLSHILL	10/8/04	5' 10"	10ST 5LB	MID	CELTIC
7	M'DONALD	SCOTT	DOUGLAS	21/08/83	DANDENONG	7/1/04	5' 8"	12ST 4LB	FWD	WIMBLEDON
31	M'STAY	JOHN		10/07/87	BELLSHILL	9/6/03	5' 7.5"	9ST 8LB	DEF	CELTIC YOUTHS
42	MITCHELL	LIAM		16/01/86	GLASGOW	13/8/04	6' 0.5"	12ST 2LB	DEF	CELTIC
10	O'DONNELL	PHILIP		25/03/72	BELLSHILL	2/1/04	5' 10"	12ST 3LB	MID	SHEFFIELD WEDNESD
14	PARTRIDGE	DAVID	WILLIAM	26/11/78	LONDON	22/7/02	6' 1"	14ST 0LB	DEF	DUNDEE UNITED
18	PATERSON	JAMES	LEE	25/09/79	BELLSHILL	14/7/04	5' 11"	13ST 6LB	MID	DUNDEE UNITED
30	QUINN	MARK	JAMES	13/05/87	GLASGOW	9/6/03	5' 10.5"	10ST 11LB	DEF	MOTHERWELL YOUTH
19	QUINN	PAUL	CHARLES	21/07/85	LANARK	28/8/00	6' 1"	11ST 4LB	DEF	MOTHERWELL YOUTH
40	REYNOLDS	MARK		07/05/87	MOTHERWELL	18/5/04	5' 11"	10ST 9LB	DEF	MOTHERWELL YOUTH
34	RUSSELL	RYAN		09/04/87	DUNFERMLINE	9/6/03	5' 8.5"	10ST 12LB	FWD	MOTHERWELL YOUTH
37	SMITH	DARREN	LEE	27/03/88	LANARK	18/5/04	6' 0"	11ST 7LB	FWD	MOTHERWELL YOUTH
36	SOUTAR	WILLIAM	THOMPSON	12/07/87	LANARK	16/1/04	5' 11"	10ST 0LB	DEF	MOTHERWELL YOUTH
20	WRIGHT	KENNETH	THOMAS	01/08/85	BELLSHILL	5/6/01	5' 10.5"	11ST 5LB	FWD	MOTHERWELL YOUTH

TICKET INFORMATION

SEASON TICKET INFORMATION – SEATED

	SEASON TICKET PRICE	STANDARD GATE ENTRY	PREMIUM GATE ENTRY
MAIN STAND			
ADULT	£280	£18	£20
JUVENILE	£100	£7	£9
STUDENT/SENIOR CITIZEN	£155	£11	£13
COOPER STAND			
ADULT	£220	£16	£18
JUVENILE (11-16)	£75	£6	£8
CHILD (UNDER 11)	-	£6	£8
STUDENT/SENIOR CITIZEN	£130	£10	£12
FAMILY ADULT + JUVENILE	£250	£20	£22
FAMILY ADULT + CHILD	£220	£20	£22
EAST STAND			
ADULT	£200	£14	£16
JUVENILE	£60	£5	£7
STUDENT	£110	£9	£11
SENIOR CITIZEN	£100	£9	£11

THE WELL'S 10 YEAR LEAGUE RECORD

SEASON	DIV	P	W	D	L	F	A	PTS
1994-95	P	36	14	12	10	50	50	54
1995-96	P	36	9	12	15	28	39	39
1996-97	P	36	9	11	16	44	55	38
1997-98	P	36	9	7	20	46	64	34
1998-99	SPL	36	10	11	15	35	54	41
1999-00	SPL	36	14	10	12	49	63	52
2000-01	SPL	38	12	7	19	42	56	43
2001-02	SPL	38	11	7	20	49	69	40
2002-03	SPL	38	7	7	24	45	71	28
2003-04	SPL	38	12	10	16	42	49	46

The well's stats 2003/04

SEASON STATS 2003/04

Date	Venue	Opponents	Att	Res	MARSHALL G.	CORRIGAN M.	PARTRIDGE D.	HAMMELL S.	CRAIGAN S.	McDONALD K.	PEARSON S.	LEITCH D.S.	CRAIG S.	BURNS A.	CLARKSON D.	McFADDEN J.	LASLEY K.	WRIGHT K.	QUINN P.	ADAMS D.	DAIR J.	FAGAN S.	O'DONNELL P.	McDONALD S.	BOLLAN G.	CORR B.J.	KINNIBURGH W.	FITZPATRICK M.	COWAN D.
UG	H	DUNDEE	6,812	0 - 3	1	2	3	4	5	6	7	8	9	10	11	12													
AUG	A	LIVINGSTON	4,497	0 - 1	1	2	3	4	5		7	8	12	10	11		6		9										
AUG	H	KILMARNOCK	5,087	2 - 1	1	2	3	4			7^1	8	13	10	12	11^1	6		5	9									
AUG	H	PARTICK THISTLE	6,193	2 - 2	1	2	3	4			7	8		10	12	11^2	6		5	9									
SEP	A	HIBERNIAN	8,387	2 - 0	1	2	3	4	5		7	8	13	10	11^2		6		9	12									
SEP	A	CELTIC	57,492	0 - 3	1	2	3	4	5		7	8	10		11		6		12	9									
SEP	H	HEARTS	5,888	1 - 1	1	2	3	4	5		7	8	10		11		6			9^1	12								
CT	A	DUNDEE UNITED	6,194	2 - 0	1	2	3	4	5		7	8	10		11		6			9^2	12								
OCT	A	RANGERS	10,824	1 - 1	1	2	3	4	5		7^1	8	10		11		6			9	12								
OV	A	ABERDEEN	6,895	3 - 0	1	2	3	4	5		7^1	8	10^1		11		6^1			9	12								
OV	A	DUNDEE	6,374	1 - 0	1	2	3	4	5		7	8	12	10^1	11		6	13	9										
NOV	H	LIVINGSTON	6,357	1 - 1	1	2	3	4	5		7	8	12	10	11^1		6		9										
NOV	H	DUNFERMLINE ATH	4,220	2 - 2	1	2^1	3	4	5		7^1	8	13	10	11		6		9	12									
NOV	A	KILMARNOCK	6,320	0 - 2	1	2	3	4	5		7	8	14	10	11		6	13	9	12									
EC	A	PARTICK THISTLE	4,124	0 - 1	1	2	3	4	5		7	8		10	11		6	13	9	12									
DEC	H	HIBERNIAN	4,533	0 - 1	1	2		4	5		7	8		10	11		6		12	9	3								
DEC	H	CELTIC	10,513	0 - 2	1	2		4	5		7	8		10	11		6		12	9	3								
DEC	A	HEARTS	10,046	0 - 0	1	2		4	5		12	8	13	10	11		6		3	9	7	14							
AN	H	DUNDEE UNITED	5,549	3 - 1	1	2		4	5			8		10	11^3		6		3	9	7	12							
JAN	A	RANGERS	48,925	0 - 1	1	2		4	5			8		10	11		6		3	9	7	12	13						
JAN	A	DUNFERMLINE ATH	5,270	0 - 1		2		4	5			8		10	11		6		3	9	7			12		1			
FEB	H	DUNDEE	4,247	5 - 3	1	2		4	5			8		10^1	11^1		6^1		3	9	7^2		13	12					
FEB	A	LIVINGSTON	3,624	1 - 3	1	2		4	5			8		10	11		6	13	3	9^1	7			12					
FEB	H	KILMARNOCK	5,163	1 - 0	1	2		4	5			8		10	11		6	13	3^1	9	7			12					
FEB	H	ABERDEEN	5,220	1 - 0	1	2		4	5		12	8		10	11		6	13	3	9	7	14^1							
FEB	H	PARTICK THISTLE	5,814	3 - 0	1	2		4^1	5		12	8		10	11^1		6	13	3	9	7	14							
MAR	A	CELTIC	57,580	1 - 1	1	2		4	5			8		10	11		6		12	3	9	13	7^1						
MAR	A	HIBERNIAN	5,568	3 - 3	1	2		4	5			8^1		10	11		6^1		3	9^1	12	7	13						
MAR	A	DUNDEE UNITED	7,585	0 - 1	1	2		4	5		12	8		10	11		6		3	9	7								
APR	H	RANGERS	8,967	0 - 1	1	2		4	5		12	8		10	11		6		3	9	7								
APR	H	HEARTS	5,500	1 - 1	1	2		4	5		12	8		10	11^1		6		3	9	7								
APR	H	DUNFERMLINE ATH	3,920	1 - 0	1	2		4	5		12	8		10	11		6		3	9^1	7		13						
APR	A	ABERDEEN	7,246	2 - 0		2		4	5		12	8		10^1	11^1		6		3	9	7				1				
APR	A	DUNFERMLINE ATH	4,250	0 - 3		2		4	5			8		10	11		6		3	9	7		13	12	1				
MAY	A	RANGERS	47,579	0 - 4	1	2		4	5			8		10	11		6		3	9	7		13	12					
MAY	H	DUNDEE UNITED	5,722	0 - 1	1	2		4	5		12	8		10	11		6		3	9	7								
MAY	H	CELTIC	7,749	1 - 1		2		4	5			8		10	11^1		6	14		9	7		13	12	1				
MAY	A	HEARTS	11,619	2 - 3		2		4	5			8^1		10	11^1		6		3	9	7		13	12	1				
TOTAL FULL APPEARANCES					33	38	15	37	36	1	17	20	16	29	32	2	33	2	24	31	19	9	7	10	1	5		1	
TOTAL SUB APPEARANCES										3	1		8	4	6	1		12	2		10	4	2	5	2		1	1	1
TOTAL GOALS SCORED						1		1			4		3	2	11	3	3	1	1	7	2	1		2				

bold figures denote goalscorers; † denotes opponents' own goals.

LEADING GOALSCORERS:

Season	Div	Goals	Player
94-95	P	16	T. Coyne
95-96	P	5	W. Falconer
96-97	P	11	T. Coyne
97-98	P	15	T. Coyne
98-99	SPL	7	O. Coyle, J. Spencer
99-00	SPL	11	J. Spencer
00-01	SPL	10	S. Elliott
01-02	SPL	10	S. Elliott, J. McFadden
02-03	SPL	13	J. McFadden
03-04	SPL	11	D. Clarkson

MILESTONES:

YEAR OF FORMATION: 1886
MOST CAPPED PLAYER: Tommy Coyne (Republic of Ireland)
NO. OF CAPS: 13
MOST LEAGUE POINTS IN A SEASON:
66 (Division 1 – Season 1931/32)
MOST LEAGUE GOALS SCORED BY A PLAYER IN A SEASON:
William McFadyen (Season 1931/32)
NO. OF GOALS SCORED: 52
RECORD ATTENDANCE:
35,632 (-v- Rangers – Scottish Cup, 12.3.1952)
RECORD VICTORY: †12-1 (-v- Dundee United – Division 2, 23.1.1954)
RECORD DEFEAT: 0-8 (-v- Aberdeen – Premier Division, 26.3.1979)

MOTHERWELL PLAYING KITS SEASON 2004/05

FIRST KIT   SECOND KIT   THIRD KIT

RANGERS
Ibrox Stadium,150 Edmiston Drive,
Glasgow, G51 2XD
CHAIRMAN
David E. Murray
DIRECTORS
John McClelland, R. Campbell Ogilvie,
Daniel P. Levy, Donald Wilson, David C. King,
Martin Bain, David Jolliffe, Nick Peel,
John Greig & Alastair Johnston
ASSOCIATE DIRECTOR
Ian Russell
COMPANY SECRETARY
David Jolliffe
DIRECTOR OF FOOTBALL BUSINESS
Martin Bain (0141) 580 8569
HEAD OF FOOTBALL ADMINISTRATION
Andrew Dickson
MANAGER
Alex McLeish
ASSISTANT MANAGER
Andy Watson
FIRST TEAM COACH
Jan Wouters
GOALKEEPING COACH
Billy Thomson
RESERVE COACH
John Brown
HEAD OF YOUTH DEVELOPMENT
George Adams
COMMUNITY COACH
Craig Mulholland
CLUB DOCTOR
Dr. Ian McGuinness
PHYSIOTHERAPIST
David Henderson
PUBLIC RELATIONS EXECUTIVE
Carol Patton
**OPERATIONS EXECUTIVE/
FOOTBALL SAFETY OFFICERS'
ASSOCIATION REPRESENTATIVE**
Laurence MacIntyre M.B.E. (0141) 580 8630
GROUNDSMAN
David Roxburgh
KIT PERSON
Jim Bell
STADIUM MANAGER
Ross MacAskill
MATCHDAY PROGRAMME EDITOR
Lindsay Herron (Rangers Media Editor in Chief)
RETAIL DIRECTOR
Nick Peel
TELEPHONES
Main Switchboard (0141) 580 8500
Football Administration (0141) 580 8609
Fax–Football Administration (0141) 580 8947
Ticket Centre 0870 600 1993
Fax (0141) 580 8504
Customer Services 0870 600 1972
Hospitality 0870 600 1964
Commercial 0870 600 1899
Retail/Mail Order 0870 599 1997
Fax Enquiries 0870 600 1978
E-MAIL & INTERNET ADDRESS
dorahowie@rangers.co.uk
www.rangers.co.uk
CLUB SHOPS
1873 SUPERSTORE, Ibrox Stadium, Glasgow
G51. Open until 10.00p.m. on Matchdays
and 9.30a.m.-5.30p.m. Mon to Sat
Sunday 11.00a.m. to 5.00pm.
THE RANGERS SHOP, 84-92 Sauchiehall Street,
Glasgow, G2. Open 9.00a.m.-5.30p.m. Mon
to Sat and Sun Noon-4.00p.m.
THE RANGERS SHOP, Unit G5,
St. Enoch's Shopping Centre, Glasgow
ADDITIONAL SHOPS LOCATED IN:
Edinburgh, East Kilbride, Clydebank, Paisley,
Stirling, Falkirk, Ayr, Kirkcaldy, Inverness,
Livingston, Belfast, Ballymena, Glasgow &
Prestwick Airports
OFFICIAL SUPPORTERS CLUB
Worldwide Alliance. Argyle House,
Ibrox Stadium,Glasgow, G51 2XD
TEAM CAPTAIN
Stefan Klos
SHIRT SPONSOR
Carling
KIT SUPPLIER
Diadora

LIST OF PLAYERS 2004/05

SQUAD NO.	PLAYERS SURNAME	FIRST NAME	MIDDLE NAME	DATE OF BIRTH	PLACE OF BIRTH	DATE SIGNED	HEIGHT FT INS	WEIGHT ST LBS	POSITION ON PITCH	PREVIOUS CLUB
40	ADAM	CHARLES	GRAHAM	10/12/85	DUNDEE	23/1/03	6' 1"	13ST 0LB	MID	RANGERS YOUTHS
53	AGNEW	SCOTT		11/07/87	IRVINE	3/7/03	5' 6.5"	9ST 9LB	MID	RANGERS YOUTHS
5	ANDREWS	MARVIN		22/12/75	SAN JUAN	21/7/04	6' 2"	14ST 7LB	DEF	LIVINGSTON
7	ARVELADZE	SHOTA		22/02/73	TBILISI	11/9/01	5' 11"	11ST 12LB	FWD	AJAX
18	BALL	MICHAEL		02/10/79	LIVERPOOL	20/8/01	5' 11"	12ST 4LB	DEF	EVERTON
4	BOUMSONG	JEAN-ALAIN		14/12/79	DOUALA	7/7/04	6' 3"	14ST 2LB	DEF	AUXERRE
50	BOYD	DARRYL	RODDIE	14/04/87	GLASGOW	3/7/03	5' 8"	10ST 2LB	FWD	RANGERS YOUTHS
32	BRIGHTON	TOM		28/03/84	IRVINE	4/9/00	6' 1"	11ST 10LB	MID	RANGERS YOUTHS
17	BURKE	CHRISTOPHER		02/12/83	GLASGOW	5/7/00	5' 8.5"	10ST 10LB	MID	RANGERS YOUTHS
46	CAMPBELL	STEVEN		20/08/86	KIRKCALDY	4/6/02	5' 10"	10ST 8LB	DEF	RANGERS YOUTHS
-	CARCARY	DEREK		11/07/86	GLASGOW	20/8/04	5' 6"	9ST 10LB	FWD	QUEEN'S PARK
34	COYLE	FRASER		19/02/85	GLASGOW	14/1/02	5' 9"	11ST 6LB	DEF	RANGERS YOUTHS
56	CROOKS	JASON		31/01/88	GLASGOW	30/1/04	5' 9.5"	10ST 12LB	FWD	RANGERS YOUTHS
42	DAVIDSON	ROBERT		25/03/86	RUTHERGLEN	4/6/02	5' 8.5"	11ST 9LB	FWD	RANGERS YOUTHS
41	DICK	ANDREW	JAMES	25/02/86	CARLISLE	10/6/02	6' 1.5"	10ST 6LB	MID	RANGERS YOUTHS
58	EMSLIE	PAUL	STEPHEN	13/03/88	ABERDEEN	14/6/04	5' 10"	10ST 10LB	MID	RANGERS YOUTHS
38	FETAI	BAJRAM		07/09/85	JUGOSLAVIEN	22/2/04	5' 11"	11ST 5LB	FWD	B93 COPENHAGEN
60	FRIZZEL	CRAIG		30/06/88	EDINBURGH	18/8/04	5' 11.5"	11ST 11LB	FWD	RANGERS YOUTHS
-	GIACOMI	ROBERT		01/08/86	TORONTO	31/8/04	6' 4"	13ST 0LB	GK	MARKHAM LIGHTNING
51	GILMOUR	BRIAN	THOMAS	08/05/87	IRVINE	3/7/03	5' 6"	9ST 4LB	MID	RANGERS YOUTHS
27	HUGHES	STEPHEN		14/11/82	MOTHERWELL	12/7/99	5' 11"	10ST 10LB	MID	RANGERS 'S' FORM
20	HUTTON	ALAN		30/11/84	GLASGOW	4/9/00	6' 0"	12ST 1LB	DEF	RANGERS YOUTHS
48	JACMOT	WARREN		17/02/87	LYON	3/7/03	5' 9.5"	10ST 10LB	DEF	AS ST. PRIESTE
49	JOHNSTON	JOHN	BUCHANAN	26/03/87	GREENOCK	3/7/03	6' 0"	10ST 8LB	FWD	RANGERS YOUTHS
36	KALENGA	MARC	GARY	18/03/85	TOULOUSE	7/10/03	6' 0"	12ST 11LB	MID	AUXERRE
15	KHIZANISHVILI	ZURAB		06/10/81	TBILISI	3/7/03	6' 0"	13ST 5LB	DEF	DUNDEE
1	KLOS	STEFAN		16/08/71	DORTMUND	23/12/98	6' 11.5"	13ST 3LB	GK	BV09 BORUSSIA DORTMUND
55	LENNON	STEVEN		20/01/88	IRVINE	30/1/04	5' 7"	9ST 7LB	MID	RANGERS YOUTHS
26	LOVENKRANDS	PETER		29/01/80	HORSHOLM	14/6/00	5' 10"	11ST 9LB	FWD	AB COPENHAGEN
54	LOWING	ALAN	ALEXANDER	07/01/88	RUTHERGLEN	20/5/04	5' 10"	10ST 9LB	DEF	RANGERS YOUTHS
12	MALCOLM	ROBERT		12/11/80	GLASGOW	1/7/97	5' 11.5"	13ST 9LB	DEF	RANGERS 'S' FORM
47	M°COLL	ALEXANDER	CAMPBELL	07/02/87	STIRLING	30/1/04	5' 10"	12ST 4LB	DEF	RANGERS YOUTHS
45	M°CORMACK	ROSS		18/08/86	GLASGOW	4/6/02	5' 9"	11ST 10LB	FWD	RANGERS YOUTHS
22	M°GREGOR	ALLAN	JAMES	31/01/82	EDINBURGH	14/7/98	6' 3"	13ST 10LB	GK	RANGERS YOUTHS
39	M°KENZIE	GARY		15/10/85	LANARK	3/7/03	6' 3"	13ST 4LB	DEF	RANGERS YOUTHS
35	M°LEAN	BRIAN	STUART	28/02/85	RUTHERGLEN	1/6/01	6' 2"	12ST 3LB	DEF	RANGERS YOUTHS
14	MLADENOVIC	DRAGAN		16/02/76	KRAJELVO	21/7/04	6' 3.5"	13ST 1LB	MID	RED STAR BELGRADE
3	MOORE	CRAIG	ANDREW	12/12/75	ADELAIDE	31/3/99	6' 0"	13ST 0LB	DEF	CRYSTAL PALACE
31	NAMOUCHI	HAMED		14/02/84	CANNES	15/9/03	6' 1"	13ST 2LB	MID	CANNES
10	NOVO	IGNACIO	JAVIER	26/03/79	EL FERROL	9/7/04	5' 9"	10ST 8LB	FWD	DUNDEE
9	PRSO	DADO		05/11/74	ZADAR	7/7/04	6' 3"	14ST 0LB	FWD	AS MONACO
11	RAE	ALEXANDER		30/09/69	GLASGOW	5/7/04	5' 9"	11ST 6LB	MID	WOLVERHAMPTON WANDERERS
8	RAE	GAVIN	PAUL	28/11/77	ABERDEEN	2/1/04	6' 0"	13ST 6LB	MID	DUNDEE
52	REDFORD	CALUM		26/05/87	GLASGOW	3/7/03	5' 11"	12ST 0LB	GK	RANGERS 'S' FORM
2	RICKSEN	FERNANDO		27/07/76	HEERLEN	5/7/00	5' 9"	11ST 4LB	DEF	AZ ALKMAR
44	ROBINSON	LEE	DAVID	02/07/86	SUNDERLAND	30/1/04	5' 11"	12ST 0LB	GK	ESH WINNING
21	ROSS	MAURICE		03/02/81	DUNDEE	1/7/97	6' 0"	12ST 4LB	DEF	RANGERS S.A.B.C.
30	SMITH	GRAEME		08/06/83	EDINBURGH	13/7/99	6' 0"	13ST 5LB	GK	RANGERS 'S' FORM
37	SMITH	STEVEN		30/08/85	BELLSHILL	1/6/02	5' 9.5"	10ST 13LB	DEF	RANGERS YOUTHS
19	THOMPSON	STEVEN		14/10/78	PAISLEY	1/1/03	6' 2"	13ST 4LB	FWD	DUNDEE UNITED
59	URE	MARTIN		06/06/88	IRVINE	23/7/04	5' 9"	10ST 13LB	DEF	RANGERS YOUTHS
16	VANOLI	PAOLO		12/08/72	VARESE	5/8/03	6' 0"	13ST 1LB	DEF	BOLOGNA
24	VIGNAL	GREGORY		19/07/81	MONTPELLIER	6/8/04	6' 0"	12ST 2LB	DEF	LIVERPOOL
33	WALKER	ALEXANDER		25/04/84	BELLSHILL	1/7/00	5' 11.5"	12ST 4LB	DEF	RANGERS YOUTHS
43	WATSON	GRAEME		06/05/86	GLASGOW	4/6/03	5' 8"	10ST 6LB	DEF	RANGERS YOUTHS
-	WOODS	SAMUEL		06/02/88	ASCOT	27/8/04	5' 8"	9ST 12LB	MID	HUTCHISON VALE

TICKET INFORMATION

SEASON TICKET INFORMATION – SEATED

		Block	Adult/Conc./Juv.
MAIN STAND (Front)		F/G/O/P	£387/275/184
		H	£551/387/214
		J/K/M/N	£525/367/214
		L (Section MLF)	£581/326/–
MAIN STAND (Rear)		E	£495/347/214
		C/D/Q/R	£403/286/184
		A/B/S/T	£372/255/184
MEMBERS CLUB		Hospitality area only	
GOVAN (Rear)		3/4/5	£541/377/214
		2/6	£495/347/214
		1/7	£454/321/214
GOVAN (Front)		2/3/4/5/6	£408/286/184
		1/7/East	£387/275/184
ENCLOSURE		SE 1/2/3 SW 3/4/5	£387/275/184
		SE 4/5 SW1/2	£398/281/184
COPLAND (Rear)		1/2/3/4/5	£387/275/184
COPLAND (Front)		1/2/3/4/5	£377/265/184
LEAGUE ADMISSION PRICES		ADULT	£22/20
		CONCS/JUV	£11

THE GERS' 10 YEAR LEAGUE RECORD

SEASON	DIV	P	W	D	L	F	A	PTS
1994-95	P	36	20	9	7	60	35	69
1995-96	P	36	27	6	3	85	25	87
1996-97	P	36	25	5	6	85	33	80
1997-98	P	36	21	9	6	76	38	72
1998-99	SPL	36	23	8	5	78	31	77
1999-00	SPL	36	28	6	2	96	26	90
2000-01	SPL	38	26	4	8	76	36	82
2001-02	SPL	38	25	10	3	82	27	85
2002-03	SPL	38	31	4	3	101	28	97
2003-04	SPL	38	25	6	7	76	33	81

SEASON STATS 2003/04

Column headers (players, left to right): KLOS S., RICKSEN F., MOORE C., KHIZANISHVILI Z., BALL M., ROSS M., FERGUSON B., ARTETA M., DE BOER R., MOLS M., LOVENKRANDS P., VANOLI P., MALCOLM R., THOMPSON S., BERG H., NERLINGER C., CAPUCHO N., ARVELADZE S., BURKE C., COSTA E., OSTENSTAD E., HUGHES S., DUFFY D., RAE G., NAMOUCH H., DE BOER F., HUTTON A., FETAI B., WALKER A., ADAMS C., MGREGOR A., MCCORMACK R., MYKENZIE G., DAVIDSON R.

DATE	VENUE	OPPONENTS	ATT	RES
AUG	H	KILMARNOCK	49,108	4 - 0
AUG	A	ABERDEEN	16,348	3 - 2
AUG	H	HIBERNIAN	49,642	†5 - 2
AUG	A	DUNDEE UNITED	11,111	3 - 1
SEP	H	DUNFERMLINE ATH	49,072	4 - 0
SEP	A	HEARTS	14,732	4 - 0
SEP	H	DUNDEE	49,548	3 - 1
OCT	H	CELTIC	49,825	0 - 1
OCT	A	MOTHERWELL	10,824	1 - 1
OCT	A	LIVINGSTON	7,689	0 - 0
NOV	H	PARTICK THISTLE	49,551	3 - 1
NOV	A	KILMARNOCK	12,204	3 - 2
NOV	H	ABERDEEN	49,962	3 - 0
NOV	A	HIBERNIAN	11,116	1 - 0
DEC	H	DUNDEE UNITED	49,307	2 - 1
DEC	A	DUNFERMLINE ATH	8,592	0 - 2
DEC	H	HEARTS	49,592	2 - 1
DEC	A	DUNDEE	10,948	†2 - 0
JAN	A	CELTIC	59,042	0 - 3
JAN	H	MOTHERWELL	48,925	1 - 0
JAN	H	LIVINGSTON	48,638	1 - 0
FEB	A	PARTICK THISTLE	8,220	1 - 0
FEB	H	KILMARNOCK	46,900	2 - 0
FEB	A	ABERDEEN	15,815	1 - 1
FEB	H	HIBERNIAN	49,698	3 - 0
FEB	A	DUNDEE UNITED	10,497	0 - 2
MAR	A	HEARTS	14,598	1 - 1
MAR	H	DUNDEE	49,364	4 - 0
MAR	H	DUNFERMLINE ATH	47,487	4 - 1
MAR	H	CELTIC	49,909	1 - 2
APR	A	MOTHERWELL	8,967	1 - 0
APR	A	LIVINGSTON	6,092	1 - 1
APR	H	PARTICK THISTLE	49,279	2 - 0
APR	A	DUNDEE UNITED	8,339	3 - 3
MAY	H	MOTHERWELL	47,579	4 - 0
MAY	A	CELTIC	59,180	0 - 1
MAY	H	HEARTS	47,467	0 - 1
MAY	A	DUNFERMLINE ATH	6,719	3 - 2

TOTAL FULL APPEARANCES: 34 29 16 25 30 10 3 23 12 29 22 14 8 20 11 18 17 11 13 2 17 9 4 15 11 1 4 1

TOTAL SUB APPEARANCES: 1 1 1 2 10 4 6 3 9 6 7 3 4 2 9 1 9 5 1 3 1 2 1 1 2 1 1 2 1

TOTAL GOALS SCORED: 1 2 1 1 8 2 9 8 1 8 1 5 12 3 3 2 3 2 1 1

Bold figures denote goalscorers. † denotes opponent's own goal.

LEADING GOALSCORERS:

SEASON	DIV	GOALS	PLAYER
94-95	P	13	M. Hateley
95-96	P	17	G. Durie
96-97	P	16	B. Laudrup
97-98	P	32	M. Negri
98-99	P	18	R. Wallace
99-00	SPL	17	J. Albertz
00-01	SPL	11	T. A. Flo
01-02	SPL	17	T. A. Flo
02-03	SPL	16	R. de Boer, B. Ferguson
03-04	SPL	12	S. Arveladze

MILESTONES:

YEAR OF FORMATION: 1873
MOST CAPPED PLAYER: Alistair McCoist
NO. OF CAPS: 58
MOST LEAGUE POINTS IN A SEASON:
76 (Division 1 - Season 1920/21) (2 Points for a Win)
97 (Scottish Premier League - Season 2002/2003) (3 Points for a Win)
MOST LEAGUE GOALS SCORED BY A PLAYER IN A SEASON:
Sam English (Season 1931/32)
NO. OF GOALS SCORED: 44
RECORD ATTENDANCE: 118,567 (-v- Celtic – 2.1.1939)
RECORD VICTORY: 14-2 (-v- Blairgowrie – Scottish Cup, 20.1.1934)
RECORD DEFEAT: 2-10 (-v- Airdrieonians – 1886)

RANGERS PLAYING KITS SEASON 2004/05

FIRST KIT   SECOND KIT   THIRD KIT

Aberdeen: Pittodrie Stadium

You can reach Pittodrie Stadium by these routes:
BUSES: The following buses all depart from the city centre to within a hundred yards of the ground: Nos. 1, 2, and 11.
TRAINS: The main Aberdeen station is in the centre of the city and the above buses will then take fans to the ground.
CARS: Motor vehicles coming from the city centre should travel along Union Street, then turn into King Street and the park will be on your right, about half a mile further on. Parking on Beach Boulevard and Beach Esplanade.

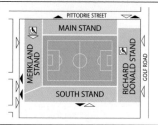

CAPACITY: 21,474 (All Seated)
PITCH DIMENSIONS: 110 yds x 72 yds
FACILITIES FOR DISABLED SUPPORTERS:
There are a total of 26 wheelchair spaces in the home support areas. 20 are located at the front of the Richard Donald stand and 6 at the front of the Merkland Family Stand. There are 7 spaces available in the away support (section Q) in the South Stand.
Please telephone 087 1983 1903.

Celtic: Celtic Park

The following routes may be used to reach Celtic Park:
BUSES: The following buses all leave from the city centre and pass within 50 yards of the ground. Nos. 43, 62, and 64.
TRAINS: There is a frequent train service from Glasgow Central Low Level station to Bridgeton Cross Station and this is only a ten minute walk from the ground. There is also a train from Queen Street Station (lower level) to Bellgrove Rail Station, approximately 20 minutes walk from the ground.
CARS: From the city centre, motor vehicles should travel along London Road and this will take you to the ground. Parking spaces are available in various areas close to the ground. On matchdays all car parking is strictly limited and is only available to those in possession of a valid car park pass.

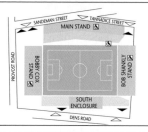

CAPACITY: 60,355 (All Seated)
PITCH DIMENSIONS: 115 yds x 75 yds
FACILITIES FOR DISABLED SUPPORTERS:
There is provision for 142 wheelchair positions for disabled supporters and their helpers. These are split into 87 in the North Stand, at the front of the lower terracing, 10 in the East Stand, lower terracing and 37 in the South Stand, lower terracing. Celtic fans should contact the club for availability. There is also a provision for 6 away positions in the lower East Stand.

Dundee: Dens Park

The following routes may be used to reach Dens Park:
BUSES: There is a frequent service of buses from the city centre. Nos. 1A and 1B leave from Albert Square and Nos. 18, 19 and 21 leave from Commercial Street.
TRAINS: Trains from all over the country pass through the mainline Dundee station and fans can then proceed to the ground by the above buses from stops situated close to the station.
CARS: Cars may be parked in the car park (Densfield Park) and local streets adjacent to the ground.

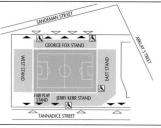

CAPACITY: 11,506 (All Seated)
PITCH DIMENSIONS: 113 yds x 74 yds
FACILITIES FOR DISABLED SUPPORTERS:
There is provision for disabled supporters in both the Bobby Cox & Bob Shankly Stands

Dundee United: Tannadice Park

Tannadice Park can be reached by the following routes:
BUSES: The following buses leave from the city centre at frequent intervals Nos. 1a, 18, 19 and 21 from Meadowside and No. 22 from Littlewoods Store, High Street.
TRAINS: Trains from all over the country pass through the main Dundee station and fans can then proceed to the ground by the above bus services from stops situated within walking distance of the station.
CARS: There is parking in the streets adjacent to the ground.

CAPACITY: 14,223 (All Seated)
PITCH DIMENSIONS: 110 yds x 72 yds
FACILITIES FOR DISABLED SUPPORTERS:
George Fox Stand – Lower Tier – Home Supporters.
East Stand – Lower Tier – Home Supporters.
West Stand – Away Supporters.

Dunfermline Athletic: East End Park

East End Park may be reached by the following routes:
TRAINS: There is a regular train service from Edinburgh to either Dunfermline Town or Dunfermline Queen Margaret Stations. The ground is a 15 minute walk from either station.
BUSES: Buses destined for Kelty, Perth, St. Andrews and Kirkcaldy all pass close to East End Park.
CARS: Car Parking is available in a large car park adjoining the East End of the ground and there are also facilities in various side streets. Multi-storey car parking approximately 10 minutes walk from the ground.

CAPACITY: 11,998 (All Seated)
PITCH DIMENSIONS: 115 yds x 70 yds
FACILITIES FOR DISABLED SUPPORTERS:
12 spaces in East Stand for Away Supporters. 12 spaces in the Norrie McCathie Stand for Home Supporters. 24 seats for helpers.

Hearts: Tynecastle Stadium

Tynecastle Stadium can be reached by the following routes:
BUSES: A frequent service of buses leaves from the city centre, Nos. 1, 2, 3, 4, 33, 34, 35 and 44 all pass the ground.
TRAINS: Haymarket Station is about half a mile from the ground.
CARS: Car Parking facilities exist in the adjacent side streets in Robertson Avenue and also the Westfield area.

CAPACITY: 17,700 (All Seated)
PITCH DIMENSIONS: 107 yds x 74 yds
FACILITIES FOR DISABLED SUPPORTERS:
There are 15 spaces for visiting fans at the Roseburn Stand. Regarding facilities for home supporters, fans should contact the club in advance for availability.

Hibernian: Easter Road Stadium

Easter Road Stadium can be reached by the following routes:
BUSES: The following Lothian Regional Transport buses depart Princes Street every few minutes and stop in London Road at Easter Road (Nos. 1, 4, 15, 26 and 44). The No. 1 bus travels down Easter Road and stops near the Stadium. The following First Bus Service stop on London Road, at the top of Easter Road (66, 106, 113, 124, 129, X5).
TRAINS: Edinburgh Waverley is served by trains from all over the country and adjoins Princes Street. The Stadium is about a 20/25 minute walk from Princes Street.
CARS: There are no special parking arrangements for cars in the immediate vicinity of the Stadium. Parking is controlled by a Temporary Traffic Regulation Order (coned areas). Persons with disabilities displaying Orange Badges on their vehicles will be permitted to park on the south side of St. Clair Street under the direction of Parking Attendants/Police.

CAPACITY: 17,458 (All Seated)
PITCH DIMENSIONS: 115 yds x 70 yds
FACILITIES FOR DISABLED SUPPORTERS:
Home Supporters: Famous Five (North) Stand / Wheelchair Disabled and Hearing Impaired.
West Stand / Wheelchair and Ambulant Disabled and Visually Impaired
Away Supporters: South Stand / Wheelchair and Ambulant Disabled and Hearing and Visually Impaired.

Inverness C T: Pittodrie Stadium

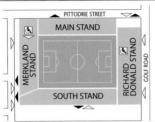

You can reach Pittodrie Stadium by these routes:
BUSES: The following buses all depart from the city centre to within a hundred yards of the ground: Nos. 1, 2, and 11.
TRAINS: The main Aberdeen station is in the centre of the city and the above buses will then take fans to the ground.
CARS: Motor vehicles coming from the city centre should travel along Union Street, then turn into King Street and the park will be on your right, about half a mile further on. Parking on Beach Boulevard and Beach Esplanade.

CAPACITY: 21,474 (All Seated)
PITCH DIMENSIONS: 110 yds x 72 yds
FACILITIES FOR DISABLED SUPPORTERS:
There are a total of 26 wheelchair spaces in the home support areas. 20 are located at the front of the Richard Donald stand and 6 at the front of the Merkland Family Stand. There are 7 spaces available in the away support (section Q) in the South Stand. Please telephone 01463 222880.

Kilmarnock: Rugby Park

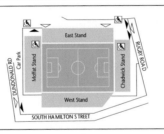

Rugby Park can be reached by the following routes:
BUSES: The main bus station, which is served by buses from all over the country, is ten minutes walk from the ground, but there are three local services which run from here to within a two minute walk of the park. These are the Kilmarnock/Saltcoats, Kilmarnock/Ardrossan and Kilmarnock/Largs.
TRAINS: Kilmarnock Station is well served by trains from Glasgow and the West Coast, and the station is only 15 minutes walk from the ground.
CARS: Car parking is available in the club car park by permit only. Entry ONLY from Dundonald Road. Visiting supporters enter ONLY from Rugby Road Entrance.

CAPACITY: 18,128 (All Seated)
PITCH DIMENSIONS: 112 yds x 74 yds
FACILITIES FOR DISABLED SUPPORTERS:
Contact: Grace Jamieson, Secretary, Persons with a Disability Association Tel: (01563) 555933

Livingston: Almondvale Stadium

Almondvale Stadium can be reached by the following routes:
BUSES: By bus to terminus at Almondvale Shopping Centre. Follow direction signs for St. John's Hospital or Almondvale Stadium and it is a short 5 minute walk.
TRAINS: To either Livingston North or South Stations, and by taxi to stadium. Approximate cost is £2.00.
CARS: Leave M8 at Livingston Junction (East). Follow signs for St. John's Hospital or the Almondvale Stadium.

CAPACITY: 10,005 (All Seated)
PITCH DIMENSIONS: 107yds x 75yds
FACILITIES FOR DISABLED SUPPORTERS:
By prior arrangement with Secretary.

Motherwell: Fir Park

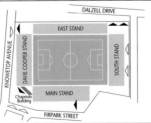

The following routes can be used to reach Fir Park:
BUSES: Fir Park is less than a quarter of a mile from the main thoroughfare through the town and numerous buses serving Lanarkshire and Glasgow all pass along this road.
TRAINS: Motherwell Station is a twenty minute walk from Fir Park, while the station at Airbles Road is only ten minutes away. East Coast access is via Motherwell Central Station on the Glasgow/London East Coast line. Travel from West Coast and Glasgow areas is via the low level Glasgow Central line to Airbles and Motherwell Central. This is a regular service on a 30 minute basis (8 mins & 38 mins past).
CARS: Controlled supervised car parking is available in the immediate area of Fir Park. Car park season tickets are available for closest proximity car parks. Away fan car parking is extensive in the grounds of Motherwell College on a day rate basis of £3.00.

CAPACITY: 13,757 (All Seated)
PITCH DIMENSIONS: 113 yds x 72 yds
FACILITIES FOR DISABLED SUPPORTERS:
Area between Main Stand and South Stand. Prior arrangement must be made with the Secretary and a ticket obtained.

Rangers: Ibrox Stadium

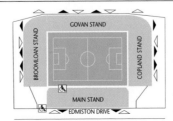

You can reach Ibrox Stadium by these routes:
BUSES: The following buses all pass within 300 yards of the Stadium and can be boarded from Glasgow city centre:- Nos. 4, 9A, 23, 23A, 52, 53, 53A, 54A, 54B, 65, 89 and 91.
UNDERGROUND: GGPTE Underground station is Ibrox, which is two minutes walk from the Stadium.
CARS: Motor Vehicles can head for the Stadium from the city centre by joining the M8 Motorway from Waterloo Street. Take the B768 turn-off for Govan. This will then take you to the ground. A limited number of parking spaces will be available in the Albion Car Park.

CAPACITY: 50,444 (All Seated)
PITCH DIMENSIONS: 115yds x 75yds
FACILITIES FOR DISABLED SUPPORTERS:
Special area within stadium and also special toilet facilities provided. The club also have a Rangers Disabled Supporters' Club. Contact: David Milne, Secretary, Disabled Supporters' Club, c/o Ibrox Stadium, Glasgow, G51 2XD. This is free of charge.

Airdrie Unite

AIRDRIE UNITED

Excelsior Stadium, Broomfield Park,
Airdrie, ML6 8QZ

ALL CORRESPONDENCE ADDRESSED TO:
Secretary, Airdrie United F.C.
60 St. Enoch Square,
Glasgow, G1 4AG

CHAIRMAN
James W. Ballantyne

DIRECTORS
Ann Marie Ballantyne, Gavin W. Speirs,
Mrs. Rose Mary Ballantyne, John Ballantyne
& W. Gardner Speirs

HONORARY PRESIDENT
Ian McMillan

SECRETARY
Ms. Ann Marie Ballantyne

MANAGER
Sandy Stewart

PLAYER/ASSISTANT MANAGER
Kenny Black

YOUTH CO-ORDINATOR
Jimmy Boyle

YOUTH TEAM COACHES
Jimmy Boyle (U17)

**FOOTBALL SAFETY OFFICERS'
ASSOCIATION REPRESENTATIVE**
Alistair Cameron

COMMERCIAL/LOTTERY MANAGER
Les Jones
Mobile 07949 976116

STADIUM MANAGER
Alistair Cameron
Tel (01236) 622000

CLUB DOCTOR
Dr. Brian Dunn, M.B., CLB, M.R.C.P.(UK)

PHYSIOTHERAPIST
Ian Constable

GROUNDSMAN
John McGuire

KIT PERSON
John Donnelly

**COMMERCIAL DIRECTOR &
MEDIA LIAISON OFFICER**
James W. Ballantyne

MATCHDAY PROGRAMME EDITOR
John O'Brien
(B) (0141) 285 4618
(H) (01236) 763824

SEASON TICKET ADMINISTRATOR
Scott Gilkison

TELEPHONES
Ground (Match Days Only)
(01236) 622000
Fax (0141) 221 1497
Sec. Bus. (07710) 230775

E-MAIL & INTERNET ADDRESS
www.airdrieunitedfc.com
jim@airdrieunitedfc.com
annmarie@airdrieunitedfc.com

CLUB SHOP
Situated at Ground
Open on Home Match Days and also on
Sundays between 2-4.30pm, Other opening
times listed on website (01236) 770147

FANS REPRESENTATIVE
Veronica McGregor

TEAM CAPTAIN
Stephen Docherty

SHIRT SPONSOR
Pertemps

KIT SUPPLIER
Pro Star

LIST OF PLAYERS 2004/05

PLAYERS SURNAME	FIRST NAME	MIDDLE NAME	DATE OF BIRTH	PLACE OF BIRTH	DATE SIGNED	HEIGHT FT INS	WEIGHT ST LBS	POSITION ON PITCH	PREVIOUS CLUB
BARKEY	KEVIN		05/02/85	GLASGOW	30/07/04	5 8	10 7	MIDFIELD	MOTHERWELL
BARTON	ROSS	JOHN	16/10/89	BELLSHILL	03/09/04	5 7	8 0	DEFENDER	FALKIRK FORM D UND...
BLACK	KENNETH	GEORGE	29/11/63	STENHOUSEMUIR	30/07/04	5 9	12 12	MIDFIELD	EDINBURGH UNIVERSI...
BROWN	ANDREW	KENNETH	24/04/88	BROXBURN	13/09/04	5 11	10 4	MIDFIELD	FALKIRK FORM D UNDER ...
BURRELL	MARK	WILLIAM	10/01/88	LANARK	07/09/04	5 10	9 0	GOALKEEPER	MOTHERWELL
CAINE	DAVID		22/07/89	BELLSHILL	22/08/04	5 8	9 7	MIDFIELD	AIRDRIE UNITED B.C.
CHRISTIE	KEVIN		01/04/76	ABERDEEN	28/05/04	6 1	13 4	MIDFIELD	FALKIRK
COYLE	OWEN	COLUMBA	14/07/66	PAISLEY	23/07/04	5 11	10 4	FORWARD	DUNDEE UNITED
CULLEN	PAUL	FRANCIS	15/04/88	LANARK	23/08/04	5 9	9 7	DEFENDER	HAMILTON ACAD. FORM D UND...
DOCHERTY	STEPHEN		18/02/76	GLASGOW	26/07/02	5 10	12 0	DEF/MID	AIRDRIEONIANS
DUNN	DAVID	HUGH	01/11/81	BELLSHILL	31/01/03	5 11	12 1	MIDFIELD	CLYDE
FENNESSEY	THOMAS	HARTY	26/03/88	COATBRIDGE	26/08/04	5 11	10 7	MIDFIELD	DUNDEE UNITED
GALLACHER	CHRISTOPHER		23/08/88	BELLSHILL	26/08/04	5 8	9 7	MIDFIELD	HEART OF MIDLOTHIAN
GALLAGHER	MARK		23/09/88	GLASGOW	23/08/04	5 10.5	10 12	DEFENDER	CLYDE FORM S
GEMMELL	MICHAEL		01/07/86	EDINBURGH	29/07/03	5 10	10 10	MIDFIELD	GAIRDOCH UNITED
GORDON	PAUL	ROSS	26/04/88	GLASGOW	23/08/04	6 1	11 0	FORWARD	ST. MIRREN FORM D UNDER 1...
GOW	ALAN		09/10/82	GLASGOW	30/08/02	6 0	12 0	MIDFIELD	CLYDEBANK
GRANT	BARRY		08/09/87	BELLSHILL	21/10/03	5 6	9 0	MIDFIELD	MOTHERWELL
HARDIE	MARTIN		22/04/76	ALEXANDRIA	04/08/04	6 0	11 0	MID/FWD	KILMARNOCK
HOEY	THOMAS	GAVIN	14/04/86	GLASGOW	06/07/04	5 11	11 7	MIDFIELD	ARSENAL B.C.
HOLLIS	LEE	JAMES	12/03/86	GLASGOW	11/08/03	6 0	11 0	GOALKEEPER	HILLWOOD B.C.
LOVERING	PAUL	JAMES	25/11/75	GLASGOW	28/05/04	5 10	11 3	DEFENDER	ST. JOHNSTONE
McDOUGALL	STEVEN	DAVID	17/06/86	PAISLEY	11/08/03	5 11	10 6	FORWARD	RANGERS
McGEOWN	MARK		10/05/70	PAISLEY	26/07/02	5 10.5	12 0	GOALKEEPER	STRANRAER
McGOWAN	NEIL	WILLIAM	15/04/77	GLASGOW	29/08/02	5 10	11 4	DEFENDER	K.A. ICELAND
McKENNA	STEPHEN		25/11/85	GLASGOW	28/05/04	6 1	12 4	MIDFIELD	RANGERS
McKEOWN	STEPHEN	JAMES	17/07/81	RUTHERGLEN	29/08/02	5 10	12 10	FORWARD	AIRDRIEONIANS
McLAREN	LIAM		25/06/88	GLASGOW	26/08/04	6 0	10 3	GOALKEEPER	DUNFERMLINE ATHLETI...
McLAREN	WILLIAM		06/11/84	GLASGOW	23/02/04	5 9	9 0	MIDFIELD	BENBURB JUNIORS
McMANUS	ALLAN	WILLIAM	17/11/74	PAISLEY	06/06/03	6 1	13 4	DEFENDER	AYR UNITED
MONAGHAN	DARREN		01/02/88	GLASGOW	26/08/04	5 8	9 9	DEFENDER	MOTHERWELL
O'HARE	STEVEN	PAUL	30/04/88	LANARK	03/09/04	5 6	9 6	MIDFIELD	AIRDRIE UNITED B.C.
QUINTILIANI	GIANPIERO		29/04/88	BELLSHILL	08/09/04	5 11	11 0	FORWARD	MOTHERWELL
ROBERTS	MARK	KINGSLEY	29/10/75	IRVINE	16/07/03	5 11	11 10	FORWARD	ST. MIRREN
STEWART	ALEXANDER		14/10/65	BELLSHILL	30/07/04	5 7	11 7	DEFENDER	AIRDRIEONIANS
SWEENEY	KEVIN		26/05/88	GLASGOW	23/08/04	5 6	8 2	MIDFIELD	MANCHESTER UNITED B.C.
VARBILLE	JEROME		01/06/74	VERNOUX	20/09/02	6 1	12 13	FORWARD	AIRDRIEONIANS
WILSON	CHRISTOPHER		02/02/88	GLASGOW	26/08/04	5 10	10 2	DEFENDER	MOTHERWELL
WILSON	MARVYN		01/12/73	BELLSHILL	01/08/03	5 8	11 8	MIDFIELD	AYR UNITED
WILSON	RYAN	CHARLES	05/01/89	NEWCASTLE	03/09/04	5 9	10 0	FORWARD	FALKIRK FORM D UNDER 16
WILSON	WILLIAM	STEWART	19/08/72	GLASGOW	14/07/04	5 8	10 2	DEFENDER	EAST FIFE

TICKET INFORMATION

SEASON TICKET PRICES

SEATED	ADULT	£245 RESERVED SEAT
	ADULT	£225 UNRESERVED SEAT
	OAP/UNEMPLOYED	£125/100 RESERVED/UNRESERVED SEAT
	JUVENILE (12-16)	£85
	CHILD UNDER 12	£25 WITH PARENT
	CHILD OVER 12	£50 WITH PARENT
	DISABLED	£50

LEAGUE ADMISSION PRICES

SEATED	ADULT	£14
	JUVENILE/OAP/ UNEMPLOYED (WITH UB40)	£6
	PARENT & CHILD	£18

THE DIAMONDS' 10 YEAR LEAGUE RECOR

SEASON	DIV	P	W	D	L	F	A	PTS
1994-95	F	36	8	11	17	33	47	35
1995-96	F	36	10	10	16	39	58	40
1996-97	F	36	7	7	22	31	59	28
1997-98	S	36	16	12	8	48	31	60
1998-99	F	36	11	13	12	36	38	46
1999-00	F	36	1	7	28	17	82	10
2000-01	S	36	12	11	13	42	43	47
2001-02	S	36	14	9	13	44	45	51
2002-03	S	36	14	12	10	51	44	54
2003-04	S	36	20	10	6	64	36	70

The diamonds' stats 2003/04

SEASON STATS 2003/04

DATE	VENUE	OPPONENTS	ATT	RES	McGEOWN M.	WILSON W.	DUNN D.	STEWART A.	McMANUS A.	McGOWAN N.	VAREILLE J.	WILSON M.	McKEOWN S.	DOCHERTY S.	ROBERTS M.	RONALD P.	GOW A.	BLACK K.	WILSON S.	GLANCY M.	SINGBO F.	McLAREN W.	COYLE O.	CHRISTIE K.	LOVERING P.	McKENNA S.
AUG	A	MORTON	3,806	1-3	1	2	3	4	5	6	7	8	9^1	10	11	12	14									
AUG	H	ALLOA ATHLETIC	1,445	1-0	1	2		4		6	7^1	8		10	9	14	11	3	5	15						
AUG	A	HAMILTON ACADEMICAL	2,007	1-2	1		12	4	2	6	7^1	8			11	10	9	3	5	14						
AUG	H	DUMBARTON	1,468	2-0	1	2	10^1			6	7	4			9	8	14	3	5	11^1	16					
SEP	A	EAST FIFE	885	1-3	1	2	10	12	4	6	7	8			9		15	3	5	11^1						
SEP	H	ARBROATH	1,385	2-1	1	3	10^1	4	5	6		8		2^1	9	16	7			11	14					
SEP	A	BERWICK RANGERS	752	1-0	1	3		4	5	6	14	8	15	2	9		7^1			12	11	10				
OCT	A	FORFAR ATHLETIC	650	1-1	1	3	10	4	5	6	15	8	16	2	9		7^1			11	14					
OCT	A	ALLOA ATHLETIC	636	4-1	1	2		4	5	3	7^1	8	14	10^1	9^1	12	11^1			6	15					
OCT	H	STENHOUSEMUIR	1,406	2-0	1	2	12	4	5	3	7^1	8	15^1	10	9		11			6	16					
NOV	H	MORTON	3,159	1-6	1	2	10			3	7	8	14^1	4	9		11		5	15	6					
NOV	H	EAST FIFE	1,418	1-1	1	2	3	4		6	7	8	9	10^1	11	12		5	15		16					
NOV	A	DUMBARTON	1,361	0-2	1	2	6	4		3	7	8				12		5	11		16					
DEC	A	ARBROATH	405	1-1	1	3	10	4		7	8	14	2	11	6^1	15				16			9			
DEC	H	BERWICK RANGERS	1,254	1-1	1	11		5	3	15	8	7	2	10	6	14				16	4		9^1			
DEC	H	FORFAR ATHLETIC	1,072	3-3	1	6		4	3	15	8	10	2	16	7	11^2		5					9^1			
DEC	A	STENHOUSEMUIR	1,005	1-0	1	14	4	5	3	15	8	7	2	10	6	11^1							9			
JAN	H	ARBROATH	1,267	0-1	1		4	5	3	14	8	7	2	10	6	11				15	16		9			
FEB	A	EAST FIFE	793	1-0	1	6^1	5	4	7		8		10									11	9	2	3	
FEB	H	DUMBARTON	1,378	1-1	1	6		5	4	7^1	14		8	15		10				16		11	9	2	3	
FEB	H	STENHOUSEMUIR	1,324	4-0	1	6		4		7^4	14	16	8	15		10		5			11	9	2	3		
MAR	H	HAMILTON ACADEMICAL	1,634	3-0	1	6		4		7	14	16	8	15		10		5			11	9^3	2	3		
MAR	H	ALLOA ATHLETIC	1,542	2-1	1	6	12	4		7		16	8	15		10		5			11^2	9	2	3		
MAR	A	MORTON	3,252	1-1	1	12	6		5	4	7	14		8	15		10^1				11	9	2	3		
MAR	A	HAMILTON ACADEMICAL	2,559	1-0	1	2	6		5	4	7	14	15	8	10					16	11	9^1		3		
MAR	A	BERWICK RANGERS	502	1-1	1	2	6		5	4	7		15	8	10					16	11^1	9	12	3		
MAR	A	FORFAR ATHLETIC	710	3-1	1		6		5	4	7	14	15	8	10	16					11^2	9	2^1	3		
MAR	A	DUMBARTON	1,543	2-1	1	12	6		5	4		14	15	8	10						7^1	11^1	9	2	3	
MAR	H	EAST FIFE	1,597	2-1	1	2	6^1		5	4		14	15	8			10				7	11^1	9		3	
APR	H	BERWICK RANGERS	1,546	6-0	1	2		5	4	15	6	14	8^1		10^2					12	7	11	9^3		3	
APR	A	ARBROATH	1,074	4-0	1	2		4			15	8	6^1		16		10		5^1		7	11	9		3^1	14
APR	A	STENHOUSEMUIR	1,197	3-0	1	2		4			15	8	6		16		10^1		5		7	11	9^1	12	3^1	
APR	H	FORFAR ATHLETIC	1,959	2-2	1	2		4			15	8	6		16		10		5		7	11^1	9^1	12	3	
MAY	H	HAMILTON ACADEMICAL	2,936	1-1	1		6		5	4	15	8	14		16		10^1				7	11	9	2	3	
MAY	A	ALLOA ATHLETIC	1,635	1-0	1		6		5	4	15	8		14	16		10				7	11	9^1	2	3	
MAY	H	MORTON	5,704	2-0	1	2	6		5	4	7	8	14		15		10^1			12		11^1	9		3	
TOTAL FULL APPEARANCES					36	21	25	13	28	32	21	25	10	27	19	7	26	4	16	14	3	18	23	10	18	
TOTAL SUB APPEARANCES					2	3	1	1			12	8	18		11	6	6		3	12	3	3		3		1
TOTAL GOALS SCORED							4				9		4	4	1	1	12		1	3		10	12	1		2

Bold figures denote goalscorers. † denotes opponent's own goal.

LEADING GOALSCORERS:

SEASON	DIV	GOALS	PLAYER
94-95	F	9	K. Eadie
95-96	F	11	J. Grady
96-97	F	8	J. Grady
97-98	S	13	C. McDonald
98-99	F	9	C. McDonald
99-00	F	5	I. Cameron
00-01	S	8	A. Burke
01-02	S	9	A. Burke
02-03	S	18	J. Vareille
03-04	S	12	A. Gow/O. Coyle

MILESTONES:

YEAR OF FORMATION:
1965 (From seasons 1965/66 to 2001/02 known as Clydebank F.C.)

MOST LEAGUE POINTS IN A SEASON:
58 (Division 1 – Season 1976/77) (2 Points for a Win)
70 (Second Division – Season 2003/04) (3 Points for a Win)

MOST LEAGUE GOALS SCORED BY A PLAYER IN A SEASON:
Ken Eadie (Season 1990/91)
NO. OF GOALS SCORED: 29

RECORD ATTENDANCE:
14,900 (-v- Hibernian – 10.2.1965 at Kilbowie Park)
5,703 (-v- Morton – 15.5.2004 at Excelsior Stadium)

RECORD VICTORY: 8-1 (-v- Arbroath – Division 1, 3.1.1977)
RECORD DEFEAT: 1-9 (-v- Gala Fairydean – Scottish Cup, 15.9.1965)

AIRDRIE UNITED PLAYING KITS SEASON 2004/05

FIRST KIT | SECOND KIT | THIRD KIT

CLYDE FC
Broadwood Stadium,
Cumbernauld, G68 9NE
CHAIRMAN

VICE-CHAIRMAN

DIRECTORS
Gerard W. Dunn, M.A., Harry McCall, B.A.,
C.Eng., M.I.C.E., John D. Taylor, A.C.I.B.,
Leonard McGuire, Francis G. Dunn,
James Murray & John G. Alexander
HONORARY PRESIDENT
William B. Carmichael
HONORARY VICE-PRESIDENT
William J. Dunn
SECRETARY
John D. Taylor, A.C.I.B.
Bus. (01236) 451511
(H) (0141) 633 1013
OFFICE ADMINISTRATOR
Mrs. Lynn Calder
MANAGER
Billy Reid
ASSISTANT MANAGER
Stuart Balmer
COMMUNITY COACH
Jim Strathdee
YOUTH COACHES
Chris Hillcoat (U19),
Gary O'Rourke (U13)
WOMENS DEVELOPMENT COACH
David Mark
COMMERCIAL MANAGER
Jack Rolland
CLUB DOCTORS
Dr. Michael McGavigan,
Dr. Michael McLaughlin & Dr. Frank Dunn
PHYSIOTHERAPISTS
Iain McKinlay & Avril Downs
**FOOTBALL SAFETY OFFICERS'
ASSOCIATION REPRESENTATIVE**
Peter Eadie
MEDIA LIAISON PERSON John Ruddy
STADIUM MANAGER Peter Eadie
KIT PERSON Bill Munro
MATCHDAY PROGRAMME EDITOR
John D. Taylor
TELEPHONES
Ground (01236) 451511
Fax (01236) 733490
E-MAIL & INTERNET ADDRESS
info@clydefc.co.uk
www.clydefc.co.uk
CLUB SHOP
Situated at Ground
Open on Home Matchdays 1 hour before and
for 1 hour after match. Online Shop -
www.clydefc.co.uk
SUPPORTERS CLUB
Castlemilk Branch, Eric Steel (0141) 569 3625
Glasgow Branch, Andy Peters (0141) 423 1671
Rod MacKenzie (0141) 771 1385
TEAM CAPTAIN John Potter
SHIRT SPONSOR
First choice playing kit: The Walker Group
Second choice playing kit:
DM Design Kitchens & Bedrooms
KIT SUPPLIER TFG

LIST OF PLAYERS 2004/05

PLAYERS SURNAME	FIRST NAME	MIDDLE NAME	DATE OF BIRTH	PLACE OF BIRTH	DATE SIGNED	HEIGHT FT INS		WEIGHT ST LBS		POSITION ON PITCH	PREVIOUS CLUB
ARBUCKLE	GARY		16/08/84	GLASGOW	27/07/04	5	11	12	6	FORWARD	CELTIC
BALMER	STUART	MURRAY	20/09/69	FALKIRK	06/08/04	6	1	13	12	DEFENDER	BOSTON UNITED
BOLLAN	GARY		24/03/73	DUNDEE	07/08/04	5	10	13	10	DEFENDER	MOTHERWELL
BRADLEY	KEVIN		18/06/86	GLASGOW	29/05/03	5	6	8	7	FORWARD	CLYDE YOUTHS
BRYSON	CRAIG	JAMES	06/11/86	RUTHERGLEN	02/02/04	5	7	9	7	MIDFIELD	EAST KILBRIDE THISTLE JU
CONWAY	AARON		29/03/85	DUNDEE	27/08/04	5	11	11	7	FORWARD	DUNDEE UNITED
DEVLIN	MARTIN	LIAM	17/07/86	GLASGOW	29/08/04	5	10	10	5	MIDFIELD	MOTHERWELL
DORNAN	SCOTT	THOMAS	30/04/87	GLASGOW	10/09/04	5	10	9	7	DEFENDER	CLYDE FORM D UNDE
FLAHERTY	PAUL		13/12/87	BELLSHILL	03/06/04	5	11	9	7	MIDFIELD	CLYDE FORM S
GIBSON	JAMES	ROBERT	19/02/80	BELLSHILL	21/08/03	5	7	11	3	MIDFIELD	RANGERS
GILHANEY	MARK		04/11/84	LANARK	05/06/02	5	7	10	5	FORWARD	CAMBUSLANG RANGERS JUN
HALLIWELL	BRYN	STEVEN	01/10/80	EPSOM	12/06/00	6	1	12	10	GOALKEEPER	WIMBLEDON
HARRIS	ROBERT		28/08/87	GLASGOW	08/06/04	5	8	9	0	DEFENDER	RANGERS
HARTY	IAN	McGUINNESS	08/04/78	BELLSHILL	21/05/03	5	9	12	6	FORWARD	STRANRAER
MALONE	EDWARD	JOSEPH	06/04/85	EDINBURGH	24/08/04	5	11	10	7	MIDFIELD	ST. JOHNSTONE
MARSIGLIA	MICHAEL		25/12/75	LA CIOTAT	17/09/04	6	1	11	12	MIDFIELD	FC CARTAGENA
McCAFFERTY	SEAMUS	PATRICK	08/04/87	GLASGOW	08/09/04	5	9	10	7	GOALKEEPER	PARTICK THISTLE
McCRACKEN	GRAEME		23/07/86	COATBRIDGE	05/07/04	5	10	10	6	MIDFIELD	CLYDE YOUTHS
McKEEVER	JOHN	PAUL	18/11/87	GLASGOW	03/06/04	5	7	8	7	MIDFIELD	CLYDE FORM S
McNAUGHT	DAVID	ANDREW	24/03/88	ALEXANDRIA	03/06/04	5	10	10	7	FORWARD	CLYDE FORM D UNDER
MENSING	SIMON	ROSS	27/06/82	WOLFENBUTTL	26/10/01	6	0	13	3	DEFENDER	WIMBLEDON
MORRISON	ALLAN	JAMES	31/03/82	IRVINE	23/08/02	6	1	13	6	GOALKEEPER	CARLISLE UNITED
NAPIER	MARC		05/10/88	LANARK	31/08/04	5	8	10	9	DEFENDER	CARLUKE B.C.
POLLOCK	ROSS		14/04/88	GLASGOW	18/09/04	5	9	10	0	DEFENDER	MANCHESTER UNITED
POTTER	JOHN	PAUL	15/12/79	DUNFERMLINE	27/03/02	6	1	13	2	DEFENDER	DUNFERMLINE ATHLET
RENNY	ANDREW		18/09/87	GLASGOW	02/09/04	5	11	12	7	DEFENDER	PARTICK THISTLE
SHERIDAN	DARREN	STEPHEN	08/12/67	MANCHESTER	06/08/04	5	6.5	11	0	MIDFIELD	OLDHAM ATHLETIC
THORBURN	MICHAEL		13/07/88	LANARK	28/08/04	6	0	9	8	FORWARD	LESMAHAGOW B.C.
WALKER	ALEXANDER		25/04/84	BELLSHILL	20/08/04	5	11.5	12	4	MIDFIELD	RANGERS
WILFORD	ARON		14/01/82	SCARBOROUGH	02/08/04	6	3	14	2	FORWARD	LINCOLN CITY
WILSON	SCOTT	WILLIAM	20/04/82	BELLSHILL	31/08/04	6	3	11	2	DEFENDER	AIRDRIE UNITED

TICKET INFORMATION

SEASON TICKET INFORMATION

SEATED		
	ADULT	£260
	OAP/STUDENTS	£130
	JUVENILE (U18)	£60
	JUVENILE (U12)	£30

LEAGUE ADMISSION PRICES

SEATED		
	ADULT	£14
	OAP/STUDENT	£7
	UNDER 18	£5
	PARENT & UP TO 2 CHILDREN	£18

THE BULLY WEE'S 10 YEAR LEAGUE RECOR

SEASON	DIV	P	W	D	L	F	A	PTS
1994-95	S	36	14	10	12	53	48	52
1995-96	S	36	11	12	13	47	45	45
1996-97	S	36	14	10	12	42	39	52
1997-98	S	36	10	12	14	40	53	42
1998-99	S	36	15	8	13	46	42	53
1999-00	S	36	18	11	7	65	37	65
2000-01	F	36	11	14	11	44	46	47
2001-02	F	36	13	10	13	51	56	49
2002-03	F	36	21	9	6	66	37	72
2003-04	F	36	20	9	7	64	40	69

SEASON STATS 2003/04

DATE	VENUE	OPPONENTS	ATT	RES	MORRISON A.	MENSING S.	McLAUGHLIN M.	KERNAGHAN A.	FRASER J.	ROSS J.	HAGEN D.	MILLEN A.	KEOGH P.	HARTY I.	McCONALOGUE S.	POTTER J.	GILHANEY M.	SMITH A.	HALLIWELL B.	GIBSON J.	DOYLE P.	McGROARTY C.	MARSHALL C.	McCLUSKEY S.	FOTHERINGHAM K.	McCANN H. A.
UG	H	AYR UNITED	1,067	3-0	1	2	3[1]	4	5	6	7	8	9[2]	10	11	12		14	15							
AUG	A	INVERNESS CAL TH	1,839	0-0		2	3		5	6	7	8		10	11	4	9	12	1							
AUG	H	BRECHIN CITY	1,063	2-1		2	3		5	6	7[1]	8			10[1]	11	4	12	9	1	14	15				
AUG	A	ST. MIRREN	3,010	1-2					5	6	7	8	9		3	10[1]	12	1	4	2	11					
SEP	H	ST. JOHNSTONE	1,468	2-0			3	12	4	5	6	8	9[1]	11[1]		2	10	14	1		7					
SEP	H	FALKIRK	2,758	1-2			3	12	4	5	6	14	8	9	11[1]	2	10	15	1		7					
SEP	A	QUEEN OF THE SOUTH	1,952	1-4			3	10	4	5	6	15	8		9	11[1]	2	12	14	1	7					
CT	H	ROSS COUNTY	1,056	†2-2			3		4	15	6		8	9	12	11[1]	2	10	14	1	5					
OCT	H	RAITH ROVERS	1,765	1-0			3	4	5	6	15	8	9	14	11	2	12		1	10[1]						
NOV	H	AYR UNITED	1,653	2-2	1		3	4	5		7	8	9[2]	14	10	2	15				11	6				
NOV	H	INVERNESS CAL TH	734	1-0	1	16	3	4	5	6	7	8	9		11[1]	2	12	15			10					
NOV	A	ST. JOHNSTONE	2,474	0-3	1	3		4	5	6	7	8	9		11	2	12	15			10	14				
NOV	H	ST. MIRREN	1,811	2-0	1	2	3	4		6	11	8	9[1]	16	10		12[1]			5		7	14			
NOV	H	QUEEN OF THE SOUTH	1,271	3-1	1	2	3	4		6	7	14		11[1]		12	9[2]			5		10	8			
NOV	A	FALKIRK	2,898	2-0	1	3	5[1]	4	2	6	7	14		11	15	12	9[1]			10			8			
EC	H	RAITH ROVERS	1,375	0-0	1	3	5	4	2	6	7	14		11	15	12	9			10			8			
DEC	A	ROSS COUNTY	2,721	1-0	1	2	5	4		6	7			11[1]		12	9			10		3	8			
DEC	H	AYR UNITED	1,049	2-1	1	2	3[1]	4		6	7	5		11[1]		12	9			10			8			
DEC	A	BRECHIN CITY	808	3-1	1	3	5	4	2	6	7		16	11[1]	14	12	9[1]			10[1]			8			
AN	A	ST. MIRREN	3,355	3-2	1	3	5[1]		2	6	7		16	11[1]		12	9[1]			10	15		8	4		
JAN	H	FALKIRK	3,137	4-2	1	3	5[1]		2	6	7		16[1]	11[1]		12	9			10	15		8[1]	4		
FEB	H	ROSS COUNTY	1,139	1-0	1	3	5	4		6	7		15	11[1]		12	9			10			8	2		
FEB	A	RAITH ROVERS	1,871	3-0	1	3	5	4	14	6	7		15	11[2]			9			10	16		8[1]	2		
MAR	H	ST. JOHNSTONE	1,518	2-3	1	3	5	4		6	7		14[1]	11		12	9[1]			10			8	2	16	
MAR	A	QUEEN OF THE SOUTH	2,169	2-1		3	5	4		6	16		14	11		12	9	1		10			8	2	7[1]	
MAR	H	BRECHIN CITY	1,037	0-0		3	5	4		6	15		10	11	14	12	9	1					8	2	7	
MAR	A	INVERNESS CAL TH	2,645	1-3		2	5		6	7		14	11	15		12	9	1		10			8	4	3[1]	
MAR	A	ST. JOHNSTONE	3,512	3-1	19	2	5		6	16		12	11[1]	7[1]		9[1]	1		10			8	4	3	
MAR	H	ST. MIRREN	1,786	2-2		2	5		6[1]	7		14	11[1]	15		9	1		10	16		8	4	3	
APR	H	QUEEN OF THE SOUTH	1,207	2-0		2			6[1]			14	11	7[1]		12	9	1		10		8	4	5	3	
APR	A	FALKIRK	2,536	1-1		2			6	16		12	11	7		14	9[1]	1		10		8	4	5	3	
APR	H	RAITH ROVERS	1,533	4-1		2	5		6	15		14[1]	11	7		12	9	1	10[2]			8	4[1]	3		
APR	A	ROSS COUNTY	3,220	0-0		2	5		6	15		12	11			7	9	1	10			8	4	14	3	
MAY	H	AYR UNITED	1,816	1-1		2	5		6			7[1]	11	14		12	9	1	10			8	4	15	3	
MAY	H	INVERNESS CAL TH	4,722	1-2			5	4		6		14	11[1]			12	9	1	10			8	2	16	3	
MAY	A	BRECHIN CITY	1,268	5-2			5		6			11[3]	12	7		15	9[2]	1	10	16		8	2	4	3	
TOTAL FULL APPEARANCES					16	30	29	22	16	35	22	14	10	29	17	11	6	24	20	26	1	12	24	17	9	6
TOTAL SUB APPEARANCES					1	1	2		2		9	3	15	5	7	1	27	9		1	6		2		4	
TOTAL GOALS SCORED							5		2	1			12	15	7		2	10		4			2	1	2	

Bold figures denote goalscorers. † denotes opponent's own goal.

LEADING GOALSCORERS:

SEASON	DIV	GOALS	PLAYER
-95	S	10	J. Dickson
-96	S	21	E. Annand
-97	S	21	E. Annand
-98	S	8	P. Brownlie
-99	S	12	S. Convery
-00	S	18	B. Carrigan
-01	F	7	A. Kane
-02	F	11	P. Keogh
-03	F	12	P. Keogh
-04	F	15	I. Harty

MILESTONES:

YEAR OF FORMATION: 1877
MOST CAPPED PLAYER: Tommy Ring
NO. OF CAPS: 12
MOST LEAGUE POINTS IN A SEASON:
64 (Division 2 – Season 1956/57) (2 Points for a Win)
72 (First Division – Season 2002/03) (3 Points for a Win)
MOST LEAGUE GOALS SCORED BY A PLAYER IN A SEASON:
Bill Boyd (Season 1932/33)
NO. OF GOALS SCORED: 32
RECORD ATTENDANCE:
52,000 (-v- Rangers – 21.11.1908 – at Shawfield Stadium)
7,382 (-v- Celtic – 14.8.1996 (Coca-Cola Cup) – at Broadwood Stadium)
RECORD VICTORY: 11-1 (-v- Cowdenbeath – Division 2, 6.10.1951)
RECORD DEFEAT: 0-11 (-v- Dumbarton and Rangers, Scottish Cup)

CLYDE PLAYING KITS SEASON 2004/05

FIRST KIT | SECOND KIT | THIRD KIT

FALKIRK FC
The Falkirk Stadium,
Westfield,
Falkirk, FK2 9DX

CHAIRMAN
Campbell Christie, C.B.E.

DIRECTORS
W. Martin Ritchie O.B.E., Ann M. Joyce,
Graham Crawford, Douglas Paterson &
Michael M^cA. White

SECRETARY
Alexander Blackwood

GENERAL SECRETARY
Michael M^cA. White

GENERAL MANAGER
Crawford B. Baptie

PLAYER/HEAD COACH
John Hughes

FIRST TEAM COACH
Brian Rice

YOUTH INCOME GENERATING MANAGER
Alexander Totten

COMMUNITY COACH
Tom Elliott

YOUTH DEVELOPMENT COACH
Eddie May

YOUTH CO-ORDINATORS
Eddie May & Jim McCafferty

YOUTH TEAM COACHES
Eddie May & Paul Kane (U19),
Kevin Hoggan & Alan Sneddon (U17),
Richard Fox & Larry Haggart (U15),
Jim Henderson (U14),
Alan Bateman (U13)

CLUB DOCTORS
Dr. R. Gillies Sinclair &
Dr. Robert Deuchar

PHYSIOTHERAPISTS
Stuart Yule & David McKenzie

**FOOTBALL SAFETY OFFICERS'
ASSOCIATION REPRESENTATIVES**
Crawford Baptie & Tom McGunnigle
(01324) 624121

GROUNDSMAN
James Dawson

MEDIA LIAISON OFFICER
Crawford Baptie (01324) 624121

MATCHDAY PROGRAMME EDITOR
Gordon McFarlane (07801) 798916

TELEPHONES
Ground/Commercial/
Ticket Office/Information Service
(01324) 624121
Fax (01324) 612418

E-MAIL & INTERNET ADDRESS
alexb@falkirkfc.co.uk
www.falkirkfc.co.uk

CLUB SHOP
47 Glebe Street, Falkirk, FK1 1HX
Tel (01324) 639366
Open Mon. – Sat. 9.30 a.m. – 12 Noon
and 1.00 p.m. – 5.00 p.m.
Closed on Wednesday

OFFICIAL SUPPORTERS CLUB
Association of Falkirk F.C. Supporters
Clubs–Chairman: Gordon McFarlane
Tel (01324) 638104

TEAM CAPTAIN
Kevin James

VICE-CAPTAIN
Scott MacKenzie

SHIRT SPONSOR
Budweiser Budvar

KIT SUPPLIER
TFG

LIST OF PLAYERS 2004/05

PLAYERS SURNAME	FIRST NAME	MIDDLE NAME	DATE OF BIRTH	PLACE OF BIRTH	DATE SIGNED	HEIGHT FT INS		WEIGHT ST LBS		POSITION ON PITCH	PREVIOUS CLUB
ALLISON	BRIAN		23/06/88	EDINBURGH	03/08/04	5	10	11	7	DEFENDER	ROYSTON B.C.
BARR	DARREN		17/03/85	GLASGOW	12/07/02	5	10	10	4	MIDFIELD	FALKIRK FORM D UNDER
BOYLE	NICHOLAS	JAMES	28/05/87	GLASGOW	27/07/04	5	9	10	7	MIDFIELD	FALKIRK FORM S
CAMPBELL	MARK	THOMAS	04/02/78	IRVINE	09/06/04	6	2	14	1	DEFENDER	AYR UNITED
CHURCHILL	GRAEME		20/07/87	GLASGOW	27/07/04	6	0	11	0	FORWARD	FALKIRK FORM D UNDER
CREANEY	PHILIP		12/02/83	BELLSHILL	09/06/00	5	11.5	11	5	MIDFIELD	FALKIRK FORM S
DAVIDSON	ALAN	MARTIN	10/01/85	FALKIRK	22/08/03	6	2	12	4	DEFENDER	RAITH ROVERS
DUFFY	DARRYL	ALEXANDER	16/04/84	GLASGOW	05/07/04	5	11	12	1	FORWARD	RANGERS
FERGUSON	ALLAN	THOMAS	21/03/69	LANARK	04/07/02	5	11	13	0	GOALKEEPER	AIRDRIEONIANS
HAYMAN	ROSS		07/08/86	GLASGOW	07/08/03	5	9	10	3	DEFENDER	FALKIRK FORM S
HENRY	JOHN		31/12/71	VALE OF LEVEN	19/05/04	5	10	10	5	MIDFIELD	AIRDRIEONIANS
HILL	DARREN		03/12/81	FALKIRK	07/07/98	6	1.5	12	3	GOALKEEPER	FALKIRK B.C.
HUGHES	JOHN		09/09/64	EDINBURGH	27/05/04	6	0	13	10	DEFENDER	AYR UNITED
HUTCHISON	JOHN	CHARLES	14/05/85	BELLSHILL	29/07/03	6	2	12	9	GOALKEEPER	HIBERNIAN
JAMES	KEVIN	FRANCIS	03/12/75	EDINBURGH	25/05/04	6	7	14	7	DEFENDER	AIRDRIEONIANS
KANTE	MANUEL		21/08/86	VILLEPINTE	26/08/04	6	1	12	0	MIDFIELD	AS BEAUVAIS OISE
LATAPY	RUSSELL	NIGEL	02/08/68	TRINIDAD & TOBAGO	02/06/04	5	7	11	4	MIDFIELD	DUNDEE UNITED
LAWRIE	ANDREW		24/11/78	GALASHIELS	18/06/96	6	0	12	6	DEFENDER	FALKIRK FORM D UNDER
LIGGETT	GARY		28/09/87	CRAIGAVON	20/09/04	6	0	12	7	FORWARD	GLENAVON
McALONEY	PAUL		31/01/86	BELLSHILL	08/08/03	5	11	11	2	MIDFIELD	LIVINGSTON
McIVER	MARK		10/05/88	BELLSHILL	27/07/04	6	0	10	10	GOALKEEPER	CELTIC
McKENZIE	SCOTT		07/07/70	GLASGOW	23/08/02	5	9	11	2	MIDFIELD	ST. MIRREN
McSWEEN	IAN		07/06/84	EDINBURGH	10/07/01	5	11.5	11	0	FORWARD	FALKIRK FORM D UNDER
MANSON	STEPHEN		25/02/86	EDINBURGH	07/08/03	5	9	10	2	FORWARD	HIBERNIAN
MAUCHLINE	SCOTT		08/07/87	FALKIRK	27/07/04	5	11	11	2	MIDFIELD	FALKIRK FORM S
MAY	EDWARD	SKILLION	30/08/67	EDINBURGH	27/05/04	5	10	11	7	DEFENDER	BERWICK RANGERS
McFANESPIE	KIERAN		11/09/79	GOSPORT	22/07/03	5	8	11	2	MIDFIELD	PLYMOUTH ARGYLE
McBREEN	DANIEL	JAMES	23/04/77	BURNLEY	10/09/04	6	1	13	0	FORWARD	FC UNIVERSITATEA CRAIOV
McPHERSON	CRAIG		27/03/71	GREENOCK	19/05/04	5	10	11	6	MIDFIELD	AIRDRIEONIANS
McSTAY	RYAN	MICHAEL	04/12/85	BELLSHILL	12/07/02	6	1	10	0	MIDFIELD	FALKIRK FORM D UNDER
MOUTINHO	PEDRO	DA SILVA	09/09/79	PORTO	29/07/04	5	11	12	8	FORWARD	F.C. PENAFIEL
NEILSON	ART	CHRIS ARCHIBALD	20/03/86	STIRLING	03/03/04	5	11	10	8	MIDFIELD	RANGERS
NICHOLLS	DAVID		05/04/72	BELLSHILL	09/08/03	5	10	12	7	MIDFIELD	DUNFERMLINE ATHLETIC
O'NEIL	JOHN	THOMAS	06/07/71	BELLSHILL	29/08/03	5	8	12	0	MIDFIELD	HIBERNIAN
RAHIM	BRENT		08/08/78	TRINIDAD & TOBAGO	08/08/03	5	10	12	0	MIDFIELD	LEVSKI SOFIA
RAMSAY	MARK		24/01/86	DUNFERMLINE	07/08/03	5	7	10	0	MIDFIELD	FALKIRK FORM D UNDER 1
SCALLY	NEIL		14/08/78	PAISLEY	19/05/04	5	11	12	7	MIDFIELD	DUMBARTON
SCOBBIE	THOMAS		31/03/88	FALKIRK	27/07/04	6	0	11	0	DEFENDER	FALKIRK FORM D UNDER 1
SHARP	JAMES		02/01/76	READING	18/07/03	6	1	14	4	MIDFIELD	HARTLEPOOL UNITED
THOMSON	ANDREW		01/04/71	MOTHERWELL	04/06/04	5	11	11	11	FORWARD	PARTICK THISTLE
TWADDLE	MARC	IAN	27/08/86	GLASGOW	22/08/03	6	1	12	0	MIDFIELD	RANGERS

TICKET INFORMATION

SEASON TICKET PRICES SEATED

MAIN STAND
PRIME SEATS	£275
ADULT	£225
CONCESSION	£135
PRIMARY SCHOOL CHILD	£50

LEAGUE ADMISSION PRICES SEATED

MAIN STAND
ADULT	£15
CONCESSION	£10

TEMP STAND
ADULT	£14
CONCESSION	£7

THE BAIRNS' 10 YEAR LEAGUE RECORD

SEASON	DIV	P	W	D	L	F	A	PTS
1994-95	P	36	12	12	12	48	47	48
1995-96	P	36	6	6	24	31	60	24
1996-97	F	36	15	9	12	42	39	54
1997-98	F	36	19	8	9	56	41	65
1998-99	F	36	20	6	10	60	38	66
1999-00	F	36	20	8	8	67	40	68
2000-01	F	36	16	8	12	57	59	56
2001-02	F	36	10	9	17	49	73	39
2002-03	F	36	25	6	5	80	32	81
2003-04	F	36	15	10	11	43	37	55

SEASON STATS 2003/04

DATE	VENUE	OPPONENTS	ATT	RES	HILL D.	LAWRIE A.	McPHERSON C.	McKENZIE S.	HUGHES J.	SHARP J.	RAHIM B.	NICHOLLS D.	LEE J.	LATAPY R.	McMENAMIN C.	McLAREN A.	SCALLY N.	RODGERS A.	MAY E.	O'NEIL J.	XAUSA D.	McFANESPIE K.	HENRY J.	JAMES K.	FERGUSON A.	McCLUSKEY S.	COLQUHOUN D.	CHRISTIE K.	McSTAY R.	McSWEEN I.	BARR D.	RAMSAY M.	TWADDLE M.	CREANEY P.	MANSON S.
-AUG	H	INVERNESS CAL TH	2,619	2-1	1	2	3	4	5	6	7	8	**9**	10	**11**	12			15																
-AUG	A	AYR UNITED	2,519	1-1	1	2	3		5	6	7	8	**9**	10	11		4			12	16														
-AUG	H	QUEEN OF THE SOUTH	2,202	0-0	1	2	3		5	6	7	8	9	10			4			12	14														
-AUG	A	RAITH ROVERS	4,222	1-0	1	5	3		6	2	8		9	10	11		14	15		4	**7**	12													
-SEP	H	ROSS COUNTY	2,970	0-2	1	5			6		8	9	10		2		14		4	7	11	3	16												
-SEP	A	CLYDE	2,758	2-1	1	2	3	5	16	4	14	10	9		15	11	7				8²	6													
-SEP	H	ST. JOHNSTONE	3,887	0-3	1	2	3	5	15	4	10	9		11	7	12	8	6																	
OCT	A	ST. MIRREN	3,105	0-0		2	3	5	11		10	14		7	9		8	6	1	4															
-OCT	H	BRECHIN CITY	2,442	3-0		2	3	4	5	11		10	16	14	7¹	9	15	8²	6	1															
-OCT	H	AYR UNITED	2,609	0-1		2	3	4	5	10		11		14	7	9	15	8	6	1		16													
NOV	A	INVERNESS CAL TH	2,223	2-1	2¹	3	4	5	7	14	**9**	10	12		8	11		15	6	1															
NOV	A	ROSS COUNTY	3,206	2-1	2¹	3	4	5	7	12	**9**	10	11		8		14		6	1															
-NOV	H	RAITH ROVERS	3,237	3-2	2	3	4	5	7¹	6	9	10	11²	15	8		14			1	16														
-NOV	A	ST. JOHNSTONE	4,185	4-0	2	3	5	7	4	9	10¹	11¹	16	8	15	12¹		6¹	1																
-NOV	H	CLYDE	2,898	0-2	2	3	7	4	15	9	10	11	5	8	12	14		6	1																
DEC	A	BRECHIN CITY	1,043	†2-2	2	3	7	4	15	9¹	11		8	10	12	6	1	5																	
-DEC	H	ST. MIRREN	2,581	0-0	2	3	4	7	12	9	14		8	10	11	6	1	5																	
-DEC	A	QUEEN OF THE SOUTH	4,075	0-2	3	12	5	4	2	9	10	11	7	8		6	16																		
JAN	A	RAITH ROVERS	2,885	0-2	17	5	3	2	9	10	4	7	8	11	6	1	14																		
-JAN	H	ROSS COUNTY	2,482	2-0	1	2	3	4	5	6	10¹	12	7	8	11	9¹	14	15																	
-JAN	A	CLYDE	3,137	2-4	1	2	3	4	6	14	15	10	7	8	11¹	9¹																			
-FEB	A	ST. MIRREN	2,934	1-1	2	3	4	5¹	6	15	14	9	10	7	12	11	8																		
-FEB	H	BRECHIN CITY	2,060	5-0	2	3	4	5¹	6	8	14	9¹	10²	11¹	7	12	1	16																	
-MAR	H	INVERNESS CAL TH	2,268	2-1	2	3	4	6	8	14	9¹	10	11	7	12¹	1		15																	
MAR	A	AYR UNITED	2,048	3-2	1	2	3	4	5	6	15	8¹	9¹	10	11¹	7	12																		
-MAR	H	ST. JOHNSTONE	2,799	0-1	1	2	3	4	5	6	8	9	10	11	7	12	15	14																	
-MAR	H	QUEEN OF THE SOUTH	2,098	0-2	1	2	3	4	5	6	8	9	10	11	7	12	14	15																	
-MAR	A	ROSS COUNTY	2,931	1-1	1	2	3¹	4	6	8	9	10	11	7	12																				
-MAR	H	RAITH ROVERS	2,386	1-0	1	12	3	4	5	6	2	9	10	11	7¹	8	15																		
-APR	A	ST. JOHNSTONE	2,535	1-2	2	3	4	5	6	8	12	9	10¹	7	11	1	14	15																	
-APR	H	CLYDE	2,536	1-1	2	3	4	5	6	8	12	10¹	7	1	9	11																			
-APR	H	BRECHIN CITY	768	1-0	1	2	3	4	5	6	8	12	10¹	7	9	14	11	15																	
-APR	H	ST. MIRREN	2,386	1-0	1	2	3	4	5	6	8	9	10	7¹	12	16	11	14																	
-MAY	A	INVERNESS CAL TH	2,631	0-0	1	2	3	4	5	6	9	10	7	8	12	11	15																		
-MAY	H	AYR UNITED	2,077	0-0	1	2	3	4	5	6	9	10	8	7	11	12																			
-MAY	A	QUEEN OF THE SOUTH	2,751	0-1	1	2	3	4	5	6	9	7	11	10	8	15	14	16																	

					HILL D.	LAWRIE A.	McPHERSON C.	McKENZIE S.	HUGHES J.	SHARP J.	RAHIM B.	NICHOLLS D.	LEE J.	LATAPY R.	McMENAMIN C.	McLAREN A.	SCALLY N.	RODGERS A.	MAY E.	O'NEIL J.	XAUSA D.	McFANESPIE K.	HENRY J.	JAMES K.	FERGUSON A.	McCLUSKEY S.	COLQUHOUN D.	CHRISTIE K.	McSTAY R.	McSWEEN I.	BARR D.	RAMSAY M.	TWADDLE M.	CREANEY P.	MANSON S.
TOTAL FULL APPEARANCES					19	34	35	26	27	30	19	13	27	32	13	1	12	2	2	30	10	12	5	13	17	1	7	2		2	5				
TOTAL SUB APPEARANCES					1	1		1				7	9	2		4	1	8	4	2		5	14	2		8			4	5	1	2	3	1	1
TOTAL GOALS SCORED						2	1		2	1		1	8	7	4		2			4		3	4	1		2								

bold figures denote goalscorers. † denotes opponent's own goal.

LEADING GOALSCORERS:

SEASON	DIV	GOALS	PLAYER
94-95	P	9	C. McDonald
95-96	P	6	P. McGrillen
96-97	F	8	M. McGraw
97-98	F	12	D. Moss
98-99	F	17	M. Keith
99-00	F	14	S. Crabbe
00-01	F	11	G. Hutchison
01-02	F	11	L. Miller
02-03	F	20	O. Coyle
03-04	F	8	J. Lee

MILESTONES:

YEAR OF FORMATION: 1876
MOST CAPPED PLAYER: Alex H. Parker
NO. OF CAPS: 14
MOST LEAGUE POINTS IN A SEASON:
66 (First Division – Season 1993/94) (2 Points for a Win) and
81 (First Division – Season 2002/03) (3 Points for a Win)
MOST LEAGUE GOALS SCORED BY A PLAYER IN A SEASON:
Evelyn Morrison (Season 1928/29)
NO. OF GOALS SCORED: 43
RECORD ATTENDANCE: 23,100 (-v- Celtic – 21.2.1953)
RECORD VICTORY: 12-1 (-v- Laurieston – Scottish Cup, 23.3.1893)
RECORD DEFEAT: 1-11 (-v- Airdrieonians – Division A, 28.4.1951)

FALKIRK PLAYING KITS SEASON 2004/05

FIRST KIT SECOND KIT THIRD KIT

HAMILTON ACADEMICAL
New Douglas Park, Cadzow Avenue,
Hamilton, ML3 0FT
CHAIRMAN
Ronnie MacDonald
VICE CHAIRMAN
Leslie Gray
DIRECTORS
Kenneth Blake, Brian Cairney, George W. Fairley,
Denis Gowans, Arthur Lynch,
Ronald J. McKinnon & Scott A. Struthers
HONARY PRESIDENTS
Dr. Alexander A. Wilson & Jan W. Stepek
CHIEF EXECUTIVE
George W. Fairley
SECRETARY & YOUTH CO-ORDINATOR
Scott A. Struthers, B.A.(Hons)
MANAGER
Allan Maitland
ASSISTANT MANAGER
Dennis McDaid
FIRST TEAM COACH
Jimmy McQuade
RESERVE COACH
James Ward
GOALKEEPING COACH
Steve Harvey
DIRECTOR OF YOUTH DEVELOPMENT
Leslie Gray
YOUTH DEVELOPMENT COACH
John Bean
YOUTH TEAM COACHES
Gerry McGregor & John Bean (U19),
John Joyce (U17), John Bean (U15),
Murdo McKinnon (U14), Steve Harvey (U13)
CHIEF SCOUT Brian Byrne
COMMERCIAL MANAGER
Arthur Lynch (01698) 368656
STADIUM MANAGER
Denis Gowans (01698) 368652
PHYSIOTHERAPIST
Michael Valentine
**FOOTBALL SAFETY OFFICERS'
ASSOCIATION REPRESENTATIVES**
Scott A. Struthers & Denis Gowans
Tel (01698) 368650
MEDIA LIAISON OFFICER
Scott A. Struthers
MATCHDAY PROGRAMME EDITORS
Scott A. Struthers & Arthur Lynch
GROUNDSMAN Willie Roberts
KIT PERSON Jim Kennedy
TELEPHONES
Ground (01698) 368650
Sec Bus. (01698) 368655
(Fax-Office) (01698) 285422
E-MAIL ADDRESS
scott.sas@btopenworld.com
CLUB SHOP
"The Acciesshop",
Hamilton Academical F.C.,
New Douglas Park, Cadzow Avenue,
Hamilton, ML3 0FT
OFFICIAL SUPPORTERS CLUB
Jim Galloway, Secretary, HAFC Supporters
Club, 3 Pitcairn Terrace, Burnbank, Hamilton
CLUB CAPTAIN
Steven Convery
TEAM CAPTAIN
Steven Thomson
SHIRT SPONSOR
First Choice - Cullen Packaging
Second Choice - Gleeson
Third Choice - Hawkhead Carpets
KIT SUPPLIER
TFG

LIST OF PLAYERS 2004/05

PLAYERS SURNAME	FIRST NAME	MIDDLE NAME	DATE OF BIRTH	PLACE OF BIRTH	DATE SIGNED	HEIGHT FT INS		WEIGHT ST LBS		POSITION ON PITCH	PREVIOUS CLUB
AITKEN	CHRISTOPHER	IAN	31/03/81	GLASGOW	30/06/03	5	9	11	6	MIDFIELD	NEILSTON JUNIORS
ANDERSON	DEREK	FINDLAY	12/02/87	BELLSHILL	03/09/04	6	0.5	11	5	FORWARD	CLYDE FORM S
ANSON	SCOTT	ROBERT	29/04/89	GLASGOW	07/09/04	6	1	10	10	FORWARD	HAMILTON ACAD. FORM D U'16
ARBUCKLE	ANDREW	PAUL	06/02/85	MUNSTER	31/07/03	5	9	11	0	DEFENDER	HAMILTON ACAD. FORM D U'16
BLACKADDER	RYAN	ROBERT	11/10/83	KIRKCALDY	30/01/04	5	9	11	10	MIDFIELD	RAITH ROVERS
BUCKLEY	SEAN	PATRICK	07/07/87	VALE OF LEVEN	15/09/04	6	0	13	5	FORWARD	CELTIC FORM D
CARRIGAN	BRIAN	ERIC	26/09/79	GLASGOW	30/06/03	5	8	11	5	FORWARD	RAITH ROVERS
CONNOLLY	STEPHEN	PATRICK	29/11/83	GLASGOW	07/09/04	5	6	9	4	MIDFIELD	HAMILTON ACAD. FORM D U'16
CONVERY	STEVEN		27/10/72	GLASGOW	30/06/03	5	11	12	1	FORWARD	CLYDE
CORCORAN	MARK	CHRISTIAN	30/11/80	PERTH	03/07/03	5	10	11	3	FORWARD	LINLITHGOW ROSE JUNIORS
DIMILTA	DAVID	VITO	05/05/88	GLASGOW	07/09/04	5	5	9	2	MIDFIELD	HAMILTON ACAD. FORM D U'16
EASTON	BRIAN	NEIL	05/03/88	GLASGOW	07/09/04	6	0	12	0	MIDFIELD	WEIRS B.C.
FERGUSON	DEREK		31/07/67	GLASGOW	03/07/03	5	8.5	11	12	MIDFIELD	ALLOA ATHLETIC
FYFE	IAIN	STUART	03/04/82	ADELAIDE	29/07/04	6	2	13	4	MIDFIELD	SYDNEY OLYMPIC
GIBSON	DANIEL	ROBERT	15/03/88	KIRKCALDY	07/09/04	5	8	9	11	FORWARD	HAMILTON ACAD. FORM D U'16
GLACKIN	RONALD		06/04/87	RUTHERGLEN	03/09/04	5	9	11	4	FORWARD	CLYDE FORM D UNDER 16
HALLIDAY	ROBERT	LYNCH	14/01/86	GLASGOW	10/08/04	5	10	10	0	MIDFIELD	CLYDE
HAMILTON	DAVID	WILLIAM	30/06/80	MOTHERWELL	07/07/04	6	0.5	12	7	MIDFIELD	POLLOK JUNIORS
HARRISON	GREGG		27/05/88	GLASGOW	07/09/04	5	10	10	5	MIDFIELD	HAMILTON ACAD. FORM D U'16
HODGE	SANDY	GEORGE	04/10/80	LANARK	22/08/03	6	3	13	5	MIDFIELD	QUEEN OF THE SOUTH
INGLIS	RAYMOND	SCOTT	31/03/88	GLASGOW	07/09/04	6	1	10	0	DEFENDER	HAMILTON ACAD. FORM D U'16
IRONS	STUART		18/10/87	RUTHERGLEN	03/09/04	5	10	10	12	MIDFIELD	RAITH ROVERS FORM D U'16
JELLEMA	RAYMOND	JAMES GARDINER	27/09/85	IRVINE	04/06/04	5	11	11	11	GOALKEEPER	PRESTAYR B.C.
JOYCE	CRAIG		28/03/88	GLASGOW	07/09/04	5	7	9	0	MIDFIELD	HAMILTON ACAD. FORM D U'16
KEOGH	PATRICK	SEBASTIAN	07/05/76	GLASGOW	10/06/04	6	2	14	7	FORWARD	CLYDE
LAWLEY	JAMES		23/10/87	LANARK	03/09/04	5	8.5	9	13	MIDFIELD	HAMILTON ACAD. FORM D U'16
LIVINGSTONE	MICHAEL		18/10/88	MELBOURNE	07/09/04	5	9	10	8	MIDFIELD	FALKIRK FORM D UNDER 16
LUMSDEN	TODD		06/02/84	CONSETT	30/06/03	6	2	12	5	DEFENDER	ALBION ROVERS
McALPINE	MARK	IAN	26/06/88	GLASGOW	07/09/04	5	5	9	7	FORWARD	HAMILTON ACAD. FORM D U'16
McARTHUR	JAMES		07/10/87	GLASGOW	07/09/04	5	6	10	0	FORWARD	CLYDE FORM D UNDER 15
McAVEETY	PHILLIP		06/04/89	GLASGOW	07/09/04	5	8	10	0	MIDFIELD	HAMILTON ACAD. FORM D U'16
McCLUSKEY	WILLIAM	JOHN	16/03/89	GLASGOW	07/09/04	5	10	10	5	MIDFIELD	HAMILTON ACAD. FORM D U'16
McEWAN	DAVID		26/02/82	LANARK	14/02/04	6	0	12	10	GOALKEEPER	LIVINGSTON
McGEOGHEGAN	JAMIE		20/01/87	GLASGOW	07/09/04	6	0.5	9	8	FORWARD	CELTIC FORM D UNDER 16
McGREGOR	RYAN	JAMES	04/10/87	GLASGOW	03/09/04	6	0	10	1	MIDFIELD	CLYDE FORM D UNDER 15
McINALLY	MARK	JOHN	25/10/87	GLASGOW	03/09/04	5	8	9	6	FORWARD	LIVINGSTON FORM D UNDER 15
McKEEVER	FRANCIS	GERARD	11/03/89	GLASGOW	07/09/04	5	7	9	0	MIDFIELD	HAMILTON ACAD. FORM D U'16
McLAUCHLAN	GERARD		08/03/89	GLASGOW	07/09/04	6	1.5	10	12	DEFENDER	HAMILTON ACAD. FORM D U'16
McLAUGHLIN	MARK		02/12/75	GREENOCK	10/06/04	6	2	13	5	DEFENDER	CLYDE
McLEAN	PAUL	JAMES	06/09/88	GLASGOW	07/09/04	5	6	9	0	MIDFIELD	CLYDE FORM D UNDER 16
McLENAGHAN	GARY	ALEXANDER	25/05/87	BELLSHILL	03/09/04	6	2	11	4	GOALKEEPER	EAST STIRLINGSHIRE FORM S
McLEOD	PAUL		22/05/87	BELLSHILL	03/09/04	5	10	11	2	FORWARD	DUNDEE UNITED FORM D U'15
McPHEE	BRIAN		23/10/70	GLASGOW	23/11/01	5	10	11	10	FORWARD	LIVINGSTON
MURPHY	CRAIG	MATTHEW	19/12/86	GLASGOW	03/09/04	5	3.5	9	0	DEFENDER	CLYDE FORM D UNDER 16
MURRAY	DAVID	ANTHONY	25/09/89	GLASGOW	07/09/04	5	7	9	0	DEFENDER	HAMILTON ACAD. FORM D U'16
NICOLL	KEVIN		16/06/86	GLASGOW	03/09/04	6	1	11	7	DEFENDER	CLYDE FORM D UNDER 16
O'DONNELL	PAUL	DAVID	27/07/89	PAISLEY	07/09/04	5	10	10	0	MIDFIELD	HAMILTON ACAD. FORM D U'16
O'DONNELL	RYAN	PAUL	05/07/85	GLASGOW	03/09/04	5	10.5	10	1	FORWARD	ABERDEEN FORM D U'16
REID	CHRISTOPHER	THOMAS DUNCAN	13/08/87	GLASGOW	15/09/04	5	6.5	8	11	MIDFIELD	ST. JOHNSTONE FORM D U'16
RENFREW	MARK		01/08/89	PAISLEY	07/09/04	5	8	9	6	FORWARD	HAMILTON ACAD. FORM D U'16
SIM	ANDREW		04/02/87	LANARK	17/08/04	5	7	3.5	7	9	FORWARD	HAMILTON ACAD. FORM D U'16
STEVENSON	ANTHONY		24/07/88	GLASGOW	03/09/04	5	9	11	10	DEFENDER	CLYDE FORM S
THOMSON	STEVEN	WILLIAM	19/04/73	GLASGOW	30/06/03	6	2	12	7	DEFENDER	ALLOA ATHLETIC
TOUGH	GRAHAM	ROBERT	22/10/87	BELLSHILL	03/09/04	6	0.5	11	13	DEFENDER	CLYDE FORM D UNDER 15
TUNBRIDGE	SCOTT	ROBERT	26/06/82	ADELAIDE	29/07/04	6	0	13	3	FORWARD	CUMBERLAND UNITED
WADDELL	RICHARD		04/02/81	FALKIRK	24/03/04	5	11	10	7	FORWARD	PARTICK THISTLE
WALKER	ROBERT		16/06/82	GLASGOW	31/08/03	6	0	13	0	DEFENDER	MARYHILL JUNIORS

TICKET INFORMATION

SEASON TICKET PRICES

SEATED		
	ADULT	£180
	YOUTH/OAP	£90
	JUVENILE (U-14)	£50
	FAMILY (M+F ADULTS & 2 U-14)	£230

LEAGUE ADMISSION PRICES

WEST (MAIN) STAND

SEATED		
	ADULT	£12
	JUVENILE (U-16)/OAP	£6

NORTH STAND

SEATED		
	ADULT	£12
	JUVENILE (U-16)/OAP	£6

THE ACCIES' 10 YEAR LEAGUE RECORD

SEASON	DIV	P	W	D	L	F	A	PTS
1994-95	F	36	14	7	15	42	48	49
1995-96	F	36	10	6	20	40	57	36
1996-97	S	36	22	8	6	75	28	74
1997-98	F	36	9	11	16	43	56	38
1998-99	F	36	6	10	20	30	62	28
1999-00*	S	36	10	14	12	39	44	29
2000-01	T	36	22	10	4	75	30	76
2001-02	S	36	13	9	14	49	44	48
2002-03	S	36	12	11	13	43	48	47
2003-04	S	36	18	8	10	70	47	62

* 15 POINTS DEDUCTED FOR FAILING TO FULFIL FIXTURE AGAINST STENHOUSEMUIR F.C. ON SATURDAY, 1ST APRIL.

SEASON STATS 2003/04

DATE	VENUE	OPPONENTS	ATT	RES	M'EWAN D.	FITTER J.	FORBES B.	THOMSON S.W.	LUMSDEN T.	MAXWELL D.R.	CARRIGAN B.	AITKEN C.	CONWERY S.	McPHEE B.	CORCORAN M.	SHERRY J.	WADDELL A.	WHITEFORD A.	PATERSON N.	ARBUCKLE A.	HODGE S.	GRIBBEN D.	BAILEY J.	JELLEMA R.	QUITONGO J.	DONNELLY C.	ANDERSON D.	WALKER R.	FERGUSON D.	GEMMELL J.	BLACKADDER R.	WADDELL R.
-AUG	H	FORFAR ATHLETIC	1,271	1-2	1	2	3	4	5	6	7	8	9	10^1	11	12	14	15														
-AUG	A	BERWICK RANGERS	552	1-3	1	2		4	5	6	7	8	9	10	11			14	3^1	15	16											
-AUG	H	AIRDRIE UNITED	2,007	2-1	1			4	5		7^1	8	9^1	10	11	6		2		14	3	16											
-AUG	A	ARBROATH	650	2-2	1			4^1	5		7^1	8	9	10	11	6		2	14	12	3	15											
-SEP	H	STENHOUSEMUIR	934	2-0	1		14	4	5		7	8^1	12	10	11	6		2			3^1	16	9										
-SEP	A	MORTON	3,225	1-1	1		14	4	5		7	8	11^1	10	15	6		2			3	16	9										
-SEP	A	EAST FIFE	1,123	2-2	1		11	4	5		7	8		10	12	6	14^1	2			3	15	9^1										
-OCT	H	ALLOA ATHLETIC	1,016	3-4	1		11	4	5		7^1	8^1			9^1	6	12	2		16	3	10	17										
-OCT	A	DUMBARTON	890	3-0	1	2		4^1	5		7	8	9		11^1			16		6	3				10^1	12							
-OCT	H	BERWICK RANGERS	1,143	2-2	1	2	14	4	5		7^1	8^1	9		11					6	3	16			10								
-NOV	A	FORFAR ATHLETIC	558	3-4	1	2	14	4	5		7^1	8		10	11					6	3	12^1			9^1	16							
-NOV	A	STENHOUSEMUIR	576	3-0	1		11	4	5			7		10^3					16	8	3	15	14		6		2						
-NOV	H	ARBROATH	1,286	2-0	1			4	5		7^2	8	9	10	14					6	3	12		11	15		2						
-DEC	H	MORTON	1,905	1-2	1			4	5		7^1	8	15	10	12	11				6	3	14		9			2						
-DEC	A	EAST FIFE	584	3-2	1			4	5		7	8^1	15	10^2	14	11				6	3			9			2						
-DEC	A	ALLOA ATHLETIC	504	3-1	1			4	5		8	7^2		10	12	11			16	6	3	14		9^1			2						
-JAN	H	FORFAR ATHLETIC	1,099	2-1	1			4	5		7^1	8		10^1	14			2		6	3			9	16					11	15		
-JAN	A	MORTON	2,942	2-2	1			4	5^1		7^1	8	14	10	12	11				6	3			9							15		
-JAN	H	EAST FIFE	1,429	1-0	1			4	5		7	8		10	12	11		2		6	3			9^1				16			15		
-FEB	H	STENHOUSEMUIR	1,111	0-1	1			4	5		7		9	10	11	6					3			15			2	8			12	14	
-FEB	A	ARBROATH	502	2-0	1			4	5		7	8^1		10	16	11				6	3	12		9^1			2				15		
-FEB	A	DUMBARTON	1,015	0-2	1			4	5		7	8		10	11	6			14		3	16					2				9		
-MAR	A	AIRDRIE UNITED	1,634	0-3	1			4	5		8	7		10	11		2			6	3	15					12	9			14		
-MAR	A	BERWICK RANGERS	468	4-2	1			4	5^1		7	8^1		10^1	15				16		3			9^1		14	2				11		
-MAR	H	DUMBARTON	949	2-0	1			4	5		7	8		10^1	15	12				6	3	9^1				14	2				11		
-MAR	H	AIRDRIE UNITED	2,559	0-1	1			4	5		7	8		10	16	12				6	3	9					2				11		
-MAR	H	ALLOA ATHLETIC	831	0-1	1			4	5		7	12			11	8		15		6	3	9				14	2				10		
-MAR	H	ARBROATH	1,041	2-2	1			4	5		7^1			10		8				6	3				16		2^1	14	15	9			11
-APR	A	EAST FIFE	489	3-2	1			4	5		7	8		10^2	12	6				15	3			14			2^1			9			11
-APR	A	STENHOUSEMUIR	296	2-0	1			4	5		14	9		10^2	11	8				6	3	16		7			2						15
-APR	H	MORTON	2,692	6-1	1			4	5		7^1	8^1		10^2	11^1						3	16		12			2^1			14			9
-APR	H	DUMBARTON	1,343	2-1	1			4^1	5		7	8		10	11	6					3	16					2			12^1			9
-APR	A	ALLOA ATHLETIC	579	1-1	1			4	5		7	8		10^1	11	6					3	12		15			2			14			9
-MAY	A	AIRDRIE UNITED	2,936	1-1	1			4			8			10^1	11	6					5			12		7	15		2	14	9	3	
-MAY	H	BERWICK RANGERS	1,591	2-0	1			4					8^1	10	11		6^1				5			12		7	15		2	14	9	3	
-MAY	A	FORFAR ATHLETIC	1,496	4-0	1			4	12		7^2	8		10^2		15				6	5			14			2				9	3	
TOTAL FULL APPEARANCES					36	5	4	36	33	2	30	32	12	31	22	22		12		23	31	4	4	14	1	21	3				10	8
TOTAL SUB APPEARANCES						4			1		1	1	4		13	4	5	5	3	6	1	19	3	1	4	8	1	2	1	8	5	1
TOTAL GOALS SCORED							3	2			14	8	4	19	3	1	2	1						2	2	5				3	1

ll bold figures denote goalscorers. † denotes opponent's own goal.

LEADING GOALSCORERS:

SEASON	DIV	GOALS	PLAYER
94-95	F	20	P. Duffield
95-96	F	11	P. Hartley
96-97	S	31	P. Ritchie
97-98	F	7	P. Ritchie
98-99	F	11	G. Wales
99-00	S	6	D. Henderson, N. Henderson
00-01	T	24	D. McFarlane
01-02	S	12	M. Moore
02-03	S	11	B. McPhee
03-04	S	19	B. McPhee

MILESTONES:

YEAR OF FORMATION: 1874
MOST CAPPED PLAYER: Colin Miller (Canada)
NO. OF CAPS: 29
MOST LEAGUE POINTS IN A SEASON:
57 (First Division – Season 1991/92) (2 Points for a Win)
76 (Third Division – Season 2000/01) (3 Points for a Win)
MOST LEAGUE GOALS SCORED BY A PLAYER IN A SEASON:
David Wilson (Season 1936/37)
NO. OF GOALS SCORED: 35
RECORD ATTENDANCE:
28,690 (-v- Hearts – Scottish Cup 3.3.1937 at Douglas Park)
4,280 (-v- Sunderland – Opening of new ground 28.7.2001)
RECORD VICTORY: 10-2 (-v- Cowdenbeath – Division 1, 15.10.1932)
RECORD DEFEAT: 1-11 (-v- Hibernian – Division 1, 6.11.1965)

HAMILTON ACADEMICAL PLAYING KITS SEASON 2004/05

FIRST KIT · SECOND KIT · THIRD KIT

PARTICK THISTLE
Firhill Stadium, 80 Firhill Road,
Glasgow, G20 7AL
CHAIRMAN
Thomas Hughes
VICE-CHAIRMAN
Allan Cowan
DIRECTORS
James Oliver, T. Brown McMaster,
Edward Prentice, Norman Springford
Gordon D. Peden & Ronald S. Gilfillan
HON. VICE-PRESIDENT
Robert W. Reid
ASSOCIATE DIRECTORS
Robert W. Reid, Les Hope & John Lambie
CHIEF EXECUTIVE/SECRETARY
Alan C. Dick
JOINT MANAGERS
Gerry Britton and Derek Whyte
FIRST TEAM COACH
John McLaughlan
GOALKEEPING COACH
Tom Scott
YOUTH TEAM COACHES
Ally Dawson (U19), Pat Barkey & Steve Adam
(U17), John Hamilton & Paul Gillan (U15),
Neil Ross & Scott Allison (U13)
YOUTH CO-ORDINATOR/CHIEF SCOUT
John Arrol
CLUB DOCTOR
Dr Alan W. Robertson
PHYSIOTHERAPIST
George Hannah
STADIUM MANAGER & CHIEF OF SECURITY
Alan C. Dick
GROUNDSMAN
George Furze
KIT PERSON
Rikki Roughan
CHIEF STEWARD
Brian McKigen
**FOOTBALL SAFETY OFFICERS'
ASSOCIATION REPRESENTATIVE**
Alan C. Dick (0141) 579 1971
COMMERCIAL MANAGER
Amanda Barrie (0141) 579 1971
LOTTERY MANAGER
Bobby Briggs
MEDIA LIAISON OFFICER
Alan C. Dick
MATCHDAY PROGRAMME EDITOR
Tom Hosie
SHOP MANAGERESS
Liz Gordon
TELEPHONES
Ground/Ticket Office/Commercial
(0141) 579 1971
Fax (0141) 945 1525
Jagsline (09068) 666474
E-MAIL AND INTERNET ADDRESS
mail@ptfc.co.uk
www.ptfc.co.uk
CLUB SHOP
80 Firhill Road, Glasgow, G20 7AL
Tel (0141) 579 1971.
Open each matchday and every Tuesday from
12.30p.m. - 4.30p.m. Upstairs office shop
open daily from 9.00 a.m. - 4.30 p.m.
OFFICIAL SUPPORTERS CLUB
c/o Firhill Stadium, 80 Firhill Road, Glasgow,
G20 7AL
TEAM CAPTAIN
Grant Murray
SHIRT SPONSOR
D.H. Morris
KIT SUPPLIER
TFG

LIST OF PLAYERS 2004/05

PLAYERS SURNAME	FIRST NAME	MIDDLE NAME	DATE OF BIRTH	PLACE OF BIRTH	DATE SIGNED	HEIGHT FT INS		WEIGHT ST LBS		POSITION ON PITCH	PREVIOUS CLUB
ANIS	JEAN-YVES		30/11/80	OUME - IVORY COAST	04/08/03	5	11	10	12	DEFENDER	CHELSEA
ARTHUR	KENNETH		07/12/78	BELLSHILL	01/06/97	6	3	13	8	GOALKEEPER	POSSILPARK Y.M.C.A.
BARRON	DAVID		10/09/87	GREENOCK	09/01/04	5	10	12	7	MIDFIELD	PARTICK THISTLE FORM D U' 1
BENNETT	NEIL	ROBERT	29/10/80	DEWSBURY	29/07/04	6	1	12	13	GOALKEEPER	ALBION ROVERS
BRITTON	GERARD	JOSEPH	20/10/70	GLASGOW	31/07/04	6	0	11	13	FORWARD	LIVINGSTON
CAMERON	IAN		23/05/88	GLASGOW	28/07/04	5	10	10	8	MIDFIELD	PARTICK THISTLE FORM D U' 1
CARTER	JONATHAN		02/12/87	GLASGOW	10/06/04	6	1	12	5	DEFENDER	PARTICK THISTLE FORM D U' 1
CASSIDY	PAUL	JOHN	18/11/86	GLASGOW	02/07/03	5	11	10	7	MIDFIELD	PARTICK THISTLE FORM D U' 1
DOWIE	ANDREW	JOHN	25/03/83	BELLSHILL	23/07/04	6	1	12	6	DEFENDER	RANGERS
ESCALAS	JUAN	ALBERTO RAMON	02/12/76	MALLORCA	29/07/04	5	10	12	2	FORWARD	TALAVERA C.F.
FERGUSON	WILLIAM		02/08/87	GLASGOW	28/11/03	5	9	11	3	FORWARD	PARTICK THISTLE YOUTH
FLEMING	DEREK	ADAM	05/12/73	FALKIRK	21/06/01	5	8	10	5	MIDFIELD	LIVINGSTON
FULTON	STEPHEN		10/08/70	GREENOCK	09/07/04	5	10	11	12	MIDFIELD	KILMARNOCK
GEMMELL	JOHN	O'NEILL	06/09/84	GLASGOW	03/06/03	6	2	12	7	FORWARD	QUEEN'S PARK
GIBSON	ANDREW	STEWART	02/03/82	GLASGOW	03/07/00	5	10	10	9	MID/FWD	PARTICK THISTLE B.C.
GIBSON	WILLIAM		01/08/81	BELLSHILL	09/07/04	5	10.5	11	13	MIDFIELD	RANGERS
HASWELL	KENNETH	ANDREW	29/02/88	GLASGOW	10/06/04	6	1	11	11	DEFENDER	CELTIC FORM D UNDER 16
HINDS	LEIGH	MICHAEL	17/08/78	BECKENHAM	31/07/04	5	10	12	1	FORWARD	ABERDEEN
HOWIE	WILLIAM		09/07/82	RUTHERGLEN	21/05/99	5	9	10	1	MIDFIELD	PARTICK THISTLE B.C.
MADASCHI	ADRIAN	ANTHONY	11/07/82	PERTH - AUSTRALIA	20/10/03	6	2	12	5	DEFENDER	ATALANTA BERGAMO
M°CURLEY	STEFAN	JOHN	18/05/87	GLASGOW	19/08/04	5	10	11	3	GOALKEEPER	DUNDEE UNITED
M°GOLDRICK	JOHN	LOWE	30/06/88	BELLSHILL	04/06/04	5	11	11	4	FORWARD	PARTICK THISTLE FORM D U' 16
M°KEOWN	FRANK		18/08/86	GLASGOW	04/08/04	6	1	12	1	DEFENDER	RAITH ROVERS
MILNE	KENNETH		26/08/79	STIRLING	17/06/02	6	2.5	12	8	FORWARD	HEART OF MIDLOTHIAN
MITCHELL	JAMES	M°GILVRAY	06/01/76	GLASGOW	18/05/02	5	7	10	0	MIDFIELD	CLYDE
MURRAY	GRANT	ROBERT	29/08/75	EDINBURGH	23/06/03	5	10	12	0	DEFENDER	ST. JOHNSTONE
NIVEN	DAVID		27/12/87	GLASGOW	07/01/04	5	10	12	13	MIDFIELD	PARTICK THISTLE FORM D U' 16
ONE	ARMAND		15/03/83	PARIS	06/08/04	6	5	12	7	FORWARD	ORVAULT F.C.
PANTHER	EMMANUEL	UGOCHUKWU EZENWA	11/05/84	GLASGOW	18/06/03	5	11	13	1	MIDFIELD	LIVINGSTON
PINKOWSKI	STEVEN		09/06/83	BELLSHILL	05/01/04	5	10	12	8	GOALKEEPER	LINLITHGOW ROSE JUNIORS
ROSS	ANDREW	CAMERON	18/09/82	IRVINE	02/07/03	5	10	10	7	MIDFIELD	CHELSEA
ROSS	IAN		27/08/74	BROXBURN	21/01/03	5	10	11	10	MIDFIELD	ST. MIRREN
SHIELDS	MATTHEW	JOHN	17/02/86	GLASGOW	30/08/02	5	9	10	2	FORWARD	PARTICK THISTLE FORM S
STEWART	MARK	GORDON	22/06/88	GLASGOW	10/06/04	5	7	10	6	FORWARD	CELTIC FORM D UNDER 16
STRACHAN	ADAM		24/02/87	GLASGOW	26/11/03	5	10.5	11	0	FORWARD	PARTICK THISTLE FORM D U' 16
WILKINSON	ANDREW	GORDON	06/08/84	DUDLEY	16/07/04	6	0	12	8	DEFENDER	STOKE CITY
WILSON	DAVID		22/01/86	GLASGOW	02/07/03	5	11	12	3	DEFENDER	RANGERS

TICKET INFORMATION

SEASON TICKET INFORMATION

SEATED
ADULT	OAP/U16/STUDENT	U12
£225	£115	£60

LEAGUE ADMISSION INFORMATION

SEATED
ADULT	OAP/U16/STUDENT
£13	£7

STANDING
ADULT	OAP/U16/STUDENT
£12	£6

THE JAGS' 10 YEAR LEAGUE RECORD

SEASON	DIV	P	W	D	L	F	A	PTS
1994-95	P	36	10	13	13	40	50	43
1995-96	P	36	8	6	22	29	62	30
1996-97	F	36	12	12	12	49	48	48
1997-98	F	36	8	12	16	45	55	36
1998-99	S	36	12	7	17	36	45	43
1999-00	S	36	12	10	14	42	44	46
2000-01	S	36	22	9	5	66	32	75
2001-02	F	36	19	9	8	61	38	66
2002-03	SPL	38	8	11	19	37	58	35
2003-04	SPL	38	6	8	24	39	67	26

50

SEASON STATS 2003/04

DATE	VENUE	OPPONENTS	ATT	RES	MIKKELSEN J.	LILLEY D.	MURRAY G.	WHYTE D.	BONNES S.	TAYLOR S.	ROWSON D.	McBRIDE J.P.	MILNE K.	GRADY J.	THOMSON A.	BRITTON G.	ROSS I.	ANIS J-Y.	PANTHER E.	FORREST E.	MITCHELL J.	WADDELL R.	ROSS A.	GEMMELL J.	ARTHUR K.	FLEMING D.	MADASCHI A.	HOWIE W.	LANGFIELD J.	GIBSON A.	GIBSON W.	CADETE J.	ENGLISH T.	CHIARINI D.	STRACHAN A.	PINKOWSKI S.
-AUG	H	LIVINGSTON	4,220	1-1	1	2	3	4	5	6	7	8	9¹	10	11	12	13																			
-AUG	A	KILMARNOCK	6,778	1-2	1	2	3	4	5	6	7	8	9	10¹	11	14		12	13																	
-AUG	H	CELTIC	9,045	1-2	1		3	4	13		7	8		10¹	11	9	6	5			2	12														
-AUG	A	MOTHERWELL	6,193	2-2	1	2	3	4	8¹	7		10	12	9¹	6	5					14	11	13													
-SEP	A	ABERDEEN	10,597	1-2	1	2		4		11	7	6	5	10	13	9		12			3	8¹			14											
-SEP	H	DUNDEE UNITED	4,711	0-2	2	3			11	7		5	10	12	9	6	4				8				1											
-SEP	A	DUNFERMLINE ATHLETIC	4,684	1-2		3	4	11	13	7	8	5	10¹		12				2	9		6		1	14											
OCT	H	HIBERNIAN	4,125	0-1		3	4		13	7		5	10	12	9		2			11		8		1	6											
-OCT	A	DUNDEE	6,497	0-1		3	4		13	7		5	10		9		2			11	12	8	14	1	6											
-OCT	H	HEARTS	4,814	1-4	2	3	4	10	9	7		6			11	12		13			8	14¹		1		5										
NOV	A	RANGERS	49,551	1-3	2	3	4			7	8	5	10¹				14			9	11	12	13	1	6											
NOV	A	LIVINGSTON	4,397	0-2	2	3	4			7	9	5	10		13					11		8		1	6	12	14									
-NOV	H	KILMARNOCK	4,445	2-4		3	4		12	7		6	10¹		9					11¹				1	13	5	8										
-NOV	A	CELTIC	58,194	1-3		3	4		13		9	6	10¹				2	12		11		8	14	1	7	5										
DEC	H	MOTHERWELL	4,124	1-0	2	3	4		13		9¹	6	10							11		8		1	7	5	12									
-DEC	A	ABERDEEN	5,189	0-3	2	3	4		14		9	6	10				13			11	8	12	1	7	5											
-DEC	A	DUNDEE UNITED	6,440	0-0	2	3	13			9	5	10	11				14			8		12		1	6	4										
-DEC	H	DUNFERMLINE ATHLETIC	4,377	4-1	2	3	13		7		5	10²	11¹		14			12		9		8¹		1	6	4										
JAN	A	HIBERNIAN	8,875	2-3	2	3	13		7		5	10¹	11			12		14		9		8		1	6	4¹										
-JAN	H	DUNDEE	4,690	1-2	2	3	13		7¹	12	5	10	11				14	9						6	4		1									
-JAN	A	HEARTS	10,264	0-2	2	3			7	9	5	10	13		8				11	14				6	4		1	12								
FEB	H	RANGERS	8,220	0-1		3		12	7	8	5	10	13	9	6	2					11	14			1	4										
-FEB	H	LIVINGSTON	3,011	†5-2		3		11	7	8		10¹	13¹	9²	6	2		14							1	4				12	5						
-FEB	A	KILMARNOCK	5,818	1-2		3	11¹		7	8		10	12	9	5					13	6		1	4				2								
-FEB	H	CELTIC	8,131	1-4		3			7	8	5	10		9¹	6					11			1	4				12	2	13						
-FEB	A	MOTHERWELL	5,814	0-3		3			7		5	10		9	6					11			1	4			8	2	12	13						
MAR	A	ABERDEEN	7,395	0-0		3	11		7				9	6	5			8					4			1	13	2	10	14	12					
-MAR	H	DUNDEE UNITED	3,510	1-1		3	11		7¹		5		9	6	4			10				13			1	12	2	14		8						
-MAR	A	DUNFERMLINE ATHLETIC	4,351	0-1		3			7	13	5		11		9									1	14	2	12		8							
-MAR	H	HIBERNIAN	3,155	1-1		3	10		7		5		11¹	13	6	4					9				12		1	2		8						
APR	A	DUNDEE	5,084	1-2		3	10		7			12	11¹	14	6	4					9			5		13	1	2		8						
-APR	H	HEARTS	4,043	1-0		3			7	8		10	11¹	13		4					9			6	5	12	1	2								
-APR	A	RANGERS	49,279	0-2		3	14		7	8		10	11	13	4						9			6	5	12	1	2								
-APR	H	DUNDEE	2,727	0-1		3			13	7	9		10		11		4				12			3	5	6	1	2			8	14				
MAY	H	ABERDEEN	2,839	2-0		3				7			10¹		14		4				11¹		13	1	6	5	8		12	2					9	
MAY	A	HIBERNIAN	5,380	2-1		3				7			10¹			4					11¹		12	1	6	5	8		9	2					13	
MAY	A	LIVINGSTON	2,706	2-2		3				7			10¹		14		4				11		13	1	6	5¹	8		9	2					12	
-MAY	H	KILMARNOCK	4,124	2-2		3				7			10²		14		13	12			11		8		4	5			9	2					6	1
TOTAL FULL APPEARANCES					5	15	36	15	11	6	35	19	25	32	13	15	15	20		3	30	3	11	22	20	23	5	10	4	16	1		5	2	1	
TOTAL SUB APPEARANCES							9	7		2		1	8	12	3	4	8	2		2	4	8	5		4	1	5		7			4	2	1	3
TOTAL GOALS SCORED							1		1	2		1	1	15	5	4					4	1	1					2						

Bold figures denote goalscorers. † denotes opponent's own goal.

LEADING GOALSCORERS:

SEASON	DIV	GOALS	PLAYER
94-95	P	7	W. Foster
95-96	P	5	A. Lyons, R. McDonald
96-97	F	11	D. Moss
97-98	F	6	J. Stirling
98-99	S	10	R. Dunn
99-00	S	5	R. Dunn
00-01	S	16	S. McLean
01-02	F	12	G. Britton
02-03	P	16	A. Burns
03-04	P	15	J. Grady

MILESTONES:

YEAR OF FORMATION: 1876
MOST CAPPED PLAYER: Alan Rough
NO. OF CAPS: 53
MOST LEAGUE POINTS IN A SEASON:
57 (First Division – Season 1991/92) (2 Points for a Win)
75 (Second Division – Season 2000/01) (3 Points for a Win)
MOST LEAGUE GOALS SCORED BY A PLAYER IN A SEASON:
Alex Hair (Season 1926/27)
NO. OF GOALS SCORED: 41
RECORD ATTENDANCE: 49,838 (-v- Rangers – 18.2.1922)
RECORD VICTORY: 16-0 (-v- Royal Albert – Scottish Cup, 17.1.1931)
RECORD DEFEAT: 0-10 (-v- Queen's Park – Scottish Cup, 3.12.1881)

PARTICK THISTLE PLAYING KITS SEASON 2004/05

FIRST KIT | SECOND KIT | THIRD KIT

Queen of the South

QUEEN OF THE SOUTH
Palmerston Park, Terregles Street,
Dumfries, DG2 9BA
CHAIRMAN
David Rae
VICE-CHAIRMAN
Thomas G. Harkness
DIRECTORS
Keith M. Houliston, Craig Paterson &
William Hewitson
SECRETARY
Richard Shaw, M.B.E.
OFFICER ADMINISTRATOR
Margaret Bell
MANAGER
Ian Scott
ASSISTANT MANAGER
Warren Pearson
COACHING STAFF
Gordon Hyslop, Fred Smith, George Paterson,
Tim Leighfield, Keith Middlemiss,
Neil Muirhead, Alan Goodwin, Alan Murray
YOUTH TEAM COACHES
U15 – George Paterson, Tim Leighfield & Mark Turner
U14 – Neil Muirhead, Keith Middlemiss & Alan Goodwin
U13 – Alan Murray & David McCann
CLUB DOCTORS
Dr. Andrew Downie & Dr. Bill Balfour
PHYSIOTHERAPIST
Kenneth Crichton
FOOTBALL SAFETY OFFICERS'
ASSOCIATION REPRESENTATIVE
George Galbraith (01387) 254853
CHIEF SCOUT
Iain McChesney
GROUNDSMAN
Kevin McCormick
KIT PERSON
George Paterson
COMMERCIAL MANAGER
Margaret Heuchan (H) (01556) 504569
(B) (01387) 254853
BUSINESS DEVELOPMENT MANAGER
Kenny Crichton
LOTTERY MANAGER Ian Heuchan
MEDIA LIAISON OFFICER
Bill Goldie (01387) 265569
(M) 07733 203171
MATCHDAY PROGRAMME EDITOR
Bruce Wright
(B)(01387) 262960 (H)(01387) 252400
TELEPHONES
Ground/Ticket Office/Information Service
(01387) 254853
Football Office Only (01387) 251666
Restaurant (01387) 252241
Fax (01387) 240470
E-MAIL & INTERNET ADDRESS
admin@qosfc.com
www.qosfc.co.uk
CLUB SHOP
Contact: John Paterson
Palmerston Park, Terregles Street,
Dumfries, DG2 9BA (01387) 254853
Open 9.00am – 4.00pm Mon. to Fri. and
1.30pm – 5.00pm on home match days.
Also available online - www.qosfc.co.uk
OFFICIAL SUPPORTERS CLUB
c/o Palmerston Park, Terregles Street,
Dumfries, DG2 9BA
TEAM CAPTAIN
Steven Bowey
SHIRT SPONSOR
Barron Wright Partnership
KIT SUPPLIER
Nike

LIST OF PLAYERS 2004/05

PLAYERS SURNAME	FIRST NAME	MIDDLE NAME	DATE OF BIRTH	PLACE OF BIRTH	DATE SIGNED	HEIGHT FT INS		WEIGHT ST LBS		POSITION ON PITCH	PREVIOUS CLUB
ARMSTRONG	CHRISTOPHER		08/11/84	LITTLE THORPE	06/08/04	6	2	14	0	FORWARD	ROCHDALE
BAGAN	DAVID		26/04/77	IRVINE	16/07/03	5	6	10	7	MIDFIELD	INVERNESS CALEDONIAN THISTLE
BATY	JAMES	LEA	28/08/87	DUMFRIES	28/07/04	5	7	8	5	MIDFIELD	QUEEN OF THE SOUTH FORM S
BEATTIE	ROSS		17/07/86	DUMFRIES	20/06/03	5	7	9	0	MIDFIELD	KILMARNOCK
BOWEY	STEVEN		10/07/74	DURHAM	14/02/02	5	9	11	2	MIDFIELD	GATESHEAD
BROWN	MARK	ALEXANDER	21/11/87	GLASGOW	17/09/04	5	7	10	4	MIDFIELD	STENHOUSEMUIR
BURNS	PAUL		18/05/84	IRVINE	17/06/02	5	9	9	7	MIDFIELD	QUEEN OF THE SOUTH FORM S
CAMPBELL	GARETH		05/10/87	IRVINE	31/08/04	5	10	11	5	DEFENDER	ABERDEEN
CLUCKIE	STUART		10/04/86	DUMFRIES	19/06/03	6	1	11	8	MIDFIELD	QUEEN OF THE SOUTH FORM S
CRAIG	DAVID	WILLIAM	11/06/69	GLASGOW	06/09/04	6	2	13	0	DEFENDER	AYR UNITED
CUNLIFFE	MARTIN		24/02/87	DUMFRIES	30/08/04	5	10	10	2	MIDFIELD	KILMARNOCK
ENGLISH	THOMAS		25/12/83	EASINGTON	02/07/04	5	10	11	13	DEFENDER	PARTICK THISTLE
FERGUSON	JAMIE		12/12/87	IRVINE	26/08/04	6	2	11	7	DEFENDER	AUCHINLECK TALBOT B.C.
GEORGE	LEE	MICHAEL	20/04/85	SUNDERLAND	17/09/04	5	10	10	7	FORWARD	BLYTH SPARTANS
GIBB	GRAHAM	SAMUEL	11/07/88	BELLSHILL	09/09/04	5	10	12	7	MIDFIELD	RANGERS EAST B.C.
GIBSON	WILLIAM		06/08/84	DUMFRIES	27/09/00	5	10	10	0	MIDFIELD	MAXWELLTOWN THISTLE
HAYES	SCOTT	PATRICK	16/02/87	IRVINE	17/09/04	5	9	10	7	FORWARD	TROON KAY PARK
HILL	STUART	DAVID	26/05/86	CARLISLE	28/07/04	6	4	12	7	DEFENDER	QUEEN OF THE SOUTH D U/16
INGLIS	ALAN	STUART	20/02/87	CARLISLE	17/09/04	5	11	11	0	MIDFIELD	FALKIRK
JACONELLI	EMILIO		05/06/83	LANARK	28/06/04	5	8	12	5	FORWARD	KILMARNOCK
MARTIN	DARREN		16/05/88	DUMFRIES	09/09/04	5	8	9	2	GOALKEEPER	LOCHAR THISTLE
MAXWELL	RICHARD	GRAEME	16/06/87	DUMFRIES	03/09/03	5	11	10	3	DEFENDER	QUEEN OF THE SOUTH FORM S
M°CARRON	KEVIN	QUAIL	24/03/88	GLASGOW	14/09/04	5	8	9	5	MIDFIELD	LENZIE B.C.
M°COLLIGAN	BRIAN		31/10/80	GLASGOW	06/06/02	5	9	10	0	MIDFIELD	CLYDEBANK
M°FARLANE	GORDON	JAMES	02/05/89	IRVINE	10/09/04	5	7	9	8	FORWARD	VALSPAR
M°LAUGHLIN	BRIAN		14/05/74	BELLSHILL	05/06/04	5	4	9	7	MIDFIELD	ST. JOHNSTONE
M°NIVEN	DAVID		27/05/78	LEEDS	06/07/04	5	9	14	0	FORWARD	LEIGH R.M.I.
MURRAY	MARC		15/06/88	BELLSHILL	09/09/04	6	0	12	0	DEFENDER	MANCHESTER UNITED B.C.
PATON	ERIC	JOHN	01/08/78	GLASGOW	06/06/04	5	10	12	0	MIDFIELD	CLYDEBANK
PAYNE	STEPHEN		23/12/83	EDINBURGH	08/01/04	5	11	11	1	DEFENDER	ABERDEEN
REDPATH	GARY	WILLIAM	02/09/88	DUMFRIES	12/08/04	5	8	9	1	MIDFIELD	LOCHAR THISTLE YOUTHS
REID	BRIAN	ROBERTSON	15/06/70	PAISLEY	11/08/03	6	3	14	2	DEFENDER	FALKIRK
ROBERTSON	SCOTT		26/11/87	IRVINE	16/07/04	6	2	11	5	MIDFIELD	TROON KAY PARK
RUDD	CRAIG		30/05/87	DUMFRIES	31/07/04	6	1	11	0	FORWARD	MAXWELLTOWN THISTLE
SAMSON	CRAIG	IAN	01/04/84	IRVINE	22/07/04	6	2	12	7	GOALKEEPER	KILMARNOCK
SCOTT	CHRISTOPHER		11/01/85	SOUTH SHIELDS	05/07/04	5	10	11	3	DEFENDER	SUNDERLAND
SCOTT	COLIN	GEORGE	19/05/70	GLASGOW	03/11/00	6	2	14	0	GOALKEEPER	CLYDEBANK
THOMSON	JAMES		15/05/71	STIRLING	23/05/01	6	4	14	0	DEFENDER	ARBROATH
WHORLOW	MARK		03/07/86	DUMFRIES	19/06/03	5	10	11	0	MIDFIELD	QUEEN OF THE SOUTH D U/16
WOOD	GARRY	PRINGLE GILLAN	18/09/76	EDINBURGH	05/08/03	5	11	12	2	FORWARD	BERWICK RANGERS
WRIGHT	GRAHAM	JOHN	21/01/86	DUMFRIES	30/01/04	6	1	11	5	GOALKEEPER	QUEEN OF THE SOUTH FORM S

THE DOONHAMERS' 10 YEAR LEAGUE RECORD

SEASON	DIV	P	W	D	L	F	A	PTS
1994-95	S	36	11	11	14	46	51	44
1995-96	S	36	11	10	15	54	67	43
1996-97	S	36	13	8	15	55	57	47
1997-98	S	36	15	9	12	57	51	54
1998-99	S	36	13	9	14	50	45	48
1999-00	S	36	8	9	19	45	75	33
2000-01	S	36	13	7	16	52	59	46
2001-02	S	36	20	7	9	64	42	67
2002-03	F	36	12	12	12	45	48	48
2003-04	F	36	15	9	12	46	48	54

The doonhamers' stats 2003/04

SEASON STATS 2003/04

DATE	VENUE	OPPONENTS	ATT	RES	DODDS J.	PATON E.	McALPINE J.	ALLAN D.	AITKEN A.	BAGAN D.	O'CONNOR S.	BOWEY S.	WOOD G.	LYLE D.	GIBSON W.	BURKE A.	REID B.	THOMSON J.	BURNS P.	SCOTT C.	TALBOT P.	McCOLLIGAN B.	JACONELLI E.	ROBERTSON K.	McMULLAN P.	PAYNE S.	SAMSON C.
AUG	A	ST. JOHNSTONE	2,939	1-4	1	2	3	4	5	6	7	8[1]	9	10	11	15											
AUG	H	ROSS COUNTY	1,734	1-0	1	2	3	4	16	7	15	8	9	10[1]	11	14	5	6									
AUG	A	FALKIRK	2,202	0-0	1	2	3	4		7	14	8	9	10	11		5	6									
AUG	A	AYR UNITED	2,143	4-1	1	2[1]	3	4		7	14[2]	8	9	10	11	16[1]	5	6	15								
SEP	H	RAITH ROVERS	2,142	0-2	1	2	3	4		7	15	8	9	10	11	16	5	6	17								
SEP	A	ST. MIRREN	2,681	2-1		2	3	4		7		8	14			9[1]	5	6	17	1	11						
SEP	H	CLYDE	1,952	4-1		2[1]	3	15	4	7[1]	8	14				9[2]	5	6	10	1	11	11					
OCT	A	BRECHIN CITY	621	1-0		2	3	17	4	7[1]	8	14				9	5	6	10	1	11	16					
OCT	H	INVERNESS CAL TH	3,547	3-2		2	11	3	4[1]	7[2]	8	14				9	5	6	10	1							
OCT	A	ROSS COUNTY	2,962	0-1		2	11	3	4	7	8		14	17		9	5	6	10	1							
NOV	H	ST. JOHNSTONE	3,159	1-1		2	3		14	4	7	8	16	15		9	5	6	10	1		11[1]					
NOV	A	RAITH ROVERS	1,944	1-0		2	3	15		4	8	7				9[1]	5	6	10	1		11					
NOV	H	AYR UNITED	3,555	1-0		2	3		14	4	8	7	15			9[1]	5	6	10	1		11					
NOV	A	CLYDE	1,271	1-3	12	2	3		6	4	8	7[1]	17			9	5		10	1		11	16				
DEC	H	ST. MIRREN	2,473	1-2		2	3		17	4		9	15	11		10[1]	5	6	7			8	16	1			
DEC	A	INVERNESS CAL TH	1,745	1-4		2			3	4	14	8	7[1]	10			9	5	6		17	11	1				
DEC	H	BRECHIN CITY	1,736	1-0	1	2		14	3	4	7	8	15[1]			9	5	6	11			16					
DEC	A	ST. JOHNSTONE	1,999	2-2	1	2			3	4	7[1]	8	10	17		9	5[1]	6				11					
DEC	H	FALKIRK	4,075	2-0	1	2				7[1]	8	10[1]	14			9	5	6	4			11					
JAN	A	AYR UNITED	2,303	1-1	1	2			3	4	7	8[1]	10			9	5	6	14			11	15				
JAN	H	RAITH ROVERS	2,089	1-1	1	2	15		3		8					9	5	6	4			11	17		10	16	
JAN	A	ST. MIRREN	2,540	1-3	1	2	3		5	4[1]	7	8	6			9			10			14	16		11	15	
FEB	A	BRECHIN CITY	642	1-2	1	2			15	4	7	8[1]				14	5	6	10			11	9		3	17	
FEB	H	INVERNESS CAL TH	2,021	2-1		2	11	6	3	4	7[1]	8[1]				14	5		10			9	16				1
MAR	H	ROSS COUNTY	2,047	1-1		2		6	3	4		8[1]	16		11	9	5		7			10	17				1
MAR	H	CLYDE	2,169	1-2		2	11	4	3		8	9				14[1]	5	6	7			10	17	16			1
MAR	A	FALKIRK	2,098	2-0		2		6	3	4	7	8				9[2]	5		10		16				15	11	1
MAR	A	RAITH ROVERS	1,482	1-3			14	6	3	4	7[1]	8				9	5	2	10			17			16	11	1
MAR	H	AYR UNITED	1,831	0-0		2	11	4	3	14	7	8				9		6	5		15	16				10	1
APR	A	CLYDE	1,207	0-2		2		6	3	16	7	8		11		9	5				4	10	17				
APR	H	ST. MIRREN	2,211	1-0		2		6	3	7		8[1]		11		9	5				4	10	17	16			1
APR	A	INVERNESS CAL TH	2,126	1-4		2		6	3			8		11		16[1]	5	14	10		4	9			7		1
APR	H	BRECHIN CITY	1,352	2-2		2		6	3		15	8		11		9[1]	5				4	10[1]		14	16		1
MAY	H	ST. JOHNSTONE	1,629	1-1		2		3		7		8		11		9	5	6			4	10[1]					1
MAY	A	ROSS COUNTY	2,842	2-1		2			7	14	8[1]			11		9[1]	5	6	15	1	4	10					
MAY	H	FALKIRK	2,751	1-0		2	15		3	7	15			11		9	5	6	8		4	10[1]					1
TOTAL FULL APPEARANCES					12	35	19	15	24	29	19	33	16	8	14	27	33	26	23	10	3	18	11	2	3	4	12
TOTAL SUB APPEARANCES					1		3	3	6	2	8			6	7	2	7		1	6		1	5	6		9	6
TOTAL GOALS SCORED						2			2	12	7	4	1			13	1					1	3				

bold figures denote goalscorers. † denotes opponent's own goal.

LEADING GOALSCORERS:

SEASON	DIV	GOALS	PLAYER
94-95	S	9	D. Campbell, S. Mallan
95-96	S	12	S. Mallan
96-97	S	13	S. Mallan
97-98	S	11	T. Bryce
98-99	S	15	S. Mallan
99-00	S	13	S. Mallan
00-01	S	16	P. Weatherson
01-02	S	19	J. O'Neil
02-03	F	9	J. O'Neil
03-04	F	13	A. Burke

MILESTONES:

YEAR OF FORMATION: 1919
MOST CAPPED PLAYER: William Houliston
NO. OF CAPS: 3
MOST LEAGUE POINTS IN A SEASON:
55 (Second Division – Season 1985/86) (2 Points for a Win)
67 (Second Division – Season 2001/02) (3 Points for a Win)
MOST LEAGUE GOALS SCORED BY A PLAYER IN A SEASON:
Jimmy Gray (Season 1927/28)
NO. OF GOALS SCORED: 37
RECORD ATTENDANCE: 26,552 (-v- Hearts – Scottish Cup, 23.2.1952)
RECORD VICTORY: 11-1 (-v- Stranraer – Scottish Cup, 16.1.1932)
RECORD DEFEAT: 2-10 (-v- Dundee – Division 1, 1.12.1962)

QUEEN OF THE SOUTH PLAYING KITS SEASON 2004/05

FIRST KIT · SECOND KIT · THIRD KIT

RAITH ROVERS
FOOTBALL CLUB

RAITH ROVERS
Stark's Park, Pratt Street,
Kirkcaldy, Fife, KY1 1SA

CHAIRMAN

VICE-CHAIRMAN
Mario Caira

DIRECTORS
Eric W. Drysdale, William H. Gray,
Colin C. McGowan & Alex Short

HONORARY PRESIDENT
John Urquhart

SECRETARY
Eric W. Drysdale

GENERAL MANAGER/
OFFICE ADMINISTRATOR
Bob Mullen

MANAGER
Gordon Dalziel

RESERVE COACH
Shaun Dennis

HEAD OF YOUTH DEVELOPMENT
Francisco (Paquito) Ortiz

YOUTH DEVELOPMENT COACHES
Roy Davidson & John Gavin

YOUTH TEAM COACHES
George Gemmill & Ged Chapman (U17)

CLUB DOCTOR
Dr. Robert Robertson

PHYSIOTHERAPISTS
Natural Remedy Clinic

FOOTBALL SAFETY OFFICERS'
ASSOCIATION REPRESENTATIVE
Bill Brown (01592) 263514

GROUNDSMAN
John Murray

KIT PERSON
Linda Patrick

COMMERCIAL/LOTTERY MANAGER
John Drysdale (M) 07962 023683

MEDIA LIAISON PERSON
Keith Lusack

DISABILITY LIAISON
Elizabeth Drysdale

MATCHDAY PROGRAMME EDITORS
Tom Bell & Mike Melville

CLUB PHOTOGRAPHER
Tony Fimister (01592) 201645

HOSPITALITY MANAGER
Tom Smith

TELEPHONES
Ground (01592) 263514
Fax (01592) 642833

E-MAIL & INTERNET ADDRESS
office@raithroversfc.com
www.raithroversfc.com

CLUB SHOP
South Stand Shop situated within stand.
Open during Office hours 9.00 a.m. to 5.00
p.m. and on home match days
2.00 p.m. to 5.00 p.m.

OFFICIAL SUPPORTERS CLUB
c/o Fraser Hamilton, 22 Tower Terrace,
Kirkcaldy, Fife

TEAM CAPTAIN
Ian Davidson

VICE CAPTAIN
Darren Brady

SHIRT SPONSOR
Bar Itza

KIT SUPPLIER
XARA

LIST OF PLAYERS 2004/05

PLAYERS SURNAME	FIRST NAME	MIDDLE NAME	DATE OF BIRTH	PLACE OF BIRTH	DATE SIGNED	HEIGHT FT INS		WEIGHT ST LBS		POSITION ON PITCH	PREVIOUS CLUB
BARTHOLOME	ANTHONY		10/12/82	ST. ETIENNE	20/08/04	6	2	13	5	DEFENDER	VALENCE
BENAISSA	AMAR		11/11/82	CHOISY LE ROI - FRANCE	02/07/04	6	1	12	1	MIDFIELD	AS CHOISY LE ROI
BERTHELOT	DAVID		29/09/77	A VILLEPINTE	13/07/04	6	4	13	0	GOALKEEPER	LOUANS CUISEAUX
BOYLE	JOHN		22/10/86	BELLSHILL	24/07/03	5	9	10	0	MIDFIELD	RAITH ROVERS FORM D U'1
BRADY	DARREN		04/11/81	GLASGOW	09/06/04	5	11	11	0	MIDFIELD	LIVINGSTON
CAMPBELL	RICHARD		15/01/88	EDINBURGH	01/09/04	6	2	11	6	DEFENDER	EDINA HIBS
DALY	WESLEY	JAMES PATRICK	07/03/84	LONDON	20/08/04	5	7	11	9	MIDFIELD	QUEENS PARK RANGERS
DAVIDSON	IAN		14/01/84	KIRKCALDY	29/07/04	6	0	10	7	DEFENDER	SCARBOROUGH
EBANDA	HERVE		14/02/79	PARIS	28/07/04	6	0	12	8	FORWARD	BEAUCARE
ELOUDI	MEHDI		13/07/83	PARIS	02/07/04	6	0	10	7	MIDFIELD	U.S. IVRY
EWART	SCOT		23/09/88	BELLSHILL	17/08/04	5	6	10	8	FORWARD	EAST KILBRIDE BURGH U'16
FITZPATRICK	STEPHEN		22/04/88	FALKIRK	08/09/04	5	8	10	7	FORWARD	HEART OF MIDLOTHIAN
FOX	MARK		31/05/87	BELLSHILL	31/08/04	5	9	9	0	MIDFIELD	RAITH ROVERS FORM D U'1
FREW	MICHAEL	ANTHONY	11/01/86	DUNFERMLINE	31/08/04	5	5	9	2	MIDFIELD	BALLINGRY ROVERS JUNIORS
GILFILLAN	JAMIE		28/08/86	KIRKCALDY	30/08/04	5	10	11	7	FORWARD	KIRKCALDY Y.M.C.A. JUNIOR
GORDON	STEVEN		30/09/88	EDINBURGH	17/08/04	6	1	11	6	DEFENDER	ST. JOHNSTONE
HAJOVSKY	TOMAS		10/12/82	BOJNICE - SLOVAKIA	30/07/04	6	5	14	2	DEFENDER	SK TATRAN POSTOMA
HALL	STUART	MATTHEW	09/02/87	KIRKCALDY	20/08/04	6	1	11	0	GOALKEEPER	BALLINGRY ROVERS JUNIOR
HENDERSON	RICHARD		22/08/87	DUNDEE	13/03/04	5	8	9	0	MIDFIELD	LOCHEE HARP JUNIORS
HOWITT	KYLE		16/06/87	DUNDEE	13/07/04	5	8	9	5	MIDFIELD	LINLITHGOW B.C.
LEIPER	COLIN		05/02/87	KIRKCALDY	01/09/04	6	2	11	0	MIDFIELD	WHITBURN JUNIORS
MALCOLM	CRAIG		30/12/86	BELLSHILL	24/07/03	5	10	11	0	MID / FWD	RAITH ROVERS FORM D U'1
MARTIN	JOHN		04/05/85	KIRKCALDY	18/08/04	5	11	11	7	FORWARD	BALLINGRY ROVERS JUNIOR
MAXWELL	DANIEL	RYAN	14/06/83	LARNE	21/08/04	5	9	11	2	MIDFIELD	HAMILTON ACADEMICAL
McALPINE	JOSEPH	CHARLES	12/09/81	GLASGOW	30/07/04	5	10	11	9	MIDFIELD	QUEEN OF THE SOUTH
McKNIGHT	JOHN		21/11/88	BANGOUR	17/08/04	5	10	11	2	MIDFIELD	POLBETH B.C.
McLEOD	STUART		26/08/88	BANGOUR	17/08/04	5	7	10	4	MIDFIELD	BATHGATE B.C.
McMURRAY	JOHN	MICHAEL	20/06/88	LANARK	17/08/04	5	8	11	0	DEFENDER	HARELEESHILL B.C.
McQUADE	PAUL		17/05/87	KIRKCALDY	05/08/04	5	7	11	7	MIDFIELD	DUNDONALD BLUEBELL JUNIOR
MENDY	MAURICE		24/09/82	PIKINE - SENEGAL	28/07/04	5	10	10	3	DEFENDER	A.S. ORLY
MILLAR	PAUL	THOMAS	21/09/85	STIRLING	31/08/04	5	10	11	7	MIDFIELD	DERBY COUNTY
NESS	DARYL		14/03/88	EDINBURGH	17/08/04	6	1	10	8	DEFENDER	SALVESEN B.C.
O'MARA	CRAIG		20/02/89	EDINBURGH	22/09/04	5	7	10	9	MIDFIELD	LIVINGSTON
OCOWAN	PETER		20/02/84	ZVOLEN - SLOVAKIA	12/08/04	5	10	11	13	MIDFIELD	NITRA - SLOVAKIA
OUATTARA	MOUSSA		27/02/83	PARIS	31/07/04	5	9	11	9	MIDFIELD	AS ORLY
PERRY	JACK	JOSEPH	26/10/84	ISLINGTON	20/08/04	6	0	12	7	DEFENDER	QUEENS PARK RANGERS
POUNOUSSAMY	RUDY	JEAN FRANCOIS	10/08/78	SAINT-DENIS	28/07/04	6	1	11	9	GOALKEEPER	F.C. CAPRICORNE
RAFFELL	BRUCE	JOHN	19/03/86	ABERDEEN	24/08/04	5	10	9	7	MIDFIELD	DUNDEE NORTH END JUNIORS
RINTOUL	JORDAN		27/02/88	FALKIRK	17/08/04	5	10	11	4	MIDFIELD	FALKIRK FORM D UNDER 14
RIVAS	FRANCISCO	ORTIZ	12/08/69	GRANADA	04/07/02	5	10	12	0	MIDFIELD	U.D. LAS PALMAS
SACKO	HAMED		11/12/80	BAMAKO - MALI	02/07/04	5	11	11	11	FORWARD	PARIS F.C.
SMART	JONATHAN		01/02/81	DUNDEE	10/06/04	6	3	13	4	DEFENDER	DEE CLUB
STEWART	MICHAEL		26/07/84	DUNDEE	20/08/04	5	9	10	1	MIDFIELD	DUNDEE NORTH END JUNIORS
TAGRO	BAROAN		05/10/77	COTE D'IVOIN	20/08/04	5	5	9	10	MIDFIELD	CARSHALTON ATHLETIC
TCHIMBAKALA	JULES		15/01/71	POINTE-NOIRE (CONGO)	23/06/04	5	10	10	12	MIDFIELD	PARIS F.C.
WILSON	DEREK		01/01/88	BANGOUR	17/08/04	5	10	10	10	MIDFIELD	LINLITHGOW B.C.
WOODS	DEAN		17/05/88	EDINBURGH	31/08/04	5	11	11	10	FORWARD	HEART OF MIDLOTHIAN
YOUNG	LLOYD	PAUL	26/12/85	DUNDEE	13/01/04	5	8	9	7	MIDFIELD	LOCHEE HARP JUNIORS

TICKET INFORMATION

SEASON TICKET PRICES

SEATED

MAIN STAND/ SOUTH STAND	ADULT	£220
	JUVENILE/OAP	£100
	CHILD (PRIMARY SCHOOL)	£50
	PARENT & JUVENILE	£270

LEAGUE ADMISSION PRICES

SEATED

| MAIN STAND/ SOUTH STAND/NORTH STAND | ADULT | £12 |
| | JUVENILE/OAP | £6 |

THE ROVERS' 10 YEAR LEAGUE RECORD

SEASON	DIV	P	W	D	L	F	A	PTS
1994-95	F	36	19	12	5	54	32	69
1995-96	P	36	12	7	17	41	57	43
1996-97	P	36	6	7	23	29	73	25
1997-98	F	36	17	9	10	51	33	60
1998-99	F	36	8	11	17	37	57	35
1999-00	F	36	17	8	11	55	40	59
2000-01	F	36	10	8	18	41	55	38
2001-02	F	36	8	11	17	50	62	35
2002-03	S	36	16	11	9	53	36	59
2003-04	F	36	8	10	18	37	57	34

SEASON STATS 2003/04

Player columns (left to right): GONZALEZ R., PATINO C., CALDERON A., TALIO V., DENNIS S., BRADY D., STANLEY C., RIVAS F., SUTTON J., BRITTAIN R., PREST M., BROWN I., BLACKADDER R., PEERS M., MARTIN J., HENRY J., STANIC G., EVANS D., HAWLEY K., ROBB S., JACK M., LANGFIELD J., CARRANZA L.A., BOYLE J., YOUNG L., PEREIRA GOMEZ R., BERTHELOT D., BORNES J., NIETO J., FERRERO S., MILLAR P., MALCOLM C., SMART J., DOW A., CAPIN MARTINO S., MAXWELL D., O'REILLY C., GLYNN D., IRONS S., RAFFELL B., LEIPER C.

DATE	VENUE	OPPONENTS	ATT	RES
-AUG	H	ST. MIRREN	3,090	1 - 1
-AUG	A	BRECHIN CITY	1,013	3 - 0
-AUG	H	AYR UNITED	2,337	1 - 1
-AUG	H	FALKIRK	4,222	0 - 1
-SEP	A	QUEEN OF THE SOUTH	2,142	2 - 0
-SEP	A	ST. JOHNSTONE	2,983	1 - 0
-SEP	H	ROSS COUNTY	2,292	1 - 7
OCT	A	INVERNESS CAL TH	1,707	1 - 2
-OCT	H	CLYDE	1,765	0 - 1
-OCT	H	BRECHIN CITY	1,685	2 - 1
NOV	A	ST. MIRREN	3,005	1 - 2
NOV	H	QUEEN OF THE SOUTH	1,944	0 - 1
-NOV	A	FALKIRK	3,237	2 - 3
-NOV	A	ROSS COUNTY	2,803	2 - 3
-NOV	H	ST. JOHNSTONE	1,996	1 - 4
DEC	A	CLYDE	1,375	0 - 0
-DEC	H	INVERNESS CAL TH	1,432	1 - 3
-DEC	A	AYR UNITED	1,791	0 - 1
JAN	H	FALKIRK	2,885	2 - 0
-JAN	A	QUEEN OF THE SOUTH	2,089	1 - 1
-JAN	A	ST. JOHNSTONE	2,576	2 - 5
-FEB	H	ROSS COUNTY	1,562	0 - 0
-FEB	A	INVERNESS CAL TH	1,879	0 - 3
-FEB	H	CLYDE	1,871	0 - 3
-MAR	H	ST. MIRREN	1,882	2 - 0
-MAR	A	BRECHIN CITY	925	1 - 1
-MAR	H	AYR UNITED	2,231	2 - 1
-MAR	H	QUEEN OF THE SOUTH	1,482	† 3 - 1
-MAR	A	FALKIRK	2,386	0 - 1
-APR	A	ROSS COUNTY	2,414	1 - 1
-APR	H	ST. JOHNSTONE	2,676	1 - 1
-APR	H	CLYDE	1,533	1 - 4
-APR	H	INVERNESS CAL TH	1,748	0 - 1
-MAY	A	ST. MIRREN	2,372	1 - 1
-MAY	H	BRECHIN CITY	2,311	1 - 1
-MAY	A	AYR UNITED	1,283	0 - 1

TOTAL FULL APPEARANCES: 17 20 26 9 23 24 18 33 20 9 8 13 8 2 1 28 2 4 8 6 5 2 3 9 10 14 13 11 12 1 1 9 9 11 2 2 1

TOTAL SUB APPEARANCES: 1 3 1 5 2 1 4 3 3 9 3 4 1 1 6 7 3 1 12 5 1 1 4 3 1 5 2 1 1 1

TOTAL GOALS SCORED: 1 3 1 1 2 13 1 1 1 2 6 3 1

Bold figures denote goalscorers. † denotes opponent's own goal.

LEADING GOALSCORERS:

SEASON	DIV	GOALS	PLAYER
94-95	F	15	G. Dalziel
95-96	P	9	C. Cameron
96-97	P	5	P. Duffield, D. Lennon
97-98	F	10	P. Hartley, K. Wright
98-99	F	8	C. Dargo
99-00	F	12	C. Dargo
00-01	F	9	P. Tosh
01-02	F	19	I. Novo
02-03	S	7	K. Hawley
03-04	F	13	J. Sutton

MILESTONES:

YEAR OF FORMATION: 1883
MOST CAPPED PLAYER: David Morris
NO. OF CAPS: 6
MOST LEAGUE POINTS IN A SEASON:
65 (First Division - Season 1992/93) (2 Points for a Win)
69 (First Division - Season 1994/95) (3 Points for a Win)
MOST LEAGUE GOALS SCORED BY A PLAYER IN A SEASON:
Norman Heywood (Season 1937/38)
NO. OF GOALS SCORED: 42
RECORD ATTENDANCE: 31,306 (-v- Hearts – Scottish Cup, 7.2.1953)
RECORD VICTORY: 10-1 (-v- Coldstream – Scottish Cup, 13.2.1954)
RECORD DEFEAT: 2-11 (-v- Morton – Division 2, 18.3.1936)

RAITH ROVERS PLAYING KITS SEASON 2004/05

FIRST KIT   SECOND KIT   THIRD KIT

ROSS COUNTY
Victoria Park Stadium, Jubilee Road,
Dingwall, Ross-shire, IV15 9QZ
CHAIRMAN
Roy J. MacGregor
VICE-CHAIRMAN
Gordon M. R. MacRae
DIRECTORS
Thomas A. Mackenzie, Andrew R. Duncan,
Alastair I. Kennedy, Ronald M. Fraser, Michael
B. Kydd, John MacGregor & Peter C. Swanson
MANAGEMENT COMMITTEE
Donald MacBean, David R. Patience
& Calum Grant
CHIEF EXECUTIVE
Alastair Kennedy
SECRETARY
Donald MacBean
OFFICE ADMINISTRATOR
Marie Ewan
MANAGER
Alexander N. Smith
FIRST TEAM COACH
Jimmy Bone
GOALKEEPING COACH
Stuart Garden
DIRECTOR OF YOUTH DEVELOPMENT
Calum Grant
COMMUNITY COACH
Gavin Levey
YOUTH DEVELOPMENT COACH
Brian Irvine
YOUTH COACHES
Gardner Spiers & Brian Irvine (U19)
Peter Budge, Martin Rae & Andrew Naismith (U17)
Rod Houston & Muir Morton (U15)
Graeme Sutherland & Stephen McLean (U13)
CLUB DOCTOR
Dr. Colin Fettes
PHYSIOTHERAPISTS
Dougie Sim & Jan Campbell
KIT PERSON
Susan Wilson
**FOOTBALL SAFETY OFFICERS'
ASSOCIATION REPRESENTATIVE**
David R. Patience (01463) 222893
STADIUM MANAGER/GROUNDSMAN
David Fraser
COMMERCIAL/LOTTERY MANAGER
Duncan Chisholm
MEDIA LIAISON OFFICER
Alastair Kennedy (01349) 860860
MATCHDAY PROGRAMME EDITOR
Bryan Munro (01463) 230721
bryan.munro@lineone.net
TELEPHONES
Ground/Ticket Office (01349) 860860
Fax (01349) 866277
Youth Department (01349) 860862
E-MAIL & INTERNET ADDRESS
donnie@rosscountyfootballclub.co.uk
www.rosscountyfootballclub.co.uk
CLUB SHOP
Official Ross County F.C. merchandising
available from the Club Shop situated at the
ground. Merchandise also available online -
www.rosscountydiect.com
OFFICIAL SUPPORTERS CLUB
George Shiels, 4 Tulloch Place, Dingwall
(01349) 865135
TEAM CAPTAIN
Jim Lauchlan
SHIRT SPONSOR
McLean Electrical Ltd
KIT SUPPLIER
XARA

LIST OF PLAYERS 2004/05

PLAYERS SURNAME	FIRST NAME	MIDDLE NAME	DATE OF BIRTH	PLACE OF BIRTH	DATE SIGNED	HEIGHT FT INS		WEIGHT ST LBS		POSITION ON PITCH	PREVIOUS CLUB
ADAM	CHARLES	GRAHAM	10/12/85	DUNDEE	31/08/04	6	1	13	0	MIDFIELD	RANGERS
ALLAN	DAVID	WILLIAM	21/08/89	WICK	03/08/04	5	8	10	2	FORWARD	ROSS COUNTY FORM D U' 14
BEGG	SCOTT		15/08/88	WICK	24/08/04	5	9	9	4	DEFENDER	ROSS COUNTY FORM D U' 15
BELL	DANIEL		12/07/89	INVERNESS	26/07/04	5	6	8	9	GOALKEEPER	ROSS COUNTY FORM D U' 15
BUNYAN	GRAEME		16/07/88	IRVINE	02/07/04	5	9	9	3	MIDFIELD	ROSS COUNTY FORM D U' 14
BURKE	ALEXANDER		11/11/77	GLASGOW	02/06/04	5	9	10	12	FORWARD	QUEEN OF THE SOUTH
CAMERON	JOHN		12/04/89	INVERNESS	26/07/04	5	8	9	12	FORWARD	ROSS COUNTY FORM D U' 15
CANNING	MARTIN		03/12/81	GLASGOW	28/07/99	6	2.5	12	10	DEFENDER	CLYDEBANK
CLARK	CAMERON	JAMES	15/05/89	ABERDEEN	24/08/04	5	9	8	7	DEFENDER	ROSS COUNTY FORM D U' 15
COWIE	DON		15/02/83	INVERNESS	23/08/00	5	5	8	5	MIDFIELD	ROSS COUNTY FORM S
CUNNINGHAM	STEVEN		15/10/89	WICK	10/08/04	5	8	9	6	MIDFIELD	ROSS COUNTY FORM D U' 15
DOCHERTY	DARREN		23/11/87	VALE OF LEVEN	10/08/04	5	11	10	5	MIDFIELD	LIVINGSTON
DUGUID	KEVIN		22/08/88	ABERDEEN	13/08/04	5	8.5	9	0	MIDFIELD	ROSS COUNTY FORM D U' 15
DUNNETT	MICHAEL	THOMSON	13/03/86	INVERNESS	27/05/03	5	10	10	6	MIDFIELD	ROSS COUNTY FORM D U' 16
FERGUSON	PAUL		19/05/87	EDINBURGH	05/07/04	5	11	9	12	GOALKEEPER	ROSS COUNTY FORM D U' 16
GARDEN	STUART	ROBERTSON	10/02/72	DUNDEE	12/07/04	5	11.5	12	3	GOALKEEPER	NOTTS COUNTY
GRANT	ALAN		28/03/88	INVERNESS	26/07/04	5	10	10	12	FORWARD	ROSS COUNTY FORM D U' 16
GUNN	CRAIG		17/07/87	WICK	02/07/04	5	11	10	7	FORWARD	CAITHNESS UNITED
HIGGINS	SEAN		29/10/84	GLASGOW	07/08/02	5	8.5	10	1	FORWARD	ST. JOHNSTONE
HOOKS	NEAL		03/07/87	HEXHAM	10/08/04	6	0	12	2	MIDFIELD	CRAMLINGTON B.C.
KERR	SHAUN	STEVEN	23/04/86	BIRKENHEAD	27/05/03	5	11	11	5	FORWARD	ROSS COUNTY FORM D U' 16
KILGANNON	SEAN		08/03/81	STIRLING	12/07/04	5	11	11	8	MIDFIELD	DUNFERMLINE ATHLETIC
LAUCHLAN	JAMES	HARLEY	02/02/77	GLASGOW	02/01/04	6	1	12	7	DEFENDER	LIVINGSTON
LAWRIE	BLAIR	JOHN	02/07/86	INVERNESS	27/05/03	5	6	8	7	MIDFIELD	ROSS COUNTY FORM D U' 16
LOMBARDI	MICHELE		02/07/86	IRVINE	02/07/04	5	10	11	5	FORWARD	ABERDEEN
McADIE	RICHARD	WILLIAM	09/04/87	WICK	02/07/04	5	8	10	7	MIDFIELD	ROSS COUNTY FORM D U' 16
McDONALD	NEIL	McLEOD	15/06/87	DUNFERMLINE	22/08/03	5	10	11	7	DEFENDER	DUNFERMLINE ATHLETIC
McFARLANE	MARTIN		06/09/88	ABERDEEN	30/08/04	6	3	11	7	GOALKEEPER	ROSS COUNTY FORM D U' 15
MACKAY	STEVEN		26/06/81	INVERGORDON	29/07/02	5	11	12	3	DEF / MID	NAIRN COUNTY
MAIN	JORDAN		19/02/88	ABERDEEN	03/08/04	5	7	9	7	DEFENDER	ROSS COUNTY FORM D U' 16
MALCOLM	STUART	ROSS	20/08/79	EDINBURGH	26/07/03	6	3	13	0	DEFENDER	PLYMOUTH ARGYLE
MALIN	JOSEPH		13/07/88	BELLSHILL	02/07/04	5	10	10	1	GOALKEEPER	CELTIC
McCULLOCH	MARK	ROSS	19/05/75	INVERNESS	29/07/02	5	11	13	7	MIDFIELD	PARTICK THISTLE
McCUNNIE	JAMIE		15/04/83	BELLSHILL	18/07/03	5	10	11	0	DEFENDER	DUNDEE UNITED
McGARRY	STEVEN	THOMAS	28/09/79	PAISLEY	29/07/04	5	9	10	0	FORWARD	ST. MIRREN
McGRAW	ALLAN		15/06/87	GLASGOW	10/08/04	5	10	10	12	DEFENDER	PARTICK THISTLE
McINTYRE	IAN		23/02/88	IRVINE	05/07/04	5	11	10	7	GOALKEEPER	RANGERS
McKELLAR	SCOTT		30/07/87	GREENOCK	20/08/04	5	10	10	0	DEFENDER	PARTICK THISTLE
McKINLAY	KEVIN	DONALD	28/02/86	STIRLING	17/09/04	6	0	11	0	MID / FWD	CHELSEA
McNAB	GORDON		21/08/88	INVERNESS	31/07/04	5	9	10	10	MIDFIELD	ROSS COUNTY FORM D U' 16
McSWEGAN	GARY	JOHN	24/09/70	GLASGOW	29/07/04	5	7.5	12	8	FORWARD	KILMARNOCK
MOFFAT	ADAM	JOHN WILLIAM	15/05/86	GLASGOW	30/08/03	5	11	11	9	DEFENDER	RANGERS
MOORE	DANIEL		11/10/88	INVERNESS	07/08/04	5	10.5	11	8	MIDFIELD	ROSS COUNTY FORM D U' 16
MURPHY	CHRISTOPHER		02/04/88	LIVERPOOL	31/07/04	5	9	10	7	FORWARD	ROSS COUNTY FORM D U' 16
NAISMITH	ADAM	ANDREW	26/08/89	INVERNESS	26/07/04	5	4.5	9	2	DEFENDER	ROSS COUNTY FORM D U' 15
NICOLSON	MARK		25/06/88	INVERNESS	31/07/04	6	1	11	9	MIDFIELD	ROSS COUNTY FORM D U' 16
RANKIN	JOHN		27/06/83	BELLSHILL	10/07/03	5	10	10	8	MIDFIELD	MANCHESTER UNITED
RENWICK	ALAN	McFARLANE	14/10/88	INVERNESS	26/07/04	5	6	9	0	GOALKEEPER	ROSS COUNTY FORM D U' 16
ROBERTSON	JOHN	ALEXANDER	28/03/76	IRVINE	05/07/04	6	0	12	4	DEFENDER	ST. JOHNSTONE
SINCLAIR	SHAUN		26/02/87	WICK	02/07/04	5	10	9	7	DEFENDER	ABERDEEN
SKINNER	STEPHEN		25/04/88	INVERNESS	26/07/04	6	1	12	6	DEFENDER	ROSS COUNTY FORM D U' 16
STEVEN	SCOTT	MACKAY	12/03/88	WICK	30/08/04	5	10	10	2	MID / FWD	ROSS COUNTY FORM D U' 16
STEWART	COLIN		10/01/80	MIDDLESBROUGH	18/07/03	3	2	12	12	GOALKEEPER	KILMARNOCK
TAYLOR	STUART		26/11/74	GLASGOW	05/07/04	6	1	11	10	MIDFIELD	ST. JOHNSTONE
URQUHART	JOHN	JAMES ALEXANDER	24/03/88	ABERDEEN	26/07/04	5	9	9	10	MIDFIELD	ROSS COUNTY FORM D U' 16
WINTERS	DAVID		07/03/82	PAISLEY	09/07/03	5	11	11	10	FORWARD	DUNDEE UNITED
YOUNG	BRYAN		02/09/86	PAISLEY	21/08/03	5	7	10	0	MIDFIELD	KILMARNOCK

TICKET INFORMATION

SEASON TICKET PRICES

SEATED
ADULT	£195
JUVENILE (U-18)/OAP	£110
JUVENILE (U-12)	£80

FAMILY SECTION
ADULT/OAP	£170/£100
JUVENILE (U-16)	£55
JUVENILE (U-12)	£40

STANDING
ADULT/OAP	£160/£80
JUVENILE (U-16)	£45
JUVENILE (U-12)	£30

LEAGUE ADMISSION PRICES

SEATED
ADULT	£14
JUVENILE/OAP	£8

STANDING
ADULT	£12
JUVENILE/OAP	£7

THE COUNTY'S 10 YEAR LEAGUE RECORD

SEASON	DIV	P	W	D	L	F	A	PTS	
1994-95	T	36	18	6	12	59	44	60	
1995-96	T	36	12	17	7	56	39	53	
1996-97	T	36	20	7	9	58	41	67	
1997-98	T	36	19	10	7	71	36	67	
1998-99	T	36	24	5	7	87	42	77	
1999-00	S	36	18	8	10	57	39	62	
2000-01	F	36	11	10	15	48	52	43	
2001-02	F	36	14	10	12	51	43	52	
2002-03	F	36	9	8	19	42	46	35	
2003-04	F	36	12	13	11	49	41	49	

SEASON STATS 2003/04

Players (column headers): STEWART C., McCUNNIE J., MACKAY S., TAIT J., MALCOLM S., McCULLOCH M., RANKIN J., HANNAH D., HIGGINS S., ROBERTSON H., WINTERS D., COWIE D., GETHINS C., HAMILTON J., WEBB S., BAYNE G., McGARRY S., O'DONNELL S., FRIDGE L., SMITH G., CANNING M., LAUCHLAN J., OGUNMADE D., McDONALD N.

DATE	VENUE	OPPONENTS	ATT	RES	STEWART C.	McCUNNIE J.	MACKAY S.	TAIT J.	MALCOLM S.	McCULLOCH M.	RANKIN J.	HANNAH D.	HIGGINS S.	ROBERTSON H.	WINTERS D.	COWIE D.	GETHINS C.	HAMILTON J.	WEBB S.	BAYNE G.	McGARRY S.	O'DONNELL S.	FRIDGE L.	SMITH G.	CANNING M.	LAUCHLAN J.	OGUNMADE D.	McDONALD N.
-AUG	H	BRECHIN CITY	2,662	4-0	1	2	3[1]	4[1]	5	6	7	8	9	10[1]	11	14	15	16[1]										
-AUG	A	QUEEN OF THE SOUTH	1,734	0-1	1	2	3	4	5	6	7	8	9	15	11		16	10	13									
-AUG	H	ST. MIRREN	3,053	†2-0	1	2	3	4	5	6	7	8	14		11[1]	10	16	15		9								
-AUG	H	INVERNESS CAL TH	5,020	1-1	1	2	3	4	5	6	7	8[1]	9	10	11	14	16	15										
-SEP	A	FALKIRK	2,970	2-0	1	2	3	4	5	6	7[1]	8	9	10	11[1]	14			16	15								
-SEP	H	AYR UNITED	2,911	2-2	1	2		3	5	6	7	8	9[2]	10	11	4		14			15	13						
-SEP	A	RAITH ROVERS	2,292	7-1	1	2	3		5	4	7		9[1]	13	11[3]	14		6	16[1]	10[1]	8[1]							
-OCT	A	CLYDE	1,056	2-2	1	2	3		5	6	7[1]		9	4	11	14		15		16	10	8[1]						
-OCT	H	ST. JOHNSTONE	3,195	0-3	1	2	3	13	5	6	7	8	9		11		15			16	10	4						
-OCT	H	QUEEN OF THE SOUTH	2,962	1-0	1	2		4	5	6	7	8		10	11	13	16		3[1]	9		14						
-NOV	A	BRECHIN CITY	564	2-4	1	2		4	5	6	7	8	14	10	11	13			3	9[2]	15							
-NOV	H	FALKIRK	3,206	1-2	1	2	3		5	6	7	8	9	10[1]	15	4	13			11	16							
-NOV	A	INVERNESS CAL TH	3,523	3-3	1	2	3		5	6		8	16	10	11[1]		14		4	9[1]	15[1]	7						
-NOV	H	RAITH ROVERS	2,803	3-2	1	2	13		5	8	7		16	3	11[2]	14	10[1]		6	9		4						
-NOV	A	AYR UNITED	977	3-1	1	2			6	7[2]	8		3	11	14	10	15	5	9	16	4[1]							
-DEC	A	ST. JOHNSTONE	2,478	1-1	1	2		5	6	7	8		3	11		16	10[1]		9		4	12						
-DEC	H	CLYDE	2,721	0-1	2			5	6	7	8		3	15	14	11	10		9	16	4							
-DEC	H	BRECHIN CITY	2,545	2-1	4			5	14	7	8	9[1]	3		11			6	16	10[1]	15		1	2				
-DEC	A	ST. MIRREN	3,550	1-1	2			5	13	7[1]	8	9	3	15	11		6	16	10		1	4						
-JAN	H	INVERNESS CAL TH	6,020	1-0	2			4	7	8	9	3	11		15[1]		5	16	10	14	1	6						
-JAN	A	FALKIRK	2,482	0-2	2			4	7	8		3	11	14	16	9	5		15	10	1	6						
-JAN	H	AYR UNITED	2,732	1-1	2			5	4	7	8		3	11		16	15		9[1]	10	14	1	6					
-FEB	A	RAITH ROVERS	1,562	0-0	2	3		5	10	7	8		15	13	11	9	4	16			1	6						
-FEB	A	CLYDE	1,139	0-1	2	3		5	4	7	8	16	11				9	15	10		1	12	6					
-FEB	H	ST. JOHNSTONE	3,050	2-0	2	3		4	7	8	9[1]	15[1]			16	10	11	14	1	5	6							
-MAR	A	QUEEN OF THE SOUTH	2,047	1-1	2	3		4	7	8	9	15		16	11	10[1]	14	1	5	6								
-MAR	H	ST. MIRREN	2,819	1-0	2	3		13	4	7	8	15[1]		9	11	10	14	1	5	6								
-MAR	H	FALKIRK	2,931	1-1	2	3		4	7	8	15	11		16	9[1]	10	14	1	5	6								
-MAR	A	INVERNESS CAL TH	4,019	0-1	2	3		4	7	8	11		15	9	10	14	1	5	6									
-APR	H	RAITH ROVERS	2,414	1-1	2	3	4	13	7	8		9[1]		14	10	11	1	5	6	15								
-APR	A	AYR UNITED	1,535	2-1	2	3		4	7	8	15	14	9[1]		10[1]	11	1	5	6									
-APR	A	ST. JOHNSTONE	2,169	†1-1	2			4	7	8	16	15	14	9	10	11	1	5	6	3								
-APR	H	CLYDE	3,220	0-0	2	3		4	7	8	16	15	14	9	10	11	1	5	6									
-MAY	A	BRECHIN CITY	464	0-1	2			3	7	8	9	11	4	16	14	10	1	5	6	15								
-MAY	H	QUEEN OF THE SOUTH	2,842	1-2	2			3	7	8	16	4	11	9[1]	10	14	1	5	6	15								
-MAY	A	ST. MIRREN	2,291	0-2			4	2	7		16	15	8	11	9	3	10	1	5	6	14							
TOTAL FULL APPEARANCES					16	35	20	8	23	33	35	32	15	18	22	8	6	12	12	16	19	14	20	14	17		1	
TOTAL SUB APPEARANCES							1	1	1	3		11	2	11	15	13	10	2	9	9	11	1		1		4	
TOTAL GOALS SCORED						1	1		5	1	5	2	10		2	5	1	6	5	3							

All bold figures denote goalscorers. † denotes opponent's own goal.

LEADING GOALSCORERS:

SEASON	DIV	GOALS	PLAYER
94-95	T	12	B. Grant
95-96	T	15	C. Milne
96-97	T	22	D. Adams
97-98	T	16	D. Adams
98-99	T	17	S. Ferguson, N. Tarrant
99-00	S	13	G. Shaw
00-01	F	14	A. Bone
01-02	F	14	S. Hislop
02-03	F	6	G. Bayne, S. Ferguson
03-04	F	10	D. Winters

MILESTONES:

YEAR OF FORMATION: 1929
MOST LEAGUE POINTS IN A SEASON:
77 (Third Division – Season 1998/99) (3 Points for a Win)
MOST LEAGUE GOALS SCORED BY A PLAYER IN A SEASON:
Derek Adams (Season 1996/97)
NO. OF GOALS SCORED: 22
RECORD ATTENDANCE:
8,000 (-v- Rangers – Scottish Cup, 28.2.66)
RECORD VICTORY:
13-2 (-v- Fraserburgh – Highland League, 1965)
RECORD DEFEAT:
1-10 (-v- Inverness Thistle – Highland League)

ROSS COUNTY PLAYING KITS SEASON 2004/05

FIRST KIT | SECOND KIT | THIRD KIT

ST. JOHNSTONE
McDiarmid Park, Crieff Road,
Perth, PH1 2SJ

CHAIRMAN
Geoffrey S. Brown

DIRECTORS
Douglas B. McIntyre, A. Stewart M. Duff,
Steve Brown, Steve Park, Charles Gallagher

MANAGING DIRECTOR/SECRETARY
A. Stewart M. Duff

MANAGER
John Connolly

FIRST TEAM COACH
Jim Weir

YOUTH FOOTBALL CO-ORDINATOR
Tommy Campbell

YOUTH COACHES
U19/ Tommy Campbell
U17/ Derek Barron
U15/ Derek Simpson
U14/ Derek Black

COMMUNITY COACH
Atholl Henderson

CLUB DOCTOR
Dr. Alistair McCracken

PHYSIOTHERAPIST
Nick Summersgill

GROUNDSMAN
Chris Smith

STADIUM MANAGER
Jimmy Hogg

**FOOTBALL SAFETY OFFICERS'
ASSOCIATION REPRESENTATIVES**
A. Stewart M. Duff & George Smith
(01738) 459090

SALES EXECUTIVE
Susan Weir

MEDIA LIAISON OFFICER
A. Stewart M. Duff

MATCHDAY PROGRAMME EDITOR
David Low

TELEPHONES
Ground (01738) 459090
Ticket Office (01738) 455000
Fax (01738) 625771
Clubcall (09068) 121559

E-MAIL & INTERNET ADDRESS
anyone@saints.sol.co.uk
www.stjohnstonefc.co.uk

CLUB SHOP
Open Mon-Fri at Main Reception
at Ground. A shop is also open on matchdays
and is situated at Ormond (South) Stand

OFFICIAL SUPPORTERS CLUB
157 Dunkeld Road, Perth
Tel: (01738) 442022

TEAM CAPTAIN
David Hannah

SHIRT SPONSOR
Megabus.com

KIT SUPPLIER
XARA

LIST OF PLAYERS 2004/05

PLAYERS SURNAME	FIRST NAME	MIDDLE NAME	DATE OF BIRTH	PLACE OF BIRTH	DATE SIGNED	HEIGHT FT INS	WEIGHT ST LBS	POSITION ON PITCH	PREVIOUS CLUB
ANDERSON	STEVEN	JAMES STUART	19/12/85	EDINBURGH	25/08/04	5 11	11 4	DEFENDER	DUNDEE UNITED
BATCHELOR	BLAIR		24/03/88	FALKIRK	30/06/04	5 7	10 7	MIDFIELD	ST.JOHNSTONE FORM D U 16
BAXTER	MARK		16/04/85	PERTH	04/07/01	5 7	9 4	DEFENDER	ST. JOHNSTONE FORM S
BERNARD	PAUL	ROBERT JAMES	30/12/72	EDINBURGH	22/07/03	6 0	13 0	MIDFIELD	PLYMOUTH ARGYLE
CUTHBERT	KEVIN	SCOTT	08/09/82	PERTH	21/09/98	5 11	10 6	GOALKEEPER	ST. JOHNSTONE B.C.
DYER	WILLIAM		25/02/87	GLASGOW	29/06/04	5 11	10 0	DEFENDER	RANGERS EAST B.C.
FORSYTH	ROSS	DAVID JAMES	20/11/82	GLASGOW	09/07/99	5 10	11 7	DEFENDER	ST. JOHNSTONE FORM S
FOTHERINGHAM	KEVIN	GEORGE	13/08/75	DUNFERMLINE	25/08/04	5 11	12 4	DEFENDER	CLYDE
FOTHERINGHAM	MARTYN	FRASER	23/03/83	PERTH	09/07/99	5 10	11 6	MIDFIELD	FORFAR B.C.
FRASER	STEPHEN		01/03/85	GLASGOW	02/07/03	5 11	10 0	DEFENDER	ST.JOHNSTONE FORM D U 16
HANNAH	DAVID		04/08/73	COATBRIDGE	12/06/04	5 11.5	11 10	MIDFIELD	ROSS COUNTY
HARDY	LEE		26/11/81	BLACKPOOL	10/06/04	6 0	12 7	MIDFIELD	AYR UNITED
HAUGEN	PETER	MARTIN	28/09/87	EDINBURGH	30/06/04	5 10	12 0	MIDFIELD	ST. JOHNSTONE B.C.
HAY	CHRISTOPHER	DRUMMOND	28/08/74	GLASGOW	29/08/02	5 11	12 6	FORWARD	HUDDERSFIELD TOWN
JACKSON	ANDREW	STEVEN	09/01/88	FALKIRK	08/07/04	5 10	9 7	FORWARD	ST.JOHNSTONE FORM D U 16
McDONALD	PETER	IAN RONALD	17/11/80	GLASGOW	06/07/04	5 9.5	11 8	FORWARD	RANGERS
MAHOOD	ALAN	SCOTT	26/03/73	KILWINNING	31/08/04	5 8	11 5	MIDFIELD	KILMARNOCK
MAXWELL	IAN		02/05/75	GLASGOW	16/05/02	6 3	12 5	DEFENDER	ROSS COUNTY
McCANN	RYAN		21/09/81	BELLSHILL	31/08/04	5 11	11 10	MIDFIELD	HARTLEPOOL UNITED
McCONALOGUE	STEPHEN		16/06/81	GLASGOW	06/07/04	5 9	11 7	FORWARD	CLYDE
McGREGOR	ALLAN	JAMES	31/01/82	EDINBURGH	10/08/04	6 3	13 10	GOALKEEPER	RANGERS
McMANUS	STEVEN		24/04/87	PERTH	02/07/03	5 8	10 7	MID / FWD	ST. JOHNSTONE FORM S
MOON	KEVIN	JOHN	08/06/87	PERTH	30/06/04	5 7	9 0	MIDFIELD	ST. JOHNSTONE FORM S
MOORE	MICHAEL	JORDAN	24/03/81	PAISLEY	08/07/04	6 2	12 7	FORWARD	STRANRAER
RUTKIEWICZ	KEVIN		10/05/80	GLASGOW	02/07/04	6 1	12 7	DEFENDER	ABERDEEN
SHEERIN	PAUL	GEORGE	28/08/74	EDINBURGH	30/07/04	5 10	12 8	MIDFIELD	ABERDEEN
STEVENSON	RYAN	CAIRNS	24/08/84	IRVINE	28/03/02	5 11	13 7	MIDFIELD	CHELSEA
TAIT	JORDAN	ALEXANDER	27/09/79	BERWICK UPON TWEED	29/07/04	5 11	12 0	DEFENDER	AYR UNITED
WEBB	SEAN	MICHAEL	04/01/83	DUNGANNON	05/06/04	6 2	12 7	DEFENDER	ROSS COUNTY
WEIR	JAMES	McINTOSH	15/06/69	MOTHERWELL	10/06/04	6 1	12 5	DEFENDER	HEART OF MIDLOTHIAN

TICKET INFORMATION

SEASON TICKET PRICES

WEST STAND

Executive	£295
Adult	£250
OAP/Juvenile	£175

EAST STAND

Adult	£230
OAP/Juvenile	£80/£40
Parent & Juvenile	£200

LEAGUE ADMISSION PRICES

WEST STAND

Adult	£18
OAP/Juvenile	£10

EAST STAND

Adult	£16
OAP	£5
Juvenile	£4

THE SAINTS' 10 YEAR LEAGUE RECORD

SEASON	DIV	P	W	D	L	F	A	PTS	
1994-95	F	36	14	14	8	59	39	56	
1995-96	F	36	19	8	9	60	36	65	
1996-97	F	36	24	8	4	74	23	80	
1997-98	P	36	13	9	14	38	42	48	
1998-99	SPL	36	15	12	9	39	38	57	
1999-00	SPL	36	10	12	14	36	44	42	
2000-01	SPL	38	9	13	16	40	56	40	
2001-02	SPL	38	5	6	27	24	62	21	
2002-03	F	36	20	7	9	49	29	67	
2003-04	F	36	15	12	9	59	45	57	

SEASON STATS 2003/04

DATE	VENUE	OPPONENTS	ATT	RES	CUTHBERT K.	ROBERTSON J.	FORSYTH R.	DONNELLY S.	DODS D.	MAXWELL I.	PARKER K.	REILLY M.	PAATELAINEN M-M.	FOTHERINGHAM M.	BERNARD P.	STEVENSON R.	BAXTER M.	MALONE E.	LOVERING P.	FERRY M.	HAY C.	ROBERTSON M.	McLAUGHLIN B.	McDONALD P.	NELSON C.	McQUILKEN J.	VATA R.	WEIR J.	TAYLOR S.	FRASER S.
-AUG	H	QUEEN OF THE SOUTH	2,939	4-1	1	2	3	4	5	6	7²	8	9	10¹	11		14	16	17¹											
-AUG	A	ST. MIRREN	3,613	1-1	1	2		4	5	6	7¹	8	9	14	10	11	15					3								
-AUG	H	INVERNESS CAL TH	3,031	1-2	1	2		4	5	6	7¹		9		10		14	11	3	8	16									
-AUG	H	BRECHIN CITY	2,219	3-1	1	2	12	10	5¹	6	7	8	9²		4		3	11				14	17							
-SEP	A	CLYDE	1,468	0-2	1	2		10	5	6	7	8	9		4		3	17				11	14							
-SEP	H	RAITH ROVERS	2,983	0-1	1	2		10	5	6	7	8	9		4		17	3				11	14							
-SEP	A	FALKIRK	3,887	3-0	1	2	3	10	5	6	14	8	9¹		4			16				11	7²							
-OCT	H	AYR UNITED	1,906	1-1	1	2	3	10	5	6	14	8	9		4		11					4	7¹							
-OCT	A	ROSS COUNTY	3,195	3-0	1	2	3	10	5	6	14	8	9³		4						16	11	12	7						
-OCT	H	ST. MIRREN	2,677	1-0	1	2	3	10	5	6	14	8	9		4							11¹	12	7						
-NOV	A	QUEEN OF THE SOUTH	3,159	1-1	1	2	3	10	5	6	7		9		4						8	11¹	14							
-NOV	H	CLYDE	2,474	3-0	1	2	3	10²	5	6	14		9	17	4						12	8	11	7¹						
-NOV	A	BRECHIN CITY	1,434	1-0	1	2	3	10	5	6			9		4		16	17			12	8	11	7¹						
-NOV	A	FALKIRK	4,185	0-4	1	2	3	10	5	6	14		9		4	8	16				12		11	7						
-NOV	A	RAITH ROVERS	1,996	4-1	1	2	3	10					9¹		4	5	8			7¹			11¹	14¹						
-DEC	H	ROSS COUNTY	2,478	1-1	1	2	3	10	5	6	14		9¹		4	8					7		11	12						
-DEC	A	AYR UNITED	1,203	1-1	1	2	3	10	5	6			9		4¹	8					12		11	7						
-DEC	H	QUEEN OF THE SOUTH	1,999	†2-2		2	3	10	5	6	14		9¹	16	4	8				12			11	7	1					
-DEC	A	INVERNESS CAL TH	2,949	0-1		2		10	5	6	14	12	9		4	8			3		16		11	7	1					
-JAN	H	BRECHIN CITY	2,171	2-2		2			4	5	6	7	8	9¹	16			3			12		11	10¹	1					
-JAN	H	RAITH ROVERS	2,576	5-2		2	16			6		8	9								7²		11¹	17¹	1	3	4	5	10¹	
-FEB	H	AYR UNITED	2,067	3-0		2	14	9¹		6¹	16	8				17				7			11		1	3¹	4	5	10	
-FEB	A	ROSS COUNTY	3,050	0-2				9	12	6	17	8	14		10	2				7			11		1	3	4	5		
-MAR	H	CLYDE	1,518	3-2	1	2		7²		6	8	9	10¹					14								3	4	5		
-MAR	A	FALKIRK	2,799	1-0	1	2		7				9			10								14¹			3	4	5		
--MAR	H	INVERNESS CAL TH	2,913	3-2	1	2		7¹		6	10¹	8	9¹			17		14								3	4	5		
-MAR	A	ST. MIRREN	2,180	1-1	1	2¹		7		6	10	8	9			16		14								3	4	5		
-MAR	H	CLYDE	3,512	1-1	1	2	17	7		6	16¹	8	9	10				14								3	4	5		
-MAR	A	BRECHIN CITY	822	2-0	1			7	5	6	8	9				2¹					11¹	14				3	4			10
-APR	H	FALKIRK	2,535	2-1	1		12	7	5	6	16	8				14				2	9²		11			3	4			10
-APR	A	RAITH ROVERS	2,676	1-1	1			7¹	5	6	16	8	9								2		11	14		3	4			10
²-APR	A	ROSS COUNTY	2,169	1-1	1		3	7	5	6	16	8	14		4	12					9¹		11			2				10
-APR	A	AYR UNITED	1,119	1-1	1			7	5	6	16	8								2	9¹		14	10		3	4	11		
-MAY	H	QUEEN OF THE SOUTH	1,629	1-1	1		3	10¹				9	8			7	14	2								4	5	11	6		
-MAY	H	ST. MIRREN	2,363	1-3	1		3	10	14	6	9¹	8			4		2						11			7	5		16	
-MAY	A	INVERNESS CAL TH	6,092	1-3		4	10				9¹	17		8		7	2	14			12		11		1	3		5		6
TOTAL FULL APPEARANCES					29	27	18	35	24	33	13	25	28	3	24	8	11	5	4	1	10	8	23	11	7	15	15	9	8	2
TOTAL SUB APPEARANCES						4	1	2			19	2	5	4	1		5	6	5	1			14	1		7	4			1
TOTAL GOALS SCORED						1		8	1	1	8		11	1	2			1			1	9	1	3	8		1		1

Bold figures denote goalscorers. † denotes opponent's own goal.

LEADING GOALSCORERS:

SEASON	DIV	GOALS	PLAYER
94-95	F	19	G. O'Boyle
95-96	F	21	G. O'Boyle
96-97	F	19	R. Grant
97-98	P	10	G. O'Boyle
98-99	SPL	4	G. Bollan, R. Grant, M. Simao
99-00	SPL	10	N. Lowndes
00-01	SPL	9	K. Parker
01-02	SPL	5	P. Hartley
02-03	F	9	C. Hay
03-04	F	11	M-M. Paatelainen

MILESTONES:

YEAR OF FORMATION: 1884
MOST CAPPED PLAYER: Nick Dasovic (Canada)
NO. OF CAPS: 26
MOST LEAGUE POINTS IN A SEASON:
59 (Second Division – Season 1987/88) (2 Points for a Win)
80 (First Division – Season 1996/97) (3 Points for a Win)
MOST LEAGUE GOALS SCORED BY A PLAYER IN A SEASON:
Jimmy Benson (Season 1931/32)
NO. OF GOALS SCORED: 38
RECORD ATTENDANCE:
29,972 (-v- Dundee 10.2.1951 at Muirton Park)
10,545 (-v- Dundee – SPL, 23.05.1999 at McDiarmid Park)
RECORD VICTORY: 8-1 (-v- Partick Thistle – League Cup, 16.8.1969)
RECORD DEFEAT: 1-10 (-v- Third Lanark – Scottish Cup, 24.1.1903)

ST. JOHNSTONE PLAYING KITS SEASON 2004/05

FIRST KIT   SECOND KIT   THIRD KIT

LIST OF PLAYERS 2004/05

PLAYERS SURNAME	FIRST NAME	MIDDLE NAME	DATE OF BIRTH	PLACE OF BIRTH	DATE SIGNED	HEIGHT FT INS	WEIGHT ST LBS	POSITION ON PITCH	PREVIOUS CLUB
ALLEN	ROSS		21/04/88	GLASGOW	08/09/04	5 9	8 7	FORWARD	ST. MIRREN FORM D UNDER 15
ANDERSON	STEPHEN		24/03/87	PAISLEY	12/06/04	5 10	12 11	FORWARD	LINWOOD RANGERS B.C.
BAIRD	ALAN		29/01/89	IRVINE	08/09/04	5 8.5	8 6	FORWARD	ST. MIRREN FORM D UNDER 15
BAIRD	JOHN	DAVID	22/08/85	RUTHERGLEN	23/07/04	5 7	10 5	FORWARD	CLYDE
BAIRD	STEPHEN		21/01/88	IRVINE	19/08/04	5 10	9 0	MIDFIELD	ST. MIRREN FORM D UNDER 15
BROADFOOT	KIRK		08/08/84	IRVINE	01/07/02	6 2	14 1	DEFENDER	HIBERNIAN
COPLAND	KEVIN		04/01/87	PAISLEY	12/06/04	5 5	10 3	DEFENDER	ST. MIRREN FORM D UNDER 15
CRILLY	MARK	PATRICK	23/05/80	GLASGOW	28/05/03	5 11	11 7	MIDFIELD	STIRLING ALBION
DEMPSIE	MARK	WILLIAM	19/10/80	BELLSHILL	22/01/03	6 0	12 10	DEFENDER	HIBERNIAN
DOWNIE	SCOTT		15/02/89	BELLSHILL	08/09/04	5 9	8 3	MIDFIELD	ST. MIRREN FORM D UNDER 15
ELLIS	LAURENCE		07/11/79	EDINBURGH	02/06/03	5 11	10 7	DEFENDER	RAITH ROVERS
FULTON	MICHAEL	GRAHAM	26/06/88	IRVINE	19/08/04	5 10	9 2	FORWARD	ST. MIRREN FORM D UNDER 16
GEMMILL	SCOTT		09/06/87	RUTHERGLEN	17/07/03	5 10	10 0	FORWARD	ST. MIRREN FORM D UNDER 16
GILLESPIE	GARY		10/04/87	PAISLEY	17/07/03	5 10	11 4	MIDFIELD	ST. MIRREN FORM D UNDER 16
GILLIES	RICHARD	CHARLES	24/08/76	GLASGOW	23/06/00	5 10	12 2	FORWARD	ABERDEEN
GORDON	BRIAN	ANDREW PETER	29/01/86	GLASGOW	31/08/02	6 1	11 8	DEFENDER	ST. MIRREN B.C.
HARKNESS	MATTHEW		23/03/87	GLASGOW	12/06/04	5 10	10 4	DEFENDER	ST MIRREN FORM S
HINCHCLIFFE	CRAIG	PETER	05/05/72	GLASGOW	26/06/03	5 11	12 6	GOALKEEPER	ARBROATH
LAPPIN	SIMON		25/01/83	GLASGOW	07/10/99	5 11	10 0	MIDFIELD	ST. MIRREN B.C.
LINDSAY	MICHAEL	JAMES	15/06/89	IRVINE	26/08/04	5 9	9 9	DEFENDER	ST. MIRREN FORM D UNDER 16
LOVE	ANDREW	ROBERT JOHN	16/05/88	DUMBARTON	19/08/04	5 7	9 5	MIDFIELD	ST. MIRREN FORM D UNDER 16
MCPHERSON	ANGUS	IAN	11/10/68	GLASGOW	10/07/03	5 10	11 6	DEFENDER	DUNFERMLINE ATHLETIC
MARINI	SANTINO	DONATO	26/04/87	BELLSHILL	12/06/04	5 11	9 0	FORWARD	ST. MIRREN FORM D UNDER 16
MARR	CRAIG	ANDREW	23/03/88	PAISLEY	19/08/04	5 10	11 2	FORWARD	ST. MIRREN FORM D UNDER 16
MARTIN	DAVID		02/02/87	PAISLEY	18/07/03	5 9	10 7	DEFENDER	RANGERS
MCAUSLAND	MARC		13/08/88	PAISLEY	19/08/04	6 0	10 3	DEFENDER	ST. MIRREN FORM S
MCCAY	RYAN	JOHN JAMES	04/05/86	PAISLEY	31/08/02	5 8	10 8	MIDFIELD	ST. MIRREN FORM S
MCCOLGAN	DANIEL		11/05/89	IRVINE	26/08/04	5 8	9 0	GOALKEEPER	ST. MIRREN FORM D UNDER 16
MCFARLANE	SCOTT		30/07/87	PAISLEY	01/06/04	5 6	9 0	FORWARD	ST. MIRREN FORM D UNDER 16
MCGINTY	BRIAN		10/12/76	EAST KILBRIDE	31/10/01	6 1	12 7	FORWARD	CUMNOCK JUNIORS
MCGOWNE	KEVIN		16/12/69	KILMARNOCK	10/07/03	6 1	13 0	DEFENDER	PARTICK THISTLE
MCGREGOR	CALUM		15/01/89	IRVINE	08/09/04	5 10	9 3	DEFENDER	ST. MIRREN FORM D UNDER 16
MCGREGOR	JAKE	JOHN	05/05/88	EDINBURGH	19/08/04	5 6	9 7	MIDFIELD	ST. MIRREN FORM D UNDER 16
MCKENNA	DAVID		19/09/86	PAISLEY	31/03/03	5 8	11 4	FORWARD	ST. MIRREN FORM D UNDER 16
MCLACHLAN	SHAUN	PATRICK	04/01/89	PAISLEY	19/08/04	5 8	9 0	FORWARD	ST. MIRREN FORM D UNDER 16
MCMAHON	CRAIG	THOMAS	01/10/88	PAISLEY	26/08/04	5 10	10 0	GOALKEEPER	ST. MIRREN FORM D UNDER 16
MCMENAMIN	CHRISTOPHER		02/01/89	GLASGOW	19/08/04	5 11	11 0	MIDFIELD	ST. MIRREN FORM D UNDER 15
MCWILLIAM	GRAHAM		07/02/86	PAISLEY	31/08/02	6 2	13 3	DEFENDER	ST. MIRREN FORM D UNDER 16
MILLEN	ANDREW	FRANK	10/06/65	GLASGOW	03/01/04	5 11	11 4	DEFENDER	CLYDE
MILNE	IAN	MCGARRY	09/01/87	PAISLEY	12/06/04	5 8	8 8	DEFENDER	ST. MIRREN FORM D UNDER 16
MOLLOY	CRAIG		26/04/86	GREENOCK	31/08/02	5 7	10 3	MIDFIELD	ST. MIRREN FORM D UNDER 16
MUIR	ALAN		05/11/86	PAISLEY	31/03/03	5 9	9 9	MIDFIELD	ST. MIRREN FORM D UNDER 16
MURRAY	HUGH		08/01/79	BELLSHILL	23/08/02	5 10	11 9	MIDFIELD	MANSFIELD TOWN
O'NEIL	JOHN	JOSEPH	03/01/74	BELLSHILL	28/05/03	5 11	12 0	MIDFIELD	QUEEN OF THE SOUTH
PAATELAINEN	MIKA-MATTI	PETTERI	03/02/67	HELSINKI	07/07/04	6 0	14 0	FORWARD	ST. JOHNSTONE
REILLY	MARK	FRANCIS	30/03/69	BELLSHILL	10/06/04	5 8	11 8	MIDFIELD	ST. JOHNSTONE
ROBINSON	ROBERT		11/04/88	ALEXANDRIA	08/09/04	5 9	12 0	DEFENDER	ST. MIRREN FORM D UNDER 16
RUSSELL	ALLAN	JOHN	13/12/80	GLASGOW	08/08/03	6 0	12 1	MIDFIELD	HAMILTON ACADEMICAL
SMITH	GRAEME		19/05/86	PAISLEY	19/08/04	5 10	10 3	MIDFIELD	ST. MIRREN FORM D UNDER 16
SMITH	WALLACE	CHRISTOPHER	05/03/86	GLASGOW	03/06/04	6 3	13 0	GOALKEEPER	ST. MIRREN FORM D UNDER 16
VAN ZANTEN	DAVID		08/05/82	DUBLIN	28/07/03	5 10	11 0	DEFENDER	CELTIC
WARDROP	GRAEME		02/01/87	GLASGOW	12/06/04	5 11	10 7	GOALKEEPER	ST. MIRREN FORM D UNDER 16
WHITE	JOHN	JAMES	07/08/87	PAISLEY	12/06/04	5 10	11 0	MIDFIELD	ST. MIRREN FORM D UNDER 16
WOODS	STEPHEN	GERARD	23/02/70	GLASGOW	02/07/03	6 2	13 5	GOALKEEPER	MOTHERWELL

TICKET INFORMATION

SEASON TICKET PRICES

MAIN STAND/LOWER ENCLOSURE
Adult £210
Juvenile/OAP £130

**LDV NORTH STAND/
REID KERR COLLEGE FAMILY STAND**
Adult £190
OAP £120
Juvenile £70

LEAGUE ADMISSION PRICES

MAIN STAND
Adult £13
Juvenile/OAP £7

LOWER ENCLOSURE
Adult £13
Juvenile/OAP £7

LDV NORTH STAND
Adult £12
Juvenile/OAP £7
1 Parent & 1 Juvenile £16

REID KERR COLLEGE FAMILY STAND
Adult £12
Juvenile/OAP £7
1 Parent & 1 Juvenile £16

THE BUDDIES' 10 YEAR LEAGUE RECORD

SEASON	DIV	P	W	D	L	F	A	PTS
1994-95	F	36	8	12	16	34	50	36
1995-96	F	36	13	8	15	46	51	47
1996-97	F	36	17	7	12	48	41	58
1997-98	F	36	11	8	17	41	53	41
1998-99	F	36	14	10	12	42	43	52
1999-00	F	36	23	7	6	75	39	76
2000-01	SPL	38	8	6	24	32	72	30
2001-02	F	36	11	12	13	43	53	45
2002-03	F	36	9	10	17	42	71	37
2003-04	F	36	9	14	13	39	46	41

SEASON STATS 2003/04

DATE	VENUE	OPPONENTS	ATT	RES	HINCHCLIFFE C.	McPHERSON A.	ELLIS L.	McGOWNE K.	BROADFOOT K.	CRILLY M.	GILLIES R.	O'NEIL J.	McGINTY B.	DUNN R.	LAPPIN S.	VAN ZANTEN D.	RUSSELL A.	GEMMILL S.	TWADDLE K.	DEMPSIE M.	LAVETY B.	MUIR A.	WALKER S.	MURRAY H.	ANNAND E.	McKNIGHT P.	McKENNA D.	MILLEN A.	WOODS S.	McGRORTY C.	MOLLOY C.	McCAY R.
9-AUG	A	RAITH ROVERS	3,090	1-1	1	2	3	4	5	6	7^1	8	9	10	11	12	14			15												
16-AUG	H	ST. JOHNSTONE	3,613	1-1	1	2	3	5	4	6	7	8^1		10	11	12	9															
23-AUG	A	ROSS COUNTY	3,053	0-2	1	5	3	4	8	6	7	10			11	2	9		15	12												
30-AUG	H	CLYDE	3,010	2-1	1	5	3	4		6	7	8		10	11	2	9^2		12	14	15											
13-SEP	A	BRECHIN CITY	956	1-1	1		3	5	4	11	7^1	8			2		9			10			6	12	14							
20-SEP	H	QUEEN OF THE SOUTH	2,681	1-2	1		3	5	4	11	7^1	8		12		2	9		14	10			6	15								
27-SEP	A	INVERNESS CAL TH	1,896	0-2	1	4	3	5	8		7					2	9		11	15	14		6	10	12							
4-OCT	H	FALKIRK	3,105	0-0	1	4	3	5	8	11	7			10		2	14		15	12			6	9								
18-OCT	A	AYR UNITED	2,447	2-0	1	4	3	5	8^2		7	16	10	15		2							6	9	12							
25-OCT	H	ST. JOHNSTONE	2,677	0-1	1	4	3	5		11	7	8	10	15		2	9		12				6	16								
1-NOV	H	RAITH ROVERS	3,005	2-1	1	4	3	5	6	11	7^1	8^1	10	14		2	9		15	12												
8-NOV	H	BRECHIN CITY	2,801	0-0	1		3	5	6	11	7	8	10	14		2	9		4	12				16								
14-NOV	A	CLYDE	1,811	0-2	1		3	5	6	11	7	8	10	15		2	9		4	12			14									
22-NOV	H	INVERNESS CAL TH	2,204	0-4	1		3	5	6	15	12	8	16	7	11	2	9		4				10									
3-DEC	A	QUEEN OF THE SOUTH	2,473	2-1	1		3	5	6		7^1		9	12	11	2	10^1		4				8			15						
6-DEC	H	AYR UNITED	2,567	3-2	1		3	5	6		7^2		9	12	11^1	2	10		4	14			8			15						
13-DEC	A	FALKIRK	2,581	0-0	1		3		5		8		9	7	11	2			4	10			6			12						
27-DEC	H	ROSS COUNTY	3,550	1-1	1		3	5		12	7^1	14	9	10	11	2	15		6				8				4					
3-JAN	H	CLYDE	3,355	2-3			3	5	15	12	7	14	9	10^1	11	2			6				8				4^1	1			
17-JAN	A	BRECHIN CITY	878	0-2			5	15	14	7	10			11		2			6	9			8				16	4	1	3		
24-JAN	H	QUEEN OF THE SOUTH	2,540	3-1			5	14		7	10^2	9^1	15	11		2			6				8				4	1	3			
31-JAN	A	INVERNESS CAL TH	1,913	1-1			5	16		7	10	9	14	11^1		2			6				8				4	1	3			
14-FEB	H	FALKIRK	2,934	1-1			5			7	10	9	12	11	2	15			6				8^1				4	1	3			
21-FEB	A	AYR UNITED	2,252	0-2			5	14		7	10	9	12	11	2	15			6				8				4	1	3			
6-MAR	A	RAITH ROVERS	1,882	0-2			5			7	16	10	9	11	2	9			6				8			15	4	1	3			
13-MAR	A	ROSS COUNTY	2,819	0-1			5	8			15	10	9	12	11	2	14			6			7				4	1	3			
16-MAR	H	ST. JOHNSTONE	2,180	1-1	1			5		14	7	10	9		11	2	15			6			8^1				4	1	3			
20-MAR	H	BRECHIN CITY	2,221	†3-3	1		12	5	11^1	7	10		9^1			2	16			6			8				14	4		3		
27-MAR	A	CLYDE	1,786	1-2	1		5	6		10	7	9	12		11^1	2	15^1			8				4						3		
3-APR	H	INVERNESS CAL TH	2,272	0-0	1		5	6		10	7		12	15	11	2	9			8	16						4		3			
10-APR	A	QUEEN OF THE SOUTH	2,211	0-1	1	15	5	6		7	12	10		9	11	2	14			8							4		3			
17-APR	H	AYR UNITED	3,211	4-1	1		5	3			7	16	12^1		11^1	2^2	10			6	15		8	9			4					
24-APR	A	FALKIRK	2,386	0-1	1		5	3			7	14	12	16	11	2				6			8	9			4					
1-MAY	H	RAITH ROVERS	2,372	1-1	1		14	5	3^1		7		10			2				6			8	9			12	4			15	
8-MAY	A	ST. JOHNSTONE	2,363	3-1	1		3	5		6	7	10	9^3		11	2				16			8				14	4			15	
15-MAY	H	ROSS COUNTY	2,291	2-0	1		3	5^1		6	7	10	9^1		14	12				16			8	4							2	11
TOTAL FULL APPEARANCES					28	9	21	29	28	18	33	23	23	11	23	32	17		1	20	4		1	27	6		1	19	8	12	1	1
TOTAL SUB APPEARANCES						2	1	3	7	2	3	6	5	16	1	3	9		3	2	3		9	3		3	3	4	8		1	1
TOTAL GOALS SCORED						1	3	1	8	4	6	2	4	2	4					2				1							

All bold figures denote goalscorers. † denotes opponent's own goal.

LEADING GOALSCORERS:

SEASON	DIV	GOALS	PLAYER
94-95	F	7	B. Lavety
95-96	F	11	B. Lavety
96-97	F	15	M. Yardley
97-98	F	9	J. Mendes
98-99	F	11	M. Yardley
99-00	F	19	M. Yardley
00-01	SPL	10	R. Gillies
01-02	F	6	R. Gillies, B. McGinty
02-03	F	12	M. Cameron
03-04	F	8	R. Gillies

MILESTONES:

YEAR OF FORMATION: 1877
MOST CAPPED PLAYERS: Iain Munro & Billy Thomson
NO. OF CAPS: 7
MOST LEAGUE POINTS IN A SEASON:
62 (Division 2 – Season 1967/68) (2 Points for a Win)
76 (First Division – Season 1999/2000) (3 Points for a Win)
MOST LEAGUE GOALS SCORED BY A PLAYER IN A SEASON:
Dunky Walker (Season 1921/22)
NO. OF GOALS SCORED: 45
RECORD ATTENDANCE: 47,438 (-v- Celtic 7.3.1925)
RECORD VICTORY: 15-0 (-v- Glasgow University – Scottish Cup, 30.1.60)
RECORD DEFEAT: 0-9 (-v- Rangers – Division 1, 4.12.1897)

ST. MIRREN PLAYING KITS SEASON 2004/05

FIRST KIT · SECOND KIT · THIRD KIT

Airdrie United: Excelsior Stadium

Excelsior Stadium can be reached by the following routes:
TRAINS: From Glasgow Queen Street to Airdrie there is a train every 15 minutes. From the station beyond Airdrie, Drumgelloch, there is a train every 30 minutes, then a 10 minute walk to the stadium.
BUSES: Nos 260 or 15 from Airdrie Town Centre.
CARS: From Glasgow or Edinburgh leave the M8 at Newhouse junction (A73) and the stadium is 2½ miles north of Newhouse. From Cumbernauld, the stadium is 6 miles south on the A73.

CAPACITY: 10,170 (All Seated)
PITCH DIMENSIONS: 115 yds x 74 yds
FACILITIES FOR DISABLED SUPPORTERS:
Disabled facilities are provided in the North, East & South Stands.

Clyde: Broadwood Stadium

The following routes may be used to reach Broadwood Stadium:
BUSES: From Buchanan Street Bus Station in Glasgow, fans should board Bus No. 36A (Glasgow to Westfield) or X3.
TRAINS: There are regular trains from Queen Street Station, Glasgow to Croy Station. The Stadium is a 15 minute walk from here.
CARS: From Glasgow City Centre, fans should take the Stepps By-Pass joining the A80 towards Stirling. Take Broadwood turn-off to Stadium.

CAPACITY: 8,006 (All Seated)
PITCH DIMENSIONS: 112 yds x 76 yds
FACILITIES FOR DISABLED SUPPORTERS:
Facilities available in OKI, West and South Stands.

Falkirk: The Falkirk Stadium

The Falkirk Stadium can be reached by the following routes.
TRAINS: Take the main Edinburgh-Glasgow service and alight at Grahamston Station. The stadium is approximately 20 minutes walk from here. Alternatively, the bus route from the town centre is the Falkirk to Grangemouth route which is approximately one mile from the stadium.
BUSES: The following buses run from Callendar Riggs Bus Station which is in the centre of the town. Bus numbers 3 & 4 (destination Grangemouth) and also numbers 6 and 7 (destination Bo'ness) stop outside the stadium. The Bus Station is appox. 5 min's from Grahamston Railway Station.
CARS: Cars from Glasgow and the west should take the M80 then the M876 before joining the M9. Leave the M9 at the exit for B.P. Grangemouth then turn right at end of the slip road. Follow the road for approximately 200 yards to the Earlsgate roundabout before going under the motorway at the roundabout and then following the Grangemouth to Falkirk Road. The Falkirk Stadium is on the left hand side. Cars travelling from Edinburgh and the east should leave the M9 at Junction 5 and proceed along the road to Falkirk for about 1 mile and the stadium is on your right hand side. There are Car Parking facilities available for both Home and Away fans at the stadium which can hold approximately 500 cars. Supporters will be directed to the appropriate parking areas by the police and stewards on duty.

CAPACITY: 4,851 (All Seated)
PITCH DIMENSIONS: 115 yds x 74 yds
FACILITIES FOR DISABLED SUPPORTERS:
Accommodation for disabled in new Stand. Toilet facilities also provided.

Hamilton Academical: New Douglas Park

The following routes may be used to reach New Douglas Park:
TRAINS: Hamilton West Station is situated adjacent to the ground. Normally there are 2 trains per hour to Glasgow, Lanark (change at Motherwell) and Motherwell. A path connects the station to the ground.
BUSES: Buses from across Lanarkshire and Glasgow pass close to the ground. Buses from across Scotland and the UK call at Hamilton Bus Station 1mile away.
CARS: Exit M74 at Junction 5 (A725 Coatbridge – East Kilbride Road goes through this interchange as well). Follow signs for Hamilton Racecourse and Football Traffic.Turn right at lights at Racecourse and first right again into New Park Street. Stadium is on the left.

CAPACITY: 5,396 (All Seated)
PITCH DIMENSIONS: 115 yds x 75 yds
FACILITIES FOR DISABLED SUPPORTERS:
Available trackside and in front row of Main (West) Stand.

Partick Thistle: Firhill Stadium

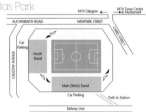

The following routes may be used to reach Firhill Stadium:
TRAINS: The nearest railway stations are Glasgow Queen Street and Glasgow Central and buses from the centre of the city pass within 100 yards of the ground.
BUSES: Buses from the city centre all pass near the ground: No's. 40, 61, 109 and 119 and the frequency of the buses is just under 10 minutes from Hope Street.
CARS: Street parking near the ground is somewhat limited. Supporters Buses can park in Panmure Street under Police direction.
UNDERGROUND: The nearest Strathclyde PTE Underground station is St.George's Cross and supporters walking from here should pass through Cromwell Street into Maryhill Road and walk up this road as far as Firhill Street. The ground is on the right. The Kelvinbridge Underground Station is also not far from the ground and supporters from here should walk along Great Western Road as far as Napiershall Street and then follow this into Maryhill Road.

CAPACITY: 13,141; Seated 10,921; Standing 2,220
PITCH DIMENSIONS: 115 yds x 75 yds
FACILITIES FOR DISABLED SUPPORTERS:
Covered places are available for 17 supporters in front of the Main Stand (North area). A total of 14 spaces are available in front of the North Stand for visiting disabled fans. Prior arrangement must be made with the Secretary and a ticket obtained.

Queen of the south: Palmerston Park

Palmerston Park can be reached by the following routes:

TRAINS: There is a reasonable service to Dumfries Station from Glasgow on Saturdays, but the service is more limited in midweek. The station is about ³/₄ mile from the ground.

BUSES: Buses from Glasgow, Edinburgh, Ayr and Stranraer all pass within a short distance of the park.

CARS: The car park may be reached from Portland Drive or King Street and has a capacity for approximately 174 cars. Please note that the car park is closed 30 minutes prior to kick-off.

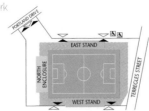

CAPACITY: 6,412; Seated 3,509, Standing 2,903
PITCH DIMENSIONS: 112 yds x 73 yds
FACILITIES FOR DISABLED SUPPORTERS: Situated in East Stand including toilets.

Raith Rovers: Stark's Park

The following routes may be used to reach Stark's Park:

TRAINS: Kirkcaldy railway station is served by trains from Dundee, Edinburgh and Glasgow (via Edinburgh) and the ground is within 10–15 minutes walking distance of the station.

BUSES: The main bus station in Kirkcaldy is also within 15 minutes walking distance of the ground, but the Edinburgh, Dunfermline and Leven services pass close by the park.

CARS: Car parking is available in the Esplanade, which is on the south side of the ground and in Beveridge Park, which is on the north side of the ground. Follow signs for Football traffic.

CAPACITY: 8,473 (All Seated)
PITCH DIMENSIONS: 113 yds x 70 yds
FACILITIES FOR DISABLED SUPPORTERS: By prior arrangement with Disability Liaison Officer or General Manager.
North Stand – Away Supporters. South Stand – Home Supporters. Limited disabled parking immediately adjacent to North Stand. By prior arrangement, Matchday Hospitality can be arranged for disabled supporters.

Ross County: Victoria Park Stadium

The following routes may be used to reach Victoria Park Stadium:

TRAINS: The nearest mainline station is Inverness and fans travelling from the south should alight and board a train that takes them direct to Dingwall Station.

BUSES: Regular buses on a daily basis from Glasgow, Edinburgh and Perth.

CARS: The major trunk roads, A9 and A96, connect Dingwall with the North, the South and the East.

CAPACITY: 6,900, Seated 3,000, Standing 3,900
PITCH DIMENSIONS: 115 yds x 75 yds
FACILITIES FOR DISABLED SUPPORTERS: Areas in Main Stand and Terracing. Toilet facilities are also available.

St. Johnstone: McDiarmid Park

The following routes can be used to reach McDiarmid Park:

TRAINS: Perth Station is well served by trains from all parts of the country. The station is about 40 minutes walk from the park.

BUSES: Local services nos. 1 and 2 pass near the ground. Both leave from Mill Street in the town centre.

CARS: The car park at the park holds 1,500 cars and 100 coaches. Vehicles should follow signs A9 to Inverness on Perth City by-pass, then follow "Football Stadium" signs at Inveralmond Roundabout South onto slip road adjacent to McDiarmid Park. Vehicle charges are £2.00 for cars and no charge for coaches.

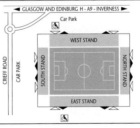

CAPACITY: 10,723 (All Seated)
PITCH DIMENSIONS: 115 yds x 74 yds
FACILITIES FOR DISABLED SUPPORTERS: Entrance via south end of West Stand and south end of East Stand. Visiting disabled fans should contact the club in advance. Headphones available in West and North Stands for blind and partially sighted supporters.

St. Mirren: St. Mirren Park

St. Mirren Park can be reached by the following routes:

TRAINS: There is a frequent train service from Glasgow Central Station and all coastal routes pass through Gilmour Street. The ground is about half a mile from the station.

BUSES: All SMT coastal services, plus buses to Johnstone and Kilbarchan, pass within 300 yards of the ground.

CARS: The only facilities for car parking are in the streets surrounding the ground.

CAPACITY: 10,752: (All Seated)
PITCH DIMENSIONS: 112 yds x 73 yds
FACILITIES FOR DISABLED SUPPORTERS: Full wheelchair facilities available for visiting supporters in the Caledonia Stand.

ALLOA ATHLETIC
Recreation Park,
Clackmannan Road, Alloa, FK10 1RY
CHAIRMAN
David R. Murray
VICE-CHAIRMAN
Ian Henderson
DIRECTORS
Ewen G. Cameron,
Robert F. Hopkins & Patrick Lawlor
HONORARY PRESIDENT
George Ormiston
HONORARY DIRECTOR
Ronald J. Todd
SECRETARY
Ewen G. Cameron
OFFICE ADMINISTRATOR
Jean Davison
MANAGER
Tom Hendrie
FIRST TEAM COACH
Gareth Evans
HEAD OF YOUTH DEVELOPMENT
Hugh McCann
YOUTH CO-ORDINATOR
Robert Wilson
YOUTH TEAM COACHES
Hugh McCann (U19)
Derek Brown / Robert Campbell (U17)
Tom McPake / Stuart M°Gregor (U15)
Robert Hutton / Alistair Jenkins (U14)
CLUB DOCTOR
Dr. Clarke Mullen
PHYSIOTHERAPIST
Vanessa Smith
**FOOTBALL SAFETY OFFICERS'
ASSOCIATION REPRESENTATIVE**
Robert Wilson (01259) 722695
GROUNDSMAN
John Robertson
KIT PERSON
Nicol Campbell
COMMERCIAL MANAGER
Mike Mulraney
Bus. (01259) 722695
Home (01259) 720444
Mobile (07770) 440795
MATCHDAY PROGRAMME EDITOR
John Glencross
Bus. (01786) 464402
Home (01786) 817362
Mobile (07754) 173150
TELEPHONES
Ground (01259) 722695
Fax (01259) 210886
Sec. Bus. (01324) 619708 / 626996
Sec. Home (01259) 722696
E-MAIL & INTERNET ADDRESS
fcadmin@alloaathletic.co.uk
www.alloaathletic.co.uk
CLUB SHOP
Situated adjacent to Refreshment Kiosk
CLUB SHOP MANAGER
Jean Davison Tel: (01259) 722696
OFFICIAL SUPPORTERS CLUB
c/o Recreation Park,
Clackmannan Road, Alloa, FK10 1RY
Contact: Charlotte Glass
Tel: (01259) 216758
TEAM CAPTAIN
Iain Nicolson
SHIRT SPONSOR
Machine Tool Engineers (E.K) Ltd
KIT SUPPLIER
Pendle

LIST OF PLAYERS 2004/05

PLAYERS SURNAME	FIRST NAME	MIDDLE NAME	DATE OF BIRTH	PLACE OF BIRTH	DATE SIGNED	HEIGHT FT INS		WEIGHT ST LBS		POSITION ON PITCH	PREVIOUS CLUB
BARCLAY	CRAIG		24/08/86	EDINBURGH	20/07/04	5	9	11	0	DEFENDER	ALLOA ATHLETIC FORM D U'
BOLOCHOWECKYJ	MICHAEL		04/05/84	EDINBURGH	23/07/04	6	1	11	0	DEFENDER	ROSS COUNTY
BROWN	ANDREW	STEWART	11/10/76	EDINBURGH	10/06/04	6	4	14	0	FORWARD	STENHOUSEMUIR
BROWN	DANIEL	MICHAEL	16/11/88	STIRLING	12/08/04	5	8	10	0	MIDFIELD	ST. JOHNSTONE
BRUCE	HARRY		15/03/86	STIRLING	20/07/04	5	9	10	0	MIDFIELD	ALLOA ATHLETIC FORM D U'
CALLAGHAN	STUART		20/07/76	CALDERBANK	03/06/03	5	9	11	7	MIDFIELD	HAMILTON ACADEMICAL
CARR	JAMIE		22/03/88	GLASGOW	31/08/04	5	11	11	2	DEFENDER	ALLOA ATHLETIC FORM D U'
CHALMERS	ADAM		25/04/86	STIRLING	20/07/04	6	1	11	2	DEFENDER	ALLOA ATHLETIC FORM D U'
COMRIE	ALAN	M°IVER	05/11/87	STIRLING	20/07/04	5	8	10	0	MIDFIELD	FALKIRK
CUNNINGHAM	DEAN		02/03/88	KIRKCALDY	12/08/04	5	9	10	0	MIDFIELD	ABERDOUR B.C.
DALY	MICHAEL		24/11/85	GLASGOW	21/08/03	6	0	12	0	MIDFIELD	CLYDE
ENWOOD	STEVEN		01/01/88	EDINBURGH	12/08/04	5	10	10	7	DEFENDER	ROYSTON B.C.
EVANS	BARRY		03/07/86	STIRLING	20/07/04	5	9	10	4	MIDFIELD	ALLOA ATHLETIC FORM D U'
EVANS	GARETH	JOHN	14/01/67	COVENTRY	13/06/03	5	7.5	11	7	FORWARD	AIRDRIEONIANS
EVANS	JAMES		27/01/82	GLASGOW	25/06/03	6	0	12	10	GOALKEEPER	BOLTON WANDERERS
FERGUSON	ALEXANDER	BROWN	04/06/81	FALKIRK	16/07/02	5	11	12	6	MIDFIELD	EAST STIRLINGSHIRE
FOSTER	BARRY	JOHN	09/02/87	DUNFERMLINE	12/08/04	6	1	11	7	DEFENDER	DUNFERMLINE ATHLETIC
FUSCO	SCOTT	MURRAY	26/06/88	EDINBURGH	12/08/04	6	1	10	0	DEFENDER	ALLOA ATHLETIC FORM D U'
GIBSON	MICHAEL	NORMAN	25/10/84	EDINBURGH	31/07/04	5	6	10	7	MIDFIELD	ROSS COUNTY
GILMOUR	ROBERT		13/04/88	BO'NESS	12/08/04	6	2	10	7	GOALKEEPER	ALLOA ATHLETIC FORM D U'
GOODSIR	ANDREW		23/07/88	FALKIRK	22/09/04	6	0	10	7	DEFENDER	SYGENTA
HAMILTON	ROSS		17/06/80	FALKIRK	31/07/00	6	1	12	8	FORWARD	STENHOUSEMUIR
HANEY	GEORGE		05/08/86	STIRLING	20/07/04	5	9	10	7	FORWARD	ALLOA ATHLETIC FORM D U'
HARDIE	JOHN		18/01/88	GLASGOW	12/08/04	6	2	11	0	FORWARD	ALLOA ATHLETIC FORM D U'
HILL	DOUGLAS		16/01/85	EDINBURGH	24/07/04	6	0	12	2	DEFENDER	FALKIRK
JACK	MARTIN		07/02/89	BROXBURN	18/08/04	6	0	10	12	FORWARD	BANKTON UNDER 16'S
KELLY	FRANCIS		29/11/88	GLASGOW	12/08/04	5	7	10	0	MIDFIELD	ALLOA ATHLETIC FORM D U'
KNOX	JAMIE		11/01/86	EDINBURGH	20/07/04	5	11	12	2	MIDFIELD	SALVESEN B.C.
LEARMONTH	STEVEN	JAMES	25/05/86	FALKIRK	20/07/04	5	10	10	7	DEFENDER	B.P. UNDER 19'S
M°INNES	JOSEPH		13/09/88	EDINBURGH	12/08/04	6	1	11	0	DEFENDER	ROYSTON B.C.
M°LEOD	ROSS		12/04/85	GLASGOW	06/08/04	6	2	12	7	DEFENDER	HEART OF MIDLOTHIAN
MANSON	ELLIOT	GARROW	13/09/89	FALKIRK	12/08/04	5	9	10	7	MIDFIELD	LIVINGSTON
M°DERMOTT	MICHAEL	ROBERT	30/07/79	EDINBURGH	23/07/04	5	9	11	0	MIDFIELD	BONNYRIGG ROSE JUNIORS
M°GIVERN	GUY	VINCENT	14/02/88	DECHMONT	12/08/04	5	4	9	10	DEFENDER	MURIESTON BLUE B.C.
M°GLYNN	GARY	DOMINIC	24/11/77	FALKIRK	18/06/03	5	11	12	0	GOALKEEPER	MONTROSE
M°LAUGHLIN	PAUL		20/02/84	GLASGOW	01/08/04	6	0	12	7	DEFENDER	HEART OF MIDLOTHIAN
M°MILLAN	ALEXANDER		12/01/84	RUTHERGLEN	29/07/04	5	9	10	10	FORWARD	CLYDEBANK JUNIORS
MORTIMER	PAUL	THOMAS	14/02/80	FALKIRK	23/07/04	6	1	12	10	DEFENDER	EAST FIFE
MUIR	ROSS	JOHN EDWARDSON	11/03/88	STIRLING	18/08/04	6	2	12	0	FORWARD	EAST STIRLINGSHIRE B.C.
NICHOLAS	STEVEN	ARTHUR	08/07/81	STIRLING	09/06/04	5	10	11	0	FORWARD	EAST FIFE
NICOLSON	IAIN		13/10/76	GLASGOW	30/06/03	5	11	12	4	DEFENDER	AYR UNITED
O'RAW	MICHAEL		15/04/86	EDINBURGH	20/08/04	6	0	11	0	MIDFIELD	ALLOA ATHLETIC FORM D U' 1
RIDDICK	DARREN		20/01/88	DUMFRIES	12/08/04	5	10	10	7	MIDFIELD	GREIG PARK RANGERS
STANTON	JOHN		05/03/86	EDINBURGH	20/07/04	6	1	11	10	FORWARD	ALLOA ATHLETIC FORM D U' 1
STANTON	PATRICK	THOMAS	26/01/88	EDINBURGH	12/08/04	5	10	10	7	MIDFIELD	BANKTON B.C.
STEVENSON	JAMES		13/07/84	GLASGOW	02/02/04	5	9	10	0	FORWARD	REAL MALLORCA
SWANEY	SCOTT		12/10/87	EDINBURGH	20/07/04	5	11	10	7	DEFENDER	DUNFERMLINE ATHLETIC
TIROPOULOS	ROBERT		01/02/86	ALEXANDRIA	21/08/03	6	0	11	7	GOALKEEPER	FALKIRK
TOWNSLEY	CHRISTOPHER	JAMES	04/03/85	EDINBURGH	23/07/04	6	1	11	8	DEFENDER	ROSS COUNTY
WALKER	RICHARD	ALAN	08/07/82	EDINBURGH	13/06/01	5	11	11	0	FORWARD	WHITEHILL WELFARE COLTS
WALKER	THOMAS		06/02/88	BROXBURN	12/08/04	5	11	10	7	FORWARD	ALLOA ATHLETIC FORM D U'
WESTWATER	KEVIN		25/07/86	FALKIRK	22/08/03	6	1	12	0	DEFENDER	B.P. UNDER 16'S
WILLIAMS	JOHN		29/03/88	EDINBURGH	12/08/04	5	11	10	8	DEFENDER	ROYSTON B.C.
WOOD	RYAN		06/04/86	STIRLING	20/07/04	5	10	11	3	FORWARD	ALLOA ATHLETIC FORM D U' 1

TICKET INFORMATION

SEASON TICKET PRICES

SEATED	ADULT	£150
	JUVENILE/OAP	£80
STANDING	ADULT	£140
	JUVENILE/OAP	£70

LEAGUE ADMISSION PRICES

SEATED	ADULT	£10
	JUVENILE/OAP	£6
STANDING	ADULT	£9
	JUVENILE/OAP	£5

THE WASPS' 10 YEAR LEAGUE RECORD

SEASON	DIV	P	W	D	L	F	A	PTS
1994-95	T	36	15	9	12	50	45	54
1995-96	T	36	6	11	19	26	58	29
1996-97	T	36	16	7	13	50	47	55
1997-98	T	36	24	4	8	78	39	76
1998-99	S	36	13	7	16	65	56	46
1999-00	S	36	17	13	6	58	38	64
2000-01	F	36	7	11	18	38	61	32
2001-02	S	36	15	14	7	55	33	59
2002-03	F	36	9	8	19	39	72	35
2003-04	S	36	12	8	16	55	55	44

SEASON STATS 2003/04

Bold figures denote goalscorers. † denotes opponent's own goal.

DATE	VENUE	OPPONENTS	ATT	RES	McGLYNN G.	NICOLSON I.	SEATON A.	VALENTINE C.	McGOWAN J.	FERGUSON A.B.	WALKER R.	HAMILTON R.	CRABBE S.	CALLAGHAN S.	LITTLE I.	EVANS G.	KELBIE K.	McLAUGHLIN P.	JANCZYK N.	WATSON M.	WALKER S.	EVANS J.	BOLOCHOWECKYJ M.	DALY M.	STEVENSON J.	CLARK D.
AUG	H	DUMBARTON	446	†1-2	1	2	3	4	5	6	7	8	9	10	11	12	14	15								
AUG	A	AIRDRIE UNITED	1,445	0-1	1	2	3		5	6	7	8		10	11	9	14	4								
AUG	H	STENHOUSEMUIR	447	2-2	1	2	3	4	5	6	7	9[1]	12	10	11[1]		14		8	16						
AUG	A	BERWICK RANGERS	405	2-3	1	2	3	4		6	7	9	12	10[2]	11		14	5	8							
SEP	H	ARBROATH	358	2-2	1	2[1]	3	4	5	6	7	9[1]		10	11		14		8							
SEP	A	EAST FIFE	595	1-0	1	3		2	5	6	7[1]	9	12	10	11				8		4	20				
SEP	H	FORFAR ATHLETIC	378	1-1		2	3	4	5	8	7	9	12	10[1]	11		14	16			6	1				
OCT	H	HAMILTON ACADEMICAL	1,016	4-3		2	3	4	5		7	9	12	10	11[3]				8[1]		6	1				
OCT	H	AIRDRIE UNITED	636	1-4	1	2	3	4	5		7	9	12	10	11				8[1]		6					
OCT	H	MORTON	1,118	0-1	1	2		4	5		7	9	12	10				15	8	14	6					
NOV	A	DUMBARTON	742	0-1	1	2		4	5	3	7			10	11				8	14	6					
NOV	A	ARBROATH	448	1-3	1	2	3	4	5		7			10	11[1]	15			8		6					
NOV	H	BERWICK RANGERS	391	2-3	1	2	3	4	5	12	7	9		10	11[2]	15			8		6					
DEC	H	EAST FIFE	405	2-0	1	2[1]	3	4	5	8	7	9[1]	15	10	11	16		14			6					
DEC	A	FORFAR ATHLETIC	502	1-1	1	2	3	4	5	8[1]	7	9		10	11						6					
DEC	H	HAMILTON ACADEMICAL	504	1-3	1	2	3		4	8[1]	7	9	15	10	11		4	14			6					
JAN	A	STENHOUSEMUIR	402	3-1	1	2[1]	3	4	6	8	7	9[1]		10	11[1]								5			
JAN	H	DUMBARTON	423	3-0	1	3		4	6	2	7	9[1]		10	11[1]							20	5	8[1]		
JAN	A	EAST FIFE	647	1-0		2	3	4	6	8[1]	7	9		10	11	16					1		5	15		
JAN	H	FORFAR ATHLETIC	321	4-0	1	2	3	4	6	8	7[1]	9[3]		10	11								5	15		
FEB	H	ARBROATH	442	4-0	1	2	3	4	6[1]	8	7	9[1]		10[1]	11								5	15	14[1]	
FEB	A	BERWICK RANGERS	445	1-3	1	2	3	4	6[1]	8	7	9		10	11								5	15	14	
FEB	H	MORTON	1,145	3-3	1	2		3	6	8	7[1]	9		10[1]	11[1]								5	4	14	
MAR	A	AIRDRIE UNITED	1,542	1-2	1	2		4	6	3	7	9	12	10			14	15					5	8[1]	11	
MAR	H	STENHOUSEMUIR	444	1-0	1	2	3	4	6	8	7	9[1]		10	11			16					5	12	14	
MAR	A	HAMILTON ACADEMICAL	831	1-0	1	2	3	4	6[1]	8	7	9		10	11								5		14	
MAR	A	ARBROATH	449	1-2	1	2		4		3	7			10	11			6					5	8	9[1]	
MAR	H	BERWICK RANGERS	365	4-2	1	2		4	6[1]	3	7	9[1]		10[1]	11								5[1]	8		
MAR	A	MORTON	2,436	2-2	1	2		4	6	3	7[1]	9[1]		10	11								5	8		
APR	H	EAST FIFE	567	1-1	1	2		4	6	3	7	9[1]		10	11								5	8	14	16
APR	A	FORFAR ATHLETIC	411	0-2	1			4	6	2	7	9		10	11								5	8	14	3
APR	A	MORTON	2,618	1-2	1	2		4	6	8	7	9		10[1]	11								5		14	3
APR	H	HAMILTON ACADEMICAL	579	1-1		2		4	6	8	7[1]	9		10	11						1		5	15	14	3
MAY	A	STENHOUSEMUIR	480	1-0		2		4	6	8	7	9		10	11								5	15		3[1]
MAY	H	AIRDRIE UNITED	1,635	0-1	1	2		4	6	8	7	9		10	11								5	15	14	3
MAY	A	DUMBARTON	1,494	1-3	1	2			6[1]	8	7	9		10	11			4					5	14	12	3
TOTAL FULL APPEARANCES					32	35	20	33	34	33	35	35	1	35	33	1		8	10		11	4	20	8	2	6
TOTAL SUB APPEARANCES									1				9		1	5	8	4	2	4		2		9	11	1
TOTAL GOALS SCORED						3			5	3	5	13		6	11			2					1	2	2	1

LEADING GOALSCORERS:

SEASON	DIV	GOALS	PLAYER
94-95	T	13	B. Moffat
95-96	T	5	B. Moffat, S. Rixon
96-97	T	12	W. Irvine
97-98	T	18	W. Irvine
98-99	S	15	M. Cameron, W. Irvine
99-00	S	15	M. Cameron
00-01	F	9	R. Hamilton
01-02	S	14	G. Hutchison
02-03	F	8	R. Sloan
03-04	S	13	R. Hamilton

MILESTONES:

YEAR OF FORMATION: 1883
MOST CAPPED PLAYER: Jock Hepburn
NO. OF CAPS: 1
MOST LEAGUE POINTS IN A SEASON:
60 (Division 2 – Season 1921/22)(2 Points for a Win)
76 (Third Division – Season 1997/98)(3 Points for a Win)
MOST LEAGUE GOALS SCORED BY A PLAYER IN A SEASON:
William Crilley (Season 1921/22)
NO. OF GOALS SCORED: 49
RECORD ATTENDANCE: 13,000 (-v- Dunfermline Athletic – 26.2.1939)
RECORD VICTORY: 9-2 (-v- Forfar Athletic – Division 2, 18.3.1933)
RECORD DEFEAT: 0-10 (-v- Dundee – Division 2 and Third Lanark – League Cup)

ALLOA ATHLETIC PLAYING KITS SEASON 2004/05

FIRST KIT | SECOND KIT | THIRD KIT

ARBROATH
Gayfield Park,
Arbroath, Angus, DD11 1QB

PRESIDENT
John D. Christison

VICE-PRESIDENT
Michael Caird

COMMITTEE
R. Alan Ripley (Treasurer),
Malcolm L. Fairweather,
Dr. Gary J. Callon,
Mark R. Davies & Ian J. Angus

HONORARY PRESIDENTS
I. Stirling, G. Johnston, B. Pearson,
J. King, J. Leslie, D. Ferguson,
J. Milne, W. Smith & C. Kinnear

HONORARY PATRONS
Earl of Airlie, Lord Inchcape & Lord Fraser

SECRETARY
Dr. Gary J. Callon

OFFICE ADMINISTRATOR
Mike Cargill

MANAGER
Harry Cairney

ASSISTANT MANAGER
Stuart Sorbie

FIRST TEAM COACH/RESERVE COACH
Jake Ferrier

U-19 YOUTH TEAM COACH
Mike Cargill

U-17 YOUTH TEAM COACHES
Mike Cargill & Willie Anderson

CLUB DOCTOR
Dr. Dick Spiers

PHYSIOTHERAPIST
Ian Barrett

CHIROPODIST
Alexander McKinnon

**FOOTBALL SAFETY OFFICERS'
ASSOCIATION REPRESENTATIVE**
William Scorgie (Bus)(01241) 878778

COMMERCIAL MANAGER
Malcolm Fairweather
Bus. (01241) 434765

STADIUM MANAGER
Michael Caird

GROUNDSMAN
Tim Twiss

KIT MANAGER
Margaret Reid

MATCHDAY PROGRAMME EDITOR
Ian Angus

TELEPHONES
Ground/Ticket Office/Club Shop
(01241) 872157
Fax (01241) 431125
Sec. Home (01241) 872394
Sec. Bus. 07802 747558

E-MAIL & INTERNET ADDRESS
afc@gayfield.fsnet.co.uk
garycallon@onetel.com
www.arbroathfc.co.uk

CLUB SHOP
Contact: Karen Fleming
Gayfield Park, Arbroath, DD11 1QB.
Open on home matchdays.

TEAM CAPTAIN
John M'Glashan

SHIRT SPONSOR
AllStar's International

KIT SUPPLIER
ERREA

LIST OF PLAYERS 2004/05

PLAYERS SURNAME	FIRST NAME	MIDDLE NAME	DATE OF BIRTH	PLACE OF BIRTH	DATE SIGNED	HEIGHT FT INS		WEIGHT ST LBS		POSITION ON PITCH	PREVIOUS CLUB
ANDERSON	CRAIG	DUNCAN	21/02/88	DUNDEE	19/06/04	5	8	10	0	MIDFIELD	ARBROATH FORM D U' 16
ANDERSON	GRAHAM		25/07/88	DUNDEE	15/06/04	6	1	11	5	DEFENDER	ARBROATH FORM D U' 16
BEITH	GAVIN		07/10/81	DUNDEE	18/06/04	5	10	10	0	MIDFIELD	BRECHIN CITY
BISHOP	JAMES	DAVID GEORGE	14/01/85	DUNDEE	06/07/04	6	1	12	6	DEFENDER	DUNFERMLINE ATHLETIC
BRAZIL	ALAN		05/07/85	EDINBURGH	20/07/04	5	10	13	0	FORWARD	ASTON VILLA
BURNETT	MARC		04/02/88	DUNDEE	07/09/04	5	11	10	13	FORWARD	DUNDEE
CAIRD	ALEXANDER		11/06/88	DUNDEE	04/09/04	5	11	10	0	FORWARD	BRECHIN CITY FORM S
CARGILL	CHRISTOPHER	JAMES	30/05/86	DUNDEE	15/06/04	6	4	14	0	GOALKEEPER	ARBROATH FORM D U' 16
COLLIER	JAMES	STEWART	17/12/86	ABERDEEN	01/06/04	6	1	13	0	FORWARD	ABERDEEN
COOK	STEVEN		13/06/85	DUNDEE	01/06/04	5	10	11	0	MIDFIELD	DUNDEE
CUSICK	JOHN	JAMES	16/01/75	KIRKCALDY	27/07/04	5	8	11	0	MIDFIELD	EAST FIFE
DONALDSON	EUAN	GORDON	20/08/75	FALKIRK	13/07/04	5	11	11	6	DEFENDER	EAST FIFE
DUNCAN	GRAEME		16/03/88	DUNDEE	15/06/04	6	2	11	7	DEFENDER	ARBROATH FORM D U' 16
FARQUHARSON	PAUL		16/10/84	DUNDEE	06/07/04	5	9	11	0	MIDFIELD	ARBROATH SPORTING CLUB JUNIORS
GAULD	IAIN	ALAN	23/12/89	DUNDEE	04/09/04	6	1	12	0	DEFENDER	BRECHIN CITY B.C.
GORDON	ROSS	M'DONALD	19/11/88	DUNDEE	19/06/04	5	7	9	3	DEFENDER	ARBROATH FORM D U' 16
HENDERSON	ANDREW		30/01/88	DUNDEE	15/06/04	6	2	11	0	FORWARD	ATHLETICO BLAIR
HENSLEE	GREIG		13/01/83	DUNDEE	28/05/04	5	10	12	1	MIDFIELD	ARBROATH FORM S
HYND	KENNETH	SHAW	17/04/88	PERTH	04/09/04	5	8	10	0	MIDFIELD	F.C. LUNCARTY
INGLIS	NEIL	DAVID	10/09/74	GLASGOW	06/07/04	6	1	12	2	GOALKEEPER	BERWICK RANGERS
JOHNSTON	MATTHEW	RICHARD	16/01/86	ARBROATH	07/08/04	6	1.5	12	0	DEFENDER	ARBROATH LADS CLUB
JONES	LEE		04/10/88	PLYMOUTH	15/06/04	5	9	10	7	DEFENDER	ARBROATH FORM D U' 16
KERR	STUART	JAMES	08/05/88	DUNDEE	08/09/04	5	10	10	0	DEFENDER	DUNDEE
KIRK	GREG	DAVID	18/08/86	DUNDEE	15/06/04	6	2	12	0	MID / FWD	MARYFIELD UNITED
LAWRENCE	DARRAN	ANDREW	01/12/88	GERMANY	04/09/04	5	10	10	5	GOALKEEPER	DEE CLUB
M'DONALD	STUART		15/05/81	GLASGOW	27/07/04	5	10	12	0	MIDFIELD	CUMNOCK JUNIORS
MARTIN	JAMIE	ANDREW	10/01/86	DUNDEE	07/08/04	6	3	12	4	DEFENDER	DUNDEE UNITED
MASSON	TERRY		03/07/88	DUNDEE	08/09/04	5	8	9	5	MIDFIELD	DUNDEE
M'AULAY	JOHN		28/04/72	GLASGOW	01/07/04	5	9	12	0	DEFENDER	CLYDE
M'GLASHAN	JOHN		03/06/67	DUNDEE	29/05/04	6	2	13	0	MIDFIELD	ROSS COUNTY
M'INTOSH	KRISTOPHER		11/02/87	DUNDEE	30/08/04	5	10	10	0	MIDFIELD	BRECHIN CITY FORM S
M'KIBBEN	PHILIP	NEIL	04/04/87	ABERDEEN	30/08/04	5	11.5	11	0	MIDFIELD	ALBION B.C.
M'LEAN	DUNCAN		07/08/83	DUNDEE	08/06/04	5	10	11	6	FORWARD	DUNDEE
M'LEOD	CHRISTOPHER		28/01/84	EDINBURGH	28/08/04	6	2	12	7	DEFENDER	RANGERS
M'MULLAN	KEVIN	ANDREW	15/06/83	KIRKCALDY	25/05/04	5	10	11	0	DEFENDER	NEWBURGH JUNIORS
MILLER	GREG	ALLAN	01/04/76	GLASGOW	18/06/04	5	8	11	1	MIDFIELD	BRECHIN CITY
NEILSON	PAUL		27/03/88	DUNDEE	08/09/04	5	8	10	5	MIDFIELD	THE DEE CLUB
O'LEARY	MARC	BLAIR	11/02/86	DUNDEE	30/08/04	5	10	11	0	MIDFIELD	MARYFIELD UNITED U' 16'S
RENNIE	STEVEN		03/08/81	STIRLING	30/06/03	6	2	12	7	DEFENDER	FALKIRK
RUSSELL	NICHOLAS	JOHN GORDON	31/01/87	DUNDEE	30/08/04	6	2	12	0	GOALKEEPER	BRECHIN CITY FORM S
STEWART	NEIL		28/03/88	DUNDEE	11/09/04	5	9	9	0	FORWARD	ARBROATH FORM S
SWANKIE	GAVIN		22/11/83	ARBROATH	20/02/01	5	10	10	12	FORWARD	ARBROATH FORM S
TRAYNOR	JOHN	BRIAN	06/08/86	DUNDEE	30/08/04	5	10	10	0	MIDFIELD	BRECHIN CITY
WARREN	GARRY	STEWART	01/07/86	DUNDEE	30/08/04	5	11	10	0	FORWARD	ARBROATH FORM S
WEBSTER	MARTIN	JAMES	07/05/87	DUNDEE	30/08/04	6	0	10	5	FORWARD	BRECHIN CITY FORM S
WOODCOCK	TIMOTHY	MARTIN	04/02/84	DUNDEE	25/05/04	6	0	12	0	GOALKEEPER	ARBROATH FORM S

TICKET INFORMATION

SEASON TICKET PRICES
SEATED	ADULT	£160
	JUVENILE/OAP	£75
STANDING	ADULT	£160
	JUVENILE/OAP	£75
	JUVENILE UNDER 12 YEARS	£30

LEAGUE ADMISSION PRICES
SEATED	ADULT	£10
	JUVENILE/OAP	£6
STANDING	ADULT	£9
	JUVENILE/OAP/ UNEMPLOYED WITH UB40	£5
	PARENT & CHILD	£12

THE RED LICHTIES' 10 YEAR LEAGUE RECORD

SEASON	DIV	P	W	D	L	F	A	PTS
1994-95	T	36	13	5	18	51	62	44
1995-96	T	36	13	13	10	41	41	52
1996-97	T	36	6	13	17	31	52	31
1997-98	T	36	20	8	8	67	39	68
1998-99	S	36	12	8	16	37	52	44
1999-00	S	36	11	14	11	52	55	47
2000-01	S	36	15	13	8	54	38	58
2001-02	F	36	14	6	16	42	59	48
2002-03	F	36	3	6	27	30	77	15
2003-04	S	36	11	10	15	41	57	43

SEASON STATS 2003/04

Bold figures denote goalscorers. † denotes opponent's own goal.

	VENUE	OPPONENTS	ATT	RES	PEAT M.	McMULLEN K.	KING D.	RENNIE S.	DENHAM G.	CUSICK J.	CARGILL A.	DOW A.	GRAHAM J.R.	McGLASHAN J.	KERRIGAN S.	MITCHELL A.	SWANKIE G.	HENSLEE G.	BROWNE P.	FARQUHARSON P.	HERKES J.	McFAULAY J.	NEWALL C.	DURNO P.	GRAHAM E.	KIRK S.	SHAW G.	DIACK I.	McCULLOCH M.	WATSON C.	MILLER G.	McLEAN D.	COLLIER J.	WOODCOCK T.
AUG	H	BERWICK RANGERS	565	1-0	1	2	3	4		5	6	7	8[1]	9	10	11		14	15	12														
AUG	A	DUMBARTON	1,070	1-1	1		3	4	5	6	7[1]	8	9	10	11	12	14								2					16				
AUG	H	FORFAR ATHLETIC	856	0-0	1	2	3	4		6	7	8	9	10		11	14	5		12														
AUG	H	HAMILTON ACADEMICAL	650	2-2		2	3	4		6[1]	7	8	9	10[1]	12	1	14	5	16	11														
SEP	A	ALLOA ATHLETIC	358	2-2	1	2	3	4		6		8	9[1]	10	11	12	15[1]			7	16													
SEP	A	AIRDRIE UNITED	1,385	1-2	1	2	3	4		6	7[1]	8	9	10	11	12	5		15	14														
SEP	H	MORTON	1,116	0-4	1	14	4		6		8	3	9	10	2	5		15	11	12	7													
OCT	A	STENHOUSEMUIR	344	0-1	1	2	3	4			8	9	10			7	5	14	6		11	12	16											
OCT	H	EAST FIFE	705	0-1	1	2	3	4		7	6		10			9	5	11	14	15	8													
OCT	H	DUMBARTON	506	2-1	1	2	3		7[1]	6	9	10[1]	15		8	5	11	12			4		14											
NOV	A	BERWICK RANGERS	383	0-3	1	2	3	4		7	6	9	10	14	16	8	5	11	12															
NOV	H	ALLOA ATHLETIC	448	3-1	1	2	3	4		7[1]	6[1]	9	10[1]		11	8	5	14	12															
NOV	A	HAMILTON ACADEMICAL	1,286	0-2	1	2	3	4		7	6	9	10		8	5	14		15						11									
DEC	H	AIRDRIE UNITED	405	1-1	1	2	3	4		6	7		10		11	8	5	14	12									9[1]						
DEC	A	MORTON	2,707	4-6	1	2	3	4		6	7[2]		10[1]		11	8	5	16	12							15[1]		9						
DEC	H	STENHOUSEMUIR	402	2-1	1	2	3	4		7	6		10[1]		11	15	5	14										9[1]		8				
DEC	A	EAST FIFE	811	1-0		2	3		7			10		1	11	4	5	16	6	12								9[1]		8				
JAN	H	BERWICK RANGERS	411	1-2	1	16	3	4		5[1]	7	6	10		11						2							9	8	14				
JAN	A	AIRDRIE UNITED	1,267	1-0	1	7[1]	3	4		5	6				11		12	16			2		15					9	8					
JAN	H	MORTON	805	2-2	1	2	3	4		5[1]	6				14	15	12				10							9	8		7	11[1]		
FEB	A	ALLOA ATHLETIC	442	0-4	1		3	4			6				12	15	5	14			2							9	8		7	11		
FEB	H	HAMILTON ACADEMICAL	502	0-2	1	2	3	4			7		16	10			15		12		5							9	6		8	11		
FEB	H	EAST FIFE	596	0-0	1	2	3	4		5	7		11	10			15				12							9	6		8	14		
MAR	A	DUMBARTON	828	0-1	1	2	5	4		8		9			15	10		16	6									14	3		7	11		
MAR	H	FORFAR ATHLETIC	702	0-1	1	2	5	4		6			10		11	8			15									9	3		7	12		
MAR	A	FORFAR ATHLETIC	682	2-2	1	2	5	4		6			10[1]		11	8	16											9[1]	3		7			
MAR	H	ALLOA ATHLETIC	449	2-1	1	2	5	4		6			10[1]		11	8			15									9[1]	3		7	12		
MAR	A	HAMILTON ACADEMICAL	1,041	2-2	1	2	5	4		6			10[1]		11	8			16									9[1]	3		7	12		
MAR	A	STENHOUSEMUIR	307	3-0	1	2	5		6[1]	8[1]			10		11	14			15									9	3		7	4[1]		
APR	A	MORTON	2,493	0-1	1	2			6	8			10		11	5	15				12	14						3		7	9			
APR	H	AIRDRIE UNITED	1,074	0-4	1	2			6	8			10		12	5	16											9	3		7	11	15	
APR	A	EAST FIFE	762	2-1	1	2	5		6	7			10		12	11	16						3					8		14	9[2]			
APR	H	STENHOUSEMUIR	511	1-1	1	2	5		6	7			10		12	8							3					9	3			11[1]		18
MAY	A	FORFAR ATHLETIC	707	2-1		2	5	4		7			10[1]		8				12		14							9[1]	3		6	11		1
MAY	A	DUMBARTON	553	0-3	1	2	5		6	7			10[1]		14	15			16									9	3		8	11		
MAY	A	BERWICK RANGERS	506	3-1	1	2	5		6[1]				10[1]		12	7	14		4									9	3		8	11[1]		
TOTAL FULL APPEARANCES					33	32	33	32	3	24	25	18	14	34	3	2	16	20	17		7	8			3	2		21	21		15	12		1
TOTAL SUB APPEARANCES						2							1		3		14	11	4	12	8	10	3	8	3	1	1	1	1	1	4	1	1
TOTAL GOALS SCORED						1				5	7	2	1	10				1							1			7		6			

LEADING GOALSCORERS:

SEASON	DIV	GOALS	PLAYER
95	T	11	S. Tosh
96	T	8	S. McCormick, D. Pew
97	T	5	B. Grant
98	T	16	W. Spence
99	S	12	C. McGlashan
00	S	16	C. McGlashan
01	S	10	S. Mallan
02	F	6	G. Bayne, J. McGlashan, S. Mallan
03	F	4	J. Cusick, M. McDowell
04	S	10	J. McGlashan

MILESTONES:

YEAR OF FORMATION: 1878
MOST CAPPED PLAYER: Ned Doig
NO. OF CAPS: 2
MOST LEAGUE POINTS IN A SEASON:
57 (Division 2 – Season 1966/67) (2 Points for a Win)
68 (Third Division – Season 1997/98) (3 Points for a Win)
MOST LEAGUE GOALS SCORED BY A PLAYER IN A SEASON:
David Easson (Season 1958/59)
NO. OF GOALS SCORED: 45
RECORD ATTENDANCE: 13,510 (-v- Rangers – Scottish Cup, 23.2.1952)
RECORD VICTORY: 36-0 (-v- Bon Accord – Scottish Cup, 12.9.1885)
RECORD DEFEAT: 1-9 (-v- Celtic – League Cup, 25.8.1993)

ARBROATH PLAYING KITS SEASON 2004/05

FIRST KIT | SECOND KIT | THIRD KIT

LIST OF PLAYERS 2004/05

PLAYERS SURNAME	FIRST NAME	MIDDLE NAME	DATE OF BIRTH	PLACE OF BIRTH	DATE SIGNED	HEIGHT FT INS		WEIGHT ST LBS		POSITION ON PITCH	PREVIOUS CLUB
BROWN	GRAEME	ROBERT	08/11/80	JOHANNESBURG	12/01/04	5	11	11	0	FORWARD	COWDENBEATH
BURGESS	ROBERT	GEORGE	11/03/85	IRVINE	09/07/02	6	0	11	4	DEFENDER	AYR UNITED FORM S
CARGILL	ANDREW		02/09/75	DUNDEE	12/06/04	5	6.5	10	8	MIDFIELD	ARBROATH
CHAPLAIN	SCOTT		09/10/83	BELLSHILL	27/07/00	5	9	11	7	MIDFIELD	RANGERS
CONNOLLY	PATRICK	MARTIN	25/06/70	GLASGOW	21/06/04	5	9.5	11	0	FORWARD	ST. JOHNSTONE
CONWAY	CRAIG	IAN	02/05/85	IRVINE	03/03/04	5	9	11	4	MIDFIELD	IRVINE MEADOW JUNIORS
CRAWFORD	STEVEN		16/12/86	IRVINE	22/07/04	5	9	11	0	DEFENDER	CUMNOCK JUNIORS
DUNLOP	MICHAEL		05/11/82	GLASGOW	07/07/03	6	1	11	12	DEFENDER	RENFREW JUNIORS
DUNNING	ALLAN		02/09/80	GLASGOW	06/08/04	6	1	12	0	FORWARD	QUEEN'S PARK
FERGUSON	ANDREW	DAVID	24/03/85	GLASGOW	23/01/02	6	0	11	13	FORWARD	AYR UNITED FORM S
FERGUSON	STEVEN		18/05/77	EDINBURGH	17/07/03	5	9	12	1	MIDFIELD	ROSS COUNTY
FRASER	NEIL	KENNETH	12/04/88	PAISLEY	17/09/04	5	9	9	7	DEFENDER	ST. MIRREN
HENDERSON	DARREN	RONALD	12/10/66	KILMARNOCK	29/05/04	5	11	12	11	MIDFIELD	FORFAR ATHLETIC
HILLCOAT	JOHN	GEORGE	16/12/70	PAISLEY	23/05/03	6	0	12	6	GOALKEEPER	STRANRAER
KEAN	STEWART		04/03/83	IRVINE	15/01/00	5	9	11	8	FORWARD	CRAIGMARK BURNTONIANS
LYLE	WILLIAM		14/04/84	IRVINE	27/07/00	5	10	10	7	DEFENDER	AYR UNITED FORM S
McAULAY	CALLUM	JAMES	14/06/88	IRVINE	13/08/04	5	7	11	0	DEFENDER	WHITTLETS B.C.
McGRADY	STUART	IAN	08/04/85	IRVINE	08/08/03	5	10	10	2	DEF / MID	AYR UNITED FORM S
McLAUGHLIN	BARRY	JOHN	19/04/73	PAISLEY	08/07/04	6	1	13	1	DEFENDER	KILMARNOCK
McVICAR	NEILL	CRAIG	21/02/87	IRVINE	20/08/04	5	9	10	7	FORWARD	ARDROSSAN WINTON ROVERS
MIDDLETON	ALAN		01/01/88	IRVINE	13/08/04	6	1	11	6	MIDFIELD	RANGERS
MULLEN	BOYD		02/01/86	IRVINE	18/01/02	5	9	9	7	MIDFIELD	AYR UNITED FORM S
O'NEILL	MICHAEL	ANDREW MARTIN	05/07/69	PORTADOWN	22/07/04	5	11.5	12	0	MIDFIELD	GLENTORAN
QUIGLEY	DARREN	NELSON	31/07/88	IRVINE	10/06/04	5	9	10	0	FORWARD	AYR UNITED FORM S
RAMSAY	DOUGLAS		26/04/79	IRVINE	21/08/03	5	11	12	9	MIDFIELD	MOTHERWELL
ROY	LUDOVIC		18/08/77	TOURS	07/07/03	6	1	13	0	GOALKEEPER	ST. MIRREN
SMYTH	MARC		27/12/82	EDINBURGH	14/09/01	6	0	11	7	DEFENDER	GLENAFTON ATHLETIC JN
TEMPLETON	PAUL	JOSEPH JOHNSTON	11/04/87	IRVINE	20/08/04	5	9	10	0	MIDFIELD	ARDROSSAN WINTON ROVERS
WEIR	ROBBIE		21/02/88	IRVINE	10/06/04	5	10	12	0	FORWARD	AYR UNITED FORM S
WILDE	NICOLAS		08/05/88	IRVINE	19/08/04	6	0	10	3	DEFENDER	RANGERS

THE HONEST MEN'S 10 YEAR LEAGUE REC

SEASON	DIV	P	W	D	L	F	A	PTS
1994-95	F	36	6	11	19	31	58	29
1995-96	S	36	11	12	13	40	40	45
1996-97	S	36	23	8	5	61	33	77
1997-98	F	36	10	10	16	40	56	40
1998-99	F	36	19	5	12	66	42	62
1999-00	F	36	10	8	18	42	52	38
2000-01	F	36	19	12	5	73	41	69
2001-02	F	36	13	13	10	53	44	52
2002-03	F	36	12	9	15	34	44	45
2003-04	F	36	6	13	17	37	58	31

SEASON STATS 2003/04

Bold figures denote goalscorers (shown as superscript). † denotes opponent's own goal.

DATE	VENUE	OPPONENTS	ATT	RES	ROY L.	SMYTH M.	KERR C.	LATTA J.	CAMPBELL M.	RAMSAY D.	CHAPLAIN S.	BLACK A.	KEAN S.	WHALEN S.	McGRADY S.	LYLE W.	McCOLL M.	CONWAY C.	CRAIG D.	FERGUSON S.	DUNLOP M.	MULLEN B.	FERGUSON A.	HILLCOAT J.	BURGESS R.	HARDY L.	KINNIBURGH W.	CRAWFORD S.	BROWN G.	DOYLE J.	MILLER S.	TAIT J.
9-AUG	A	CLYDE	1,067	0-3	1	2	3	4	5	6	7	8	9	10	11	12			15	16												
16-AUG	H	FALKIRK	2,519	1-1	1	4	3		5	8	11		9^1	10		2			6	7	14		15	16								
23-AUG	A	RAITH ROVERS	2,337	1-1	1	4	3		5	8	7					2	12		6	16	6		11	15	10^1							
30-AUG	H	QUEEN OF THE SOUTH	2,143	1-4	1	4	3		5^1	8			9	16	2	12			6	7	11		15	10								
13-SEP	A	INVERNESS CAL TH	1,476	0-1	1	7			5	4	10	9		11		2	15		6	8	3		16									
20-SEP	H	ROSS COUNTY	2,911	2-2	1	4	12		5	11	7^1	10	9^1		3	2			6	8												
27-SEP	H	BRECHIN CITY	1,427	3-2	1	4			5	11	7^1	10	9	3		2	16		6^1	8	14^1											
4-OCT	A	ST. JOHNSTONE	1,906	1-1	1	4	14		5	11	7	10^1		3		2			6	8			9									
18-OCT	H	ST. MIRREN	2,447	0-2	1	4	14		5	11	7	10		3		2	16		6	8			9		1							
25-OCT	A	FALKIRK	2,609	1-0	1	4	14		5	11	7		9			2	16		6	8	3		10^1									
1-NOV	H	CLYDE	1,653	2-2	1	4			15	5	11	7^1	9^1			2	16		6	8	3		10									
8-NOV	H	INVERNESS CAL TH	1,464	0-3	1	5	3	15	4	7			9	10	14	2	11		6	8							12					
16-NOV	A	QUEEN OF THE SOUTH	3,555	0-1	1	4			8	7	15	9				2			6		11		10	17		3	5					
22-NOV	A	BRECHIN CITY	508	1-3	1	4			8	7		9	16			2		15	6		11^1		10		12	3	5					
29-NOV	H	ROSS COUNTY	977	1-3	1	8			5	2	7	11	9	10					6		15		16		12	3^1	4					
6-DEC	A	ST. MIRREN	2,567	2-3	1	2			8	7	4	9^1	10					15	6		3	14	16^1		5	11						
13-DEC	H	ST. JOHNSTONE	1,203	1-1	1	2			8^1	7	4	9			14		16		6		3		10			11	5					
20-DEC	H	CLYDE	1,049	1-2	1	2			8	7^1	4	9			14		16		6		3		10			11	5					
29-DEC	H	RAITH ROVERS	1,791	1-0	1	2			8	4	9			7	12	16	15		6		10^1					11	5	3				
3-JAN	H	QUEEN OF THE SOUTH	2,303	1-1	1	2			8	4	9			7	12	16			6		10^1					11	5	3				
17-JAN	A	INVERNESS CAL TH	1,443	1-2	1	4			5	8	7	10			15	2	11		6		16					3			9	14^1		
24-JAN	A	ROSS COUNTY	2,732	1-1	1	4			8	7		10^1		14		2			6		16					3			9	11	15	
31-JAN	H	BRECHIN CITY	1,512	1-2	1				7	12	10			14	2				6		3		16			5	11		9^1	4	8	
4-FEB	A	ST. JOHNSTONE	2,067	0-3	1	2			8	4	10		12	7					6		3		16			5	11		9	15		
21-FEB	H	ST. MIRREN	2,252	2-0	1	4			5	8	14	7	9^1			2			6		10^1		11			16						3
6-MAR	H	FALKIRK	2,048	2-3	1	4			5	8	14	7	9^1	15		2			6		10		11^1			16						3
13-MAR	A	RAITH ROVERS	2,231	1-2	1	4			5	8	14	7	9			2			6		10		11^1			16				15		3
20-MAR	H	INVERNESS CAL TH	1,207	1-1	1	14			5	8	4	7	9			2			6		12		16			11^1			10			3
27-MAR	A	QUEEN OF THE SOUTH	1,831	0-0	1	14			5	8	4	7	9			2			6		16		11			10			15			3
5-APR	A	BRECHIN CITY	519	3-0	1	14^1			5	8	4	7^1	9^1			2			6		16		11			10						3
10-APR	H	ROSS COUNTY	1,535	1-2	1	8			5		4	7	9			2	15		6		14	16	11			10^1						3
17-APR	A	ST. MIRREN	3,211	1-4	1	8			5		4	7	9^1			2			6		12		11			10						3
24-APR	H	ST. JOHNSTONE	1,119	†1-1	1	4			5			7	9		12				6		3		16			11			10	8	14	2
1-MAY	A	CLYDE	1,816	1-1	1	6			5^1		4	7	9			2	15				3		16			14	11		10	8		
8-MAY	A	FALKIRK	2,077	0-0	1	6			5		14	7	9			2	15				8		16			11			10	4		
15-MAY	H	RAITH ROVERS	1,283	1-0	1	12			5		8	14	7	9		6					10^1		11			4	3					
TOTAL FULL APPEARANCES					35	31	5	1	25	29	29	17	36	7	11	26	2		32	9	18		16	1	4	24	7	1	12	6	1	11
TOTAL SUB APPEARANCES					4	4	2		5	2		2		9	5	12	8			5	5		15	1	4				3	1	5	
TOTAL GOALS SCORED						1			2	1	4	1	9	1					1		2		7			4			2	1	

Bold figures denote goalscorers. † denotes opponent's own goal.

MILESTONES:

YEAR OF FORMATION: 1910
MOST CAPPED PLAYER: Jim Nisbett
NO. OF CAPS: 3
MOST LEAGUE POINTS IN A SEASON:
61 (Second Division – Season 1987/88) (2 Points for a Win)
77 (Second Division – Season 1996/97) (3 Points for a Win)
MOST LEAGUE GOALS SCORED BY A PLAYER IN A SEASON:
Jimmy Smith (Season 1927/28)
NO. OF GOALS SCORED: 66
RECORD ATTENDANCE: 25,225 (-v- Rangers – 13.9.1969)
RECORD VICTORY: 11-1 (-v- Dumbarton – League Cup, 13.8.1952)
RECORD DEFEAT: 0-9 (-v- Rangers, Heart of Midlothian, Third Lanark – Division 1)

AYR UNITED PLAYING KITS SEASON 2004/05

FIRST KIT | SECOND KIT | THIRD KIT

BERWICK RANGERS
Shielfield Park, Shielfield Terrace,
Tweedmouth, Berwick-Upon-Tweed, TD15 2EF

CHAIRMAN
Robert L. Wilson

VICE-CHAIRMAN
W. Moray McLaren

DIRECTORS
John H. Hush, Peter McAskill,
John G. Robertson, Ian R. Smith,
John Bell, Robert J. Darling & Craig Forsyth

HONORARY PRESIDENT
Rt. Hon. Alan Beith M.P.

CLUB SECRETARY
Dennis J. McCleary

TREASURER & OFFICE ADMINISTRATOR
, Neil Simpson

MANAGER
Sandy Clark

DIRECTOR OF FOOTBALL & YOUTH DEVELOPMENT DIRECTOR/COACH
Ian R. Smith

YOUTH COACHES
Andy Raeburn (U19)
Neil Oliver (U17)

STADIUM MANAGER & GROUNDSMAN
Ross Aitchison

HONORARY PARAMEDIC
Paul Ross BAEMT-P, IHCD, SRP

PHYSIO STAFF
Ian Smith & Jamie Dougal

CHIEF STEWARD
John Dodds

FOOTBALL SAFETY OFFICERS' ASSOCIATION REPRESENTATIVE
Craig Forsyth

KIT PERSON
Ian Oliver

COMMERCIAL MANAGER
Conrad Turner (01289) 307969

MEDIA LIAISON OFFICER
Paul Smith (0131) 449 6834

MATCHDAY PROGRAMME EDITOR
Dennis McCleary (01289) 307623

TELEPHONES
Ground/Ticket Office (01289) 307424
Fax (01289) 309424
Club Sec. Home (01289) 307623
Manager Bus: (0131) 449 6834
24 Hour Hotline (09068) 800697

E-MAIL & INTERNET ADDRESS
dennis@mccleary133.fsnet.co.uk
berwickranger@btopenworld.com
www.berwickrangers.co.uk

CLUB SHOP
Supporters Shop situated within
the ground. Open during first
team home matchdays.

OFFICIAL SUPPORTERS CLUB
c/o Shielfield Park, Tweedmouth,
Berwick-Upon-Tweed, TD15 2EF
(01289) 307424

TEAM CAPTAIN
Martin Neil

SHIRT SPONSOR
Haggerston Castle Holiday Park

KIT SUPPLIER
Pro Star

LIST OF PLAYERS 2004/05

PLAYERS SURNAME	FIRST NAME	MIDDLE NAME	DATE OF BIRTH	PLACE OF BIRTH	DATE SIGNED	HEIGHT FT INS		WEIGHT ST LBS		POSITION ON PITCH	PREVIOUS CLUB
AINSLIE	KIERAN		04/03/89	ASHINGTON	20/08/04	5	11.5	11	0	DEFENDER	BERWICK RANGERS JNRS
BAIN	CHRISTOPHER		24/01/86	EDINBURGH	26/07/04	6	2	11	12	MIDFIELD	TYNECASTLE HEARTS
BENZIE	DEAN		29/03/86	EDINBURGH	26/07/04	6	1	11	2	FORWARD	ST. BERNARDS
BIRRELL	JAMIE		07/04/86	EDINBURGH	02/06/04	5	11	11	0	MIDFIELD	TYNECASTLE HEARTS
BLYTH	FINLAY		15/06/88	ASHINGTON	20/08/04	5	7	9	2	FORWARD	LOWICK F.C.
BRACKS	KEVIN		01/10/86	EDINBURGH	26/07/04	5	11	12	6	DEFENDER	HIBERNIAN
BROWN	DAVID	ALAN	16/09/88	BERWICK UPON TWEED	20/08/04	5	8	12	0	FORWARD	BERWICK RANGERS JNRS
BURKE	MARK		29/03/87	EDINBURGH	26/07/04	5	11	12	5	DEF / MID	HEART OF MIDLOTHIAN
CONNELL	GRAHAM		31/10/74	GLASGOW	21/06/02	5	10	11	7	MIDFIELD	QUEEN OF THE SOUTH
CONNELLY	GORDON		01/11/76	GLASGOW	04/07/02	6	0	12	7	MIDFIELD	QUEEN OF THE SOUTH
COWAN	MARK		16/01/71	EDINBURGH	17/06/03	6	0	13	0	DEFENDER	ALLOA ATHLETIC
DOUGAL	JOHN		29/06/88	EDINBURGH	20/08/04	5	7	9	6	FORWARD	EYEMOUTH AMATEURS
FORREST	GORDON	IAIN	14/01/77	DUNFERMLINE	12/06/00	5	9	10	10	DEFENDER	EAST FIFE
GASS	GRANT	JAMES	18/08/87	EDINBURGH	30/07/04	5	11	10	3	MIDFIELD	ABERDEEN
GLENNIE	DAVID		02/04/87	EDINBURGH	30/07/04	5	8	10	2	DEFENDER	MUSSELBURGH ATHLETIC JNRS
GODFREY	ROSS		21/01/77	EDINBURGH	20/08/04	6	0	13	0	GOALKEEPER	BATHGATE THISTLE
GORDON	KEVIN	MERVYN	01/05/77	TRANENT	29/01/04	5	10	10	12	MID / FWD	COWDENBEATH
HAMPSHIRE	PAUL	CHRISTOPHER	20/09/81	EDINBURGH	24/06/03	5	11	11	0	MIDFIELD	RAITH ROVERS
HORN	ROBERT	DAVID	03/08/77	EDINBURGH	02/06/04	6	0	12	7	DEFENDER	FORFAR ATHLETIC
HUTCHISON	GARETH	WILLIAM MᶜKAY	04/06/72	EDINBURGH	05/06/03	5	11	11	10	FORWARD	ALLOA ATHLETIC
LACKENBY	SCOTT		04/01/89	GALASHIELS	20/08/04	6	1	12	0	DEFENDER	DUNBAR
LALLEY	CHRISTOPHER	JAMES	19/05/86	GLASGOW	26/07/04	6	2	12	10	DEFENDER	BALLOCH EASTFIELD
LAMB	GED		04/11/88	GALASHIELS	20/08/04	5	6	8	7	MIDFIELD	SALVESEN B.C.
LITTLE	IAN	JAMES	10/12/73	EDINBURGH	25/05/04	5	8	10	10	FORWARD	ALLOA ATHLETIC
LOUGH	KEITH	WILLIAM EDWARD	08/11/87	EDINBURGH	25/08/04	6	1	10	10	FORWARD	COLDSTREAM
LUCAS	SCOTT		28/05/86	EDINBURGH	26/07/04	6	0	11	2	MIDFIELD	TYNECASTLE HEARTS
MASTERS	ROBERT		06/08/86	EDINBURGH	26/07/04	6	2	11	0	MIDFIELD	VALE OF LEITHEN
MᶜCANN	GAVIN	JOHN	15/03/86	BANGOUR	12/08/04	5	11	10	10	GOALKEEPER	DUNDEE UNITED
MᶜCATHIE	PAUL		22/06/88	EDINBURGH	25/08/04	5	10	11	0	DEFENDER	ROSEBURN COLTS
MᶜNICOLL	GRANT		07/09/77	EDINBURGH	30/07/97	5	11	11	1	DEFENDER	HEART OF MIDLOTHIAN
MᶜPARTLIN	JAMES		19/11/86	EDINBURGH	26/07/04	5	9	10	6	DEF / MID	SPARTANS
MᶜQUADE	DANIEL		10/06/86	EDINBURGH	26/07/04	6	1	11	4	DEFENDER	REDPATH ALBION
MOFFAT	CHRISTOPHER		29/01/86	EDINBURGH	26/07/04	5	8	10	1	MID / FWD	EDINA HEARTS
MURIE	DAVID		02/08/76	EDINBURGH	14/06/01	5	9	11	0	DEFENDER	MORTON
NEIL	MARTIN		16/04/70	ASHINGTON	17/11/94	5	8	11	4	MIDFIELD	BOLTON WANDERERS
O'CONNOR	GARY		07/04/74	NEWTONGRANGE	02/06/04	6	3	14	0	GOALKEEPER	EAST FIFE
PEOPLES	CALLUM	STUART	21/05/89	GALASHIELS	20/08/04	5	10	10	12	MIDFIELD	HEART OF MIDLOTHIAN
PUNTON	BEN		07/01/89	BERWICK UPON TWEED	20/08/04	6	1	11	7	DEFENDER	BERWICK RANGERS JNRS
RAEBURN	RYAN		15/12/87	EDINBURGH	25/08/04	5	10	10	10	FORWARD	CIVIL SERVICE STROLLERS
ROBERTSON	JAMES		10/06/88	EDINBURGH	20/08/04	5	11	11	0	MIDFIELD	SALVESEN B.C.
SCOTT	DEAN		01/07/87	EDINBURGH	26/07/04	5	9	11	6	DEFENDER	LIVINGSTON
SEATON	ANDREW	MURRAY	16/09/77	EDINBURGH	25/05/04	5	10	12	0	DEFENDER	ALLOA ATHLETIC
SENIOR	DAVID		20/03/89	ASHINGTON	20/08/04	5	9	10	10	DEFENDER	BERWICK RANGERS JNRS
SIMPSON	SEAN		12/03/89	ASHINGTON	20/08/04	5	10	11	12	FORWARD	BERWICK RANGERS JNRS
SMITH	DARREN		04/06/80	EDINBURGH	16/10/98	5	7	10	2	MIDFIELD	BERWICK RANGERS COLTS
SMITH	ELLIOTT	HARVEY	23/12/83	EDINBURGH	08/06/04	5	10	11	0	DEFENDER	MONTROSE
STALKER	RUSSELL		27/07/88	ALNWICK	20/08/04	6	0	11	12	GOALKEEPER	BELFORD B.C.
TAIT	MARTYN		18/01/88	ASHINGTON	20/08/04	6	0	12	2	MIDFIELD	BERWICK RANGERS JNRS
WINDRAM	JACK		29/04/88	EDINBURGH	20/08/04	5	8	9	0	FORWARD	EYEMOUTH UNDER 17'S
YOUNG	CHRISTOPHER	DAVID	16/01/88	EDINBURGH	20/08/04	5	11	12	3	DEFENDER	AYTON AMATEURS
YOUNGER	MARK		16/11/88	EDINBURGH	20/08/04	5	9	8	8	DEFENDER	EYEMOUTH JUNIORS

TICKET INFORMATION

SEASON TICKET PRICES
TICKETS FOR SEATED OR STANDING VALID FOR ALL
BELL'S SECOND DIVISION GAMES

SEATED & ADULT £150
STANDING CONCESSIONS £75
(INCLUDES JUVENILE/OAP/UNEMPLOYED WITH UB40/REGISTERED DISABLED)
SCHOOLCHILD SEASON TICKETS AVAILABLE VIA LOCAL SCHOOLS EQUATES TO
£2 PER LEAGUE GAME

LEAGUE ADMISSION PRICES
SEATED & ADULT £10
STANDING CONCESSIONS £5

N.B. ALL FANS FOR STAND ENTER VIA EITHER GROUND 'A' OR 'B' AND
TRANSFER TO STAND(S).

THE BORDERERS' 10 YEAR LEAGUE RECORD

SEASON	DIV	P	W	D	L	F	A	PTS
1994-95	S	36	15	10	11	52	46	55
1995-96	S	36	18	6	12	64	47	60
1996-97	S	36	4	11	21	32	75	23
1997-98	T	36	10	12	14	47	55	42
1998-99	T	36	12	14	10	53	49	50
1999-00	T	36	19	9	8	53	30	66
2000-01	S	36	14	12	10	51	44	54
2001-02	S	36	12	11	13	44	52	47
2002-03	S	36	13	10	13	43	48	49
2003-04	S	36	14	6	16	61	67	48

The borderers' stats 2003/04

SEASON STATS 2003/04

DATE	VENUE	OPPONENTS	ATT	RES	INGLIS N.	MURIE D.	NEILL A.	COWAN M.	McNICOLL G.	HAMPSHIRE P.	CONNELLY G.	FORREST G.	McALLISTER J.	HUTCHISON G.	BENNETT J.N.	McCORMICK M.	BIRRELL J.	WALDIE C.	CONNELL G.	McCUTCHEON G.	SMITH D.	GODFREY R.	BLACKLEY D.	HILLAND P.	ROBERTSON M.	NEIL M.	KERRIGAN S.	GORDON K.	ELLIOTT B.	NOON D.	BRACKS K.	BAIN C.	McDONALD S.
9-AUG	A	ARBROATH	565	0-1	1	2	3	4	5	6	7	8	9	10	11	12	15																
16-AUG	H	HAMILTON ACADEMICAL	552	3-1	1	2	5	4		11^1	6			9	3		7	8	10^2	14	16												
23-AUG	A	EAST FIFE	692	1-3			5	4^1	2	11	15	6	14	9	3		7	8	10		1	13											
30-AUG	H	ALLOA ATHLETIC	405	3-2		2	5		4	11	7	6^2		9^1	3			8	10	15	1		12										
13-SEP	A	DUMBARTON	751	1-1		2		4	5	11	7			9^1	8		12	6	10		1	13	3										
20-SEP	H	STENHOUSEMUIR	393	3-0		2		4	5	11	7			9^2	3		6	8	10^1		1	14	12	13										
27-SEP	A	AIRDRIE UNITED	752	0-1		2		4	5	11	7		15	9	3		6	8	10		1												
4-OCT	H	MORTON	2,896	3-1		2		4	5	11	7^1			9^1	3		6	8	10^1		1	13												
18-OCT	A	FORFAR ATHLETIC	423	0-4		2		4	5	11	7			9	3		6	8	10		1	14	12	13										
25-OCT	A	HAMILTON ACADEMICAL	1,143	2-2		2		5	4	11	7^1			9	6		8	10^1			1		3											
1-NOV	H	ARBROATH	383	3-0		2		5	4	11	7			9^3	6		12	8	10		1		3	13	15									
8-NOV	H	DUMBARTON	395	1-4		2		5	4	11	7			9	6		8	10^1			1		3	15										
16-NOV	A	ALLOA ATHLETIC	391	3-2	1	2	4	5		11^1	14			9^1	3^1		6	8	10^1				12		7									
29-NOV	H	STENHOUSEMUIR	330	2-1	1	2		5	4^1	11	7			9	3	14	7	8	10	13						6	15							
6-DEC	A	AIRDRIE UNITED	1,254	1-1	1	2		5	4	11				9^1	3	14	7	8	10	13						6	15							
13-DEC	H	MORTON	882	2-3	1	2	12	5	4	11				9	3	14	7	8	10^1	13						6^1								
27-DEC	A	FORFAR ATHLETIC	603	5-1	1	2	4	5		11	7^1	8^3		9	3	14			10^1	13						6	15							
3-JAN	H	EAST FIFE	501	0-1	1	2	4	5		11	7	8		9	3				10	13						6	15							
17-JAN	A	ARBROATH	411	2-1	1	2	3	5	4	11	7	8		9					10^2	15						6	14							
24-JAN	A	STENHOUSEMUIR	337	1-3	1	2	3	5^1	4	11	7	8		9			13	10	15							6	14							
7-FEB	H	DUMBARTON	722	1-4	1	2		5^1	4	11	7	6		9	3		8	10	13									14	15					
14-FEB	A	ALLOA ATHLETIC	445	3-1	1	2		5	4	14	7	8^1		9^2	3		6	10	11							12		15						
21-FEB	H	FORFAR ATHLETIC	435	3-1	1	2		5^1	4		7	8^1		9^1	3		6	10	11									15						
6-MAR	H	HAMILTON ACADEMICAL	468	2-4	1	2	13	5	4	14^1	7	8		9^1	3		6	10	11									15						
13-MAR	A	EAST FIFE	498	2-2	1	2		5		4	11	7	8		9^1	12		6	10					3^1		13	15							
16-MAR	H	AIRDRIE UNITED	502	1-1	1	2		5		4	11	7			9	12		6	10					3^1		8	15							
23-MAR	A	MORTON	2,300	1-2	1	2		5		4	11	7			9	12		6	10	14			3			8	15							
27-MAR	A	ALLOA ATHLETIC	365	2-4	1	2		5		4	11	7			9^2	12		6	10	13			3			8		15						
30-MAR	H	DUMBARTON	354	1-2	1	2		5		4	13	12	7		9	3^1		6	10	11						8	15							
3-APR	A	AIRDRIE UNITED	1,546	0-6	1	2		5		4	11	7	6		9	3		8	12				10					15						
10-APR	H	STENHOUSEMUIR	392	3-0	1	2		5		4	11^1	7	8^1		9	3		6	10^1	13								14	15					
17-APR	A	FORFAR ATHLETIC	465	2-1	1	2		5		4	11	7	8		9^1	3			10^1									6						
24-APR	H	MORTON	1,175	2-0	1	2		5		4	11	7	8		9^1	3			10^1									6	14	15				
1-MAY	A	EAST FIFE	490	1-1	1	2	5		4	11				9^1	3		14	10	8									6	7					
8-MAY	A	HAMILTON ACADEMICAL	1,591	0-2	1	2	5	12	4	11	13			9	3			10	8									6	7	14				
15-MAY	H	ARBROATH	506	1-3		2		5	4	11				9^1	3			8	1									6	7	10	12	14	15
TOTAL FULL APPEARANCES					25	35	20	24	32	32	27	18	1	36	30		11	25	33	7	11	9	16	3	1								
TOTAL SUB APPEARANCES						2	1		3	4		2		4	1	2	2	1	12	1	5	4	3	4	6	10	5		1	1	1		
TOTAL GOALS SCORED						4		1	4	3	8	22	2	14				2	1														

All bold figures denote goalscorers. † denotes opponent's own goal.

LEADING GOALSCORERS:

SEASON	DIV	GOALS	PLAYER
94-95	S	16	W. Hawke
95-96	S	13	W. Irvine
96-97	S	6	P. Forrester
97-98	T	10	P. Forrester
98-99	T	12	M. Leask
99-00	T	14	M. Anthony
00-01	S	14	G. Wood
01-02	S	9	G. Wood
02-03	S	12	A. Burke, G. Wood
03-04	S	22	G. Hutchison

MILESTONES:

YEAR OF FORMATION: 1881

MOST LEAGUE POINTS IN A SEASON:
54 (Second Division – Season 1978/79)(2 Points for a Win)
66 (Third Division – Season 1999/2000)(3 Points for a Win)

MOST LEAGUE GOALS SCORED BY A PLAYER IN A SEASON:
Ken Bowron (Season 1963/64)

NO. OF GOALS SCORED: 33

RECORD ATTENDANCE: 13,365 (-v- Rangers – 28.1.1967)

RECORD VICTORY:
8-1 (-v- Forfar Athletic (H) – Division 2, 25.12.1965)
8-1 (-v- Vale of Leithen – Scottish Cup at Innerleithen, 17.12.1966)

RECORD DEFEAT: 1-9 (-v- Hamilton Academical – First Division, 9.8.1980)

BERWICK RANGERS PLAYING KITS SEASON 2004/05

FIRST KIT   SECOND KIT   THIRD KIT

BRECHIN CITY
Glebe Park, Trinity Road,
Brechin, Angus, DD9 6BJ
CHAIRMAN
David H. Birse
VICE-CHAIRMAN
Hugh A. Campbell Adamson
DIRECTORS
Martin G. Smith (Treasurer),
Calum I. McK. Brown,
Kenneth W. Ferguson, Stephen D. Mitchell,
Angus A. Fairlie & Andrew Allison
HON. LIFE PRESIDENT
David H. Will C.B.E
HON. LIFE MEMBERS
David K. Lindsay &
George C. Johnston
SECRETARY
Kenneth W. Ferguson
MANAGER
Richard M. Campbell
ASSISTANT MANAGER
Ian Campbell
FIRST TEAM COACH
Bert Paton
COACHING STAFF
Norman Ross
KIT PERSON
Alan Grieve
CLUB DOCTOR
Dr. Alan Dawson
PHYSIOTHERAPIST
Tom Gilmartin
OFFICE ADMINISTRATOR
Ken Ferguson
**FOOTBALL SAFETY OFFICERS'
ASSOCIATION REPRESENTATIVE**
Calum Brown (01307) 461222
CHIEF STEWARD Alan Boath
GROUNDSMAN Alex Laing
**COMMERCIAL MANAGER/
MEDIA LIAISON OFFICER/
MATCHDAY PROGRAMME EDITOR**
Steve Mitchell (01356) 626336
LOTTERY MANAGER Angus Fairlie
TELEPHONES
Ground (Matchdays Only) (01356) 622856
Sec. Bus. (01356) 625285
Sec. Mobile 07803 089060
Sec. Home (01356) 625691
Sec. Home Fax (01356) 625667
Sec. Bus. Fax (01356) 625524
E-MAIL/INTERNET ADDRESS
ken.ferguson@brechincityfc.com
www.brechincity.co.uk
CLUB SHOP
Glebe Park, Brechin, Angus, DD9 6BJ
Open during home match days. Merchandise
available online - www.brechincity.co.uk
OFFICIAL SUPPORTERS CLUB
c/o Glebe Park, Brechin,
Angus, DD9 6BJ
TEAM CAPTAIN
Paul Deas
SHIRT SPONSOR
Delson Contracts
KIT SUPPLIER
Paulas Benara

LIST OF PLAYERS 2004/05

PLAYERS SURNAME	FIRST NAME	MIDDLE NAME	DATE OF BIRTH	PLACE OF BIRTH	DATE SIGNED	HEIGHT FT INS		WEIGHT ST LBS		POSITION ON PITCH	PREVIOUS CLUB
BLACK	RODDY		22/02/78	DUNDEE	31/07/03	5	10	12	0	MIDFIELD	CARNOUSTIE PANMURE JNRS
BYERS	KEVIN		23/08/79	KIRKCALDY	09/06/04	5	10	11	4	MIDFIELD	FORFAR ATHLETIC
DEAS	PAUL	ANDREW	22/02/72	PERTH	24/01/03	5	11	12	1	DEFENDER	ROSS COUNTY
DENNIS	SHAUN		20/12/69	KIRKCALDY	30/06/04	6	1	15	0	DEFENDER	RAITH ROVERS
GIBSON	GRAHAM		19/07/80	KIRKCALDY	12/03/02	6	3	11	6	FORWARD	LOCHORE WELFARE JNRS
HAMPSHIRE	STEVEN	GARY	17/10/79	EDINBURGH	30/08/03	5	11	11	7	MIDFIELD	DUNFERMLINE ATHLETIC
HAY	DAVID	ALEXANDER	02/01/80	EDINBURGH	19/07/02	6	4	14	0	GOALKEEPER	EAST STIRLINGSHIRE
JACKSON	CHRISTOPHER	ROBERT	29/10/73	EDINBURGH	05/06/02	5	9.5	11	8	MIDFIELD	STENHOUSEMUIR
JOHNSON	IAN	GRANT	24/03/72	DUNDEE	22/07/03	5	11	11	3	MIDFIELD	MONTROSE
KING	CHARLES	ALEXANDER	15/11/79	EDINBURGH	18/07/01	5	7	10	2	FORWARD	LIVINGSTON
McNICOL	SCOTT		25/02/83	BRISBANE	23/07/04	5	10	12	2	MIDFIELD	FORFAR ATHLETIC
McCULLOCH	SCOTT	ANDERSON JAMES	29/11/75	CUMNOCK	03/07/03	6	0	14	10	DEFENDER	FORFAR ATHLETIC
McFLEISH	KEVIN	MICHAEL	03/12/80	EDINBURGH	31/08/03	5	10	12	0	MIDFIELD	DUNFERMLINE ATHLETIC
MITCHELL	ALISTAIR	ROBERT	03/12/68	KIRKCALDY	03/07/03	5	7	11	8	FORWARD	ST. MIRREN
NELSON	CRAIG	ROBERT	28/05/71	COATBRIDGE	20/08/04	6	1	13	4	GOALKEEPER	ST. JOHNSTONE
RITCHIE	PAUL	MICHAEL	25/01/69	ST. ANDREWS	19/06/04	6	1	13	5	FORWARD	INVERNESS CALEDONIAN THISTLE
SMITH	JAMES		11/07/78	GLASGOW	21/09/01	6	3	13	0	DEFENDER	PARTICK THISTLE
TEMPLEMAN	CHRISTOPHER		12/01/80	KIRKCALDY	18/07/01	6	5	15	2	FORWARD	STIRLING ALBION
WALKER	SCOTT	EDWARD	05/03/75	GLASGOW	30/06/04	6	3	12	10	DEFENDER	HARTLEPOOL UNITED
WHITE	DAVID	WILLIAM	09/08/79	EDINBURGH	03/07/03	6	1.5	11	12	DEFENDER	COWDENBEATH
WINTER	CRAIG	JOHN	30/06/76	DUNFERMLINE	12/03/04	5	11	12	0	MIDFIELD	COWDENBEATH

TICKET INFORMATION

SEASON TICKET INFORMATION

SEATED	ADULT	£150
	PARENT & JUVENILE (UNDER 12)	£165
	OAP	£85
	JUVENILE	£45

LEAGUE ADMISSION PRICES

SEATED	ADULT	£9
	JUVENILE/OAP	£4
ENCLOSURE	ADULT	£9
	JUVENILE/OAP	£4
STANDING	ADULT	£9
	JUVENILE/OAP	£4
	PARENT & JUVENILE	£12

THE CITY'S 10 YEAR LEAGUE RECORD

SEASON	DIV	P	W	D	L	F	A	PTS
1994-95	S	36	6	6	24	22	60	24
1995-96	T	36	18	9	9	41	21	63
1996-97	S	36	10	11	15	36	49	41
1997-98	S	36	7	11	18	42	73	32
1998-99	T	36	17	8	11	47	43	59
1999-00	T	36	10	8	18	42	51	38
2000-01	T	36	22	6	8	71	36	72
2001-02	T	36	22	7	7	67	38	73
2002-03	S	36	16	7	13	63	59	55
2003-04	F	36	6	9	21	37	73	27

SEASON STATS 2003/04

DATE	VENUE	OPPONENTS	ATT	RES	BUDINAUCKAS K.	DAVIDSON I.	McCULLOCH S.	DEAS P.	WHITE D.	FOTHERINGHAM K.	MITCHELL A.	JOHNSON I.G.	TEMPLEMAN C.	GIBSON G.	BLACK R.	MILLER G.	STEIN J.	SHIELDS D.	CLARK D.	JACKSON C.	KING C.	HAY D.	McCULLOCH M.	JABLONSKI N.	SOUTAR D.	HAMPSHIRE S.	SMITH J.	McLEISH K.	MILLAR M.	BOYLAN C.	BETH G.	WALKER S.	DUFFY D.	DOWIE A.	WINTER C.
AUG	A	ROSS COUNTY	2,662	0-4	1	2	3	4	5	6	7	8	9	10	11	12		14		16															
AUG	H	RAITH ROVERS	1,013	0-3	1	2	3		4	6			9	12			7	11	15	5	8		10	18											
AUG	A	CLYDE	1,063	1-2	14	5	4	4	12	3	6	9	10		2	17					1	8	11[1]												
AUG	A	ST. JOHNSTONE	2,219	1-3	4	14	8	5	6	3		9	12[1]		2						16		11	10	1	7									
SEP	H	ST. MIRREN	956	1-1		4	3	5	6[1]	11		12	9		2						14		16	8	1	10		7							
SEP	H	INVERNESS CAL TH	652	0-2		4	3	5		11	8	12	7		16						10		14	6	1	9	2								
SEP	A	AYR UNITED	1,427	2-3		10	3	5		11	8	12	15		2						7[1]		14	6	1	9[1]	4								
OCT	H	QUEEN OF THE SOUTH	621	0-1		10	3	5	15	11	8	12			2						7		6	1	9	4									
OCT	A	FALKIRK	2,442	0-3		3	4	5		8		9	15		14	11	12				7		6		1	10	2								
OCT	A	RAITH ROVERS	1,685	1-2		4	3	5	12[1]	8		10	14		2	16					7		11		1	9	6								
NOV	H	ROSS COUNTY	564	4-2		12	3	5[2]		6	8	9	16		14						7		2	1	10	4[1]	11[1]								
NOV	A	ST. MIRREN	2,801	0-0		12	3	5		6	8	9									7	18	2	1	10	4	11	15							
NOV	H	ST. JOHNSTONE	1,434	0-1		3	5	14	11	4	9	15		16							7	1	8		10	6		2							
NOV	H	AYR UNITED	508	3-1		14	3	5		4	10[1]	12	16								7	1	8		9[1]	6	11[1]	2							
NOV	A	INVERNESS CAL TH	1,393	0-5		6	3	5		4	10	12	16	15							7	1	8		9	11	2								
DEC	H	FALKIRK	1,043	2-2		12	3	5		11[1]	4	15	10								7		14	1	9	6	8	2[1]							
DEC	A	QUEEN OF THE SOUTH	1,736	0-1		5	3	6	11		14	9		14					2		7	1	8			10		16							
DEC	A	ROSS COUNTY	2,545	1-2		3	5	6	11		12[1]	10		14							7		8	9	2	15									
DEC	H	CLYDE	808	1-3		5		6	9	8	11	10									4	1	7[1]	3	12	2	16	15							
JAN	A	ST. JOHNSTONE	2,171	2-2		12	3		6	7[1]	11	9	15								16	1	10[1]	4	8	2		5							
JAN	H	ST. MIRREN	878	2-0		3[1]	6		8	4		15	16	12							7	1	9	5[1]		2	11	10							
JAN	H	INVERNESS CAL TH	669	2-4		8	5		11	7	11	14	12	3							12	1	9	4	16	2		10[2]	6						
JAN	A	AYR UNITED	1,512	2-1		3	5		11	8	14	12									7[1]	1	9	4	2[1]			10	6						
FEB	H	QUEEN OF THE SOUTH	642	2-1		3	5		8	9		11		6							7[1]	1	2	14		15	16[1]	10	4						
FEB	A	FALKIRK	2,060	0-5		12	3	5		8	6	14		16						12	7	1	10	2		11		9	4						
MAR	H	RAITH ROVERS	925	1-1	1	5	6	4		3									15		7		9	12	11	8	14	10[1]	2						
MAR	A	CLYDE	1,037	0-0		5	3		11	4											7	1	9	15	12	2	14	10	6	8					
MAR	A	ST. MIRREN	2,221	3-3		5[1]			11	6	14[1]								12		7	1	9	2	15	3		10	4	8[1]					
MAR	H	ST. JOHNSTONE	822	0-2		3		12	11	6	9	15									7	1	10	5	14	2			4	8					
APR	H	AYR UNITED	519	0-3		6	3	5		8	10	12									1		9	2	14	7	16		4	11					
APR	A	INVERNESS CAL TH	1,198	0-1	18	6	3	5		8	7										12	1	9	2		11	16		4	10					
APR	H	FALKIRK	768	0-1	1	6	3		16		9	14	15								11		5	8	2	7			4	10					
APR	A	QUEEN OF THE SOUTH	1,352	2-2	1	6	3	5		11	9	16[1]	15								7		2		10	14			4	8[1]					
MAY	H	ROSS COUNTY	464	1-0	1	6	3		11		9	10[1]	16								7		5	14	2	15			4	8					
MAY	A	RAITH ROVERS	2,311	1-1	1		3	5	14	10	9	11[1]	6								7		2	12		16			4	8					
MAY	H	CLYDE	1,268	2-5	1	14	5			6	9[2]	10	3								7		11	2		16			4	8					
TOTAL FULL APPEARANCES					8	3	22	32	27	8	27	25	22	11	5	7	2		3	1	27	16	4	14	12	27	26	11	19	1	2	1	8	15	10
TOTAL SUB APPEARANCES					1	1	8			1	4	2			11	16	5	10	4	2	3		5	2	3	1			2	9	1	12	2		
TOTAL GOALS SCORED						2			2	2	2		5	4							3			1			4	2	2	2		1		3	2

bold figures denote goalscorers. † denotes opponent's own goal.

LEADING GOALSCORERS:

SEASON	DIV	GOALS	PLAYER
94-95	S	6	G. Price, R. Smith
95-96	T	8	A. Ross
96-97	S	7	S. Kerrigan
97-98	S	7	C. Feroz
98-99	T	5	J. Dickson
99-00	T	11	B. Honeyman
00-01	T	22	R. Grant
01-02	T	15	C. Templeman
02-03	S	21	C. Templeman
03-04	F	5	C. Templeman

MILESTONES:

YEAR OF FORMATION: 1906

MOST LEAGUE POINTS IN A SEASON:
55 (Second Division – Season 1982/83) (2 Points for a Win)
73 (Third Division – Season 2001/02) (3 Points for a Win)

MOST LEAGUE GOALS SCORED BY A PLAYER IN A SEASON:
Ronald McIntosh (Season 1959/60)

NO. OF GOALS SCORED: 26

RECORD ATTENDANCE:
8,122 (-v- Aberdeen – 3.2.1973)

RECORD VICTORY: 12-1 (-v- Thornhill – Scottish Cup, 28.1.1926)

RECORD DEFEAT: 0-10 (-v- Airdrieonians, Albion Rovers and Cowdenbeath – Division 2, 1937/38)

BRECHIN CITY PLAYING KITS SEASON 2004/05

FIRST KIT | SECOND KIT | THIRD KIT

DUMBARTON

DUMBARTON
Strathclyde Homes Stadium, Dumbarton
Castle, Castle Road, Dumbarton, G82 1JJ
CHAIRMAN
John G. MacFarlane
MANAGING DIRECTOR
Neil Rankine
DIRECTORS
Colin J. Hosie, John Benn,
Callum L. Hosie,
Donald McK. MacIntyre,
Sidney S. Collumbine
ASSOCIATE DIRECTORS
Alan T. Jardine, Andrew Gemmell &
James Todd
HON. PRESIDENTS
Ian A. Bell, J.P., R. Campbell Ward, C.A.
& Douglas S. Dalgleish
CLUB SECRETARY
J. David Prophet
COMPANY SECRETARY
John Benn M.Sc.
OFFICE ADMINISTRATOR
Freida McMahon
DIRECTOR OF FOOTBALL
Sidney S. Collumbine
Bus. (01324) 611777
Mob. (07710) 079459
Fax (01324) 635590
MANAGER
Brian Fairley
ASSISTANT MANAGER
Allan McGonigal
**FIRST TEAM COACH/
GOALKEEPING COACH**
Alan Banner
COACH
Alan Fraser
CLUB DOCTOR Neil MacKay, MBC, HB
SPORTS THERAPIST
Jaki West, Chartered Physiotherapist BSC
(Hons) MCSP.SR
CHIEF SCOUT Willie Hughes
GROUND MAINTENANCE Apex Groundcare
KIT PERSON Steven Hunter
COMMERCIAL MANAGER
John Sharp (01389) 762569
LOTTERY MANAGER
George Park (01389) 763651
**FOOTBALL SAFETY OFFICERS'
ASSOCIATION REPRESENTATIVE**
Martin Love
Home (01389) 602866
Bus. (07713) 151023
MEDIA LIAISON OFFICERS
Colin J. Hosie & John Benn
MATCHDAY PROGRAMME EDITOR
Graeme Robertson (0131) 441 5451
TELEPHONES
Ground (01389) 762569
Sec. Home (01389) 602567
Sec. Bus (01389) 723510
Sec. Mobile (07796) 881002
Fax (01389) 762629
E-MAIL & INTERNET ADDRESS
club@dumbartonfootballclub.com
david_prophet58@hotmail.com
www.dumbartonfootballclub.com
CLUB SHOP
Situated in ground. Open on home match-
days and 10.00 a.m. – 4.00 p.m. Mon-Fri
OFFICIAL SUPPORTERS CLUB
c/o Dumbarton FC,
Strathclyde Homes Stadium, Castle Road,
Dumbarton, G82 1JJ
TEAM CAPTAIN
Paul Ronald
SHIRT SPONSOR
Laphroaig
KIT SUPPLIER
Vandanel

LIST OF PLAYERS 2004/05

PLAYERS SURNAME	FIRST NAME	MIDDLE NAME	DATE OF BIRTH	PLACE OF BIRTH	DATE SIGNED	HEIGHT FT INS	WEIGHT ST LBS	POSITION ON PITCH	PREVIOUS CLUB
ALLAN	DEREK		24/12/74	IRVINE	24/05/04	6 0	12 12	DEFENDER	QUEEN OF THE SOUTH
ANDERSON	KARL	WILLIAM	26/03/82	IRVINE	01/09/04	5 11	11 0	DEFENDER	KNIGHTSWOOD JUVENILES
ANNAND	EDWARD		24/03/73	GLASGOW	28/08/04	5 11	13 1	FORWARD	ST. MIRREN
BINNIE	JOSEPH	NEIL	25/12/67	STIRLING	08/08/04	6 2	13 6	GOALKEEPER	BO'NESS UNITED JUNIORS
BONAR	STEVEN	ANDREW	20/05/79	GLASGOW	30/03/00	5 9.5	10 6	MIDFIELD	ALBION ROVERS
BORRIS	RYAN	EDWARD	07/06/83	PAISLEY	07/06/04	5 11	11 0	FORWARD	ST. PETERS JUVENILES
BOYLE	CHRISTOPHER	THOMAS	10/06/82	IRVINE	11/06/03	5 7	10 7	MIDFIELD	KILMARNOCK
BRADLEY	MARK		10/08/76	GLASGOW	06/06/03	5 8	10 7	MIDFIELD	BERWICK RANGERS
BRITTAIN	CRAIG		10/01/74	GLASGOW	14/06/97	5 5	10 0	DEFENDER	ASHFIELD JUNIORS
DILLON	JOHN	PETER	16/12/78	VALE OF LEVEN	30/07/99	5 7	10 5	MIDFIELD	CLYDE
DOBBINS	IAN	ALEXANDER	24/08/83	BELLSHILL	29/08/03	6 2	12 7	DEFENDER	HAMILTON ACADEMICAL
DONALD	BARRY		24/12/78	GLASGOW	31/01/03	6 1	12 0	MIDFIELD	QUEEN OF THE SOUTH
DUNN	ROBERT		28/06/79	GLASGOW	07/06/04	5 10	11 0	MID / FWD	ST. MIRREN
GRINDLAY	STEPHEN	JOHN	13/03/82	VALE OF LEVEN	02/08/02	6 2	13 12	GOALKEEPER	DUMBARTON ACADEMY
HERD	GORDON	ROBERT WALKER	28/06/81	FALKIRK	31/08/04	5 10	12 7	FORWARD	LINLITHGOW ROSE JUNIORS
HOLMES	GRAEME		26/03/84	MOTHERWELL	27/08/04	5 9	10 4	MIDFIELD	DUNDEE UNITED
M'EWAN	CRAIG	GEORGE	03/10/77	GLASGOW	15/08/03	5 8.5	11 4	DEFENDER	AYR UNITED
M'KINSTRY	JAMES	ANTHONY	03/07/79	GLASGOW	07/07/03	5 10	12 1	DEFENDER	PARTICK THISTLE
RODGERS	ANDREW		18/10/83	FALKIRK	14/06/04	5 10.5	11 0	FORWARD	FALKIRK
RONALD	PAUL		19/07/71	GLASGOW	31/01/04	6 2	12 10	FORWARD	AIRDRIE UNITED
RUSSELL	IAIN	THOMAS	14/11/82	DUMFRIES	31/01/03	5 10	11 0	FORWARD	MOTHERWELL
WIGHT	JOHN	CAMPBELL	11/12/73	ALEXANDRIA	04/08/00	6 0	13 0	GOALKEEPER	BEITH JUNIORS

TICKET INFORMATION

SEASON TICKET PRICES
SEATED

ADULT	£135
JUVENILE 13-16 YEARS/OAP	£70
PARENT & JUVENILE	£170
JUVENILE UP TO 12 YEARS	£45
PREMIER SEAT	£150
PARENT + 2 CHILDREN	£200
PARENT + 3 CHILDREN	£230*
2PARENTS + 1 CHILD	£295
2PARENTS + 2 CHILDREN	£330*
2PARENTS + 3 CHILDREN	£360*

*ANY ADDITIONAL CHILD ABOVE QUANTITY OF THREE ADD £30 PER CHILD

LEAGUE ADMISSION PRICES
SEATED

ADULT	£10
JUVENILE/OAP	£5

THE SONS' 10 YEAR LEAGUE RECORD

SEASON	DIV	P	W	D	L	F	A	PTS	P
1994-95	S	36	17	9	10	57	35	60	
1995-96	F	36	3	2	31	23	94	11	1
1996-97	S	36	9	8	19	44	66	35	
1997-98	T	36	7	10	19	42	61	31	1
1998-99	T	36	16	9	11	53	40	57	
1999-00	T	36	15	8	13	53	51	53	
2000-01	T	36	13	6	17	46	49	45	
2001-02	T	36	18	7	11	59	48	61	
2002-03	S	36	13	9	14	48	47	48	
2003-04	S	36	18	6	12	56	41	60	

SEASON STATS 2003/04

DATE	VENUE	OPPONENTS	ATT	RES	GRINDLAY S.	McKINSTRY J.	BRITTAIN C.	OKOLI J.	DUFFY C.	SMITH D.	BONAR S.	BRADLEY M.	FLANNERY P.	RUSSELL I.	DILLON J.	BOYLE C.	ENGLISH I.	HERD G.	DONALD B.	McEWAN C.	COLLINS N.	OBIDILE E.	WIGHT J.	DOBBINS I.	ROBERTSON K.	RENICKS S.	MALLAN S.	RODGERS A.	RONALD P.	LAIDLER S.	SKJELBRED B.
9-AUG	A	ALLOA ATHLETIC	446	2 - 1	1	2	3	4	5	6	7	8^{1}	9^{1}	10	11	12	14	15														
16-AUG	H	ARBROATH	1,070	1 - 1	1	2	3	4	5	16	7	12	9^{1}		11	6	10			8	14											
23-AUG	A	MORTON	3,410	2 - 2	1	2	3		5		7	12	9^{1}		11	6^{1}	10			8	14	4										
30-AUG	A	AIRDRIE UNITED	1,468	0 - 2	1	2	3		5		7	12	9		11	6	10			8	15	4	16									
13-SEP	H	BERWICK RANGERS	751	1 - 1	1	2	3		5		7	8		10	16	11^{1}	6			14		4	9	18								
20-SEP	H	FORFAR ATHLETIC	449	1 - 3	1	2	3		5		7	12	9	10	15	6			8		14^{1}	11		4								
27-SEP	H	STENHOUSEMUIR	730	0 - 1		2	3		5		8	12	9	10	14	11				4	7			6	1	15						
4-OCT	A	EAST FIFE	518	0 - 1		4	3			6	7	8	15	10	11	12					9			5	1	2						
18-OCT	H	HAMILTON ACADEMICAL	890	0 - 3	1	2	3			6		14	9	16	11	8	10			15	4	7	5									
25-OCT	A	ARBROATH	506	1 - 2	1	4				6	7		15	10	11		9		8	2^{1}	5	16		3								
1-NOV	A	ALLOA ATHLETIC	742	1 - 0	1	4	3				7	8		15	11	6	10			2^{1}	5	9										
8-NOV	A	BERWICK RANGERS	395	4 - 1	1	3			5		7^{1}	8		15	11^{2}	6	10^{1}			2	4	9	12									
16-NOV	H	AIRDRIE UNITED	1,361	2 - 0	1	4					7	8		15	11^{2}	6	10		14	2	5	9		3								
6-DEC	A	STENHOUSEMUIR	447	1 - 3	1	4	3				7	8^{1}		10	11	12			6	2	5				9							
13-DEC	H	EAST FIFE	683	3 - 1	1	4	3				7^{1}	8		10^{1}	11^{1}				6	2	5		12		9							
3-JAN	H	MORTON	2,011	1 - 0	1	4	3				7	8		10^{1}	11	12			6	2	5				16	15	9					
10-JAN	H	FORFAR ATHLETIC	781	2 - 1	1	4	3				7	8		10	11^{1}	12			6	2	5				16	15	9^{1}					
17-JAN	A	ALLOA ATHLETIC	423	0 - 3	1	4	3				7	8		10	11			15		6	2	5			16	9						
24-JAN	A	FORFAR ATHLETIC	540	0 - 1	1	4	3	14			7	8		10	11			15		6	2	5			16	9						
7-FEB	H	BERWICK RANGERS	722	4 - 1	1	4	3^{1}				7	8		16^{1}	11	12		10^{1}	6	2^{1}	5						9					
14-FEB	A	AIRDRIE UNITED	1,378	1 - 1	1	4	3				7	8		16	11	12		9	6	2	5						15^{1}	10				
21-FEB	H	HAMILTON ACADEMICAL	1,015	2 - 0	1	4	3				7^{1}	8		11^{1}	12	6		15		2	5						9	10				
6-MAR	A	ARBROATH	828	1 - 0	1	4	3				7	8		10	11			15		2	5						9^{1}	6				
9-MAR	A	HAMILTON ACADEMICAL	949	0 - 2	1	4	3				7	8		15	6	2	5			14	16						9					
13-MAR	A	MORTON	3,028	2 - 3	1	4	3				7^{1}	8		14	6	2^{1}	5				15		9	16								
16-MAR	A	EAST FIFE	439	3 - 1	1	4	3				7			8^{1}	11	15^{1}		12^{1}	6	2	5						10	9	14			
23-MAR	H	STENHOUSEMUIR	552	4 - 0	1	4	3				7^{1}			10^{2}	11	6^{1}			2	5		12		15	16	8						
27-MAR	H	AIRDRIE UNITED	1,543	1 - 2	1	4	3				7			10	11	6		9^{1}	2	5		12					8	14	16			
30-MAR	A	BERWICK RANGERS	354	2 - 1	1	2	3				7			10^{1}	11	6^{1}		9	8	5		4	15						16			
3-APR	A	STENHOUSEMUIR	387	2 - 1	1	2	3				7			10	12^{1}	11		9	6	5		4					16	8^{1}				
10-APR	H	FORFAR ATHLETIC	1,007	1 - 1	1	2	3				7			10	11	6		9^{1}	8	5		4	14						12	15		
17-APR	A	HAMILTON ACADEMICAL	1,343	1 - 2	1	2	3				7			10	12	11		9	6	5^{1}		4	15				8		16			
24-APR	H	EAST FIFE	841	1 - 0	1	2	3				7			10^{1}	11	12		14	6	5							8	15	9			
1-MAY	H	MORTON	1,882	3 - 0	1	4	3				7			10^{1}	11	12		9^{1}	8		5		2				8^{1}	15	16			
8-MAY	A	ARBROATH	553	3 - 0	1	4	3				7			10	11	12		9^{2}			5		2				8^{1}	15	16			
15-MAY	H	ALLOA ATHLETIC	1,494	3 - 1	1	4				2				10	11			9^{1}			5		3				16^{1}	8				7^{1}
TOTAL FULL APPEARANCES					34	36	32	2	8	4	35	18	8	26	31	17	8	11	24	19	29	8		12	2	7	3	7	13	6	2
TOTAL SUB APPEARANCES						1	1				6	2	7	5	11	9	2	4	1	2	1	5		11	2	4	1	6	6		
TOTAL GOALS SCORED						1					5	2	3	10	8	4	1	8		4	2						4	3		1

all bold figures denote goalscorers. † denotes opponent's own goal.

LEADING GOALSCORERS:

SEASON	DIV	GOALS	PLAYER
1994-95	S	17	M. Mooney
1995-96	F	5	M. Mooney
1996-97	S	7	H. Ward
1997-98	T	10	C. McKinnon
1998-99	T	17	P. Flannery
1999-00	T	14	P. Flannery
2000-01	T	17	P. Flannery
2001-02	T	18	P. Flannery
2002-03	S	8	P. Flannery, G. McCutcheon
2003-04	S	10	I. Russell

MILESTONES:

YEAR OF FORMATION: 1872
MOST CAPPED PLAYERS: J. Lindsay and J.McAulay
NO. OF CAPS: 8 each
MOST LEAGUE POINTS IN A SEASON:
53 (First Division – Season 1986/87) (2 Points for a Win)
61 (Third Division – Season 2001/02) (3 Points for a Win)
MOST LEAGUE GOALS SCORED BY A PLAYER IN A SEASON:
Kenneth Wilson (Season 1971/72)
NO. OF GOALS SCORED: 38
RECORD ATTENDANCE: 18,001 (-v- Raith Rovers – 2.3.1957 at Boghead Park) 2,011 (-v- Morton – 3.1.2004 at Strathclyde Homes Stadium)
RECORD VICTORY: 13-2 (-v- Kirkintilloch – Scottish Cup)
RECORD DEFEAT: 1-11 (-v- Ayr United/Albion Rovers)

DUMBARTON PLAYING KITS SEASON 2004/05

FIRST KIT   SECOND KIT   THIRD KIT

Forfar Athletic

LIST OF PLAYERS 2004/05

PLAYERS SURNAME	FIRST NAME	MIDDLE NAME	DATE OF BIRTH	PLACE OF BIRTH	DATE SIGNED	HEIGHT FT INS		WEIGHT ST LBS		POSITION ON PITCH	PREVIOUS CLUB
ANDERSON	DAVID	WILLIAM	21/04/86	DUNDEE	28/07/04	6	0	11	8	DEFENDER	BRECHIN CITY
BOOTH	MARK		07/03/80	COATBRIDGE	15/06/04	5	10	12	0	MIDFIELD	STENHOUSEMUIR
BROWN	MICHAEL		07/11/79	STRANRAER	06/06/01	6	1	12	8	GOALKEEPER	PARTICK THISTLE
BROWNHILL	MYLES	GORDON	03/08/86	ABERDEEN	24/08/04	5	9	8	11	MIDFIELD	BRECHIN CITY
CAMERON	DOUGLAS		08/02/83	DUNDEE	30/08/04	5	10	12	0	MIDFIELD	DUNDEE
CLARK	NEIL		12/04/84	DUNDEE	30/08/04	5	11	11	10	MIDFIELD	DUNDEE
DAVIDSON	HUGH	NORMAN	03/08/80	DUNDEE	06/06/03	5	11.5	12	6	MIDFIELD	DUNDEE UNITED
DUNCAN	GREIG	RUSSELL	22/12/87	DUNDEE	24/08/04	5	11	10	5	FORWARD	DOUGLAS B.C.
DUNCAN	RYAN	RICHARD	17/08/87	DUNDEE	28/07/04	5	9	11	5	FORWARD	DUNDEE WEST B.C.
DUNN	DAVID	WALTER	01/03/84	EDINBURGH	20/07/04	6	2	11	10	DEFENDER	HEART OF MIDLOTHIAN
FERRIE	NEAL		23/11/81	DUNDEE	07/06/00	6	0	11	4	GOALKEEPER	DUNDEE UNITED
FLORENCE	STEVEN		28/10/71	DUNDEE	18/07/03	5	6	11	0	DEFENDER	ARBROATH
FORREST	EDWARD	ALEXANDER	17/12/78	EDINBURGH	15/06/04	6	0	12	0	DEFENDER	PARTICK THISTLE
FORSYTH	ROSS		10/10/86	DUNDEE	24/08/04	5	11	10	10	MIDFIELD	BRECHIN CITY
GIBB	LIAM	ROBERT	07/03/85	DUNDEE	30/08/04	5	9	9	7	FORWARD	BROUGHTY ATHLETIC JNRS
GUNN	EWAN	BRYSON	15/01/87	DUNDEE	24/08/04	5	11	11	5	MIDFIELD	DOUGLAS B.C.
HAMILTON	STEVEN	JAMES	19/03/75	BAILLIESTON	15/06/04	5	9	12	0	DEFENDER	STENHOUSEMUIR
KANE	DAVID	DARREN	30/07/87	DUNDEE	28/07/04	5	7	10	6	MIDFIELD	FAIRMUIR B.C.
KING	DAVID	WILLIAM	13/07/79	FALKIRK	28/05/04	6	0	12	0	MIDFIELD	ARBROATH
KING	MATHU		26/03/84	BELLSHILL	02/07/04	5	11	10	7	FORWARD	HEART OF MIDLOTHIAN
LOWING	DAVID		04/09/83	PAISLEY	02/07/04	6	0	10	0	DEFENDER	ST. MIRREN
LUNAN	PAUL	JAMES	20/09/82	DUNDEE	04/08/01	5	10	10	0	MIDFIELD	DUNDEE VIOLET JUNIORS
MAHER	MARTIN	NEIL	05/11/83	PERTH	04/06/03	5	10.5	11	6	MIDFIELD	ST. JOHNSTONE
MARTIN	KRAIG	JOHN	22/06/87	DUNDEE	24/08/04	5	10	12	3	GOALKEEPER	BRECHIN CITY
M'CLUNE	DAVID	JAMES	08/02/83	GLASGOW	03/07/03	5	7	10	0	DEFENDER	ST. JOHNSTONE
M'KENZIE	DARYL		24/06/85	DUNDEE	30/08/04	6	1	11	4	DEFENDER	LOCHEE HARP
MENZIES	RYAN	KENNETH	07/05/85	PERTH	30/08/04	5	11	11	7	MIDFIELD	BLAIRGOWRIE JUNIORS
MITCHELL	BRAD	LEE	17/03/87	DUNDEE	24/08/04	5	10	12	8	MIDFIELD	DOUGLAS B.C.
RATTRAY	ALAN	RAYMOND	08/06/79	DUNDEE	16/11/96	5	10	11	0	DEFENDER	DUNDEE VIOLET JUNIORS
SCOTT	DARREN	KEVIN	20/01/85	DUNDEE	30/08/04	6	2	10	9	FORWARD	LOCHEE HARP
SELLARS	BARRY	MICHAEL	06/12/75	ARBROATH	02/11/00	6	1	12	10	MIDFIELD	CLYDE
SHIELDS	PAUL	MARTIN	15/08/81	DUNFERMLINE	24/07/03	6	0	12	0	FORWARD	CLYDE
SMART	KYLE		25/09/87	DUNDEE	28/07/04	5	8	11	5	DEFENDER	DUNDEE WEST B.C.
STEIN	JAY		13/01/79	DUNFERMLINE	15/06/04	5	9	10	7	MIDFIELD	EAST FIFE
THAIN	GARY		02/02/87	DUNDEE	24/08/04	5	11	13	2	GOALKEEPER	DUNDEE WEST B.C.
THOMSON	ANDREW	WILLIAM	19/09/86	DUNDEE	28/07/04	5	10	12	5	MIDFIELD	BRECHIN CITY
TOSH	PAUL	JAMES	18/10/73	ARBROATH	28/06/01	6	1	13	4	FORWARD	RAITH ROVERS
TOVEY	SCOTT	PAUL WILLIAM	24/07/87	DUNDEE	28/07/04	6	2	12	4	DEFENDER	DUNDEE WEST B.C.
WILCOX	COLIN	JAMES	12/07/87	PERTH	24/08/04	6	0	10	12	DEFENDER	BRECHIN CITY

THE LOONS' 10 YEAR LEAGUE RECORD

SEASON	DIV	P	W	D	L	F	A	PTS
1994-95	T	36	25	5	6	67	33	80
1995-96	S	36	11	7	18	37	61	40
1996-97	T	36	19	10	7	74	45	67
1997-98	S	36	12	10	14	51	61	46
1998-99	S	36	8	7	21	48	70	31
1999-00	T	36	17	10	9	64	40	61
2000-01	S	36	10	10	16	48	52	40
2001-02	S	36	15	8	13	51	47	53
2002-03	S	36	14	9	13	55	53	51
2003-04	S	36	12	11	13	49	57	47

SEASON STATS 2003/04

TE	VENUE	OPPONENTS	ATT	RES	FERRIE N.	RATTRAY A.	LOWING D.	HORN R.	STEWART D.	McCLUNE D.	LUNAN P.	SELLARS B.	TOSH P.	DAVIDSON H.	SHIELDS P.	FLORENCE S.	MAHER M.	HENDERSON D.	BROWN M.	TAYLOR S.	BYERS K.	VELLA S.	WILLIAMS D.	OGUNMADE D.	FORBES B.	FERRY M.	KING M.	McNICOL S.	BREMNER K.
AUG	A	HAMILTON ACADEMICAL	1,271	2-1	1	2	3	4	5	6	7	8	9¹	10	11¹	12	14	16											
-AUG	H	EAST FIFE	708	0-1		2	3	4	5	6	7	8		10	11		15			1	9	14							
-AUG	A	ARBROATH	856	0-0			3	4	5	6	2	8	9	10	11			7		1	16								
-AUG	A	STENHOUSEMUIR	383	0-2			3	4	5	6	2		9	10	11	12	7	8		1	15						4	14	
-SEP	H	MORTON	1,006	2-3			3		5	6	2	9	8¹	11	12	15	10¹	1			14	4		7					
-SEP	H	DUMBARTON	449	3-1		3	12	5	4	2	15	9¹	8	11¹		14	10¹	1			6			7					
-SEP	A	ALLOA ATHLETIC	378	1-1		4	3		5	2	7	9¹	8	11		14	10	1		16	6			15					
OCT	H	AIRDRIE UNITED	650	1-1		2	3	4	5		7¹	9	8	11			10	1	16	6			15						
-OCT	A	BERWICK RANGERS	423	4-0		3		4	5	2	7	9²	8	11¹			10	1	16¹	6			15					
-OCT	A	EAST FIFE	671	3-2		3		4	5	2	7	9¹	8	11²	12		10	1		6			16					
NOV	H	HAMILTON ACADEMICAL	558	4-3	18	3¹		5	4	2	7	9²	8			14	10	1	11¹	6								
NOV	A	MORTON	3,327	1-1	1	3		5		4	2	7	9	8	14		10¹		11	6								
-NOV	H	STENHOUSEMUIR	478	†2-0		3		5	4	2	7	9¹	8	11		10	1	15		6								
DEC	H	ALLOA ATHLETIC	502	1-1			12	5	4	2	7	9	8¹	11		3	10	1		6			15					
-DEC	A	AIRDRIE UNITED	1,072	3-3		3	14	5	4	2	7¹	9	8¹	11		15	10	1	16	6								
-DEC	H	BERWICK RANGERS	603	1-5		3	16	4	10	2	7	9¹	8	11		14		1	14	6	5							
-JAN	A	DUMBARTON	781	1-2		2	3	4		5	10¹	6	9	8	11		7		1	15	14			16				
-JAN	A	HAMILTON ACADEMICAL	1,099	1-2	18	3	12	5		4	2	7	9	8	15			10	1						6¹	11		
-JAN	H	DUMBARTON	540	1-0	1		3	5		4	2		9¹	8	16	12	14	10		7					6	11		
-JAN	A	ALLOA ATHLETIC	321	0-4	1	2	3	5		4	16		9	8	14			10		15	7				6	11		
FEB	H	MORTON	958	2-1		2		5		4	3	7	9¹	8	16			10	1		12				6¹	11		
-FEB	A	STENHOUSEMUIR	335	2-0		2		5			3	7	9	8	15¹		14	10	1		4				6¹	11		
-FEB	A	BERWICK RANGERS	435	1-3		2		5			3	7	9¹	8	15		14	10	1		4	16			6	11		
-MAR	H	EAST FIFE	600	1-0				5		3	2	7	9¹	8	11	12	14	10	1		4				6			
-MAR	A	ARBROATH	702	1-0				5		4	2	7	9	8	11			10¹	1						6	16	3	
-MAR	H	ARBROATH	682	2-2		2		5		4		7	9²	8			15	10	1		6				14	11	3	
-MAR	H	AIRDRIE UNITED	710	1-3		2		5		16	4	7	9	8	15		14		1		10				6¹	11	3	
-MAR	H	STENHOUSEMUIR	407	1-1		2¹		5			14	7	9			4	8	10	1						6	11	3	
-APR	A	MORTON	2,453	1-1		5				6¹	4	7			9	3	11	10	1			15			8	2		
-APR	A	DUMBARTON	1,007	1-1		5				6	4	7		16	9	3	11¹	10	1			15			14	8	2	
-APR	H	ALLOA ATHLETIC	411	2-0			10	5		6	4	7		8	9²	3	11		1						14		2	
-APR	H	BERWICK RANGERS	465	0-2			10	5		6	4	7	16	8	9		11		1		14				3	12	2	
-APR	A	AIRDRIE UNITED	1,959	2-2			6	5		11	4	7	9	8¹	10¹	3	14		1						16		2	
-MAY	H	ARBROATH	707	1-2			5	4		6		7	9¹	8	10	3	11		1						12	14	2	
MAY	A	EAST FIFE	448	0-2			11	4			9	8	10	5	7				3						15	14	2	12
-MAY	H	HAMILTON ACADEMICAL	1,496	0-4			5	4		7		9	8	11	3	15	10	1		6					12	14	2	
TOTAL FULL APPEARANCES					4	23	16	28	11	28	29	28	31	33	25	8	11	25	32	3	20	4	1	2	11	11	12		
TOTAL SUB APPEARANCES					2		5			1	2	1	1		8	6	17	1			10	5		6	3	1	7	5	1
TOTAL GOALS SCORED						2				1	1	2	18	4	9		1	4			2				4			

Bold figures denote goalscorers. † denotes opponent's own goal.

LEADING GOALSCORERS:

SEASON	DIV	GOALS	PLAYER
94-95	T	22	D. Bingham
95-96	S	12	G. Higgins
96-97	T	17	B. Honeyman
97-98	S	14	M. McLauchlan
98-99	S	10	R. Brand
99-00	T	16	S. Milne
00-01	S	9	W. Stewart
01-02	S	19	P. Tosh
02-03	S	15	M. Bavidge
03-04	S	18	P. Tosh

MILESTONES:

YEAR OF FORMATION: 1885

MOST LEAGUE POINTS IN A SEASON:
63 (Second Division – Season 1983/84) (2 Points for a Win)
80 (Third Division – Season 1994/95) (3 Points for a Win)

MOST LEAGUE GOALS SCORED BY A PLAYER IN A SEASON:
Dave Kilgour (Season 1929/30)

NO. OF GOALS SCORED: 45

RECORD ATTENDANCE:
10,800 (-v- Rangers – 7.2.1970)

RECORD VICTORY:
14-1 (-v- Lindertis – Scottish Cup, 1.9.1888)

RECORD DEFEAT:
2-12 (-v- King's Park – Division 2, 2.1.1930)

FORFAR ATHLETIC PLAYING KITS SEASON 2004/05

FIRST KIT | SECOND KIT | THIRD KIT

MORTON
Cappielow Park, Sinclair Street,
Greenock, PA15 2TY
CHAIRMAN
Douglas D. F. Rae
DIRECTORS
Iain D. Brown, James McColl,
W. Arthur M. Montford & Crawford McL. Rae
CHIEF EXECUTIVE
Gillian Donaldson (07713) 724369
COMPANY SECRETARY
Mrs Mary Davidson
MANAGER
Jim McInally
YOUTH MANAGER
Joe McLaughlin
YOUTH COACHES
Joe Harkins (U17)
Derek Collins (U15)
George Wall (U13)
CLUB DOCTORS
Dr. R. Craig Speirs, M.B., Ch.B
& Dr. Fraser Gray, M.B., Ch.B
PHYSIOTHERAPISTS
Paul Kelly & Bruce Coyle
GROUNDSMAN
Mark Farrell
STADIUM DIRECTOR
Crawford Rae
**FOOTBALL SAFETY OFFICERS'
ASSOCIATION REPRESENTATIVE**
Peter Copland
KIT PERSON
Andy Bryan
**COMMERCIAL MANAGER/
MATCHDAY PROGRAMME EDITOR**
Susan Gregory
LOTTERY MANAGER
Eugene McDade
TELEPHONES
Ground/Ticket Office
(01475) 723571
Fax (01475) 781084
E-MAIL & INTERNET ADDRESSES
info@gmfc.net
chiefexec@gmfc.net
www.gmfc.net
CLUB SHOP
Morton F.C. Cappielow Park, Sinclair Street,
Greenock PA15 2TY.
Opening Hours Mon - Fri 12 noon - 4pm.
Also open on Match days
OFFICIAL SUPPORTERS CLUB
Morton Supporters Club,
Regent Street, Greenock
TEAM CAPTAIN
Derek Collins
SHIRT SPONSOR
First & Third choice kit:
Millions – The Tiny Tasty Chewy Sweets
Second choice kit: Half Pounders
KIT SUPPLIER
Vandanel

LIST OF PLAYERS 2004/05

PLAYERS SURNAME	FIRST NAME	MIDDLE NAME	DATE OF BIRTH	PLACE OF BIRTH	DATE SIGNED	HEIGHT FT INS		WEIGHT ST LBS		POSITION ON PITCH	PREVIOUS CLUB
BALLANTYNE	GRAEME		19/01/88	BELLSHILL	28/06/04	5	9	9	7	GOALKEEPER	RANGERS
BANNERMAN	SCOTT	JOHN	21/03/79	EDINBURGH	03/08/01	5	7	11	0	DEFENDER	AIRDRIEONIANS
BLACK	CRAIG		11/05/88	GREENOCK	03/09/04	5	8	10	0	MIDFIELD	MORTON FORM D U' 16
COLLINS	DEREK	JOSEPH	15/04/69	GLASGOW	13/07/04	5	9	11	0	DEFENDER	SLIEMA WANDERERS
COYLE	CRAIG	ROBERT	06/09/80	EDINBURGH	03/08/01	5	11	12	0	GOALKEEPER	RAITH ROVERS
DIACK	IAIN	GORDON	17/02/81	GLASGOW	31/05/04	6	1	11	8	FORWARD	ARBROATH
GILBRIDE	ALAN		03/03/88	GREENOCK	17/09/04	6	2	11	0	DEFENDER	MORTON FORM D U' 16
GLASS	STEVEN	JOHN	04/08/89	PAISLEY	03/08/04	5	8	9	0	MIDFIELD	LINWOOD RANGERS
GREACEN	STEWART		31/03/82	LANARK	20/06/03	6	2	14	0	DEFENDER	FORFAR ATHLETIC
HAMILTON	STEPHEN		18/04/88	PAISLEY	25/06/04	5	9	10	7	MIDFIELD	MORTON FORM D U'16
HARKINS	PAUL		02/11/88	GLASGOW	17/09/04	5	9	9	0	MIDFIELD	GREENOCK JUNIORS COLTS
HAWKE	WARREN	ROBERT	20/09/70	DURHAM	03/06/04	5	10.5	11	4	FORWARD	QUEEN OF THE SOUTH
KEENAN	DEAN	MATTHEW	15/10/85	GLASGOW	26/05/04	5	11	11	0	MIDFIELD	POLLOK UNITED
KERR	JAMES	WILLIAM	06/02/89	PAISLEY	03/08/04	5	9	10	4	FORWARD	LINWOOD RANGERS
KERR	SCOTT		12/04/88	DUMFRIES	17/09/04	5	9	8	12	MIDFIELD	MORTON FORM D U' 16
McGREGOR	DAVID	GEORGE	09/06/81	GREENOCK	03/08/01	5	11	11	10	MIDFIELD	MORTON FORM S
McINNES	PAUL		01/01/88	GLASGOW	03/08/04	5	9	9	7	FORWARD	HILLINGTON Y.C.
McLEOD	DAVID		19/09/88	GREENOCK	17/09/04	5	6	10	2	DEFENDER	MORTON FORM D U' 14
MAISANO	JOHN	MARCEL	06/01/79	MELBOURNE	12/07/02	5	6	10	7	MIDFIELD	MARCONI STALLIONS
MAISANO	MARCO	MIGUEL	15/02/81	HAEDO - ARGENTINA	06/03/02	5	10	12	0	MIDFIELD	MARCONI STALLIONS
McALISTER	JAMES	DUNCAN	02/11/85	ROTHESAY	01/06/04	5	10	13	0	FORWARD	LINWOOD RANGERS
McCAFFERTY	KEVIN	JOHN	15/01/88	GLASGOW	17/09/04	6	0	10	7	DEFENDER	MORTON FORM D U' 16
McCLUSKEY	STUART	CAMPBELL	29/10/77	BELLSHILL	26/05/04	6	0	13	0	DEFENDER	CLYDE
McCULLOCH	MARC	RAYMOND	14/03/80	EDINBURGH	15/07/04	5	10	12	8	DEFENDER	ARBROATH
McGRORY	ALAN		24/09/88	PAISLEY	22/09/04	5	11	10	9	FORWARD	MORTON FORM D U' 16
McGURN	DAVID	EDWARD	14/09/80	GLASGOW	26/05/04	6	1	13	3	GOALKEEPER	HILLWOOD B.C.
McLEAN	KENNETH		17/11/84	GLASGOW	04/09/04	5	8	10	3	FORWARD	HILLWOOD JUVENILES
McMASTER	STEVEN		27/02/88	PAISLEY	22/09/04	5	10	11	2	DEFENDER	MORTON FORM D U' 16
MILLAR	CHRISTOPHER	ALEXANDER	30/03/83	GLASGOW	13/07/04	5	9	10	3	MIDFIELD	CELTIC
STARK	JOHN	PAUL	03/06/86	GLASGOW	24/06/04	6	2	13	0	GOALKEEPER	QUEEN'S PARK
WALKER	JASON		21/03/84	BARROW-IN-FURNESS	23/07/04	5	9	11	7	FORWARD	DUNDEE
WALKER	PAUL		20/08/77	KILWINNING	13/06/03	5	7	9	7	FORWARD	PARTICK THISTLE
WEATHERSON	PETER	JOSEPH	29/05/80	NORTH SHIELDS	24/06/03	6	0	12	10	FORWARD	QUEEN OF THE SOUTH
WILLIAMS	ALEXANDER	BOYD	15/01/83	GLASGOW	17/05/02	5	10.5	11	0	FORWARD	STIRLING ALBION

TICKET INFORMATION

**SEASON TICKET INFORMATION
SEATED
GRANDSTAND (SECTIONS A & B)**
ADULT — £180
CONCESSIONS — £90
PARENT & JUVENILE — £200

**GRANDSTAND (SECTIONS C & D –
NUMBERED SEATS)**
ADULT — £195

STANDING
ADULT — £150
CONCESSIONS — £75
CHILD (15 & UNDER) — £40
PARENT & JUVENILE — £180

**LEAGUE ADMISSION PRICES
SEATED
GRANDSTAND (SECTIONS A,B,E & F)**
ADULT — £12
CONCESSIONS — £6
PARENT & JUVENILE — £15

STANDING
ADULT — £10
CONCESSIONS — £5
CHILD (15 & UNDER) — £2
PARENT & JUVENILE — £12

THE TON'S 10 YEAR LEAGUE RECORD

SEASON	DIV	P	W	D	L	F	A	PTS
1994-95	S	36	18	10	8	55	33	64
1995-96	F	36	20	7	9	57	39	67
1996-97	F	36	12	9	15	42	41	45
1997-98	F	36	12	10	14	47	48	46
1998-99	F	36	14	7	15	45	41	49
1999-00	F	36	10	6	20	45	61	36
2000-01	F	36	9	8	19	34	61	35
2001-02	S	36	7	14	15	48	63	35
2002-03	T	36	21	9	6	67	33	72
2003-04	S	36	16	11	9	66	58	59

SEASON STATS 2003/04

DATE	VENUE	OPPONENTS	ATT	RES	COYLE C.	COLLINS D.	BOTTIGLIERI E.	McGREGOR D.	GREACEN S.	BANNERMAN S.	MILLAR C.	MAISANO J.	WILLIAMS A.	WEATHERSON P.	WALKER P.	HAWKE W.	MAISANO M.	UOTINEN J.	HENDERSON R.	CANNIE P.	ADAM J.	McALISTER J.	McLEOD C.	GAUGHAN P.	McGLINCHEY P.
9-AUG	H	AIRDRIE UNITED	3,806	3 - 1	1	2	3	4	5	6	7	8[1]	9[1]	10[1]	11	12	14	15							
16-AUG	A	STENHOUSEMUIR	1,343	2 - 0	1	2	3		5		7	8	9[1]	10[1]	11	14	6		4						
23-AUG	H	DUMBARTON	3,410	2 - 2	1	2	3		5	12	7	8	9[1]	10[1]	11	14	6	15	4						
30-AUG	H	EAST FIFE	3,270	2 - 1	1	2	3[1]	4	5	9	7	8	12	10[1]	11		6	15							
13-SEP	A	FORFAR ATHLETIC	1,006	3 - 2	1	2	3	4	5	9	7	8	14	10[1]	11[1]	12	6[1]	15							
20-SEP	H	HAMILTON ACADEMICAL	3,225	1 - 1	1	2	3	4	5	9	7	8	14[1]	10	11		6	15							
27-SEP	A	ARBROATH	1,116	4 - 0	1	2	3[1]	4	5[1]	14	7	8	9	10[2]	11	12	6	15							
OCT	H	BERWICK RANGERS	2,896	1 - 3	1	2	3	4	5	14	7	8	9	10	11[1]	12	6	15							
18-OCT	A	ALLOA ATHLETIC	1,118	1 - 0	1	2	3	4	5		7	8	9	10	11			12							
25-OCT	H	STENHOUSEMUIR	2,880	5 - 2	1	2	3	4	5	12	7	8	9[1]	10[2]			6[1]	14[1]		11					
NOV	A	AIRDRIE UNITED	3,159	6 - 1	1	2	3	4	5[2]	12	7	8[2]	9	10	11[1]		6	14	16						
NOV	H	FORFAR ATHLETIC	3,327	1 - 1	1		3	4	5[1]	8	7		9	10	11		6	12	2	14					
16-NOV	A	EAST FIFE	1,757	0 - 0	1		3	4	5		7	8	9	10	11		6		2						
DEC	A	HAMILTON ACADEMICAL	1,905	2 - 1	1		3	4	5	12	7	8	9[2]	10	11		6		2	15					
DEC	H	ARBROATH	2,707	6 - 4	1		3	4	5	2[1]	7[1]	8	9[1]	10[1]	11[1]		6[1]			15					
13-DEC	A	BERWICK RANGERS	882	3 - 2	1		3	4	5	2	7	8[2]	9	10	11[1]		6			14					
JAN	A	DUMBARTON	2,011	0 - 1	1	2	3	4		7	12	8	9	10	11		6		5			14	16		
24-JAN	H	HAMILTON ACADEMICAL	2,942	2 - 2	1	2	3	4			7	8	9[2]	10	11	15	6	12		14			5		
31-JAN	A	ARBROATH	805	2 - 2	1		3	4			7	8	9[1]	10[1]	11		6	12			5	2			
FEB	A	FORFAR ATHLETIC	958	1 - 2	1	2	3	4			7	8	9[1]	10	11	15	6				16	5	12		
14-FEB	H	EAST FIFE	2,894	1 - 1	1	2	3		4	6[1]	7	8	9	10	11	15	14					5		16	
21-FEB	A	ALLOA ATHLETIC	1,145	3 - 3	1	2[1]	3	12	4	6	7	8[1]	9	10				11[1]				14	5		
MAR	A	STENHOUSEMUIR	1,217	1 - 0	1	2	3	4	5		7[1]		9				8	6	10	14	11		16	12	
MAR	H	AIRDRIE UNITED	3,252	1 - 1	1	2	12	4	5		7	8[1]	9		11		6		3	10			16		14
13-MAR	H	DUMBARTON	3,028	3 - 2	1	2	3		5[1]		7[1]	8	9[1]		11			4	12	10	16			15	
23-MAR	H	BERWICK RANGERS	2,300	2 - 1	1	2	3		5[1]	16	7	8	9		11			4	14[1]	10				12	
27-MAR	A	EAST FIFE	1,114	0 - 1	1	2	3		5	8	7		9		11			4	10		16			12	
30-MAR	H	ALLOA ATHLETIC	2,436	2 - 2	1	2	3		5[1]	8	7		14	9	11			4	10[1]				5		
APR	H	ARBROATH	2,493	1 - 0	1	2	3		5	8	7		12	9[1]	11	16		6	4	10					
APR	H	FORFAR ATHLETIC	2,453	1 - 1	1		3		5	6	7		12	9[1]	11		2	8	4	10					
10-APR	A	HAMILTON ACADEMICAL	2,692	1 - 6	1	2	3		5	6[1]	7	8	9	10	12		11	15	4	14					
17-APR	H	ALLOA ATHLETIC	2,618	2 - 1	1	2	16	3	5	6	7	8	12	10	11[1]				15	4	9[1]				
24-APR	A	BERWICK RANGERS	1,175	0 - 2	1	2	3	4	5		7	8	12	10	11		6	14		9		16			
MAY	A	DUMBARTON	1,882	0 - 3	1	2			4	5	7	8		10	11		6	3	9	16	14		12		
16-MAY	H	STENHOUSEMUIR	3,456	1 - 4	1			4	5	2	7	8	9	10[1]	11	12	16	6	3	15					
15-MAY	A	AIRDRIE UNITED	5,704	0 - 2	1	2	11	4	5		7		14	9	12	10	6		3	8		15			
TOTAL FULL APPEARANCES					36	28	32	25	32	17	35	29	26	31	31	1	28	5	20	11	2	1	5	1	
TOTAL SUB APPEARANCES						2	1		8	1		9		2		11	3	15	1	10	3	8	1	2	7
TOTAL GOALS SCORED						1	2		7	3	3	7	15	14	6		3	1	1	3					

bold figures denote goalscorers. † denotes opponent's own goal.

MILESTONES:

YEAR OF FORMATION: 1874
MOST CAPPED PLAYER: Jimmy Cowan
NO. OF CAPS: 25
MOST LEAGUE POINTS IN A SEASON:
69 (Division 2 – Season 1966/67) (2 Points for a win)
72 (Third Division - Season 2002/03) (3 Points for a win)
MOST LEAGUE GOALS SCORED BY A PLAYER IN A SEASON:
Allan McGraw (Season 1963/64)
NO. OF GOALS SCORED: 58
RECORD ATTENDANCE: 23,500 (-v- Celtic – 1922)
RECORD VICTORY: 11-0 (-v- Carfin Shamrock – Scottish Cup, 13.11.1886)
RECORD DEFEAT: 1-10 (-v- Port Glasgow Athletic, 5.5.1884)

MORTON PLAYING KITS SEASON 2004/05

FIRST KIT SECOND KIT THIRD KIT

STIRLING ALBION
Forthbank Stadium, Springkerse,
Stirling, FK7 7UJ

CHAIRMAN
Peter McKenzie

VICE-CHAIRMAN
Peter Gardiner, C.A.

DIRECTORS
Duncan B. MacGregor
& John L. Smith

SECRETARY
Mrs. Marlyn Hallam

COACH
Allan Moore

FIRST TEAM COACHES
David Gemmell & Mark McNally

DIRECTOR OF YOUTH DEVELOPMENT
John L. Smith

YOUTH CO-ORDINATOR/
YOUTH DEVELOPMENT COACH
Stuart Taylor

YOUTH COACHES
U19 Youth Team Coach
David Gemmell

U15 Youth Team Coach
Paul Donnelly

U14 Youth Team Coaches
Mike Kerr & Paul Chalmers

U13 Youth Team Coaches
Ian McConnell & Tommy Smith

CLUB DOCTOR
Dr. Duncan MacGregor

PHYSIOTHERAPIST
Michael McLaughlan

FOOTBALL SAFETY OFFICERS'
ASSOCIATION REPRESENTATIVE
Alistair Caw (01786) 812520

GROUND MAINTENANCE
Greentech, Bandbeath Ind. Est., Throsk

COMMERCIAL MANAGER/
MEDIA LIAISON
Mrs. Marlyn Hallam
Tel (01786) 450399

KIT PERSON
Stuart McColl

MATCHDAY PROGRAMME EDITOR
Allan Grieve (01259) 751152
email: ADGrieve@aol.com

TELEPHONES
Ground/Ticket Office
(01786) 450399
Fax (01786) 448400

E-MAIL ADDRESS
stirlingalbion.footballclub@virgin.net

CLUB SHOP
Situated at Forthbank Stadium.
Open Mon. – Fri. and
Home Match Days.

OFFICIAL SUPPORTERS CLUB
Stephen Torrance, Secretary,
Forthbank Stadium, Springkerse,
Stirling, FK7 7UJ

TEAM CAPTAIN
George Rowe

SHIRT SPONSOR
Prudential

KIT SUPPLIER
Vandanel

LIST OF PLAYERS 2004/05

PLAYERS SURNAME	FIRST NAME	MIDDLE NAME	DATE OF BIRTH	PLACE OF BIRTH	DATE SIGNED	HEIGHT FT INS		WEIGHT ST LBS		POSITION ON PITCH	PREVIOUS CLUB
ALLAN	JAMES		21/09/79	GLASGOW	22/07/04	5	10	11	3	MIDFIELD	GRETNA
BELL	ANDREW	ROBERT	16/01/87	GLASGOW	30/08/04	5	11	10	6	MIDFIELD	KILMARNOCK
BERRY	MARK	RICHARD	27/03/85	BRADFORD	29/08/03	5	8	9	0	DEFENDER	STIRLING ALBION FORM D
BROPHY	CHRISTOPHER		16/03/87	GLASGOW	17/08/04	5	6	9	6	FORWARD	STIRLING ALBION FORM D
BRYCE	GRAHAM		21/06/88	BELLSHILL	28/08/04	5	8.5	10	0	DEFENDER	DUNDEE UNITED
CASEY	SCOTT		08/06/88	GLASGOW	28/08/04	6	2	11	6	DEFENDER	DUNDEE UNITED
CAWLEY	DANIEL	JAMES	06/07/89	GLASGOW	28/08/04	6	2	11	6	GOALKEEPER	STIRLING ALBION FORM D
CHALMERS	CHRISTOPHER	JOHN WILLIAM	20/01/88	GLASGOW	23/08/04	5	10	10	4	FORWARD	DUNDEE UNITED
CHRISTIE	SCOTT	JAMES	13/11/87	FALKIRK	24/12/03	5	10	9	0	GOALKEEPER	STIRLING ALBION FORM D
CLARK	CHARLES		20/03/86	STIRLING	10/09/04	5	10	9	7	GOALKEEPER	CLYDE
CONROY	MICHAEL		20/05/87	STIRLING	28/08/04	5	6	11	2	DEFENDER	STIRLING ALBION FORM D
CUMMINGS	DARREN	DAVID	15/03/85	FALKIRK	14/08/02	5	9	10	7	FORWARD	STIRLING ALBION FORM D
CURRIE	DEREK		04/12/89	STIRLING	28/08/04	5	8	10	0	DEF / MID	STIRLING ALBION FORM D
DEVINE	STEWART		11/04/84	EDINBURGH	13/07/00	5	10	10	2	MIDFIELD	STIRLING ALBION YOUTH
DONALDSON	STUART	HAIG	14/09/89	STIRLING	28/08/04	5	7	8	7	FORWARD	STIRLING ALBION FORM D
DONNELLY	PAUL		23/09/87	BANGOUR	17/08/04	5	8	9	0	MIDFIELD	STIRLING ALBION FORM D
FERGUSON	CRAIG	WILLIAM	03/02/81	GLASGOW	22/07/03	6	2	14	0	MIDFIELD	MARYHILL B.C. U'21'S
FORBES	DAVID		03/02/87	GLASGOW	17/08/04	5	11	10	3	MIDFIELD	STIRLING ALBION FORM D
FOTHERINGHAM	KEVIN	CAMPBELL	11/03/89	STIRLING	28/08/04	5	5	8	4	MIDFIELD	STIRLING ALBION FORM D
GETHINS	CONOR		01/11/83	LIFFORD	16/07/04	5	7	9	0	FORWARD	ROSS COUNTY
GLANCY	MARTIN	PAUL	24/03/76	GLASGOW	06/08/04	5	8	11	0	FORWARD	BATHGATE THISTLE JUNIORS
HAY	PAUL		14/11/80	GLASGOW	16/03/01	5	10	11	7	MIDFIELD	CLYDE
HOGARTH	MYLES		30/03/75	FALKIRK	11/03/03	6	2.5	12	7	GOALKEEPER	ALLOA ATHLETIC
HONEYMAN	DAVID	LEE	01/02/88	RINTELN - GERMANY	28/08/04	5	10	10	7	FORWARD	DUNDEE UNITED
HUGHES	MARC		01/07/87	BANGOUR	28/08/04	5	7	10	5	MIDFIELD	STIRLING ALBION FORM D
HUTCHISON	STEVEN		01/08/85	STIRLING	23/07/01	5	11	10	7	FORWARD	RANGERS
LOCHHEAD	CHRISTOPHER		06/05/85	GLASGOW	29/08/03	5	8	10	0	MIDFIELD	STIRLING ALBION FORM D
McDONALD	KEVIN	GRAHAM	05/02/83	GLASGOW	08/06/04	5	11	11	0	MIDFIELD	MOTHERWELL
McCLYMONT	GRAHAM	JAMES	16/06/89	STIRLING	28/08/04	5	8.5	11	0	FORWARD	STIRLING ALBION FORM D
McKINLAY	LEWIS	ALEXANDER	28/11/89	STIRLING	23/08/04	6	0	10	6	MIDFIELD	STIRLING ALBION FORM D
McLEAN	DAVID	JOHN	27/10/87	STIRLING	28/08/04	5	8	9	6	DEFENDER	STIRLING ALBION FORM D
McLEAN	SCOTT	JAMES	17/06/76	EAST KILBRIDE	18/07/03	5	11.5	13	6	FORWARD	ST. MIRREN
McNALLY	MARK		10/03/71	MOTHERWELL	25/07/02	5	11	12	7	DEFENDER	CLYDEBANK
McSKIMMING	ROBERT	SCOTT	25/02/87	BELLSHILL	23/08/04	5	7	10	0	MIDFIELD	RAITH ROVERS
MILLAR	JOHN	J.	18/06/87	STIRLING	28/08/04	5	10	11	8	MIDFIELD	STIRLING ALBION FORM D
MOOTY	JAMES		07/03/89	BELLSHILL	27/08/04	5	7	8	2	MIDFIELD	MOTHERWELL
NAPOLI	PATRICE		24/06/86	FALKIRK	29/08/03	5	6	9	10	MIDFIELD	CLYDE FORM D UNDER 16
NEVILLE	BARRY		18/04/85	GLASGOW	08/06/04	5	11	11	5	DEFENDER	MOTHERWELL
NUGENT	PAUL	BRIAN	04/04/83	ALEXANDRIA	30/11/01	5	11	11	0	DEFENDER	CLYDE
O'BRIEN	DAVID		24/01/84	STIRLING	20/07/01	5	10	10	8	MIDFIELD	DENNY AMATEURS
O'DONNELL	ANTHONY	STEPHEN	01/10/87	BLACKPOOL	28/08/04	5	11	10	5	FORWARD	STIRLING ALBION B.C.
O'LEARY	CRAIG		23/08/86	GLASGOW	17/08/04	5	11	12	7	DEFENDER	QUEEN'S PARK FORM D U16
PENDER	DOUGLAS		12/02/87	VALE OF LEVEN	28/08/04	5	7	10	6	DEFENDER	STIRLING ALBION B.C.
PRENTICE	MITCHELL	JAMES	02/03/83	WOLLONGONG	17/09/04	6	0	11	3	MIDFIELD	NORTH SYDNEY SOCCER CLUB
ROSS	STUART		14/03/86	FALKIRK	29/08/03	6	2	11	0	DEFENDER	RAITH ROVERS
ROWE	JOHN	GEORGE	23/08/68	GLASGOW	25/07/02	6	0	13	0	DEFENDER	ARBROATH
ROYCROFT	SEAN		29/08/85	STIRLING	29/08/03	6	0	11	0	FORWARD	STIRLING ALBION FORM D U16
SCOTLAND	CHRISTOPHER	JAMES	22/03/85	STIRLING	14/08/02	5	11.5	12	0	DEFENDER	STIRLING ALBION FORM D U16
SHADDICK	SAM	RYAN	06/06/89	STIRLING	28/08/04	5	8	9	12	MIDFIELD	STIRLING ALBION FORM D U15
SHAW	KEVIN	O'DONNELL	03/07/86	FALKIRK	31/08/04	5	11	11	0	MIDFIELD	CLYDE FORM D UNDER 16
TAGGART	NATHAN		28/06/87	GLASGOW	30/08/04	5	6	10	7	MIDFIELD	STIRLING ALBION FORM D U16
TAYLOR	BARRIE		26/04/88	STIRLING	28/08/04	5	11.5	11	0	MIDFIELD	DUNDEE UNITED
THOMSON	DAVID	ANGUS ALEXANDER	15/05/88	STIRLING	28/08/04	5	11	10	7	GOALKEEPER	ALLOA ATHLETIC FORM D U16
TRAYNOR	MARC	MICHAEL	30/10/89	STIRLING	28/08/04	5	7	8	7	MIDFIELD	STIRLING ALBION FORM D U15
WILSON	DOUGLAS	JOHN	27/05/84	STIRLING	20/07/01	5	7	9	3	MIDFIELD	STIRLING ALBION FORM D U16
WRIGHT	GARY	CRAIG	19/04/89	FALKIRK	28/08/04	5	8	7	7	MIDFIELD	STENHOUSEMUIR FORM D U15

TICKET INFORMATION

SEASON TICKET PRICES

SEATED		
	ADULT	£160
	JUVENILE/OAP	£100
	YOUNG RED	£85

LEAGUE ADMISSION PRICES

SEATED		
	ADULT	£9
	JUVENILE	£6

STANDING		
	ADULT	£8
	JUVENILE/OAP	£5

THE ALBION'S 10 YEAR LEAGUE RECORD

SEASON	DIV	P	W	D	L	F	A	PTS
1994-95	S	36	17	7	12	54	43	58
1995-96	S	36	24	9	3	83	30	81
1996-97	F	36	12	10	14	54	61	46
1997-98	F	36	8	10	18	40	56	34
1998-99	S	36	12	8	16	50	63	44
1999-00	S	36	11	7	18	60	72	40
2000-01	S	36	5	17	14	34	50	32
2001-02	T	36	9	10	17	45	68	37
2002-03	T	36	15	11	10	50	44	56
2003-04	T	36	23	8	5	78	27	77

SEASON STATS 2003/04

DATE	VENUE	OPPONENTS	ATT	RES	HOGARTH M.	NUGENT P.	ANDERSON D.	McNALLY M.	ROWE J.G.	HAY P.	FERGUSON C.	McLEAN S.	ELLIOT B.	DEVINE S.	O'BRIEN D.	WILSON D.	DAVIDSON R.	SMITH A.	GIBSON A.	MORRISON S.	McKINNON C.	SCOTLAND C.	KELLY G.	LYLE D.	BEVERIDGE R.
-AUG	H	COWDENBEATH	576	0-0	1	2	3	4	5	6	7	8	9	10	11	12	14	15							
-AUG	A	STRANRAER	436	1-0	1	2	3	4	5	6	7	9			11	12	10^1		8	16					
-AUG	H	EAST STIRLINGSHIRE	581	5-1	1	2	3	4	5	16^1	6	9^1	12	8^1	11		10^2		7						
-AUG	A	QUEEN'S PARK	638	2-0		2	3	4	5	6	15	9^1	14	8	11^1		10		7	1					
-SEP	H	PETERHEAD	711	3-1	1	2	3	4	5	14		9^2	12	8			15	11	6	7	10^1				
-SEP	A	ALBION ROVERS	685	2-1	1	2	3	4	5			9^1	12	11	12		10	6	7		8^1				
-SEP	A	GRETNA	482	1-0	1	2	3	4	5	14		9	12		11		10	6	7		8^1				
OCT	H	ELGIN CITY	648	3-0	1	2	3	4	5	14		9^1	12	16^1	11^1		10	6	7		8				
-OCT	H	MONTROSE	490	3-0	1	2	3	4	5	16	15	9	12^1		11		10^1	6	7		8^1				
-OCT	A	MONTROSE	338	3-2	1		3	4	5	2		9	12	11	14		10	6	7^1		8^2				
-OCT	H	STRANRAER	924	1-0	1		3	4	5	2		9	12	11	14		10	6	7		8^1				
NOV	A	COWDENBEATH	468	0-2	1		3	4	5	2	12	9	10		11	15	14	6	7		8				
NOV	A	PETERHEAD	589	2-2	1		3	4	5	2	14	9^1			11		10^2	6	7		8				
-NOV	H	QUEEN'S PARK	590	1-0	1			4	5	3	14^1	9	12		11	15	10	6	7		8	2			
-DEC	A	ALBION ROVERS	392	3-0	1		3	4	5	2	14^1	9^1			11^1	12	10^1	6	7			8			
-DEC	H	GRETNA	682	0-1	1	16	3	4	5	2		9	15		11	12	10	6	7			8			
-DEC	A	ELGIN CITY	478	†2-0	1	2	3	4	5	12	14	9^1			11		10	6	7			8			
-JAN	A	EAST STIRLINGSHIRE	495	†4-2	1	2	3	4	5		16	9^1	10		11	12^1		6				8^1	7			
-JAN	H	COWDENBEATH	790	1-1	1	2	3	4	5	16		9	14		11	7		6			12		8	10^1	
-JAN	H	ALBION ROVERS	629	3-0	1	2	3	4	5			9^1	12	16	11^1	7	14	6					8	10^1	
-FEB	A	PETERHEAD	651	0-2	1	2	3	4	5			9		15	11	7	16	14					8	10	
-FEB	A	QUEEN'S PARK	742	4-1	1	4	3		5	2		9^1			14	11^1	7		6			8^1		12	10^1	16
-FEB	A	MONTROSE	466	4-1	1	4	3		5^1	2	15				14	11^1	7	9^1	6			8		12	10^1	
-MAR	A	GRETNA	758	0-1	1	2	3	4	5	7		12			16	11		9	6			8		14	10	
-MAR	A	STRANRAER	685	1-1	1				5	2		9			3	11		10	6			8^1	4	12	7	
-MAR	H	ELGIN CITY	527	†6-1	1	2	14		5^1	7	16	9^3			3	11		12	6			8	4		10^1	
-MAR	H	EAST STIRLINGSHIRE	739	6-0	1	2			5^1	7	14			15	3	11^2		10	6			8	4	12	9^3	
-MAR	A	PETERHEAD	588	0-0	1	2			5	7		9	12	3	11			6				8	4	15	10	
-MAR	H	QUEEN'S PARK	797	0-0	1	2	15		5	7				3	11		16	6				8	4	14	10	
-APR	H	GRETNA	678	0-1	1	2			5	8				3	11	7	10	6				12	4	14	10	16
-APR	A	ALBION ROVERS	615	5-3			3		5	2	15	9^1			6^1	11	7	16				8^1	4	14	10^2	
-APR	H	MONTROSE	672	1-1	1		3		5	6	12				7	11	14^1	10^1	2			8	4		9	16
-APR	A	ELGIN CITY	542	1-0	1				5	2					3	11	7	14	6			8^1	4		9	10
-MAY	A	EAST STIRLINGSHIRE	779	3-0	1		15					9^2			3	11^1	7	12	6			8	4	16	10	
-MAY	H	STRANRAER	2,190	2-2	1				5	2	14^2	9			3	11	7	16	6			8	4	15	10	
-MAY	A	COWDENBEATH	692	5-0					5	2	12	9^4			3	11^1	7	16	6			8	4	15	10	
TOTAL FULL APPEARANCES					35	22	25	22	36	24	4	30	3	20	31	11	21	30	15	1	26	13	7	19	1
TOTAL SUB APPEARANCES						1	3			7	15	1	16	6	4	8	11	2	1		2			12	3
TOTAL GOALS SCORED							3	1	3	21	1	3	10	1	9			1			11		1	10

all bold figures denote goalscorers. † denotes opponent's own goal.

LEADING GOALSCORERS:

SEASON	DIV	GOALS	PLAYER
1994-95	S	15	W. Watters
1995-96	S	25	S. McCormick
1996-97	F	9	A. Bone
1997-98	F	13	A. Bone
1998-99	S	20	A. Bone
1999-00	S	17	A. Graham
2000-01	S	5	C. Feroz, A. Graham
2001-02	T	17	A. Williams
2002-03	T	10	S. Nicholas
2003-04	T	21	S. McLean

MILESTONES:

YEAR OF FORMATION: 1945
MOST LEAGUE POINTS IN A SEASON:
59 (Division 2 – Season 1964/65)(2 Points for a Win)
81 (Second Division – Season 1995/96)(3 Points for a Win)
MOST LEAGUE GOALS SCORED BY A PLAYER IN A SEASON:
Joe Hughes (Season 1969/70)
NO. OF GOALS SCORED: 26
RECORD ATTENDANCE: 26,400
(-v- Celtic – Scottish Cup, 11.3.1959 at Annfield Park)
3,808 (-v- Aberdeen – Scottish Cup, 17.2.1996 at Forthbank Stadium)
RECORD VICTORY: 20-0 (-v- Selkirk – Scottish Cup, 8.12.1984)
RECORD DEFEAT: 0-9 (-v- Dundee United – Division 1, 30.12.1967)

STIRLING ALBION PLAYING KITS SEASON 2004/05

FIRST KIT | SECOND KIT | THIRD KIT

STRANRAER
Stair Park, London Road,
Stranraer, DG9 8BS
CHAIRMAN
James Bark
VICE-CHAIRMAN
James T. Robertson
COMMITTEE
George F. Compton,
James Hannah, Alexander McKie,
Nigel C. Redhead, R. A. Graham Rodgers,
Barry Critchley & Robert J. Clanachan
HONORARY PRESIDENT
John Carruth
HONORARY VICE-PRESIDENTS
Ian Porter, George Binnie,
Robert G. Rice & Peter Muir
SECRETARY
R. A. Graham Rodgers
MANAGER
Neil Watt
ASSISTANT MANAGER
Stuart Millar
RESERVE COACH
Tom McAllister
COACHING STAFF
Barney Duffy
YOUTH COACHES
John Pollock & Nish Walker
CLUB DOCTORS
Dr. Ranald Spicer, Dr. Niall Balmer
& Dr. Paul Carnaghan
PHYSIOTHERAPIST
Walter Cannon
**FOOTBALL SAFETY OFFICERS'
ASSOCIATION REPRESENTATIVE**
Alex Connor
GROUNDSMAN
Murray Gibson
COMMERCIAL MANAGER
David McMillan
LOTTERY MANAGER Bill Paton
MATCHDAY PROGRAMME EDITOR
R. A. Graham Rodgers
(01776) 702194
TELEPHONES
Ground (01776) 703271
Fax (01776) 702194
Sec. Home/Ticket Office/
Information Service (01776) 702194
E-MAIL & INTERNET ADDRESS
grodgers_sfc@yahoo.co.uk
www.stranraerfc.com
CLUB SHOP
Situated at Ground
2.30p.m-3.00pm and half time
on Matchdays
OFFICIAL SUPPORTERS CLUB
Situated in Social Club, North Strand Street,
Stranraer. Tel (01776) 704121
CLUB CAPTAIN
Derek Wingate
TEAM CAPTAIN
Allan Jenkins
SHIRT SPONSOR
Stena Line
KIT SUPPLIER
Nike

LIST OF PLAYERS 2004/05

PLAYERS SURNAME	FIRST NAME	MIDDLE NAME	DATE OF BIRTH	PLACE OF BIRTH	DATE SIGNED	HEIGHT FT INS		WEIGHT ST LBS		POSITION ON PITCH	PREVIOUS CLUB
AITKEN	STEPHEN	SMITH	25/09/76	GLASGOW	10/07/01	5	8	11	1	MIDFIELD	MORTON
CRAWFORD	BRIAN		27/07/78	LANARK	25/11/03	5	10	11	10	FORWARD	STENHOUSEMUIR
CRUICKSHANK	CHRISTOPHER		25/08/80	GLASGOW	25/06/03	5	11	12	0	DEFENDER	MARYHILL JUNIORS
DONNACHIE	STEPHEN		16/02/82	BELLSHILL	20/08/04	5	10	10	7	FORWARD	BELLSHILL ATHLETIC JNR
FINLAYSON	KEVIN	CHARLES	07/12/79	GLASGOW	10/07/01	5	10	10	11	FORWARD	QUEEN'S PARK
FRASER	JOHN		17/01/78	DUNFERMLINE	05/08/04	5	10	11	4	MIDFIELD	CLYDE
GAUGHAN	KEVIN		06/03/78	GLASGOW	26/01/04	6	1	13	0	DEFENDER	STENHOUSEMUIR
GAUGHAN	PAUL		27/09/80	GLASGOW	05/08/04	6	2	14	7	DEFENDER	MORTON
GRAHAM	DAVID		02/06/83	STIRLING	19/06/03	5	9	11	0	FORWARD	STENHOUSEMUIR
GUY	GRAHAM		15/08/83	BELLSHILL	25/06/03	6	0	11	0	DEFENDER	ST. MIRREN
HENDERSON	MURRAY		15/06/80	LANARK	19/06/03	6	3	13	0	DEFENDER	BALMORE AMATEURS
JENKINS	ALLAN	DAVID	07/10/81	STRANRAER	03/09/98	6	1	13	0	MIDFIELD	AYR BOSWELL
McALLISTER	THOMAS	JAMES	21/02/71	GLASGOW	06/08/04	6	0	12	0	MIDFIELD	MARYHILL JUNIORS
McCAULAY	MARTIN	JOHN ANDREW	05/06/85	DUMFRIES	18/04/04	5	11	11	0	GOALKEEPER	GIRVAN JUNIORS
McCONDICHIE	ANDREW	MORRISON	21/08/77	GLASGOW	21/06/03	5	10.5	12	3	GOALKEEPER	MARYHILL JUNIORS
McCUTCHEON	GARY	KYLE	08/10/78	DUMFRIES	08/06/04	5	6	11	5	FORWARD	BERWICK RANGERS
McGINTY	MARTIN		24/09/84	GLASGOW	20/08/04	5	10	10	9	MIDFIELD	POLLOK JUNIORS
McPHEE	GARY		01/10/79	GLASGOW	25/06/03	5	10	11	0	MIDFIELD	CUMBERNAULD UNITED JNR
MEECHAN	KENNETH		16/02/72	GREENOCK	26/06/03	6	0	14	0	GOALKEEPER	LARGS THISTLE JUNIORS
SHARP	LEE		22/05/75	GLASGOW	01/08/02	5	9	12	0	MIDFIELD	AYR UNITED
SWIFT	STEPHEN		21/07/80	GLASGOW	15/07/03	5	11	11	7	DEFENDER	LINLITHGOW ROSE JNRS
TURNBULL	DAVID		05/09/80	DURBAN	02/08/03	6	1	12	0	FORWARD	MARYHILL JUNIORS
WINGATE	DEREK		26/09/75	GLASGOW	10/07/01	6	2	13	0	DEFENDER	BENBURB JUNIORS
WRIGHT	FRASER		23/12/79	EAST KILBRIDE	03/09/98	5	10	11	10	DEFENDER	ST. MIRREN B.C.

TICKET INFORMATION

SEASON TICKET PRICES

SEATED	ADULT	£135
	JUVENILE/OAP	£70
STANDING	ADULT	£115
	JUVENILE/OAP	£60

LEAGUE ADMISSION PRICES

SEATED	ADULT	£10
	JUVENILE/OAP	£5
STANDING	ADULT	£9
	JUVENILE/OAP	£4.50

THE BLUES' 10 YEAR LEAGUE RECORD

SEASON	DIV	P	W	D	L	F	A	PTS	P
1994-95	F	36	4	5	27	25	81	17	1
1995-96	S	36	8	18	10	38	43	42	
1996-97	S	36	9	9	18	29	51	36	
1997-98	S	36	18	7	11	62	44	61	
1998-99	F	36	5	2	29	29	74	17	1
1999-00	S	36	9	18	9	47	46	45	
2000-01	S	36	15	9	12	51	50	54	
2001-02	S	36	10	15	11	48	51	45	
2002-03	S	36	12	8	16	49	57	44	
2003-04	T	36	24	7	5	87	30	79	

SEASON STATS 2003/04

DATE	VENUE	OPPONENTS	ATT	RES	McCONDICHIE A.	SWIFT S.	WRIGHT F.	WINGATE D.	HENDERSON M.	JENKINS A.	FINLAYSON K.	McALLISTER T.	MOORE M.	KERR P.	SHARP L.	AITKEN S.	TURNBULL D.	GUY G.	ESSLER A.	GRANT A.	CRUICKSHANK C.	McPHEE G.	MARSHALL S.	GRAHAM D.	CRAWFORD B.	COLLINS L.	GAUGHAN K.
-UG	A	ALBION ROVERS	323	1-1	1	2	3	4	5	6	7	8	9	10^1	11	14	16										
-AUG	H	STIRLING ALBION	436	0-1	1	2		4	5	6	7	8	9	10		14		3	11	12	16						
-AUG	A	GRETNA	367	1-1	1	2		4		6	7		9	12	11	8				10^1	3	5	16				
-AUG	A	PETERHEAD	813	2-1	1	2	3	4	5	6	7		9		11	8					14	15^1		10^1			
-SEP	H	EAST STIRLINGSHIRE	358	4-0	1	2	3	4	5	6	7^2		9^2		11	8	16			12				10			
-SEP	H	ELGIN CITY	370	4-3	1	2^1	3	4	5	6^1	7		9^1		11^1	8	14			12	16			10			
-SEP	A	MONTROSE	273	4-2	1	2	3	4	5	6	7		9^4		11	8				12		15		10			
-OCT	A	COWDENBEATH	232	1-0	1	2	3	4	5	6	7		9^1	16	11	8					14	15		10			
-OCT	H	QUEEN'S PARK	464	1-0	1	2	3	4	5	6	7		9	16	11	8								10^1			
-OCT	A	STIRLING ALBION	924	0-1	1	2	3	4	5	6	7		9	16	11	8				12		15		10			
-NOV	H	ALBION ROVERS	447	5-0	1	2^2	3	4	5^1	6	7		9^1	16	11	8								10^1			
-NOV	A	EAST STIRLINGSHIRE	245	4-1	1	2	3	4	5	6^2	7		9^1		11	8	14			12		15		10^1			
-NOV	H	PETERHEAD	428	0-2	1	2	3	4	5	6	7	15	9	16	11	8				12				10			
-NOV	A	ELGIN CITY	410	3-1	1	2^1	3	4	5	6	7		9^1		11	8						15		10^1	14		
-DEC	H	MONTROSE	409	2-0	1	2	3	4	5	6	7^1		9		11	8								10	14^1		
-DEC	H	COWDENBEATH	395	†2-0	1	2^1	3	4	5	6	7				11	8	16			12	15			10	9		
-JAN	A	GRETNA	534	1-2	1	2	3	4	5	14	7		9^1		11	8				12				10			6
-JAN	A	QUEEN'S PARK	473	4-0	1	2	3	4	5^1	6^1	7		9^1		11	8^1	16				14			10			
-JAN	H	ELGIN CITY	393	6-0	1	2	3	4	5	6	7^2	14	9^4		11	8				12		15		10			
-JAN	A	MONTROSE	349	4-1	1	2	3^1	4	5	6^1	7		9		11	8	14							10^2			
-FEB	H	EAST STIRLINGSHIRE	405	7-1	1	2	3	4	5	6	7^2		9^1		11	8								10^4			
-FEB	A	PETERHEAD	615	0-2	1	2	3	4	5	6	7		9		11	8	14							10			
-FEB	A	ALBION ROVERS	428	4-1	1	2	3	4	5^1	6	7				11^1	8	14							10^1	9^1		
-FEB	H	QUEEN'S PARK	435	3-1	1	2	3	4	5	6	7^2	12			11^1	8								10	9		15
-MAR	H	STIRLING ALBION	685	1-1	1	2	3	4	5	6	7	14^1			11	8								10	9		
-MAR	A	COWDENBEATH	210	2-1	1	2	3	4^1	5	6			9		11	8								10	14^1	7	
-MAR	A	GRETNA	736	0-0	1	2	3	4	5	6	12		9		11	8					16			10		7	
-MAR	A	EAST STIRLINGSHIRE	181	2-1	1	2	3	4	5^1	6	14		9^1		11	8								10		7	
-MAR	H	PETERHEAD	434	1-1	1	2	3	4	5	6	7		9		11	8								10^1			
-APR	H	MONTROSE	378	6-0	1	2^2	3	4	5^1	6	7	15	9^1		11	8								10^1	12^1	16	
-APR	A	ELGIN CITY	663	0-0	1	2	3	4	5	6	7		9		11									10	12	8	
-APR	A	QUEEN'S PARK	564	2-0	1	2	3	4	5	6	7	15	9^1		11									10^1	12	8	16
-APR	H	COWDENBEATH	457	1-0	1	2	3	4	5	6^1	7				11	8	12	15						10	9		
-MAY	H	GRETNA	697	3-2	1	2	3	4	5	6	7				11	8	9^1							10^2	12		
-MAY	A	STIRLING ALBION	2,190	2-2	1	2	3^1	4	5	6	7		9^1		11	8								10	12		
-MAY	H	ALBION ROVERS	1,321	4-0	1	2	3	4	5	6	7^1	15	9^1		11	8	14							10^2	12		
TOTAL FULL APPEARANCES					36	36	34	36	35	35	32	3	30	2	35	31	1	1	2	1	1	1		30	2	11	
TOTAL SUB APPEARANCES									1	1	7	1	6	2		13	1	9	5	2	6	2		9	1	2	
TOTAL GOALS SCORED						7	2	1	5	6	10		24	1	3	1		1	1	2				19	3	1	

Bold figures denote goalscorers. † denotes opponent's own goal.

LEADING GOALSCORERS:

MILESTONES:

YEAR OF FORMATION: 1870

MOST LEAGUE POINTS IN A SEASON:
56 (Second Division – Season 1993/94) (2 Points for a Win)
79 (Third Division – Season 2003/04) (3 Points for a Win)

MOST LEAGUE GOALS SCORED BY A PLAYER IN A SEASON:
Derek Frye (Season 1977/78)

NO. OF GOALS SCORED: 27

RECORD ATTENDANCE:
6,500 (-v- Rangers – 24.1.1948)

RECORD VICTORY:
7-0 (-v- Brechin City – Division 2, 6.2.1965)

RECORD DEFEAT: 1-11 (-v- Queen of the South – Scottish Cup, 16.1.1932)

STRANRAER PLAYING KITS SEASON 2004/05

FIRST KIT   SECOND KIT   THIRD KIT

Alloa Athletic: Recreation Park

Recreation Park can be reached by the following routes:
TRAINS: The nearest railway station is Stirling, which is seven miles away. Fans would have to connect with an inter-linking bus service to reach the ground from here.
BUSES: There are three main services which stop outside the ground. These are the Dunfermline–Stirling, Stirling–Clackmannan and Falkirk–Alloa buses.
CARS: Car Parking is available in the car park adjacent to the ground and this can hold 175 vehicles.

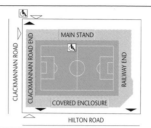

CAPACITY: 3,100; Seated 400, Standing 2,700
PITCH DIMENSIONS: 110 yds x 75 yds
FACILITIES FOR DISABLED SUPPORTERS:
Accommodation for wheelchairs and invalid carriages in front of Stand. Disabled toilets are also available.

Arbroath: Gayfield Park

The following routes may be used to reach Gayfield Park:
BUSES: Arbroath is on the main route from both Glasgow and Edinburgh to Aberdeen. Buses from these three cities, plus Stirling, Dundee and Perth all stop at Arbroath Bus Station at hourly intervals. There is also a local service between Dundee–Arbroath and Montrose and this service is half hourly until 7.00 p.m. Between 7.00 p.m. and 10.45 p.m. the service is hourly. The bus station is 10 minutes walk from the ground.
TRAINS: Arbroath is on the Inter-City 125 route from London to Aberdeen and there are frequent local services between Arbroath, Dundee and Edinburgh. Trains also travel north from Glasgow, Stirling and Perth. The station is a 15 minute walk from the ground.
CARS: There is free parking for 500 cars just next to the ground in Queen's Drive.

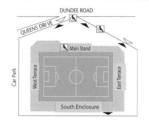

CAPACITY: 4,165; Seated 860, Standing 3,305
PITCH DIMENSIONS: 115 yds x 71 yds
FACILITIES FOR DISABLED SUPPORTERS:
Enclosure at east and west ends of Stand with wide steps to take a wheelchair. Toilet facilities are also available.

Ayr United: Somerset Park

Somerset Park can be reached by the following routes:
TRAINS: There is a half hourly train service from Glasgow to either Ayr or Newton-on-Ayr. The ground is a ten minute walk from both stations.
BUSES: There are several buses from the town centre with a frequency approximately every five minutes. Fans should board buses bound for Dalmilling, Whitletts or any bus passing Ayr Racecourse. The ground is only a ten minute walk from the town centre.
CARS: A77 to Ayr and at Whitletts Roundabout, take third exit (A719) and follow until after Ayr Racecourse. Take first right at traffic lights then left and right into Somerset Road. Car parking facilities are available at Craigie Road, Ayr Racecourse and also at Somerset Road car parks.

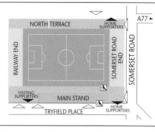

CAPACITY: 10,185; Seated 1,597, Standing 8,588
PITCH DIMENSIONS: 110 yds x 72 yds
FACILITIES FOR DISABLED SUPPORTERS:
Enclosure and toilet facilities for wheelchairs. Match commentary available for blind persons at all first team matches.

Berwick Rangers: Shielfield Park

Shielfield Park can be reached by the following routes:
The ground is approximately 1½ miles south of Berwick town centre and is situated in Shielfield Terrace, Tweedmouth (signposted).
TRAINS: The railway station is Berwick, which is situated on the East Coast line and a frequent service operates at various stages during the day. The ground is 1½ miles (approx.) from the station and a taxi service operates from there or alternatively, fans can take the local bus service as detailed.
BUSES: The local bus route from the town centre is the Prior Park service and the nearest stop is Shielfield Terrace, only yards from the ground.
CARS: There is a large car park at the rear of the ground.

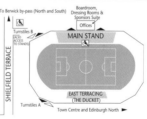

CAPACITY: 4,131; Seated 1,366, Standing 2,765
PITCH DIMENSIONS: 110 yds x 70 yds
FACILITIES FOR DISABLED SUPPORTERS:
Supporters should enter via gate adjacent to ground turnstiles (see ground plan) or via official entrance.

Brechin City: Glebe Park

The following routes may be used to reach Glebe Park:
TRAINS: The nearest railway station is Montrose, which is eight miles away. There is a regular Inter-City service from all parts of the country and fans alighting at Montrose can then catch a connecting bus service to Brechin.
BUSES: Brechin bus station is only a few hundred yards from the ground and buses on the Aberdeen–Dundee and Montrose–Edzell routes stop here.
CARS: Car parking is available in the Brechin City car park, which is capable of holding 50 vehicles. There are also a number of side streets which may be used for this purpose.

CAPACITY: 3,060; Seated 1,518, Standing 1,542
PITCH DIMENSIONS: 110 yds x 67 yds
FACILITIES FOR DISABLED SUPPORTERS:
Section of Terracing designated for disabled supporters. Disabled access from both ends of the Ground.

Dumbarton: Strathclyde Homes Stadium

Strathclyde Homes Stadium can be reached by the following routes:
TRAINS: The train service from Glasgow Queen Street and Glasgow Central Low Level both pass through Dumbarton East Station (fans best choice) situated just under a ten minute walk from the ground.
BUSES: There are two main services which pass close to the ground. These are bound for Helensburgh and Balloch from Glasgow.
CARS: Follow A82 then A814 Helensburgh/Dumbarton sign post. Follow road for about 1 mile. Pass under Dumbarton East Railway Bridge and take second right – Victoria Street (also signposted Dumbarton Castle). The car park at the stadium holds 400 cars and 6 coaches.

CAPACITY: 2,020 (All Seated)
PITCH DIMENSIONS: 114 yds x 75 yds
FACILITIES FOR DISABLED SUPPORTERS:
20 Wheelchair spaces are accommodated at the front of the stand. Contact the Club Secretary in advance regarding availability.

Forfar Athletic: Station Park

Station Park can be reached by the following routes:
BUSES: There is a regular service of buses departing from Dundee City Centre into Forfar. The bus station in the town is about half a mile from the ground. There is also a local service.
TRAINS: The nearest railway station is Dundee (14 miles away) and fans who travel to here should then board a bus for Forfar from the city centre. Arbroath station is also about 14 miles away.
CARS: There are car parking facilities in adjacent streets to the ground and also in the Market Muir car park.

CAPACITY: 5,177 Seated 739, Standing 4,438
PITCH DIMENSIONS: 113 yds x 70 yds
FACILITIES FOR DISABLED SUPPORTERS:
Ramp entrance via Main Stand.

Morton: Cappielow Park

Cappielow Park may be reached by the following routes:
BUSES: Services from Glasgow stop just outside the park. There are also services from Port Glasgow and Gourock.
TRAINS: The nearest local station is Cartsdyke and is a five minute walk from the ground. There are two to three trains every hour from Glasgow and from Gourock.
CARS: Car parking is available adjacent to the ground.

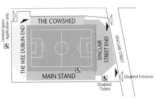

CAPACITY: 11,589; Seating 6,039, Standing 5,550
PITCH DIMENSIONS: 110 yds x 70 yds
FACILITIES FOR DISABLED SUPPORTERS:
Seating facilities below Grandstand. Disabled toilets located at Main Entrance. Disabled Access and facilities within Club Hospitality areas.

Stirling Albion: Forthbank Stadium

Forthbank Stadium can be reached by the following routes:
TRAINS: The nearest station is Stirling Railway Station, which is approximately 2 miles from the ground.
BUSES: From Goosecroft Bus Station, Stirling.
CARS: Follow signs for A91 St. Andrews/Alloa. Car Parking is available in the club car park. Home support in West Car Park and visiting support in East Car Park.

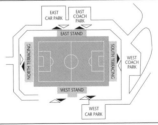

CAPACITY: 3,808, Seated 2,508, Standing 1,300
PITCH DIMENSIONS: 110 yds x 74 yds
FACILITIES FOR DISABLED SUPPORTERS:
Disabled access, toilets and spaces for 36.

Stranraer: Stair Park

Stair Park can be reached by the following routes:
TRAINS: There is a regular service of trains from Ayr and the station is only 1 mile from the ground.
BUSES: Two services pass the park. These are the buses from Glenluce to Portroadie and the Dumfries–Stranraer service.
CARS: Car parking is available in the Public Park at the ground, where there is space for approximately 50 vehicles and also in the side streets around the park. Signs for away supporters will be displayed and parking situated at Stranraer Academy, McMasters Road.

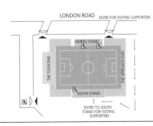

CAPACITY: 5,600; Seated 1,830, Standing 3,770
PITCH DIMENSIONS: 110 yds x 70 yds
FACILITIES FOR DISABLED SUPPORTERS:
By prior arrangement with Club Secretary.

ALBION ROVERS
Cliftonhill Stadium, Main Street,
Coatbridge, ML5 3RB

CHAIRMAN
Andrew Dick, M.Sc., B.Sc., C.Eng.

VICE-CHAIRMAN
David T. Shanks, B.Sc.

DIRECTORS
Robert Watt, David Wright & Thomas Young

**GENERAL MANAGER/OFFICE
ADMINISTRATOR**
John Reynolds

SECRETARY
David T. Shanks, B.Sc.

MANAGER
Kevin McAllister

ASSISTANT MANAGER
Scott Crabbe

**DIRECTOR OF YOUTH DEVELOPMENT/
YOUTH CO-ORDINATOR**
Jimmy Lindsay

U19 YOUTH TEAM COACH
Jimmy Lindsay

U17 YOUTH TEAM COACH
Derek Kelly

U16 YOUTH TEAM COACH
Willie McNab

U15 YOUTH TEAM COACH
John Bell

PHYSIOTHERAPIST
Derek Kelly

**FOOTBALL SAFETY OFFICERS'
ASSOCIATION REPRESENTATIVE**
John Reynolds 07719 736287

GROUNDSMAN
Hugh McBride

KIT PERSON
Wilma McBride

COMMERCIAL MANAGER
Jim Mercer

MATCHDAY PROGRAMME EDITOR
Bill Walker 07855 492122

CLUB STEWARD
Chic Young

TELEPHONES
Ground (01236) 606334/607041
Fax (01236) 606334
Sec. Home (01236) 421686
Sec. Bus. (01236) 762775

E-MAIL & INTERNET ADDRESS
jimmy_lindsay66@hotmail.com
www.albionrovers.com

CLUB SHOP
Cliftonhill Stadium, Main Street,
Coatbridge, ML5 3RB. Open one hour prior to
kick-off at first team home matches.

OFFICIAL SUPPORTERS CLUB
John Smith, 45 Blair Road, Coatbridge
(01236) 420417

TEAM CAPTAIN
Jim Mercer

SHIRT SPONSOR
Reigart

KIT SUPPLIER
Pro Star

LIST OF PLAYERS 2004/05

PLAYERS SURNAME	FIRST NAME	MIDDLE NAME	DATE OF BIRTH	PLACE OF BIRTH	DATE SIGNED	HEIGHT FT INS		WEIGHT ST LBS		POSITION ON PITCH	PREVIOUS CLUB
BENSON	SCOTT	THOMAS	10/01/88	GLASGOW	07/07/04	6	0	10	0	FORWARD	HIBERNIAN
BLACK	DANIEL		22/01/86	NEW PLYMOUTH	08/07/03	6	0	12	5	DEFENDER	HEART OF MIDLOTHIAN FC
BOYLE	JOSEPH		16/05/83	GLASGOW	30/07/04	6	1	12	1	MIDFIELD	PARTICK THISTLE
BRADFORD	JOHN		15/12/79	IRVINE	11/07/02	6	0	12	2	FORWARD	AYR UNITED
CARR	MATTHEW		04/09/87	GLASGOW	21/01/04	6	1	11	0	GOALKEEPER	CELTIC
CLEARY	ALLAN		12/09/87	EDINBURGH	07/07/04	6	2	9	0	DEFENDER	HIBERNIAN
CONNOLLY	CHARLES		18/07/85	GLASGOW	30/01/03	6	0	10	4	DEFENDER	CUMBERNAULD UNITED JM
CRABBE	SCOTT		12/08/68	EDINBURGH	10/06/04	5	9	11	8	MIDFIELD	ALLOA ATHLETIC
DOCHERTY	MARK		15/05/88	BELLSHILL	08/09/04	5	8	9	7	DEFENDER	ALBION ROVERS FORM D U
DOUGLAS	IAN		03/08/87	BROXBURN	07/07/04	5	9	9	6	FORWARD	FALKIRK
FAHEY	CHRISTOPHER		28/06/78	COATBRIDGE	30/07/04	6	0	12	6	GOALKEEPER	LARKHALL THISTLE JUNI
FLEMING	GARRY		17/05/87	VALE OF LEVEN	09/07/03	5	8	9	0	FORWARD	CELTIC FORM D
HADDOW	MARK	LYLE	14/01/86	LANARK	17/01/04	6	1	11	6	DEFENDER	RAITH ROVERS
HALLIDAY	KEVIN		30/04/88	BELLSHILL	08/09/04	6	0	10	0	DEFENDER	MOTHERWELL FORM D U
HARDIE	CRAIG		16/07/88	GLASGOW	07/07/04	5	9	12	0	MIDFIELD	HEART OF MIDLOTHIAN
KERR	STEVEN		30/04/86	GLASGOW	25/07/02	5	10	10	6	DEFENDER	STENHOUSEMUIR
LARKIN	STEPHEN		02/03/88	BELLSHILL	18/09/04	5	8	10	2	FORWARD	BURNBANK
McALLISTER	KEVIN		08/11/62	FALKIRK	09/08/02	5	5	11	0	FORWARD	FALKIRK
McCAUL	GRAEME		05/10/84	EDINBURGH	11/07/02	5	11	11	2	MIDFIELD	HEART OF MIDLOTHIAN
McGOWAN	JAMIE		05/12/70	MORECAMBE	07/07/04	6	0	11	11	MIDFIELD	ALLOA ATHLETIC
McINALLY	MICHAEL		05/01/87	EDINBURGH	07/07/04	5	10	10	0	GOALKEEPER	HIBERNIAN
McINULTY	SEAN		26/01/88	BELLSHILL	08/07/04	6	0	10	0	DEFENDER	HIBERNIAN
McKENNA	KEVIN		24/01/88	BELLSHILL	21/08/04	5	10	10	4	GOALKEEPER	DUNDEE UNITED
McKENZIE	MARC		11/07/85	GLASGOW	17/07/02	5	6	9	11	FORWARD	RAITH ROVERS FORM D
McLAREN	GRAEME		08/09/83	STIRLING		5	11	10	9	DEFENDER	EAST STIRLINGSHIRE
McMAHON	GERARD		05/06/87	BELLSHILL	04/09/04	6	0	10	8	DEFENDER	ST. MIRREN FORM D U'
McMANUS	PAUL	JOHN	26/12/82	KIRKCALDY	29/07/03	5	10	10	5	FORWARD	RAITH ROVERS
MEIKLEJOHN	GERARD		16/01/88	GLASGOW	07/07/04	5	9	10	0	FORWARD	ALBION ROVERS FORM D H
MERCER	JAMES		30/07/74	GLASGOW	13/07/02	6	5	14	3	MIDFIELD	ARBROATH
PATERSON	ANDREW		05/05/72	GLASGOW	17/07/02	5	9.5	11	10	DEFENDER	STRANRAER
PATERSON	SCOTT		21/04/88	BELLSHILL	07/07/04	5	9	10	0	DEFENDER	ALBION ROVERS FORM D L'
PATRICK	RICKY		14/03/86	KIRKCALDY	09/07/03	5	10	10	5	MIDFIELD	HIBERNIAN FORM D
PEAT	MARK		13/03/82	BELLSHILL	29/07/04	6	2	13	7	GOALKEEPER	ARBROATH
POTTER	KERR	ALAN	13/08/86	EDINBURGH	09/07/03	6	0	10	0	DEFENDER	HEART OF MIDLOTHIAN FORM
PRESTON	FRASER		18/04/87	EDINBURGH	02/09/04	5	10	10	0	DEFENDER	FALKIRK FORM S
QUINN	RICHARD	JAMES	16/03/88	IRVINE	31/08/04	5	9	10	2	MIDFIELD	ALBION ROVERS FORM D U
REID	GRAEME		05/02/88	BELLSHILL		5	5	8	7	MIDFIELD	ALBION ROVERS FORM D U
RICHARDSON	GARY	STEVEN	13/05/86	LANARK	17/01/04	5	9	11	0	MIDFIELD	RAITH ROVERS
SCOTT	DAVID	ROBERT	20/05/88	BELLSHILL	31/08/04	5	9	10	8	GOALKEEPER	ALBION ROVERS FORM D U
SELKIRK	ANDREW		12/09/86	GLASGOW	17/07/02	5	10	10	6	FORWARD	ALBION ROVERS FORM D U
SILVESTRO	CHRISTOPHER		16/03/79	BELLSHILL	30/07/04	5	7	11	4	MIDFIELD	GLENBOIG
SMITH	JORDAN		02/02/82	BELLSHILL	29/07/99	6	2	13	0	DEFENDER	ALBION ROVERS FORM SI
STEWART	PAUL		19/09/88	GLASGOW	21/09/04	5	5	9	0	FORWARD	HIBERNIAN
STIRLING	JERED		13/10/76	STIRLING	19/07/02	6	0	13	0	DEFENDER	STRANRAER
STUART	PAUL	NEIL	22/01/88	GLASGOW	24/01/04	6	0	11	5	FORWARD	ALBION ROVERS FORM D U'
VALENTINE	JAMES	McINNES	24/07/85	BROXBURN	17/07/02	5	9	10	0	MIDFIELD	RAITH ROVERS FORM D U'
WALLACE	NEIL		13/06/87	EDINBURGH	07/07/04	5	9	10	0	DEFENDER	HEART OF MIDLOTHIAN
YARDLEY	MARK		14/09/69	LIVINGSTON	29/01/03	6	2	16	8	FORWARD	ST. MIRREN
YOUNG	JAMES		15/06/88	GLASGOW	07/07/04	5	7	9	0	MIDFIELD	KILMARNOCK

TICKET INFORMATION

SEASON TICKET PRICES

SEATED	ADULT	£100
	OAP/UNEMPLOYED	£60
	12-16 YEARS UNACCOMPANIED	£30
	UNDER 12'S	£20
	(WHEN ACCOMPANIED BY A PAYING ADULT)	

LEAGUE ADMISSION PRICES

SEATED	ADULT	£8
	OAP/UNEMPLOYED	£4
STANDING	ADULT	£8
	OAP/UNEMPLOYED	£4

THE WEE ROVERS' 10 YEAR LEAGUE RECO

SEASON	DIV	P	W	D	L	F	A	PTS
1994-95	T	36	5	3	28	27	82	18
1995-96	T	36	7	8	21	37	74	29
1996-97	T	36	13	10	13	50	47	49
1997-98	T	36	13	5	18	60	73	44
1998-99	T	36	12	8	16	43	63	44
1999-00	T	36	5	7	24	33	75	22
2000-01	T	36	12	9	15	38	43	45
2001-02	T	36	16	11	9	51	42	59
2002-03	T	36	20	10	6	62	36	70
2003-04	T	36	12	4	20	66	75	40

SEASON STATS 2003/04

DATE	VENUE	OPPONENTS	ATT	RES	FAHEY C.	McCAUL G.	STIRLING J.	SMITH J.	CORMACK P.	McCAIG J.	McALLISTER K.	FARRELL D.	McMANUS P.	DIACK I.	MERCER J.	YARDLEY M.	PATERSON A.	McBRIDE K.	SKINNER S.	CONNOLLY C.	BENNETT N.	SWEENEY S.	McKENZIE M.	MOLLOY M.	DENHAM G.	BRADFORD J.	KERR C.	PATRICK R.	LOW A.	CRABBE S.	SELKIRK A.	CARR M.	POTTER K.	VALENTINE J.	SILVESTRO C.	KERR S.
-AUG	H	STRANRAER	323	1-1	1	2	3	4	5	6	7	8	9^1	10	11	12																				
-AUG	A	COWDENBEATH	362	4-1	1	8	3	4		6	7	5	10^1	14	11^1	9^2	2	16																		
-AUG	H	QUEEN'S PARK	627	3-1	1	8	3	12^1	6	5	7	4^1	10	15	11	9^1	2	14																		
-AUG	A	GRETNA	385	1-3	1		3	4	5	6	12	8	10	7^1		9	2	11		15																
-SEP	H	ELGIN CITY	394	1-2	1	8	3		5	6	7	4	10^1	16	11	9	2	14	15																	
-SEP	H	MONTROSE	262	0-1	1	8	3			7	4		10	9	11		2		15																	
-SEP	A	STIRLING ALBION	685	1-2	1	7	3	8	6	5	14	4	10	15	11	9^1	2																			
-SEP	H	PETERHEAD	283	2-0	8				5	7	6		10^1	3	11	9^1	2	14			1	4	15	16												
-OCT	H	EAST STIRLINGSHIRE	256	5-0	8^1				5	7	4		10^2	3	11	9^1	2	14^1			1	6		15												
-OCT	A	ELGIN CITY	681	5-1	8		3^1		12	5	7^1	6	10^1	16	11^1	11^1	2				1	4														
-OCT	H	COWDENBEATH	415	1-2	8	3			5	7	6		10	16	11	9	2	15^1			1	4														
-NOV	A	STRANRAER	447	0-5	8		2	5	14	7	6		10	16	11	9	12	3			1	4														
-NOV	A	MONTROSE	267	0-1	8	3	12		5	7	6		10	14	11		2	9			1	4		15												
-NOV	H	GRETNA	357	1-3	8	3^1	4	12	5	7			10		11		2	6			1		15	9												
-DEC	H	STIRLING ALBION	392	0-3	8	12	4	3					10		11	9	2	6	15	1	5	14	7													
-DEC	A	PETERHEAD	485	1-2	7	6	8	3					10^1		11	9			2	1	4			5	15											
-DEC	A	EAST STIRLINGSHIRE	175	† 4-3	7	6^1	8	3	5				10		11^1	9^1	12	14	2	1	4			15												
-JAN	A	QUEEN'S PARK	454	1-1	7	6	4	5					10^1		11	9			2	1		14		12	3	8										
-JAN	A	STIRLING ALBION	629	0-3		3	6						14		11				2	1	4	7		10		8	16									
-FEB	H	MONTROSE	192	3-0	6	14	5^1						10^1		11^1	9			2	1	4	16		15	3	8	7									
-FEB	A	GRETNA	418	0-3		6	5						10		11		2		17	1	4	15			3	8	7	9								
-FEB	H	STRANRAER	428	1-4		6	5						10		11		2			1	4	7		12^1	3	8	14	9								
-FEB	H	ELGIN CITY	425	2-1		6	5						10^1		11		2			1	4			14	3	8^1	7	9								
-MAR	A	COWDENBEATH	248	1-1		6^1	5	15					10				2			1	4			11	3	8	7	9								
-MAR	H	EAST STIRLINGSHIRE	179	5-1		3		5	4			6	10^1		11^2	9^1	2			1				7^1	15		12	8	16								
-MAR	H	QUEEN'S PARK	491	† 3-1		3	5	6					10^2		11	9	2			1	4			7	12		14	8								
-MAR	H	PETERHEAD	253	3-3		3^1	5		6				10		11^1	9^1	2			1	4			7			12	8								
-MAR	A	MONTROSE	339	1-3		3	5	6	4				10^1		11	9	2			1		16		7				8	15							
-MAR	H	GRETNA	287	† 1-2		3	5		4				10		11	9	2			1	6			7				8								
-APR	A	PETERHEAD	440	0-5		3	5	12	4			6	10		11	9	2							7		8	14			1	16					
-APR	H	STIRLING ALBION	615	3-5	1	3	6	5	4				10		11^2	9^1	2							7		8					16					
-APR	H	ELGIN CITY	212	1-2	1	3	6	5					10^1		11	9	2		17		15			7		8					4				
-APR	A	EAST STIRLINGSHIRE	223	8-1		3^1	6				14	10^2			11^1	9	2			1	5	12^1		7^2				8^1		4	16					
-MAY	A	QUEEN'S PARK	516	1-0		3	4						10		11	9	2			1	4	16^1		7		15	8				6				
-MAY	H	COWDENBEATH	307	2-4		3^1	4	12							11		2			1	5^1	9		7		10	8				6				
-MAY	A	STRANRAER	1,321	0-4		3	5	11		6							2			1		15		9		7		10		4		8	16			
TOTAL FULL APPEARANCES					9	18	31	27	17	21	12	16	33	5	33	26	29	5		5	26	21	3	2	1	14	6	12	4	13		1	3		3
TOTAL SUB APPEARANCES							2	2	4	2	2	1	8		1	2		7	2	3	1			11	3		6	2	1	6		2		2	1		1
TOTAL GOALS SCORED						1	7	2			1	1	18	1	10	11		2				1	2				4		1	1					

Bold figures denote goalscorers. † denotes opponents's own goals.

LEADING GOALSCORERS:

SEASON	DIV	GOALS	PLAYER
94-95	T	7	M. Scott
95-96	T	12	G. Young
96-97	T	11	W. Watters
97-98	T	13	W. Watters
98-99	T	10	D. Lorimer
99-00	T	7	I. Diack
00-01	T	6	M. Booth
01-02	T	11	C. McLean
02-03	T	10	J. Mercer
03-04	T	18	P. McManus

MILESTONES:

YEAR OF FORMATION: 1882
MOST CAPPED PLAYER: John White
NO. OF CAPS: 1
MOST LEAGUE POINTS IN A SEASON:
54 (Division 2 – Season 1929/30)(2 Points for a win)
70 (Third Division – Season 2002/03)(3 Points for a win)
MOST LEAGUE GOALS SCORED BY A PLAYER IN A SEASON:
John Renwick (Season 1932/33)
NO. OF GOALS SCORED: 41
RECORD ATTENDANCE: 27,381 (-v- Rangers 8.2.1936)
RECORD VICTORY: 12-0 (-v- Airdriehill – Scottish Cup, 3.9.1887)
RECORD DEFEAT: 1-11 (-v- Partick Thistle – League Cup, 11.8.1993)

ALBION ROVERS PLAYING KITS SEASON 2004/05

FIRST KIT   SECOND KIT   THIRD KIT

COWDENBEATH
Central Park, High Street,
Cowdenbeath, KY4 9QQ
CHAIRMAN
Gordon McDougall
VICE-CHAIRMAN
Albert V. Tait
DIRECTORS
Ian Fraser, Brian Watson,
Dr. Robert Brownlie, John Johnston, Robert
Johnston, Graham Thompson , Joseph
Macnamara & Thomas W. Ogilvie
HON. LIFE MEMBER
Brenda Solomon
**GENERAL/COMMERCIAL/
LOTTERY MANAGER**
Joseph Macnamara
SECRETARY
Thomas Ogilvie
OFFICE ADMINISTRATOR
Kathryn Nellies
MANAGER
David Baikie
ASSISTANT MANAGER
Graeme Irons
YOUTH TEAM COACHES
David Liddle & Steven McLeish (U19)
Gary McAlpine, Carlo Crolla & David Stewart (U17)
James Ward (U15)
Brian Welsh, Gary Miller (U14)
Philip Kidd, Steven Forrest (U13)
Tom Blackley (U12)
WOMEN'S DEVELOPMENT COACH
Graham Thompson
GOALKEEPING COACH
David Westwood
CHIEF SCOUT
Owen Coll
CLUB DOCTOR
Dr. Robert Brownlie
PHYSIOTHERAPIST
Neil Bryson
**FOOTBALL SAFETY OFFICERS'
ASSOCIATION REPRESENTATIVE**
Aaron Turnbull
GROUNDSMAN
Gordon McDougall Jnr.
KIT PERSON
Bert Johnston
MATCHDAY PROGRAMME EDITOR
Andrew Mullen (01383) 611644
TELEPHONES
Ground/Ticket Office/Information Service
(01383) 610166
Sec. Home (01383) 513013
Sec. Bus (01383) 313400
Fax (01383) 512132
E-MAIL & INTERNET ADDRESS
bluebrazil@cowdenbeathfc.com
www.cowdenbeathfc.com
CLUB SHOP
Situated at Stadium. Open 10.00 a.m. – 3.00 p.m.
and on Home Match Days
OFFICIAL SUPPORTERS CLUB
Central Park, High Street, Cowdenbeath, KY4 9QQ
TEAM CAPTAIN
Innes Ritchie
SHIRT SPONSOR
Gladyer Inn
KIT SUPPLIER
Paulas Benara

LIST OF PLAYERS 2004/05

PLAYERS SURNAME	FIRST NAME	MIDDLE NAME	DATE OF BIRTH	PLACE OF BIRTH	DATE SIGNED	HEIGHT FT INS		WEIGHT ST LBS		POSITION ON PITCH	PREVIOUS CLUB
ALLAN	REES		11/05/87	EDINBURGH	02/08/04	5	8	11	7	DEFENDER	SALVESEN B.C.
ANDERSON	ALEXANDER		23/05/87	DUNFERMLINE	02/08/04	5	10	11	7	DEFENDER	ROSYTH RECREATION
ANDERSON	CRAIG		05/05/88	EDINBURGH	02/08/04	5	10	10	0	MIDFIELD	HUTCHISON VALE
BAIN	JONATHAN		28/01/86	EDINBURGH	13/05/03	6	0	11	0	DEFENDER	WARDIEVALE B.C.
BATHGATE	STEPHEN		01/02/87	KIRKCALDY	21/08/03	6	0	10	5	FORWARD	RAITH ROVERS FORM D U'
BLACK	LEE		07/04/85	BELLSHILL	30/08/04	5	11	10	7	FORWARD	CROSSGATES PRIMROSE JN
BOUGLAS	DALE		23/01/87	DUNFERMLINE	21/08/03	5	10	10	0	DEFENDER	RAITH ROVERS FORM D U'
BUCHANAN	LIAM		27/03/85	EDINBURGH	02/07/02	5	8	10	8	MIDFIELD	HEART OF MIDLOTHIAN
BURNS	JOHN	PAUL	11/03/78	KIRKCALDY	21/07/04	5	8	12	0	MIDFIELD	GLENROTHES JUNIORS
CAMPBELL	ANDREW	MARK	15/03/79	EDINBURGH	24/10/01	6	0	12	7	DEFENDER	ARNISTON RANGERS JN
CARLIN	ANDREW		06/01/81	GLASGOW	06/04/03	6	1	14	8	GOALKEEPER	STENHOUSEMUIR
CRAIG	STEVEN	WILLIAM	21/10/82	GLASGOW	28/08/04	6	2	12	10	FORWARD	GLASGOW UNIVERSITY
CROLLA	JACOB	AARON	08/10/87	KIRKCALDY	14/05/04	5	11	9	10	FORWARD	RAITH ROVERS FORM D U'
CROOKSTON	MICHAEL	DOUGLAS	24/11/88	KIRKCALDY	14/08/04	5	9	9	6	FORWARD	CAIRNEYHILL Y.F.C.
DOYLE	DARREN		24/01/87	KIRKCALDY	30/08/04	6	0	11	0	FORWARD	DUNDONALD BLUEBELL JN
FINDLAY	SCOTT		16/10/83	PERTH	28/08/04	6	4	14	7	GOALKEEPER	FORFAR ATHLETIC
FLEMING	ALLAN		06/05/84	DUNFERMLINE	26/01/02	6	3	11	10	GOALKEEPER	MUSSELBURGH WINDS
FRASER	KENNETH		28/01/88	DUNFERMLINE	02/08/04	5	11	11	8	DEFENDER	DUNFERMLINE ATHLETIC
FUSCO	GARY		01/06/82	EDINBURGH	22/07/02	6	1	11	5	MIDFIELD	MUSSELBURGH ATHLETIC JN
FYFE	ROBERT	JAMES	03/05/88	DUNFERMLINE	02/08/04	6	0	11	0	DEFENDER	DUNFERMLINE ATHLETIC
GIBSON	NEIL		14/05/86	DUNFERMLINE	20/08/04	5	10	12	8	DEFENDER	ST. JOHNSTONE
GILBERTSON	JOHN		19/12/86	EDINBURGH	13/05/03	6	1	11	7	GOALKEEPER	WARDIEVALE B.C.
GOLLAN	KEVIN		17/01/87	MELBOURNE	21/08/03	5	9	9	5	MIDFIELD	CROSSFORD UNDER 16'S
GRAY	LIAM		22/02/87	EDINBURGH	26/08/04	5	10	11	7	GOALKEEPER	HIBERNIAN
GRIBBEN	DARREN		27/03/86	BELLSHILL	11/09/04	5	11	10	12	FORWARD	HAMILTON ACADEMICAL
GUILD	GRAEME		10/05/88	KIRKCALDY	04/08/04	5	8	9	8	MIDFIELD	COWDENBEATH FORM D U'
JAHN	SIMON		14/11/87	BROXBURN	21/08/03	5	9	11	0	FORWARD	CAIRNEYHILL B.C.
JOHNSON	DARYL		17/05/87	EDINBURGH	26/08/04	5	9	11	0	DEFENDER	LOANHEAD B.C.
KELLY	JOHN	PAUL	26/04/85	EDINBURGH	26/01/04	5	6	10	9	MIDFIELD	WYCOMBE WANDERERS
KILLIN	GRANT		16/05/85	EDINBURGH	21/08/04	5	9	11	2	FORWARD	PENICUIK ATHLETIC JUNC
LAWRIE	GREIG	IAN	06/07/86	DUNFERMLINE	14/08/04	6	0	12	0	DEFENDER	DUNFERMLINE COLTS
MAUCHLEN	IAN		11/06/79	IRVINE	24/07/01	5	7	10	10	MID / FWD	OAKLEY UNITED JUNIORS
M'AVINUE	PAUL		25/01/88	LILLE	04/08/04	6	0	11	0	DEFENDER	COWDENBEATH FORM D U'
M'CAFFERY	JONATHAN		21/09/87	GLASGOW	10/11/03	5	6	9	0	DEFENDER	RAITH ROVERS FORM D U'
M'CALLUM	RYAN		20/12/86	EDINBURGH	13/05/03	6	1	11	0	FORWARD	FERNIESIDE B.C.
M'CONNACHIE	SCOTT		09/08/88	EDINBURGH	02/08/04	5	10	10	4	DEFENDER	COWDENBEATH FORM D U'
M'EWEN	MARK		05/01/86	EDINBURGH	13/05/03	6	1	11	0	MIDFIELD	WARDIEVALE B.C.
M'GREGOR	DARREN		07/08/85	EDINBURGH	16/08/03	5	11	12	0	DEFENDER	LEITH ATHLETIC
M'HALE	PAUL		30/09/81	STIRLING	14/07/04	5	9	10	12	MIDFIELD	SAUCHIE JUNIORS
M'ILVEAN	ROSS		13/09/88	DUNFERMLINE	14/08/04	6	0	10	6	DEFENDER	ROSYTH RECREATION JN
M'KEOWN	JOHN	PATON	21/04/81	GLASGOW	19/07/03	6	4.5	14	0	DEFENDER	DUMBARTON
MILLER	DARREN		25/05/83	BELLSHILL	10/08/04	6	0	12	6	MIDFIELD	ARDRIE UNITED
MOWAT	DAVID		17/12/83	THURSO	16/01/03	6	0	11	0	DEFENDER	WICK ACADEMY
MUNRO	DANIEL		30/04/86	EDINBURGH	13/05/03	5	11	10	7	DEFENDER	LEITH ATHLETIC
PATERSON	ROSS		10/05/88	DUMFRIES	09/08/04	5	9	10	1	MIDFIELD	HIBERNIAN
REID	COLIN		17/05/88	LIVINGSTON	04/08/04	6	1	12	1	DEFENDER	DUNFERMLINE ATHLETIC
RICHARDSON	STUART		26/08/88	EDINBURGH	14/08/04	5	9	10	0	MIDFIELD	ABERDOUR B.C.
RITCHIE	INNES		24/08/73	EDINBURGH	16/09/03	6	1	14	4	DEFENDER	ARBROATH
ROWBOTHAM	MARK		19/06/88	KIRKCALDY	02/08/04	6	0	11	0	GOALKEEPER	COWDENBEATH FORM D U'
SANDEMAN	ROY		03/02/87	EDINBURGH	02/08/04	5	11	11	0	MIDFIELD	HUTCHISON VALE B.C.
SCOTT	CRAIG		15/08/87	EDINBURGH	21/07/04	5	6.5	9	0	FORWARD	BAYSWATER CITY S.C.
SHAND	CALVIN	DAVID	09/11/83	EDINBURGH	18/07/03	6	0	11	6	DEFENDER	HIBERNIAN
SHIELDS	DENE		16/09/82	EDINBURGH	08/01/04	6	0	12	8	FORWARD	BRECHIN CITY
STEVENSON	MARK		05/04/88	EDINBURGH	04/08/04	6	1	10	12	FORWARD	HUTCHISON VALE B.C.
STEWART	SEAN	DAVID	01/07/88	DUNFERMLINE	02/08/04	5	10	10	5	MIDFIELD	COWDENBEATH FORM D U'
THOMAS	JAMIE		25/02/87	EDINBURGH	02/08/04	6	1	10	5	MIDFIELD	HIBERNIAN
WILLIAMS	DAVID		29/09/81	GLASGOW	26/07/04	6	0	12	2	MIDFIELD	FORFAR ATHLETIC

TICKET INFORMATION

SEASON TICKET PRICES

SEATED	ADULT	£145 (INCLUDING ALL CUP TIES)
	JUVENILE/OAP	£60

LEAGUE ADMISSION PRICES

SEATED	ADULT	£9
	JUVENILE/OAP	£3.50
STANDING	ADULT	£8
	JUVENILE/OAP	£3

THE BLUE BRAZIL'S 10 YEAR LEAGUE RECORD

SEASON	DIV	P	W	D	L	F	A	PTS
1994-95	T	36	11	7	18	48	60	40
1995-96	T	36	10	8	18	45	59	38
1996-97	T	36	10	9	17	38	51	39
1997-98	T	36	12	2	22	33	57	38
1998-99	T	36	8	7	21	34	65	31
1999-00	T	36	15	9	12	59	43	54
2000-01	T	36	23	7	6	58	31	76
2001-02	S	36	11	11	14	49	51	44
2002-03	S	36	8	12	16	46	57	36
2003-04	T	36	15	10	11	46	39	55

The blue brazil's stats 2003/04

SEASON STATS 2003/04

DATE	VENUE	OPPONENTS	ATT	RES	CARLIN A.	SHAND C.	McINALLY D.	CAMPBELL A.	McKEOWN J.	MOWAT D.	GILFILLAN B.	MORRIS I.	BROWN G.	GORDON K.	BOYLE S.	MATHESON R.	FALLON J.	MOFFAT A.	WINTER C.	BUCHANAN L.	MAUCHLEN I.	SHIELDS D.	RITCHIE I.	FUSCO G.	SLAVEN J.	STEWART S.	McGUINNESS L.	SKINNER S.	ORHUE P.	McCALLUM R.	KELLY J.P.	BRISTOW S.	FLEMING A.	BATHGATE S.
-AUG	A	STIRLING ALBION	576	0-0	1	2	3	4	5	6	7	8	9	10	11	12	14	16																
-AUG	H	ALBION ROVERS	362	1-4	1	2	3	4	12	5	15	11	10						7	9	6	8	16¹											
-AUG	A	MONTROSE	338	3-1	1	2	3	15	5	6	4	10¹	9¹				14		11	8¹	16	7												
-AUG	A	EAST STIRLINGSHIRE	296	1-1	1	2	3		5	6	4	11¹	9	10		12			7	8		16												
-SEP	H	QUEEN'S PARK	339	0-1	1	2	3		5	6	4	11	9	12		14			8			7	10	16										
-SEP	H	GRETNA	235	0-1	1	2	3		5	6	4		9	10		7		15	8	16	14	11												
-SEP	A	ELGIN CITY	665	4-0	1	16	3		5	2	4		9			14			8	11¹		10²	6¹	7	15									
-OCT	H	STRANRAER	232	0-1	1	2	3		5	7	4		9	14		11			8			10	6		16									
-OCT	A	PETERHEAD	542	1-0	1	2	3		5	16	4¹					12	9		8	11		10	6	15		7								
-OCT	A	ALBION ROVERS	415	2-1	1	2	3		5	12	4			16			9		8	11		10	6	14¹		7¹								
-NOV	H	STIRLING ALBION	468	2-0	1		3	2	5	11	4¹		9				12		8	16¹	15		6	10		7								
-NOV	H	QUEEN'S PARK	554	0-0	1	2	3		5	11	4		9				14		8		15	10	6	7		12								
-NOV	H	EAST STIRLINGSHIRE	330	2-1	1	2	3		5	11	4						12		8	16	14	9²	6	10		7								
-DEC	A	GRETNA	401	0-1	1		3	16	5	2	4		9	12					8		7	10	6	11										
-DEC	H	ELGIN CITY	242	3-2	1		3		5	14	4		9¹	7					8	15	2¹	10¹	6	12		11								
-DEC	A	STRANRAER	395	0-2	1	2	3		5	14	4		9	14					8		7	10	6	12		15								
-DEC	H	PETERHEAD	308	2-0	1	2	3¹	12		5	4		16¹	10		14			8		7	9	6	11										
-JAN	H	MONTROSE	282	3-3	1	2	3		5	11			12²	10					8	16	7	9¹	6	4		15								
-JAN	A	STIRLING ALBION	790	1-1	1	2	3		5	4			12							7	9¹	6	8			11	10	15						
-JAN	H	GRETNA	290	1-2	1	2	3	4	5	7			14							12	9	6	8			11	10¹		16					
-FEB	H	QUEEN'S PARK	275	5-1	1		3		5	2	4								15²	12	9²	8				11	10¹		14	7				
-FEB	A	EAST STIRLINGSHIRE	308	1-0	1	2	11		5	3	4								8	15	7	9	6¹			12	10		16					
-FEB	A	PETERHEAD	619	0-0	1		12	2	5	3	4								8	15	7	9	6	11			10							
-MAR	H	ALBION ROVERS	248	1-1	1	2	3	6	5	11	4								8	14¹	7	9		12			10		15					
-MAR	H	STRANRAER	210	1-2	1	2	3		5	11	4								8¹	10	16	9	6	7			14		15					
-MAR	A	MONTROSE	349	0-0		2	11	3	5	8	4									7	9¹	6				15	10	16			1			
-MAR	A	ELGIN CITY	312	0-0		2	11	3		5	4								14	12	9	6	8			10		15	7					
-MAR	A	QUEEN'S PARK	508	2-1		2	11	3	5	10	4¹								12	7		6¹	8			15		14	9					
-MAR	H	EAST STIRLINGSHIRE	289	2-0		2	15	3		5	4¹								10¹		9	6	8			11	12		7		1	16		
-APR	H	ELGIN CITY	218	2-0		2	14	3	5	7	4								10¹		9	6¹	8			11		12	15		1			
-APR	A	GRETNA	429	1-0		2	14	3	5	7	4¹								10	12	9	6	8			11			15		1			
-APR	H	PETERHEAD	238	0-3		2		3	5	7	4								10	12	9	6	8			11		16	15		1			
-APR	A	STRANRAER	457	0-1		2	10	3	5	7	4								14		9	6	8			11		15	12		1			
-MAY	H	MONTROSE	229	0-0		2	12	3	5	10	4								14		9	6	8			11		15	7		1			
-MAY	A	ALBION ROVERS	307	†4-2		2	11	3	5	7	4¹								12		9²	6	8			10		14			1			
-MAY	H	STIRLING ALBION	692	0-5		2	11	3	5	10	4								12	7	9	6	8				15	18			1			
TOTAL FULL APPEARANCES					33	30	29	18	32	33	32	5	12	7	1	3	3		21	8	14	30	29	22	4	11	8	1	4	3			
TOTAL SUB APPEARANCES						1	5	3	1	3	1		2	8		6	4	2		17	10	1	1	5	2	1	5	1	1	12	6	1	1	1
TOTAL GOALS SCORED							1				6	2	5						2	8	1	12	4	1		1		2				

II bold figures denote goalscorers. † denotes opponent's own goals.

LEADING GOALSCORERS:

SEASON	DIV	GOALS	PLAYER
94-95	T	23	M. Yardley
95-96	T	11	D. Scott
96-97	T	6	G. Wood
97-98	T	6	W. Stewart
98-99	T	7	W. Stewart
99-00	T	13	M. McDowell
00-01	T	10	M. McDowell
01-02	S	17	G. Brown
02-03	S	10	G. Brown, K. Gordon
03-04	T	12	D. Shields

MILESTONES:

YEAR OF FORMATION: 1881
MOST CAPPED PLAYER: Jim Paterson
NO. OF CAPS: 3
MOST LEAGUE POINTS IN A SEASON:
60 (Division 2 – Season 1938/39)(2 Points for a Win)
76 (Third Division – Season 2000/01)(3 Points for a Win)
MOST LEAGUE GOALS SCORED BY A PLAYER IN A SEASON:
Rab Walls (Season 1938/39)
NO. OF GOALS SCORED: 54
RECORD ATTENDANCE: 25,586 (-v- Rangers – 21.9.1949)
RECORD VICTORY: 12-0 (-v- Johnstone – Scottish Cup, 21.1.1928)
RECORD DEFEAT: 1-11 (-v- Clyde – Division 2, 6.10.1951)

COWDENBEATH PLAYING KITS SEASON 2004/05

FIRST KIT   SECOND KIT   THIRD KIT

LIST OF PLAYERS 2004/05

PLAYERS SURNAME	FIRST NAME	MIDDLE NAME	DATE OF BIRTH	PLACE OF BIRTH	DATE SIGNED	HEIGHT FT INS	WEIGHT ST LBS	POSITION ON PITCH	PREVIOUS CLUB
BAIN	KEVIN		19/09/72	KIRKCALDY	30/01/04	6 0	12 7	MIDFIELD	PETERHEAD
BISSETT	CALLUM	JAMES	01/04/86	KIRKCALDY	07/05/04	6 2	11 5	MIDFIELD	BLUE BRAZIL B.C. U' 16'S
BRASH	KRISTOFER		01/03/83	DUNDEE	15/06/04	5 9	9 7	MIDFIELD	PETERHEAD
BROWN	MARK	JAMES	26/01/86	KIRKCALDY	29/07/04	6 2	12 2	DEFENDER	ARBROATH
BYLE	LESLIE		29/08/82	GLASGOW	01/08/03	5 10	11 7	MIDFIELD	HIBERNIAN
COLQUHOUN	DEREK		23/03/85	EDINBURGH	02/09/04	6 1	12 0	MIDFIELD	FALKIRK
CONDIE	CRAIG	JOHN	27/06/86	KIRKCALDY	02/01/04	5 10	11 7	DEFENDER	LOMOND COLTS
CRAWFORD	ROBERT	EDWARD	26/01/87	DUNFERMLINE	28/04/04	5 11	11 2	MIDFIELD	DUNFERMLINE ATHLETIC
DAMMER	KYLE	EWAN	27/09/87	KIRKCALDY	18/06/04	6 3	13 6	DEFENDER	THORNTON B.C.
DICKSON	MARTIN	JOSEPH	19/04/86	KIRKCALDY	28/04/04	5 9	10 4	DEFENDER	COWDENBEATH FORM D U'16
DODDS	JOHN	GEORGE	16/12/81	EDINBURGH	24/05/04	6 3	14 7	GOALKEEPER	QUEEN OF THE SOUTH
DUNCAN	FRASER	TOM DAVID	08/03/83	STIRLING	31/08/04	6 3	13 0	DEFENDER	SAUCHIE JUNIORS
FAIRBAIRN	BRIAN		07/04/83	BROXBURN	21/07/03	5 10	11 7	FORWARD	GRETNA
FERGUSON	JOHN	NEIL	12/03/86	GLASGOW	30/04/04	5 8	10 10	FORWARD	DUNFERMLINE ATHLETIC
GARDINER	ROSS	MURRAY	29/09/86	KIRKCALDY	30/01/04	6 1	11 7	GOALKEEPER	LOMOND COLTS
HALL	MICHAEL		11/12/74	EDINBURGH	16/05/02	6 3	13 0	DEFENDER	EAST STIRLINGSHIRE
HERKES	JAMES		28/02/78	KIRKCALDY	16/01/04	5 11	11 7	FORWARD	ARBROATH
HODGE	ROBERT		31/03/87	KIRKCALDY	28/04/04	6 0	11 2	FORWARD	THORNTON Y.F.C. U' 15'S
JOHNSTON	CRAIG		29/06/85	PERTH	21/07/04	6 0	12 0	DEFENDER	ST. JOHNSTONE
KELLY	GARY	PATRICK	01/09/81	FALKIRK	17/06/04	5 11	11 9	MIDFIELD	STIRLING ALBION
LINTON	SAMUEL	PETER	10/05/86	KIRKCALDY	28/06/04	6 2	12 7	DEFENDER	HIBERNIAN
LOGIE	ROBERT	WILLIAM	23/09/87	PERTH	29/07/04	6 2	13 6	GOALKEEPER	DUNFERMLINE ATHLETIC
LUMSDEN	CRAIG	McDONALD	26/04/84	KIRKCALDY	11/07/02	6 1	12 0	DEFENDER	DUNFERMLINE ATHLETIC
McDONALD	GREIG	JAMES	12/05/82	DUNFERMLINE	06/03/03	6 1	13 0	DEFENDER	DUNFERMLINE ATHLETIC
McDONALD	IAN		07/03/78	NEWCASTLE UPON TYNE	03/07/03	6 1	13 10	DEFENDER	COWDENBEATH
McKAY	GRANT	JOHN	24/05/86	KIRKCALDY	30/04/04	5 10	11 0	DEFENDER	DUNFERMLINE ATHLETIC
McKENZIE	JAMIE	WILLIAM	25/02/86	KIRKCALDY	28/08/04	5 8	10 0	MIDFIELD	ST. JOHNSTONE
McLAUGHLIN	WILLIAM	SCOTT	16/08/86	KIRKCALDY	28/04/04	6 0	12 0	MIDFIELD	KINGHORN ROYALS
MILLS	GRAEME		30/01/87	KIRKCALDY	28/06/04	5 9	10 0	MIDFIELD	THORNTON Y.F.C.
MITCHELL	JONATHON	ANDREW	22/06/81	DUNDEE	03/07/03	5 10	11 7	MIDFIELD	TAYPORT JUNIORS
MORRISON	SCOTT	JOHN	22/10/81	GLASGOW	02/07/04	6 2	12 0	GOALKEEPER	DRYMEN UNITED
MORRISON	SHAUN		03/04/86	KIRKCALDY	07/05/04	5 8	11 0	FORWARD	BLUE BRAZIL B.C. U' 16'S
OLIVER	MARK	BRUCE	29/06/86	PERTH	03/08/04	6 1	11 2	MIDFIELD	NEWBURGH JUNIORS
PALICZKA	SEAN		25/04/84	GALASHIELS	24/05/04	5 10	10 7	FORWARD	INNERLEVEN VALE
RENWICK	MICHAEL	JOHN	29/02/76	EDINBURGH	13/08/04	5 10	12 0	DEFENDER	GLENAVON
SIMPSON	GREGOR		02/08/87	KIRKCALDY	26/08/04	5 10	13 0	MIDFIELD	EAST FIFE FORM S
STEELE	KEVIN	JAMES	11/10/81	DUNDEE	09/08/04	5 10	11 7	FORWARD	COVE RANGERS
TARDITI	STEPHEN		23/02/85	BELLSHILL	30/07/04	6 4	15 7	FORWARD	ABERDEEN

THE FIFERS' 10 YEAR LEAGUE RECORD

SEASON	DIV	P	W	D	L	F	A	PTS	F
1994-95	S	36	11	10	15	48	56	43	
1995-96	S	36	19	10	7	50	29	67	
1996-97	F	36	2	8	26	28	92	14	
1997-98	S	36	14	6	16	51	59	48	
1998-99	S	36	12	6	18	42	64	42	
1999-00	T	36	17	8	11	45	39	59	
2000-01	T	36	15	8	13	49	46	53	
2001-02	T	36	11	7	18	39	56	40	
2002-03	T	36	20	11	5	73	37	71	
2003-04	S	36	11	8	17	38	45	41	

SEASON STATS 2003/04

DATE	VENUE	OPPONENTS	ATT	RES	O'CONNOR G.	KELLY P.	MILLER C.	MORTIMER P.	HALL M.	BYLE L.	McMILLAN C.	McDONALD G.	DEUCHAR K.	STEWART W.	DONALDSON E.	RUSSELL G.	LYNES C.	FAIRBAIRN B.	LOVE G.	MITCHELL J.	GILBERT G.	LUMSDEN C.	BLAIR B.	McDONALD I.	NICHOLAS S.	GRAHAM M.	STEIN J.	HERKES J.	MATHIE G.	BAIN K.
9-AUG	H	STENHOUSEMUIR	568	3-2	1	2	3	4	5	6	7	8^1	9^1	10	11	12	15	16^1												
16-AUG	A	FORFAR ATHLETIC	708	1-0	1	6	3	4	5	8	7	12^1	9	10	11	2			16	14										
23-AUG	H	BERWICK RANGERS	692	3-1	1	6	3		5		2	8	9^1	10	11	4		16^1	7	12^1										
30-AUG	A	MORTON	3,270	1-2	1	6	3		5		2	8	9	10	11^1	4		16	12	7	14									
13-SEP	H	AIRDRIE UNITED	885	3-1	1	6	3	12	5		7	8^1	9^1		11^1	2				10		15	16	4						
20-SEP	H	ALLOA ATHLETIC	595	3-1	1	6	3		5		7	8	9		11	2				10		15	16	4	14					
27-SEP	A	HAMILTON ACADEMICAL	1,123	2-2	1	6					2	8^1	9	10	11^1					16	7	15		3						
4-OCT	H	DUMBARTON	518	1-0	1	6					2	8	9							16^1	10	7	16	4	3	14				
18-OCT	A	ARBROATH	705	1-0	1	8		12	5		2		9	10	3			14			7	16	4	6	11^1					
25-OCT	H	FORFAR ATHLETIC	671	2-3	1				5^1		2	8^1	9	16	3		6	15			10	11	4	12	7					
1-NOV	A	STENHOUSEMUIR	532	0-3	1				5		2	8	9	15	3		6	16			10	11	4	14	7					
8-NOV	A	AIRDRIE UNITED	1,418	1-1	1	8			5		2		9^1	10	3	11		16			14	15	4	6	7					
16-NOV	H	MORTON	1,757	0-0	1	8		12	5		2	14	9	7	3					16		11	4	6	10					
2-DEC	A	ALLOA ATHLETIC	405	0-2	1	14			5		2	8	9	7	3	11		15				4	6	10						
6-DEC	H	HAMILTON ACADEMICAL	584	2-3				14	5^1		2	8	9	16	3			15			7	11	4	6	10^1	1				
13-DEC	A	DUMBARTON	683	1-3			2	6	5		7	8^1	9	16	3			15				11	4	12	10	1				
27-DEC	A	ARBROATH	811	0-1	1	6		4	5		7	8	9	11	3	2		15		16		14		10						
3-JAN	A	BERWICK RANGERS	501	2-0	1	6			5		11^1	4^1	9	16	3			15			7	2	8		10					
17-JAN	H	STENHOUSEMUIR	536	1-0	1	8			5		2	4	16^1	10	3	9					7	12	6	11	14					
24-JAN	H	ALLOA ATHLETIC	647	0-1	1	8			5		2	12	9	10	3	4					7	15	6	11	14					
31-JAN	A	HAMILTON ACADEMICAL	1,429	0-1	1	6	3				2	4	9		11					16	7						10	15	5	14
7-FEB	H	AIRDRIE UNITED	793	0-1	1	6	3				2	4	9	16	11							8					10	7	5	
14-FEB	A	MORTON	2,894	1-1	1	8	3				2	4	9^1	10	11						14	15					7	5	6	
21-FEB	A	ARBROATH	596	0-0	1	8	3				2	4	9	10	11							15	16				7	5	6	
6-MAR	A	FORFAR ATHLETIC	600	0-1	1	8					2	4	9	10	3							15					11	7	5	6
13-MAR	H	BERWICK RANGERS	498	2-2	1	8					2	4	9^2		3					10		15					11	7	5	6
16-MAR	H	DUMBARTON	439	1-3	1	8					2	4	9		3					10^1		15					11	7	5	6
27-MAR	H	MORTON	1,114	1-0	1	14					2	10	9^1	16							7	4	8	3			11	12	5	6
31-MAR	A	AIRDRIE UNITED	1,597	1-2	1	8		12			6	4	9	7							10	16	2	3			11^1		5	
3-APR	H	HAMILTON ACADEMICAL	489	2-3	1						2^1		9^1				6			16	7	4	8	3			11	5	10	
10-APR	A	ALLOA ATHLETIC	567	1-1	1			12^1			7	4	9		15					16	11	2	6	3			10	5	8	
17-APR	H	ARBROATH	762	†1-2	1						6	7	4	9	2					16		10		3			11	15	5	8
24-APR	A	DUMBARTON	841	0-1	1						4	7	6	16	11						15	10	2	3			9	5	8	
-MAY	A	BERWICK RANGERS	490	1-1	1						4	3	7	8	16^1	11					15	14	10	2	6		9	5		
-MAY	H	FORFAR ATHLETIC	448	2-0	1						4	3	7^1	8^1	16	11						9	10	2	6		14	5		
5-MAY	A	STENHOUSEMUIR	826	1-0	1						4	3	7	8^1	16	11						9	10	2	6		14	5		
TOTAL FULL APPEARANCES					34	24	6	9	27	2	36	31	31	14	31	9	3	10	1	14	11	21	15	9	10	2	12	8	16	10
TOTAL SUB APPEARANCES						1		7				3	5	7	1		1	3		20	2	10	11	2	7		1	1	7	1
TOTAL GOALS SCORED						1	2				3	9	11		3			1		3		1	2	1					

bold figures denote goalscorers. † denotes opponent's own goal.

LEADING GOALSCORERS:

SEASON	DIV	GOALS	PLAYER
94-95	S	14	R. Scott
95-96	S	11	R. Scott
96-97	F	4	M. Dyer, P. Ronald
97-98	S	11	M. Dyer
98-99	S	13	B. Moffat
99-00	T	11	B. Moffat
00-01	T	8	S. Kerrigan
01-02	T	11	P. McManus
02-03	T	20	K. Deuchar
03-04	S	11	K. Deuchar

MILESTONES:

YEAR OF FORMATION: 1903
MOST CAPPED PLAYER: George Aitken
NO. OF CAPS: 5
MOST LEAGUE POINTS IN A SEASON:
57 (Division 2 – Season 1929/30)(2 Points for a Win)
71 (Third Division – Season 2002/03)(3 Points for a Win)
MOST LEAGUE GOALS SCORED BY A PLAYER IN A SEASON:
Henry Morris (Season 1947/48)
NO. OF GOALS SCORED: 41
RECORD ATTENDANCE: 22,515 (-v- Raith Rovers – 2.1.1950 at
Bayview Park – old Stadium)
1,996 (-v- Queen's Park – 10.5.2003 at Bayview Stadium – new Stadium)
RECORD VICTORY: 13-2 (-v- Edinburgh City – Division 2, 11.12.1937)
RECORD DEFEAT: 0-9 (-v- Heart of Midlothian – Division 1, 5.10.1957)

EAST FIFE PLAYING KITS SEASON 2004/05

FIRST KIT | SECOND KIT | THIRD KIT

East Stirlingshire

EST. 1881

EAST STIRLINGSHIRE
Firs Park,
Firs Street,
Falkirk, FK2 7AY

CHAIRMAN
Alan J. Mackin

VICE-CHAIRMAN
Douglas W. Morrison

DIRECTORS
Alexander M. McCabe,
John M. D. Morton
& Alexander S.H. Forsyth

CHIEF EXECUTIVE/SECRETARY
Leslie G. Thomson

HEAD COACH
Dennis Newall

ASSISTANT COACH
Greg Denham

PHYSIOTHERAPIST
David Jenkins

**FOOTBALL SAFETY OFFICERS'
ASSOCIATION REPRESENTATIVE**
Malcolm Newbiggin

GROUNDSMAN/KIT PERSON
James Wilson

**MATCHDAY PROGRAMME EDITOR/
MEDIA LIAISON OFFICER**
Leslie G. Thomson
(01324) 623583

TELEPHONES
Ground (01324) 623583
Fax (01324) 637862
Sec. Home (01324) 551099
Sec. Mobile 07739 209648
Head Coach (at Ground)
(01324) 623583 (evenings only)

E-MAIL & INTERNET ADDRESS
lestshirefc@aol.com
www.east-stirlingshire-fc.co.uk

CLUB SHOP
Situated at ground.
Open Mon-Fri 10.00a.m. till 3.00p.m.
(except Wednesday)
and on all home matchdays

TEAM CAPTAIN
Graham McGhee

SHIRT SPONSOR
First Choice:
Littlewoods Football Pools - *be lucky*
Second Choice:
Meikle & Co – HR Consultants

KIT SUPPLIER
Pro Star

LIST OF PLAYERS 2004/05

PLAYERS SURNAME	FIRST NAME	MIDDLE NAME	DATE OF BIRTH	PLACE OF BIRTH	DATE SIGNED	HEIGHT FT INS	WEIGHT ST LBS	POSITION ON PITCH	PREVIOUS CLUB
BALDWIN	CHRISTOPHER	JOHN	31/01/84	EDINBURGH	30/05/03	5 9	11 0	DEFENDER	SALVESEN B.C.
DENHAM	GREIG	PATERSON	05/10/75	GLASGOW	28/07/04	6 2	13 3	DEFENDER	KILBIRNIE LADESIDE JNRS
DONALDSON	ROSS		27/06/77	BELLSHILL	28/07/04	5 10	12 10	FORWARD	RUTHERGLEN GLENCAIRN JNRS
DUNBAR	JAMES		09/01/84	GLASGOW	29/07/04	5 9	11 0	FORWARD	CUMNOCK JUNIORS
FINDLAY	GRANT		24/10/85	GLASGOW	31/07/04	6 1	12 0	FORWARD	CHRYSTON JUVENILES
GILPIN	ROSS	SCOTT	22/04/85	EDINBURGH	30/01/04	5 10	11 4	GOALKEEPER	MONTROSE
HARVEY	DAVID		25/01/85	BELLSHILL	28/07/04	5 10	10 4	DEFENDER	FALKIRK
LIVINGSTONE	SCOTT	ALAN	05/04/80	FALKIRK	31/08/02	6 0	11 2	MIDFIELD	STIRLING ALBION
MACKAY	JAMIE	ANDREW	02/09/81	GLASGOW	28/07/04	6 0	13 0	DEFENDER	DUMBARTON
M°AULEY	SEAN		27/02/80	EDINBURGH	30/03/01	5 8	10 10	MIDFIELD	CLYDE
M°GHEE	GRAHAM	HENRY	24/09/81	COATBRIDGE	03/01/01	6 1	12 8	DEFENDER	CLYDE
MILLER	CHRISTOPHER	THOMAS	19/11/82	PAISLEY	28/07/04	5 8	12 6	DEFENDER	STENHOUSEMUIR
MITCHELL	ANTHONY	MARTIN	10/01/79	GLASGOW	28/07/04	6 1	12 8	GOALKEEPER	ARBROATH
MOFFAT	ALAN	JOHN	24/02/77	STIRLING	28/07/04	5 11	12 0	MID / FWD	FAULDHOUSE UNITED JNRS
NEWALL	CHRISTOPHER		12/03/80	GLASGOW	31/01/04	6 2	12 0	DEFENDER	ARBROATH
OATES	STEPHEN	JOHN	02/01/84	FALKIRK	30/05/03	6 0	9 7	MIDFIELD	ZENECA JUVENILES
PARKS	GORDON	JOHN	19/11/72	GLASGOW	28/07/04	5 11	12 2	FORWARD	QUEEN'S PARK
QUINN	KENNETH		19/12/71	GLASGOW	28/07/04	5 10	11 1	MIDFIELD	WISHAW JUNIORS
ROBERTSON	JOSEPH		12/04/77	GLASGOW	31/08/04	5 9	11 8	MIDFIELD	YOKER ATHLETIC JUNIORS
ROSS	PAUL		06/01/85	GLASGOW	28/07/04	5 8	10 0	MIDFIELD	ST. MIRREN
STUART	WILLIAM	GIBB	28/01/83	PAISLEY	17/08/04	5 10	11 2	MIDFIELD	STIRLING ALBION
THYWISSEN	CARL	ERICH	28/02/78	LEICESTER	06/08/04	6 2	13 0	MIDFIELD	FOSSUM I.F.
TULLOCH	BARRY	ALEXANDER	30/01/84	GLASGOW	02/09/04	6 2	12 0	FORWARD	COWDENBEATH
URE	DEREK		20/07/84	FALKIRK	19/02/02	5 9	10 0	FORWARD	ZENECA JUVENILES

TICKET INFORMATION

SEASON TICKET PRICES

SEATED OR STANDING	ADULT	£120
	CONCESSIONS *	£60
	FAMILY TICKET	£150

LEAGUE ADMISSION PRICES

SEATED	ADULT	£10
	JUVENILE/OAP	£4
STANDING	ADULT	£8
	CONCESSIONS*	£4

* CONCESSIONARY TICKETS ALLOW OAPS, JUVENILES, UB40 HOLDERS, STUDENTS AND PEOPLE WITH LONG TERM ILLNESS TO BE ADMITTED TO GROUND AT THE STATED CONCESSIONARY PRICE. PRODUCTION OF DSS BENEFIT BOOK OR SIMILAR DOCUMENTARY PROOF REQUIRED.

THE SHIRE'S 10 YEAR LEAGUE RECORD

SEASON	DIV	P	W	D	L	F	A	PTS
1994-95	T	36	18	5	13	61	50	59
1995-96	T	36	11	11	14	58	62	44
1996-97	T	36	8	9	19	36	58	33
1997-98	T	36	17	6	13	50	48	57
1998-99	T	36	9	13	14	50	48	40
1999-00	T	36	11	7	18	28	50	40
2000-01	T	36	10	7	19	37	69	37
2001-02	T	36	12	4	20	51	58	40
2002-03	T	36	2	7	27	32	105	13
2003-04	T	36	2	2	32	30	118	8

Player columns (left to right): CONNOLLY J., PENMAN C., POLWART D., LIVINGSTONE S., MAUGHAN R., McGHEE G., BOYLE G., MACKAY J., KELLY S., ORMISTON D., BALDWIN C., LEISHMAN J., RODDEN P., McLAREN G., McCANN K., McCULLOCH G., REID C., McAULEY S., HARE R., URE D., TODD C., OATES S., IRVINE S., OGILVIE F., MULHOLLAND B., FORD K., CARNACHAN G., NEWALL C., LYNCH C., MILLER D., GILPIN R., KANE P., REID M.

Match results and appearances — block 1

DATE	VENUE	OPPONENTS	ATT	RES	CONNOLLY J.	PENMAN C.	POLWART D.	LIVINGSTONE S.	MAUGHAN R.	McGHEE G.	BOYLE G.	MACKAY J.	KELLY S.	ORMISTON D.	BALDWIN C.	LEISHMAN J.	RODDEN P.	McLAREN G.	McCANN K.	McCULLOCH G.
9-AUG	A	ELGIN CITY	604	1 - 3	1	2	3	4¹	5	6	7	8	9	10	11	12	14			
16-AUG	H	MONTROSE	182	1 - 1	1		4	7	2	6	14	8	9¹	10	11		12	3	5	
23-AUG	A	STIRLING ALBION	581	1 - 5	1		4¹	7	2	6		8	9	10	11	15	12	3	5	16
30-AUG	H	COWDENBEATH	296	1 - 1	1		4	7	2	6			10	9¹		11	12	3		
13-SEP	A	STRANRAER	358	0 - 4	1		11	7	2	6		4		9		10	12	3	5	14
20-SEP	A	PETERHEAD	520	0 - 2	1		4	7	2	6			10	9	11		14	3	5	
27-SEP	H	QUEEN'S PARK	281	1 - 2	1		4			6			9	7	11		10	3	5	2
4-OCT	A	ALBION ROVERS	256	0 - 5			4		2	6	15	14	7		11		9	3		
18-OCT	H	GRETNA	198	0 - 1	1		3	7		6	14	8	10		11		12			
25-OCT	A	MONTROSE	246	1 - 5	1		3	7		6	14	8	10		11		12	15		
1-NOV	H	ELGIN CITY	239	3 - 1	1		14	7	2	6			15¹		11	8	10	3		
8-NOV	H	STRANRAER	245	1 - 4	1		11		2	6	16		12			8	10¹	3		
14-NOV	A	COWDENBEATH	330	†1 - 2	1		16	7	2	6			14		11	8	10	3		
29-NOV	H	PETERHEAD	178	1 - 3	1			7	2	3	12		10¹			11		4		
6-DEC	A	QUEEN'S PARK	439	0 - 3	1			7	2	6	12	14	10			11		5		
13-DEC	H	ALBION ROVERS	175	3 - 4	1			7	2	6			10¹		11	8¹		5		
27-DEC	A	GRETNA	532	1 - 2	1			7	2	3		4	9¹		11	14		6		
10-JAN	H	STIRLING ALBION	495	2 - 4	1			7	2	3		4			11			6		
17-JAN	A	ELGIN CITY	432	0 - 3	1		3	7	2	6		4	15		11	8				
24-JAN	A	PETERHEAD	553	0 - 6	1		3	15	2	6		4	14		11	12				
7-FEB	A	STRANRAER	405	1 - 7			3		2	12		8	15				6			
14-FEB	H	COWDENBEATH	308	0 - 1			16	14	2	6		8			11		15	3		
21-FEB	H	GRETNA	187	2 - 4			12	7		6					11¹			3		
2-MAR	H	QUEEN'S PARK	235	2 - 4				7		6			16		11			3		
6-MAR	H	MONTROSE	195	1 - 4			15	2	6				9¹		7			3		
9-MAR	A	ALBION ROVERS	179	1 - 5			4	2	6		14	11					3			
13-MAR	A	STIRLING ALBION	739	0 - 6			9	4	6			15	16		3		2	14		
24-MAR	H	STRANRAER	181	1 - 2				7	2	5			12		11		3			
27-MAR	A	COWDENBEATH	289	0 - 2				7	2	6			14		11		3			
3-APR	A	QUEEN'S PARK	404	0 - 1				7	2	6					11	12	3			
10-APR	H	PETERHEAD	243	0 - 3				6	2	5			10			8	9	3		
17-APR	A	GRETNA	311	1 - 5				7		5			14			12	10	3		
24-APR	H	ALBION ROVERS	223	1 - 8				2		6			10¹			7	16	12		
1-MAY	H	STIRLING ALBION	779	0 - 3				7		5			9		11	10	12	3		
8-MAY	A	MONTROSE	360	0 - 1				2		6			10		7	15	3			
15-MAY	H	ELGIN CITY	363	† 2 - 1				2		6			10		7	3				
TOTAL FULL APPEARANCES					19	1	14	29	26	35	1	12	20	7	23	14	7	30	5	1
TOTAL SUB APPEARANCES							4	3		1	7	3	11		1	6	12	2		
TOTAL GOALS SCORED							1	1					7	1	1	1				

Appearances — block 2

DATE	OPPONENTS	REID C.	McAULEY S.	HARE R.	URE D.	TODD C.	OATES S.	IRVINE S.	OGILVIE F.	MULHOLLAND B.	FORD K.	CARNACHAN G.	NEWALL C.	LYNCH C.	MILLER D.	GILPIN R.	KANE P.	REID M.
9-AUG	ELGIN CITY																	
16-AUG	MONTROSE																	
23-AUG	STIRLING ALBION																	
30-AUG	COWDENBEATH	5	8															
13-SEP	STRANRAER		8	16														
20-SEP	PETERHEAD		8															
27-SEP	QUEEN'S PARK		8	15	12¹	18												
4-OCT	ALBION ROVERS	5	8	12	10	1												
18-OCT	GRETNA	5	4	2	9													
25-OCT	MONTROSE	5	4	2	9¹													
1-NOV	ELGIN CITY	12	4	9²	5													
8-NOV	STRANRAER	15	4	9	5	7												
14-NOV	COWDENBEATH	12	4	9	5													
29-NOV	PETERHEAD	16	8	6	9		5	15										
6-DEC	QUEEN'S PARK	8	4	9		3	15											
13-DEC	ALBION ROVERS		4	9¹			3	15	16									
27-DEC	GRETNA	5							8	10								
10-JAN	STIRLING ALBION	5		12	10²				8	9								
17-JAN	ELGIN CITY		12		10				9	5								
24-JAN	PETERHEAD		8		10	5			7	9								
7-FEB	STRANRAER	11¹	4	10	1				7	9		5						
14-FEB	COWDENBEATH		4		10	1			7	9		5						
21-FEB	GRETNA	2¹	8	4	10	1			9		5	16						
2-MAR	QUEEN'S PARK	2	8²	4	10	1			9		5		12					
6-MAR	MONTROSE	14	8		10	1			11		5	16	4				14	
9-MAR	ALBION ROVERS		10¹	1					7	16	5	9	8					
13-MAR	STIRLING ALBION		10	1					7		5	11	8					
24-MAR	STRANRAER	10		9	4					6		8¹	1					
27-MAR	COWDENBEATH	10		9	1	4			12		5	8						
3-APR	QUEEN'S PARK	10		9	1	4			15		5	8	16					
10-APR	PETERHEAD	7		12	1	4			11			15						
17-APR	GRETNA	8		9	1	4			11		2	6¹	15					
24-APR	ALBION ROVERS	8		9	1	4			3		5	11	15					
1-MAY	STIRLING ALBION	6			4				8		2	14	1					
8-MAY	MONTROSE	8		9	4				11		5		1					
15-MAY	ELGIN CITY	8		9¹	4				11		5		1					
TOTAL FULL APPEARANCES		9	24	11	26	13	16	1	13	9	1	15	2	8	4			
TOTAL SUB APPEARANCES		2	2	5	4	2	1		2	1	3	1		2	3		3	1
TOTAL GOALS SCORED		1	3	9								2						

Bold figures denote goalscorers. † denotes opponent's own gnd.

EADING GOALSCORERS:

EASON	DIV	GOALS	PLAYER
04-95	T	16	M. Geraghty
05-96	T	21	P. Dwyer
96-97	T	9	G. Inglis
97-98	T	13	D. Watt
98-99	T	8	W. McNeill
99-00	T	9	G. Higgins, S. Laidlaw
00-01	T	16	S. Hislop
1-02	T	11	K. Gordon
2-03	T	5	J. Leishman, D. Ure
3-04	T	9	D. Ure

MILESTONES:

YEAR OF FORMATION: 1881
MOST CAPPED PLAYER: Humphrey Jones
NO. OF CAPS: 5 (for Wales)
MOST LEAGUE POINTS IN A SEASON:
55 (Division 2 – Season 1931/32) (2 Points for a Win)
59 (Third Division – Season 1994/95) (3 Points for a Win)
MOST LEAGUE GOALS SCORED BY A PLAYER IN A SEASON:
Malcolm Morrison (Season 1938/39)
NO. OF GOALS SCORED: 36
RECORD ATTENDANCE: 11,500 (-v- Hibernian – 10.2.1969)
RECORD VICTORY: 10-1 (-v- Stenhousemuir – Scottish Cup, 1.9.1888)
RECORD DEFEAT: 1-12 (-v- Dundee United – Division 2, 13.4.1936)

EAST STIRLINGSHIRE PLAYING KITS SEASON 2004/05

FIRST KIT   SECOND KIT   THIRD KIT

LIST OF PLAYERS 2004/05

PLAYERS SURNAME	FIRST NAME	MIDDLE NAME	DATE OF BIRTH	PLACE OF BIRTH	DATE SIGNED	HEIGHT FT INS	WEIGHT ST LBS	POSITION ON PITCH	PREVIOUS CLUB
ALLISON	JOHN	CLARK	05/06/70	DUNFERMLINE	17/07/03	5 8	11 3	MIDFIELD	EAST FIFE
BLACK	STEPHEN	THOMAS	14/05/83	ABERDEEN	27/07/04	5 10	11 7	MIDFIELD	HIBERNIAN
BONE	ALEXANDER	SYME FREW	26/12/71	STIRLING	27/05/03	5 9	11 7	FORWARD	PETERHEAD
BREMNER	FRASER		24/03/85	ELGIN	09/07/03	5 11	11 7	MIDFIELD	ELGIN CITY FORM S
CHARLESWORTH	MARTIN		18/04/88	INVERNESS	30/07/04	5 11	10 7	FORWARD	ELGIN CITY FORM D U' 16
CUMMING	STUART	ALEXANDER	30/01/85	ABERDEEN	26/07/04	5 11	11 7	DEFENDER	BLACKBURN ROVERS
DEMPSIE	ALLAN	HENRY	05/11/82	BELLSHILL	10/06/04	5 11	11 0	DEFENDER	HIBERNIAN
DICKSON	HUGH		28/08/81	DOWNPATRICK	17/10/03	6 1	12 7	DEFENDER	LINFIELD
DUFF	MURRAY	THOMAS	25/05/87	EDINBURGH	31/08/04	5 11	10 4	MIDFIELD	EAST END VILLA
GRAY	ALEXANDER	CHARLES	21/03/88	ABERDEEN	11/08/04	5 6	9 9	DEFENDER	ELGIN CITY FORM S
HARTY	MARTIN	JOHN	11/07/82	BELLSHILL	14/07/04	6 2	11 5	FORWARD	STENHOUSEMUIR
HIND	DAVID	SCOTT	15/02/82	INVERNESS	30/03/01	6 1	11 7	DEFENDER	INVERNESS CALEDONIAN THISTLE
KACZAN	PAUL		03/02/83	BELLSHILL	29/07/04	6 1	12 0	DEF / MID	PARTICK THISTLE
KELLY	DARRYN	PAUL	19/01/88	GREENOCK	10/08/04	6 0	10 0	DEFENDER	BANCHORY B.C.
KNIGHT	STUART		24/10/87	PETERHEAD	31/08/04	6 1	12 8	GOALKEEPER	ELGIN CITY FORM S
LENNOX	ANTHONY		29/04/88	GLASGOW	25/08/04	5 11	11 0	FORWARD	SHEDDOCKSLY B.C.
MARTIN	WILLIAM	M°LEAN	21/08/81	GLASGOW	30/06/03	6 1	12 0	MID / FWD	QUEEN'S PARK
M°DONALD	JASON	NORMAN	15/01/87	ABERDEEN	11/08/04	5 6.5	11 6	MIDFIELD	ABERDEEN
M°KENDRICK	KYLE		02/04/88	ABERDEEN	22/09/04	6 0	11 10	DEFENDER	ALBION B.C.
M°KENZIE	JAMIE		29/11/80	BELLSHILL	06/02/04	5 8	11 6	MIDFIELD	STENHOUSEMUIR
M°KENZIE	STUART		06/01/88	ABERDEEN	10/08/04	6 1	10 4	GOALKEEPER	ALBION B.C.
M°MILLAN	ALLISTER	SCOTT	08/08/76	GLASGOW	31/08/03	6 1	13 10	DEFENDER	IRVINE MEADOW JUNIOR
NAPIER	PAUL	ALEXANDER	17/06/87	ABERDEEN	25/08/04	5 5	9 0	MIDFIELD	BANKS O' DEE JUNIORS
NELSON	ADAM	EDGAR	24/07/84	EDINBURGH	26/07/04	5 11	12 0	MIDFIELD	BLACKBURN ROVERS
PIRIE	MARTIN	JAMES	01/06/72	ABERDEEN	26/07/00	6 2	13 9	GOALKEEPER	PETERHEAD
RALPH	JAMIE	INNES	21/02/88	FRASERBURGH	11/08/04	5 11	10 3	DEFENDER	ALBION B.C.
READ	CALLUM	DANIEL	05/01/88	NORTHAMPTON	25/08/04	5 11	11 10	DEFENDER	ELGIN CITY FORM S
REID	PHILIP	GEORGE	03/04/87	ABERDEEN	26/07/04	6 0	11 0	FORWARD	MOTHERWELL
RENTON	KEIRON	DESMOND	13/02/84	EDINBURGH	26/07/04	6 2	13 0	GOALKEEPER	BLACKBURN ROVERS
ROBERTSON	DAVID	ALEXANDER	17/10/68	ABERDEEN	29/07/04	5 11	13 0	DEFENDER	MONTROSE
RODDIE	ANDREW	ROBERT	04/11/71	GLASGOW	08/06/04	5 11	11 0	FORWARD	PETERHEAD
TEASDALE	MICHAEL	JOSEPH	28/07/69	ELGIN	26/03/02	6 0	13 0	DEF / MID	INVERNESS CALEDONIAN THISTLE
VIGURS	IAIN	ANGUS	07/05/88	ABERDEEN	31/08/04	5 6	10 2	DEFENDER	ALBION B.C.
VIGURS	PATRICK	SCOTT	06/08/86	DARTFORD	31/08/04	6 0	11 5	MIDFIELD	ELGIN CITY FORM X
WOOD	GARRY	JOHN	27/01/88	ABERDEEN	05/08/04	6 0	12 5	MIDFIELD	ALBION B.C.

TICKET INFORMATION

SEASON TICKET PRICES

SEATED

	ADULT	£162
	JUVENILE /OAP	£90
STANDING		
	ADULT	£126
	JUVENILE /OAP	£54

LEAGUE ADMISSION PRICES

SEATED

	ADULT	£10
	JUVENILE /OAP	£6
STANDING		
	ADULT	£8
	JUVENILE /OAP	£4

THE BLACK AND WHITES' 10 YEAR LEAGUE RECO

SEASON	DIV	P	W	D	L	F	A	PTS
SEASON 2000-01 WAS THE CLUB'S FIRST SEASON IN MEMBERSHIP OF SFL								
2000-01	T	36	5	7	24	29	65	22
2001-02	T	36	13	8	15	45	47	47
2002-03	T	36	5	13	18	33	63	28
2003-04	T	36	6	7	23	48	93	25

The black and whites' stats 2003/04

SEASON STATS 2003/04

DATE	VENUE	OPPONENTS	ATT	RES	PIRIE M.	HIND D.	GALLAGHER J.	WHITE J.	COULTER R.	ALLISON J.	MARTIN W.	McLEAN C.	McCORMICK S.	STEELE K.	MURPHY J.S.	McLEAN N.	OGBOKE C.	BONE A.	McMULLAN R.	CAMPBELL C.	McMILLAN A.	TEASDALE M.	HAMILTON P.	DICKSON H.	GORAM A.	DEMPSIE A.	BREMNER F.	TULLY B.	DONALD M.	ADDICOAT W.	McKENZIE J.	VIGURS I.	REID P	DICKSON M.	CHARLESWORTH M.	READ C.	ANDERSON R.	RALPH J.	THOMSON R.	WOOD G.
9-AUG	H	EAST STIRLINGSHIRE	604	3-1	1	2	3	4	5	6^1	7	8		9	10	11	12	16^2																						
16-AUG	A	QUEEN'S PARK	556	2-5	1	2	3	4	5	6	7		8^1	10	11	12	9^1	14		16																				
23-AUG	H	PETERHEAD	748	2-3	1	2		4	5	6	7^1			10	11		9^1	8		12	3																			
30-AUG	A	MONTROSE	324	3-3	1	2		4	5^1	6	7			10^1	11	14	9^1	8			3																			
6-SEP	A	ALBION ROVERS	394	2-1	1	2	14	4	5		7^2	8		10	6		9	16			11	3																		
13-SEP	H	GRETNA	529	3-3	1	2	12	4	5	6	7			10			9^1	11^2	15	8	3																			
20-SEP	A	STRANRAER	370	3-4	1	2			5	6	7^1	11		10	14		9^1	16^1	15	8	3	4																		
27-SEP	H	COWDENBEATH	665	0-4				4	5	6	7	16	11		2	10	9	14	8	3		1																		
4-OCT	A	STIRLING ALBION	648	0-3			3		5	6	7	8		10	9	15		11	4		1	2																		
18-OCT	H	ALBION ROVERS	681	1-5	8			4	5	6	7		10	16		9	11^1	3			2	1																		
25-OCT	H	QUEEN'S PARK	548	2-2	8			4^1		6	7^1		10	16		9	11	3	5		2	1																		
1-NOV	A	EAST STIRLINGSHIRE	239	1-3	8			4^1		6	7	15	10	16		9	11	3	5		2	1																		
8-NOV	A	GRETNA	451	2-2	8			4		6	7	14	10	9^1	16	11	2	5^1		1	3	15																		
15-NOV	H	MONTROSE	475	2-3	8			4		6	7^1	15	10	9	16^1	11	2	5		14	1	3																		
29-NOV	H	STRANRAER	410	1-3	1	14		4		6	7	15	10	16	9	11	2		8		3	5^1																		
6-DEC	A	COWDENBEATH	242	2-3	1		12	4		6	7^1	15	10	16	9	11	2	8			3	5^1																		
13-DEC	H	STIRLING ALBION	478	0-2	1	12		3	4	6	7		10	15	9	11	2	8				5	16																	
3-JAN	A	PETERHEAD	714	1-5	1	16			6		7	8	15	10		9	11	2		4		5^1																		
17-JAN	H	EAST STIRLINGSHIRE	432	3-0	1	8^2			6		7	16	14	10	9		15	2		4		5^1	11																	
24-JAN	A	STRANRAER	393	0-6	1	8		12	6	7		14	10	9			2		4		5	16	11																	
7-FEB	H	GRETNA	383	1-1	1	8		2	6		15	10	9	7			3		5^1	16	11	4																	
14-FEB	A	MONTROSE	312	3-4	1	8		12	2	6	16	15	9^3	7	10		3	5			11	4																		
21-FEB	H	ALBION ROVERS	425	1-2	1	8		2	6	11			9^1	7	10		3	5			4																			
6-MAR	A	QUEEN'S PARK	444	0-4	1	8		2	6	11	10		9	7	3	14		5			4																			
10-MAR	A	STIRLING ALBION	527	1-6	1	8		12	2	6	7	10	16	9^1	11	4		2	3		5																			
13-MAR	H	PETERHEAD	675	1-0	1	4		2	15	11	12	9^1	7	10	6		5	3		8																				
16-MAR	H	COWDENBEATH	312	1-0	1	4		2	15	11	14	9^1	7	10	6		5	3		8																				
20-MAR	A	GRETNA	360	1-2	1	4		2	15	10^1	12	9	7		6		5	3		8																				
27-MAR	H	MONTROSE	499	2-1		4		2	10	11^1	3	9^1	7	8	1		12	5	15		6	14																		
3-APR	A	COWDENBEATH	218	0-2	1	4		2	10	11	12	3	9	7	8		5				6	16																		
10-APR	H	STRANRAER	663	0-0	1	4		2	7	11	12	9	15	10			5	3		8		6	16																	
17-APR	A	ALBION ROVERS	212	2-1	1	4		2	7	11		9^1	15	14			5	3		8		6^1	16																	
24-APR	H	STIRLING ALBION	542	0-1	1	4		2	15	11		16	14	10			5	3	7	8		6	9																	
1-MAY	A	PETERHEAD	616	1-3	1				10		8	9^1	11	2			5	3	7	4		6	15	14																
8-MAY	H	QUEEN'S PARK	421	1-3	1				11		10	9		8			5	7^1	4		6		2	14	12	15														
15-MAY	A	EAST STIRLINGSHIRE	363	1-2	1				10^1		6	9		8			5	2	7				3	11	12				4	16	14									
TOTAL FULL APPEARANCES					28	28	3	13	16	32	30	2	14	9	6		19	9	30	18	28	19	1	3	18	5	21	4	17		4	14	1	2	1				1	
TOTAL SUB APPEARANCES					3	2	3	1		4			2	13	1	7	10	3	10		2				2		4			2	4	1	1	1	1		1	1	
TOTAL GOALS SCORED					2			2	1	1	8	2	2				6	15	1			1	5							1								

In bold figures denote goalscorers. † denotes opponent's own goal.

MILESTONES:

YEAR OF FORMATION: 1893
MOST CAPPED PLAYER: Douglas Grant (Scotland Amateur Internationalist)
MOST LEAGUE POINTS IN A SEASON:
55 (Highland League - Season 1967/68) (2 Points for a Win)
81 (Highland League - Season 1989/90) (3 Points for a Win)
47 (SFL Third Division - Season 2001/02) (3 Points for a Win)
MOST LEAGUE GOALS SCORED BY A PLAYER IN A SEASON:
Alex Bone (Season 2003/04)
No. OF GOALS SCORED: 15
RECORD ATTENDANCE: 12,608 (-v- Arbroath – 17.2.1968)
RECORD VICTORY: 18-1 (-v- Brora Rangers – North of Scotland Cup – 6.2.1960)
RECORD DEFEAT: 1-14 (-v- Heart of Midlothian – Scottish Cup – 4.2.1939)

ELGIN CITY PLAYING KITS SEASON 2004/05

FIRST KIT — SECOND KIT — THIRD KIT

GRETNA F.C.

Gretna

GRETNA
Raydale Park, Dominion Road,
Gretna, DG16 5AP.
PRESIDENT
Brian Fulton
HON. LIFE PRESIDENT
Tom Kerr
HON. LIFE MEMBERS
Charles Apperley, Ian Dalgliesh,
John Smith & Jack Gass
CHAIRMAN
Ron MacGregor MA(Hons), FtHM
DIRECTORS
Brooks Mileson, Helen MacGregor,
Paul Grootendorst &
Mark C. Hampson (Non-Executive)
MANAGING DIRECTOR
Brooks Mileson
SECRETARY
Mrs Helen MacGregor MSR, DCR
GENERAL MANAGER
Colin Carter
MANAGER
Rowan Alexander
ASSISTANT MANAGER/RESERVE COACH
David Irons
**HEAD OF YOUTH FOOTBALL/
SCHOOLS DEVELOPMENT COACH**
Danny Lennon
FITNESS COACH
David Holdsworth
GOALKEEPING COACHES
Alan Main & David Wylie
YOUTH COACHES
Danny Lennon (U19)
David Farrell (U17)
James Gordon (U16)
Derek McWilliams (U15)
David McLenaghan (14)
Neil Graham (U13)
COMMERCIAL MANAGERS
Brooks Mileson & Colin Carter
CLUB DOCTOR
Dr Kenneth McQueen & Dr. Fiona Vernon
PHYSIOTHERAPISTS
Billy Bentley & Gael Moffat
**GROUNDSMAN/FOOTBALL SAFETY OFFICERS'
ASSOCIATION REPRESENTATIVE**
Paul Barnett
MEDIA LIAISON OFFICER
Ron MacGregor
MATCHDAY PROGRAMME EDITOR
Jon Tait
TELEPHONES
Ground (01461) 337602
Ground Fax (01461) 338047
Sec.Home & Fax (01387) 811820
E-MAIL & INTERNET ADDRESS
info@gretnafootballclub.co.uk
www.gretnafootballclub.co.uk
CLUB SHOP
Situated at Ground. (01461) 337602
Open on Home Matchdays
1.00 p.m. to 5.00 p.m.
Contact: Alan Watson (01387) 251550
SUPPORTERS CLUB
Secretary: Richard Wharton
31 Lindisfarne Street, Carlisle CA1 2ND
Tel No. (01228) 547761
TEAM CAPTAIN
Michael Galloway
SHIRT SPONSOR
First Choice: Wm. Armstrong Group
Second Choice: Kwik-Fit Insurance Services
KIT SUPPLIER
Nike

LIST OF PLAYERS 2004/05

PLAYERS SURNAME	FIRST NAME	MIDDLE NAME	DATE OF BIRTH	PLACE OF BIRTH	DATE SIGNED	HEIGHT FT INS	WEIGHT ST LBS	POSITION ON PITCH	PREVIOUS CLUB
AITKEN	ANDREW	ROBERT	02/02/78	DUMFRIES	18/05/04	6 0	12 7	DEFENDER	QUEEN OF THE SOUTH
BAIN	JAMIE	DONALD	16/08/86	EDINBURGH	29/06/04	6 1	10 4	DEFENDER	COWDENBEATH
BALDACCHINO	RYAN		13/01/81	LEICESTER	02/01/04	5 10	10 8	MIDFIELD	CARLISLE UNITED
BANKS	MARTIN	WALES	23/05/88	PAISLEY	28/07/04	5 11	10 0	MIDFIELD	ST. MIRREN FORM D U' 15
BELL	MARTIN		21/12/84	DUMFRIES	27/08/03	5 11	11 0	DEFENDER	KELLO ROVERS JUNIORS
BERKELEY	MATTHEW	ANTHONY	03/08/87	MANCHESTER	14/09/04	5 11	10 10	FORWARD	BURNLEY
BINGHAM	DAVID	THOMAS	03/09/70	DUNFERMLINE	16/06/04	5 10	10 13	FORWARD	INVERNESS CALEDONIAN THISTLE
BIRCH	MARK		05/01/77	STOKE ON TRENT	21/08/03	5 11	13 2	DEFENDER	CARLISLE UNITED
BONNAR	GEORGE		10/09/86	BROXBURN	29/06/04	5 11	10 9	DEFENDER	FALKIRK FORM D U' 16
BOYD	MARK	EDWARD	22/10/81	CARLISLE	30/07/04	5 9	12 6	MIDFIELD	CARLISLE UNITED
BOYLE	DANIEL		08/11/88	GLASGOW	28/07/04	5 11	10 3	DEFENDER	HILLINGTON Y.C.
BRYAN	ANTHONY		13/04/86	GLASGOW	24/06/04	6 3	12 0	DEFENDER	LENNOX B.C.
CALLAGHAN	JAMES		12/12/88	GLASGOW	28/07/04	5 10	10 7	MIDFIELD	HILLINGTON Y.C.
CAMERON	MARTIN	GEORGE	16/06/78	DUNFERMLINE	14/07/04	6 1	14 0	FORWARD	ST. MIRREN
CLANNACHAN	STUART		22/04/88	GLASGOW	28/07/04	5 10	10 7	MIDFIELD	CHERRIE B.C.
COSGROVE	STEPHEN		29/12/80	GLASGOW	29/08/03	5 9	10 7	MIDFIELD	CLYDE
COSH	CHRISTOPHER	JOHN	09/01/88	ALEXANDRIA	28/07/04	5 11	11 0	DEFENDER	ALLOA ATHLETIC FORM D U' 16
COYLE	RYAN		02/12/88	GLASGOW	28/07/04	5 8	10 10	DEFENDER	ERSKINE B.C.
CUMERSKY	IAN		09/12/85	CARLISLE	01/08/02	5 9	9 10	MIDFIELD	CARLISLE UNITED
CUNNINGHAM	THOMAS		15/06/88	GLASGOW	28/07/04	5 5	8 7	FORWARD	HILLINGTON Y.C.
DEUCHAR	KENNETH	ROBERT	06/07/80	STIRLING	08/07/04	6 3	13 10	FORWARD	EAST FIFE
DUNGLINSON	DANIEL	SCOTT	24/05/87	DUMFRIES	24/06/04	5 7	9 7	MIDFIELD	FALKIRK
ELLIS	PHILLIP	DAVID	09/10/87	LONDON	09/07/04	5 10	9 0	FORWARD	BASILDON
GALLOWAY	MICHAEL	ANTHONY	13/10/74	NOTTINGHAM	01/01/03	5 10	12 8	MIDFIELD	CARLISLE UNITED
GILFILLAN	BRYAN	JAMES	14/09/84	CARDENDEN	21/08/04	6 0	11 2	DEFENDER	COWDENBEATH
GORDON	WAYNE		10/07/84	MUNSTER	31/07/02	5 10	10 0	MIDFIELD	GRETNA
GRAINGER	DANIEL	LESLIE	28/07/86	CARLISLE	19/10/02	6 0	12 0	DEFENDER	PENRITH
HALLIGAN	STEWART		05/03/88	GLASGOW	28/07/04	5 8	10 6	MIDFIELD	RANGERS EAST B.C.
HART	CHRIS	JOHN	19/01/88	GLASGOW	16/08/04	5 10	10 4	FORWARD	GLENIFFER
HENDERSON	NIALL	JOSEPH	07/02/88	CRAIGAVON	28/07/04	5 9	10 3	MIDFIELD	LURGAN TOWN
HOLDSWORTH	DAVID	GARY	08/11/68	WALTHAMSTOW	24/07/03	6 0	13 6	DEFENDER	SCARBOROUGH
IRONS	DAVID	JOHN	18/07/61	GLASGOW	31/07/02	5 11	11 4	DEFENDER	ANNAN ATHLETIC
JONES	BARRY		30/11/88	GLASGOW	16/08/04	6 2	10 0	GOALKEEPER	ERSKINE B.C.
LAMB	PATRICK	FRANCIS	26/03/87	GLASGOW	14/09/04	5 8	11 3	FORWARD	KILMARNOCK
LENNON	DANIEL	JOSEPH	06/04/70	WHITBURN	18/07/03	5 7	10 10	MIDFIELD	PARTICK THISTLE
LITTLE	LIAM	JOHN	27/07/86	WHANGARI - NEW ZEALAND	29/06/04	6 3	12 6	GOALKEEPER	PICTON RANGERS
MADDISON	LEE	ROBERT	05/10/72	BRISTOL	29/08/03	6 2	12 11	DEFENDER	CARLISLE UNITED
MAIN	ALAN	DAVID	05/12/67	ELGIN	28/07/04	5 11.5	13 9	GOALKEEPER	LIVINGSTON
MARSHALL	SCOTT		23/02/88	GLASGOW	28/07/04	5 8	10 0	DEF / MID	RANGERS EAST B.C.
MATHIESON	DAVID	JAMES	18/01/78	DUMFRIES	02/08/02	6 0	12 10	GOALKEEPER	QUEEN OF THE SOUTH
McBRIDE	MARTIN	ANTHONY	21/05/86	GLASGOW	24/06/04	5 11	11 0	MIDFIELD	PARTICK THISTLE
McDOUGALL	JAMES		17/01/88	RUTHERGLEN	28/07/04	6 1	10 0	MIDFIELD	RANGERS EAST B.C.
McGILL	MARK		27/02/89	GLASGOW	28/07/04	5 8	9 7	DEFENDER	QUEEN'S PARK FORM D U' 15
McGUFFIE	RYAN		22/07/80	DUMFRIES	05/08/02	6 2	12 6	DEF / MID	NEWCASTLE UNITED
McLAREN	JOHN		20/08/88	GLASGOW	28/07/04	5 11	10 9	FORWARD	ERSKINE B.C.
McQUILKEN	JAMES	CHARLES	03/10/74	GLASGOW	09/07/04	5 10	11 6	DEFENDER	ST. JOHNSTONE
MONTGOMERY	KEVIN	DONALD	03/01/86	GLASGOW	24/06/04	5 10	11 0	GOALKEEPER	PARTICK THISTLE
MULGREW	BRYAN	ANTHONY	15/11/87	GLASGOW	14/09/04	5 11	10 5	DEFENDER	BENBURB JUNIORS
MURRAY	ROSS	WILLIAM	30/05/86	IRVINE	14/09/04	5 10	9 6	FORWARD	QUEEN OF THE SOUTH FORM D U'
ORR	ALLAN	JAMES WILLIAM	12/05/88	GLASGOW	08/09/04	5 7	10 0	FORWARD	RANGERS
PATTERSON	LIAM	COLIN ALLAN	16/08/86	DUMFRIES	24/06/04	6 1	12 0	DEFENDER	UNATTACHED
PROKAS	RICHARD		22/01/76	PENRITH	05/08/03	5 10	12 0	MIDFIELD	WORKINGTON TOWN
SIDESERF	MARK		11/08/88	GLASGOW	28/07/04	5 8	8 0	DEFENDER	RANGERS EAST B. C.
SKELTON	GAVIN	RICHARD	27/03/81	CARLISLE	31/07/02	5 10	12 10	DEFENDER	GRETNA
SMITH	ANDREW	MARK	27/11/68	ABERDEEN	27/05/04	6 1	10 8	FORWARD	CLYDE
SPENCE	COLIN	WILLIAM	02/03/84	IRVINE	02/08/03	5 9	10 5	MIDFIELD	BONNYTON THISTLE
STEVENS	IAN		21/10/66	MALTA	05/09/03	5 11	13 6	FORWARD	A.F.C. BARROW
SUMMERSGILL	CRAIG	WILLIAM	02/10/85	HEXHAM	13/01/04	6 3	13 0	GOALKEEPER	HALTWHISTLE
TOWNSLEY	DEREK	JOHNSTONE	21/01/73	CARLISLE	19/01/04	6 5	14 7	MIDFIELD	OXFORD UNITED
WAKE	BRIAN	CHRISTOPHER	13/08/82	STOCKTON-ON-TEES	01/01/04	6 0	11 8	FORWARD	CARLISLE UNITED

TICKET INFORMATION

SEASON TICKET PRICES

SEATED
	ADULT	£135
	JUVENILE /OAP	£68

STANDING
	ADULT	£117
	JUVENILE /OAP	£59

LEAGUE ADMISSION PRICES

SEATED
	ADULT	£8
	JUVENILE /OAP	£4

STANDING
	ADULT	£7
	JUVENILE /OAP	£3.50

THE BLACK AND WHITES' 10 YEAR LEAGUE RECORD

SEASON	DIV	P	W	D	L	F	A	PTS
SEASON 2002-03 WAS THE CLUB'S FIRST SEASON IN MEMBERSHIP OF SFL								
2002-03	T	36	11	12	13	50	50	45
2003-04	T	36	20	8	8	59	39	68

SEASON STATS 2003/04

DATE	VENUE	OPPONENTS	ATT	RES	MATHIESON D.	KNOX K.	SKELTON G.	PROKAS R.	O'NEILL P.	HOLDSWORTH D.	SKINNER S.	GALLOWAY M.	CAMERON M.	COHEN G.	ALLAN J.	McGUFFIE R.	GORDON W.	ROBB R.	GRAINGER D.	IRONS D.	COSGROVE S.	BIRCH M.	BALDACCHINO R.	HORE J.	ECCLES M.	MADDISON L.	STEVENS I.	WAKE B.	LENNON D.	TOWNSLEY D.	MAY K.	SUMMERSGILL C.	SPENCE C.
AUG	H	QUEEN'S PARK	420	1-1	1	2	3	4	5	6	7	8	9^1	10	11	14	15																
3-AUG	A	PETERHEAD	464	0-2	1	7	11	4	5	6		8	9	10						15	2	3	12	16								
3-AUG	H	STRANRAER	367	1-1	1		3			6		8	9	10		4				5	2^1	7			11	14							
0-AUG	H	ALBION ROVERS	385	3-1	1		12			6		8	9^3	10		4			15	5	2	7			11	3							
3-SEP	A	ELGIN CITY	529	3-3	1		3			6		8	9^2	7	15	4^1	16			5	12	2			11	10							
0-SEP	A	COWDENBEATH	235	†1-0	1		14			6		8	9	10		4	15			5	2	7			11	3							
7-SEP	H	STIRLING ALBION	482	0-1	1		14					8	9	16		4	10			5	2	7			3	15							
OCT	H	MONTROSE	356	1-1	1		11	4		6		8	9^1	10						5	2	7			3	14							
8-OCT	A	EAST STIRLINGSHIRE	198	1-0	1		11	4		6		8	9	14						5	2	7			3	10^1							
5-OCT	H	PETERHEAD	425	3-2	1		11^1	4		6		8	9^2	14						5	2	7		15	3	10							
NOV	A	QUEEN'S PARK	522	1-0	1		11	4		6		8	9^1	15		16				5	2	7			3	10							
NOV	H	ELGIN CITY	451	2-2	1		11	4		6		8	9^2			16				5	2	7			3	10							
4-NOV	A	ALBION ROVERS	357	3-1	1		11^1	4		6		8	9	14						5	2	7			3	10^2							
DEC	H	COWDENBEATH	401	1-0	1		11	4		6		8	9							5	2	7^1			3	10							
DEC	A	STIRLING ALBION	682	1-0	1		11	4		6		8	9	15		14				5	2	7			3	10^1							
3-DEC	A	MONTROSE	438	0-2	1		11	4		6		8	15	9		14				5	2	7			3	10							
7-DEC	H	EAST STIRLINGSHIRE	532	2-1	1		11	4		6		8				10				5		15^1			2	7				3	9^1			
JAN	A	STRANRAER	534	2-1	1		3			6		8^1		10		16	11			5	12	2^1			7				9	14			
7-JAN	H	QUEEN'S PARK	419	0-1	1		11	4		6		8	15	10		16				5	2	7			3				9	12			
4-JAN	A	COWDENBEATH	290	2-1	1		11	4		6		8^1	15	10		2				5		7			3				9^1				
FEB	A	ELGIN CITY	383	1-1	1		11	4				8	9			2				5		7^1			3	10				6			
4-FEB	H	ALBION ROVERS	418	3-0	1		12			6		8	9^2	16		2				5		7			3	10^1			4	11^1			
1-FEB	A	EAST STIRLINGSHIRE	187	4-2	1					6		8^1	9^3	12		2				5		7			3	10			4	11			
8-FEB	H	MONTROSE	635	1-2	1					6		8	9^1	12		2	16			5		7			3	10^1							
MAR	H	STIRLING ALBION	758	1-0	1		11	4		6		8	9	12		2	16			5		7			3	10^1							
MAR	A	PETERHEAD	556	1-2	1		11	4				8	9	12		2				5		7			3	14			10	6^1			
3-MAR	H	STRANRAER	736	0-0	1		11	4				8	9	12		2				5		7			3				10	6			
0-MAR	H	ELGIN CITY	360	2-1	1		11	4				8	9	12		2				5^1		7			3^1	14			10	6			
7-MAR	A	ALBION ROVERS	287	2-1	1		11	4		6		8	9	10						5		7^1			3				12^1	14	15	2	
8-APR	A	STIRLING ALBION	678	1-0	1		11	4				8		15						5	2	7			3				9	12	14	6^1	
0-APR	H	COWDENBEATH	429	0-1	1		11	4				8		10		15	16			5	2	7			3				9	12	6		
7-APR	H	EAST STIRLINGSHIRE	311	†5-1	1		11	4				8		10		15				5	2	7		16	3	9^1			12	6^3			
4-APR	A	MONTROSE	395	4-1	1		3	4						12						5	2	7			14	9	10^2			8^2	15		
MAY	A	STRANRAER	697	2-3	1		11	4					12			8	16			5	2	7			3	9	10^1			6	15		
3-MAY	H	PETERHEAD	418	3-2	1		11	4		6		8		12						5	2^1	7^1			3	9^1				10			
5-MAY	A	QUEEN'S PARK	541	1-1			3	14		6		8	9			2	16					7							15^1	10	5	4	
TOTAL FULL APPEARANCES					35	2	30	27	2	27	1	34	24	14	2	19	4	1	1	32	23	33	1	5	29	23	6	3	15	1	1	1	1
TOTAL SUB APPEARANCES						1	1	3				1	2	12	4	7	15			1		4				5	5	5	4		2		
TOTAL GOALS SCORED							2					3	17			1	1			1		3			4	1			10	5			9

All bold figures denote goalscorers. † denotes opponent's own goal.

LEADING GOALSCORERS:

SEASON 2002-03 WAS THE CLUB'S FIRST SEASON IN MEMBERSHIP OF SFL

SEASON	DIV	GOALS	PLAYER
02-03	T	10	M. Dobie
03-04	T	17	M. Cameron

MILESTONES:

YEAR OF FORMATION: 1946
MOST LEAGUE POINTS IN A SEASON:
95 (Northern League (Champions) - Season 1990/91) (3 Points for a Win)
68 (SFL Third Division – Season 2003/04 – 3 Points for a Win)
MOST LEAGUE GOALS SCORED BY A PLAYER IN A SEASON:
Dennis "Touchy" Smith (Season 1950/51)
No. OF GOALS SCORED: 101
RECORD ATTENDANCE:
2,307 (-v- Rochdale – F.A. Cup 1991)
RECORD VICTORY: 20-0 (-v- Silloth – Carlisle & District League 1962)
RECORD DEFEAT: 2-9 (-v- Ashton United – Unibond League Division 1 – 28.10.2000)

GRETNA PLAYING KITS SEASON 2004/05

FIRST KIT • SECOND KIT • THIRD KIT

MONTROSE

Links Park Stadium, Wellington Street,
Montrose, DD10 8QD

CHAIRMAN
John F. Paton

VICE-CHAIRMAN
Robert Ritchie

DIRECTORS
John D. Crawford, David I. Tait,
Malcolm J. Watters, John Ednie

ASSOCIATE DIRECTORS
Andrew G. Stephen &
David G. Skene

HONORARY PRESIDENT
William Johnston, M.B.E., J.P.

SECRETARY/LOTTERY MANAGER
John D. Crawford

OFFICE ADMINISTRATOR
Andrew G. Stephen

MANAGER
Henry Hall

FIRST TEAM COACH
Ian Gilzean

FITNESS COACH
David Brown

GOALKEEPING COACH
Jim Butter

YOUTH CO-ORDINATOR
Andrew G. Stephen

YOUTH DEVELOPMENT COACH
David Brown

CHIEF SCOUT Ian Cochrane

COMMERCIAL MANAGER
Mrs Glynis Crawford
(B)(01674) 673200 (H)(01674) 673758

**FOOTBALL SAFETY OFFICERS'
ASSOCIATION REPRESENTATIVE**
John Ednie

PHYSIOTHERAPIST Fiona Fairlie

GROUNDSMAN Ron Marquis

KIT PERSON Brian Leiper

MATCHDAY PROGRAMME EDITOR
Andrew Stephen
(B) (01356) 626766 (H) (01674) 672314

TELEPHONES
Ground/Commercial (01674) 673200
Sec. Home (01674) 673758
Sec. Bus. (01674) 672064
Ground Fax (01674) 677311

E-MAIL & INTERNET ADDRESS
info@johncrawford.co.uk
www.montrosefc.co.uk

CLUB SHOP
Situated at Stadium (01674) 673200
Open 2.00pm - 5.00pm on home matchdays

OFFICIAL SUPPORTERS CLUB
c/o Simon Bradford, Secretary
16 Mount Avenue, Montrose

CLUB CAPTAIN
Jim Butter

TEAM CAPTAIN
Steven Kerrigan

SHIRT SPONSOR
Bon Accord Glass

KIT SUPPLIER
Vandanel

LIST OF PLAYERS 2004/05

PLAYERS SURNAME	FIRST NAME	MIDDLE NAME	DATE OF BIRTH	PLACE OF BIRTH	DATE SIGNED	HEIGHT FT INS		WEIGHT ST LBS		POSITION ON PITCH	PREVIOUS CLUB
BARBOUR	MICHAEL		19/07/85	ABERDEEN	31/08/04	6	5	13	11	DEFENDER	STONEHAVEN JUNIORS
BREMNER	KIT		07/06/84	HIGH WYCOMBE	31/08/04	5	11	11	5	MIDFIELD	BROUGHTY ATHLETIC JNRS
BUDD	ALAN	DOUGLAS	23/02/84	KIRKCALDY	30/08/03	5	10	12	0	MIDFIELD	GLENROTHES JUNIORS
BUTTER	JAMES	ROSS	14/12/66	DUNDEE	23/07/04	6	1	12	12	GOALKEEPER	EAST FIFE
DODDS	KERR		05/05/85	EDINBURGH	27/08/04	5	9	10	8	DEFENDER	ROSS COUNTY
DONACHIE	BARRY	JAMES	21/12/79	DUNDEE	18/01/03	5	8	12	0	MIDFIELD	BRECHIN CITY
DOYLE	PAUL		26/09/84	BELLSHILL	27/08/04	5	10.5	11	6	DEFENDER	CLYDE
FERGUSON	STUART		09/11/80	BANGOUR	03/08/00	5	10	10	5	DEF / MID	FORFAR ATHLETIC
GREENHILL	DAVID		08/07/85	EDINBURGH	27/08/04	5	7	9	7	MIDFIELD	CLYDE
HALL	EUAN	STUART	19/08/85	DUNDEE	23/12/03	5	8	10	10	MIDFIELD	ST. JOHNSTONE
HANKINSON	MICHAEL	RICHARD	04/07/83	DUNDEE	31/08/02	6	1	11	7	GOALKEEPER	TAYPORT JUNIORS
KERRIGAN	STEVEN	PAUL	29/09/70	WOLVERHAMPTON	30/05/01	5	10	11	7	FORWARD	EAST FIFE
LANNEN	SHAUN	FRANCIS	19/03/85	DUNDEE	30/08/02	5	10	11	7	DEFENDER	LOCHEE HARP JUNIORS
MORRICE	KRISTOFER	MARTIN	20/08/87	FORFAR	31/08/04	5	8	12	0	MIDFIELD	KIRRIEMUIR THISTLE JNRS
O'REILLY	CRAIG		20/09/87	EDINBURGH	20/08/04	6	2	11	7	FORWARD	RAITH ROVERS
SHARP	GRAEME		03/05/84	FRASERBURGH	31/01/03	5	10	10	7	MIDFIELD	BANCHORY ST. TERNAN JNRS
SMART	CRAIG		26/11/78	KIRKCALDY	29/07/03	5	9	11	7	FORWARD	HILL O' BEATH HAWTHORN JNRS
SMITH	DARYN	ANDREW	09/10/80	BELFAST	28/07/04	5	10	9	12	MIDFIELD	PETERHEAD
SPINK	DARREN		08/01/81	ARBROATH	22/09/03	6	0	12	7	MIDFIELD	ARBROATH
STEPHEN	NEIL	ANDREW	03/07/84	DUNDEE	30/01/04	6	2	12	7	DEFENDER	DUNDEE NORTH END JNRS
WATSON	CALUM	NEIL	18/02/84	MONTROSE	04/03/04	5	11	12	4	FORWARD	MONTROSE ROSELEA JNRS
WEBSTER	KEVIN	SCOTT	21/01/83	DUNDEE	29/03/02	5	9	10	0	MIDFIELD	DUNDEE
WOOD	MARTIN		20/08/82	ABERDEEN	15/07/03	5	10	12	7	FORWARD	ROSS COUNTY

TICKET INFORMATION

SEASON TICKET PRICES

SEATED	ADULT	£130
OR STANDING	JUVENILE/OAP	£70
	FAMILY (1 ADULT & 1 JUVENILE)	£150

LEAGUE ADMISSION PRICES

SEATED		
OR STANDING	ADULT	£8
	JUVENILE/OAP	£4
	FAMILY (1 ADULT AND 1 JUVENILE)	£10

THE GABLE ENDIES' 10 YEAR LEAGUE RECORD

SEASON	DIV	P	W	D	L	F	A	PTS	P
1994-95	T	36	20	7	9	69	32	67	
1995-96	S	36	5	5	26	33	86	20	1
1996-97	T	36	12	7	17	46	62	43	
1997-98	T	36	10	8	18	53	80	38	
1998-99	T	36	8	6	22	42	74	30	1
1999-00	T	36	10	7	19	39	54	37	
2000-01	T	36	6	8	22	31	65	26	
2001-02	T	36	16	7	13	43	39	55	
2002-03	T	36	7	12	17	35	61	33	
2003-04	T	36	12	12	12	52	63	48	

The gable endies' stats 2003/04

SEASON STATS 2003/04

Bold figures denote goalscorers. † denotes opponent's own goal.

DATE	VENUE	OPPONENTS	ATT	RES	BUTTER J.	DONACHIE B.	FERGUSON S.	CONWAY F.	SIMPSON M	SMITH G.	GIBSON K.	FARNAN C.	SMART C.	WOOD M.	KERRIGAN S.	SHARP G.	HENDERSON R.	WEBSTER K.	THOMSON G.	MICHIE S.	WATT J.	MCQUILLAN J.	BLACK R.	BRASH K.	HANKINSON M.	SPINK D.	SMITH E.	HALL E.	COULSTON D.	BUDD A.	STEPHEN N.
9-AUG	H	PETERHEAD	411	0 - 1	1	2	3	4	5	6	7	8	9	10	11			14	15	16											
16-AUG	A	EAST STIRLINGSHIRE	182	1 - 1	1	2	3	4	5		7¹	8		10	11	12			15	6	9	14									
23-AUG	H	COWDENBEATH	338	1 - 3	1	2	3	6	5	4	8			10	12	15	7	11	9¹	14											
30-AUG	H	ELGIN CITY	324	3 - 3	1	2	3	6	5	8¹			12	14	10¹			7		9		4	11¹								
13-SEP	A	ALBION ROVERS	262	1 - 0	1	2	3	6	5	14	15	8		10¹				7		9	12	4	11								
20-SEP	A	QUEEN'S PARK	490	1 - 1		2	3	6	5		16	7		10	12			9¹	14	4		11	1	8							
27-SEP	H	STRANRAER	273	2 - 4			3		5	7¹				10¹	14			9	12	4	8	11	1	6	2						
4-OCT	A	GRETNA	356	1 - 1	1		3	5¹		4	8			10	14	7		9	12	6					2						
11-OCT	A	STIRLING ALBION	490	0 - 3			3		5	15	8	6		10	12	7		9				18	11								
18-OCT	H	STIRLING ALBION	338	2 - 3	14	3			5	12	8²	10	11		16	7		9	4	6		1	2								
25-OCT	H	EAST STIRLINGSHIRE	246	5 - 1		2	3			12	8	9	6¹	14		7		10¹	15	5	11²	1	4¹								
1-NOV	A	PETERHEAD	540	0 - 0				4	15	10	9	8	14			7		12	5	11	6										
8-NOV	H	ALBION ROVERS	267	1 - 0	1	2	3		8			10	6¹	15		7		9	16	5	11		4								
15-NOV	A	ELGIN CITY	475	3 - 2	1	2	3		8	12¹		10	6¹	14		7		9¹	15	5	11		4								
2-DEC	H	QUEEN'S PARK	279	0 - 0	1	2	3		8	12	7	10	6		11			15		9	5	16	4								
6-DEC	A	STRANRAER	409	0 - 2	1	2	3	12		6	8	10			14	7		9		5	11		4	15							
13-DEC	H	GRETNA	438	2 - 0	1	2	3		8	15	10	14	6	16		7		9¹		5	11¹		4								
3-JAN	A	COWDENBEATH	282	3 - 3	1	2	3	4		12	8¹	10	6¹	11	9	14				5			7¹								
17-JAN	H	PETERHEAD	512	2 - 1	1	2	3		8¹	10	6	11	14	7		9¹				5			4								
24-JAN	A	QUEEN'S PARK	443	1 - 1	1	2	3		8	11	10	6¹	14	15	7			9		5			16	4							
31-JAN	H	STRANRAER	349	1 - 4	1	2	3	12	8¹	14	10	6	11		7			9		5			4	16							
7-FEB	A	ALBION ROVERS	192	0 - 3	1	2	3		8		7	10	11	14				9		5			6	4	15	16					
14-FEB	H	ELGIN CITY	312	4 - 3	1	2	3	12	8¹		6	10	11¹	14		7		9²		5			4								
21-FEB	H	STIRLING ALBION	466	1 - 4	1	2	3	12	8		6	10	11	14		7¹		9		5			15	4							
28-FEB	A	GRETNA	635	2 - 1		2	3		6	10	11²	9	8	14		7				5			4								
6-MAR	A	EAST STIRLINGSHIRE	195	4 - 1		2	3		12		11	10¹	8	7		14		9²		5			4¹	16							
13-MAR	H	COWDENBEATH	349	1 - 1	1	2	3		8		12	6	7	10		9¹				5			4	16	11						
20-MAR	H	ALBION ROVERS	339	3 - 1	1	2	3	4		11	10	6	12			7		9²		5			8¹								
27-MAR	A	ELGIN CITY	499	1 - 2	1	2	3		8		10	6	11	16	7			9	5¹				4	14	15						
3-APR	A	STRANRAER	378	0 - 6	1	2	3		6		11	10	8			7		9		5			15	4	14	16					
10-APR	H	QUEEN'S PARK	388	1 - 1	1		3		2		8¹	10	6	15	12	7		9		5					11	4					
17-APR	A	STIRLING ALBION	672	1 - 1	1	2	3		4		8	6	11	10	7			9¹		5			15	14	16						
24-APR	H	GRETNA	395	1 - 4	1	2	3		4		10¹	6	14	12	7			9		5			8	11	15						
1-MAY	A	COWDENBEATH	229	0 - 0		2	3				10	6	7	14	12			9		5			1	8	11			4			
8-MAY	H	EAST STIRLINGSHIRE	360	1 - 0		2	3				8¹	10	6	11	12	7		9		5								14			
15-MAY	A	PETERHEAD	604	2 - 1	1		3				8	10	6	14	9¹	7¹				5			15	4	11			2	16		
TOTAL FULL APPEARANCES					30	31	36	6	10	9	19	6	24	26	32	13	4	26	2	30	1	33	10	3	6	5	28	1	2	2	1
TOTAL SUB APPEARANCES					1					1	4	4	7	2	3			16	16	6		1	9		1		1	5		9	4	2
TOTAL GOALS SCORED							1			5	1	8	2	8	1	1		2		14		1	4						4	

Bold figures denote goalscorers. † denotes opponent's own goal.

LEADING GOALSCORERS:

SEASON	DIV	GOALS	PLAYER
94-95	T	19	C. McGlashan
95-96	S	16	C. McGlashan
96-97	T	11	C. McGlashan
97-98	T	20	C. McGlashan
98-99	T	7	S. Taylor
99-00	T	12	S. Taylor
00-01	T	7	J. Mitchell
01-02	T	13	S. Laidlaw
02-03	T	8	S. Kerrigan
03-04	T	14	S. Michie

MILESTONES:

YEAR OF FORMATION: 1879

MOST CAPPED PLAYER: Sandy Keiller

NO. OF CAPS: 6 (2 whilst with Montrose)

MOST LEAGUE POINTS IN A SEASON:
53 (Division 2 - Season 1974/75) &
(Second Division - Season 1984/85) (2 Points for a win)
67 (Third Division - Season 1994/95) (3 Points for a win)

MOST LEAGUE GOALS SCORED BY A PLAYER IN A SEASON:
Brian Third

NO. OF GOALS SCORED: 28 (Season 1972/73)

RECORD ATTENDANCE: 8,983 (-v- Dundee – 17.3.1973)

RECORD VICTORY: 12-0 (-v- Vale of Leithen – Scottish Cup, 4.1.1975)

RECORD DEFEAT: 0-13 (-v- Aberdeen, 17.3.1951)

MONTROSE PLAYING KITS SEASON 2004/05

FIRST KIT   SECOND KIT   THIRD KIT

PETERHEAD

Balmoor Stadium,
Lord Catto Park,
Balmoor Terrace,
Peterhead, AB42 1EU

CHAIRMAN
Roger Taylor

VICE-CHAIRMAN
Rodger G. Morrison

DIRECTORS
George Watson
& Gerry Gaffney

COMMITTEE
Dave Watson,
Arthur Duncan
& George Moore

SECRETARY
George Moore

GENERAL MANAGER
Dave Watson 07774 615820

OFFICE ADMINISTRATOR/ TREASURER
Shona Aird

MANAGER
Iain Stewart

ASSISTANT MANAGER
Paul Mathers

CLUB DOCTOR
Dr. Ian Small

PHYSIOTHERAPIST
Sandy Rennie

GROUNDSMAN
Bill Spence

KIT PERSON
Robert Buchan

FOOTBALL SAFETY OFFICERS' ASSOCIATION REPRESENTATIVE
Arthur Duncan
(01779) 477201

MEDIA LIAISON OFFICERS
Dave Watson
(01224) 771100
& George Moore
(01224) 820851

MATCHDAY PROGRAMME EDITOR
George Moore

TELEPHONES
Ground (01779) 478256
Sec. Bus. (01224) 820851
Sec. Home (01779) 476870
Sec. Mob 07740 105457
Fax (01779) 490682

E-MAIL & INTERNET ADDRESS
georgemoore@tiscali.co.uk
www.peterheadfc.org.uk

OFFICIAL SUPPORTERS CLUB
c/o Balmoor Stadium,
Peterhead, AB42 1EU

TEAM CAPTAIN
Robert Raeside

SHIRT SPONSOR
Gillanders Motors

KIT SUPPLIER
ProStar

Peterhead

LIST OF PLAYERS 2004/05

PLAYERS SURNAME	FIRST NAME	MIDDLE NAME	DATE OF BIRTH	PLACE OF BIRTH	DATE SIGNED	HEIGHT FT INS		WEIGHT ST LBS		POSITION ON PITCH	PREVIOUS CLUB
BAIN	CLARK	ROSS	25/10/84	ABERDEEN	21/05/04	5	7	10	10	MIDFIELD	COVE RANGERS
BAVIDGE	MARTIN	MITCHELL	30/04/80	ABERDEEN	24/07/03	6	1	13	7	FORWARD	FORFAR ATHLETIC
BUCHAN	MARTIN	JAMES	03/04/77	MANCHESTER	23/01/04	5	11	12	7	MIDFIELD	STOCKPORT COUNTY
BUCHANAN	ROSS	ALEXANDER	20/11/80	ABERDEEN	23/08/03	6	2	13	10	GOALKEEPER	LONGSIDE JUNIORS
CAMPBELL	CRAIG		10/12/83	DINGWALL	27/07/04	5	10	11	0	FORWARD	ROSS COUNTY
DUNCAN	ROBERT		08/03/83	PETERHEAD	01/08/03	5	11	11	0	FORWARD	ABERDEEN
FARQUHAR	JOHN	GRAHAM	31/07/85	ABERDEEN	28/08/04	5	11	10	7	GOALKEEPER	WILSONS X1 JUNIOR
GIBSON	KEITH		01/05/81	DUNDEE	26/03/04	6	0	12	4	MIDFIELD	MONTROSE
GOOD	IAIN	DAVID	09/08/77	GLASGOW	24/07/03	6	1	12	0	DEFENDER	FORFAR ATHLETIC
HAGEN	DAVID	JAMES	05/05/73	EDINBURGH	10/06/04	5	11	13	12	FORWARD	CLYDE
MATHERS	PAUL		17/01/70	ABERDEEN	30/05/02	6	0	12	7	GOALKEEPER	BERWICK RANGERS
M°SKIMMING	SHAUN	PETER	29/05/70	STRANRAER	06/08/02	5	11	11	7	MIDFIELD	ATLANTA SILVERBACK
MICHIE	SCOTT	DAVID	22/08/83	ABERDEEN	08/07/04	5	10	11	7	FORWARD	ABERDEEN
MILNE	DANIEL	DEAN	05/01/86	ABERDEEN	09/08/03	5	10	10	7	MIDFIELD	ALBION B.C.
PERRY	MARK	GEORGE	07/02/71	ABERDEEN	31/01/03	6	1	12	10	DEFENDER	ROSS COUNTY
RAESIDE	ROBERT		07/07/72	PETERSBURG - S.A.	09/08/02	6	2	13	10	DEFENDER	ALLOA ATHLETIC
ROBERTSON	COLIN	DAVID	13/07/85	ABERDEEN	30/08/04	5	10	11	0	MIDFIELD	WILSONS X1 JUNIOR
ROBERTSON	SCOTT		07/04/85	DUNDEE	28/08/04	6	0	11	4	MIDFIELD	DUNDEE
SEIVWRIGHT	JAMES	COLLIE	14/10/85	ABERDEEN	28/08/04	6	1	11	0	DEFENDER	WILSONS X1 JUNIOR
SHAND	RICHARD		03/05/85	ABERDEEN	12/08/03	5	8	10	7	MIDFIELD	DUNDEE UNITED
STEEL	WILLIAM	ROBERT	05/12/85	ABERDEEN	28/08/04	5	7	10	7	MIDFIELD	WILSONS X1 JUNIOR
STEWART	GRAEME	JOHN	02/04/82	ABERDEEN	11/07/03	6	1	12	8	MIDFIELD	INVERNESS CALEDONIAN TH
STEWART	IAIN	ANGUS	23/10/69	DUNDEE	27/06/02	5	7	10	5	FORWARD	INVERNESS CALEDONIAN TH
TULLY	CRAIG		07/01/76	STIRLING	21/05/04	6	0	12	10	DEFENDER	ELGIN CITY
YOUNGSON	ALLAN		29/09/84	ABERDEEN	08/06/04	5	9	11	3	DEF / MID	DUNDEE

TICKET INFORMATION

SEASON TICKET PRICES
SEATED

ADULT	£130
ADULT & JUVENILE	£195
OAP	£65

STANDING

ADULT	£110
JUVENILE /OAP	£55

LEAGUE ADMISSION PRICES
SEATED

ADULT	£8
JUVENILE /OAP	£4

STANDING

ADULT	£8
JUVENILE /OAP	£4

THE BLUE TOON'S 10 YEAR LEAGUE RECO

SEASON	DIV	P	W	D	L	F	A	PTS
SEASON 2000-01 WAS THE CLUB'S FIRST SEASON IN MEMBERSHIP OF S								
2000-01	T	36	13	10	13	46	46	49
2001-02	T	36	17	5	14	63	52	56
2002-03	T	36	20	8	8	76	37	68
2003-04	T	36	18	7	11	67	37	61

SEASON STATS 2003/04

Player columns (in order): MATHERS P., McGUINNESS K., McSKIMMING S., RAESIDE R., PERRY M., BAIN K., TINDAL K., DUNCAN R., GRANT R., BAVIDGE M., RODDIE A., STEWART I., JOHNSTON M., MACKAY S., BETH G., STEWART D., SMITH D., GOOD I., STEWART G., BRASH K., BUCHAN M.J., ROBERTSON S., MILNE D., BUCHANAN R., GIBSON K., SHAND R.

DATE	VENUE	OPPONENTS	ATT	RES
AUG	A	MONTROSE	411	1 - 0
AUG	H	GRETNA	464	2 - 0
AUG	A	ELGIN CITY	748	3 - 2
AUG	H	STRANRAER	813	1 - 2
SEP	A	STIRLING ALBION	711	1 - 3
SEP	H	EAST STIRLINGSHIRE	520	2 - 0
SEP	A	ALBION ROVERS	283	0 - 2
OCT	A	QUEEN'S PARK	395	2 - 0
OCT	H	COWDENBEATH	542	0 - 1
OCT	A	GRETNA	425	2 - 3
NOV	H	MONTROSE	540	0 - 0
NOV	H	STIRLING ALBION	589	2 - 2
NOV	A	STRANRAER	428	2 - 0
NOV	A	EAST STIRLINGSHIRE	178	3 - 1
DEC	H	ALBION ROVERS	485	2 - 1
DEC	H	QUEEN'S PARK	535	4 - 1
DEC	A	COWDENBEATH	308	0 - 2
JAN	H	ELGIN CITY	714	5 - 1
JAN	A	MONTROSE	512	1 - 2
JAN	H	EAST STIRLINGSHIRE	553	6 - 0
FEB	A	STIRLING ALBION	651	2 - 0
FEB	H	STRANRAER	615	2 - 0
FEB	H	COWDENBEATH	619	0 - 0
FEB	A	QUEEN'S PARK	581	0 - 1
MAR	H	GRETNA	556	2 - 1
MAR	A	ELGIN CITY	675	0 - 1
MAR	A	ALBION ROVERS	253	3 - 3
MAR	H	STIRLING ALBION	588	0 - 0
MAR	A	STRANRAER	434	1 - 1
APR	H	ALBION ROVERS	440	5 - 0
APR	A	EAST STIRLINGSHIRE	243	3 - 0
APR	A	COWDENBEATH	238	3 - 0
APR	H	QUEEN'S PARK	631	1 - 1
MAY	H	ELGIN CITY	616	3 - 1
MAY	A	GRETNA	418	2 - 3
MAY	H	MONTROSE	604	1 - 2

	TOTAL FULL APPEARANCES	TOTAL SUB APPEARANCES	TOTAL GOALS SCORED
MATHERS P.	33	3	
McGUINNESS K.	20	2	6
McSKIMMING S.	20	1	1
RAESIDE R.	30		
PERRY M.	33	2	2
BAIN K.	11	4	1
TINDAL K.	17	8	
DUNCAN R.	20	4	
GRANT R.	3	1	
BAVIDGE M.	33	2	16
RODDIE A.	25	4	3
STEWART I.	17	5	6
JOHNSTON M.	28	8	18
MACKAY S.	11	3	2
BETH G.	9	9	2
STEWART D.	1	12	
SMITH D.	11	1	1
GOOD I.	22	3	1
STEWART G.	4	4	1
BRASH K.	6		
BUCHAN M.J.	15	4	3
ROBERTSON S.	16		3
MILNE D.	1		
BUCHANAN R.	3		
GIBSON K.	6		1
SHAND R.	1		

Bold figures denote goalscorers. † denotes opponent's own goal.

LEADING GOALSCORERS:

SEASON	DIV	GOALS	PLAYER
SEASON 2000-01 WAS THE CLUB'S FIRST SEASON IN MEMBERSHIP OF SFL			
2000-01	T	11	C. Yeats
2001-02	T	19	I. Stewart
2002-03	T	21	I. Stewart
2003-04	T	18	M. Johnston

MILESTONES:

YEAR OF FORMATION: 1891

MOST LEAGUE POINTS IN A SEASON:
89 (Highland League – Season 1989/90 (3 Points for a Win))
68 (SFL Third Division – Season 2002/03 (3 Points for a Win))

MOST LEAGUE GOALS SCORED BY A PLAYER IN A SEASON:
Iain Stewart (Season 2001/02)

NO. OF GOALS SCORED: 23

RECORD ATTENDANCE:
6,310 (-v- Celtic – 1948 at Recreation Park)
2,200 (-v- Aberdeen – 6.7.2002 – at Balmoor Stadium)

RECORD VICTORY: 17-0 (-v- Fort William – Season 1998/99)

RECORD DEFEAT: 0-13 (-v- Aberdeen, Scottish Cup, Season 1923/24)

PETERHEAD PLAYING KITS SEASON 2004/05

FIRST KIT · SECOND KIT · THIRD KIT

Queen's Park

QUEENS PARK
The National Stadium,
Hampden Park, Mount Florida,
Glasgow, G42 9BA
HON. PATRON
The Lord Macfarlane of Bearsden KT
PRESIDENT
David Gordon, B.Acc., A.C.M.A.
COMMITTEE
A. Kenneth C. Harvey, Malcolm D. Mackay,
David McNeil, Garry M. Templeman
(Treasurer), James M. Hastie LL.B,
Dr. Alan S. Hutchison B.Sc., M.B., ChB.,
F.R.C.P. Glas, F.R.C., P.A.T.H., David B.
Stirling, Ross Caven MBA, M.Sc, B.Sc &
James Nicholson
SECRETARY
Alistair MacKay
OFFICE ADMINISTRATORS
Mrs. Janice Balmain & Mrs. Susan Kennedy
COACH
William Stark
ASSISTANT COACH
Robert Dickson
COACHING STAFF
Keith MacKenzie, Robert Kelly, Michael
Jamieson, Steve Adam,
Chic McCarry, Barry McNab,
Brian Hamilton, Pat Barkie, Peter McLean,
Billy Ogilvie, Alan Simpson & Willie Neil
GOALKEEPING COACH
Ronnie Cant
HEAD OF YOUTH DEVELOPMENT
Ian Cairns
YOUTH DEVELOPMENT COACH
Tommy Wilson
YOUTH TEAM COACHES
Keith MacKenzie, Robert Kelly
& Chic McCarry (U19)
Barry McNab, Michael Jamieson
& Brian Hamilton (U17)
Peter McLean (U15)
Billy Ogilvie (U14)
Willie Neil & Alan Simpson (U13)
CLUB DOCTOR
Dr. Alan S. Hutchison
PHYSIOTHERAPISTS
Robert C. Findlay & Andrew Myles
GROUNDSMEN
Steve Bache & Scott McCreadie
FOOTBALL SAFETY OFFICERS'
ASSOCIATION REPRESENTATIVE/
MEDIA LIAISON OFFICER
Alistair MacKay (0141) 632 1275
KIT PERSON
Billy Ogilvie
COMMERCIAL DIRECTOR
Ross Caven (0141) 632 1275
MATCHDAY PROGRAMME EDITORS
David B. Stirling & Logan Taylor
TELEPHONES
Office (0141) 632 1275
Stadium Operations (0141) 620 4000
Fax (0141) 636 1612
Sec.Home (0141) 6380905
Sec.Bus (0141) 6321275
E-MAIL & INTERNET ADDRESS
secretary@queensparkfc.co.uk
www.queensparkfc.co.uk
CLUB SHOP
Home matches only – Hampden Park
(Kiosk within BT Scotland Stand).
Open 2.15p.m. – 3.00p.m. and
4.45pm – 5.00pm on home match days.
Mail Orders may be obtained through the
Secretary of the Official Supporters Club.
OFFICIAL SUPPORTERS CLUB
c/o Secretary, Keith McAllister,
58 Brunton Street,
Glasgow, G44 3NQ
CLUB CAPTAIN
Danny Ferry
SHIRT SPONSOR
Barr Irn Bru – Original and Best
KIT SUPPLIER
DIADORA

LIST OF PLAYERS 2004/05

PLAYERS SURNAME	FIRST NAME	MIDDLE NAME	DATE OF BIRTH	PLACE OF BIRTH	DATE SIGNED	HEIGHT FT INS		WEIGHT ST LBS		POSITION ON PITCH	PREVIOUS CLUB
AGOSTINI	DAMIANO	PIETRO	22/11/78	IRVINE	13/03/98	6	1	13	7	DEFENDER	EAST FIFE
ALLAN	RICHARD		04/02/88	PAISLEY	26/08/04	5	10	10	2	MIDFIELD	QUEEN'S PARK FORM D U' 16
ANDERSON	ALEX		24/06/88	GLASGOW	26/08/04	5	7	10	6	DEFENDER	PARTICK THISTLE
AUSTIN	WILLIAM	MICHAEL	04/01/88	KETTERING	26/08/04	5	11	11	0	DEFENDER	QUEEN'S PARK FORM D U' 16
BLAIR	BRIAN		10/03/83	RUTHERGLEN	28/07/04	6	2	12	0	MIDFIELD	EAST FIFE
BONNAR	MARTIN	MICHAEL	12/01/79	BELLSHILL	02/08/04	5	9.5	10	7	MID / FWD	CUMNOCK JUNIORS
CAMPBELL	ROSS		17/03/87	GLASGOW	27/08/04	6	0	11	2	MIDFIELD	QUEEN'S PARK FORM D U' 15
CANNING	STEVEN		06/05/83	GLASGOW	31/07/01	5	11	12	2	MIDFIELD	QUEEN'S PARK FORM X
CARROLL	FRANK	ANDREW	30/01/81	GLASGOW	13/07/99	5	8	11	10	FORWARD	BENBURB JUVENILES
CHISHOLM	GRANT		16/05/86	GLASGOW	27/08/04	5	10	11	0	DEFENDER	CLYDE
CLARK	ROSS		07/02/83	RUTHERGLEN	31/07/01	5	9	11	0	MIDFIELD	QUEEN'S PARK FORM X
CLARKE	DAVID		22/06/83	RUTHERGLEN	28/07/04	5	9.5	10	5	FORWARD	MOTHERWELL
CLOSE	GARY		29/09/88	BELLSHILL	26/08/04	5	10	10	0	DEFENDER	QUEEN'S PARK FORM D U' 16
COLQUHOUN	CHRISTOPHER		06/01/88	GLASGOW	26/08/04	5	11	10	2	FORWARD	ST. MIRREN FORM D U' 16
CRAWFORD	DAVID		30/06/85	GLASGOW	28/08/03	6	2	11	7	GOALKEEPER	DUNDEE B.C.
CUSHLEY	EDWARD		11/02/88	BELLSHILL	26/08/04	5	8	9	4	MIDFIELD	HAMILTON ACAD. FORM D U' 16
DAILY	JAMES		11/10/87	GLASGOW	27/08/04	6	2	11	4	DEFENDER	QUEEN'S PARK B.C.
FELVUS	BRYAN		16/01/86	BELLSHILL	30/06/04	5	6	10	4	FORWARD	HAMILTON ACAD. FORM D U' 16
FERRY	DANIEL		31/01/77	GLASGOW	23/06/95	5	8	10	0	DEF / MID	QUEEN'S PARK U' 18'S
GALLOWAY	STEPHEN		02/05/88	PAISLEY	27/08/04	5	9	10	3	FORWARD	ST. MIRREN B.C.
GIBBONS	PAUL		31/03/88	BELLSHILL	03/09/04	5	10	11	0	GOALKEEPER	PARTICK THISTLE
GIBSON	STEPHEN		17/10/87	GLASGOW	27/08/04	5	10	12	0	MIDFIELD	QUEEN'S PARK FORM D U' 15
GRAHAM	ALASTAIR	SLOWEY	11/08/66	GLASGOW	29/07/03	6	3	14	10	FORWARD	HAMILTON ACADEMICAL
HARTY	ALAN		28/03/88	BELLSHILL	27/08/04	5	11	12	0	DEFENDER	QUEEN'S PARK FORM D U' 16
HARVEY	PAUL	EDWARD	28/08/88	GLASGOW	30/08/03	5	9	11	7	MIDFIELD	AIRDRIE UNITED
HASTIE	MARK		29/06/88	IRVINE	27/08/04	5	6	8	6	MIDFIELD	QUEEN'S PARK FORM D U' 16
KETTLEWELL	STUART		04/06/84	GLASGOW	16/08/02	6	0	11	0	MIDFIELD	LENZIE YOUTH CLUB
LENNON	SEAN		25/10/87	BELLSHILL	27/08/04	5	7	9	6	MIDFIELD	QUEEN'S PARK FORM D U' 16
LIVINGSTON	ANTHONY		15/08/86	GLASGOW	28/08/03	5	8	10	5	MIDFIELD	QUEEN'S PARK FORM D U' 16
M'BRIDE	JOSEPH		01/05/88	GLASGOW	27/08/04	5	7	8	6	MIDFIELD	QUEEN'S PARK FORM D U' 16
M'BRIDE	SEAN		01/05/88	GLASGOW	27/08/04	5	7	8	4	MIDFIELD	QUEEN'S PARK FORM D U' 16
M'CAIG	MATTHEW		24/03/88	GLASGOW	27/08/04	5	9	12	6	MIDFIELD	KILMARNOCK
M'CALLUM	DAVID	JOHN	07/09/77	BELLSHILL	31/01/03	5	10	10	10	MIDFIELD	PARTICK THISTLE
M'CLORY	PAUL		26/11/87	BELLSHILL	27/08/04	5	6	9	1	FORWARD	QUEEN'S PARK FORM D U' 15
M'CUE	BRIAN		24/01/85	GLASGOW	18/08/03	6	3	14	2	GOALKEEPER	DUNFERMLINE ATHLETIC
M'ELHINNEY	JOHN		11/08/86	GLASGOW	28/08/03	6	0	11	0	DEFENDER	QUEEN'S PARK FORM D U' 16
M'GINTY	ANDREW		19/07/84	GLASGOW	16/08/02	6	0	12	0	DEFENDER	CUMBERNAULD UNITED. JNRS
M'GOVERN	STEVEN		20/02/82	GLASGOW	30/06/04	6	3	12	7	GOALKEEPER	ARTHURLIE JUNIORS
M'LAREN	MARK		03/05/88	GLASGOW	27/08/04	5	9	9	6	DEFENDER	PARTICK THISTLE FORM D U' 16
M'LAUGHLIN	DAVID		20/02/87	GLASGOW	27/08/04	6	1	11	0	FORWARD	MOTHERWELL
M'NULTY	JOHN		12/01/88	RUTHERGLEN	27/08/04	5	9	10	6	DEFENDER	PARTICK THISTLE
M'SKIMMING	ROSS		06/03/87	GLASGOW	27/08/04	5	8	9	10	MIDFIELD	KILMARNOCK
MOLLOY	SHAUN		14/06/85	GLASGOW	28/07/04	6	0	12	7	DEFENDER	DUNDEE UNITED
MORGAN	KEVIN		17/05/88	VALE OF LEVEN	27/08/04	6	2	11	3	GOALKEEPER	QUEEN'S PARK FORM D U' 16
PHILIP	JOHN		19/10/87	GLASGOW	27/08/04	5	6	9	4	MIDFIELD	QUEEN'S PARK B.C.
QUINN	ANTHONY	THOMAS	09/09/81	GLASGOW	30/06/04	6	2	13	5	MIDFIELD	KIRKINTILLOCH ROB ROY JNRS
REILLY	STEVEN	JAMES	29/08/81	GLASGOW	22/07/03	6	0	12	10	DEFENDER	STIRLING ALBION
RUSHFORD	GAVIN	DAVID	05/05/86	GLASGOW	28/07/04	5	11	10	7	DEFENDER	PARTICK THISTLE
RUSSELL	ROBERT		29/06/86	GLASGOW	28/08/03	5	8	10	0	MIDFIELD	QUEEN'S PARK FORM D U' 16
SINCLAIR	RICHARD		20/05/82	GLASGOW	25/05/00	5	10	12	0	DEFENDER	QUEEN'S PARK FORM S
SLOAN	THOMAS		16/08/86	IRVINE	28/07/04	5	10	11	0	MID / FWD	ARDROSSAN WINTON ROVERS JNR
TROUTEN	ALAN		08/11/85	RUTHERGLEN	30/06/04	5	7	10	3	MIDFIELD	MORTON
WATERS	DAVID	ANTHONY	01/10/88	GLASGOW	27/08/04	5	9	8	0	MIDFIELD	QUEEN'S PARK FORM D U' 16
WATERS	LOUIS	GERARD	04/04/84	GLASGOW	30/06/04	6	2	12	0	DEFENDER	QUEEN'S PARK FORM S
WEATHERSTON	DAVID		25/08/86	PAISLEY	30/06/04	5	9	10	0	FORWARD	QUEEN'S PARK B.C.
WEIR	JOHN		05/04/85	GLASGOW	28/08/03	6	1	12	0	MIDFIELD	QUEEN'S PARK FORM D U' 16
WHELAN	JONATHAN		10/10/72	LIVERPOOL	30/11/01	6	0	12	3	MIDFIELD	BERWICK RANGERS
WINTER	ROSS		31/08/87	BELLSHILL	27/08/04	6	2	12	4	GOALKEEPER	QUEEN'S PARK FORM D U' 16

TICKET INFORMATION

SEASON TICKET PRICES

BT SCOTLAND STAND	ADULT	£115
	JUVENILE	
	(OVER 12 AND UNDER 16) / OAP	£40
	PARENT & JUVENILE	£125
	FOR EACH ADDITIONAL JUVENILE	£10
	JUVENILE (UNDER 12)	£25

LEAGUE ADMISSION PRICES

BT SCOTLAND STAND	ADULT	£8
	JUVENILE (U16)/OAP	£2
	PARENT & JUVENILE	£9
	JUVENILE/OAP	£1

THE SPIDERS' 10 YEAR LEAGUE RECORD

SEASON	DIV	P	W	D	L	F	A	PTS
1994-95	T	36	12	6	18	46	57	42
1995-96	T	36	12	12	12	40	43	48
1996-97	T	36	9	9	18	46	59	36
1997-98	T	36	10	11	15	42	55	41
1998-99	T	36	11	11	14	41	46	44
1999-00	T	36	20	9	7	54	37	69
2000-01	S	36	10	10	16	28	40	40
2001-02	T	36	9	8	19	38	53	35
2002-03	T	36	7	11	18	39	51	32
2003-04	T	36	10	11	15	41	53	41

SEASON STATS 2003/04

DATE	VENUE	OPPONENTS	ATT	RES	SCRIMGOUR D.	DUNNING A.	CLARK R.	SINCLAIR R.	AGOSTINI D.	CONLIN R.	REILLY S.	HARVEY P.	GRAHAM A.	WHELAN J.	MENELAWS D.	FERRY D.	CARROLL F.	MOFFAT S.	FALLON S.	KETTLEWELL S.	CANNING S.	CARCARY D.	McAULEY S.	THOMPSON J.	GALLAGHER P.	McCALLUM D.	CRAWFORD D.	STEWART D.	BONNAR M.	WEATHERSTON D.	QUINN A.T.	TROUTEN A.	McCUE B.
9-AUG	A	GRETNA	420	1-1	1	2	3	4	5	6	7	8	9	10	11	12	14¹	15															
16-AUG	H	ELGIN CITY	556	5-2	1	2	7	4	5		8³		9	10²	11	3		15	6	12		14											
23-AUG	A	ALBION ROVERS	627	1-3	1	2		4			8		9	10	11	3		5	6	7	12¹	14	16										
30-AUG	H	STIRLING ALBION	638	0-2	1	14	7	4					10	12	2		5	6		8	11	9	3	15									
13-SEP	A	COWDENBEATH	339	1-0	1		7	5			8	12	9	10		2		3	6		4¹	15	11										
20-SEP	H	MONTROSE	490	1-1	1		7	5			4	16	9	10	12	2		3	6		8		11¹	15									
27-SEP	A	EAST STIRLINGSHIRE	281	2-1	1		7	5			10	8	9	14	12			4	6		2		11²		16	3							
4-OCT	H	PETERHEAD	395	0-2	1		7	5			8	4	9	10					6		2	14	11	16	3								
18-OCT	A	STRANRAER	464	0-1	1		8	4	5				9	14	2	12		6	10	7		11		3									
25-OCT	A	ELGIN CITY	548	2-2	1		8	4	5		7		10	9	2	11		6			12¹	3	15¹										
1-NOV	H	GRETNA	522	0-1	1		16	4	5		8		9	10	2	15		6	14			11	3	7									
8-NOV	H	COWDENBEATH	554	0-0	1		7	4	5				9	10	2		3	6	8	12	15	11	16										
15-NOV	A	STIRLING ALBION	590	0-1	1		7		5				9	10	2	14	6	8			11	3											
2-DEC	A	MONTROSE	279	0-0	1			4	14			8	9	15	12	5		6	7	2		11	3	10									
6-DEC	H	EAST STIRLINGSHIRE	439	3-0	1		7				8	9¹	10		2	3		6	14	4		11²	12	15									
13-DEC	A	PETERHEAD	535	1-4	1		3		14	5	8	9¹	4		2	10			7	6		11		12		20							
3-JAN	H	ALBION ROVERS	454	1-1			15		5		7	8	9	12		2	4	6		3		11		10¹	14	1							
10-JAN	A	STRANRAER	473	0-4				5			4	8	9	14		2	12	6	7	10		16		11			3						
17-JAN	A	GRETNA	419	1-0	1		4		5		8¹	11				6	15		7								3						
24-JAN	H	MONTROSE	443	1-1	1		4		5		8¹	7			2	9		6	16			11		14			3						
7-FEB	A	COWDENBEATH	275	1-5	1		4		5		8	7	12	10¹		2	9		6	16		11	14				3						
14-FEB	H	STIRLING ALBION	742	1-4	1		4	5			8	7		10		2	9		12	14	16	11			6		3¹						
21-FEB	A	STRANRAER	435	1-3	1		3	5			8		9	15		2		4		7	11¹			10		6	14						
28-FEB	H	PETERHEAD	581	†1-0	1	4	6		16		8		10		2			14	7	11				3		5	15						
2-MAR	A	EAST STIRLINGSHIRE	235	4-2	1	4	6		5		8¹	15	9¹	10		2	14		12	7	11¹			3¹									
6-MAR	H	ELGIN CITY	444	4-0	1	4	6				8	12¹	10		2	9		15	7¹	11²				3			14						
13-MAR	A	ALBION ROVERS	491	1-3	1	4	6				8		10		2	9¹		14	7	11				3		15	12						
20-MAR	H	COWDENBEATH	508	1-2	1	4	6				8	14			2	9¹		12	10	11				3		5						
27-MAR	A	STIRLING ALBION	797	0-0	1	4	6				8	12				9		7	10	11				3		5	16					
3-APR	H	EAST STIRLINGSHIRE	404	1-0	1	4¹	6				8	11				9		7	10	12				3		5	2	14					
10-APR	A	MONTROSE	388	1-1	1	4	6	16			8	7		15		14		11	10	9¹				3		5	2						
17-APR	A	STRANRAER	564	0-2	1	4		2	14		8¹	7		10		12		6	11	9				3		5	15						
24-APR	H	PETERHEAD	631	1-1	1		5	2			8	6		10		9		7	11					3			4	14	16				
1-MAY	H	ALBION ROVERS	516	0-1	1	14	6	5	2		8		10			9		7	11					3			4	12					
8-MAY	A	ELGIN CITY	421	3-1	1		5				7		10²			9		2	8¹	11				3		4	6	14	12	15			
15-MAY	H	GRETNA	541	1-1	1		6	5	4		7		10			9		2	8	11				3¹			16	14			20		
TOTAL FULL APPEARANCES					35	12	27	20	20	1	27	19	20	26	3	24	17	8	20	15	25	16	13	5	4	18	1	13	7				
TOTAL SUB APPEARANCES						2	2	1	3	1	6	1	7	3	2	7	3	1	12	3	6	4	4	6	1	1	2	6	5	2	1	1	
TOTAL GOALS SCORED					1						7	1	3	5		3				4	5	6			2		2	1				

In bold figures denote goalscorers. † denotes opponent's own goal.

LEADING GOALSCORERS:

SEASON	DIV	GOALS	PLAYER
94-95	T	8	S. McCormick
95-96	T	6	S. Edgar, K. McGoldrick
96-97	T	7	D. Ferry
97-98	T	8	S. Edgar, J. Mercer
98-99	T	7	S. Edgar
99-00	T	13	M. Gallagher
00-01	S	7	M. Gallagher
01-02	T	5	S. Canning, R. Jackson
02-03	T	8	J. Gemmell
03-04	T	7	S. Reilly

MILESTONES:

YEAR OF FORMATION: 1867
MOST CAPPED PLAYER: Walter Arnott
NO. OF CAPS: 14
MOST LEAGUE POINTS IN A SEASON:
57 (Division 2 – Season 1922/23)(2 Points for a Win)
69 (Third Division – Season 1999/2000)(3 Points for a Win)
MOST LEAGUE GOALS SCORED BY A PLAYER IN A SEASON:
William Martin (Season 1937/38)
NO. OF GOALS SCORED: 30
GROUND RECORD ATTENDANCE:
149,547 (Scotland v England – 17.4.1937)
CLUB RECORD ATTENDANCE: 95,772 (-v- Rangers – 18.1.1930)
RECORD VICTORY: 16-0 (-v- St. Peters – Scottish Cup, 29.8.1885)
RECORD DEFEAT: 0-9 (-v- Motherwell – Division 1, 29.4.1930)

QUEEN'S PARK PLAYING KITS SEASON 2004/05

FIRST KIT   SECOND KIT   THIRD KIT

Stenhousemuir

STENHOUSEMUIR
Ochilview Park, Gladstone Road,
Stenhousemuir, FK5 4QL

CHAIRMAN
Michael R. Laing

VICE-CHAIRMAN
David O. Reid

DIRECTORS
Martin I. McNairney, Gordon T. Cook,
Bill Darroch, Alan J. McNeill & A. Terry Bulloch

SECRETARY
David O. Reid

OFFICE ADMINISTRATOR
Margaret Kilpatrick

CO-MANAGERS / RESERVE COACHES
Des McKeown and Tony Smith

FITNESS COACH
Martin McBride

GOALKEPPING COACH
Kevin McKeown

DIRECTOR OF YOUTH DEVELOPMENT
Bill Darroch

FOOTBALL DEVELOPMENT OFFICER
Tony Smith

COMMUNITY COACH
Scott Murphy

YOUTH TEAM COACHES
George Mawhinnie & Stuart Orr (U19),
John Morrison (U17),
Tommy Whiteside (U15)
Jim Blair (U13)
Tom Beattie (U12)

CLUB DOCTOR
Dr. Jonathon Sharp

PHYSIOTHERAPIST
Alan Davidson

COMMERCIAL DEPARTMENT
Contact Club

GROUNDSMAN Michael Ellis

KIT PERSON Jim Mackay

MEDIA LIAISON OFFICER
David O. Reid (0141) 566 8231

MATCHDAY PROGRAMME EDITOR
Margaret Kilpatrick (01324) 562992

TELEPHONES
Ground (01324) 562992
Fax (01324) 562980
Sec. Home (01324) 719898
Sec. Bus. (0141) 566 8231

E-MAIL & INTERNET ADDRESS
stenhousemuir.fc@talk21.com
www.stenhousemuirfc.com

CLUB SHOP
Ochilview Park, Gladstone Road,
Stenhousemuir, FK5 4QL. (01324) 562992.
Open during first team home
Matchdays between 2.00pm until 3.00pm &
Mon, Tue, Thu & Fri 9.00am till 4.30pm.
Contact Mrs M. Kilpatrick

OFFICIAL SUPPORTERS CLUB
Ochilview Park, Gladstone Road,
Stenhousemuir, FK5 4QL

SUPPORTERS CLUB CHAIRMAN
Harry Larkin

WARRIORS ABROAD
Alan McNeill at the Club's address

TEAM CAPTAIN
Lee Collins

SHIRT SPONSOR
Professional Office Supplies Ltd

KIT SUPPLIER
The Branded Group

LIST OF PLAYERS 2004/05

PLAYERS SURNAME	FIRST NAME	MIDDLE NAME	DATE OF BIRTH	PLACE OF BIRTH	DATE SIGNED	HEIGHT FT INS		WEIGHT ST LBS		POSITION ON PITCH	PREVIOUS CLUB
ARMIT	AINSLEY		17/06/83	BROXBURN	31/08/04	5	10	12	0	FORWARD	PUMPHERSTON JUNIORS
BAIRD	GARY		28/05/89	FALKIRK	22/07/04	5	7	8	7	DEFENDER	STENHOUSEMUIR FORM D U' 15
BAXTER	ANTHONY		11/02/88	GLASGOW	22/07/04	6	0	10	7	GOALKEEPER	STENHOUSEMUIR B.C.
BODEL	CRAIG		14/02/86	BANGOUR	14/05/04	5	8	11	9	DEFENDER	STENHOUSEMUIR FORM D U' 16
BOYCE	KIERAN		12/07/87	ALEXANDRIA	12/07/04	5	10	9	0	MIDFIELD	GLENLUSSET B.C.
COLLINS	LEE		03/02/74	BELLSHILL	07/06/04	5	8	11	0	MIDFIELD	STRANRAER
CONNOLLY	AIDAN		28/01/88	GLASGOW	22/07/04	5	6	10	7	MIDFIELD	RANGERS EAST B.C.
CRAIG	JAMIE	WILLIAM	23/07/86	STIRLING	11/05/04	6	0	11	7	MIDFIELD	STENHOUSEMUIR FORM D U' 16
CURWOOD	ROSS		22/06/86	FALKIRK	14/05/04	5	11	12	0	DEFENDER	BOTHKENNAR B.C.
DAVIDSON	RYAN		22/09/82	IRVINE	20/07/04	5	11	11	2	FORWARD	STIRLING ALBION
DESMOND	STEVEN		12/09/89	FALKIRK	22/07/04	5	7	8	7	FORWARD	STENHOUSEMUIR FORM D U' 15
DEVINE	CRAIG		07/09/89	BELLSHILL	22/07/04	5	8	8	11	DEFENDER	STENHOUSEMUIR FORM D U' 15
DOCHERTY	DEAN		24/05/88	GLASGOW	22/07/04	5	5	11	4	FORWARD	STENHOUSEMUIR B.C.
DOOLIN	LIAM		29/03/88	GLASGOW	22/07/04	5	10	10	0	MIDFIELD	STRATHKELVIN AMATEURS
EASTON	STEWART		10/10/81	COATBRIDGE	06/06/02	5	9	11	2	MIDFIELD	ALBION ROVERS
FALLON	STEVEN		08/05/79	PAISLEY	20/05/04	5	8.5	12	0	DEFENDER	QUEEN'S PARK
FRASER	MURRAY		09/08/88	EDINBURGH	22/07/04	5	9	9	7	MIDFIELD	TYNECASTLE HEARTS B.C.
GAHAGAN	KEVIN		18/09/88	GLASGOW	22/07/04	5	10	10	6	MIDFIELD	STENHOUSEMUIR B.C.
GARDINER	MARK	JOHN	10/03/85	IRVINE	31/08/04	5	8	10	5	MIDFIELD	ROSS COUNTY
GEMMELL	STEVEN		26/03/88	GLASGOW	22/07/04	6	1	12	7	DEFENDER	WEIRS RECREATION
GRIFFIN	KRISTOPHER		29/11/88	GLASGOW	22/07/04	5	9	11	2	FORWARD	STENHOUSEMUIR B.C.
HANLIN	DARREN		04/01/89	BELLSHILL	22/07/04	5	10	10	1	DEFENDER	STENHOUSEMUIR FORM D U' 1
HENDERSON	ROBBIE		11/10/82	BELLSHILL	09/06/04	6	1	13	2	DEFENDER	MORTON
HIGGINS	LIAM		27/10/89	GLASGOW	22/07/04	5	6	8	0	MIDFIELD	STENHOUSEMUIR FORM D U' 1
HILL	CRAIG		01/08/87	FALKIRK	20/05/04	6	5	13	6	DEFENDER	STENHOUSEMUIR B.C.
KERRIGAN	STEVEN		09/10/72	BELLSHILL	26/03/04	6	0	12	10	FORWARD	BERWICK RANGERS
KIRKHAM	JAMES		25/03/87	STIRLING	12/07/04	6	1	12	0	GOALKEEPER	SYNGENTA JUVENILES
KNOX	KEITH		06/08/64	STRANRAER	16/01/04	6	0	12	0	DEFENDER	GRETNA
LAUCHLAN	MARTIN	THOMAS	01/10/80	RUTHERGLEN	14/07/03	5	9	11	8	MIDFIELD	ST. JOHNSTONE
LEE	ANDREW		19/02/86	BELLSHILL	14/05/04	6	0	12	7	FORWARD	STENHOUSEMUIR FORM D U' 1
LYNN	CHRISTOPHER		12/09/88	GLASGOW	26/08/04	5	10	10	0	DEFENDER	HAMILTON ACADEMICAL
McINTOSH	EWAN		31/01/88	EDINBURGH	22/07/04	5	7	10	0	MIDFIELD	TYNECASTLE HEARTS
McVICAR	CAMERON		03/01/89	GERMANY	22/07/04	5	7	9	1	DEFENDER	BONNYBRIDGE B.C.
McBRIDE	JOHN	PAUL	28/11/78	HAMILTON	29/07/04	5	10	12	0	MIDFIELD	PARTICK THISTLE
McCAMBLEY	PAUL		09/04/87	GLASGOW	25/08/04	5	9	9	7	FORWARD	HILLINGTON Y.C.
McCULLOCH	GREIG		18/04/76	GIRVAN	30/06/03	5	8	11	7	DEFENDER	BRECHIN CITY
McCULLOCH	WILLIAM		02/04/73	BAILLIESTON	04/06/03	6	1	13	7	GOALKEEPER	STRANRAER
McGREGOR	STEVEN		08/02/82	DUNDEE	07/06/04	6	1	12	7	MIDFIELD	CAMPSIE BLACK WATCH
McGRILLEN	PAUL	ALEXANDER	19/08/71	GLASGOW	12/07/04	5	9	11	0	FORWARD	BELLSHILL JUNIORS
McINALLY	DAVID		03/03/81	GLASGOW	29/07/04	5	8	10	8	MIDFIELD	COWDENBEATH
McKEOWN	KEVIN		12/10/67	GLASGOW	10/06/04	6	1	14	0	GOALKEEPER	EAST FIFE
MENZIES	CRAIG		10/07/86	PAISLEY	14/05/04	5	10	11	0	MIDFIELD	STENHOUSEMUIR FORM D U'
MILES	CRAIG		10/07/87	GLASGOW	20/05/04	5	10	11	0	FORWARD	STENHOUSEMUIR B.C.
MORRISON	BRYAN		22/03/87	GLASGOW	20/05/04	5	8	11	13	DEFENDER	STENHOUSEMUIR B.C.
MORRISON	DAVID	JAMES	02/01/86	FALKIRK	09/07/03	6	1	10	7	MIDFIELD	STENHOUSEMUIR FORM D U'
MORRISON	LEE		22/03/87	GLASGOW	20/05/04	5	8	11	1	MIDFIELD	STENHOUSEMUIR FORM D U'
MORRISON	MARK		15/08/86	DUNFERMLINE	14/05/04	5	10	10	5	DEFENDER	STENHOUSEMUIR FORM D U'
MURPHY	PAUL	DAVID	01/08/85	PETERHEAD	14/05/02	6	1	11	0	MIDFIELD	CELTIC B.C.
NISBET	SEAN		26/09/86	GLASGOW	14/05/04	5	10	10	7	MIDFIELD	CAMPSIE BLACK WATCH
O'BOYLE	JAMIE		20/11/87	GLASGOW	12/07/04	5	11	10	10	DEFENDER	STENHOUSEMUIR B.C.
ORR	DAVID		25/08/87	GLASGOW	25/08/03	6	0	10	4	GOALKEEPER	STENHOUSEMUIR FORM D U'
REILLY	STEPHEN		01/06/86	FALKIRK	14/05/04	5	4	9	11	MIDFIELD	STENHOUSEMUIR FORM D U'
RODGERS	ANTON		30/08/88	GLASGOW	22/07/04	5	8	12	0	DEFENDER	STENHOUSEMUIR B.C.
SAVAGE	JOSEPH	GERARD	22/05/84	BELLSHILL	16/01/04	6	1	11	0	FORWARD	BO'NESS UNITED JNRS
SCOTT	ADAM		29/04/88	AYLESBURY	22/07/04	5	8	9	5	MIDFIELD	CALEY B.C.
SIMPSON	ANDREW		13/08/87	RUTHERGLEN	20/05/04	5	7	10	2	MIDFIELD	STENHOUSEMUIR FORM D U'
SINCLAIR	THOMAS		22/05/87	GLASGOW	08/08/03	5	8	12	2	MIDFIELD	STENHOUSEMUIR B.C.
SMITH	ANTHONY		28/10/73	BELLSHILL	04/06/03	5	8	11	7	DEF / MID	BERWICK RANGERS
SMITH	KIERAN		28/05/89	BELLSHILL	22/07/04	6	0	10	1	DEFENDER	STENHOUSEMUIR FORM D U'
STEWART	MARTIN		29/05/89	STIRLING	22/07/04	5	7	8	13	DEFENDER	STENHOUSEMUIR FORM D U'
STRUTHERS	KEVIN		15/01/86	GREENOCK	13/09/04	5	11	11	3	FORWARD	HEART OF MIDLOTHIAN
THOM	GARY		07/10/89	FALKIRK	22/07/04	5	9	9	5	FORWARD	STENHOUSEMUIR FORM D U'
VAUGHAN	KRIS	FRANCIS	05/08/86	DUNFERMLINE	14/09/04	6	1.5	13	0	DEFENDER	DUNFERMLINE ATHLETIC
VITA	DINO		22/05/86	EDINBURGH	09/07/03	5	4	9	10	FORWARD	HEART OF MIDLOTHIAN
WHITESIDE	IAIN		15/05/87	GLASGOW	20/05/04	5	10	10	4	MIDFIELD	STENHOUSEMUIR B.C.

TICKET INFORMATION

SEASON TICKET PRICES

SEATED	ADULT	£135
	JUVENILE/OAP/STUDENT	£70
	FAMILY FLEXI - ADD £60 FOR EACH ADDITIONAL ADULT & £30 FOR EACH ADDITIONAL OAP/JUVENILE (UP TO 4 PERSONS) TO FULL PRICE SEASON TICKET	

LEAGUE ADMISSION PRICES

SEATED	ADULT	£9
	JUVENILE/OAP	£5
STANDING	ADULT	£8
	JUVENILE/OAP	£4

THE WARRIORS' 10 YEAR LEAGUE RECORD

SEASON	DIV	P	W	D	L	F	A	PTS
1994-95	S	36	14	14	8	46	39	56
1995-96	S	36	14	7	15	51	49	49
1996-97	S	36	11	11	14	49	43	44
1997-98	S	36	10	10	16	44	53	40
1998-99	T	36	19	7	10	62	42	64
1999-00	S	36	10	8	18	44	59	38
2000-01	S	36	12	6	18	45	63	42
2001-02	S	36	8	12	16	33	57	36
2002-03	S	36	12	11	13	49	51	47
2003-04	S	36	7	4	25	28	65	25

SEASON STATS 2003/04

Player columns (left to right): McCULLOCH W., HAMILTON S., McKENNA G., TULLY C., GAUGHAN K., BOOTH M., McCULLOCH G., McKENZIE J., BROWN A., McDOWELL M., LAUCHLAN M., CRAWFORD B., JOHNSTONE D., SMITH A., McGOWAN M., McCLOY B., DONNELLY K., CARR D., HARTY M., MALLAN S., BONAR P., McQUILTER R., CAIRNEY C., HARDIE A., MURPHY S., FLANNERY P., SCOTT C., WALDIE C., MILLER C., MURPHY P., KNOX J., KNOX K., COSGROVE S., KERRIGAN S., CRAIG J., MORRISON D., SAVAGE J., SINCLAIR T., EASTON S.

DATE	VENUE	OPPONENTS	ATT	RES
-AUG	A	EAST FIFE	568	2 - 3
-AUG	H	MORTON	1,343	0 - 2
-AUG	A	ALLOA ATHLETIC	447	†2 - 2
-AUG	H	FORFAR ATHLETIC	383	2 - 0
-SEP	A	HAMILTON ACADEMICAL	934	0 - 2
-SEP	H	BERWICK RANGERS	393	0 - 3
-SEP	A	DUMBARTON	730	1 - 0
-OCT	H	ARBROATH	344	†1 - 0
-OCT	A	AIRDRIE UNITED	1,406	0 - 2
-OCT	A	MORTON	2,880	2 - 5
-NOV	H	EAST FIFE	532	3 - 0
-NOV	H	HAMILTON ACADEMICAL	576	0 - 3
-NOV	A	FORFAR ATHLETIC	478	0 - 2
-NOV	A	BERWICK RANGERS	330	1 - 2
-DEC	H	DUMBARTON	447	1 - 1
-DEC	A	ARBROATH	402	1 - 2
-DEC	A	AIRDRIE UNITED	1,005	0 - 1
-JAN	H	ALLOA ATHLETIC	402	1 - 3
-JAN	A	EAST FIFE	536	0 - 1
-JAN	H	BERWICK RANGERS	337	3 - 1
-FEB	A	HAMILTON ACADEMICAL	1,111	1 - 0
-FEB	H	FORFAR ATHLETIC	335	0 - 2
-FEB	A	AIRDRIE UNITED	1,324	0 - 4
-MAR	H	MORTON	1,217	0 - 1
-MAR	A	ALLOA ATHLETIC	444	0 - 1
-MAR	A	DUMBARTON	552	0 - 4
-MAR	A	FORFAR ATHLETIC	407	1 - 1
-MAR	H	ARBROATH	307	0 - 3
-APR	H	DUMBARTON	387	1 - 2
-APR	H	HAMILTON ACADEMICAL	296	0 - 2
-APR	H	BERWICK RANGERS	392	0 - 3
-APR	H	AIRDRIE UNITED	1,197	0 - 3
-APR	A	ARBROATH	511	1 - 1
-MAY	H	ALLOA ATHLETIC	480	0 - 1
-MAY	A	MORTON	3,456	4 - 1
-MAY	H	EAST FIFE	826	0 - 1

TOTAL FULL APPEARANCES: 34 24 17 6 15 23 13 16 27 2 21 1 1 21 9 4 4 18 19 5 7 8 2 10 5 11 6 18 17 3 11 5 3 5 3

TOTAL SUB APPEARANCES: 3 5 1 5 3 5 7 3 2 3 1 2 1 7 13 1 5 2 3 4 1 1 1 3 5 1 1 2 1 1

TOTAL GOALS SCORED: 2 3 5 1 1 1 2 2 1 1 4 1 2

bold figures denote goalscorers. † denotes opponent's own goal.

MILESTONES:

YEAR OF FORMATION: 1884

MOST LEAGUE POINTS IN A SEASON:
50 (Division 2 – Season 1960/61) (2 Points for a Win)
64 (Second Division – Season 1998/99) (3 Points for a Win)

MOST LEAGUE GOALS SCORED BY A PLAYER IN A SEASON:
Evelyn Morrison (Season 1927/28) and
Robert Murray (Season 1936/37)

NO. OF GOALS SCORED: 31

RECORD ATTENDANCE: 12,500 (-v- East Fife – 11.3.1950)

RECORD VICTORY: 9-2 (-v- Dundee United – Division 2, 16.4.1937)

RECORD DEFEAT: 2-11 (-v- Dunfermline Athletic – Division 2, 27.9.1930)

STENHOUSEMUIR PLAYING KITS SEASON 2004/05

FIRST KIT   SECOND KIT   THIRD KIT

Albion Rovers: Cliftonhill Stadium

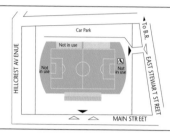

The following routes can be used to reach Cliftonhill Stadium:
BUSES: The ground is conveniently situated on the main Glasgow–Airdrie bus route and there is a stop near the ground. Local buses serving most areas of Coatbridge and Airdrie pass the ground every few minutes.
TRAINS: The nearest railway station is Coatdyke on the Glasgow–Airdrie line and the ground is a ten minute walk from there. The frequency of service is 15 minutes.
CARS: Vehicles may park in Hillcrest Avenue, Albion Street and East Stewart Street, which are all adjacent to the ground.

CAPACITY: 1,238; Seated 538, Standing 700
PITCH DIMENSIONS: 110 yds x 72 yds
FACILITIES FOR DISABLED SUPPORTERS:
Access from East Stewart Street with toilet facilities and space for wheelchairs, cars etc. Advanced contact with club advised – this area is uncovered.

Cowdenbeath: Central Park

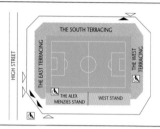

You can get to Central Park by the following routes:
TRAINS: There is a regular service of trains from Edinburgh and Glasgow (via Edinburgh) which call at Cowdenbeath and the station is only 400 yards from the ground.
BUSES: A limited Edinburgh-Cowdenbeath service stops just outside the ground on matchdays and a frequent service of Dunfermline–Ballingry buses also stop outside the ground, as does the Edinburgh-Glenrothes service.
CARS: Car parking facilities are available in the public car park adjacent to the ground for 190 cars. There are also another 300 spaces at the Stenhouse Street car park, which is 200 yards from the ground.

CAPACITY: 4,370; Seated 1,431, Standing 2,939
PITCH DIMENSIONS: 107 yds x 65 yds
FACILITIES FOR DISABLED SUPPORTERS:
Direct access from car park into designated area within ground. Toilet and catering facilities also provided.

East Fife: First 2 Finance Bayview Stadium

The First 2 Finance Bayview Stadium can be reached by the following routes:
TRAINS: The nearest railway station is Kirkcaldy (8 miles away), and fans will have to catch an inter-linking bus service from just outside the station to the ground.
BUSES: A regular service from Kirkcaldy to Leven passes close to the ground, as does the Leven to Dunfermline service. The Leven bus terminus is approximately ²/₃ mile from the ground (5 minutes walk).
CARS: There are Car Parking facilities available for both Home and Away fans at the ground.

CAPACITY: 1,992 (All Seated)
PITCH DIMENSIONS: 115 yds x 75 yds
FACILITIES FOR DISABLED SUPPORTERS:
Area available at both Home & Away Sections of the Stand. Spaces for 12 wheelchairs

East Stirlingshire: Firs Park

The following routes may be used to reach Firs Park:
TRAINS: Passengers should alight at Grahamston Station and the ground is then five minutes walk.
BUSES: All buses running from the town centre pass close by the ground. The Grangemouth via Burnbank Road and Tamfourhill via Kennard Street services both stop almost outside the ground.
CARS: Car parking is available in the adjacent side streets. There are also spaces available in the car park adjacent to the major stores around the ground.

CAPACITY: 781; Seated 245, Standing 536
PITCH DIMENSIONS: 108 yds x 71 yds
FACILITIES FOR DISABLED SUPPORTERS:
By prior arrangement with Secretary.

Elgin City: Borough Briggs

Borough Briggs can be reached by the following routes:
TRAINS: Elgin Railway Station is situated approximately one mile south of the stadium. Regular connections to and from Aberdeen and Inverness.
BUSES: Elgin Bus Station is situated in the town centre, which is only half a mile from Borough Briggs. Regular connections to and from Aberdeen and Inverness.
CARS: Elgin is situated on the A96, 38 miles east of Inverness and 67 miles west of Aberdeen. From the south, leave A9 at Aviemore and take the A95 as far as Craigellachie then take A941 to Elgin.

CAPACITY: 4,962; Seated 480, Standing 4,482
PITCH DIMENSIONS: 111 yds x 72 yds
FACILITIES FOR DISABLED SUPPORTERS:
An area is designated in the south east enclosure.

Gretna: Raydale Park

Raydale Park can be reached by the following routes:
BUSES: Buses between Carlisle and Annan and Dumfries serve Gretna.
TRAINS: Gretna Station is on the Glasgow–Carlisle line. Raydale Park is approximately one mile south-west of the station.
CARS: From the North: Leave M74 at sign for Old Blacksmith's Shop Visitor sign (B7076). Go through Springholm into Gretna Green. Turn left and left again. Go through traffic lights into Gretna. Through roundabout take B721 at Crossways Inn. After ¼ mile turn left into Dominion Road. Raydale Park is on your right. From the South: 8 miles north of Carlisle look for the Old Blacksmith's Shop Visitor Centre sign. Take B7076 to Gretna. In Gretna turn left at Crossways Inn and go on the Annan Road for ¼ mile. Turn left into Dominion Road and Raydale Park is on your right. From the West: Leave A75 at sign for Gretna (B721). Turn left into Gretna and right into Dominion Road. Raydale Park is on your right.

GRETNA F.C.

CAPACITY: 2,200; Seated 450, Standing 1,750
PITCH DIMENSIONS: 113 yds x 74 yds
FACILITIES FOR DISABLED SUPPORTERS:
Toilets and ramps in place. Further information available from Secretary.

Montrose: Links Park

Links Park can be reached by the following routes:
TRAINS: Montrose is on the Inter-City 125 route from London to Aberdeen and also on the Glasgow–Aberdeen route. There is a regular service and the station is about 15 minutes walk from the ground.
BUSES: An hourly service of buses from Aberdeen and Dundee stop in the town centre and it is a 15 minute walk from here to the ground.
CARS: Car parking is available in the car park at the ground and there are numerous side streets all round the park which can be used if necessary.

CAPACITY: 3,292; Seated 1,334, Standing 1,958
PITCH DIMENSIONS: 113 yds x 68 yds
FACILITIES FOR DISABLED SUPPORTERS:
Area set aside for wheelchairs and designated area in new stand.

Peterhead: Balmoor Stadium

Balmoor Stadium can be reached by the following routes:
TRAINS: The nearest train station is Aberdeen. From Aberdeen you would have to travel by bus to Peterhead. Travel time 1 hour.
BUSES: Buses leave Aberdeen city centre every hour for Peterhead. Travel time 1 hour.
CARS: From Aberdeen city centre: Take A90 to Peterhead, at first roundabout approaching Peterhead take a left at McDonalds to St. Fergus (still on A90). Continue on this road to next roundabout – go straight on to the next T-junction. Take right A980 back into Peterhead – continue on A980 through next roundabout and Balmoor Stadium is about ½ mile past the roundabout on the right hand side.

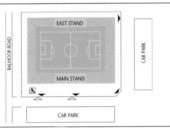

CAPACITY: 3,150; Seated 990, Standing 2,160
PITCH DIMENSIONS: 105 yds x 70 yds
FACILITIES FOR DISABLED SUPPORTERS:
Designated area in new stand.
Lift at main entrance for access to Main Stand.

Queen's Park FC: The National Stadium, Hampden Park

The following routes may be used to reach The National Stadium, Hampden Park:
TRAINS: There are two stations within five minutes walk of the ground. Mount Florida Station, on the Cathcart Circle, and King's Park Station. A 15 minute service runs from Glasgow Central.
BUSES: Services to approach Mount Florida end of Stadium: From City Centre: 5, 5A, 5B, M5, M14, 31, 37, 66, 66A, 66B, 66C; From Govan Cross: 34; From Drumchapel: 96, 97, Circular Service: 89, 90; G.C.T. Service: 1; Services to approach King's Park end of Stadium; From City Centre: 12, 12A, 74; Circular Service: 89, 90; G.C.T. Service: 19.
CARS: Car and Coach parking facilities are available in the car park in Letherby Drive, which is capable of holding 200 vehicles. Side streets can also be used. Free car parking at all Queen's Park matches.

CAPACITY: 52,025 (All Seated)
PITCH DIMENSIONS: 115 yds x 75 yds
FACILITIES FOR DISABLED SUPPORTERS:
Disabled facilities are situated in the BT Scotland Stand as follows: West Front (44 places & 44 helpers), West Section A (21 places & 21 helpers), Ambulant/Blind (55 places), East Front (44 places & 44 helpers), East Section G (21 places & 21 helpers), Ambulant/Blind (55 places)

Stenhousemuir: Ochilview Park

Ochilview Park can be reached by the following routes:
TRAINS: The nearest station is Larbert, which is about 1 mile away from the ground.
BUSES: There are regular bus services from Falkirk.
CARS: There is a large car park on the north side of the ground.

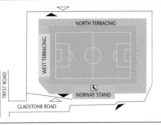

CAPACITY: 3,776; Seated 626, Standing 3,150
PITCH DIMENSIONS: 110 yds x 72 yds
FACILITIES FOR DISABLED SUPPORTERS:
Accommodation for disabled in Norway Stand.
Toilet facilities also provided.

LORENZO AMORUSO

Scottish Football 2003/2004
Month by Month Review

JULY

Lorenzo Amoruso leaves Rangers to sign for Blackburn Rovers in a £1.4 million deal.

Former Scotland striker Scott Booth rejoins Aberdeen from Dutch club Twente Enschede.

Vitesse Arnhem sign Dutch defender Bert Konterman on a free transfer from Rangers.

Dundee United sign Scotland midfielder Derek McInnes from West Bromwich Albion.

Coventry City sign Scotland Under-21 goalkeeper Scott Shearer from Albion Rovers for a nominal fee.

Dunfermline Athletic recruit brothers Darren and Derek Young from Aberdeen under Freedom of Movement.

Rangers sign Georgian international Zurab Khizanishvili on a three year contract from Dundee.

Hearts sign Australian defender Patrick Kisnorbo from South Melbourne.

Celtic defeat Lithuanian Champions FBK Kaunas 4-0 away from home in the first leg of their Champions League Second Qualifying Round tie.

Dundee sign Trinidad and Tobago defender Brent Sancho from Portland Timbers.

AUGUST

DARREN FLETCHER

Italian defender Paolo Vanoli signs for Rangers on a free transfer from Bologna.

Scotland winger Neil McCann leaves Rangers to sign for Southampton in a £1.5 million deal.

Rangers sign veteran Norwegian international defender Henning Berg on a free transfer from Blackburn Rovers.

Celtic defeat FBK Kaunas 1-0 at Parkhead to complete a 5-0 aggregate victory in their Champions League Second Qualifying Round tie.

Hibernian sign former Scotland midfielder Stephen Glass from Watford.

Rangers are held to a 1-1 draw at Ibrox by FC Copenhagen in the first leg of their Champions League Third Qualifying Round tie. Celtic all but book their place in the group stage of the tournament by beating MTK Hungaria 4-0 in Budapest.

Dundee celebrate their return to major European club competitions after a 29-year absence by defeating Vllaznia Shkoder 2-0 in Albania in the first leg of their UEFA Cup Qualifying Round tie.

Celtic's Republic of Ireland international midfielder Colin Healy joins Sunderland under Freedom of Movement.

Scotland's Under-21 side lose 3-1 to Norway in Skien in a friendly international after Simon Lynch had put them in front.

Manchester United's teenage midfielder Darren Fletcher makes his senior debut for Scotland in a 0-0 draw against Norway in Oslo in a friendly international.

Shota Arveldaze's late goal earns Rangers a 2-1 win over FC Copenhagen in Denmark, clinching a 3-2 Champions League Third Qualifying Round aggregate victory for the Scottish Champions. Celtic join them in the group stage of the tournament as they beat MTK Hungaria 1-0 at Parkhead to conclude a 5-0 aggregate success.

Dundee crush Vllaznia Shkoder 4-0 at Dens Park in the second leg of their UEFA Cup Qualifying Round tie for a 6-0 aggregate win.

Barry Ferguson leaves Rangers to sign for Blackburn Rovers in a record transfer fee for a Scottish player of £7.5 million.

Rangers sign Brazilian midfielder Emerson on a free transfer from Atletico Madrid and Norwegian striker Egil Ostenstad from Blackburn Rovers.

CELTIC'S CHRIS SUTTON HEADS HOME AGAINST MTK HUNGARIA TO SECURE A CHAMPIONS LEAGUE SPOT

Transfers in July:

David Winters (Dundee United to Ross County), Ian Johnson (Montrose to Brechin City), Martin Bavidge (Forfar Athletic to Peterhead), Peter Weatherson (Queen of the South to Morton), John Stark (Queen's Park to Morton), Ludovic Roy (St. Mirren to Ayr United), Mark Peat (Aberdeen to Arbroath), Iain Nicolson (Ayr United to Alloa Athletic), Ross Matheson (Raith Rovers to Cowdenbeath), Ryan McMullan (Albion Rovers to Elgin City), Steven McIntyre (St. Johnstone to Clyde), Greig McCulloch (Brechin City to Stenhousemuir), Mark Kerr (Falkirk to Dundee United), Craig Hinchcliffe (Arbroath to St. Mirren), Paul Hampshire (Raith Rovers to Berwick Rangers), Graham Guy (St. Mirren to Stranraer), David Greenhill (St. Johnstone to Clyde), Bryan Gilfillan (Inverness Caledonian Thistle to Cowdenbeath), Steven Ferguson (Ross County to Ayr United), Kevin McGowne (Partick Thistle to St. Mirren), Gus MacPherson (Dunfermline Athletic to St. Mirren), David Farrell (Stranraer to Albion Rovers), Robert Coulter (Stenhousemuir to Elgin City), Graeme Stewart (Inverness Caledonian Thistle to Peterhead), Collin Samuel (Falkirk to Dundee United), Owen Coyle (Falkirk to Dundee United), Martin Lauchlan (St. Johnstone to Stenhousemuir), Greig Denham (St. Mirren to Arbroath), James Allan (Queen's Park to Gretna), Martin Wood (Ross County to Montrose), David Ormiston (Gretna to East Stirlingshire), Kevin McCann (Dumbarton to East Stirlingshire), Jim Butter (East Fife to Montrose), Mark Roberts (St. Mirren to Airdrie United), David Bagan (Inverness Caledonian Thistle to Queen of the South), Neil McLean (Forfar Athletic to Elgin City), Steven McCormick (Stenhousemuir to Elgin City), Jon Tully (Rangers to Stenhousemuir), Colin Stewart (Kilmarnock to Ross County), James Sharp (Hartlepool United to Falkirk), Calvin Shand (Hibernian to Cowdenbeath), Kieran Ritchie (Dundee to Raith Rovers), Bruce Raffell (Dundee United to Raith Rovers), Scott McLean (St. Mirren to Stirling Albion), Jamie McCunnie (Dundee United to Ross County), David Martin (Rangers to St. Mirren), Danny Lennon (Partick Thistle to Gretna), Steve Florence (Arbroath to Forfar Athletic), Derek Anderson (Queen of the South to Stirling Albion), John McKeown (Dumbarton to Cowdenbeath), Jamie McGowan (St. Mirren to Alloa Athletic), Stewart McCarthy (Dundee United to Arbroath), Stephen Cole (East Stirlingshire to Alloa Athletic), Graeme McCheyne (Montrose to East Fife), Brian Fairbairn (Gretna to East Fife), Barry Elliot (Partick Thistle to Stirling Albion), Eddie Annand (Ayr United to St. Mirren), Kevin Twaddle (Hearts to St. Mirren), John Sutton (Leicester City to Raith Rovers), Jay Stein (Stenhousemuir to Brechin City), Steven Reilly (Stirling Albion to Queen's Park), Mark Peers (Liverpool to Raith Rovers), Marc McCulloch (St. Johnstone to Brechin City), Kieran McAnespie (Plymouth Argyle to Falkirk), John Fitter (Wolverhampton Wanderers to Hamilton Academical), Paul Bernard (Plymouth Argyle to St. Johnstone), Paul Shields (Clyde to Forfar Athletic), Stephen McAuley (Airdrie Utd to Queen's Park), Steven Kerrigan (Stirling Albion to Arbroath), David Holdsworth (Scarborough to Gretna), Iain Good (Forfar Athletic to Peterhead), Lee Miller (Falkirk to Bristol City), Chris Kerr (St. Mirren to Ayr United), Gary Cohen (Scarborough to Gretna), Andy Tod (Bradford City to Dunfermline Athletic).

Transfers in August:

Kevin Muscat (Rangers to Millwall), Garry Wood (Berwick Rangers to Queen of the South), Duncan Stewart (Dunfermline Athletic to Peterhead), Richard Prokas (Workington Town to Gretna), Paul O'Neill (Workington Town to Gretna), Stephen O'Donnell (Dundee United to Ross County), Darren Miller (Hamilton Academical to Airdrie United), Paul McLaughlin (Hearts to Alloa Athletic), Stephen McKenna (Rangers to Airdrie United), Thomas McHard (Livingston to St. Mirren), Kieran McGuinness (Dundee to Peterhead), Jamie MacDonald (Livingston to Stranraer), Jason Lee (Peterborough United to Falkirk), Jim Hamilton (Dunfermline Athletic to Ross County), Patrick Kelly (Partick Thistle to East Fife), Robert Duncan (Aberdeen to Peterhead), Simon Donnelly (Sheffield Wednesday to St. Johnstone), Leslie Byle (Hibernian to East Fife), Stuart McKechnie (Morton to Gretna), James McCaig (Queen of the South to Gretna), Mark Simpson (Peterhead to Montrose), Jamie Bain (Cowdenbeath to Gretna), Derek Anderson (Clyde to Hamilton Academical), David Zdrilic (Walsall to Aberdeen), Andy Smith (Raith Rovers to Clyde), Stephen Manson (Hibernian to Falkirk), Sean Lynch (Livingston to Falkirk), Scott Michie (Aberdeen to Montrose), Paul Macaloney (Livingston to Falkirk), Marc Graham (Cowdenbeath to East Fife), Ryan Davidson (Hearts to Stirling Albion), Kevin Bracks (Hibernian to Berwick Rangers), David Nicholls (Dunfermline Athletic to Falkirk), Brian Reid (Falkirk to Queen of the South), Daniel Noon (St. Johnstone to Berwick Rangers), Steven McDougall (Rangers to Airdrie United), Barry Grant (Motherwell to Airdrie United), Adam Moffat (Raith Rovers to Cowdenbeath), Tony Mitchell (Queen's Park to Arbroath), Paul Browne (Nuneaton Borough to Arbroath), Colin Waldie (Stenhousemuir to Berwick Rangers), Andy McLaren (Kilmarnock to Dundee United), Murray Watson (Aberdeen to Alloa Athletic), Daniel Ogunmade (Dundee United to Forfar Athletic), Ryan McCann (Celtic to Hartlepool United), Chris Innes (Kilmarnock to Dundee United).

JAMES McFADDEN

SEPTEMBER

Scotland striker James McFadden leaves Motherwell to join Everton in a £1.5 million deal. Former England full-back Michael Gray joins Celtic on a four month loan contract from Sunderland.

Scotland defeat the Faroe Islands 3–1 at Hampden in a European Championship qualifier with goals from Neil McCann, Paul Dickov and James McFadden.

Shaun Maloney scores the only goal of the game as Scotland's Under–21 side claim an impressive European Under–21 Championship qualifying victory over Germany in Ahlen.

Scotland's hopes of winning their European Championship Qualifying Group are all but extinguished when they lose 2–1 to Germany in Dortmund. Neil McCann scores after the Germans take a 2–0 lead.

Dundee sign former Scotland midfielder Craig Burley and Italian striker Fabrizio Ravanelli on free transfers from Derby County.

Rangers open their Champions League Group E campaign with a dramatic 2–1 win over VfB Stuttgart at Ibrox, Peter Lovenkrands claiming a late winner.

Celtic lose 2–1 to Bayern Munich in Germany in their first match in Group A of the Champions League after taking the lead through Alan Thompson.

Hearts defeat Bosnian side Zeljeznicar 2–0 at Tynecastle in the first leg of their UEFA Cup First

HOLLAND V SCOTLAND

Round tie. Dundee lose 2–1 to Perugia at Dens Park in the first leg of their UEFA Cup First Round tie. Alex McLeish signs a contract extension as Rangers manager, taking his agreement through to the summer of 2007.

Goals from Liam Miller and Chris Sutton give Celtic a 2–0 win over Lyon at Parkhead in their second Champions League Group A fixture.

Transfers in September:

Barry Wilson (Livingston to Inverness Caledonian Thistle), Gordon Greer (Blackburn Rovers to Kilmarnock), William McCann (Dundee United to Raith Rovers), Alan Inglis (Carlisle United to Falkirk), William Freeman (Charlton Athletic to Falkirk), Daniel Dunglinson (Carlisle United to Falkirk), Jason Dair (Dunfermline Athletic to Motherwell), Andy McDermott (Northern Spirit to Dunfermline Athletic).

OCTOBER

Rangers draw 1–1 with Panathinaikos in Athens to lead Group E of the Champions League after two matches.

Celtic win the opening Old Firm SPL derby of the season with John Hartson scoring the only goal of the game at Ibrox.

John Brownlie resigns as manager of Arbroath with the club second from bottom of the Bell's Second Division.

Stephen Hughes scores twice in stoppage time as Scotland's Under-21's secure a dramatic 3-2 win over Lithuania at McDiarmid Park. The Scots trailed 2-0 with just 11 minutes remaining but snatched the victory they needed to claim a European Under-21 Championship Play-Off place.

Scotland clinch a European Championship Qualifying Play-Off place when they defeat Lithuania 1-0 at Hampden with a goal from substitute Darren Fletcher.

Marcio Maximo Barcellos resigns as manager of Livingston after just nine games in charge of the club. He is replaced by former manager Davie Hay. Hearts reach the Second Round of the UEFA Cup, a goalless draw against Zeljeznicar in Bosnia earning a 2-0 aggregate First Round win for the Edinburgh club. Dundee are knocked out of the UEFA Cup in the First Round, losing 1-0 to Perugia in Italy to go out 3-1 on aggregate.

Celtic slip to another away defeat in the Champions League, losing 1-0 to Anderlecht in Brussels despite the Belgian side being reduced to 10 men.

Manchester United manager Sir Alex Ferguson enjoys his return to Ibrox as a Phil Neville goal gives his team a 1-0 win over Rangers in the Champions League.

John Sheran is dismissed as manager of Montrose with the club struggling in the bottom half of the Bell's Third Division.

Inverness Caledonian Thistle win The Bell's Cup by defeating Airdrie United 2-0 at McDiarmid Park with David Bingham and Steven Hislop scoring the vital goals for Caley Thistle.

Transfers in October:

Graeme Bunyan (Rangers to Ayr United), Steven Nicholas (Stirling Albion to East Fife), Adrian Madaschi (Atalanta Bergamo to Partick Thistle), Elliott Smith (Hearts to Montrose).

NOVEMBER

Rangers hopes of progress in the Champions League recede dramatically when they are comprehensively beaten 3-0 at Old Trafford by Manchester United.

Celtic retain genuine hope of reaching the knock-out phase of the Champions League when they defeat Anderlecht 3-1 at Parkhead.

Hearts record one of their most impressive results away from home in Europe when they defeat Bordeaux 1-0 in France in the first leg of their UEFA Cup Second Round tie.

James McFadden scores the only goal of an enthralling match at Hampden as Scotland defeat Holland 1-0 in the first leg of their European Championship Qualifying Play-Off.

Scotland's Under-21 side lose 2-0 away to Croatia in the first leg of their European Under-21 Championship Qualifying Play-Off.

Terry Christie resigns as manager of Alloa Athletic after five consecutive defeats leave the club at the bottom of the Bell's Second Division.

Garry O'Connor of Hibernian scores on his home ground but a 1-0 win over Croatia at Easter Road is not enough for Scotland's Under-21's to reach the European Under-21 Championship Finals as they lose 2-1 on aggregate.

Tom Hendrie is named as the new manager of Alloa Athletic, starting his second spell in charge of the club.

Scotland suffer a humiliating record European Championship defeat when they are crushed 6-0 by Holland in the second leg of their Play-Off tie at the Amsterdam ArenA.

Henry Hall is appointed as the new manager of Montrose.

Dundee become the second Bank of Scotland Premierleague club to be placed in administration. Celtic drop points at home in the Champions League group stage for the first time, frustrated in a goalless draw with Bayern Munich.

John Coughlin resigns as manager of St. Mirren with the club third from bottom of the Bell's First Division.

Dundee United player/coach Owen Coyle joins Airdrie United on loan for the rest of the season.

Rangers lose 1-0 to VfB Stuttgart in Germany to end their hopes of reaching the last 16 of the Champions League.

Hearts become the first Scottish club to lose a European tie having won the first leg away from home. They lose the second leg of their UEFA Cup Second Round tie 2-0 to Bordeaux at Tynecastle to go out of the tournament 2-1 on aggregate. Partick Thistle dismiss manager Gerry Collins with the club at the foot of the SPL following 10 consecutive defeats.

Transfers in November:

Gary Young (Celtic to Queen's Park), Grant Chisholm (Clyde to Queen's Park), Richard White (Rangers to Dumbarton), Goran Zujovic (Dundee to Forfar Athletic), Stuart Irvine (Livingston to East Stirlingshire), Andy Goram (Queen of the South to Elgin City), Ryan Boyd (Ayr United to Gretna), Jim McQueen (Alloa Athletic to East Fife), Jamie Buchan (Partick Thistle to Stockport County), Craig Tully (Stenhousemuir to Elgin City), Tom Cowan (Dundee to Carlisle United), Jamie Langfield (Dundee to Raith Rovers).

DECEMBER

Peter Hetherston resigns as manager of Albion

Rovers after being sent to the stand for foul and abusive language during a Scottish Cup First Round defeat to Montrose.

Rangers are unable to claim even the consolation of a UEFA Cup place, finishing bottom of Champions League Group E following a 3-1 home defeat to Panathinaikos.

Steve Kirk is named as the new manager of Arbroath, having been in caretaker charge since John Brownlie's resignation the previous month.

Celtic suffer a sixth consecutive away defeat in the Champions League, a controversial late penalty kick seeing them lose 3-2 to Lyon in France. They finish third in Group A to salvage a place in the UEFA Cup.

Kevin McAllister is named as the new player/manager of Albion Rovers.

Rangers announce they have signed a pre-contract agreement with French defender Jean-Alain Boumsong who will join them from Auxerre in six months time.

Gus MacPherson is appointed player/manager of St. Mirren. Partick Thistle name Gerry Britton and Derek Whyte as their new joint player/managers. The duo had been in temporary charge since the dismissal of Gerry Collins.

Rangers sign Scotland midfielder Gavin Rae from Dundee for £250,000.

Ian Wilson is dismissed as manager of Peterhead with the club sitting in fourth place in the Bell's Third Division.

Transfers in December:

Iain Diack (Albion Rovers to Arbroath), Lee Hardy (Leigh RMI to Ayr United), Paul Ross (Albion Rovers to St. Mirren), Craig O'Reilly (Berwick Rangers to Raith Rovers), Steven Kerrigan (Arbroath to Berwick Rangers), Alan Gourlay (Rangers to St. Mirren), Youssef Rossi (Dunfermline Athletic to Raja Casablanca), Andy Rodgers (Falkirk to Dumbarton), Marc McCulloch (Brechin City to Arbroath).

JANUARY

Celtic take a commanding 11 point lead at the top of the SPL after a 3-0 win over Rangers at Parkhead in the second Old Firm League derby of the season.

Celtic are stunned when their Republic of Ireland midfielder Liam Miller signs a pre-contract agreement with Manchester United.

Scotland midfielder Stephen Pearson leaves Motherwell to join Celtic in a £350,000 deal.

Iain Stewart is named as the new player/manager of Peterhead with goalkeeper Paul Mathers as his assistant.

John McVeigh is dismissed as manager of Stenhousemuir after five consecutive defeats

leave the club at the bottom of the Bell's Second Division. Rangers sign veteran Dutch international defender Frank de Boer on a free transfer from Galatasaray for the rest of the season.

Celtic allow their Swedish international goalkeeper Magnus Hedman to join Italian club Ancona on loan for the rest of the season.

Scotland defender Stephen Crainey leaves Celtic to join Southampton for a fee of around £400,000.

FEBRUARY

Des McKeown and Tony Smith are named as the new co-managers of Stenhousemuir.

Derek Lilley's last minute penalty kick earns Livingston a 1-0 win over Dundee at Easter Road in The CIS Insurance Cup Semi-Final, taking the West Lothian club into the first major Final of their history.

Livingston are placed into administration, the third SPL club to suffer such a fate, the day after their CIS Insurance Cup Semi-Final victory over Dundee.

Hibernian win a dramatic penalty shoot-out against Rangers at Hampden, after the sides had drawn 1-1 after extra-time, to claim a place in the Final of The CIS Insurance Cup.

Rangers impose a £10,000 fine on their Dutch international Fernando Ricksen for elbowing Hibernian striker Derek Riordan in the face during the Semi-Final at Hampden.

Scotland Under-21's lose 2-1 to Hungary in a friendly international at Livingston. Shaun Maloney had given the Scots the lead from the penalty spot.

Wales inflict a humiliating record 4-0 defeat on Scotland in a friendly international at the Millennium Stadium in Cardiff to intensify the pressure on national coach Berti Vogts.

Celtic set a new British record of 24 consecutive League victories in a single season when they defeat Partick Thistle 4-1 at Firhill, breaking the previous mark of 23 set by Morton in the old Second Division in season 1963/64.

The SPL announce that Irish-based satellite broadcaster Setanta has won the rights to exclusive live coverage of their fixtures for four years from the start of season 2004/05.

Celtic defeat Czech side Teplice 3-0 at Parkhead in the first leg of their UEFA Cup Third Round tie.

Transfers in February:

James McKenzie (Stenhousemuir to Elgin City), Nicky Wettner (Tottenham Hotspur to Gretna), Jamie Stevenson (Real Mallorca to Alloa Athletic), Paul Ronald (Airdrie United to Dumbarton), George Paterson (Morton to Stirling Albion), Chris Newall (Arbroath to East Stirlingshire), Steven Miller (Livingston to Ayr

Transfers in January:

Kevin Fotheringham (Brechin City to Clyde), Graeme Brown (Cowdenbeath to Ayr United), Ryan Blackadder (Raith Rovers to Hamilton Academical), Brian Wake (Carlisle United to Gretna), Phil O'Donnell (Sheffield Wednesday to Motherwell), Stuart McCluskey (St. Johnstone to Clyde), Jim Lauchlan (Livingston to Ross County), Chris Kerr (Ayr United to Albion Rovers), Lee Collins (Morecambe to Stranraer), Kevin Christie (Falkirk to Airdrie United), Ryan Baldacchino (Carlisle United to Gretna), Andy Millen (Clyde to St. Mirren), Colin Waldie (Berwick Rangers to Stenhousemuir), Stuart Taylor (Partick Thistle to St. Johnstone), Dene Shields (Brechin City to Cowdenbeath), Stephen Payne (Aberdeen to Queen of the South), Jamie McQuilken (Aberdeen to St. Johnstone), Danny Griffin (Dundee United to Stockport County), Dave Stewart (Forfar Athletic to Queen's Park), Jay Stein (Brechin City to East Fife), Chris Miller (East Fife to Stenhousemuir), Fabrizio Ravanelli (Dundee to Perugia), Gary Bollan (Dundee United to Motherwell), Scott Walker (Dunfermline Athletic to Hartlepool United), Dean Jones (Stenhousemuir to Raith Rovers), Keith Knox (Gretna to Stenhousemuir), James Herkes (Arbroath to East Fife), Jamie Doyle (Leicester City to Ayr United), Jamie Langfield (Raith Rovers to Partick Thistle), Eric Deloumeaux (Aberdeen to Coventry City), Derek Townsley (Oxford United to Gretna), Gary Richardson (Raith Rovers to Albion Rovers), Jamie McCaig (Gretna to Albion Rovers), Mark Haddow (Raith Rovers to Albion Rovers), Matthew Carr (Celtic to Albion Rovers), Peter Canero (Kilmarnock to Leicester City), Alan Trouten (Morton to Queen's Park), Stephen Skinner (Albion Rovers to Cowdenbeath), David McLenaghan (St. Johnstone to Gretna), Sean McKenna (Livingston to Airdrie United), Anthony Low (Inverness Caledonian Thistle to Albion Rovers), Henry Sobolewski (Ipswich Town to Ross County), Greg Shields (Kilmarnock to Dunfermline Athletic), Kevin Gaughan (Stenhousemuir to Stranraer), Jamie Buchan (Stockport County to Peterhead), Kristofer Brash (Dundee to Peterhead), Craig Burley (Dundee to Preston North End), David Lilley (Partick Thistle to Kilmarnock), Morten Hyldgaard (Hibernian to Luton Town), Hugh Robertson (Ross County to Hartlepool United), Gary Caldwell (Newcastle United to Hibernian).

United), Greg Miller (Brechin City to Arbroath), Eddie May (Berwick Rangers to Falkirk), Danny Maxwell (Hamilton Academical to Raith Rovers), Paul Lovering (St. Johnstone to Airdrie United), John Kelly (Wycombe Wanderers to Cowdenbeath), Kevin Gordon (Cowdenbeath to Berwick Rangers), Ross Gilpin (Montrose to East Stirlingshire), Scott Findlay (Livingston to Forfar Athletic), Kevin Bain (Peterhead to East Fife), Kyle Armstrong (Gretna to Queen of the South), Andrew Bonner (Stirling Albion to Albion Rovers), James Collier (Aberdeen to Arbroath), Paul Millar (Derby County to Raith Rovers), David McEwan (Livingston to Hamilton Academical), Sean Hessey (Kilmarnock to Blackpool), Andy Dow (Arbroath to Raith Rovers), Salvador Capin (Livingston to Raith Rovers).

MARCH

Celtic lose 1–0 to Teplice in the Czech Republic but reach the Fourth Round of the UEFA Cup with a 3–1 aggregate victory.

Henrik Larsson scores the only goal of the game as Celtic defeat Rangers 1–0 at Parkhead in the Tennent's Scottish Cup Quarter Finals, all but ending the Ibrox club's hopes of silverware from the season.

Celtic defeat Barcelona 1–0 at Parkhead in a pulsating first leg of their UEFA Cup Fourth Round tie. Three players are sent off – Celtic goalkeeper Robert Douglas and the Barcelona pair of Javier Saviola and Thiago Motta.

Stephen Morrison resigns as manager of East Stirlingshire after a 16th consecutive defeat leaves the club rooted to the foot of the Bell's Third Division.

Norwegian striker Egil Ostenstad is given a free transfer by Rangers.

Livingston win their first major domestic honour defeating Hibernian 2–0 in The CIS Insurance Cup Final. Derek Lilley and Jamie McAllister score the vital goals for the West Lothian club.

Celtic reach the Quarter Finals of the UEFA Cup after a remarkable rearguard action earns them a goalless draw with Barcelona in the Nou Camp Stadium in the second leg of their Fourth Round tie. After the 1–0 aggregate win, young goalkeeper David Marshall is given a new four year contract.

Dennis Newall is named as the new manager of East Stirlingshire, taking the position on an unpaid basis.

Celtic defeat Rangers 2–1 at Ibrox in the third Old Firm League fixture of the season to extend their lead at the top of the SPL to 19 points.

Scotland Under-21's lose 2–0 to Romania in a friendly international at Firhill.

John Kennedy, the Celtic defender, suffers a serious knee injury just 13 minutes into his debut for Scotland in a friendly international against Romania at Hampden. The Scots slip to another defeat, losing 2–1 with a consolation goal from James McFadden.

CELTIC ARE CROWNED BANK OF SCOTLAND
PREMIERLEAGUE CHAMPIONS

JACKIE McNAMARA OF CELTIC IS
NAMED SCOTLAND'S PLAYER OF THE
YEAR BY THE SCOTTISH FOOTBALL
WRITERS' ASSOCIATION

Transfers in March:

Craig Winter (Cowdenbeath to Brechin City), Keith Gibson (Montrose to Peterhead), Martin McKirdy (Stenhousemuir to Queen's Park), Laurent D'Jaffo (Aberdeen to Mansfield Town), Daniel Ogunmade (Dundee United to Ross County), Scott MacNicol (Dunfermline Athletic to Forfar Athletic), Gary Wales (Hearts to Gillingham).

APRIL

Celtic draw 1–1 with Spanish side Villareal in the first leg of their UEFA Cup Quarter Final at Parkhead.

In the Semi-Finals of the Tennent's Scottish Cup at Hampden, Dunfermline Athletic and Inverness Caledonian Thistle draw 1–1 while Celtic defeat Livingston 3–1 the following day.

Celtic are eliminated from the UEFA Cup when they lose 2–0 to Villareal in the second leg of their Quarter Final tie, going out 3–1 on aggregate.

Livingston confirm that their Trinidad and Tobago defender Marvin Andrews has agreed to join Rangers when his contract expires at the end of the season.

Celtic are crowned SPL Champions with six matches to spare when they defeat Kilmarnock 1–0 at Rugby Park with a goal from Stilian Petrov.

Dunfermline Athletic reach the Tennent's Scottish Cup Final after a pulsating 3–2 Semi-Final replay victory over Inverness Caledonian Thistle at Pittodrie Stadium, the first occasion that the East End Park club have reached this stage of the competition since 1968.

Bobby Williamson resigns as manager of Hibernian to replace Paul Sturrock as the new boss of English Second Division side Plymouth Argyle.

Motherwell announce they have completed the process of coming out of administration.

Chris Sutton of Celtic is named as Scotland's Player of the Year by The Scottish Professional Footballers' Association. Ian Harty of Clyde is the First Division Player of the Year, Paul Tosh of Forfar Athletic takes the Second Division award and Stranraer's Michael Moore is the Third Division prize winner. Stephen Pearson of Celtic is named SPFA Young Player of the Year.

Billy Stark is dismissed as manager of St. Johnstone as the Perth club fade out of the Bell's First Division promotion race.

Scotland Under-21's draw 2–2 with Denmark in a friendly international in Helsingor with goals from David Clarkson and Craig Beattie.

Scotland suffer a fourth consecutive defeat when they are beaten 1–0 by Denmark in a friendly international in Copenhagen.

Celtic striker Henrik Larsson announces his decision to come out of international retirement and play for Sweden at the European Championship Finals in Portugal.

Stenhousemuir are relegated from the Third Division following their 1–1 draw with Arbroath.

MAY

Despite a 1–0 victory over Ross County, Brechin City are relegated from the First Division.

John Connolly resigns as manager of Queen of the South to become the new manager of St. Johnstone.

Jackie McNamara of Celtic is named Scotland's Player of the Year by the Scottish Football Writers' Association. His team-mate Stephen Pearson is the organisation's Young Player of the Year with boss Martin O'Neill lifting the Manager of the Year prize.

Ian Scott is named as the new manager of Queen of the South.

Ian McCall agrees to extend his contract as manager of Dundee United on reduced terms to the summer of 2008.

Rangers announce they have concluded a pre-contract agreement with Croatian striker Dado Prso who will join them from Monaco in June.

On the penultimate Saturday of the season, Airdrie United clinch the Second Division Championship with a 1–0 victory at Alloa whilst Ayr United are relegated from the First Division

Antonio Calderon resigns as manager of Raith Rovers who finish third from bottom of the Bell's First Division. He is replaced by Claude Anelka, brother of French international striker Nicolas, who takes over the running of the Kirkcaldy club.

On a dramatic finale to the Bell's Scottish Football League Championship, Inverness Caledonian Thistle are crowned First Division Champions with a 3–1 home win over St. Johnstone edging out long time leaders Clyde by a point. Hamilton Academical clinch the second promotion spot in the Second Division by winning 4–0 away at Forfar. Stranraer win the Third Division Championship by defeating Albion Rovers 4–0 edging out Stirling Albion who are promoted to the Second Division as runners-up.

Alex Rae agrees to join Rangers on a free transfer when his contract with Wolverhampton Wanderers expires at the end of the season.

Celtic win the Tennent's Scottish Cup, recovering from the loss of an Andrius Skerla goal to defeat Dunfermline Athletic 3–1 in the Final at Hampden with a double from Henrik Larsson in his final competitive game for the club and a strike from Stilian Petrov.

Steve Paterson is dismissed as manager of Aberdeen after the club finish second from bottom of the SPL.

Tony Mowbray, the former Celtic defender, is named as the new manager of Hibernian.

Scotland Under-21's lose 3-1 to the Republic of Ireland in a friendly international in Galway. Craig Beattie scores for the Scots.

James McFadden scores the only goal of the game to give Scotland a much needed victory in a friendly international against Estonia in Tallinn.

Darren Fletcher becomes Scotland's youngest captain since John Lambie of Queen's Park lead the side against Ireland in 1886.

Jimmy Calderwood resigns as manager of Dunfermline Athletic to become the new manager of Aberdeen. His assistant Jimmy Nicholl also leaves East End Park to join him at Pittodrie.

Scotland complete a disappointing season on a high note with a 4-1 victory over Trinidad and Tobago in a friendly international at Easter Road with goals from Darren Fletcher, Gary Holt, Gary Caldwell and Nigel Quashie.

Transfers in May:

Bobby Mann (Inverness Caledonian Thistle to Dundee), Lee Bullen (Dunfermline Athletic to Sheffield Wednesday), Steven Milne (Dundee to Plymouth Argyle), Jon Paul McGovern (Livingston to Sheffield Wednesday), Lee Makel (Livingston to Plymouth Argyle), Dave Mackay (Dundee to Oxford United).

JUNE

The SPL clubs vote 7-5 in favour of Inverness Caledonian Thistle's proposed groundshare with Aberdeen, falling one short of the two-thirds majority required to approve the club's promotion from the First Division.

Inverness Caledonian Thistle lodge an appeal against the SPL vote with the SFA.

A second vote on the Inverness-Aberdeen groundshare proposal is requisitioned by Hearts and Hibernian, two of the clubs who backed the Highland club in the initial ballot.

Scotland goalkeeper Paul Gallacher leaves Dundee United to sign for Norwich City under Freedom of Movement.

Allan Preston is appointed new manager of Livingston after Irish businessman Pearse Flynn is granted preferred bidder status by the administrators.

Scotland striker Stevie Crawford leaves Dunfermline Athletic to sign for Plymouth Argyle under Freedom of Movement.

Davie Hay is named as the new manager of Dunfermline Athletic. Billy Kirkwood leaves his coaching role at Livingston to become Hay's assistant at East End Park.

Alan Kernaghan resigns as manager of Clyde to become assistant manager to Allan Preston at Livingston.

Partick Thistle fail to gain an interim interdict against the second SPL vote on the Inverness-Aberdeen groundshare proposal. The vote goes ahead with a 10-2 outcome in favour of the Highland club.

Transfers in June:

David Bingham (Inverness Caledonian Thistle to Gretna), Lee Mair (Dundee to Stockport County), Sean Webb (Ross County to St. Johnstone), Keith Lasley (Motherwell to Plymouth Argyle), Matthias Kou-Doumbe (Hibernian to Plymouth Argyle), Mark McLaughlin (Clyde to Hamilton Academical), Austin McCann (Clyde to Boston United), Pat Keogh (Clyde to Hamilton Academical), Mark Reilly (St. Johnstone to St. Mirren), Mixu Paatelainen (St. Johnstone to St. Mirren), Steven Boyack (Hearts to Livingston), Richie Foran (Carlisle United to Motherwell), Colin Marshall (Aston Villa to St. Johnstone), Yannick Zambernardi (Hibernian to La Louviere), Scott Severin (Hearts to Aberdeen), Simon Brown (Colchester United to Hibernian), Keigan Parker (St. Johnstone to Blackpool), Darryl Duffy (Rangers to Falkirk), Nick Colgan (Hibernian to Barnsley), Hamed Sacko (Paris FC to Raith Rovers), Mehdi Eloujdi (US Ivry to Raith Rovers), Amar Benaissa (Choisy Le Roi to Raith Rovers), Chris Scott (Sunderland to Queen of the South), Tommy English (Partick Thistle to Queen of the South).

Scottish Premier League & Scottish Football League
Final Tables 2003/2004

BANK OF SCOTLAND PREMIERLEAGUE

	P	W	D	L	F	A	PTS
CELTIC	38	31	5	2	105	25	98
RANGERS	38	25	6	7	76	33	81
HEARTS	38	19	11	8	56	40	68
DUNFERMLINE ATHLETIC	38	14	11	13	45	52	53
DUNDEE UNITED	38	13	10	15	47	60	49
MOTHERWELL	38	12	10	16	42	49	46
DUNDEE	38	12	10	16	48	57	46
HIBERNIAN	38	11	11	16	41	60	44
LIVINGSTON	38	10	13	15	48	57	43
KILMARNOCK	38	12	6	20	51	74	42
ABERDEEN	38	9	7	22	39	63	34
PARTICK THISTLE	38	6	8	24	39	67	26

BELL'S SFL FIRST DIVISION

	P	W	D	L	F	A	PTS
INVERNESS CAL TH	36	21	7	8	67	33	70
CLYDE	36	20	9	7	64	40	69
ST. JOHNSTONE	36	15	12	9	59	45	57
FALKIRK	36	15	10	11	43	37	55
QUEEN OF THE SOUTH	36	15	9	12	46	48	54
ROSS COUNTY	36	12	13	11	49	41	49
ST. MIRREN	36	9	14	13	39	46	41
RAITH ROVERS	36	8	10	18	37	57	34
AYR UNITED	36	6	13	17	37	58	31
BRECHIN CITY	36	6	9	21	37	73	27

BELL'S SFL SECOND DIVISION

	P	W	D	L	F	A	PTS
AIRDRIE UNITED	36	20	10	6	64	36	70
HAMILTON ACADEMICAL	36	18	8	10	70	47	62
DUMBARTON	36	18	6	12	56	41	60
MORTON	36	16	11	9	66	58	59
BERWICK RANGERS	36	14	6	16	61	67	48
FORFAR ATHLETIC	36	12	11	13	49	57	47
ALLOA ATHLETIC	36	12	8	16	55	55	44
ARBROATH	36	11	10	15	41	57	43
EAST FIFE	36	11	8	17	38	45	41
STENHOUSEMUIR	36	7	4	25	28	65	25

BELL'S SFL THIRD DIVISION

	P	W	D	L	F	A	PTS
STRANRAER	36	24	7	5	87	30	79
STIRLING ALBION	36	23	8	5	78	27	77
GRETNA	36	20	8	8	59	39	68
PETERHEAD	36	18	7	11	67	37	61
COWDENBEATH	36	15	10	11	46	39	55
MONTROSE	36	12	12	12	52	63	48
QUEEN'S PARK	36	10	11	15	41	53	41
ALBION ROVERS	36	12	4	20	66	75	40
ELGIN CITY	36	6	7	23	48	93	25
EAST STIRLINGSHIRE	36	2	2	32	30	118	8

Scottish Premier League & Scottish Football League
Reserve & Youth Leagues - Final Tables 2003/2004

THE SCOTTISH PREMIER LEAGUE UNDER-21 LEAGUE

	P	W	D	L	F	A	PTS
CELTIC	33	24	5	4	80	24	77
HEARTS	33	20	6	7	57	27	66
RANGERS	33	19	6	8	58	39	63
DUNFERMLINE ATHLETIC	33	15	9	9	52	39	54
DUNDEE UNITED	33	13	7	13	54	58	46
ABERDEEN	33	13	6	14	44	54	45
KILMARNOCK	33	12	8	13	47	58	44
PARTICK THISTLE	33	11	7	15	42	53	40
LIVINGSTON	33	9	10	14	39	46	37
HIBERNIAN	33	8	8	17	41	45	32
DUNDEE	33	6	8	19	42	77	26
MOTHERWELL	33	4	8	21	27	63	20

SFL RESERVE LEAGUE EAST

	P	W	D	L	F	A	PTS
ST. JOHNSTONE	12	8	3	1	30	7	27
MONTROSE	12	6	2	4	22	13	20
FORFAR ATHLETIC	12	5	2	5	20	19	17
RAITH ROVERS	12	3	5	4	14	17	14
ARBROATH	12	4	2	6	17	24	14
EAST FIFE	12	3	5	4	12	19	14
COWDENBEATH	12	2	3	7	8	24	9

SFL RESERVE LEAGUE WEST

	P	W	D	L	F	A	PTS
GRETNA	15	10	4	1	32	14	34
MORTON	15	10	2	3	34	14	32
FALKIRK	15	9	2	4	36	14	29
QUEEN'S PARK	15	4	4	7	17	24	16
AYR UNITED	15	3	5	7	12	30	14
ALBION ROVERS	15	0	1	14	10	45	1

THE SCOTTISH PREMIER LEAGUE UNDER-19 YOUTH DIVISION

	P	W	D	L	F	A	PTS
CELTIC	22	16	3	3	66	19	51
RANGERS	22	15	4	3	41	22	49
HEARTS	22	14	3	5	43	17	45
LIVINGSTON	22	12	5	5	31	27	41
ABERDEEN	22	9	5	8	42	36	32
DUNDEE UNITED	22	9	4	9	32	37	31
DUNDEE	22	9	3	10	34	33	30
KILMARNOCK	22	6	7	9	30	36	25
MOTHERWELL	22	4	9	9	19	28	21
HIBERNIAN	22	6	3	13	28	41	21
DUNFERMLINE ATHLETIC	22	6	0	16	24	42	18
PARTICK THISTLE	22	1	4	17	13	65	7

SFL UNDER 19 YOUTH DIVISION

	P	W	D	L	F	A	PTS
ROSS COUNTY	15	12	0	3	46	18	36
ST. MIRREN	15	11	2	2	51	15	35
STIRLING ALBION	15	11	1	3	43	22	34
QUEEN'S PARK	15	10	2	3	37	23	32
FALKIRK	15	10	1	4	49	28	31
COWDENBEATH	15	8	3	4	36	18	27
AIRDRIE UNITED	15	8	3	4	38	28	27
STENHOUSEMUIR	15	7	1	7	22	18	22
ALBION ROVERS	15	7	1	7	27	30	22
EAST FIFE	15	6	2	7	20	24	20
ALLOA ATHLETIC	15	5	1	9	30	30	16
FORFAR ATHLETIC	15	3	3	9	17	33	12
ARBROATH	15	3	2	10	23	47	11
PETERHEAD	15	2	3	10	16	41	9
BRECHIN CITY	15	2	1	12	19	54	7
ELGIN CITY	15	1	2	12	10	55	5

SFL UNDER 17 YOUTH DIVISION

	P	W	D	L	F	A	PTS
FALKIRK	16	15	0	1	58	21	45
AYR UNITED	16	11	1	4	52	22	34
STENHOUSEMUIR	16	10	3	3	50	32	33
HAMILTON ACADEMICAL	16	8	4	4	46	26	28
RAITH ROVERS	16	8	4	4	28	18	28
INVERNESS CAL TH	16	8	3	5	47	33	27
ST. JOHNSTONE	16	8	3	5	43	32	27
CLYDE	16	9	0	7	42	36	27
ST. MIRREN	16	6	5	5	36	24	23
QUEEN OF THE SOUTH	16	7	2	7	36	29	23
QUEEN'S PARK	16	6	4	6	33	30	22
STIRLING ALBION	16	6	3	7	40	48	21
COWDENBEATH	16	5	1	10	25	49	16
ALBION ROVERS	16	4	2	10	20	38	14
AIRDRIE UNITED	16	3	2	11	22	43	11
ARBROATH	16	3	1	12	20	47	10
GRETNA	16	0	0	16	17	87	0

The CIS Insurance Cup Competition
Season 2003/2004

FIRST ROUND
Tuesday, 2nd September, 2003

EAST FIFE 0 AIRDRIE UNITED 2
M. Roberts, P. Ronald

East Fife: G. O'Connor, G. Russell, C. Miller,
(I. McDonald), C. Lumsden, M. Hall, P. Kelly, (B. Blair),
J. Mitchell, G. McDonald, K. Deuchar, B. Fairbairn,
E. Donaldson, (G. Gilbert)
Substitutes not used: G. Love, K. McKeown
Airdrie United: M. McGeown, W. Wilson, K. Black,
A. McManus, S. Wilson, N. McGowan, J. Vareille, (P. Ronald),
M. Wilson, M. Roberts, (A. Gow), D. Dunn, M. Glancy
Substitutes not used: D. Miller, S. McKenna, P. Cherrie
Referee: Iain Brines **Attendance:** 766

ARBROATH 1 RAITH ROVERS 0
J. Cusick

Arbroath: M. Peat, K. McMullan, (J. McAulay), D. King,
S. Rennie, P. Browne, J. Cusick, J. Herkes, (G. Henslee),
A. Dow, R. Graham, J. McGlashan, S. Kerrigan, (G. Swankie)
Substitutes not used: E. Graham, A. Mitchell
Raith Rovers: R. Gonzalez, V. Talio, G. Stanic,
(R. Blackadder), I. Brown, (M. Peers), S. Dennis, D. Brady,
R. Brittain, J. Henry, K. Hawley, A. Calderon, D. Evans, (M. Prest)
Substitutes not used: J. Sutton, R. Carroll
Referee: Alan Freeland **Attendance:** 879

INVERNESS CT 1 QUEEN'S PARK 2
P. Ritchie S. Reilly, A. Graham

Inverness Cal. Thistle: M. Brown, R. Tokely,
(D. Proctor), S. Golabek, R. Mann, S. McCaffrey,
R. Duncan, B. Wilson, S. Hislop, (D. Thomson),
P. Ritchie, R. Hart, R. McBain
Substitutes not used: G. Munro, A. Low, A. Ridgers
Queen's Park: D. Scrimgour, R. Sinclair, D. Ferry,
J. Whelan, S. Moffat, S. Fallon, R. Clark, (P. Gallagher),
S. Reilly, A. Graham, S. Canning, S. McAuley, (D. Carcary)
Substitutes not used: R. Conlin, J. Thomson, B. McCue
Referee: Garry Mitchell **Attendance:** 968

AYR UNITED 1 DUMBARTON 2
M. Smyth P. Flannery, S. Bonar

Ayr United: L. Roy, W. Lyle, S. McGrady, M. Smyth,
M. Campbell, (B. Mullen), (C. Conway), D. Craig, S. Ferguson,
D. Ramsay, S. Kean, (A. Ferguson), S. Whalen, S. Chaplain
Substitutes not used: C. Kerr, J. Hillcoat
Dumbarton: S. Grindlay, J. McKinstry, C. Brittain,
N. Collins, I. Dobbins, D. Smith, (B. Donald), C. McEwan,
M. Bradley, E. Obidile, P. Flannery, (S. Bonar), C. Boyle
Substitutes not used: J. Dillon, S. Renicks, J. Wight
Referee: Eddie Mack **Attendance:** 1,048

EAST STIRLINGSHIRE 1 ROSS COUNTY 2
P. Rodden D. Cowie, S. Mackay

East Stirlingshire: J. Connolly, R. Maughan, G. McLaren,
D. Polwart, K. McCann, G. McGhee, S. Livingstone,
S. McAuley, (P. Rodden), D. Ormiston, S. Kelly,
(G. McCulloch), C. Baldwin, (G. Boyle)
Substitutes not used: C. Reid, C. Todd
Ross County: C. Stewart, J. McCunnie, S. Mackay, J. Tait,
(D. Cowie), S. Malcolm, M. McCulloch, J. Rankin,
D. Hannah, G. Bayne, J. Hamilton, (D. Winters),
H. Robertson, (S. McGarry)
Substitutes not used: S. O'Donnell, L. Fridge
Referee: Andrew Hunter **Attendance:** 208

ELGIN CITY 0 BRECHIN CITY 4
K. Fotheringham, D. White,
G. Gibson, C. Templeman

Elgin City: M. Pirie, D. Hind, A. McMillan, J. White,
R. Coulter, J. Allison, W. Martin, C. Ogboke,
(S. McCormick), A. Bone, K. Steele, C. Campbell
Substitutes not used: J. Gallagher, S. Murphy,
R. McMullan, P. Hamilton
Brechin City: D. Hay, G. Miller, S. McCulloch,
N. Jablonski, (K. McLeish), D. White, K. Fotheringham,
C. King, A. Mitchell, (D. Clark), S. Hampshire,
(C. Templeman), G. Gibson, J. Stein
Substitutes not used: M. McCulloch, P. Deas
Referee: John Underhill **Attendance:** 486

GRETNA 1 PETERHEAD 2
D. Smith (o.g.) I. Stewart (2)

Gretna: D. Mathieson, M. Birch, L. Maddison, R. McGuffie,
D. Irons, D. Holdsworth, R. Baldacchino, M. Galloway,
M. Cameron, G. Cohen, (S. Cosgrove), M. Eccles, (G. Skelton)
Substitutes not used: K. Knox, P. O'Neill, C. Summersgill
Peterhead: P. Mathers, D. Smith, S. McSkimming, R. Raeside,
M. Perry, K. Bain, (M. Johnston), S. Mackay, (R. Grant),
I. Stewart, G. Beith, (R. Duncan), M. Bavidge, A. Roddie
Substitutes not used: I. Good, J. Farquhar
Referee: Cammy Melville **Attendance:** 386

ST. MIRREN 0 ST. JOHNSTONE 2 (AET)
D. Dods, M-M. Paatelainen

St. Mirren: C. Hinchcliffe, D. Van Zanten, L. Ellis, K. Broadfoot,
A. MacPherson, R. Dunn, (K. Twaddle), R. Gillies, J. O'Neil,
A. Russell, B. Lavety, (S. Gemmill), B. McGinty, (A. Muir)
Substitutes not used: G. McWilliam, S. Woods
St. Johnstone: K. Cuthbert, J. Robertson, M. Baxter,
P. Bernard, D. Dods, I. Maxwell, K. Parker, M. Reilly,
(M. Robertson), M-M. Paatelainen, S. Donnelly, E. Malone,
Substitutes not used: R. Forsyth, M. Fotheringham,
B. McLaughlin, C. Nelson
Referee: Willie Young **Attendance:** 2,590

HAMILTON ACADEMICAL 3
B. McPhee (2), C. Aitken

ALBION ROVERS 2
P. McManus,
K. McAllister

Hamilton Academical: D. McEwan, A. Arbuckle, (J. Fitter),
S. Hodge, S.W. Thomson, A. Whiteford, J. Sherry, B. Carrigan,
C. Aitken, M. Corcoran, (N. Paterson), B. McPhee, J. Bailey
Substitutes not used: D. Gribben, A. Waddell, R. Jellema
Albion Rovers: C. Fahey, A. Paterson, D. Farrell, J. Smith,
P. Cormack, J. McCaig, K. McAllister, G. McCaul, I. Diack,
P. McManus, S. Skinner, (K. McBride)
Substitutes not used:
A. Selkirk, M. McKenzie, G. Robertson, K. Swain
Referee: Steve Conroy
Attendance: 824

MONTROSE 2
C. Smart, S. Kerrigan

STIRLING ALBION 0

Montrose: J. Butter, B. Donachie, S. Ferguson, J. McQuillan,
M. Simpson, F. Conway, K. Webster, M. Wood, (S. Michie),
C. Smart, S. Kerrigan, R. Black, (C. Farnan)
Substitutes not used: G. Sharp, R. Henderson, M. Hankinson
Stirling Albion: M. Hogarth, P. Nugent, D. Anderson, M. McNally,
J.G. Rowe, C. Ferguson, (C. McKinnon), A. Gibson, S. Devine,
S. McLean, B. Elliot, D. O'Brien, (R. Davidson)
Substitutes not used: P. Hay, D. Wilson, S. Morrison
Referee: Craig Mackay **Attendance:** 252

COWDENBEATH 3
D. McInally (2), I. Morris

ALLOA ATHLETIC 0

Cowdenbeath: A. Carlin, C. Shand, D. McInally, B. Gilfillan,
J. McKeown, D. Mowat, I. Mauchlen, (K. Gordon), C. Winter,
G. Brown, D. Shields, (R. Matheson), I. Morris
Substitutes not used: A. Moffat, A. Campbell, A. Fleming
Alloa Athletic: G. McGlynn, I. Nicolson, A. Seaton, C. Valentine,
P. McLaughlin, A.B. Ferguson, R. Walker, N. Janczyk, S. Crabbe,
(M. Watson), K. Kelbie, (G. Evans), I. Little
Substitutes not used: G. Gillan, R. Hamilton, J. Evans
Referee: Charlie Richmond
Attendance: 288

STENHOUSEMUIR 1
M. Harty

QUEEN OF THE SOUTH 2
G. Wood, D. Bagan

Stenhousemuir: W. McCulloch, G. McCulloch, K. Gaughan,
S. Hamilton, B. McCloy, (D. Johnstone), J. McKenzie, M. Lauchlan,
(G. McKenna), K. Donnelly, S. Mallan, D. Carr, (A. Brown), M. Harty
Substitutes not used: M. McGowan, N. Parry
Queen of the South: J. Dodds, D. Bagan, J. McAlpine, D. Allan,
B. Reid, J. Thomson, S. O'Connor, S. Bowey, G. Wood, (W. Gibson),
D. Lyle, A. Burke, (P. Burns)
Substitutes not used: E. Paton, A. Aitken, C. Scott
Referee: John Rowbotham **Attendance:** 415

FORFAR ATHLETIC 1
D. Henderson

BERWICK RANGERS 0

Forfar Athletic: M. Brown, P. Lunan, (D. Ogunmade), D. Lowing,
R. Horn, D. Stewart, D. McClune, K. Byers, D. Henderson, P. Tosh,
H. Davidson, P. Shields
Substitutes not used: S. Florence, C. Hodge, M. Maher, N. Ferrie
Berwick Rangers: R. Godfrey, D. Murie, P. Hilland, M. Cowan,
G. McNicoll, G. Connell, J. McAllister, (D. Smith), J.N. Bennett,
G. Hutchison, G. McCutcheon, P. Hampshire
Substitutes not used: D. Blackley, C. Waldie, J. Birrell, W. Scott
Referee: John Gilmour **Attendance:** 407

Wednesday, 3rd September, 2003

MORTON 2
E. Bottiglieri, S. Bannerman

STRANRAER 0

Morton: C. Coyle, D. Collins, E. Bottiglieri, D. MacGregor,
S. Greacen, M. Maisano, C. Miller, J. Maisano, (J. Uotinen),
S. Bannerman, P. Weatherson, P. Walker, (A. Williams)
Substitutes not used: W. Hawke, R. Henderson, D. McGurn
Stranraer: A. McCondichie, S. Swift, F. Wright, D. Wingate,
M. Henderson, A. Jenkins, K. Finlayson, S. Aitken, (G. McPhee),
M. Moore, (P. Kerr), A. Grant, (D. Graham), L. Sharp
Substitutes not used: C. Cruickshank, K. Meechan
Referee: Craig Thomson
Attendance: 2,758

SECOND ROUND
Tuesday, 23rd September, 2003

BRECHIN CITY 1
S. Hampshire

KILMARNOCK 0

Brechin City: D. Soutar, J. Smith, P. Deas, D. White, S. McCulloch,
N. Jablonski, G. Miller, (D. Clark), I.G. Johnson, S. Hampshire,
(G. Gibson), C. King, (C. Templeman), A. Mitchell
Substitutes not used: M. McCulloch, D. Hay
Kilmarnock: F. Dubourdeau, G. Shields, F. Dindeleux,
B. McLaughlin, (S. Murray), S. Hessey, J. Fowler, (P. Di Giacomo),
C. Nish, (G. McSwegan), S. Fulton, P. Canero, K. Boyd, M. Hardie
Substitutes not used: C. Samson, A. Mahood
Referee: Craig Mackay
Attendance: 813

HIBERNIAN 9
S. Dobbie (3),
G. O'Connor (2)
I. Murray, D. Riordan,
S. Brown, S. Kerrigan (o.g.)

MONTROSE 0

Hibernian: D. Andersson, C. Murdock, R. Edge, A. Orman,
(S. Whittaker), M. Kouo–Doumbe, I. Murray, S. Glass, G. Brebner,
T. McManus, (S. Brown), G. O'Connor, S. Dobbie, (D. Riordan)
Substitutes not used: M. Hyldgaard, J. Wiss
Montrose: M. Hankinson, B. Donachie, S. Ferguson, J. McQuillan,
M. Simpson, G. Smith, (G. Sharp), K. Gibson, (K. Brash), C. Farnan,
S. Michie, S. Kerrigan, R. Black
Substitutes not used: J. Watt, R. Henderson, R. Gilpin
Referee: Kevin Toner
Attendance: 5,032

FORFAR ATHLETIC 3
(AET – 3-3 After 90 Minutes)
P. Tosh (2),
D. Henderson

MOTHERWELL 3
S. Craig, K. Lasley,
S. Pearson

Forfar Athletic won 4-2 on Kicks from the Penalty Mark

Forfar Athletic: M. Brown, P. Lunan, (D. Williams), A. Rattray,
D. McClune, (D. Lowing), D. Stewart, K. Byers, B. Sellars, H. Davidson,
P. Tosh, D. Henderson, (M. Maher), P. Shields
Substitutes not used: S. Taylor, N. Ferrie
Motherwell: G. Marshall, M. Corrigan, D. Partridge, S. Hammell,
S. Craigan, K. Lasley, (J. Dair), S. Pearson, D.S. Leitch, D. Adams,
S. Craig, (K. Wright), D. Clarkson
Substitutes not used: P. Quinn, K. MacDonald, B.J. Corr
Referee: Dougie McDonald
Attendance: 1,110

ABERDEEN 3   **DUMBARTON 1**

D. Zdrilic (2), L. Hinds   E. Obidile

Aberdeen: D. Preece, A. Diamond, J. McQuilken, (S. Muirhead), R. Anderson, K. McNaughton, M. Heikkinen, (E. Deloumeaux), S. Tosh, M. Hart, P. Sheerin, D. Zdrilic, L. Hinds, (M. Bird)
Substitutes not used: D. Mackie, D. Hutton
Dumbarton: S. Grindlay, J. McKinstry, C. Brittain, N. Collins, C. Duffy, I. Dobbins, S. Bonar, B. Donald, (P. Flannery), E. Obidile, M. Bradley, (I. Russell), C. Boyle, (J. Dillon)
Substitutes not used: S. Renicks, J. Wight
Referee: Willie Young **Attendance:** 3,944

ROSS COUNTY 0   **QUEEN OF THE SOUTH 3**

A. Burke (2), P. Burns

Ross County: C. Stewart, J. McCunnie, S. Mackay, J. Tait, (S. O'Donnell), S. Malcolm, M. McCulloch, J. Rankin, D. Cowie, S. Higgins, (J. Hamilton), H. Robertson, S. McGarry, (G. Bayne)
Substitutes not used: S. Webb, L. Fridge
Queen of the South: C. Scott, E. Paton, J. McAlpine, D. Bagan, (B. McColligan), B. Reid, J. Thomson, S. O'Connor, S. Bowey, A. Burke, (G. Wood), P. Burns, P. Talbot, (A. Aitken)
Substitutes not used: E. Jaconelli, J. Dodds
Referee: Garry Mitchell **Attendance:** 959

DUNDEE UNITED 3   **MORTON 1**

A. McLaren,   P. Weatherson
J. McIntyre (2)

Dundee United: A. Bullock, A. Archibald, C. Innes, D. Griffin, J. Paterson, (M. Kerr), S. Duff, D. McInnes, C. Miller, A. McLaren, (C. Samuel), J. Scotland, (W. Dodds), J. McIntyre
Substitutes not used: D. McCracken, P. Gallacher
Morton: C. Coyle, D. Collins, E. Bottigilieri, D. MacGregor, S. Greacen, M. Maisano, C. Miller, (J. Uotinen), J. Maisano, A. Williams, (W. Hawke), P. Weatherson, P. Walker, (S. Bannerman)
Substitutes not used: P. Gaughan, D. McGurn
Referee: John Rowbotham **Attendance:** 5,638

QUEEN'S PARK 1   **LIVINGSTON 3**

R. Clark   F. Quino, L. Makel (2)

Queen's Park: D. Scrimgour, R. Clark, S. Reilly, S. Moffat, R. Sinclair, S. Fallon, S. Canning, P. Harvey, (P. Gallagher), A. Graham, J. Whelan, (D. McCallum), S. McAuley
Substitutes not used: J. Thompson, D. Menelaws, B. McCue
Livingston: R. McKenzie, D. McNamee, J. McAllister, O. Rubio, E. Dorado, B. Kerr, L. Makel, F. Quino, (J.P. McGovern), B. O'Brien, D. Fernandez, (D. Lilley), F. Pasquinelli, (G. Ipoua)
Substitutes not used: S. McLaughlin, K. Montgomery
Referee: John Underhill **Attendance:** 1,011

ST. JOHNSTONE 3   **HAMILTON ACADEMICAL 2**

(AET – 2-2 After 90 Minutes)
S. Donnelly,   B. Carrigan,
B. McLaughlin,   M. Corcoran
M-M. Paatelainen

St. Johnstone: K. Cuthbert, J. Robertson, R. Forsyth, P. Bernard, D. Dods, I. Maxwell, K. Parker, (M-M. Paatelainen), M. Reilly, M. Robertson, S. Donnelly, (P. MacDonald), B. McLaughlin, (E. Malone)
Substitutes not used: M. Baxter, C. Nelson
Hamilton Academical: D. McEwan, A. Whiteford, S. Hodge, S.W. Thomson, T. Lumsden, (M. Corcoran), J. Sherry, (N. Paterson), B. Carrigan, C. Aitken, J. Bailey, (B. Forbes), B. McPhee, S. Convery
Substitutes not used: D. Gribben, R. Jellema
Referee: Tom Brown **Attendance:** 1,471

ARBROATH 3   **FALKIRK 4**

(AET – 2-2 After 90 Minutes)
J. McGlashan (2),   C. McMenamin,
R. Graham   A. Rodgers,
    D. Nicholls (2)

Arbroath: M. Peat, K. McMullan, (C. Newell), A. Dow, S. Rennie, P. Browne, G. Henslee, G. Swankie, (P. Durno), A. Cargill, R. Graham, J. McGlashan, J. Herkes, (J. McAulay)
Substitutes not used:
E. Graham, A. Mitchell
Falkirk: D. Hill, A. Lawrie, C. McPherson, D. Nicholls, S. MacKenzie, K. James, (J. Sharp), J. O'Neil, J. Henry, C. McMenamin, R. Latapy, (B. Rahim), A. Rodgers
Substitutes not used:
N. Scally, D. Colquhoun, A. Ferguson
Referee: Craig Thomson
Attendance: 923

CLYDE 2   **AIRDRIE UNITED 1**

A. Millen, M. Gilhaney   M. Glancy

Clyde: B. Halliwell, J. Potter, S. Mensing, A. Kernaghan, J. Fraser, J. Ross, D. Hagen, A. Millen, I. Harty, M. McLaughlin, S. McConalogue, (M. Gilhaney)
Substitutes not used:
C. Marshall, A. Smith, P. Doyle, A. Morrison
Airdrie United: M. McGeown, S. Docherty, W. Wilson, (J. Vareille), A. Stewart, (F. Singbo), A. McManus, N. McGowan, A. Gow, M. Wilson, M. Roberts, D. Dunn, M. Glancy
Substitutes not used: S. Wilson, D. Miller, L. Hollis
Referee: Michael McCurry
Attendance: 1,401

Wednesday, 24th September, 2003

DUNFERMLINE ATHLETIC 2   **COWDENBEATH 0**

S. Crawford, C. Brewster
Dunfermline Athletic: D. Stillie, L. Bullen, G. Dempsey, (R. Byrne), Darren Young, A. Skerla, S. Kilgannon, B. Nicholson, G. Mason, S. Crawford, C. Brewster, (B. Mehmet), A. Tod
Substitutes not used:
D. Grondin, S. MacNicol, S.Y. Thomson
Cowdenbeath: A. Carlin, D. Mowat, D. McInally, B. Gilfillan, J. McKeown, I. Ritchie, D. Shields, (G. Fusco), C. Winter, G. Brown, K. Gordon, L. Buchanan, (I. Mauchlen)
Substitutes not used:
R. Matheson, J. Slaven, A. Fleming
Referee: Hugh Dallas
Attendance: 3,582

PETERHEAD 2   **PARTICK THISTLE 2**

(AET –1-1 After 90 Minutes)
S. Mackay, I. Stewart   J. Mitchell, K. Milne

Partick Thistle won 4-3 on Kicks from the Penalty Mark

Peterhead: P. Mathers, K. McGuinness, (D. Smith), S. McSkimming, R. Raeside, M. Perry, K. Bain, (G. Stewart), S. Mackay, I. Stewart, R. Grant, (D. Stewart), M. Johnston, G. Beith
Substitutes not used: I. Good, J. Farquhar
Partick Thistle: K. Arthur, D. Lilley, (S. Bonnes), G. Murray, D. Whyte, K. Milne, S. Taylor, D. Rowson, J. Mitchell, R. Waddell, (E. Forrest), J. Grady, (G. Britton), A. Thomson
Substitutes not used: J.P. McBride, K. Budinauckas
Referee: Ian Fyfe
Attendance: 1,352

THIRD ROUND
Tuesday, 28th October, 2003

HIBERNIAN 2   **QUEEN OF THE SOUTH 1**
D. Riordan (2)   A. Burke

Hibernian: D. Andersson, C. Murdock, R. Edge, (A. Reid), A. Orman,
M. Kouo–Doumbe, I. Murray, S. Glass, G. Brebner, (S. Whittaker), G.
O'Connor, D. Riordan, T. McManus
Substitutes not used: S. Dobbie, K. Thomson, M. Hyldgaard
Queen of the South: C. Scott, E. Paton, A. Aitken, D. Bagan, B. Reid,
J. Thomson, S. O'Connor, S. Bowey, A. Burke, P. Burns, J. McAlpine, (G. Wood)
Substitutes not used: B. McColligan, W. Gibson, D. Lyle, J. Dodds
Referee: Michael McCurry **Attendance:** 7,613

RANGERS 6   **FORFAR ATHLETIC 0**
C. Nerlinger (3),
P. Lovenkrands,
N. Capucho, E. Ostenstad

Rangers: A. McGregor, M. Ross, (D. Duffy), C. Moore,
Z. Khizanishvili, P. Vanoli, (F. Ricksen), E. Costa, S. Hughes,
C. Nerlinger, N. Capucho, E. Ostenstad, P. Lovenkrands, (C. Burke)
Substitutes not used: H. Berg, J. Christiansen
Forfar Athletic: M. Brown, P. Lunan, (M. Maher), A. Rattray,
R. Horn, (D. McClune), D. Stewart, (D. Lowing), K. Byers, B. Sellars,
H. Davidson, P. Tosh, D. Henderson, P. Shields
Substitutes not used: S. Taylor, N. Ferrie
Referee: Stuart Dougal **Attendance:** 26,330

ST. JOHNSTONE 3   **DUNFERMLINE ATHLETIC 2**
S. Donnelly, D. Dods,   S. Crawford,
P. MacDonald   Darren Young

St. Johnstone: K. Cuthbert, J. Robertson, R. Forsyth, P. Bernard, D. Dods,
I. Maxwell, P. MacDonald, (C. Hay), M. Robertson, K. Parker, S. Donnelly,
B. McLaughlin, (E. Malone)
Substitutes not used: M–M. Paatelainen, R. Stevenson, C. Nelson
Dunfermline Athletic: D. Stillie, L. Bullen, (G. Dempsey),
S.M. Thomson, D. Grondin, S. Wilson, Darren Young, B. Nicholson,
G. Mason, S. Kilgannon, (A. Labonte), S. Crawford, C. Brewster
Substitutes not used: R. Byrne, M. Ruitenbeek
Referee: John Underhill **Attendance:** 2,680

ABERDEEN 5   **BRECHIN CITY 0**
S. Tosh, S. Booth,
S. Muirhead, P. Sheerin,
L. Hinds

Aberdeen: D. Preece, P. McGuire, (K. Rutkiewicz), E. Deloumeaux,
R. Anderson, S. Muirhead, M. Heikkinen, (F. Tiernan), S. Tosh, C. Clark,
(L. Hinds), P. Sheerin, S. Booth, D. Mackie
Substitutes not used: D. Hutton, R. Foster
Brechin City: D. Soutar, J. Smith, (G. Miller), S. McCulloch,
(M. McCulloch), D. White, P. Deas, K. Fotheringham, C. King, A. Mitchell,
S. Hampshire, N. Jablonski, J. Stein, (C. Templeman)
Substitutes not used: G. Gibson, D. Hay
Referee: Kenny Clark **Attendance:** 3,631

Wednesday, 29th October, 2003

HEARTS 2   **FALKIRK 1**
M. De Vries, A. Kirk   R. Latapy

Hearts: C. Gordon, K. McKenna, P. Kisnorbo, S. Pressley, R. Neilson,
J–L. Valois, S. Severin, S. Simmons, (D. Wyness), P. Hartley, M. De Vries, A. Kirk
Substitutes not used: A. Maybury, H.A. McCann, N. Macfarlane, Moilanen

Falkirk: A. Ferguson, A. Lawrie, C. McPherson, S. MacKenzie,
J. Hughes, K. James, J. Sharp, D. Nicholls, (K. McAnespie), D. Xausa,
R. Latapy, (B. Rahim), C. McMenamin, (D. Colquhoun)
Substitutes not used: N. Scally, D. Hill
Referee: John Rowbotham **Attendance:** 8,687

CLYDE 2   **DUNDEE 5**
P. Keogh, M. Gilhaney   I. Novo, L. Wilkie,
                  F. Ravanelli (3)

Clyde: B. Halliwell, S. Mensing, M. McLaughlin, A. Kernaghan,
J. Fraser, J. Ross, (C. Marshall), D. Hagen, A. Millen, P. Keogh,
J. Gibson, (M. Gilhaney), S. McConalogue, (I. Harty)
Substitutes not used: J. Potter, A. Morrison
Dundee: J. Speroni, D. Mackay, C. Macdonald, L. Mair, L. Wilkie,
B. Smith, C. Burley, (M. Fotheringham), G. Brady, J. Sara, F. Caballero,
(F. Ravanelli), I. Novo, (R. Linn)
Substitutes not used: L.A. Carranza, J. Langfield
Referee: Dougie McDonald **Attendance:** 1,701

DUNDEE UNITED 0   **LIVINGSTON 1**
                  P. Gallacher (o.g)

Dundee United: P. Gallacher, A. Archibald, C. Innes,
D. McCracken, M. Wilson, (C. Samuel), J. Paterson, (B. Robson),
M. Kerr, C. Easton, A. McLaren, W. Dodds, (O. Coyle), J. McIntyre
Substitutes not used: D. Griffin, P. Jarvie
Livingston: R. McKenzie, D. McNamee, J. McAllister, (B. O'Brien),
O. Rubio, M. Andrews, E. Dorado, L. Makel, (F. Quino), B. Kerr,
S. Lovell, D. Fernandez, D. Lilley
Substitutes not used: J.P. McGovern, J. Camacho, K. Montgomery
Referee: Willie Young **Attendance:** 2,899

Thursday, 4th December, 2003

PARTICK THISTLE 0   **CELTIC 2**
                  C. Beattie, J. Smith

Partick Thistle: K. Arthur, J–Y. Anis, G. Murray, D. Whyte, D. Lilley,
K. Milne, A. Ross, D. Fleming, (S. Taylor), J.P. McBride, (W. Howie),
J. Grady, (J. Gemmell), J. Mitchell
Substitutes not used: A. Madaschi, K. Budinauckas
Celtic: D. Marshall, J. Mjallby, J. Kennedy, J. McNamara,
(U. Laursen), M. Sylla, S. Crainey, M. Gray, P. Lambert, (S. Guppy),
J. Smith, S. Maloney, C. Beattie
Substitutes not used: S. Varga, L. Miller, M. Hedman
Referee: Michael McCurry **Attendance:** 5,700

FOURTH ROUND
Tuesday, 2nd December, 2003

ABERDEEN 2   **LIVINGSTON 3**
(AET – 2–2 After 90 Minutes)
S. Tosh (2)   D. Lilley, F. Pasquinelli,
                  L. Makel

Aberdeen: D. Preece, A. Diamond, E. Deloumeaux, R. Anderson,
K. McNaughton, (C. Clark), M. Heikkinen, (P. Sheerin), S. Tosh,
K. Rutkiewicz, S. Muirhead, (D. Mackie), S. Booth, D. Zdrilic
Substitutes not used: L. Hinds, R. Esson
Livingston: R. McKenzie, D. McNamee, (J.P. McGovern),
J. McAllister, (F. Quino), O. Rubio, M. Andrews, E. Dorado, L. Makel,
B. O'Brien, S. Lovell, D. Fernandez, (F. Pasquinelli), D. Lilley
Substitutes not used: J. Camacho, A. Main
Referee: Stuart Dougal **Attendance:** 6,090

CIS Insurance Cup

Winners 2004

Wednesday, 3rd December, 2003

RANGERS 3   **ST. JOHNSTONE 0**
C. Burke, E. Ostenstad,
M. Mols

Rangers: A. McGregor, F. Ricksen, R. Malcolm, Z. Khizanishvili, P. Vanoli,
S. Hughes, E. Costa, C. Burke, (M. Ross), E. Ostenstad, (N. Capucho),
M. Mols, P. Lovenkrands
Substitutes not used: W. Gibson, A. Hutton, G. Smith
St. Johnstone: K. Cuthbert, J. Robertson, (R. Stevenson), R. Forsyth,
P. Bernard, D. Dods, I. Maxwell, P. Karper, (M-M. Paatelainen), M. Robertson,
P. MacDonald, S. Donnelly, B. McLaughlin, (E. Malone)
Substitutes not used: C. Hay, C. Nelson
Referee: Dougie McDonald **Attendance:** 28,395

DUNDEE 1   **HEARTS 0**   **(AET)**
R. Linn

Dundee: J. Speroni, D. Mackay, J. Hernandez, L. Mair, L. Wilkie, B. Smith,
M. Fotheringham, G. Rae, (B. Sancho), G. Brady, S. Lovell, (R. Linn), I. Novo
Substitutes not used: T. Hutchinson, D. Cameron, J. McCafferty
Hearts: C. Gordon, A. Maybury, P. Kisnorbo, A. Webster, R. Neilson,
N. Macfarlane, M. Stamp, (J-L. Valois), D. Wyness, (S. Severin),
P. Hartley, M. De Vries, (K. McKenna), A. Kirk
Substitutes not used: G. Wales, T. Moilanen
Referee: Willie Young **Attendance:** 7,130

Thursday, 18th December, 2003

HIBERNIAN 2   **CELTIC 1**
G. Brebner, K. Thomson   S. Varga

Hibernian: D. Andersson, J. Baillie, G. Smith, S. Whittaker,
M. Kouo-Doumbe, K. Thomson, G. Brebner, T. McManus,
(S. Dobbie), D. Riordan, G. O'Connor, S. Brown
Substitutes not used: K. Nicol, A. Reid, J. Shields, M. Hyldgaard
Celtic: R. Douglas, P. Lambert, (C. Beattie), S. Varga, R. Wallace, S. Crainey,
D. Balde, H. Larsson, A. Thompson, C. Sutton, (S. Maloney), J. Kennedy, L. Miller
Substitutes not used: U. Laursen, S. Guppy, D. Marshall
Referee: John Rowbotham **Attendance:** 9,246

SEMI-FINALS
Tuesday, 3rd February 2004
Easter Road Stadium, Edinburgh

DUNDEE 0   **LIVINGSTON 1**
          D. Lilley

Dundee: J. Speroni, D. Mackay, J. Hernandez, L. Mair, B. Sancho, B. Smith,
M. Fotheringham, N. Barrett, G. Brady, S. Lovell, (S. Milne), I. Novo
Substitutes not used: J. McCafferty, S. Kneissl, T. Hutchinson, S. Robb
Livingston: R. McKenzie, D. McNamee, J. McAllister, O. Rubio, (F. Pasquinelli),
M. Andrews, E. Dorado, L. Makel, B. O'Brien, S. Lovell, D. Fernandez, D. Lilley
Substitutes not used: J. Camacho, J.P. McGovern, F. Quino, A. Main
Referee: Michael McCurry **Attendance:** 7,231

Thursday, 5th February, 2004
The National Stadium, Hampden Park, Glasgow

HIBERNIAN 1   **RANGERS 1**
(AET – 1–1 After 90 Minutes)
S. Dobbie   M. Mols
Hibernian won 4–3 on Kicks from the Penalty Mark

Hibernian: D. Andersson, C. Murdock, R. Edge, (S. Dobbie),
G. Caldwell, M. Kouo-Doumbe, K. Thomson, J. Wiss, (S. Whittaker),
A. Reid, (T. McManus), D. Riordan, G. O'Connor, S. Brown
Substitutes not used: K. Nicol, A. Brown
Rangers: S. Klos, F. Ricksen, C. Moore, F. de Boer, M. Ball, M. Ross,
(P. Vanoli), M. Arteta, (Z. Khizanishvili), C. Nerlinger, R. de Boer,
(E. Ostenstad), M. Mols, S. Arveladze
Substitutes not used: N. Capucho, A. McGregor
Referee: Kenny Clark **Attendance:** 27,954

FINAL
Sunday, 14th March, 2004
The National Stadium, Hampden Park, Glasgow

HIBERNIAN 0   **LIVINGSTON 2**

Hibernian: D. Andersson, C. Murdock, G. Smith, (T. McManus),
R. Edge, M. Kouo-Doumbe, G. Caldwell, K. Thomson, A. Reid,
(S. Dobbie), D. Riordan, G. O'Connor, S. Brown
Substitutes not used: S. Whittaker, K. Nicol, A. Brown
Livingston: R. McKenzie, D. McNamee, (S. McLaughlin),
J. McAllister, O. Rubio, M. Andrews, E. Dorado, L. Makel, B. O'Brien,
(J.P. McGovern), S. Lovell, D. Fernandez, (F. Pasquinelli), D. Lilley
Substitutes not used: W. Snowdon, A. Main
Scorers: D. Lilley, J. McAllister
Referee: Willie Young **Attendance:** 45,443

THE CIS INSURANCE CUP 2003/04
ROUND BY ROUND GOALS ANALYSIS

GAME	NO. OF GOALS SCORED	TIES PLAYED	AVERAGE PER
FIRST ROUND	37	14	2.6
SECOND ROUND	52	12	4.3
THIRD ROUND	32	8	4
FOURTH ROUND	12	4	3
SEMI-FINALS	3	2	1.5
FINAL	2	1	2

TOTAL NO. OF GOALS SCORED	138
TOTAL NO. OF TIES PLAYED	41
AVERAGE GOALS PER GAME	3.4

Tennent's Scottish Cup Competition
Season 2003/2004

FIRST ROUND
Saturday, 22nd November, 2003

FORFAR ATHLETIC 1   **EAST FIFE 1**
A. Rattray   M. Hall

Forfar Athletic: M. Brown, P. Lunan, A. Rattray, D. McClune, R. Horn, K. Byers, B. Sellars, H. Davidson, P. Tosh, (D. Williams), D. Henderson, (M. Maher), P. Shields
Substitutes not used: N. Ferrie, S. Vella, D. Lowing
East Fife: G. O'Connor, C. McMillan, (B. Fairbairn), E. Donaldson, C. Lumsden, M. Hall, B. Blair, W. Stewart, (J. Mitchell), G. McDonald, K. Deuchar, S. Nicholas, G. Gilbert
Substitutes not used: M. Graham, C. Condie, C. Miller
Referee: Tom Brown **Attendance:** 651

ELGIN CITY 1   **PETERHEAD 2**
C. Campbell   M. Bavidge (2)

Elgin City: A. Goram, (M. Pirie), C. Campbell, A. Dempsie, J. White, C. Tully, J. Allison, (C. Ogboke), W. Martin, H. Dickson, A. Bone, N. McLean, R. McMullan
Substitutes not used: A. McMillan, K. Steele, D. Hind
Peterhead: P. Mathers, S. Mackay, S. McSkimming, (D. Stewart), K. Bain, M. Perry, I. Good, G. Stewart, (D. Smith), R. Duncan, (I. Stewart), M. Johnston, M. Bavidge, A. Roddie
Substitutes not used: J. Farquhar, J. Watt
Referee: Calum Murray **Attendance:** 726

GRETNA 4   **DUMBARTON 0**
I. Stevens, G. Skelton,
D. Holdsworth, W. Gordon

Gretna: D. Mathieson, M. Birch, L. Maddison, R. Prokas, D. Irons, D. Holdsworth, R. Baldacchino, (W. Gordon), M. Galloway, (S. Cosgrove), M. Cameron, (J. Allan), I. Stevens, G. Skelton
Substitutes not used: D. Wylie, G. Cohen
Dumbarton: S. Grindlay, (R. White), C. McEwan, C. Brittain, J. McKinstry, N. Collins, C. Boyle, S. Bonar, M. Bradley, E. Obidile, I. English, (I. Russell), J. Dillon, (I. Dobbins)
Substitutes not used: B. Donald, D. Smith
Referee: Eddie Smith **Attendance:** 652

MONTROSE 1   **ALBION ROVERS 1**
M. Wood   J. Mercer

Montrose: J. Butter, B. Donachie, S. Ferguson, E. Smith, J. McQuillan, S. Kerrigan, K. Webster, K. Gibson, (C. Smart), S. Michie, M. Wood, (C. Farnan), R. Black, (G. Sharp)
Substitutes not used: M. Hankinson, M. Simpson
Albion Rovers: N. Bennett, A. Paterson, J. Stirling, (J. Valentine), J. Smith, J. McCaig, K. McBride, K. McAllister, G. McCaul, M. Yardley, P. McManus, J. Mercer
Substitutes not used:
C. Fahey, P. Cormack, M. Molloy, M. McKenzie
Referee: Chris Boyle **Attendance:** 367

STIRLING ALBION 3   **QUEEN'S PARK 1**
J.G. Rowe, D. O'Brien,   S. McAuley
G. Kelly

Stirling Albion: M. Hogarth, P. Hay, D. Anderson, M. McNally, J.G. Rowe, A. Smith, (C. Scotland), D. Wilson, C. Ferguson, (G. Kelly), S. McLean, (R. Beveridge), B. Elliot, D. O'Brien
Substitutes not used: S. Morrison, C. Geddes
Queen's Park: D. Scrimgour, R. Clark, J. Thompson, S. Fallon, D. Agostini, S. Moffat, (D. Ferry), S. Reilly, J. Whelan, S. Kettlewell, A. Graham, (D. Carcary), S. McAuley, (F. Carroll)
Substitutes not used: D. Crawford, P. Gallagher
Referee: Martin Sproule **Attendance:** 617

SPARTANS 6   **BUCKIE THISTLE 1**
K. McLeod (2), P. Johnson,   F. More
C. Manson, P. Hobbins (2)

Spartans: K. Brown, J. Rae, S. Fowlie, P. Johnson, (R. Vinter), M. Burns, I. Thomson, (D. Tough), K. McLeod, (I. Crawford), J. Johnston, P. Hobbins, C. Manson, D. Henretty
Substitutes not used: C. Graham, J. McPartlin
Buckie Thistle: K. Main, J. Shewan, P. Lamberton, M. Slater, K. Small, (R. Smith), D. Munro, P. Catto, (N. Davidson), S. Taylor, C. Milne, F. More, (J. Coutts), M. MacDonald
Substitutes not used: A. Wilson, R. Taylor
Referee: Brian Winter **Attendance:** 358

COWDENBEATH 5   **EDINBURGH CITY 2**
J. Seeley (o.g.), B. Gilfillan,   C. Gordon, T. Moriarty
I. Mauchlen, G. Fusco,
D. Shields

Cowdenbeath: A. Carlin, C. Shand, (K. Gordon), D. McInally, B. Gilfillan, (L. Buchanan), J. McKeown, I. Ritchie, I. Mauchlen, C. Winter, D. Shields, G. Fusco, (J. Fallon), D. Mowat
Substitutes not used: A. Fleming, G. Brown
Edinburgh City: A. MacKintosh, N. Ferry, T. Moriarty, J. Seeley, B. Foster, R. McNamara, S. Godden, A. Donachie, (G. Burgess), C. Nye, (C. Gordon), G. McColl, C. Seeley, (D. Whyte)
Substitutes not used: S. Vannet, N. McCardle
Referee: Jamie Downie **Attendance:** 293

CLACHNACUDDIN 0   **STRANRAER 2**
A. Jenkins, M. Moore

Clachnacuddin: M. Rae, D. Mackay, S. MacLeod, S. MacDonald, D. Matheson, G. Morrison, (C. Campbell), A. Lewis, (C. Mitchell), N. MacCuish, I. Polworth, (B. McCraw), D. Ross, Michael Sanderson
Substitutes not used: Martin Sanderson, D. Brennan
Stranraer: A. McCondichie, S. Swift, F. Wright, D. Wingate, M. Henderson, A. Jenkins, K. Finlayson, (S. Marshall), S. Aitken, M. Moore, D. Graham, L. Sharp
Substitutes not used: K. Meechan, P. Kerr, T. McAllister, W.J. MacDonald
Referee: Andrew Hunter **Attendance:** 408

FIRST ROUND REPLAYS
Saturday, 29th November, 2003

ALBION ROVERS 1   **MONTROSE 3**
J. McQuillan (o.g.)   S. Michie (2), S. Ferguson

Albion Rovers: N. Bennett, A. Paterson, (C. Connolly), P. Cormack, J. Smith, J. McCaig, (M. McKenzie), S. Sweeney, M. Molloy, (J. Valentine), K. McBride, M. Yardley, P. McManus, J. Mercer
Substitutes not used: C. Fahey, K. McAllister
Montrose: J. Butter, B. Donachie, S. Ferguson, E. Smith, J. McQuillan, S. Kerrigan, (C. Farnan), K. Webster, K. Gibson, (C. Smart), S. Michie, M. Wood, (G. Sharp), R. Black
Substitutes not used: M. Hankinson, M. Simpson
Referee: Chris Boyle **Attendance:** 230

EAST FIFE 3   **FORFAR ATHLETIC 3**
(AET – 2–2 After 90 Minutes)
R. Horn (o.g.)   P. Tosh (3)
D. McClune (o.g.)
K. Deuchar
East Fife won 4–1 on Kicks from the Penalty Mark

East Fife: G. O'Connor, C. McMillan, E. Donaldson, C. Lumsden, M. Hall, B. Blair, W. Stewart, (J. Mitchell), G. McDonald, K. Deuchar, S. Nicholas, G. Gilbert
Substitutes not used: M. Graham, C. Condie, C. Miller
Forfar Athletic: M. Brown, D. Lowing, (M. Maher), A. Rattray, D. McClune, R. Horn, K. Byers, B. Sellars, H. Davidson, P. Tosh, D. Henderson, P. Shields
Substitutes not used: N. Ferrie, S. Vella, D. Ogunmade, D. Williams
Referee: Tom Brown **Attendance:** 561

SECOND ROUND
Saturday, 20th December, 2003

INVERURIE LOCO WORKS 1
C. Ross

AIRDRIE UNITED 5
O. Coyle (2), S. McKeown, A. Stewart, M. Roberts

Inverurie Loco Works: I. Thain, K. Fraser, S. Buchan, T. Wilson, J. Young, S. Park, R. Singer, (S. McKay), A. Walker, (E. Copland), K. Coull, (A. Low), C. Ross, R. McWilliam
Substitutes not used: L. Mellough, A. Bisset
Airdrie United: M. McGeown, S. Docherty, K. Black, A. Stewart, (W. Wilson), A. McManus, P. Ronald, (W. McLaren), S. McKeown, M. Wilson, O. Coyle, M. Roberts, (M. Glancy), A. Gow
Substitutes not used: P. Cherrie, J. Vareille
Referee: Garry Mitchell **Attendance:** 1,523

PETERHEAD 0

EAST FIFE 2
G. McDonald, S. Nicholas

Peterhead: P. Mathers, D. Smith, (I. Stewart), S. McSkimming, R. Raeside, M. Perry, I. Good, K. Tindal, (R. Duncan), S. Mackay, M. Johnston, M. Bavidge, A. Roddie
Substitutes not used: J. Farquhar, K. Bain, K. McGuinness
East Fife: G. O'Connor, G. Russell, E. Donaldson, P. Mortimer, M. Hall, P. Kelly, C. McMillan, G. McDonald, K. Deuchar, (G. Gilbert), S. Nicholas, (J. Mitchell), W. Stewart, (B. Blair)
Substitutes not used: M. Graham, B. Fairbairn
Referee: John Fleming **Attendance:** 654

EAST STIRLINGSHIRE 0

COWDENBEATH 5
C. Winter, K. Gordon (2), I. Mauchlen, L. Buchanan

East Stirlingshire: J. Connolly, R. Maughan, G. McGhee, R. Hare, C. Reid, G. McLaren, (G. Boyle), S. Livingstone, (S. Irvine), J. Leishman, (J. Mackay), D. Ure, S. Kelly, C. Baldwin
Substitutes not used: P. Rodden, C. Todd
Cowdenbeath: A. Carlin, C. Shand, D. Mowat, B. Gilfillan, J. McKeown, G. Fusco, I. Mauchlen, (R. Matheson), C. Winter, D. Shields, K. Gordon, (L. Buchanan), L. McGuinness, (D. McInally)
Substitutes not used: A. Fleming, G. Brown
Referee: Steven Duff **Attendance:** 244

ALLOA ATHLETIC 3
A.B. Ferguson, R. Hamilton, R. Walker

SPARTANS 3
I. Thomson, P. Johnson, C. Manson

Alloa Athletic: G. McGlynn, I. Nicolson, I. Little, P. McLaughlin, J. McGowan, S. Walker, R. Walker, A.B. Ferguson, R. Hamilton, S. Callaghan, G. Evans, (K. Kelbie)
Substitutes not used: J. Evans, M. Watson, M. Daly, A. Seaton
Spartans: K. Brown, J. Rae, S. Fowlie, P. Johnson, M. Burns, I. Thomson, K. McLeod, J. Johnston, (I. Crawford), P. Hobbins, C. Manson, D. Henretty, (D. Tough)
Substitutes not used: C. Graham, R. Vinter, J. McPartlin
Referee: Scott MacDonald **Attendance:** 477

GRETNA 5
I. Stevens (2), G. Cohen, G. Skelton, R. Baldacchino

STENHOUSEMUIR 1
A. Brown

Gretna: D. Mathieson, M. Birch, L. Maddison, R. Prokas, (S. Cosgrove), D. Irons, D. Holdsworth, R. Baldacchino, M. Galloway, I. Stevens, G. Cohen, G. Skelton, (W. Gordon)
Substitutes not used: C. Summersgill, J. Allan, R. McGuffie
Stenhousemuir: W. McCulloch, K. Gaughan, G. McKenna, R. McQuilter, J. McKenzie, S. Murphy, M. Harty, S. Hamilton, (M. Lauchlen), A. Brown, P. Flannery, (D. Carr), P. Bonar
Substitutes not used: A. Hardie, A. Smith, G. McCulloch
Referee: Cammy Melville **Attendance:** 426

STIRLING ALBION 1
G. Kelly

ARBROATH 2
J. McGlashan (2)

Stirling Albion: M. Hogarth, P. Hay, D. Anderson, M. McNally, J.G. Rowe, A. Smith, D. Wilson, (S. Devine), G. Kelly, S. McLean, (B. Elliot), R. Davidson, (D. Cummings), D. O'Brien
Substitutes not used: S. Morrison, C. Ferguson
Arbroath: M. Peat, K. McMullan, (J. McAulay), D. King, S. Rennie, P. Browne, J. Dow, (G. Henslee), A. Cargill, M. McCulloch, I. Diack, J. McGlashan, G. Swankie, (J. Herkes)
Substitutes not used: A. Mitchell, E. Graham
Referee: Colin Hardie **Attendance:** 647

BERWICK RANGERS 4
A. Redford (o.g.), G. Hutchison (3)

HUNTLY 2
G. Farmer, R. Stainer

Berwick Rangers: N. Inglis, D. Murie, A. Neill, G. McNicoll, (P. Hilland), M. Cowan, M. Neil, C. Waldie, G. Connell, (M. McCormick), G. Hutchison, (S. Kerrigan), G. McCutcheon, P. Hampshire
Substitutes not used: R. Godfrey, M. Burke
Huntly: B. Thompson, A. Redford, S. Scott, A. Stephen, D. Henderson, (G. Green), G. McGowan, R. Craig, (R. Stainer), R. Guild, J. O'Driscoll, M. Gray, G. Farmer, (M. De Barros)
Substitutes not used: G. Pennant, A. Hendry
Referee: Eddie Mack **Attendance:** 255

Saturday, 27th December, 2003

MONTROSE 1
M. Wood

THREAVE ROVERS 0

Montrose: J. Butter, B. Donachie, S. Ferguson, E. Smith, J. McQuillan, S. Kerrigan, K. Webster, (G. Sharp), K. Gibson, C. Smart, M. Wood, (C. Farnan), R. Black, (R. Henderson)
Substitutes not used: M. Hankinson, M. Simpson
Threave Rovers: D. Gall, G. McMinn, J. Wilson, P. McGinley, S. Whiteford, J. Haney, A. Sloan, K. Neilson, C. Budrys, M. Nicol, M. Baker, (M. Adams)
Substitutes not used: R. McCombe, J. Cranson, M. Kirkpatrick, A. McGinley
Referee: John Gilmour
Attendance: 520

MORTON 4
C. Miller, A. Williams (2), P. Weatherson

VALE OF LEITHEN 0

Morton: C. Coyle, D. Collins, E. Bottiglieri, D. MacGregor, S. Greacen, (S. Bannerman), M. Maisano, (J. Adam), C. Miller, J. Maisano, A. Williams, P. Weatherson, (W. Hawke), P. Walker
Substitutes not used: D. McGurn, J. McAlister
Vale of Leithen: S. Lumsden, S. Weir, C. Lothian, G. Lothian, C. Pilon, M. Hume, J. Kayser, (C. Baxter), D. Lockhart, (D. Shanks), G. Hastie, (R. Edge), A. Morrell, S. Paliczka
Substitutes not used: C. MacKenzie, R. Clark
Referee: Mike Tumilty **Attendance:** 3,231

STRANRAER 0

HAMILTON ACADEMICAL 1
J. Quitongo

Stranraer: A. McCondichie, S. Swift, F. Wright, D. Wingate, M. Henderson, A. Jenkins, (T. McAllister), K. Finlayson, (B. Crawford), S. Aitken, M. Moore, D. Graham, L. Sharp, (A. Grant)
Substitutes not used: K. Meechan, G. Guy
Hamilton Academical: D. McEwan, R. Walker, (A. Whiteford), S. Hodge, S.W. Thomson, T. Lumsden, A. Arbuckle, B. Carrigan, C. Aitken, J. Quitongo, B. McPhee, (D. Gribben), M. Corcoran, (C. Donnelly)
Substitutes not used: R. Jellema, S. Convery
Referee: Brian Cassidy
Attendance: 820

SECOND ROUND REPLAY
Saturday, 27th December, 2003

SPARTANS 5
(AET – 3–3 After 90 Minutes)
C. Manson, K. McLeod, K. Hughes, I. Crawford, C. Valentine (o.g.)

ALLOA ATHLETIC 3
J. McGowan, S. Walker, A.B. Ferguson

Spartans: K. Brown, J. Rae, S. Fowlie, P. Johnson, M. Burns, I. Thomson, K. McLeod, (K. Hughes), J. Johnston, (I. Crawford), P. Hobbins, C. Manson, (R. Vinter), D. Henretty
Substitutes not used: C. Graham, J. McPartlin
Alloa Athletic: G. McGlynn, I. Nicolson, A. Seaton, (G. Evans), J. McGowan, S. Walker, C. Valentine, R. Walker, A.B. Ferguson, R. Hamilton, I. Little, S. Callaghan
Substitutes not used: J. Evans, K. Kelbie, M. Watson, P. McLaughlin
Referee: Scott MacDonald
Attendance: 590

DUNFERMLINE ATHLETIC 3 **DUNDEE UNITED 1**
S. Crawford (2), C. Brewster   D. McInnes

Dunfermline Athletic: D. Stillie, S. Wilson, S.M. Thomson,
A. Skerla, G. Dempsey, (A. Tod), Darren Young, B. Nicholson,
G. Mason, Derek Young, (L. Bullen), S. Crawford, (N. Hunt),
C. Brewster
Substitutes not used: S.Y. Thomson, S. MacNicol
Dundee United: P. Gallacher, A. Archibald, D. McCracken,
(J. Paterson), M. Wilson, S. Duff, C. Easton, D. McInnes, C. Miller,
(G. Holmes), A. McLaren, W. Dodds, C. Samuel, (J. Scotland)
Substitutes not used: P. Jarvie, S. Anderson
Referee: Hugh Dallas **Attendance:** 6,140

RAITH ROVERS 1   **KILMARNOCK 3**
V. Talio   G. McSwegan, G.McDonald,
                           C. Nish

Raith Rovers: R. Gonzalez, C. Patino, G. Stanic, V. Talio, (J. Martin),
A. Calderon, D. Brady, C. Stanley, F. Rivas, J. Sutton,
J. Boyle, (M. Prest), D. Evans, (R. Pereira Gomez)
Substitutes not used: J. Sweeney, F. McKeown
Kilmarnock: F. Dubourdeau, G. Shields, F. Dindeleux, G. Greer,
G. Hay, J. Fowler, S. Fulton, G. Locke, C. Nish, (K. Boyd),
G. McSwegan, (D. Invincible), G. McDonald
Substitutes not used: C. Meldrum, B. McLaughlin, S. Murray
Referee: Mike Ritchie **Attendance:** 3,610

CELTIC 2   **ROSS COUNTY 0**
J. Hartson, P. Lambert

Celtic: R. Douglas, J. McNamara, C. Sutton, D. Balde, N. Lennon,
D. Agathe, (S. Pearson), R. Wallace, (C. Beattie), P. Lambert,
S. Maloney, (S. Petrov), H. Larsson, J. Hartson
Substitutes not used: M. Hedman, S. Varga
Ross County: G. Smith, J. McCunnie, H. Robertson, M. McCulloch,
S. Webb, J. Lauchlan, J. Rankin, D. Hannah, G. Bayne, (D. Cowie),
S. O'Donnell, (S. Higgins), D. Winters, (C. Gethins)
Substitutes not used: L. Fridge, S. McGarry
Referee: Iain Brines **Attendance:** 29,615

EAST FIFE 0   **QUEEN OF THE SOUTH 1**
                          S. O'Connor

East Fife: G. O'Connor, C. McMillan, E. Donaldson, G. McDonald,
M. Hall, P. Kelly, J. Mitchell, (W. Stewart), B. Blair,
K. Deuchar, (B. Fairbairn), S. Nicholas, G. Gilbert, (J. Stein)
Queen of the South: J. Dodds, E. Paton, A. Aitken, D. Bagan,
(P. Burns), B. Reid, J. Thomson, S. O'Connor, S. Bowey, A. Burke,
G. Wood, (P. McMullan), B. McColligan
Substitutes not used: S. Robertson, E. Jaconelli, S. Payne
Referee: Alan Freeland **Attendance:** 1,063

HEARTS 2   **BERWICK RANGERS 0**
M. Cowan (o.g.), J. Hamill

Hearts: C. Gordon, A. Maybury, S. Pressley, (R. Neilson),
P. Kisnorbro, A. Webster, R. Sloan, S. Severin, N. Macfarlane,
(J. Hamill), P. Hartley, M. De Vries, A. Kirk, (D. Wyness)
Substitutes not used: T. Moilanen, G. Weir
Berwick Rangers: N. Inglis, D. Murie, P. Hampshire, (J.N. Bennett),
G. McNicoll, M. Cowan, A. Neill, (P. Hilland), G. Connelly,
(G. Connell), M. Neil, G. Hutchison, G. McCutcheon, G. Forrest
Substitutes not used: R. Godfrey, K. Bracks
Referee: Willie Young **Attendance:** 8,516

MORTON 0   **PARTICK THISTLE 3**
                          D. Rowson, J. Grady (2)

Morton: C. Coyle, D. Collins, E. Bottiglieri, D. MacGregor,
P. Gaughan, (P. Cannie), M. Maisano, (S. Bannerman),
C. Millar, J. Maisano, A. Williams, (J. Uotinen),
P. Weatherson, P. Walker
Substitutes not used: D. McGurn, R. Henderson
Partick Thistle: K. Arthur, (S. Pinkowski), D. Lilley, (E. Forrest),
G. Murray, A. Madaschi, K. Milne, I. Ross, D. Rowson, J. Mitchell,
J.P. McBride, J. Grady, A. Thomson, (S. Bonnes)
Substitutes not used: E. Panther, J. Gemmell
Referee: John Rowbotham **Attendance:** 6,613

ST. JOHNSTONE 0   **MOTHERWELL 3**
                          D. Clarkson (2), S. McDonald

St. Johnstone: C. Nelson, M. Baxter, J. McQuilken, P. Bernard,
J. Robertson, I. Maxwell, P. MacDonald, M. Reilly, M–M. Paatelainen,
(K. Parker), S. Donnelly, (C. Hay), B. McLaughlin, (S. Taylor)
Substitutes not used: K. Cuthbert, D. Dods
Motherwell: G. Marshall, M. Corrigan, S. Craigan, S. Hammell,
J. Dair, K. Lasley, (S. Fagan), P. Quinn, D.S. Leitch, D. Adams,
(P. O'Donnell), A. Burns, D. Clarkson, (S. McDonald)
Substitutes not used: B.J. Corr, W. Kinniburgh
Referee: Kevin Toner **Attendance:** 4,092

HAMILTON ACADEMICAL 2   **COWDENBEATH 0**
B. McPhee (2)

Hamilton Academical: D. McEwan, A. Whiteford, S. Hodge,
S.W. Thomson, T. Lumsden, A. Arbuckle, B. Carrigan, (D. Gribben),
C. Aitken, J. Quitongo, B. McPhee, (M. Corcoran), D. Ferguson, (J. Sherry)
Substitutes not used: R. Jellema, R. Orr
Cowdenbeath: A. Carlin, D. Mowat, D. McInally, B. Gilfillan,
(L. McGuinness), J. McKeown, (A. Campbell), I. Ritchie,
I. Mauchlen, C. Winter, D. Shields, L. Buchanan, (C. Shand),
Substitutes not used: A. Fleming, P. Orhue
Referee: Charlie Richmond **Attendance:** 1,096

CLYDE 3   **GRETNA 0**
A. Smith (2), J. Ross

Clyde: A. Morrison, (B. Halliwell), S. Mensing, S. McCluskey, A. Kernaghan,
M.McLaughlin, J.Ross, J.Fraser, C.Marshall, A.Smith, J.Gibson, I.Harty, (S.McConalogue)
Substitutes not used: P. Keogh, K. Fotheringham, M. Gilhaney
Gretna: D. Mathieson, M. Birch, G. Skelton, R. Prokas, (S. Cosgrove),
D. Irons, D. Holdsworth, R. Baldacchino, M. Galloway, (D. Lennon),
I. Stevens, G. Cohen, W. Gordon, (M. Cameron)
Substitutes not used: C. Summersgill, R. McGuffie
Referee: Ian Fyfe **Attendance:** 1,060

LIVINGSTON 1   **MONTROSE 0**
D. Fernandez

Livingston: R. McKenzie, D. McNamee, J. McAllister, E. Dorado,
M. Andrews, B. O'Brien, L. Makel, S. Lovell, D. Lilley, D. Fernandez,
F. Pasquinelli, (J.P. McGovern)
Substitutes not used: A. Main, C. McMenamin, S. McLaughlin, R. Brittain
Montrose: J. Butter, B. Donachie, S. Ferguson, E. Smith,
J. McQuillan, S. Kerrigan, K. Webster, (R. Henderson), K. Gibson,
(G. Smith), C. Smart, M. Wood, G. Sharp, (E. Hall)
Substitutes not used: M. Hankinson, C. Farnan
Referee: Craig Mackay **Attendance:** 2,657

ABERDEEN 0   **DUNDEE 0**

Aberdeen: D. Preece, A. Diamond, S. Morrison, R. Anderson,
K. Rutkiewicz, M. Heikkinen, (P. Sheerin), S. Tosh, R. Foster,
(S. Muirhead), C. Clark, S. Booth, L. Hinds, (D. Zdrilic)
Substitutes not used: R. Esson, P. McGuire
Dundee: J. Speroni, D. Mackay, J. Hernandez, L. Mair, L. Wilkie,
B. Smith, M. Fotheringham, S. Robb, G. Brady, I. Novo, (N. Jablonski),
D. McLean, (B. Sancho)
Substitutes not used: D. Soutar, C. Macdonald, D. Cameron
Referee: John Underhill **Attendance:** 11,012

INVERNESS CAL. THISTLE 5   **BRECHIN CITY 1**
P. Ritchie (3), D. Bingham,   C. King
R. McBain

Inverness Cal. Thistle: M. Brown, R. Tokely, S. Golabek, R. Mann,
S. McCaffrey, R. Duncan, D. Mackie, R. McBain, (D. Thomson),
P. Ritchie, (C. MacMillan), L. Keogh, D. Bingham, (D. MacRae)
Substitutes not used: M. Fraser, G. Munro
Brechin City: D. Hay, M. Millar, P. Deas, I.G. Johnson, D. White,
J. Smith, C. King, M. McLeish, (S. McCulloch), C. Templeman,
(G. Miller), G. Gibson, (C. Boylan), A. Mitchell
Substitutes not used: S. Vanderdeyl, D. Paterson
Referee: Craig Thomson **Attendance:** 1,412

AYR UNITED 1   **FALKIRK 2**
D. Craig   J. Lee, D. Xausa

Ayr United: L. Roy, M. Smyth, M. Dunlop, (S. McGrady), S. Chaplain,
M. Campbell, D. Craig, M. McColl, D. Ramsay, S. Kean, A. Ferguson, L. Hardy
Substitutes not used: J. Hillcoat, W. Lyle, R. Burgess, C. Conway
Falkirk: D. Hill, A. Lawrie, C. McPherson, S. MacKenzie, J. Sharp, K. James,
J. O'Neil, (N. Scally), D. Xausa, J. Lee, (D. Colquhoun), R. Latapy, K. McAnespie
Substitutes not used: J. Hutchison, R. McStay, P. Creaney
Referee: Stuart Dougal **Attendance:** 2,632

ST. MIRREN 2　　　　　**AIRDRIE UNITED 0**
B. Lavety, D. McKenna

St. Mirren: S. Woods, K. Broadfoot, S. Lappin, A. Millen,
K. McGowne, M. Dempsie, R. Gillies, (M. Crilly), J. O'Neil, R. Dunn,
(B. Lavety), B. McGinty, (D. McKenna), H. Murray
Substitutes not used: C. Smith, D. Van Zanten
Airdrie United: M. McGeown, S. Docherty, N. McGowan,
A. Stewart, A. McManus, P. Ronald, S. McKeown, (D. Dunn),
M. Wilson, (K. Christie), O. Coyle, M. Roberts, (J. Vareille), A. Gow
Substitutes not used: L. Hollis, W. McLaren
Referee: Calum Murray **Attendance:** 3,049

HIBERNIAN 0　　　　　**RANGERS 2**
　　　　　　　　　　　　　S. Arveladze, P. Lovenkrands

Hibernian: D. Andersson, C. Murdock, G. Smith, M. Kouou-Doumbe,
S. Whittaker, K. Thomson, S. Brown, G. Brebner, (K. Nicol),
D. Riordan, G. O'Connor, S. Dobbie
Substitutes not used: M. Hyldgaard, J. Baillie, A. Reid, A. Orman
Rangers: S. Klos, F. Ricksen, H. Berg, Z. Khizanishvili, P. Vanoli,
R. Malcolm, M. Arteta, N. Capucho, (M. Mols), C. Burke,
(H. Namouchi), S. Arveladze, P. Lovenkrands
Substitutes not used: A. McGregor, M. Ball, E. Ostenstad
Referee: Michael McCurry **Attendance:** 11,392

ARBROATH 1　　　　　**SPARTANS 4**
J. McGlashan　　　　　　　K. McLeod, C. Manson (2),
　　　　　　　　　　　　　P. Johnson

Arbroath: M. Peat, K. McMullan, D. King, S. Rennie, P. Browne,
(P. Farquharson), M. McCulloch, A. Cargill, G. Henslee,
(J. Herkes), I. Diack, J. McGlashan, G. Swankie, (A. Dow)
Substitutes not used: A. Mitchell, J. McAulay
Spartans: K. Brown, J. Rae, S. Fowlie, P. Johnson, M. Burns,
I. Thomson, (E. Hoy), K. McLeod, (R. Vinter), K. Hughes,
P. Hobbins, C. Manson, (I. Crawford), D. Henretty
Substitutes not used: C. Graham, J. McPartlin
Referee: Kenny Clark **Attendance:** 1,017

THIRD ROUND REPLAY
Wednesday, 21st January, 2004

DUNDEE 2　　　　　**ABERDEEN 3**
S. Robb, I. Novo　　　　　C. Clark, M. Heikkinen,
　　　　　　　　　　　　　D. Zdrilic

Dundee: J. Speroni, D. Mackay, J. Hernandez, L. Mair, L. Wilkie, B. Smith,
N. Jablonski, (S. Milne), S. Robb, G. Brady, I. Novo, R. Linn, (S. Lovell)
Substitutes not used: D. Soutar, C. Mcdonald, D. Cameron
Aberdeen: D. Preece, A. Diamond, S. Morrison, R. Anderson,
K. McNaughton, (S. Muirhead), M. Heikkinen, (P. Sheerin),
S. Tosh, C. Clark, B. Prunty, (D. Zdrilic), S. Booth, L. Hinds
Substitutes not used: R. Esson, R. Foster
Referee: John Underhill **Attendance:** 5,857

FOURTH ROUND
Saturday, 7th February, 2004

HEARTS 0　　　　　**CELTIC 3**
　　　　　　　　　　　　S. Petrov (2), H. Larsson

Hearts: C. Gordon, A. Maybury, S. Pressley, P. Kisnorbo, (A. Kirk),
A. Webster, P. Stamp, R. Sloan, (R. Neilson), N. Macfarlane,
(K. McKenna), P. Hartley, M. De Vries, D. Wyness
Substitutes not used: T. Moilanen, G. Weir
Celtic: R. Douglas, J. McNamara, S. Varga, J. Kennedy, A. Thompson,
S. Petrov, N. Lennon, S. Pearson, D. Agathe, H. Larsson, C. Sutton
Substitutes not used:
D. Marshall, J. Valgaeren, P. Lambert, S. Maloney, C. Beattie
Referee: Willie Young **Attendance:** 14,712

MOTHERWELL 3　　**QUEEN OF THE SOUTH 2**
D. Adams, A. Burns (2)　　S. O'Connor (2)

Motherwell: G. Marshall, M. Corrigan, S. Craigan, S. Hammell,
J. Dair, K. Lasley, (G. Bollan), P. Quinn, P. O'Donnell, D. Adams,
A. Burns, (S. McDonald), D. Clarkson
Substitutes not used: B.J. Corr, S. Fagan, W. Kinniburgh
Queen of the South: J. Dodds, E. Paton, J. McAlpine,
(P. McMullan), D. Bagan, B. Reid, A. Aitken, S. O'Connor, S. Bowey,
G. Wood, (E. Jaconelli), S. Payne, (B. McColligan), P. Burns
Substitutes not used: S. Robertson, A. Burke
Referee: Michael McCurry **Attendance:** 8,101

CLYDE 1　　　**DUNFERMLINE ATHLETIC 2**
M. McLaughlin　　　　N. Hunt, B. Nicholson
Match Abandoned After 57 Minutes due to Snow

Clyde: A. Morrison, S. Mensing, K. Fotheringham, S. McCluskey,
M. McLaughlin, J. Ross, D. Hagen, C. Marshall, A. Smith, J. Gibson, I. Harty
Substitutes not used:
B. Halliwell, M. Gilhaney, S. McConalogue, P. Keogh, A. Kernaghan
Dunfermline Athletic: D. Stillie, A. Tod, S.M. Thomson, A. Skerla, S. Wilson,
Darren Young, B. Nicholson, R. Byrne, N. Hunt, S. Crawford, Derek Young
Substitutes not used:
M. Ruitenbeek, G. Demspey, D. Grondin, A. Labonte, B. Mehmet
Referee: Charlie Richmond **Attendance:** 3,893

ST. MIRREN 0　　　**INVERNESS**
　　　　　　　　　　CALEDONIAN THISTLE 1
　　　　　　　　　　D. Thomson

St. Mirren: S. Woods, D. Van Zanten, (R. Dunn), C. McGroarty,
A. Millen, K. Broadfoot, M. Dempsie, R. Gillies, H. Murray, (B. Lavety),
B. McGinty, J. O'Neil, S. Lappin
Substitutes not used: C. Hinchcliffe, M. Crilly, A. Russell
Inverness Cal. Thistle: M. Brown, R. Tokely, S. Golabek, R. Mann,
G. Munro, R. Duncan, (C. Christie), D. Thomson, R. McBain,
P. Ritchie, L. Keogh, D. Bingham
Substitutes not used: M. Fraser, D. MacRae, C. MacMillan, L. MacKinnon
Referee: Tom Brown **Attendance:** 3,859

PARTICK THISTLE 5　**HAMILTON ACADEMICAL 1**
J. Mitchell, G. Britton (2),　M. Corcoran
J.P. McBride, S. Bonnes

Partick Thistle: K. Arthur, W. Gibson, I. Ross, (D. Fleming),
A. Madaschi, K. Milne, G. Murray, D. Rowson, J. Mitchell, (J-Y. Anis),
J.P. McBride, J. Grady, G. Britton, (S. Bonnes)
Substitutes not used: J. Langfield, A. Gibson
Hamilton Academical: D. McEwan, A. Whiteford, S. Hodge,
S.W. Thomson, T. Lumsden, A. Arbuckle, B. Carrigan, C. Aitken, J. Quitongo,
(R. Blackadder), B. McPhee, (S. Convery), J. Sherry, (M. Corcoran)
Substitutes not used: R. Jellema, R. Walker
Referee: Kevin Toner **Attendance:** 4,004

FALKIRK 0　　　　　**ABERDEEN 2**
　　　　　　　　　　　　D. Zdrilic, S. Booth

Falkirk: A. Ferguson, A. Lawrie, C. McPherson, S. MacKenzie,
J. Hughes, J. Sharp, J. O'Neil, D. Xausa, (J. Lee), D. Colquhoun,
R. Latapy, K. McAnespie, (D. Nicholls)
Substitutes not used: D. Hill, N. Scally, I. MacSween
Aberdeen: D. Preece, A. Diamond, S. Morrison, R. Anderson,
K. McNaughton, (P. McGuire), M. Heikkinen, S. Tosh, C. Clark,
D. Zdrilic, (S. Muirhead), S. Booth, (B. Prunty), L. Hinds
Substitutes not used: R. Esson, P. Sheerin
Referee: Kenny Clark **Attendance:** 4,747

Sunday, 8th February, 2004

KILMARNOCK 0　　　　**RANGERS 2**
　　　　　　　　　　　　R. de Boer, S. Arveladze

Kilmarnock: F. Dubourdeau, B. McLaughlin, G. Greer, G. Hay,
J. Fowler, E. Skora, D. Invincible, (S. Murray), G. Locke, (R. Dodds),
M. Hardie, G. McSwegan, G. McDonald, (K. Boyd)
Substitutes not used: C. Meldrum, C. Nish
Rangers: S. Klos, F. Ricksen, C. Moore, H. Berg, M. Ball, M. Ross,
M. Arteta, (E. Ostenstad), C. Nerlinger, (P. Vanoli), R. de Boer,
S. Arveladze, N. Capucho, (H. Namouchi)
Substitutes not used: A. McGregor, Z. Khizanishvili
Referee: Dougie McDonald **Attendance:** 11,072

SPARTANS 0　　　　**LIVINGSTON 4**
　　　　　　　　　　　D. Lilley (3), D. Fernandez

Spartans: K. Brown, J. Rae, S. Fowlie, P. Johnson, (R. Vinter),
M. Burns, I. Thomson, (J. Johnston), K. McLeod, K. Hughes,
(W. Bennett), P. Hobbins, C. Manson, D. Henretty
Substitutes not used: C. Graham, J. McPartlin
Livingston: R. McKenzie, D. McNamee, J. McAllister,
(S. McLaughlin), E. Dorado, M. Andrews, B. O'Brien, L. Makel,
S. Lovell, (R. Brittain), D. Lilley, D. Fernandez, F. Pasquinelli,
(C. McMenamin)
Substitutes not used: A. Main, O. Rubio
Referee: Craig Thomson **Attendance:** 3,000

Replayed Tie due to Match being Abandoned
Tuesday, 24th February, 2004

CLYDE 0 **DUNFERMLINE ATHLETIC 3**
B. Nicholson (2), L. Bullen

Clyde: B. Halliwell, S. Mensing, K. Fotheringham, (P. Doyle), A. Kernaghan, S. McCluskey, J. Ross, D. Hagen, C. Marshall, P. Keogh, J. Fraser, (A. Smith), I. Harty, (M. Gilhaney)
Substitutes not used: A. Morrison, S. McConalogue
Dunfermline Athletic: D. Stillie, A. Tod, S.M. Thomson, (G. Mason), A. Skerla, (D. Grondin), S. Wilson, (S. Kilgannon), L. Bullen, B. Nicholson, R. Byrne, G. Dempsey, A. Labonte, B. Mehmet.
Substitutes not used: M. Ruitenbeek, S. MacNicol
Referee: Charlie Richmond **Attendance:** 2,441

FIFTH ROUND
Saturday, 6th March, 2004

ABERDEEN 1 **LIVINGSTON 1**
S. Muirhead R. Anderson (o.g.)

Aberdeen: D. Preece, P. McGuire, S. Morrison, R. Anderson, A. Diamond, (M. Hart), M. Heikkinen, S. Tosh, (S. Muirhead), R. Foster, C. Clark, B. Prunty, (D. Zdrilic), L. Hinds
Substitutes not used: R. Esson, P. Sheerin
Livingston: R. McKenzie, D. McNamee, J. McAllister, O. Rubio, M. Andrews, E. Dorado, L. Makel, B. O'Brien, S. Lovell, D. Fernandez, D. Lilley
Substitutes not used:
A. Main, R. Brittain, S. McLaughlin, F. Pasquinelli, C. McMenamin
Referee: Dougie McDonald **Attendance:** 11,593

PARTICK THISTLE 0 **DUNFERMLINE ATHLETIC 3**
R. Byrne, B. Nicholson, C. Brewster

Partick Thistle: K. Arthur, W. Gibson, G. Murray, A. Madaschi, K. Milne, (D. Fleming), I. Ross, D. Rowson, D. Chiarini, (J. Cadete), G. Britton, S. Bonnes, (A. Gibson), J. Mitchell
Substitutes not used: J. Langfield, T. English
Dunfermline Athletic: D. Stillie, L. Bullen, A. Tod, A. Skerla, S. Wilson, Darren Young, B. Nicholson, G. Mason, (G. Dempsey), R. Byrne, S. Crawford, (Derek Young), C. Brewster, (N. Hunt)
Substitutes not used: M. Ruitenbeek, A. Labonte
Referee: Alan Freeland **Attendance:** 5,335

MOTHERWELL 0 **INVERNESS CALEDONIAN THISTLE 1**
B. Wilson

Motherwell: G. Marshall, M. Corrigan, P. Quinn, S. Hammell, S. Craigan, K. Lasley, S. Fagan, (P. O'Donnell), S. McDonald, D. Adams, A. Burns, D. Clarkson, (K. Wright)
Substitutes not used: B.J. Corr, W. Kinniburgh, K. MacDonald
Inverness Caledonian Thistle: M. Brown, R. Tokely, S. Golabek, R. Mann, S. McCaffrey, R. Duncan, B. Wilson, R. McBain, P. Ritchie, (D. Proctor), L. Keogh, D. Thomson, (G. Munro)
Substitutes not used: M. Fraser, R. Hart, C. MacMillan
Referee: Kenny Clark **Attendance:** 7,934

Sunday, 7th March, 2004

CELTIC 1 **RANGERS 0**
H. Larsson

Celtic: R. Douglas, S. Varga, J. Valgaeren, (J. Kennedy), D. Balde, A. Thompson, S. Petrov, N. Lennon, J. McNamara, S. Pearson, (C. Beattie), (M. Sylla), H. Larsson, D. Agathe
Substitutes not used: D. Marshall, P. Lambert
Rangers: S. Klos, F. Ricksen, C. Moore, F. de Boer, H. Berg, M. Ball, S. Hughes, (S. Thompson), G. Rae, M. Arteta, (R. de Boer), S. Arveladze, P. Lovenkrands
Substitutes not used: A. McGregor, M. Ross, Z. Khizanishvili
Referee: Hugh Dallas **Attendance:** 58,665

FIFTH ROUND REPLAY
Thursday, 18th March, 2004

LIVINGSTON 1 **ABERDEEN 0**
B. O'Brien

Livingston: R. McKenzie, D. McNamee, J. McAllister, O. Rubio, M. Andrews, E. Dorado, L. Makel, B. O'Brien, S. Lovell, (S. McLaughlin), D. Fernandez, D. Lilley
Substitutes not used:
A. Main, F. Pasquinelli, C. McMenamin, R. Brittain

Aberdeen: D. Preece, P. McGuire, S. Morrison, M. Hart, A. Diamond, M. Heikkinen, S. Muirhead, (R. Foster), P. Sheerin, C. Clark, (F. Tiernan), D. Zdrilic, (B. Prunty), L. Hinds
Substitutes not used: R. Esson, J. Stewart
Referee: Dougie McDonald **Attendance:** 4,487

SEMI-FINALS
Saturday, 10th April, 2004

The National Stadium, Hampden Park, Glasgow

INVERNESS CAL. THISTLE 1 **DUNFERMLINE ATHLETIC 1**
P. Ritchie C. Brewster

Inverness Cal. Thistle: M. Brown, R. Tokely, S. Golabek, R. Mann, S. McCaffrey, R. Duncan, B. Wilson, (D. Thomson), R. McBain, P. Ritchie, (S. Hislop), L. Keogh, D. Bingham, (D. Proctor)
Substitutes not used: M. Fraser, G. Munro
Dunfermline Athletic: D. Stillie, L. Bullen, A. Tod, A. Skerla, G. Mason, (D. Grondin), Darren Young, B. Nicholson, R. Byrne, (G. Dempsey), Derek Young, S. Crawford, C. Brewster
Substitutes not used: M. Ruitenbeek, A. Labonte, B. Mehmet
Referee: Hugh Dallas **Attendance:** 13,255

Sunday, 11th April, 2004

The National Stadium, Hampden Park, Glasgow

LIVINGSTON 1 **CELTIC 3**
C. McMenamin C. Sutton (2), H. Larsson

Livingston: R. McKenzie, D. McNamee, E. Dorado, O. Rubio, (R. Brittain), M. Andrews, S. McLaughlin, L. Makel, B. O'Brien, S. Lovell, (J.P. McGovern), D. Lilley, F. Pasquinelli, (C. McMenamin)
Substitutes not used: A. Main, W. Snowdon
Celtic: D. Marshall, S. Varga, J. Valgaeren, D. Balde, A. Thompson, (L. Miller), S. Petrov, N. Lennon, D. Agathe, S. Pearson, H. Larsson, (J. Mjallby), C. Sutton, (C. Beattie)
Substitutes not used: R. Douglas, P. Lambert
Referee: Kenny Clark **Attendance:** 26,152

SEMI-FINAL REPLAY
Tuesday, 20th April, 2004

Pittodrie Stadium, Aberdeen

INVERNESS CAL. THISTLE 2 **DUNFERMLINE ATHLETIC 3**
P. Ritchie, D. Bingham Darren Young, C. Brewster, B. Nicholson

Inverness Cal. Thistle: M. Brown, R. Tokely, (D. Proctor), S. Golabek, R. Mann, S. McCaffrey, R. Duncan, (D. Thomson), S. Hislop, R. McBain, P. Ritchie, (D. Mackie), L. Keogh, D. Bingham
Substitutes not used: M. Fraser, G. Munro
Dunfermline Athletic: D. Stillie, L. Bullen, G. Mason, (A. Labonte), A. Skerla, S. Wilson, Darren Young, B. Nicholson, G. Dempsey, (R. Byrne), Derek Young, S. Crawford, C. Brewster
Substitutes not used: S.Y. Thomson, A. Tod, B. Mehmet
Referee: Hugh Dallas **Attendance:** 5,728

FINAL
Saturday, 22nd May, 2004

The National Stadium, Hampden Park, Glasgow

DUNFERMLINE ATHLETIC 1 **CELTIC 3**

Dunfermline Athletic: D. Stillie, A. Labonte, G. Mason, (D. Grondin), A. Skerla, R. Byrne, (A. Tod), Darren Young, B. Nicholson, G. Dempsey, (L. Bullen), Derek Young, S. Crawford, C. Brewster
Substitutes not used:
S.Y. Thomson, B. Mehmet
Celtic: D. Marshall, J. McNamara, S. Varga, D. Balde, A. Thompson, S. Petrov, N. Lennon, D. Agathe, S. Pearson, (R. Wallace), H. Larsson, C. Sutton
Substitutes not used:
M. McGovern, P. Lambert, J. Mjallby, C. Beattie
Scorers: Dunfermline Athletic: A. Skerla
Celtic: H. Larsson(2), S. Petrov
Referee: Stuart Dougal **Attendance:** 50,846

The Bell's Cup Competition
Season 2003/2004

BELL'S CUP 2003
— Winners —

FIRST ROUND
Saturday, 2nd August, 2003

ST. MIRREN 3   **QUEEN'S PARK 2**
(AET – 2–2 After 90 Minutes)
M. Crilly, B. McGinty.   R. Clark, A. Graham,
J. O'Neil

St. Mirren: C. Hinchcliffe, D. Van Zanten, (J. O'Neil),
L. Ellis, K. McGowne, A. MacPherson, K. Broadfoot, R. Gillies,
(T. McHard), M. Crilly, B. McGinty, P. McKnight,
(R. Dunn), S. Lappin
Substitutes not used: J. Cuddihy, S. Woods
Queen's Park: D. Scrimgour, A. Dunning, (S. Canning),
D. McCallum, (D. Ferry), R. Sinclair, D. Agostini, S. Fallon,
R. Clark, S. Kettlewell, A. Graham, S. Reilly, D. Menelaws,
(S. McAuley)
Substitutes not used: S. Moffat
Referee: Willie Young **Attendance:** 1,808

ALBION ROVERS 1   **EAST FIFE 0**
I. Diack

Albion Rovers: C. Fahey, A. Paterson, (I. Diack),
J. Stirling, J. Smith, P. Cormack, J. McCaig, K. McAllister,
(C. Connolly), D. Farrell, P. McManus, (G. Robertson),
G. McCaul, J. Mercer
Substitutes not used: S. Kerr, K. Swain
East Fife: G. O'Connor, P. Kelly, C. Miller, P. Mortimer,
M. Hall, G. McDonald, (B. Blair), C. McMillan,
L. Byle, K. Deuchar, W. Stewart, (B. Fairbairn),
E. Donaldson, (J. Mitchell)
Substitutes not used: G. Russell, K. McKeown
Referee: David Somers **Attendance:** 250

COWDENBEATH 1   **ROSS COUNTY 2**
G. Brown   J. Rankin, A. Campbell (o.g.)

Cowdenbeath: A. Carlin, C. Shand, D. McInally,
A. Campbell, J. McKeown, D. Mowat, (R. Matheson),
I. Morris, (L. Buchanan), C. Winter, G. Brown, K. Gordon,
J. Fallon, (B. Gilfillan)
Substitutes not used: S. Boyle, A. Fleming
Ross County: C. Stewart, (L. Fridge), J. McCunnie,
S. Mackay, J. Tait, (S. O'Donnell), S. Malcolm,
M. McCulloch, J. Rankin, D. Hannah, S. Higgins, (G. Bayne),
H. Robertson, D. Winter
Substitutes not used: D. Cowie, C. Gethins
Referee: Brian Cassidy **Attendance:** 325

HAMILTON ACAD 2   **ST. JOHNSTONE 3**
(AET – 2–2 After 90 Minutes)
C. Aitken, B. McPhee   K. Parker, M–M. Paatelainen,
                   S. Donnelly

Hamilton Academical: D. McEwan, J. Fitter,
(A. Whiteford), B. Forbes, (R. Maxwell), S.W. Thomson,
T. Lumsden, J. Sherry, (D. Ferguson), B. Carrigan, C. Aitken,
S. Convery, B. McPhee, M. Corcoran
Substitutes not used: A. Waddell, R. Jellema
St. Johnstone: K. Cuthbert, J. Robertson, R. Forsyth,
R. Stevenson, (M. Baxter), D. Dods, I. Maxwell, K. Parker,
M. Reilly, M–M. Paatelainen, M. Fotheringham,
B. McLaughlin, (S. Donnelly)
Substitutes not used: S. McCluskey, E. Malone, C. Nelson
Referee: Stuart Dougal **Attendance:** 1,097

AIRDRIE UNITED 2   **MONTROSE 0**
S. McKeown (2)

Airdrie United: M. McGeown, W. Wilson, D. Dunn,
(M. Glancy), A. Stewart, A. McManus, N. McGowan,
J. Vareille, M. Wilson, S. McKeown, S. Docherty, (A. Gow),
M. Roberts, (P. Ronald)
Substitutes not used: S. Wilson
Montrose: J. Butter, B. Donachie, S. Ferguson, C. Farnan,
M. Simpson, G. Smith, K. Webster, (G. Sharp), K. Gibson,
C. Smart, (R. Henderson), M. Wood, G. Thomson
Substitutes not used: N. Stephen, F. Conway, M. Hankinso
Referee: Craig Thomson **Attendance:** 1,151

MORTON 4   **ARBROATH 3**
W. Hawke,   J. McGlashan (2),
P.Weatherson (3)   R. Graham

Morton: C. Coyle, D. Collins, E. Bottiglieri, D. MacGregor,
R. Henderson, S. Bannerman, (S. MacDonald), C. Miller,
J. Maisano, (J. Uotinen), W. Hawke, (P. Cannie),
P. Weatherson, P. Walker
Substitutes not used: P. Gaughan, D. McGurn
Arbroath: M. Peat, J. McAulay, (K. McMullan), D. King, A. Dow,
G. Denholm, J. Herkes, A. Cargill, G. Henslee, (J. Cusick), R. Graham
J. McGlashan, G. Swankie, (S. Kerrigan)
Substitutes not used: P. Durno, T. Woodcock
Referee: Charlie Richmond **Attendance:** 2,241

BRECHIN CITY 1   **FALKIRK 0**
C. King

Brechin City: K. Budinauckas, I. Davidson, R. Black,
(M. McCulloch), D. White, P. Deas, K. Fotheringham,
C. King, (J. Stein), I.G. Johnson, C. Templeman, D. Shields,
(G. Gibson), A. Mitchell
Substitutes not used: G. Miller, D. Hay
Falkirk: D. Hill, A. Lawrie, C. McPherson, S. MacKenzie,
J. Hughes, J. Sharp, J. Henry, K. Christie, (I. MacSween),
J. Lee, C. McMenamin, (A. Rodgers), N. Scally
Substitutes not used: P. Creaney, E. May, J. Hutchison
Referee: John Underhill **Attendance:** 938

STENHOUSEMUIR 0   **PETERHEAD 3**
                 R. Raeside, R. Grant,
                 I. Stewart

Stenhousemuir: W. McCulloch, S. Hamilton, A. Smith,
G. McCulloch, K. Gaughan, M. Booth, M. McGowan, (M. Harty),
J. McKenzie, A. Brown, (D. Johnstone), M. McDowell, M. Lauchlan
Substitutes not used: G. McKenna, D. Carr, N. Parry
Peterhead: P. Mathers, K. McGuinness, (M. Johnston),
S. McSkimming, R. Raeside, M. Perry, K. Bain, K. Tindal, M. Bavidge,
R. Grant, (I. Stewart), R. Duncan, (G. Stewart), A. Roddie
Substitutes not used: I. Good, J. Farquhar
Referee: Garry Mitchell **Attendance:** 256

AYR UNITED 1   **STIRLING ALBION 2**
(AET – 1–1 After 90 Minutes)
S. Kean   B. Elliot (2)

Ayr United: L. Roy, M. Smyth, C. Kerr, J. Latta,
M. Campbell, R. Burgess, (W. Lyle), S. Chaplain, A. Black, S.
Kean, S. Whalen, M. McColl, (C. Conway)
Substitutes not used: S. McGrady, B. Mullen, J. Hillcoat

Stirling Albion: M. Hogarth, P. Nugent, D. Anderson, M. McNally, J.G. Rowe, P. Hay, C. Ferguson, (C. McKinnon), S. Devine, S. McLean, (R. Beveridge), B. Elliot, D. O'Brien, (D. Wilson)
Substitutes not used: A. Smith, C. Scotland
Referee: Michael McCurry **Attendance:** 1,115

STRANRAER 2   QUEEN OF THE SOUTH 1
M. Moore (2)   D. Lyle

Stranraer: A. McCondichie, S. Swift, F. Wright, D. Wingate, M. Henderson, A. Jenkins, K. Finlayson, T. McAllister, M. Moore, (A. Grant), P. Kerr, (D. Turnbull), L. Sharp
Substitutes not used:
C. Cruickshank, S. Aitken, K. Meechan
Queen of the South: J. Dodds, E. Paton, S. Hodge, D. Bagan, A. Aitken, J. Thomson, S. O'Connor, S. Bowey, A. Burke, (W. Gibson), D. Lyle, J. McAlpine
Substitutes not used:
B. McColligan, D. Allan, P. Atkinson, C. Scott
Referee: Kenny Clark **Attendance:** 828

GRETNA 0   INVERNESS CAL. THISTLE 5
     D. Bingham, S. Hislop, P. Ritchie,
     R. Hart (2)

Gretna: D. Mathieson, M. Cleeland, (W. Gordon), G. Skelton, R. Robb, P. O'Neill, D. Holdsworth, M. Henney, M. Galloway, M. Cameron, G. Cohen, J. Allan, (S. Skinner)
Substitutes not used: K. Knox, D. Irons, D. Wylie
Inverness Cal. Thistle: M. Brown, R. Tokely, (D. Proctor), S. Golabek, R. Mann, S. McCaffrey, R. Duncan, R. Hart, S. Hislop, (C. Christie), P. Ritchie, (D. Thomson), R. McBain, D. Bingham
Substitutes not used: G. Munro, A. Ridgers
Referee: John Gilmour **Attendance:** 628

ALLOA ATHLETIC 1   CLYDE 2
S. Callaghan   S. McConalogue, J. Fraser

Alloa Athletic: G. McGlynn, B. Ferguson, P. McLaughlin, (R. Elliot), C. Valentine, J. McGowan, R. Hamilton, R. Walker, K. Kelbie, (G. Evans), S. Crabbe, S. Callaghan, I. Little
Substitutes not used: G. Gillan, A. Seaton, J. Evans
Clyde: B. Halliwell, S. Mensing, M. McLaughlin, J. Potter, J. Fraser, J. Ross, D. Hagen, A. Millen, P. Keogh, I. Harty, (M. Gilhaney), S. McConalogue, (C. Clark)
Substitutes not used:
A. Kernaghan, C. McBride, W. Reid
Referee: Hugh Dallas **Attendance:** 633

EAST STIRLINGSHIRE 2   RAITH ROVERS 5
S. Kelly, C. Baldwin   J. Sutton (2), M. Peers,
     M. Prest, C. Stanley

East Stirlingshire: C. Todd, R. Maughan, G. McLaren, D. Polwart, (C. Penman), C. Reid, G. McGhee, S. Livingstone, J. Mackay, S. Kelly, D. Ormiston, C. Baldwin
Substitutes not used:
G. Boyle, J. Leishman, G. McCulloch, S. Morrison
Raith Rovers: R. Gonzalez, C. Patino, A. Calderon, D. Brady, S. Dennis, C. Stanley, M. Peers, F. Rivas, J. Sutton, (J. Martin), R. Brittain, (R. Blackadder), M. Prest, (I. Brown)
Substitutes not used: A. Smith, J. Sweeney
Referee: Colin Hardie **Attendance:** 556

FORFAR ATHLETIC 4   ELGIN CITY 0
P. Tosh, P. Shields,
H. Davidson, M. Maher

Forfar Athletic: N. Ferrie, A. Rattray, D. Lowing, R. Horn, D. Stewart, D. McClune, (M. Maher), P. Lunan, B. Sellars, P. Tosh, (D. Williams), H. Davidson, P. Shields, (S. Taylor)
Substitute not used: S. Florence
Elgin City: M. Pirie, D. Hind, J. Gallagher, J. White, R. Coulter, J. Allison, W. Martin, C. McLean, (N. McLean), A. Bone, (S. McCormick), K. Steele, S. Murphy, (R. McMullen)
Substitutes not used: A. Smith, P. Hamilton
Referee: John Rowbotham **Attendance:** 444

SECOND ROUND
Tuesday, 12th August, 2003

PETERHEAD 1   INVERNESS CAL. THISTLE 2
D. Stewart   S. Hislop (2)

Peterhead: P. Mathers, K. Tindal, I. Good, R. Duncan, (M. Johnston), M. Perry, K. Bain, S. Mackay, I. Stewart, R. Grant, (G. Stewart), M. Bavidge, (D. Stewart), A. Roddie
Substitutes not used:
J. Watt, J. Farquhar
Inverness Cal. Thistle: M. Brown, R. Tokely, S. Golabek, R. Mann, S. McCaffrey, R. Duncan, R. Hart, S. Hislop, D. Bingham, (P. Ritchie), C. Christie, (D. Thomson), R. McBain
Substitutes not used:
D. Proctor, G. Munro, A. Ridgers
Referee: Alan Freeland **Attendance:** 886

FORFAR ATHLETIC 4   ALBION ROVERS 2
(AET – 2–2 After 90 Minutes)
P. Shields (3), M. Maher   P. McManus, I. Diack

Forfar Athletic: M. Brown, A. Rattray, S. Florence, (D. Lowing), R. Horn, D. Stewart, D. McClune, K. Byers, (M. Maher), B. Sellars, S. Taylor, (D. Williams), H. Davidson, P. Shields
Substitutes not used:
P. Lunan, N. Ferrie
Albion Rovers: C. Fahey, A. Paterson, J. Stirling, G. McCaul, P. Cormack, (A. Selkirk), J. McCaig, K. McBride, (C. Connolly), I. Diack, (K. McAllister), M. Yardley, P. McManus, J. Mercer
Substitutes not used:
G. Robertson, K. Swain
Referee: Craig Thomson **Attendance:** 423

ROSS COUNTY 5   DUMBARTON 0
D. Winters (3),
J. Hamilton (2)

Ross County: C. Stewart, J. McCunnie, (C. Campbell), S. Mackay, S. O'Donnell, (J. Tait), S. Malcolm, S. Webb, D. Cowie, D. Hannah, J. Hamilton, C. Gethins, (S. Higgins), D. Winters
Substitutes not used:
G. Bayne, L. Fridge
Dumbarton: S. Grindlay, J. McKinstry, C. Brittain, N. Collins, C. Duffy, D. Smith, S. Bonar, M. Bradley, P. Flannery, I. Russell, (G. Herd), (I. English), J. Dillon, (C. Boyle)
Substitutes not used:
S. Renicks, J. Wight
Referee: Ian Fyfe **Attendance:** 861

BRECHIN CITY 3   STIRLING ALBION 1
C. Templeman,   S. McLean
I.G. Johnson,
K. Fotheringham

Brechin City: K. Budinauckas, G. Miller, S. McCulloch, I.G. Johnson, D. White, K. Fotheringham, C. King, (I. Davidson), M. McCulloch, C. Templeman, D. Clark, (A. Mitchell), J. Stein, (G. Gibson)
Substitutes not used: P. Campbell, D. Hay
Stirling Albion: M. Hogarth, P. Nugent, D. Anderson, C. Scotland, (D. O'Brien), J.G. Rowe, P. Hay, (D. Wilson), C. Ferguson, S. McLean, (R. Davidson), B. Elliot, S. Devine, A. Smith
Substitutes not used: G. Kelly, C. Henny
Referee: John Rowbotham **Attendance:** 468

ST. MIRREN 2   BERWICK RANGERS 1
R. Gillies, J. O'Neil   G. McNicoll

St. Mirren: C. Hinchcliffe, A. MacPherson, L. Ellis, D. Van Zanten, G. McWilliam, M. Crilly, R. Gillies, J. O'Neil, B. McGinty, (S. Gemmill), A. Russell, (R. Dunn), S. Lappin
Substitutes not used: B. Gordon, D. McKenna, S. Woods
Berwick Rangers: N. Inglis, D. Murie, A. Neill, J.N. Bennett, G. McNicoll, G. Forrest, G. Connelly, (J. McAllister), G. Connell, P. Hampshire, M. McCormick, (D. Blackley), G. Hutchison, (D. Noon)
Substitutes not used: J. Birrell, R. Godfrey
Referee: Hugh Dallas **Attendance:** 1,747

BELL'S CUP

RAITH ROVERS 2   STRANRAER 0
A. Calderon, J. Sutton

Raith Rovers: R. Gonzalez, C. Patino, V. Talio, (A. Calderon),
D. Brady, I. Brown, C. Stanley, M. Peers, (R. Blackadder), F. Rivas,
J. Sutton, R. Brittain, M. Prest, (L. McCann)
Substitutes not used: F. McKeown, J. Sweeney
Stranraer: A. McCondichie, S. Swift, F. Wright, (G. Guy),
(D. Turnbull), D. Wingate, M. Henderson, A. Jenkins, K. Finlayson,
T. McAllister, (S. Aitken), M. Moore, P. Kerr, L. Sharp
Substitutes not used: A. Grant, K. Meechan
Referee: Iain Brines **Attendance:** 1,396

MORTON 1   AIRDRIE UNITED 2
J. Maisano   J. Vareille, M. Roberts

Morton: C. Coyle, D. Collins, E. Bottiglieri, (R. Henderson),
D. MacGregor, S. Greacen, M. Maisano, S. Bannerman, (C. Millar),
J. Maisano, (W. Hawke), A. Williams, P. Weatherson, P. Walker
Substitutes not used: J. Uotinen, D. McGurn
Airdrie United: M. McGeown, S. Docherty, K. Black, (S. Wilson),
A. Stewart, A. McManus, N. McGowan, J. Vareille, (M. Glancy),
M. Wilson, S. McKeown, (P. Ronald), A. Gow, M. Roberts
Substitutes not used: D. Dunn, L. Hollis
Referee: Willie Young **Attendance:** 3,317

CLYDE 0   ST. JOHNSTONE 1
                      K. Parker

Clyde: B. Halliwell, S. Mensing, M. McLaughlin, J. Potter, J. Fraser, J. Ross,
D. Hagen, A. Millen, P. Keogh, (M. Gilhaney), I. Harty, S. McConalogue, (J. Baird)
Substitutes not used: W. Reid, P. Doyle, A. Morrison
St. Johnstone: K. Cuthbert, J. Robertson, (M. Baxter), P. Lovering,
(R. Stevenson), S. Donnelly, D. Dods, I. Maxwell, K. Parker, M. Reilly,
M-M. Paatelainen, P. Bernard, E. Malone
Substitutes not used: S. McCluskey, M. Fotheringham, C. Nelson
Referee: Dougie McDonald **Attendance:** 1,521

THIRD ROUND
Tuesday, 26th August, 2003

INVERNESS CAL. 1   ROSS COUNTY 0
THISTLE
S. Hislop

Inverness Cal. Thistle: M. Brown, R. Tokely, S. Golabek, R. Mann,
S. McCaffrey, R. Duncan, R. Hart, S. Hislop, (D. Proctor), P. Ritchie,
R. McBain, D. Bingham, (D. Thomson)
Substitutes not used: G. Munro, L. MacKinnon, M. Fraser
Ross County: C. Stewart, J. McCunnie, S. Mackay, J. Tait,
S. Malcolm, M. McCulloch, J. Rankin, D. Hannah, S. Higgins,
(G. Bayne), J. Hamilton, (C. Gethins), D. Winters, (S. O'Donnell)
Substitutes not used: D. Cowie, L. Fridge
Referee: Willie Young **Attendance:** 2,631

ST. JOHNSTONE 1   BRECHIN CITY 2
R. Forsyth   C. Templeman, K. Fotheringham

St. Johnstone: K. Cuthbert, J. Robertson, R. Forsyth, S. Donnelly,
D. Dods, (M. Baxter), I. Maxwell, K. Parker, M. Fotheringham,
(C. Hay), M-M. Paatelainen, P. Bernard, E. Malone
Substitutes not used: M. Ferry, R. Stevenson, C. Nelson
Brechin City: D. Hay, I. Davidson, A. Mitchell, D. White, P. Deas,
K. Fotheringham, G. Miller, N. Jablonski, G. Gibson, (D. Shields),
C. Templeman, (C. Jackson), M. McCulloch, (C. King)
Substitutes not used: J. Stein, K. Budinauckas
Referee: Kenny Clark **Attendance:** 1,919

RAITH ROVERS 3   ST. MIRREN 2
M. Prest (2), J. Henry   A. Russell, J. O'Neil

Raith Rovers: R. Gonzalez, C. Patino, G. Stanic, R. Brittain, I. Brown, J. Henry,
C. Stanley, F. Rivas, J. Sutton, R. Blackadder, M. Prest, (J. Boyle)
Substitutes not used: V. Talio, M. Peers, D. Evans, R. Carroll
St. Mirren: C. Hinchcliffe, D. Van Zanten, (B. McGinty), L. Ellis,
K. McGowne, (M. Dempsie), K. Broadfoot, M. Crilly, R. Gillies,
R. Dunn, A. Russell, J. O'Neil, K. Twaddle, (S. Gemmill)
Substitutes not used: A. Muir, S. Woods
Referee: Dougie McDonald **Attendance:** 1,948

FORFAR ATHLETIC 0 AIRDRIE UNITED 2
                    S. Wilson, D. Dunn

Forfar Athletic: M. Brown, A. Rattray, D. Lowing, (S. Taylor), S. Vella, D. Stewart,
D. McClune, P. Lunan, (M. Maher), K. Byers, P. Tosh, H. Davidson, P. Shields
Substitutes not used: S. Florence, R. Horn, N. Ferrie
Airdrie United: M. McGeown, A. McManus, (W. Wilson), K. Black,
A. Stewart, S. Wilson, N. McGowan, J. Vareille, (P. Ronald),
M. Wilson, M. Roberts, D. Dunn, M. Glancy, (A. Gow)
Substitutes not used: D. Miller, P. Cherrie
Referee: John Rowbotham **Attendance:** 752

SEMI-FINALS
Tuesday, 16th September, 2003

RAITH ROVERS 0   INVERNESS CAL. THISTLE 4
                     B. Wilson (2), P. Ritchie (2)

Raith Rovers: R. Gonzalez, C. Patino, G. Stanic, D. Brady,
(A. Calderon), S. Dennis, R. Brittain, (K. Hawley), C. Stanley, F. Rivas,
J. Sutton, R. Blackadder, (S. Robb), M. Prest
Substitutes not used: J. Henry, J. Sweeney
Inverness Cal. Thistle: M. Brown, D. Proctor, S. Golabek,
R. Mann, (G. Munro), S. McCaffrey, R. Duncan, B. Wilson, R. McBain,
P. Ritchie, (S. Hislop), R. Hart, D. Bingham, (D. Thomson)
Substitutes not used: R. Tokely, A. Ridgers
Referee: Kenny Clark **Attendance:** 2,110

Wednesday, 17th September, 2003

BRECHIN CITY 1   AIRDRIE UNITED 2
(AET – 1–1 After 90 Minutes)
D. White   D. Dunn, A. Gow

Brechin City: D. Soutar, G. Miller, P. Deas, S. McCulloch, D. White,
K. Fotheringham, (G. Gibson), A. Mitchell, (J. Stein), N. Jablonski,
(C. King), C. Templeman, S. Hampshire, I.G. Johnson
Substitutes not used: K. McLeish, D. Hay
Airdrie United: M. McGeown, W. Wilson, K. Black, (F. Singbo)
A. McManus, S. Wilson, (S. Docherty) N. McGowan, J. Vareille,
M. Wilson, M. Roberts, D. Dunn, M. Glancy, (A. Gow)
Substitutes not used: P. Ronald, L. Hollis
Referee: Dougie McDonald **Attendance:** 803

FINAL
Sunday, 26th October, 2003
McDiarmid Park, Perth

INVERNESS CAL. 2   AIRDRIE UNITED 0
THISTLE

Inverness Cal. Thistle: M. Brown, R. Tokely, S. Golabek, R. Mann,
S. McCaffrey, R. Duncan, B. Wilson, R. Hart, (L. Keogh), P. Ritchie,
(S. Hislop), R. McBain, D. Bingham, (D. Thomson)
Substitutes not used: G. Munro, M. Fraser
Airdrie United: M. McGeown, S. Docherty, (F. Singbo), W. Wilson,
A. Stewart, A. McManus, S. Wilson, (P. Ronald), J. Vareille,
(S. McKeown), M. Wilson, M. Roberts, D. Dunn, A. Gow
Substitutes not used: M. Glancy, L. Hollis
Scorers: D. Bingham, S. Hislop
Referee: Willie Young **Attendance:** 5,428

THE BELLS CUP 2003/04
ROUND BY ROUND GOALS ANALYSIS

	NO. OF GOALS SCORED	TIES PLAYED	AVERAGE PER GAME
FIRST ROUND	52	14	3.7
SECOND ROUND	27	8	3.4
THIRD ROUND	11	4	2.75
SEMI-FINALS	7	2	3.5
FINAL	2	1	2

TOTAL NO. OF GOALS SCORED	**99**
TOTAL NO. OF TIES PLAYED	**29**
AVERAGE GOALS PER GAME	**3.4**

Minor Cup Competitions
Season 2003/2004

RESERVE LEAGUE CUP

FIRST ROUND

7th October, 2003

EAST FIFE	2	ARBROATH	3

14th October, 2003

ST. MIRREN	2	COWDENBEATH	1

20th October, 2003

HAMILTON ACAD	0	GRETNA	1

21st October, 2003

FALKIRK	2	FORFAR ATHLETIC	3
QUEEN'S PARK	0	ST. JOHNSTONE	2
STRANRAER	0	ALBION ROVERS	2
MORTON	0	RAITH ROVERS	2

18th November, 2003

QUEEN OF THE SOUTH	1	AYR UNITED	3

(AET – 1-1 After 90 Minutes)

SECOND ROUND

11th November, 2003

FORFAR ATHLETIC	3	ST. JOHNSTONE	5

25th November, 2003

RAITH ROVERS	2	ARBROATH	0

17th December, 2003

GRETNA	0	ALBION ROVERS	1
AYR UNITED	1	ST. MIRREN	2

SEMI-FINALS

17th February, 2004

ST. JOHNSTONE	1	RAITH ROVERS	0

24th February, 2004

ST. MIRREN	3	ALBION ROVERS	0

FINAL

Tuesday, 27th April, 2004, St. Mirren Park, Paisley

ST. MIRREN	1	ST. JOHNSTONE	3

St. Mirren: S. Woods, B. Gordon, R. McCay, M. Crilly, (A. Muir), L. Ellis, A. MacPherson, (D. Martin), J. O'Neil, C. Molloy, R. Dunn, D. McKenna, C. McGroarty.
Substitutes not used: G. McWilliam, D. Jack, C. Smith
St. Johnstone: C. Nelson, N. Gibson, (C. Johnston), S. Fraser, E. Malone, J. Weir, I. Maxwell, B. McLaughlin, K. Moon, K. Parker, M. Fotheringham, P. Connolly, (A. Jackson)
Substitutes not used: W. Dyer, R. Bowers, P. Shaw
Scorers: St. Mirren: C. Molloy
St. Johnstone: K. Parker (2), A. Jackson
Referee: Stevie O'Reilly **Attendance:** 601

TENNENT'S SCOTTISH QUALIFYING CUP (SOUTH)

PRELIMINARY ROUND

Saturday, 16th August, 2003

EDINBURGH UNIVERSITY	0	THREAVE ROVERS	1
GIRVAN	2	GLASGOW UNIVERSITY	6
NEWTON STEWART	3	ST. CUTHBERT WANDERERS	9
SPARTANS	3	SELKIRK	0
WIGTOWN AND BLADNOCH	3	CIVIL SERVICE STROLLERS	1

FIRST ROUND

Saturday, 30th August, 2003

ANNAN ATHLETIC	2	BURNTISLAND SHIPYARD	4
COLDSTREAM	0	EDINBURGH CITY	7
GALA FAIRYDEAN	3	DALBEATTIE STAR	0
HAWICK ROYAL ALBERT	1	SPARTANS	5
THREAVE ROVERS	2	GLASGOW UNIVERSITY	1
VALE OF LEITHEN	11	TARFF ROVERS	0
WHITEHILL WELFARE	0	PRESTON ATHLETIC	1
WIGTOWN AND BLADNOCH	0	ST. CUTHBERT WANDERERS	3

SECOND ROUND

Saturday, 20th September, 2003

BURNTISLAND SHIPYARD	1	VALE OF LEITHEN	3
EDINBURGH CITY	6	GALA FAIRYDEAN	0
PRESTON ATHLETIC	0	SPARTANS	1
THREAVE ROVERS	2	ST. CUTHBERT WANDERERS	1

SEMI-FINALS

Saturday, 4th October, 2003

SPARTANS	5	THREAVE ROVERS	0
VALE OF LEITHEN	1	EDINBURGH CITY	2

FINAL

Saturday, 8th November, 2003

SPARTANS	1	EDINBURGH CITY	1

(AET) Spartans won 4-2 on Kicks from the Penalty Mark

TENNENT'S SCOTTISH QUALIFYING CUP (NORTH)

FIRST ROUND

Saturday, 30th August, 2003

CLACHNACUDDIN	2	WICK ACADEMY	0
FORRES MECHANICS	1	INVERURIE LOCO WORKS	3
FORT WILLIAM	1	COVE RANGERS	0
HUNTLY	7	GOLSPIE SUTHERLAND	1
KEITH	1	FRASERBURGH	1
LOSSIEMOUTH	0	DEVERONVALE	2
NAIRN COUNTY	2	BUCKIE THISTLE	5
ROTHES	3	BRORA RANGERS	2

FIRST ROUND REPLAY

Saturday, 6th September, 2003

FRASERBURGH	3	KEITH	2

SECOND ROUND

Saturday, 20th September, 2003

CLACHNACUDDIN	1	FRASERBURGH	1
DEVERONVALE	1	BUCKIE THISTLE	3
FORT WILLIAM	0	HUNTLY	2
ROTHES	0	INVERURIE LOCO WORKS	0

SECOND ROUND REPLAYS

Saturday, 27th September, 2003

FRASERBURGH	2	CLACHNACUDDIN	6
INVERURIE LOCO WORKS	1	ROTHES	0

SEMI-FINALS

Saturday, 4th October, 2003

| HUNTLY | 2 | CLACHNACUDDIN | 4 |
| INVERURIE LOCO WORKS | 1 | BUCKIE THISTLE | 2 |

FINAL

Saturday, 1st November, 2003

| CLACHNACUDDIN | 1 | BUCKIE THISTLE | 1 |

(AET) Buckie Thistle won 6-5 on Kicks from the Penalty Mark

SCOTTISH FOOTBALL ASSOCIATION YOUTH CUP

FIRST ROUND

HUNTLY	11	LOSSIEMOUTH	1
PETERHEAD	6	FORT WILLIAM	1
ELGIN CITY	1	FORRES MECHANICS	0
KEITH	3	INVERURIE LOCO WORKS	2
COVE RANGERS	5	ROTHES	1
MONTROSE	0	HAMILTON ACADEMICAL	5
CLYDE	5	BURNTISLAND SHIPYARD	1
HEARTS	3	ARBROATH	0
SPARTANS	2	FORFAR ATHLETIC	0
AIRDRIE UNITED	3	ST. MIRREN	2
BERWICK RANGERS	0	ALBION ROVERS	3
PARTICK THISTLE	1	STIRLING ALBION	0
ALLOA ATHLETIC	0	COWDENBEATH	2
BRECHIN CITY	4	EAST FIFE	3
ST. CUTHBERT WANDERERS	2	ANNAN ATHLETIC	5
HAWICK ROYAL ALBERT	3	GIRVAN	2
DALBEATTIE STAR	1	STRANRAER	4
GALA FAIRYDEAN	1	GRETNA	2

SECOND ROUND

DEVERONVALE	2	ELGIN CITY	7
HUNTLY	5	NAIRN COUNTY	2
PETERHEAD	4	CLACHNACUDDIN	1
FRASERBURGH	4	COVE RANGERS	3
BRORA RANGERS	3	KEITH	5
BRECHIN CITY	0	STENHOUSEMUIR	3
ALBION ROVERS	3	SPARTANS	0
COWDENBEATH	1	CIVIL SERVICE STROLLERS	0
CLYDE	6	QUEEN'S PARK	1
HEARTS	3	MORTON	1
PRESTON ATHLETIC	2	ST. JOHNSTONE	3
VALE OF LEITHEN	1	PARTICK THISTLE	2
AIRDRIE UNITED	2	HAMILTON ACADEMICAL	1
GRETNA	2	STRANRAER	1
QUEEN OF THE SOUTH	11	HAWICK ROYAL ALBERT	0
NEWTON STEWART	0	ANNAN ATHLETIC	8

THIRD ROUND

| BUCKIE THISTLE | 0 | STENHOUSEMUIR | 5 |
| COWDENBEATH | 1 | CELTIC | 1 |

(Celtic won 4-2 on Kicks from the Penalty Mark)

EDINBURGH CITY	3	ELGIN CITY	1
QUEEN OF THE SOUTH	0	LIVINGSTON	7
INVERNESS C.T.	0	PARTICK THISTLE	1
GRETNA	2	AYR UNITED	3
DUNDEE UNITED	3	ST. JOHNSTONE	0
PETERHEAD	1	MOTHERWELL	3
DUNDEE	1	HEARTS	2
ANNAN ATHLETIC	0	FALKIRK	5
RANGERS	4	FRASERBURGH	0
KEITH	0	HIBERNIAN	8
ROSS COUNTY	5	ALBION ROVERS	0
HUNTLY	1	KILMARNOCK	10
ABERDEEN	2	AIRDRIE UNITED	0
CLYDE	0	DUNFERMLINE ATHLETIC	5

FOURTH ROUND

HEARTS	2	HIBERNIAN	1
MOTHERWELL	0	KILMARNOCK	2
ABERDEEN	1	AYR UNITED	0
LIVINGSTON	2	PARTICK THISTLE	0
ROSS COUNTY	5	EDINBURGH CITY	1
DUNDEE UNITED	2	RANGERS	3
DUNFERMLINE ATHLETIC	2	FALKIRK	4
CELTIC	4	STENHOUSEMUIR	1

FIFTH ROUND

ROSS COUNTY	1	KILMARNOCK	4
LIVINGSTON	0	HEARTS	1
RANGERS	4	FALKIRK	1
CELTIC	2	ABERDEEN	1

SEMI-FINALS

| HEARTS | 0 | KILMARNOCK | 2 |
| CELTIC | 0 | RANGERS | 1 |

FINAL

Monday, 10th May, 2004 – Rugby Park, Kilmarnock

| KILMARNOCK | 1 | RANGERS | 0 |

Kilmarnock: Bell, Sangster, Hamill, Cochrane, McGregor, Johnstone, Masterston, (Butcher), Naismith, Sloan, (Coyne), Boyle, Campbell
Substitutes not used: Wild, Noble, Murray
Rangers: Robinson, Jacmot, (Dick), McMillan, Watson, MacKenzie, Kalenga, Gilmour, McCormack, Davidson, Adam, Fetai, (Johnston)
Substitutes not used: Agnew, Lennon, Gallacher
Scorer: Campbell
Referee: Eddie Smith **Attendance:** 3,281

UNDER-19 YOUTH LEAGUE CUP

SECTIONAL RESULTS – SECTION 1

15th February, 2004

| AIRDRIE UNITED | 0 | ALLOA ATHLETIC | 0 |

15th February, 2004

FALKIRK	0	ALLOA ATHLETIC	0
STENHOUSEMUIR	1	ST. MIRREN	0
STIRLING ALBION	0	MORTON	5

23rd February, 2004

| QUEEN'S PARK | 2 | ALBION ROVERS | 1 |

29th February, 2004

| MORTON | 3 | QUEEN'S PARK | 0 |

6th March, 2004

| QUEEN'S PARK | 2 | ST. MIRREN | 1 |

7th March, 2004

| FALKIRK | 0 | MORTON | 4 |
| STIRLING ALBION | 2 | AIRDRIE UNITED | 0 |

14th March, 2004

| STENHOUSEMUIR | 4 | STIRLING ALBION | 0 |

17th March, 2004

| ALLOA ATHLETIC | 3 | ALBION ROVERS | 0 |

21st March, 2004

| ALBION ROVERS | 0 | MORTON | 1 |
| ALLOA ATHLETIC | 1 | ST. MIRREN | 2 |

24th March, 2004

| AIRDRIE UNITED | 0 | QUEEN'S PARK | 0 |

28th March, 2004

ST. MIRREN	3	ALBION ROVERS	1
STENHOUSEMUIR	0	FALKIRK	0
STIRLING ALBION	2	QUEEN'S PARK	4

2nd April, 2004

| ALBION ROVERS | 0 | FALKIRK | 2 |

4th April, 2004

| ALBION ROVERS | 2 | AIRDRIE UNITED | 0 |
| ALLOA ATHLETIC | 1 | STENHOUSEMUIR | 1 |

6th April, 2004

| QUEEN'S PARK | 2 | STENHOUSEMUIR | 1 |

8th April, 2004			
MORTON	0	ST. MIRREN	1
10th April, 2004			
FALKIRK	1	STIRLING ALBION	1
11th April, 2004			
STENHOUSEMUIR	1	ALBION ROVERS	0
15th April, 2004			
STIRLING ALBION	0	ALLOA ATHLETIC	3
18th April, 2004			
ALLOA ATHLETIC	1	QUEEN'S PARK	2
MORTON	0	STENHOUSEMUIR	0
ST. MIRREN	2	AIRDRIE UNITED	0
22nd April, 2004			
FALKIRK	2	AIRDRIE UNITED	1
ALBION ROVERS	1	STIRLING ALBION	1
25th April, 2004			
ST. MIRREN	5	STIRLING ALBION	2
MORTON	2	ALLOA ATHLETIC	1
29th April, 2004			
AIRDRIE UNITED	3	MORTON	2
QUEEN'S PARK	1	FALKIRK	1
2nd May, 2004			
AIRDRIE UNITED	2	STENHOUSEMUIR	0
ST. MIRREN	3	FALKIRK	1

SECTION 1 – FINAL TABLE

	P	W	L	D	F	A	PTS
ST. MIRREN	8	6	2	0	17	8	18
QUEEN'S PARK	8	5	1	2	13	10	17
MORTON	8	5	2	1	17	5	16
STENHOUSEMUIR	8	3	2	3	8	5	12
FALKIRK	8	2	2	4	7	10	10
ALLOA ATHLETIC	8	2	3	3	10	7	9
AIRDRIE UNITED	8	2	4	2	6	10	8
STIRLING ALBION	8	1	5	2	8	23	5
ALBION ROVERS	8	1	6	1	5	13	4

SECTIONAL RESULTS – SECTION 2

22nd February, 2004			
COWDENBEATH	6	ROSS COUNTY	2
ELGIN CITY	1	ARBROATH	4
FORFAR ATHLETIC	0	EAST FIFE	1
7th March, 2004			
ARBROATH	6	BRECHIN CITY	1
COWDENBEATH	3	FORFAR ATHLETIC	2
PETERHEAD	1	ROSS COUNTY	8
14th March, 2004			
EAST FIFE	3	ARBROATH	2
FORFAR ATHLETIC	5	PETERHEAD	1
ROSS COUNTY	3	ELGIN CITY	0
21st March, 2004			
BRECHIN CITY	2	EAST FIFE	0
COWDENBEATH	8	PETERHEAD	2
28th March, 2004			
EAST FIFE	1	COWDENBEATH	3
FORFAR ATHLETIC	1	ARBROATH	1
PETERHEAD	2	ELGIN CITY	1
ROSS COUNTY	5	BRECHIN CITY	0
4th April, 2004			
ARBROATH	3	PETERHEAD	1
EAST FIFE	1	ROSS COUNTY	3
ELGIN CITY	3	COWDENBEATH	3
11th April, 2004			
ROSS COUNTY	6	FORFAR ATHLETIC	0
ELGIN CITY	1	EAST FIFE	4
BRECHIN CITY	1	COWDENBEATH	1
18th April, 2004			
PETERHEAD	0	BRECHIN CITY	2
ARBROATH	1	ROSS COUNTY	3
25th April, 2004			
ARBROATH	1	COWDENBEATH	3

2nd May, 2004			
EAST FIFE	3	PETERHEAD	0
ELGIN CITY	5	FORFAR ATHLETIC	1
6th May, 2004			
BRECHIN CITY	1	FORFAR ATHLETIC	4
9th May, 2004			
BRECHIN CITY	5	ELGIN CITY	2

SECTION 2 – FINAL TABLE

	P	W	L	D	F	A	PTS
ROSS COUNTY	7	6	1	0	30	9	18
COWDENBEATH	7	5	0	2	27	12	17
EAST FIFE	7	4	3	0	13	11	12
ARBROATH	7	3	3	1	18	13	10
BRECHIN CITY	7	3	3	1	12	18	10
FORFAR ATHLETIC	7	2	4	1	13	18	7
ELGIN CITY	7	1	5	1	13	22	4
PETERHEAD	7	1	6	0	7	30	3

SEMI-FINALS

9th May, 2004			
ST. MIRREN	2	COWDENBEATH	0
ROSS COUNTY	0	QUEEN'S PARK	3

FINAL

Monday, 17th May, 2004 – St. Mirren Park, Paisley

ST. MIRREN	2	QUEEN'S PARK	3

(AET – 2-2 After 90 Minutes)

St. Mirren: C. Smith, Brian Gordon, Ben Gordon, (S. McKay), G. McWilliam, A. Muir, (G. Smith), C. Molloy, D. Martin, D. McKenna, S. Gemmill, (T. McHard), J. Baird, R. McCay
Substitutes not used: B. Taggart, A. Cowie
Queen's Park: D. Crawford, S. Lennon, (S. Gibson), A. Livingston, J. Brophy, A. Trouten, S. Molloy, R. Russell, J. Weir, J. White, (M. McLaughlin), D. Weatherston, (D. McLaughlin), B. Felvus
Substitutes not used: J. McElhinney, S. Mather
Scorers: St. Mirren: C. Molloy, J. Baird
Queen's Park: J. Weir, B. Felvus, D. McLaughlin
Referee: Steve McGeoch **Attendance:** 585

UNDER-17 YOUTH LEAGUE CUP

SEMI-FINALS

11th May, 2004			
CLYDE	2	RAITH ROVERS	1
12th May, 2004			
ST. JOHNSTONE	0	HAMILTON ACADEMICAL	1

FINAL

Wednesday, 19th May, 2004 – New Douglas Park, Hamilton

HAMILTON ACADEMICAL	1	CLYDE	1

(AET – 0-0 After 90 Minutes)
Hamilton Academical won 4-1 on Kicks from the Penalty Mark

Hamilton Academical: G. McLenaghan, A. Stevenson, J. McGeoghegan, R. McGregor, G. Tough, D. Lynch, A. Sim, (R. Porte), D. Anderson, (R. O'Donnell), P. McLeod, (S. Buckley), J. McArthur, (I. Stewart), J. Lawley, (M. McInally)
Clyde: C. Higgins, (C. Hanley), G. McDivett, (M. Kirk), M. Gallagher, R. Harris, S. Dornan, B. Lamb, (M. Napier), M. McJimpsey, (P. McLean), J.P. McKeever, P. Flaherty, D. McNaught, N. Johnston, (M. Stewart)
Scorers: Hamilton Academical: P. McLeod
Clyde: D. McNaught
Referee: Gary Hilland **Attendance:** 572

Player of the Year Awards

SCOTTISH PROFESSIONAL FOOTBALLERS ASSOCIATION

RANGER'S DEREK JOHNSTONE WON THE SPFA PLAYER OF THE YEAR IN SEASON 1977/78

CLYDE STRIKER IAN HARTY WITH HIS PFA FIRST DIVISION PLAYER OF THE YEAR AWARD

1977/78
Premier Division	**Derek Johnstone** Rangers
First Division	**Billy Pirie** Dundee
Second Division	**Dave Smith** Berwick Rangers
Young Player of the Year	**Graeme Payne** Dundee United

1978/79
Premier Division	**Paul Hegarty** Dundee United
First Division	**Brian McLaughlin** Ayr United
Second Division	**Michael Leonard** Dunfermline Athletic
Young Player of the Year	**Raymond Stewart** Dundee United

1979/80
Premier Division	**Davie Provan** Celtic
First Division	**Sandy Clark** Airdrieonians
Second Division	**Paul Leetion** Falkirk
Young Player of the Year	**John MacDonald** Rangers

1980/81
Premier Division	**Mark McGhee** Aberdeen
First Division	**Eric Sinclair** Dundee
Second Division	**Jimmy Robertson** Queen of the South
Young Player of the Year	**Charlie Nicholas** Celtic

1981/82
Premier Division	**Sandy Clark** Airdrieonians
First Division	**Brian McLaughlin** Motherwell
Second Division	**Pat Nevin** Clyde
Young Player of the Year	**Frank McAvennie** St. Mirren

1982/83
Premier Division	**Charlie Nicholas** Celtic
First Division	**Gerry McCabe** Clydebank
Second Division	**John Colquhoun** Stirling Albion
Young Player of the Year	**Paul McStay** Celtic

1983/84
Premier Division	**Willie Miller** Aberdeen
First Division	**Gerry McCabe** Clydebank
Second Division	**Jim Liddle** Forfar Athletic
Young Player of the Year	**John Robertson** Heart of Midlothian

1984/85
Premier Division	**Jim Duffy** Morton
First Division	**Gerry McCabe** Clydebank
Second Division	**Bernie Slaven** Albion Rovers
Young Player of the Year	**Craig Levein** Heart of Midlothian

1985/86
Premier Division	**Richard Gough** Dundee Utd
First Division	**John Brogan** Hamilton Academical
Second Division	**Mark Smith** Queen's Park
Young Player of the Year	**Craig Levein** Heart of Midlothian

1986/87
Premier Division	**Brian McClair** Celtic
First Division	**Jim Holmes** Morton
Second Division	**John Sludden** Ayr United
Young Player of the Year	**Robert Fleck** Rangers

1987/88
Premier Division	**Paul McStay** Celtic
First Division	**Alex Taylor** Hamilton Academical
Second Division	**Henry Templeton** Ayr Un
Young Player of the Year	**John Collins** Hibernian

1988/89
Premier Division	**Theo Snelders** Aberdeen
First Division	**Ross Jack** Dunfermline Ath
Second Division	**Paul Hunter** East Fife
Young Player of the Year	**Billy McKinlay** Dundee Ur

1989/90
Premier Division	**Jim Bett** Aberdeen
First Division	**Ken Eadie** Clydebank
Second Division	**Willie Watters** Kilmarnock
Young Player of the Year	**Scott Crabbe** Heart of Midlo

1990/91
Premier Division	**Paul Elliott** Celtic
First Division	**Simon Stainrod** Falkirk
Second Division	**Kevin Todd** Berwick Range
Young Player of the Year	**Eoin Jess** Aberdeen

1991/92
Premier Division	**Alistair McCoist** Rangers
First Division	**Gordon Dalziel** Raith Rove
Second Division	**Andrew Thomson** Queen of the South
Young Player of the Year	**Philip O'Donnell** Motherw

1992/93
Premier Division	**Andy Goram** Rangers
First Division	**Gordon Dalziel** Raith Rove
Second Division	**Alexander Ross** Brechin C.
Young Player of the Year	**Eoin Jess** Aberdeen

1993/94
Premier Division	**Mark Hateley** Rangers
First Division	**Richard Cadette** Falkirk
Second Division	**Andrew Thomson** Queen of the South
Young Player of the Year	**Philip O'Donnell** Motherw

1994/95
Premier Division	**Brian Laudrup** Rangers
First Division	**Stephen Crawford** Raith Rc
Second Division	**Derek McInnes** Greenock Mc
Third Division	**David Bingham** Forfar Athl
Young Player of the Year	**Charlie Miller** Rangers

1995/96
Premier Division	**Paul Gascoigne** Rangers
First Division	**George O'Boyle** St. Johnstc
Second Division	**Stephen McCormick** Stirling Al
Third Division	**Jason Young** Livingston
Young Player of the Year	**Jackie McNamara** Celtic

The Scottish Football Writers' Association

1996/97
Premier Division	**Paolo Di Canio** Celtic
First Division	**Roddy Grant** St. Johnstone
Second Division	**Paul Ritchie**
	Hamilton Academical
Third Division	**Iain Stewart**
	Inverness Caledonian Thistle
Young Player of the Year	**Robbie Winters**
	Dundee United

1997/98
Premier Division	**Jackie McNamara** Celtic
First Division	**James Grady** Dundee
Second Division	**Paul Lovering** Clydebank
Third Division	**Willie Irvine** Alloa Athletic
Young Player of the Year	**Gary Naysmith**
	Heart of Midlothian

1998/99
Scottish Premier League	**Henrik Larsson** Celtic
First Division	**Russell Latapy** Hibernian
Second Division	**David Bingham** Livingston
Third Division	**Neil Tarrant** Ross County
Young Player of the Year	**Barry Ferguson** Rangers

1999/2000
Scottish Premier League	**Mark Viduka** Celtic
First Division	**Stevie Crawford**
	Dunfermline Athletic
Second Division	**Brian Carrigan** Clyde
Third Division	**Steven Milne** Forfar Athletic
Young Player of the Year	**Kenny Miller** Hibernian

2000/01
Scottish Premier League	**Henrik Larsson** Celtic
First Division	**David Bingham** Livingston
Second Division	**Scott McLean** Partick Thistle
Third Division	**Steve Hislop** East Stirlingshire
Young Player of the Year	**Stilian Petrov** Celtic

2001/02
Scottish Premier League	**Lorenzo Amoruso** Rangers
First Division	**Owen Coyle** Airdrieonians
Second Division	**John O'Neil**
	Queen of the South
Third Division	**Paul McManus** East Fife
Young Player of the Year	**Kevin McNaughton** Aberdeen

2002/03
Scottish Premier League	**Barry Ferguson** Rangers
First Division	**Dennis Wyness**
	Inverness Caledonian Thistle
Second Division	**Chris Templeman** Brechin City
Third Division	**Alex Williams** Morton
Young Player of the Year	**James McFadden** Motherwell

2003/04
Scottish Premier League	**Chris Sutton** Celtic
First Division	**Ian Harty** Clyde
Second Division	**Paul Tosh** Forfar Athletic
Third Division	**Michael Moore** Stranraer
Young Player of the Year	**Stephen Pearson** Celtic

1965	**Billy McNeill** Celtic
1966	**John Greig** Rangers
1967	**Ronnie Simpson** Celtic
1968	**Gordon Wallace** Raith Rovers
1969	**Bobby Murdoch** Celtic
1970	**Pat Stanton** Hibernian
1971	**Martin Buchan** Aberdeen
1972	**Dave Smith** Rangers
1973	**George Connelly** Celtic
1974	**World Cup Squad**
1975	**Sandy Jardine** Rangers
1976	**John Greig** Rangers
1977	**Danny McGrain** Celtic
1978	**Derek Johnstone** Rangers
1979	**Andy Ritchie** Morton
1980	**Gordon Strachan** Aberdeen
1981	**Alan Rough** Partick Thistle
1982	**Paul Sturrock** Dundee United
1983	**Charlie Nicholas** Celtic
1984	**Willie Miller** Aberdeen
1985	**Hamish McAlpine** Dundee United
1986	**Sandy Jardine** Heart of Midlothian
1987	**Brian McClair** Celtic
1988	**Paul McStay** Celtic
1989	**Richard Gough** Rangers
1990	**Alex McLeish** Aberdeen
1991	**Maurice Malpas** Dundee United
1992	**Alistair McCoist** Rangers
1993	**Andy Goram** Rangers
1994	**Mark Hateley** Rangers
1995	**Brian Laudrup** Rangers
1996	**Paul Gascoigne** Rangers
1997	**Brian Laudrup** Rangers
1998	**Craig Burley** Celtic
1999	**Henrik Larsson** Celtic
2000	**Barry Ferguson** Rangers
2001	**Henrik Larsson** Celtic
2002	**Paul Lambert** Celtic
2003	**Barry Ferguson** Rangers
2004	**Jackie McNamara** Celtic

STEPHEN PEARSON, MARTIN O'NEILL & JACKIE McNAMARA WITH THEIR SFWA AWARDS

Bell's Monthly Award Winners

SEASON 2003/04

August, 2003
Player   **Peter Weatherson** Morton
Young Player   **John Sutton** Raith Rovers
First Division Manager   **John Hughes** Falkirk
Second Division Manager   **John McCormack** Morton
Third Division Manager   **Allan Moore** Stirling Albion

September, 2003
Player   **Mark Brown** Inverness C T
Young Player   **David Dunn** Airdrie United
First Division Manager   **John Robertson** Inverness C T
Second Division Manager   **Sandy Stewart** Airdrie United
Third Division Manager   **Allan Moore** Stirling Albion

October, 2003
Player   **Colin McKinnon** Stirling Albion
Young Player   **Kirk Broadfoot** St. Mirren
First Division Manager   **John Connolly** Queen of the South
Second Division Manager   **John McCormack** Morton
Third Division Manager   **Allan Moore** Stirling Albion

November, 2003
Player   **Paul Tosh** Forfar Athletic
Young Player   **David Winters** Ross County
First Division Manager   **John Hughes** Falkirk
Second Division Manager   **Raymond Stewart** Forfar Athletic
Third Division Manager   **Neil Watt** Stranraer

December, 2003
Player   **Ian Harty** Clyde
Young Player   **John Rankin** Ross County
First Division Manager   **Alan Kernaghan** Clyde
Second Division Manager   **John McCormack** Morton
Third Division Manager   **Rowan Alexander** Gretna

January, 2004
Player   **Michael Moore** Stranraer
Young Player   **Simon Lappin** St. Mirren
First Division Manager   **Dick Campbell** Brechin City
Second Division Manager   **Tom Hendrie** Alloa Athletic
Third Division Manager   **Neil Watt** Stranraer

February, 2004
Player   **Sean O'Connor** Queen of the South
Young Player   **Colin Marshall** Clyde
First Division Manager   **Alan Kernaghan** Clyde
Second Division Manager   **Sandy Stewart** Airdrie United
Third Division Manager   **Neil Watt** Stranraer

March, 2004
Player   **William McLaren** Airdrie United
Young Player   **William McLaren** Airdrie United
First Division Manager   **Antonio Calderon** Raith Rovers
Second Division Manager   **Sandy Stewart** Airdrie United
Third Division Manager   **Neil Watt** Stranraer

April, 2004
Player   **Derek Townsley** Gretna
Young Player   **William McLaren** Airdrie United
First Division Manager   **John Robertson** Inverness C T
Second Division Manager   **Allan Maitland** Hamilton Academical
Third Division Manager   **Neil Watt** Stranraer

SEASON AWARD WINNERS

Player of the Year   **Paul Ritchie** Inverness Caledonian Thistle
Young Player of the Year   **William McLaren** Airdrie United
First Division Manager of the Year   **John Robertson** Inverness Caledonian Thistle
Second Division Manager of the Year   **Sandy Stewart** Airdrie United
Third Division Manager of the Year   **Neil Watt** Stranraer
Bell's Angels   **Queen of the South F.C.**
Bell's Fan of the Year   **Ian Black** Queen of the South
Bell's Supporters Pub of the Year   **The Albert** Airdrie

Bank of Scotland
Monthly Award Winners

SEASON 2003/04

August, 2003
Player	**Michael Ball** Rangers
Young Player	**Mikel Arteta** Rangers
Manager of the Month	**Alex McLeish** Rangers

September, 2003
Player	**Shota Arveladze** Rangers
Young Player	**Zurab Khizanishvili** Rangers
Manager of the Month	**Alex McLeish** Rangers

October, 2003
Player	**Roddy McKenzie** Livingston
Young Player	**Liam Miller** Celtic
Manager of the Month	**Martin O'Neill** Celtic

November, 2003
Player	**Chris Sutton** Celtic
Young Player	**Stephen Hughes** Rangers
Manager of the Month	**Martin O'Neill** Celtic

December, 2003
Player	**Craig Brewster** Dunfermline Athletic
Young Player	**Craig Gordon** Hearts
Manager of the Month	**Steve Paterson** Aberdeen

January, 2004
Player	**Stilian Petrov** Celtic
Young Player	**David Clarkson** Motherwell
Manager of the Month	**Jim Duffy** Dundee

February, 2004
Player	**Steven Pressley** Hearts
Young Player	**Alexander Diamond** Aberdeen
Manager of the Month	**Terry Butcher** Motherwell

March, 2004
Player	**Neil Lennon** Celtic
Young Player	**David Marshall** Celtic
Manager of the Month	**Ian McCall** Dundee United

April, 2004
Player	**Barry Nicholson** Dunfermline Athletic
Young Player	**Derek Riordan** Hibernian
Manager of the Month	**Jimmy Calderwood** Dunfermline Athletic

CELTIC STRIKER CHRIS SUTTON SCOOPS
THE BANK OF SCOTLAND PREMIERLEAGUE
PLAYER OF THE SEASON AWARD

SEASON AWARD WINNERS

Player of the Year	**Chris Sutton** Celtic
Young Player of the Year	**Craig Gordon** Hearts
Manager of the Year	**Martin O'Neill** Celtic

"I never thought when I started out that I would have had as much enjoyment, made as many friends, visited as many places and had as much excitement as I have enjoyed over the past 25 years."

Willie Young

Looking back over
25 years

WOW! Can 25 years really come and go so quickly? In the same year that this august publication was making its debut, I was doing likewise as a referee on a red blaes pitch at Dawsholm Park in Glasgow in a Scottish Amateur Football League Reserve Division One match.......little did I know what I was letting myself in for!

Having played football to a reasonable standard as captain of the Ayrshire Schools' team and having played Junior football in that same county until a knee injury ended my hopes, I had to find something to do to avoid the horror of shopping trips on a Saturday afternoon with my dearly-beloathed! My cousin, Louis Thow, had been a referee for a number of years at that point and he suggested to me that refereeing would be just the ticket. I was somewhat sceptical, since I had given more than one referee a hard time during my playing days but I discovered that, a bit like a cold swimming pool, "once you're in it, its not too bad".

I did a couple of seasons in the amateur leagues and progressed into refereeing the Juniors in Ayrshire – not for the faint-hearted, let me tell you. In one of my early games, the ball was kicked out of the ground and I was less than happy with the replacement offered to me, so I shouted over to the bench to "get that balloon off" and a boy in the crowd shouted back "Who's going to referee the game, then?"

I refereed for a few seasons in Junior football before making it on to the SFA Official List as a Class 3A Official (known quite properly in those days as a "linesman"). My first appointment from The Scottish Football League in that capacity was in a game refereed by cousin Louis at East Stirlingshire –v– Raith Rovers in 1985. At this stage, refereeing was still only a hobby to me but my attitude towards it changed as I became more involved and, in particular, after I had my first taste of UEFA Cup football as a linesman in a Nantes –v– Torino game which was refereed by David Syme. After that, I applied myself more and made it my ambition to reach the top. I refereed the Scottish Junior Cup Final in 1990 in which Hill O' Beath beat Lesmahagow and at the start of the next season, I was promoted to the SFA Class One list.

The first game I refereed as a Class One Referee was Stirling Albion v Arbroath in the old Skol Cup. Prior to the start of the 2004/05 season, I had refereed 478 Scottish senior games and since I started in 1980, I have officiated at a total of 1,250 games........you could say that I've had a long apprenticeship!

My younger brother, Greig, however beat me into the pages of The Scottish Football League Review – he appeared in the first edition in season 1980/81 as a goalkeeper with Clyde, who were at that time managed by the former Scotland boss, Craig Brown. Greig's cherubic features also appeared in all their glory in the 1982/83 edition of the Review since Clyde had captured the Second Division Championship during the previous season. My much older brother, John, was a fairly useful footballer too but, like me, injury put paid to his ambitions.

We both maintain that the reason Greig was the only one of us to become a professional player is that, he was so hopeless as a boy, John and I wouldn't let him play outfield but insisted on sticking him in goals for all of our games – hence his later proficiency between the sticks for Clyde! John sat the referees' exam at the same time as me and refereed in amateur and Junior football for a number of years before making it on to the Class One list also, where he remained for several seasons before a back injury ended his refereeing days.

Greig moved south of the border with his job and played non- league football in the North of England for a number of years, including the odd FA Cup run, before taking up refereeing in England. Unfortunately, he left it too late to make it to the top level in England but he still enjoys his refereeing. Three refs in the one family (four, if you count Louis)! We must be daft – in fact, we are just football fanatics and as boys we spent many an exciting Saturday on the terracing at Somerset Park, Ayr with our parents – our mother being a fairly useful midfielder/goalkeeper herself!

During my 25 years, I have been fortunate to officiate in 68 games abroad in 27 different countries, ranging from Hong Kong to the USA, but principally in Europe. I had refereed at all of

the senior grounds in Scotland until the admission of Elgin City and Peterhead to The Scottish Football League in recent years but, with a bit of luck, I might complete the set before the end of this season. I love visiting the various grounds throughout the country where I have made many friends – I am even on speaking terms with a few spectators at certain grounds!

It has been a privilege to share an arena with some of the world's greatest players and there have been many to enjoy in the Scottish game too over the years – the dazzling skills of Gascoigne, Di Canio and Laudrup and the goalscoring proficiency of McCoist and Larsson, to name but a few.

I have refereed four Semi-Finals in the Scottish Football League Cup and four Semi-Finals in the Scottish Cup. I have had the honour of refereeing the Finals in both competitions – Hibernian –v– Livingston in 2004 and Heart of Midlothian –v– Rangers in 1998, respectively. I also refereed The Bell's Cup Final between Inverness Caledonian Thistle and Airdrie United in 2003.

As a linesman (there I go again!), I was on the FIFA List of International Linesmen for two years from 1992 and I was on their Referees' List for seven years after that before I hit the compulsory retirement age of 45. Two highlights were acting as linesman at England –v– Brazil when I incorrectly chalked off what would have been the winning Brazil goal (not too popular at home for that one!) and when I was reserve referee to Hugh Dallas at the 1999 UEFA Cup Final between Parma and Marseille in Moscow.

If you ask me about changes since I started out

– well, we've had several new clubs coming into membership of the SFL in recent years, bringing a freshness to the game. We've had foreign players coming here in greater numbers. Players generally are stronger, fitter and more athletic, the physical side of the game has diminished but less desirable aspects have emerged such as shirt pulling and simulation. Refereeing has become much more professional and, of course, we have now attracted a sponsor in the ironic shape of Specsavers, who are investing heavily in referee development.

There have been various law changes which have had a significant impact on the game – players level with the last defender are now on-side, professional fouls result in an automatic red card, back passes to goalkeepers have been outlawed, additional substitutes permitted and a six second rule imposed on goalkeepers – all with the aim of enhancing the enjoyment of the paying public. In the main, I think the changes have been successful and in my travels about the country last season, I saw enough young talent on display to suggest that the Scottish game still has the potential to produce some top class players and revive the fortunes of our national team.

I never thought when I started out that I would have had as much enjoyment, made as many friends, visited as many places and had as much excitement as I have enjoyed over the past 25 years. I am now in my 15th and final season on the Class One list and have mixed emotions – the usual excitement at the early stages of a new season tinged with the knowledge that I will have to find something else to avoid shopping trips on a Saturday afternoon when the season ends!

List of Referees
Season 2003/2004

CLASS 1 REFEREES
CATEGORY 1

CRAWFORD ALLAN
CHRIS BOYLE
IAIN BRINES
TOM BROWN
BRIAN CASSIDY
KENNY CLARK
WILLIAM COLLUM
STEVE CONROY
HUGH DALLAS
STUART DOUGAL
JAMIE DOWNIE
STEVEN DUFF
STEPHEN FINNIE
ALAN FREELAND
IAN FRICKLETON
IAN FYFE
COLIN HARDIE
ANDREW HUNTER
MICHAEL McCURRY
DOUGLAS McDONALD
SCOTT McDONALD
CRAIG MACKAY
CAMMY MELVILLE
ALAN MUIR
CALUM MURRAY
CHARLIE RICHMOND
MIKE RITCHIE
JOHN ROWBOTHAM
EDDIE SMITH
DAVID SOMERS
MARTIN SPROULE
CRAIG THOMSON
KEVIN TONER
MIKE TUMILTY
JOHN UNDERHILL
BRIAN WINTER
WILLIE YOUNG

CLASS 1 REFEREES
CATEGORY 2

RAMZAN BASHIR
ALAN BOYD
COLIN BROWN
TERRY BRUNTON
GRAHAM CHAMBERS
CRAIG CHARLESTON
GARY CHEYNE
PAUL CHEYNE
WILLIAM GILFILLAN
GARY HILLAND
WILLIE HORNBY

ANTHONY LAW
JOHN McKENDRICK
CRAIG MARSHALL
STEVEN NICHOLLS
EUAN NORRIS
MATT NORTHCROFT
STEVIE O'REILLY
THOMAS ROBERTSON
DEREK ROSE

CLASS 1
SPECIALIST ASSISTANT
REFEREES

FRANCIS ANDREWS
JAMES BEE
JOHN BICKNELL
NEIL BRAND
DEREK CLARK
FRANK COLE
STEVEN CRAVEN
MARTIN CRYANS
ALAN CUNNINGHAM
ANDY DAVIS
WILLIE DISHINGTON
MARK DOYLE
GEORGE DRUMMOND
LAWRENCE KERRIGAN
JIM LYON
STUART McAULAY
GORDON McBRIDE
BRIAN McDUFFIE
BRIAN McGARRY
GORDON MIDDLETON
RICKY MOONEY
TOM MURPHY
STEVE PULLAR
ANDREW SEYMOUR
STEWART SHEARER
CHARLIE SMITH
KEITH SORBIE
GARY SWEENEY
CHRIS YOUNG

CLASS 1
ASSISTANT REFEREES

ANDREW AIRD
STEPHEN ALLAN
JEFF BANKS
BILLY BAXTER
STUART BENNETT
WES BOULSTRIDGE
STUART CLINGAN
RODDY COBB

BRIAN COLVIN
WILLIE CONQUER
STEVEN CRICHTON
HUGH DALGETTY
COLIN DUNCAN
IAN ELMSLIE
STEVEN GEORGE
JOHN GILMOUR
RICHARD GOUGH
KEVIN GRAHAM
KEVIN GRANT
JASON HASSON
ROSS HASWELL
ALAN HOGG
TOMMY JOHNSTON
PETER KINNEY
GARY KIRKWOOD
STUART LOGAN
FRANK McDERMOTT
PAUL McDOWALL
STEVE McGEOUCH
JOHN McINALLY
DAVID McINTOSH
HUGH McINTYRE
GORDON MACKAY
CAMMY McKAY
DAVID McKENZIE
STEVEN McLEAN
BARRY McNAB
JAMES McNEIL
ANDY McWILLIAM
RUSSELL MAIN
RODNEY MARSHALL
BRIAN MARTIN
STEPHEN MARTIN
ALASTAIR MATHER
RYAN MILNE
MICHAEL MONAGHAN
NEIL MOONEY
DAVID MORAN
DEREK NICHOLLS
MORAG PIRIE
PAT RAFFERTY
ERIC ROBERTSON
GEORGE SALMOND
RICKY SMITH
BRIAN TEMPLETON
DAVID WATT
NEIL WATTERS
WILLIE WEIR
ROD WILLIAMSON
RONNIE WRIGHT
CRAIG YOUNG
EWAN YOUNG

SCOTTISH CLUBS IN EUROPE
Season 2003/2004
UEFA CHAMPIONS LEAGUE

SECOND QUALIFYING ROUND
FIRST LEG
Wednesday, 30th July, 2003,
S. Darius & S. Girenas Sport C, Kaunas

KAUNAS 0   **CELTIC 4**
Larsson, Sutton, Maloney, Miller

Kaunas: Padimanskas, Gvildys, Kancelskis, Petrenko, Regelskis, Papeckys,(Opic), Gedgaudas, Sirmelis, (Pastva), Zelmikas, Beniusis, (Karalius), Barevicius
Substitutes not used: Stonys, Sanajevas, Puotkalis, Kunevicius
Celtic: Douglas, Valgaeren, Larsson, Thompson, (Smith), Sutton, (Miller), Lambert, Agathe, Lennon, (Maloney), Petrov, Varga, Mjallby
Substitutes not used: Hedman, Sylla, McNamara, Crainey
Referee: Joaquim Paulo Paraty Da Silva (Portugal)
Attendance: 3,000

SECOND QUALIFYING ROUND
SECOND LEG
Wednesday, 6th August, 2003, Celtic Park, Glasgow

CELTIC 1   **KAUNAS 0**
Gvildys (o.g.)

Celtic: Douglas, Sylla, (Lennon), Valgaeren, Balde, Thompson, (Wallace),Sutton, Lambert, Maloney, (Beattie), Mjallby, Smith, Miller
Substitutes not used: Hedman, McNamara, Crainey, Kennedy
Kaunas: Padimanskas, Gvildys, Kancelskis, Petrenko, Beniusis, (Karalius) Opic, (Sanajevas), Regelskis, Papeckys, (Puotkalis), Gedgaudas, Barevicius, Zelmikas
Substitutes not used: Stonys, Kunevicius, Juodeikis, Sirmelis
Referee: Jacek Granat (Poland)
Attendance: 40,284 (Celtic won 5-0 on Aggregate)

THIRD QUALIFYING ROUND
FIRST LEG
Wednesday, 13th August, 2003, Puskas Ferenc, Budapest

MTK 0   **CELTIC 4**
Larsson, Agathe, Petrov, Sutton

MTK: Vegh, Molnar, (Pisont), Juhasz, Pusztai, Fuzi, Zavadszky, Halmai, Jezdimirovic, (Torghelle), Da Silva, Illes, Rednic, (Szabo)
Substitutes not used: Kovacs, Zabos, Czvitkovics, Pandur
Celtic: Douglas, Valgaeren, Balde, (Crainey), Larsson, Thompson, Sutton, Lambert, Agathe, (Sylla), Lennon, Petrov, (Miller), Varga
Substitutes not used: Hedman, McNamara, Maloney, Smith
Referee: Kim Milton Nielsen (Denmark)
Attendance: 5,000

Wednesday, 13th August, 2003, Ibrox Stadium, Glasgow

RANGERS 1   **FCK 1**
Lovenkrands   Jonsson

Rangers: Klos, Ricksen, Moore, Ferguson, Mols, R. de Boer, (Thompson), Arteta, Khizanishvili, Ball, Ross, (Capucho), Lovenkrands
Substitutes not used:
McGregor, Nerlinger, Malcolm, Vanoli, Berg
FCK: Raboczki, Urmas Rooba, Svensson, Albrechtsen, Mykland, Nielsen, Roll Larsen, Zuma, Jonsson, (Moller), Tobiasen, Norregaard
Substitutes not used:
Kihlstedt, Zivkovic, Bisgaard, Svard, Traore, Bech
Referee: Manuel Enrique Mejuto Gonzalez (Spain)
Attendance: 47,401

THIRD QUALIFYING ROUND
SECOND LEG
Wednesday, 27th August, 2003, Celtic Park, Glasgow

CELTIC 1   **MTK 0**
Sutton

Celtic: J. Hedman, Balde, (Kennedy), Larsson, (Hartson), Thompson, Sutton,Lambert, Agathe, Petrov, (Petta), Varga Crainey, Miller
Substitutes not used:
Douglas, Sylla, McNamara, Maloney
MTK: Vegh, Molnar, Komlosi, Juhasz, Halmai, Jezdimirovic Zavadszky, Pisont, (Czvitkovics), Torghelle, (Da Silva), Illes (Zabos), Fuzi
Substitutes not used:
Szantai, Rednic, Szabo, Pusztai
Referee: Wolfgang Stark (Germany)
Attendance: 41,720 (Celtic won 5-0 on Aggregate)

Wednesday, 27th August, 2003, Parken, Copenhagen

FCK 1   **RANGERS 2**
Santos   Arteta, Arveladze

FCK: Raboczki, Urmas Rooba, Svensson, Albrechtsen, Mykland, (Santos), Nielsen, Roll Larsen, Zuma, Jonsson, (Pettersson), Tobiasen, (Moller), Norregaard
Substitutes not used:
Kihlstedt, Zivkovic, Christiansen, Svard
Rangers: Klos, Ricksen, Ferguson, Arveladze, Nerlinger, Mols, (Thompson), R. de Boer, (Vanoli), Khizanishvili, Arteta, Ball, Berg, (Malcolm)
Substitutes not used:
McGregor, Capucho, Ross, Hughes
Referee: Zeljko Siric (Croatia)
Attendance: 37,000 (Rangers won 3-2 on Aggregate)

GROUP STAGE

Tuesday, 16th September, 2003, Ibrox Stadium, Glasgow

RANGERS 2   **STUTTGART 1**
Nerlinger, Lovenkrands   Kuranyi

Rangers: Klos, Ricksen, Emerson, (Capucho), Arveladze, Nerlinger, Mols, Khizanishvili, Vanoli, (Lovenkrands), Ball, Arteta, Berg
Substitutes not used: McGregor, Ostenstad, Malcolm, Ross, Hughes
Stuttgart: Hildebrand, Hinkel, Bordon, Meira, Gerber, (Szabics), Tiffert, Gleb, Heldt, (Meissner), Cacau, (Amanatidis), Soldo, Kuranyi
Substitutes not used: Heinen, Wenzel, Vranjes, Lahm
Referee: Gilles Veissiere (France)
Attendance: 47,957

Wednesday, 17th September, 2003, Olympiastadion, Munich

BAYERN MUNICH 2   **CELTIC 1**
Makaay (2)   Thompson

Bayern Munich: Kahn, Sagnol, Lizarazu, (Rau), Kovac, Makaay, Ze Roberto, Ballack, Pizarro, Salihamidzic, (Santa Cruz), Hargreaves, Linke
Substitutes not used: Schlosser, Kuffour, Demichelis, Schweinsteiger, Trochowski
Celtic: Hedman, McNamara, Balde, Larsson, Thompson, Sutton, Hartson, (Miller), Agathe, Lennon, Petrov, Varga
Substitutes not used: Douglas, Gray, Sylla, Petta, Maloney, Kennedy
Referee: Massimo de Santis (Italy)
Attendance: 48,500

Tuesday, 30th September, 2003, Celtic Park, Glasgow

CELTIC 2   **LYON 0**
Miller, Sutton

Celtic: Hedman, McNamara, Balde, Larsson, Thompson, Sutton, Hartson, (Miller), Agathe, Lennon, Petrov, Varga
Substitutes not used: Douglas, Gray, Sylla, Petta, Maloney, Kennedy
Lyon: Coupet, Deflandre, Edmilson, Diarra, Juninho, Elber, Carriere, (Essien), Reveillere, Govou, (Malouda), Muller, Dhorasoo, (Luyindula)
Substitutes not used: Vercoutre, Sartre, Berthod, Viale
Referee: Eduardo Iturralde Gonzalez (Spain)
Attendance: 58,027

Wednesday, 1st October, 2003, Apostolos Nikolaidis, Athens

PANATHINAIKOS 1   **RANGERS 1**
Konstantinidis   Emerson

Panathinaikos: Chalkias, Morris, Maric, Seitaridis, Vlaovic, (Papadopoulos), Epalle, (Konstantinidis), Zutautas, Kyrgiakos, (Goumas), Konstantinou, Fyssas, Michaelsen
Substitutes not used: Nikopolidis, Munch, Sanmartean, Basinas
Rangers: Klos, Moore, Emerson, Arveladze, (Nerlinger), Mols, Khizanishvili, Ball, Capucho, Arteta, Berg, Lovenkrands, (Vanoli)
Substitutes not used: McGregor, Ostenstad, Malcolm, Ross, Hughes
Referee: Arturo Dauden Ibanez (Spain)
Attendance: 13,718

Tuesday, 21st October, 2003, Constant van den Stock, Brussels

ANDERLECHT 1   **CELTIC 0**
Dindane

Anderlecht: Zitka, Deschacht, De Boeck, Zewlakow, Baseggio, Kolar, (Tihinen), Hasi, Wilhelmsson, (Hendrikx), Mornar, Dindane, Kompany
Substitutes not used: Peersman, Vanderhaeghe, Zetterberg, Traore, MacDonald
Celtic: Hedman, McNamara, (Valgaeren), Balde, Larsson, Thompson, Sutton, Hartson, Agathe, Lennon, (Miller), Petrov, Varga
Substitutes not used: Douglas, Gray, Sylla, Maloney, Kennedy
Referee: Fritz Stuchlik (Austria)
Attendance: 27,000

Wednesday, 22nd October, 2003, Ibrox Stadium, Glasgow

RANGERS 0   **MANCHESTER UNITED 1**
                              P. Neville

Rangers: Klos, Ricksen, Moore, Arveladze, Mols, Khizanishvili, (Ross), Vanoli, (Nerlinger), Ball, Arteta, Berg, Lovenkrands
Substitutes not used: McGregor, Emerson, Ostenstad, Capucho, Hughes

Manchester United: Howard, G. Neville, P. Neville, (Butt), Ferdinand, van Nistelrooy, Giggs, Keane, Scholes, O'Shea, Fortune, (Djemba-Djemba), Silvestre
Substitutes not used: Carroll, Ronaldo, Bellion, Forlan, Fletcher
Referee: Anders Frisk (Sweden)
Attendance: 48,730

Tuesday, 4th November, 2003, Old Trafford, Manchester

MANCHESTER UNITED 3   **RANGERS 0**
Forlan, van Nistelrooy (2)

Manchester United: Howard, G. Neville, P. Neville, Ferdinand, Ronaldo, van Nistelrooy, (Fletcher), Giggs, (Bellion), Keane, Forlan, (Kleberson), Fortune, Silvestre
Substitutes not used: Carroll, Butt, Djemba-Djemba, O'Shea
Rangers: Klos, Moore, (Ross), Arveladze, Mols, (Capucho), Khizanishvili, Vanoli, (Burke), Ball, Arteta, Berg, Lovenkrands, Hughes
Substitutes not used: McGregor, Emerson, Ostenstad, Dowie
Referee: Pierluigi Collina (Italy) **Attendance:** 66,707

Wednesday, 5th November, 2003, Celtic Park, Glasgow

CELTIC 3   **ANDERLECHT 1**
Larsson, Miller,   Dindane
Sutton

Celtic: Hedman, McNamara, Balde, Larsson, Sutton, Hartson, (Maloney), (Sylla), Agathe, Lennon, Petrov, Varga, Miller, (Gray)
Substitutes not used: Douglas, Wallace, Mjallby, Kennedy
Anderlecht: Zitka, Deschacht, Zewlakow, Baseggio, Hendrikx, (Kolar), Hasi, Wilhelmsson, Mornar, Dindane, Kompany, Tihinen
Substitutes not used:
Peersman, Ilic, Vanderhaeghe, Zetterberg, Junior, MacDonald
Referee: Kyros Vassaras (Greece) **Attendance:** 59,057

Tuesday, 25th November, 2003, Celtic Park, Glasgow

CELTIC 0   **BAYERN MUNICH 0**

Celtic: Hedman, McNamara, Balde, Larsson, Thompson, Sutton, Hartson, (Sylla), Agathe, (Miller), Lennon, Petrov, Varga
Substitutes not used: Douglas, Gray, Valgaeren, Maloney, Mjallby
Bayern Munich: Kahn, Sagnol, Lizarazu, Kuffour, Kovac, Makaay, Ballack, Jeremies, Salihamidzic, Hargreaves, Santa Cruz, (Pizarro)
Substitutes not used:
Rensing, Demichelis, Ze Roberto, Rau, Linke, Schweinsteiger
Referee: Rene H.J. Temmink (Holland) **Attendance:** 59,506

Wednesday, 26th November, 2003, Gottlieb-Daimler, Stuttgart

STUTTGART 1   **RANGERS 0**
Wenzel

Stuttgart: Hildebrand, Hinkel, Wenzel, Meira, Meissner, Gleb, (Centurion), Heldt, (Tiffert), Szabics, (Branco), Soldo, Lahm, Kuranyi
Substitutes not used: Heinen, Amanatidis, Gerber, Cacau
Rangers: Klos, Ricksen, Arveladze, Khizanishvili, Vanoli, (Mols), Ball, Capucho, Ross, (Ostenstad), Berg, Lovenkrands, (Burke), Hughes
Substitutes not used: McGregor, Emerson, Gibson, S. Smith
Referee: Manuel Enrique Mejuto Gonzalez (Spain)
Attendance: 50,348

Tuesday, 9th December, 2003, Ibrox Stadium, Glasgow

RANGERS 1
Mols

PANATHINAIKOS 3
Zutautas, Basinas,
Konstantinou

Rangers: Klos, Ricksen, Mols, Khizanishvili, (Vanoli), Ball, Capucho, Ross, (Duffy), Berg, Lovenkrands, Hughes, Burke, (Ostenstad)
Substitutes not used:
McGregor, Malcolm, Gibson, S. Smith
Panathinkaikos: Nikopolidis, Henriksen, Morris, Seitaridis, Munch, Goumas, Zutautas, Sanmartean, (Epalle), Konstantinou, Basinas, Sapanis, (Vlaovic)
Substitutes not used:
Kotsolis, Warzycha, Gitas, Konstantinidis, Michaelsen
Referee: Herbert Fandel (Germany)
Attendance: 48,588

Wednesday, 10th December, 2003, Gerland, Lyon

LYON 3
Elber, Juninho (2)

CELTIC 2
Hartson, Sutton

Lyon: Coupet, Edmilson, Cacapa, Diarra, Juninho, (Muller), Elber, (Dhorasoo), Malouda, Reveillere, Govou, Luyindula, Berthod, (Carriere)
Substitutes not used:
Vercoutre, Deflandre, Essien, Viale
Celtic: Hedman, Gray, (Wallace), Balde, Larsson, Sutton, (Kennedy), Hartson, (Sylla), Lennon, Petrov, Varga, Mjallby, Miller
Substitutes not used:
Douglas, Lambert, Maloney, Crainey
Referee: Urs Meier (Switzerland)
Attendance: 40,125

FINAL GROUP A TABLE

	P	W	D	L	F	A	PTS
LYON	6	3	1	2	7	7	10
BAYERN MUNICH	6	2	3	1	6	5	9
CELTIC	**6**	**2**	**1**	**3**	**8**	**7**	**7**
ANDERLECHT	6	2	1	3	4	6	7

FINAL GROUP E TABLE

	P	W	D	L	F	A	PTS
MANCHESTER UNITED	6	5	0	1	13	2	15
STUTTGART	6	4	0	2	9	6	12
PANATHINAIKOS	6	1	1	4	5	13	4
RANGERS	**6**	**1**	**1**	**4**	**4**	**10**	**4**

UEFA CUP

QUALIFYING ROUND
FIRST LEG
Thursday, 14th August, 2003 Loro Borici Shkoder

VLLAZNIA 0

DUNDEE 2
Lovell, Novo

Vllaznia: K. Grimaj, (Mustafa), Teli, Zmijani, Salihi, Belisha, Cungu, (Martini), Devolli, Asilani, (Luka), Ishka, Mancaku, Sinani
Substitutes not used:
Osja, Kraja, Bishja, Mashi
Dundee: Speroni, Mackay, Hernandez, Wilkie, Mair, Nemsadze, (Sancho), Novo, (Carranza), Rae, Lovell, (Sara), Smith, Brady
Substitutes not used:
Langfield, Jablonski, Boylan, Hutchinson
Referee: Jaroslav Jara (Czech Republic)
Attendance: 10,000

QUALIFYING ROUND
SECOND LEG
Thursday, 28th August, 2003 Dens Park Stadium, Dundee

DUNDEE 4
Novo (2), Sara, Rae

VLLAZNIA 0

Dundee: Speroni, Mackay, Wilkie, Mair, Hernandez, (Hutchinson), Nemsadze, (Boylan), Smith, Carranza, (Sara), Rae, Novo, Lovell
Substitutes not used: Langfield, Sancho, Robertson, Brady
Vllaznia: Grimaj, Zmijani, Luka, Teli, Osja, Salihi, Asilani, (Hoti), Belisha, Sinani, Martini, (Kraja), Cungu
Substitutes not used: Mustafa, Bishja, Mashi
Referee: Carlo Bertolini (Switzerland) **Attendance:** 8,254
(Dundee won 6–0 on Aggregate)

FIRST ROUND
FIRST LEG
Wednesday, 24th September, 2003 Dens Park Stadium, Dundee

DUNDEE 1
Wilkie

PERUGIA 2
di Loreto, Fusani

Dundee: Speroni, Mackay, Hernandez, Smith, Mair, (Cowan), Wilkie, Sara, Rae, Lovell, Nemsadze, (Brady), Novo
Substitutes not used: Langfield, Sancho, Hutchinson, Fotheringham, Macdonald
Perugia: Kalac, Ferreira, Tedesco, Grosso, (Loumpoutis), Diamoutene, Vryzas,(Do Prado), Alioui, Fusani, di Loreto, Margiotta, (Berrettoni), Gatti
Substitutes not used: Tardioli, Ignoffo, Turchi, Obodo
Referee: Zeljko Siric (Croatia) **Attendance:** 9,911

Tynecastle Stadium, Edinburgh

HEARTS 2
De Vries, Webster

ZELJEZNICAR 0

Hearts: Moilanen, Maybury, Kisnorbo, Pressley, Webster, Severin, Macfarlane, Hartley, (Hammill), De Vries, Wyness, (Weir), Boyack, (Valois)
Substitutes not used: Gordon, McKenna, Kirk, McCann
Zeljeznicar: Hasagic, Kajtaz, Alihodzic, Karic, Gredic, (Avoija), Muharemovic, Spahic, Jahic, Vuksanovic, (Biscevic), Obad, (Admir), Agic
Substitutes not used: Urosevic, Joldic, Smajlagic, Dzeko
Referee: Jack C.D. Van Hulten (Holland) **Attendance:** 15,815

FIRST ROUND
SECOND LEG
Wednesday, 15th October, 2003 Renato Curi, Perugia

PERUGIA 1
Margiotta

DUNDEE 0

Perugia: Kalac, Diamoutene, Ignoffo, di Loreto, Obodo, Loumpoutis, Ferreira,Tedesco, Bothroyd, (Do Prada), Fusani, Vryzas, (Margiotta)
Substitutes not used: Tardioli, Alioui, Ciarlora, Gatti, Berrettoni
Dundee: Speroni, Mackay, (Carranza), Wilkie, Mair, Hernandez, Nemsadze, Rae, Smith, Novo, Sara, Caballero, (McLean)
Substitutes not used: Langfield, Brady, Macdonald, Boylan, Fotheringham
Referee: Hrinak Vladimir (Slovakia)
Attendance: 6,000 (Perugia won 3–1 on Aggregate)

Wednesday, 15th October, 2003 Kosevo, Sarajevo

ZELJEZNICAR 0

HEARTS 0

Zeljeznicar: Hasagic, Biscevic, Kajtaz, Mulalic, Alihodzic, Karic, Gredic, (Joldic), Muharemovic, Jahic, Vuksanovic, (Avdija), Obad, (Dzeko)
Substitutes not used: Adilovic, Spahic, Rascic, Hadzic
Hearts: Moilanen, Maybury, Pressley, Webster, Severin, Stamp, (Hartley), De Vries, (McKenna), Valois, Macfarlane, Kisnorbo, Weir, (Wyness)
Substitutes not used: Gordon, McCann, Kirk, Simmons
Referee: Anton Stredak (Slovakia)
Attendance: 20,000 (Hearts won 2–0 on Aggregate)

SECOND ROUND
FIRST LEG
Thursday, 6th November, 2003 Chaban–Delmas, Bordeaux

BORDEAUX 0   **HEARTS 1**
                  De Vries

Bordeaux: Rame, Alicarte, Basto, Jemmali, Jurietti, (De Souza), Pochettino, Costa, Paulo Costa, (Riera), Pascal, Darcheville, Chamakh
Substitutes not used:
Roux, Caneira, Planus, Miranda, Sahnoun
Hearts: Gordon, Pressley, McKenna, Webster, Neilson, (McCann), Maybury, Wyness, Stamp, (Severin), Valois, (Hartley), Kisnorbo, De Vries
Substitutes not used:
Moilanen, Macfarlane, Kirk, Weir
Referee: Kristinn Jakobsson (Israel)
Attendance: 15,336

SECOND ROUND
SECOND LEG
Thursday, 27th November, 2003 Tynecastle Stadium, Edinburgh

HEARTS 0   **BORDEAUX 2**
                Riera, Pascal

HEARTS: Gordon, Maybury, McKenna, Webster, Stamp, De Vries, Valois, (Kirk), Macfarlane, (Simmons), Neilson, Hartley, (Severin), Kisnorbo
Substitutes not used:
Moilanen, McCann, Wyness, Sloan
Bordeaux: Rame, Caneira, Alicarte, Pochettino, Jurietti, Costa, Darcheville, (Celades), Riera, (Paulo Costa), Pascal, Planus, Chamakh, (Sahnoun)
Substitutes not used:
Roux, De Souza, Basto, Miranda
Referee: Grzegorz Gilewski (Poland)
Attendance: 17,587 (Bordeaux won 2–1 on Aggregate)

THIRD ROUND
FIRST LEG
Thursday, 26th February, 2004 Celtic Park, Glasgow

CELTIC 3   **TEPLICE 0**
Larsson (2), Sutton

Celtic: Douglas, McNamara, (Valgaeren), Balde, Larsson, Thompson, Sutton, Pearson, (Sylla), Lambert, Agathe, Petrov, Varga
Substitutes not used: Marshall, Hartson, Wallace, Beattie, Kennedy
Teplice: Pogtulka, Leitner, Rada, Tesarik, Verbir, Dolezal, Skala, Ryska, Hunal, Masek, Kowalik, (Rilke)
Substitutes not used: Kolar, Sigmund, Kuchar, Horvath
Referee: Konrad Plautz (Austria)
Attendance: 48,947

THIRD ROUND
SECOND LEG
Wednesday, 3rd March, 2004 Na Stinadlech, Teplice

TEPLICE 1   **CELTIC 0**
Masek

Teplice: Pogtulka, Leitner, (Styvar), Rada, Tesarik, Verbir, (Mares), Dolezal, Skala, Hunal, Masek, Rilke, (Ryska), Kuchar
Substitutes not used: Kolar, Kolar, Sigmund, Brozik
Celtic: Douglas, McNamara, (Valgaeren), Balde, Varga, Agathe, Lambert, Kennedy, Petrov, Thompson, Larsson, Sutton, (Pearson)
Substitutes not used: Marshall, Sylla, Wallace, Beattie, Smith
Referee: Tom Henning Ovrebo (Norway)
Attendance: 16,258 (Celtic won 3–1 on Aggregate)

FOURTH ROUND
FIRST LEG
Thursday, 11th March, 2004 Celtic Park, Glasgow

CELTIC 1   **BARCELONA 0**
Thompson

Celtic: Douglas, McNamara, Balde, Varga, Agathe, Petrov, Lennon, Pearson, Thompson, (Sylla), Larsson, Beattie, (Marshall)
Substitutes not used: Lambert, Wallace, Smith, Kennedy
Barcelona: Valdes, Reiziger, (Gerard), Puyol, Xavi, Saviola, Cocu, Ronaldinho, (Overmars), G. Garcia, L. Garcia, (Quaresma), Motta, Oleguer
Substitutes not used: Recber, Marquez, Iniesta, Lopez
Referee: Wolfgang Stark (Germany)
Attendance: 59,539

FOURTH ROUND
SECOND LEG
Thursday, 25th March, 2004 Camp Nou, Barcelona

BARCELONA 0   **CELTIC 0**

Barcelona: Valdes, Oleguer, Puyol, (Marquez), Reiziger, (Overmars), Cocu, Xavi, Gerard, G. Garcia, L. Enrique, (S. Garcia), L. Garcia, Ronaldinho
Substitutes not used: Recber, Lopez, Iniesta, Quaresma
Celtic: Marshall, Kennedy, Pearson, McNamara, (Miller), Varga, Agathe, Lennon, Petrov, Thompson, Sutton, (Sylla), Larsson
Substitutes not used: McGovern, Smith, Mjallby, Beattie, Lambert
Referee: Domenico Messina (Italy)
Attendance: 78,000 (Celtic won 1–0 on Aggregate)

QUARTER FINALS
FIRST LEG
Thursday, 8th April, 2004 Celtic Park, Glasgow

CELTIC 1   **VILLAREAL 1**
Larsson   Josico

Celtic: Marshall, Agathe, Varga, Balde, McNamara, Petrov, Lennon, Pearson, (Miller), Thompson, Sutton, Larsson
Substitutes not used:
Douglas, Valgaeren, Lambert, Mjallby, Smith, Beattie
Villareal: Reina, Javi Venta, Coloccini, Ballesteros, Arruabarrena, Jose Mari, Battaglia, Riquelme, Josico, (Marti), Roger, Anderson
Substitutes not used:
Lopez Vallejo, Victor, Calleja, Arzo, Quique Alvarez, Teo
Referee: Kyros Vassaras (Greece)
Attendance: 58,493

QUARTER FINALS
SECOND LEG
Wednesday, 14th April, 2004 El Madrigal, Villareal

VILLAREAL 2   **CELTIC 0**
Anderson, Roger

Villareal: Reina, Arruabarrena, Coloccini, Ballesteros, Belletti, Battaglia, Josico, Roger, Riquelme, Jose Mari, (Javi Venta), Anderson
Substitutes not used:
Lopez Vallejo, Marti, Victor, Guayre, Quique Alvarez, Calleja
Celtic: Marshall, McNarma, Valgaeren, Balde, Larsson, Pearson, (Wallace), Agathe, Lennon, Petrov, Varga, Miller, (Smith)
Substitutes not used: Douglas, Sylla, Lambert, Mjallby, Beattie
Referee: Massimo De Santis (Italy)
Attendance: 15,964 (Villareal won 3–1 on Aggregate)

EURO 2004 - QUALIFYING COMPETITION AND INTERNATIONAL FRIENDLY

MATCHES PLAYED BY SCOTLAND DURING SEASON 2003/04

EURO 2004
QUALIFYING COMPETITION
Saturday, 6th September, 2003 – Hampden Park, Glasgow

SCOTLAND 3   **FAROE ISLANDS 1**
N. McCann, P. Dickov,   J. Johnsson
J. McFadden

Scotland: R. Douglas, J. McNamara, G. Naysmith,
A. Webster, L. Wilkie, B. Ferguson, P. Devlin,
(J. McFadden), C. Cameron, P. Dickov, (G. Rae),
S. Crawford, (S. Thompson), N. McCann
Substitutes not used:
P. Gallacher, G. Alexander, M. Ross, S. Caldwell
Faroe Islands: J. Mikkelsen, J.I. Petersen,
P. Thorsteinsson, J.R. Jacobsen, R. Jacobsen,
F. Benjaminsen, J. Johnsson, (A. Danielsen), J.A. Borg,
(C. Holtst), J. Petersen, H. Petersen, (T. Akselsen),
O. Johannesen
Substitutes not used:
J. Knudsen, S. Olsen, A. Flotum, H. Hansen
Referee: Darko Ceferin (Slovenia) **Attendance:** 40,901

Wednesday, 10th September, 2003 –
Westfalen Stadium, Dortmund

GERMANY 2   **SCOTLAND 1**
F. Bobic, M. Ballack   N. McCann

Germany: O. Kahn, A. Friedrich, M. Rehmer, C. Worns,
C. Ramelow, F. Baumann, F. Bobic, (M. Klose),
B. Schneider, (S. Kehl), M. Ballack, T. Rau, K. Kuranyi
Substitutes not used:
J. Lehmann, B. Lauth, M. Hartmann, A. Hinkel, C. Rhan
Scotland: R. Douglas, J. McNamara, G. Naysmith, C. Dailly,
S. Pressley, B. Ferguson, J. McFadden, (G. Rae), C. Cameron,
S. Thompson, N. McCann, P. Lambert, (M. Ross)
Substitutes not used:
P. Gallacher, A. Webster, L. Wilkie, P. Devlin, P. Dickov
Referee: Anders Frisk (Sweden) **Attendance:** 67,000

Saturday, 11th October, 2003 – Hampden Park, Glasgow

SCOTLAND 1   **LITHUANIA 0**
D. Fletcher

Scotland: R. Douglas, J. McNamara, G. Naysmith, C. Dailly,
S. Pressley, B. Ferguson, G. Rae, C. Cameron, (D. Fletcher),
K. Miller, (D. Hutchison), S. Crawford, J. McFadden,
(G. Alexander)
Substitutes not used:
N. Alexander, A. Webster, L. Wilkie, K. Harper
Lithuania: G. Stauce, R. Dziaukstas, I. Dedura, N. Barasa,
D. Regelskis, (R. Beniusis), T. Zvirgzdauskas, D. Vencevicius,
(D. Maciulevicius), G. Barevicius, (D. Cesnauskis),
E. Jankauskas, T. Razanauskas, R. Poskus
Substitutes not used:
V. Zutautas, V. Alunderis, O. Buitkus, A. Skerla
Referee: Claude Colombo (France) **Attendance:** 50,343

FINAL GROUP TABLE

	P	W	D	L	F	A	PTS
GERMANY	8	5	3	0	13	4	18
SCOTLAND	**8**	**4**	**2**	**2**	**12**	**8**	**14**
ICELAND	8	4	1	3	11	9	13
LITHUANIA	8	3	1	4	7	11	10
FAROE ISLANDS	8	0	1	7	7	18	1

EURO 2004 PLAY-OFFS
Saturday, 15th November, 2003 –
Hampden Park, Glasgow

SCOTLAND 1   **NETHERLANDS 0**
J. McFadden

Scotland: R. Douglas, J. McNamara, G. Naysmith,
S. Pressley, L. Wilkie, B. Ferguson, D. Fletcher, C. Dailly,
P. Dickov, (K. Miller), J. McFadden, (D. Hutchison),
N. McCann, (S. Pearson)
Substitutes not used:
J. Gould, G. Alexander, S. Caldwell, S. Crawford
Netherlands: E. van der Sar, A. Ooijer, J. Stam, F. de Boer
G. van Bronckhorst, (C. Seedorf), P. Cocu,
A. van der Meyde, E. Davids, (R. van der Vaart),
R. van Nistelrooy, P. Kluivert, (R. Makaay), M. Overmars
Substitutes not used:
B. Zenden, M. Reiziger, R. Waterreus, P. van Hooijdonk
Referee: Terje Hauge (Norway) **Attendance:** 50,670

Wednesday, 19th November, 2003 –
Amsterdam ArenA, Amsterdam

NETHERLANDS 6   **SCOTLAND 0**
W. Sneijder, A. Ooijer,
R. van Nistelrooy (3),
F. de Boer

Netherlands: E. van der Sar, A. Ooijer, (F. de Boer),
M. Reiziger, P. Cocu, W. Bouma, (C. Seedorf), E. Davids,
A. van der Meyde, W. Sneijder, R. van Nistelrooy,
(P. Kluivert), R. van der Vaart, M. Overmars
Substitutes not used:
R. Makaay, A. Robben, R. Waterreus, P. van Hooijdonk
Scotland: R. Douglas, J. McNamara, G. Naysmith, (M. Ross),
S. Pressley, L. Wilkie, B. Ferguson, D. Fletcher, G. Rae, P. Dick
(S. Crawford), J. McFadden, N. McCann, (K. Miller)
Substitutes not used:
D. Hutchison, S. Caldwell, G. Alexander, J. Gould
Referee: Lubos Michels (Slovakia) **Attendance:** 51,00
(Netherlands won 6–1 on Aggregate)

FULL INTERNATIONAL FRIENDLY MATCHES

Wednesday, 20th August, 2003 – Ullevaal Stadium, Oslo

NORWAY 0   SCOTLAND 0

Norway: E. Johnsen, Bergdolmo, (Iversen), Lundekvam, Berg, (R. Johnsen), Basma, (Aas), Hangeland, (Andersen) Carew, (Flo), Andresen, F. Johnsen, (Solli), Solskjaer, Riise
Substitutes not used: Olsen, Strand
Scotland: R. Douglas, M. Ross, (D. Fletcher), G. Naysmith, S. Pressley, A. Webster, B. Ferguson, P. Lambert, C. Dailly, D. Hutchison, S. Crawford, (P. Devlin), C. Cameron, (G. Rae)
Substitutes not used: N. Alexander, G. Alexander, L. Wilkie, S. Maloney, B. Kerr, S. Caldwell, P. Gallacher
Referee: Mikko Vuorela (Finland) **Attendance:** 12,858

Wednesday, 18th February, 2004 – Millennium Stadium, Cardiff

WALES 4   SCOTLAND 0
Earnshaw (3), Taylor

Wales: Crossley, (Ward), Edwards, Gabbidon, Melville, (Symons), Page, Davies, (Parry), Savage, (Fletcher), Oster, Earnshaw, Speed, (Robinson), Giggs, (Taylor)
Substitutes not used: Weston, Roberts
Scotland: R. Douglas, J. McNamara, G. Naysmith, (G. Murty), C. Dailly, S. Caldwell, P. Ritchie, D. Fletcher, (A. Webster), C. Cameron, (P. Gallagher), K. Miller, P. Dickov, S. Pearson, (J. McFadden)
Substitutes not used: P. Gallacher, G. Caldwell, G. Teale
Referee: Michael Ross (Northern Ireland)
Replaced by David Redfern at Half–Time.
Attendance: 47,124

Wednesday, 31st March, 2004 – Hampden Park, Glasgow

SCOTLAND 1   ROMANIA 2
J. McFadden   Chivu, Pancu

Scotland: P. Gallacher, G. Alexander, J. Kennedy, (S. Crainey), C. Dailly, S. Pressley, G. Caldwell, G. Rae, C. Cameron, S. Thompson, (S. Crawford), K. Miller, (J. McFadden), N. McCann
Substitutes not used:
C. Gordon, S. Caldwell, P. Ritchie, R. Hughes, G. Murty, S. Shearer
Romania: B. Stelea, (B. Lobont), F. Stoican, R. Rat, A. Lencsi, C. Chivu, O. Petre, F. Cernat, (F. Soava), F. Petre, (N. Mitea), I. Ganea, A. Mutu, D. Pancu
Substitutes not used:
I. Stancu, M. Constantin, A. Cristea, I. Danciulescu
Referee: Jouni Hyytia (Finland)
Attendance: 20,433

Wednesday, 28th April, 2004 – Parken Stadium, Copenhagen

DENMARK 1   SCOTLAND 0
Sand

Denmark: Sorensen, Wieghorst, (Retov), Henriksen, (Kroldrup), Laursen, N. Jensen, (Sennels), Helveg, D. Jensen, Gronkjaer, (Rasmussen), Thomasson, (Sand), Jorgensen, (Rommedahl), C. Jensen, (Perez)
Substitutes not used:
Nielsen, Priske, Skov–Jensen, Andersen, Madsen
Scotland: P. Gallacher, G. Caldwell, S. Crainey, C. Dailly, M. Mackay, S. Pressley, D. Fletcher, G. Holt, (P. Canero), K. Kyle, J. McFadden, C. Cameron, (N. McCann)
Substitutes not used:
C. Gordon, S. Caldwell, K. Miller, G. Alexander, S. Thompson, A. Webster, D. McNamee, D. Marshall
Referee: Martin Ingvarsson (Sweden)
Replaced by Stefan Johannesson at Half–Time.
Attendance: 22,885

Thursday, 27th May, 2004 – Le Coq Arena, Tallinn

ESTONIA 0   SCOTLAND 1
                                   J. McFadden

Estonia: Kaalma, Allas, Stepanov, Jaager, Klavan, Rahn, Terehhov, (Reinumae), Reim, Viikmae, Oper, Lindpere, (Kink)
Substitutes not used:
Kaas, Saharov, Saviauk, Kristal, Zahovaiko, Teever, Grub, Post
Scotland: P. Gallacher, D. McNamee, R. Hughes, G. Caldwell, M. Mackay, S.Pressley, (A. Webster), D. Fletcher, G. Holt, K. Miller, (S. Crawford), J. McFadden, (B. Kerr), N. Quashie
Substitutes not used:
C. Gordon, S. Caldwell, J. McAllister, L. McCulloch, S. Shearer
Referee: Tonny Poulsen (Denmark) **Attendance:** 4,000

Sunday, 30th May, 2004 – Easter Road Stadium, Edinburgh

SCOTLAND 4   TRINIDAD & TOBAGO 1
D. Fletcher, G. Holt,   John
G. Caldwell, N. Quashie

Scotland: C. Gordon, J. McNamara, J. McAllister, G. Caldwell, (S. Caldwell), J. McNamee), M. Mackay, S. Pressley, D. Fletcher, G. Holt, (B. Kerr), S. Crawford, (K. Miller), J. McFadden, (A. Webster), N. Quashie, (R. Hughes)
Substitutes not used: P. Gallacher, L. McCulloch, S. Shearer
Trinidad & Tobago: Ince, Cox, Andrews, Sancho, Edwards, (Theobald), Dwarika, (Nixon), Glen, (Boucaud), John, Mason, Jones, (Rojas), Eve, (Jemmot)
Substitutes not used: King, Baptiste, Williams
Referee: Pieter Vink (Netherlands) **Attendance:** 16,187

FUTURE INTERNATIONALS
FUTURE CUP

Tuesday, 21st October, 2003 – Pittodrie Stadium, Aberdeen

SCOTLAND FUTURE 0   GERMANY "B" 1
                                          Daun

Scotland: N. Alexander, R. Stockdale, J. McAllister, B. Nicholson, (J.P. McGovern), R. Anderson, L. Wilkie, T. McManus, (K. Boyd), B. Kerr, G. O'Connor, (P. Gallagher), A. Gray, I. Murray
Substitutes not used:
D. Stillie, B. O'Brien, P. McGuire, S. Wilson, D. Soutar
Germany: Jentzsch, Korzynietz, (Muller), Bonig, (Fahrenhorst), Hertzsch, Maltritz, (Schlicke), Borowski, (Kringe), Dabrowski, Ernst, Schroth, (Benschneider), Engelhardt, (Daun), Bierofka
Substitute not used: Weidenfeller
Referee: Miroslav Liba (Czech Republic) **Attendance:** 2,417

Wednesday, 10th December, 2003– Tannadice Park, Dundee

SCOTLAND FUTURE 1   TURKEY "B" 1
S. Caldwell   Ates

Scotland: C. Gordon, (S. Shearer), G. Murty, (G. Shields), J. McAllister, S. Caldwell, A. Webster, G. Caldwell, S. Murray, P. Canero, L. McCulloch, (M. McIndoe), S. Severin, (T. McManus), S. Pearson
Substitutes not used: G. Greer, L. Mair, D. Soutar
Turkey: Tuncay, Tandogan, Mercimek, Seyhan, Cimsir, Atan, Gunes, Bolukbasi, (Kocak), Martin, (Cihan), Simsek, Ates
Substitutes not used: Sonmez, Keceli, Turan, Biryol, Polat
Referee: Mike Riley (England) **Attendance:** 1,450

FINAL GROUP TABLE

	P	W	D	L	F	A	PTS
TURKEY	4	1	3	0	4	3	6
GERMANY	4	1	2	1	5	5	5
SCOTLAND	4	0	3	1	5	6	3

EUROPEAN "UNDER-21" CHAMPIONSHIP
Tuesday, 9th September, 2003 – Wersestadion, Ahlen

GERMANY 0   **SCOTLAND 1**
S. Maloney

Germany: Wiese, Franz, Kling, Riether, Madlung, Gemiti, (Kringe), Azaouagh, Tiffert, Auer, (Jones), Feulner, (Marx), Hanke
Substitutes not used: Starke, Abel
Scotland: D. Soutar, G. Caldwell, S. Pearson, D. McCracken, S. Crainey, G. Williams, S. Duff, I. Murray, K. Kyle, M. Stewart, (D. Fletcher), S. Lynch, (S. Maloney)
Substitutes not used:
A. McGregor, A. Dowie, N . Montgomery, S. Hammell, T. McManus
Referee: Georgios Douros (Greece) **Attendance:** 4,500

Friday, 10th October, 2003 – McDiarmid Park, Perth

SCOTLAND 3   **LITHUANIA 2**
S. Hammell, S. Hughes (2)   Stankevicius, Kucys

Scotland: D. Soutar, G. Caldwell, S. Hammell, J. Kennedy, D. McCracken, G. Williams, (S. Hughes), P. Canero, (T. McManus), B. Kerr, S. Maloney, M. Stewart, S. Lynch, (P. Gallagher)
Substitutes not used: C. Gordon, A. Dowie, N. Montgomery, S. Dillon
Lithuania: Karcemarskas, Paulauskas, Stankevicius, Kilmavicius, Majus, Savenas, Kucys, Grigalevicius, (Panka), Cesnauskis, Radzinevicius, (Kavaliauskas), Radavicius, (Mikoliunas)
Substitutes not used: Grybauskas, Mikuckis, Tarvydas, Mizigurskis
Referee: Emil Bozinovski (Macedonia) **Attendance:** 5,289

FINAL GROUP TABLE

	P	W	D	L	F	A	PTS
SCOTLAND	6	4	1	1	10	6	13
GERMANY	6	4	1	1	11	5	13
LITHUANIA	6	3	0	3	10	10	9
ICELAND	6	0	0	6	2	12	0

PLAY-OFF MATCHES
16th November, 2003 – Varteks Stadium, Varazdin

CROATIA 2   **SCOTLAND 0**
Babic, Ljubojevic

Croatia: Vranjic, Buljat, Pranjic, Drpic, Lucic, Jese, Safaric, Kranjcar, (Mikulic), Ljubojevic, Babic, Petric, (Zahora)
Substitutes not used: Sarlija, Linic, Gal, Brkic, Zgela
Scotland: C. Gordon, G. Caldwell, S. Hammell, D. McCracken, J. Kennedy, B. Kerr, P. Canero, I. Murray, K. Kyle, M. Stewart, (S. Hughes), T. McManus, (S. Maloney)
Substitutes not used:
A. McGregor, S. Duff, G. Williams, G. O'Connor, S. Lynch
Referee: Iouri Basakakov (Russia) **Attendance:** 4,000

18th November, 2003 – Easter Road Stadium, Edinburgh

SCOTLAND 1   **CROATIA 0**
G. O'Connor

Scotland: C. Gordon, S. Duff, S. Hammell, G. Williams, J. Kennedy, B. Kerr, P. Canero, (N. Montgomery), I. Murray, K. Kyle, (S. Lynch), S. Maloney, (S. Hughes), G. O'Connor
Substitutes not used:
A. McGregor, T. McManus, M. Stewart, S. Dillon
Croatia: Vranjic, Buljat, Pranjic, Drpic, Lucic, Jese, Safaric, (Gal), Hikulic, Ljubojevic, (Zahora), Kranjcar, Petric, (Brkic)
Substitutes not used: Sarlija, Linic, Zgela, Cosic
Referee: Tommy Skjerven (Norway)
Attendance: 11,992

(Croatia won 2–1 on Aggregate)

UNDER-21 INTERNATIONAL FRIENDLY MATCHES
Tuesday, 19th August, 2003 – Odd Stadium, Skien

NORWAY 3   **SCOTLAND 1**
Pedersen (2), Hoff   S. Lynch

Norway: Opdal, (Kristiansen), Holm, (Paulsen), Muri, Tronseth, Hanstveit, Ludvigsen, (Andresen), Gashi, Hanssen, (Pedersen), Haugen, (Hoff), Karadas, (Brasen), Brenne, (Ystaas)
Scotland: A. McGregor, (C. Gordon), G. Caldwell, S. Hammell, D. McCracken, (A. Dowie), S. Crainey, (C. Doig), G. Williams, S. Duff, S. Pearson, (D. Noble), K. Kyle, (P. Gallagher), M. Stewart, (S. Hughes), S. Lynch, (T. McManus), (J. Kennedy)
Substitute not used: M. Brown
Referee: Jouni Hietala (Finland) **Attendance:** 1,144

Wednesday, 18th February, 2004 – City Stadium, Livingston

SCOTLAND 1   **HUNGARY 2**
S. Maloney   Csehi, Jovanczai

Scotland: G. Smith, (D. Marshall), P. Lawson, (J. Dempster), S. Lappin, (S. Morrison), J. Kennedy, A. Dowie, (A. Diamond), J. McCunnie, R. Foy, (R. Wallace), M. Wilson, (P. Sweeney), G. O'Connor, (C. Beattie), S. Maloney, (A. Reilly), B. Prunty
Hungary: Fulop, (Kovacs), Vasko, (Balogh), (Csopaki), Rodenbucher, Takacs, David, (Szijarto), Vanczak, Regedei, Nogradi, (Jovanczai), Huszti, (Sandor), Jozsi, (Csehi), Varga
Referee: Mark Courtney (Northern Ireland) **Attendance:** 1,544

Tuesday, 30th March, 2004 – Firhill Stadium, Glasgow

SCOTLAND 0   **ROMANIA 2**
Plesan, Florescu

Scotland: C. Samson, P. Lawson, S. Lappin, A. Hutton, (W. Kinniburgh), A. Dowie, M. Fotheringham, M. Wilson, (C. Burke), J. McCunnie, G. O'Connor, (K. Boyd), D. Riordan, (R. Foy), C. Beattie, (B. Prunty)
Substitutes not used: G. Smith, S. Morrison, P. Sweeney, S. Murray
Romania: Marc, Prepelita, (Arbanas) Goian, Moti, Tamas, Grigore, Cocis, Vasilache, Marica, (Codreanu), Plesan, (Marginean), Cristea, (Florescu)
Substitutes not used: Hutan, Peres
Referee: Jari Maisonlahti (Finland) **Attendance:** 1,967

Tuesday, 27th April, 2004 – Helsingor Stadion, Helsingor

DENMARK 2 **SCOTLAND 2**
Krohn–Delhi (2). D. Clarkson, C. Beattie

Denmark: Stuhr–Ellegaard, J. Poulsen, Agger, Andreasen, (Pedersen), Hogh, Kamper, (S. Poulsen), Wurtz, Svard, (Thygesen), Krohn–Delhi, Kahlenberg, Timm, (Sorensen)
Substitutes not used: Kielstrup, Rasmussen
Scotland: D. Marshall, (G. Smith), M. Wilson, S. Lappin, (S. Morrison), A. Dowie, P. Quinn, P. Sweeney, (C. Beattie), A. Hutton, (C. Burke), S. Brown, (M. Fotheringham), K. Boyd, (D. Clarkson), R. Foy, (S. Murray), P. Gallagher
Substitutes not used: P. Lawson, B. Prunty, C. Samson
Referee: Stefan Johannesson (Sweden) **Attendance:** 500

Tuesday, 25th May, 2004 – Terryland Park, Galway

REPUBLIC OF IRELAND 3 **SCOTLAND 1**
Fitzgerald (2), McCarthy C. Beattie

Republic of Ireland: Henderson, (B. Murphy), Kelly, Fitzgerald, McCarthy, Capper, K. Foley, (Brennan), Whelan, Potter, Kearney, (M. Foley), D. Murphy, (Behan), Tabb, (Zayed)
Substitutes not used: O'Brien, Dillon
Scotland: C. Samson, (G. Smith), P. Lawson, (S. Murray), S. Lappin, A. Dowie, G. Robertson, J. McCunnie, M. Wilson, S. Morrison, (P. Sweeney), K. Boyd, B. Prunty, C. Beattie, (M. Fotheringham)
Substitute not used: I. Turner
Referee: Stefan Johannesson (Sweden) **Attendance:** 2,200

UNDER-20 INTERNATIONAL FRIENDLY MATCHES
Wednesday, 17th December, 2003 –
Estadio Antonio Correia, Alcochete

PORTUGAL 1 **SCOTLAND 2**
Luis Alfonso S. Lappin, B. Prunty

Scotland: C. Samson, (I. Turner), P. Lawson, P. Sweeney, (S. Lappin), J. Dempster, W. Kinniburgh, J. McCunnie, M. Wilson, (C. Burke), M. Fotheringham, (J. Rankin), G. Weir, (S. Murray), R. Foy, (S. Morrison), B. Prunty
Referee: Antonio Costa (Portugal) **Attendance:** 150

UEFA UNDER-19 CHAMPIONSHIP
FIRST QUALIFYING ROUND
QUALIFYING GROUP 12 – HOSTED BY SCOTLAND
Saturday, 25th October, 2003 – Somerset Park, Ayr

SCOTLAND 3 **FAROE ISLANDS 1**
D. Clarkson, R. Wallace Hansen,
S. Brown

Scotland: A. Reid, P. Quinn, S. Smith, S. Low, A. Diamond, C. Adam, (F. Coyle), R. Foy, J. Winter, D. Clarkson, S. Brown, R. Wallace
Substitutes not used:
A. Brown, G. Irvine, M. Baxter, R. Wilkie, R. MacLeod, K. Wright
Faroe Islands: Nielsen, Naes, Midjord, (Thorleifson), Madsen, Djurhuus, Olsen, (Jacobsen), Hansen, Jespersen, Poulsen, Skoralid, Joensen
Substitutes not used:
Baerentsen, Olsen, Samuelsen, Nolsoe, Hojgaard
Referee: Oleg Oriekhov (Ukraine)
Attendance: 420

Monday, 27th October, 2003 –
Strathclyde Homes Stadium, Dumbarton

SCOTLAND 1 **TURKEY 1**
S. Brown Inan

Scotland: A. Reid, P. Quinn, S. Low, A. Diamond, C. Adam, R. Foy, (J. Winter), D. Clarkson, S. Brown, R. Wallace, F. Coyle, M. Baxter
Substitutes not used:
A. Brown, S. Smith, G. Irvine, R. Wilkie, R. MacLeod, K. Wright
Turkey: Kirintili, Doganay, (Aslantas), Sam, Tahtaisleyen, Teber, Sengul, Adin, (Cubukcu), Inan, Aygun, (Turan), Ozturk, Ozturk
Substitutes not used: Ozcan, Zengin, Sakar, Isikal
Referee: Olegario Benquerenca (Portugal) **Attendance:** 1,163

Wednesday, 29th October, 2003 – New Douglas Park, Hamilton

SCOTLAND 2 **MACEDONIA 0**
D. Clarkson, S. Brown

Scotland: A. Reid, P. Quinn, S. Low, A. Diamond, C. Adam, R. Foy, (R. Wilkie), J. Winter, D. Clarkson, (R. MacLeod), S. Brown, R. Wallace, (F. Coyle), M. Baxter
Substitutes not used: A. Brown, S. Smith, G. Irvine, K. Wright
Macedonia: Bosnakov, Todorovski, Osmani, Trifunovski, Sikov, Djangarovski, Jakovlevski, (Manevski), Bajrami, Kirovski, (Salihu), Stjepanovic, Tasev, (Limanov)
Substitutes not used: Zerdeski, Karakolev, Muminovic, Salevski
Referee: Anton Genov (Bulgaria) **Attendance:** 1,089

FINAL GROUP 12 TABLE

	P	W	D	L	F	A	PTS
TURKEY	3	2	1	0	9	2	7
SCOTLAND	3	2	1	0	6	2	7
MACEDONIA	3	1	0	2	5	5	3
FAROE ISLANDS	3	0	0	3	1	12	0

SECOND QUALIFYING ROUND
QUALIFYING GROUP 6 – HOSTED BY AUSTRIA
Tuesday, 25th May, 2004 – Sparkassenstadion, Gleisdorf

FINLAND 3 **SCOTLAND 2**
Taulo, Aaritalo, P. Quinn, R. Wallace
Parikka

Finland: Maenpaa, Latikka, Santala, Aaritalo, (Parikka), Savolainen, Vahasarja, (Lahitie), Kolsi, (Manninen), Taulo, Jurvainen, Tursas, Tuomanen
Substitutes not used: Moisander, Menekse, Vuorinen, Kotomaki
Scotland: D. Marshall, G. Irvine, C. Mulgrew, P. Quinn, C. Berra, C. Adam, (R. Linn), J. Winter, (S. Bell), D. Clarkson, S. Naismith, R. Wallace, S. Low, (K. Wright)
Substitutes not used: A. Brown, R. Wilkie, A. Reilly, G. McKenzie
Referee: Pavel Balaj (Romania)

Thursday, 27th May, 2004 – Hartberg Stadium, Hartberg

POLAND 3 **SCOTLAND 2**
Szymanek (2), Peszko G. McKenzie (2)

Poland: Fabianski, Stawowy, Bartczak, Latkowski, Madera, Kowalczyk, Peszko, (Blaszczykowski), Piszcek, Jasinski, Smolinski, (Kalinowski), Ilkow, (Szymanek)
Substitutes not used: Zukowski, Wasielewski, Celeban, Szczepan
Scotland: D. Marshall, G. Irvine, C. Mulgrew, P. Quinn, C. Berra, K. Wright, R. Wallace, A. Reilly, (C. Adam), G. McKenzie, R. Linn, S. Bell, (J. Winter)
Substitute not used: A. Brown
Referee: Damien Ledentu (France)

Saturday, 29th May, 2004 – Sparkassenstadion, Weiz

SCOTLAND 0   **AUSTRIA 5**
                 Gartler, Puntigam (2),
                 Thonhofer, Stuckler

Scotland: A. Brown, C. Mulgrew, P. Quinn, C. Berra, K. Wright,
J. Winter, D. Clarkson, A. Reilly, (C. Adam), G. McKenzie, R. Linn, S. Bell
Substitute not used: D. Marshall
Austria: Olejnik, Baldauf, Lindschinger, Metz, (Schicker), Osoinik,
Parager, Stuckler, Thonhofer, Puntigam, Gartler, Gercaliu
Substitutes not used: Liendl, Moosbauer, Salvatore
Referee: Pavel Balaj (Romania)

FINAL GROUP 6 TABLE

	P	W	D	L	F	A	PTS
POLAND	3	3	0	0	6	2	9
AUSTRIA	3	2	0	1	6	1	6
FINLAND	3	1	0	2	3	5	3
SCOTLAND	3	0	0	3	4	11	0

**SCOTLAND UNDER-19 NORTHERN IRELAND MILK CUP
ELITE SECTION**
Saturday, 19th July, 2003 – Coleraine Showgrounds, Coleraine

SCOTLAND 0   **PARAGUAY 1**
                 Benitez

Scotland: A. Reid, M. Baxter, F. Coyle, S. Low, I. Campbell,
(K. Wright), C. Adam, G. Irvine, J. Winter, S. Tarditi, (A. Ferguson),
R. Foster, (A. Scott), R. MacLeod
Referee: Frankie Hiles (Northern Ireland)
Attendance: 450

Monday, 21st July, 2003 – Ballymoney Showgrounds, Ballymoney

SCOTLAND 1   **POLAND 2**
K. Wright   Szewc, Bartczak

Scotland: A. Reid, S. Low, C. Adam, G. Irvine, J. Winter, R. Foster,
R. MacLeod, A. Ferguson, (S. Tarditi), K. Wright, (A. Scott), I.Campbell,
(K. Barkey), D. Pinkowski
Referee: Stephen Weatherall (Northern Ireland)
Attendance: 200

Wednesday, 23rd July, 2003 – Ballymena Showgrounds, Ballymena

SCOTLAND 0   **USA 2**
                 Karbassiyoon, Freeman

Scotland: A. Brown, M. Baxter, F. Coyle, S. Low, (I. Campbell),
J. Winter, S. Tarditi, (A. Scott), R. Foster, (A. Ferguson), R. MacLeod,
K. Barkey, K. Wright, (G. Irvine), D. Pinkowski, (C. Adam)
Referee: John Fielding (Northern Ireland)
Attendance: 335

FINAL GROUP TABLE

	P	W	D	L	F	A	PTS
PARAGUAY	3	3	0	0	3	0	9
USA	3	1	1	1	3	2	4
POLAND	3	1	1	1	3	3	4
SCOTLAND	3	0	0	3	1	5	0

PLACE MATCH
Friday, 25th July, 2003 – Mullaghacall, Portstewart

SCOTLAND 1   **WALES 1**
S. Tarditi   Garside
Wales won 4-2 on Kicks from the Penalty Mark

Scotland: A. Brown, M. Baxter, (K. Wright), F. Coyle, C. Adam,
G. Irvine, J. Winter, S. Tarditi, (A. Ferguson), R. MacLeod, K. Barkey,
D. Pinkowski, A. Scott, (R. Foster)
Referee: John Fielding (Northern Ireland)
Attendance: 100

UNDER-19 INTERNATIONAL FRIENDLY MATCHES
Saturday, 23rd August, 2003 – Municipal Stadium, Entroncamento

PORTUGAL 3   **SCOTLAND 0**
P. Pestana, H. Monteiro,
R. Costa

Scotland: A. Reid, F. Coyle, S. Smith, S. Low, A. Diamond, C. Adam,
G. Irvine, J. Winter, R. Foster, (A. Scott), R. MacLeod, D. Pinkowski,
(D. Campbell)
Referee: Joao Ferreira (Portugal)

Monday, 25th August, 2003 – Municipal Stadium, Alcanena

PORTUGAL 2   **SCOTLAND 0**
R. Felix (2)

Scotland: A. Brown, F. Coyle, S. Smith, S. Low, A. Diamond,
C. Adam, J. Winter, (R. MacLeod), S. Tarditi, (D. Campbell),
S. Anderson, A. Stewart, (A. Scott), K. Barkey
Referee: Duarte Gomes (Portugal)

**UNDER-18 INTERNATIONAL MATCHES
FOUR NATIONS TOURNAMENT, DENMARK**
Tuesday, 9th September, 2003 – Idraetspark, Nykobing Falster

BELGIUM 5   **SCOTLAND 3**
Criel (2), Kubilskis,   R. Davidson (2), J. Reilly
Wilmet, Vanderhaeghen

Scotland: E. McLean, G. Watson, C. Sives, S. Campbell, C. Reid,
C. Mulgrew, D. Campbell, S. Anderson, (S. Fletcher), R. Davidson,
K. McKinlay, (S. Naismith), M. Gardyne, (J. Reilly)
Referee: Peter Rasmussen (Denmark)

Thursday, 11th September, 2003 – Idraetspark, Nakskov

DENMARK 2 **SCOTLAND 1**
S. Campbell (o.g.). S. Naismith
Kronborg

Scotland: C. Reidford, G. Watson, C. Sives, S. Campbell, C. Reid,
C. Mulgrew, D. Campbell, R. Davidson, R. Quinn, M. Gardyne,
(K. McKinlay), S. Naismith, (G. Fraser)
Referee: Thomas Vejlgaard (Denmark)

Saturday, 13th September, 2003 – Idraetspark, Nakskov

POLAND 1 **SCOTLAND 2**
Cichy S. Campbell, G. Watson

Scotland: E. McLean, (C. Reidford), G. Watson, S. Campbell,
C. Reid, C. Mulgrew, D. Campbell, S. Anderson, R. Davidson,
R. Quinn, A. Dick, G. Fraser, (S. Naismith)
Referee: Tonny Poulsen (Denmark)

FINAL TABLE

	P	W	D	L	F	A	PTS
DENMARK	3	1	2	0	3	2	5
BELGIUM	3	1	2	0	3	4	5
SCOTLAND	**3**	**1**	**0**	**2**	**6**	**8**	**3**
POLAND	3	0	2	1	1	2	2

UNDER-18 INTERNATIONALS
SLOVAKIA CUP
Monday, 26th April, 2004 – FS Galanta

HUNGARY 0 **SCOTLAND 1**
  Scott

Scotland: E. McLean, C. Sives, M. Pelosi, D. Keogh, R. Gardiner,
D. Shaw, (T. Parratt), D. Campbell, (B. Young), D. Carcary, M. Woods,
K. McKinlay, (G. Kenneth), M. Scott

Tuesday, 27th April, 2004 – AS Trencin

SLOVAKIA 2 **SCOTLAND 2**
Bartos, Pelosi (o.g.) McKinlay, Sives
Slovakia won 4-3 on Kicks from the Penalty Mark

Scotland: E. McLean, C. Sives, M. Pelosi, D. Keogh, (T. Parratt),
R. Gardiner, D. Shaw, (J. Neill), D. Campbell, (B. Young), D. Carcary,
M. Woods, K. McKinlay, M. Scott

Thursday, 29th April, 2004 – FS Povazska Bystrica

POLAND 1 **SCOTLAND 0**
Wawrzynczok

Scotland: E. McLean, C. Sives, R. Gardiner, D. Carcary, (M. Pelosi),
M. Woods, K. McKinlay, A. Moffat, G. Kenneth, M. Scott, (J. Neill),
B.Young, (D. Campbell), T. Parratt

THIRD PLACE PLAY-OFF
Friday, 30th April, 2004 – Partizanske

FRANCE 4 **SCOTLAND 0**
Bertin d'Avernes, Ballaid,
Cambon, Vacarezza

Scotland: G. Fleming, C. Sives, (A. Moffat), M. Pelosi, D. Keogh,
R. Gardiner, D. Shaw, (M. Scott), D. Campbell, (D. Carcary), M.
Woods, K. McKinlay, G. Kenneth, (J. Neill), T. Parratt, (B. Young)

UNDER-18 INTERNATIONAL FRIENDLY MATCHES
Tuesday, 25th November, 2003 – Bayview Stadium, Methil

SCOTLAND 2 **GERMANY 0**
R. Davidson, S. Campbell

Scotland: E. McLean, G. Watson, M. Fitzpatrick, (C. Sives),
S. Campbell, C. Reid, (G. Fraser), C. Mulgrew, M. Gardyne, (B. McColl),
S. Anderson, R. Davidson, M. Woods, (S. Blair), K. McKinlay
Referee: Calum Murray (Scotland)
Attendance: 579

Thursday, 27th November, 2003 – Forthbank Stadium, Stirling

SCOTLAND 0 **GERMANY 2**
  Barje, Schrodter

Scotland: C. Reidford, (E. McLean), G. Watson, M. Fitzpatrick,
(G. Fraser), S. Campbell, C. Mulgrew, M. Gardyne, (J. Reilly),
S. Anderson, (S. Cuthbert), R. Davidson, (C. Gardiner), C. Sives,
B. McColl, S. Blair, (D. Shaw)
Referee: Crawford Allan (Scotland)
Attendance: 632

UEFA UNDER-17 CHAMPIONSHIP
FIRST QUALIFYING ROUND
QUALIFYING GROUP 3 - HOSTED BY HUNGARY
Thursday, 2nd October, 2003 – Csepel Stadium, Budapest

SCOTLAND 2　　　**NORWAY 0**
S. Fletcher (2)

Scotland: A. McNeil, S. McKeown, (J. Thomson), P. Boyle, A. McColl, S. Cuthbert, B. Gilmour, M. McGlinchey, B. Hodge, P. Reid, (K. Smith), S. Fletcher, S. Agnew
Substitutes not used:
C. Reidford, M. Quinn, B. Gilmour, J. Graham, J. McCluskey
Norway: Skeide, Driscoll, Irgens, Braaten, Matland, Haestad, Bentsen, (Skjolsvik), Ingebretsen, (Ronningene), Skjelbred, (Misje), Halvorsen, Mikkelsen
Substitutes not used: Staw, Mathisen, Eliassen, Braaten

Saturday, 4th October, 2003 – Csepel Stadium, Budapest

SCOTLAND 9　　　**SAN MARINO 0**
S. Fletcher (2), S. Agnew,
K. Smith (2), B. Hodge,
J. Graham (2), R. Snodgrass

Scotland: C. Reidford, P. Boyle, (R. Snodgrass), A. McColl, S. Cuthbert, M. McGlinchey, B. Hodge, S. Fletcher, S. Agnew, (J. Graham), K. Smith, J. Thomson, B. Gilmour, (J. McCluskey)
Substitutes not used: A. McNeil, S. McKeown, M. Quinn
San Marino: Tamagnini, Maiani, Billi, (Canini), Rastelli, Righi, Zanotti, (Palmieri), Zanotti, Cervellini, De Angelis, (Ceccoli), Canini, Simoncini
Substitutes not used: Stefanelli, Mularoni, Colombini, Bugli

Monday, 6th October, 2003 – Municipal Stadium, Vac

SCOTLAND 1　　　**HUNGARY 0**
S. Fletcher

Scotland: A. McNeil, S. McKeown, A. McColl, S. Cuthbert, M. McGlinchey, B. Hodge, S. Fletcher, (R. Snodgrass), S. Agnew, (P. Boyle), M. Quinn, K. Smith, J. McCluskey, (J. Graham)
Substitutes not used: C. Reidford, J. Thomson
Hungary: Hegedus, Okros, (Hrepka), Hibo, Vass, Petho, (Szoke), Bartha, Farkas, (Rezes) Ludanszki, Fitos, Pinter, Mathe
Substitutes not used: Boros, Juhasz, Heffler, Ivancsics

FINAL GROUP 3 TABLE

	P	W	D	L	F	A	PTS
SCOTLAND	3	3	0	0	12	0	9
NORWAY	3	1	1	1	10	4	4
HUNGARY	3	1	1	1	6	3	4
SAN MARINO	3	0	0	3	0	21	0

SECOND QUALIFYING ROUND
QUALIFYING GROUP 7 - HOSTED BY BELGIUM
Saturday, 27th March, 2004 – Royale Entente Blegnytoise, Blegny

BELGIUM 0　　　**SCOTLAND 0**

Belgium: Ruttens, Kone, Ngalula, Cortjens, Pocognoli, De Mets, Vanden Borre, (Derijck), Mirallas, Vermeulen, (Weytens), Piette, Remacle, (Defour)
Substitutes not used: Lagaer, Jacobs, Reynaert, Dembele
Scotland: A. McNeil, S. McKeown, P. Boyle, J. Kane, S. Cuthbert, B. Hodge, B. Gilmour, M. McGlinchey, C. Elliot, (J. Graham), S. Fletcher, S. Agnew
Substitutes not used:
C. Reidford, J. McCluskey, J. Thomson, R. Snodgrass, D. Richardson
Referee: Daniel Stalhammar (Sweden)

Monday, 29th March, 2004 – Stade du Pairay, Seraing

NORTHERN IRELAND 2　　　**SCOTLAND 0**
O'Connor, Carville

Northern Ireland: Tuffey, Turner, Armstrong. McCabe, (Nash), Doherty, (Melly), O'Connor, Fordyce, Catney, Rosbotham, McCordick, (Carville), McCrink
Substitutes not used: Ferry Watterson, Carson, Montgomery
Scotland: C. Reidford, S. McKeown, P. Boyle, J. Kane, B. Hodge, (R. Snodgrass), M. McGlinchey, S. Fletcher, (C. Elliot), S. Agnew, K. Smith, (J. Graham), J. McCluskey, J. Thomson
Substitutes not used: A. McNeil, S. Cuthbert, B. Gilmour, D. Richardson
Referee: Ivan Bebek (Croatia)

Wednesday, 31st March, 2004 – Royale Entente Blegnytoise, Blegny

SCOTLAND 2　　　**BELARUS 2**
Gilmour, Fletcher　　　Kisliak, Malashka

Scotland: A. McNeil, J. Kane, S. Cuthbert, B. Hodge, B. Gilmour, M . McGlinchey, S. Fletcher, J. Graham, (C. Elliot), J. Thomson, R.Snodgrass, D. Richardson
Substitutes not used:
S. McKeown, P. Boyle, S. Agnew, C. Reidford, K. Smith, J. McCluskey
Belarus: Shysheya, Charnov, Liutsko, Martynovich, Palaznik, Putsila, Hihevich, Marholenka, Kisliak, Malashka, (Bombechko), Pinchuk, (Shankou)
Substitutes not used: Hnatsiuk, Hancharov, Tsytsarau, Rekish, Kiryievich
Referee: Ivan Bebek (Croatia)

FINAL GROUP 7 TABLE

	P	W	D	L	F	A	PTS
NORTHERN IRELAND	3	3	0	0	7	2	9
BELGIUM	3	1	1	1	2	3	4
SCOTLAND	3	0	2	1	2	4	2
BELARUS	3	0	1	2	5	7	1

UNDER-17 INTERNATIONAL MATCHES
NORDIC CUP
Tuesday, 29th July, 2003 – Vang

FAROE ISLANDS 0   SCOTLAND 2
S. Fletcher, B. Gilmour

Scotland: A. McNeil, S. McKeown, P. Boyle, A. McColl, (J. Armstrong), K. Connolly, B. Gilmour, (R. Pow), B. Hodge, K. Smith, (J. Graham), S. Fletcher, (J. Johnston), S. Agnew, (J. McCluskey), M. Quinn
Referee: Thomas Vejlgaard (Denmark)

Wednesday, 30th July, 2003 – Ottestad

FINLAND 0   SCOTLAND 1
J. Graham

Scotland: A. McNeil, P. Boyle, J. Armstrong, (S. McKeown), A. McColl, K. Connolly, B. Gilmour, B. Hodge, S. Fletcher, S. Agnew, (R. Pow), J. Graham, (J. McCluskey), M. Quinn
Referee: Oddmar Andreasen (Faroe Islands)

Friday, 1st August, 2003 – Moelv

SWEDEN 1   SCOTLAND 1
Sliper   P. Boyle

Scotland: A. McNeil, S. McKeown, P. Boyle, A. McColl, K. Connolly, B. Gilmour, (J. McCluskey), B. Hodge, S. Fletcher, S. Agnew, J. Graham, (K. Smith), M. Quinn
Referee: Heikki Pajunen (Finland)

FINAL GROUP TABLE

	P	W	D	L	F	A	PTS
SCOTLAND	3	2	1	0	4	1	7
FINLAND	3	2	0	1	6	1	6
SWEDEN	3	1	1	1	4	2	4
FAROE ISLANDS	3	0	0	3	0	10	0

FINAL
Sunday, 3rd August, 2003 – Ottestad

DENMARK 1   SCOTLAND 0
Qvist

Scotland: A. McNeil, S. McKeown, P. Boyle, (J. Johnston), A. McColl, K. Connolly, (J. Thomson), B. Gilmour, B. Hodge, K. Smith, (J. McCluskey), S. Fletcher, S. Agnew, (R. Pow), M. Quinn
Referee: Michael Ryan (England)

UNDER-17 INTERNATIONAL FRIENDLY MATCHES
Monday, 19th January, 2004 – Ta 'Qali Training Grounds, Valletta

MALTA 0   SCOTLAND 3
S. Fletcher, B. Gilmour, C. Elliot

Scotland: A. McNeil, (C. Reidford), J. Thomson, (D. Martin), P. Boyle, (M. Quinn), J. Kane, S. Cuthbert, B. Hodge, (K. Connolly), B. Gilmour, (J. O'Brien), M. McGlinchey, (R. Snodgrass), C. Elliot, (J. Graham), S. Fletcher, S. Agnew, (R. Conroy)

Wednesday, 21st January, 2004 – Ta 'Qali Training Grounds, Valletta

MALTA 0   SCOTLAND 6
S. Fletcher (2), C. Elliot, A. Coakley (2), J. Thomson

Scotland: C. Reidford, (A. McNeil), (G. Kelly), D. Martin, (D. Donald), M. Quinn, (P. Boyle), J. Kane, (S. Agnew), S. Cuthbert, B. Gilmour, (J. O'Brien), M. McGlinchey, R. Snodgrass, (K. Connolly), R. Conroy, (J. Thomson), C. Elliot, (A. Coakley), S. Fletcher, (J. Graham)

SCOTLAND UNDER-16 INTERNATIONAL MATCHES
BALLYMENA INTERNATIONAL TOURNAMENT 2004
Thursday, 29th April, 2004 – Wellington Recreation, Larne

SCOTLAND 3   AUSTRIA 1
J. Crooks, P. Emslie,   Sand
S. Laird

Scotland: S. Murray, C. Mitchell, (G. Cameron), J. MacMillan, S. Laird, L. Stevenson, D. Gray, P. Emslie, S. Lennon, P. MacDonald, (I. Cameron), J. Crooks, A. Bagshaw

Friday, 30th April, 2004 – Ballymena Showgrounds, Ballymena

SCOTLAND 0   USA 2
Zimmerman (2)

Scotland: M. Curtis, G. Cameron, (D. Smith), J. MacMillan, (G. Kerr), S. Laird, L. Stevenson, I. Cameron, S. Lennon, P. Emslie, P. MacDonald, J. Crooks, D. Gray

Saturday, 1st May, 2004 – Inver Park, Larne

SCOTLAND 0   BELGIUM 0

Scotland: M. Curtis, C. Mitchell, S. Laird, G. Kerr, L. Stevenson, D. Gray, S. Lennon, (G. Rodger), P. Emslie, I. Cameron, J. Crooks, (D. Goodwillie), A. Bagshaw

FINAL GROUP TABLE

	P	W	D	L	F	A	PTS
USA	3	2	1	0	4	1	7
SCOTLAND	3	1	1	1	3	3	4
AUSTRIA	3	1	1	1	3	4	4
BELGIUM	3	0	1	2	1	2	1

THIRD PLACE PLAY-OFF
Monday, 3rd May, 2004 – Wellington Recreation, Larne

SCOTLAND 5   FINLAND 1
Gray, Smith (2), Rodger   Kangaskolkka,
I. Cameron

Scotland: S. Murray, C. Mitchell, J. MacMillan, S. Laird, G. Kerr, D. Gray, G. Cameron, I. Cameron, P. MacDonald, (L. Stevenson), D. Smith, (D. Goodwillie), G. Rodger, (J. Crooks)

All in a Player's Name

Compare the list of each clubs' players in the first Scottish Football League Review in season 1980/81, with this twenty fifth edition, and you will have a neat summary of the changes in Scottish football over that quarter of a century.

Players in season 1980/81 were predominantly Scottish, exclusively British, and when a touch of foreign influence was found, it was in the likes of Jim Bett's previous club (Belgian side Lokeren) rather than in the names of imported players.

Even the forenames of the predominantly Scots-born players reflect a different society. Ian, Bobby, Steve, Andy, Willie, Joe, John, Tom, Doug and their team-mates in the squad lists came from a generation who were probably named after members of their family, rather than pop stars and television personalities.

These are, of course, mere snapshots of Scottish society, taken at one particular time, and had The Scottish Football League Review been published in season 1950/51, thirty years before its actual birth, there would have been more players given the plain names of Jack, John, James, Bill and Bob. Perhaps more tellingly, there would have been more traditional Scottish forenames, to match the many Macs of their surnames. Over the years, Hamish, Duncan, Alexander, Donald and Archibald have become more scarce on the team lines of Scottish football, and by 1980 they were rarely spotted; even less so twenty five years later.

The influx of foreign born players has certainly expanded the lexicography of Scottish football over the last decade. Surnames and syllables now appear in squad lists that would have been unimaginable when the League Review first appeared, and while the impact on our national sport from the mass import of these exotic names is not the subject of this particular article, there is little doubt that a different dimension has been brought to our grounds.

"Not much of a player, but a great hand at Scrabble" is one of the more common wisecracks as a fan tries to pronounce the multi-consonanted name printed in the match programme. Not a few of the playing visitors to our shores have taxed the linguistic abilities of Public Address announcers, to the frequent amusement of the listening fans. Faced with announcing an otherwise straightforward substitution involving an on-coming Senegalese and an off-going Slovakian, it must be tempting for the announcer to merely intone the blindingly obvious "Number 18 replaces number 6". Shades of the infamous "Newman replaces Newman" from the pre-season friendlies of old!

There have of course, been exotic names from our own shores. At the risk of gratuitously insulting some proudly borne family names, we have to recall the likes of Bissett Harrier, a stalwart in the Brechin City side of the early 1960's; Kinnaird Ouchterlonie, an Ayr United and Dundee United stalwart immediately after the Second World War, and Rangers' Archibald McIndewar of the same era. Perhaps not so much exotic as poetic were the names sported by Sylvester O'Brien (Hamilton Academical, early 1970's), Doalty Sweeney at Aberdeen a decade later, and from the 1950's, Vernon Wentzell of Kilmarnock. No doubt Aloysius McGowan was called Ally by his St. Johnstone team-mates of the early 1950's, but that abbreviation poorly served such a distinctive forename.

There have, of course, been some interesting combinations of surnames on Scottish League teamsheets down the years. In recent times, Byers and Sellars regularly appeared together for Forfar Athletic, while Whyte and Mackay formed the left wing partnership which added spirit to a few Queen Park performances in the early 1970's. Around that time, Albion Rovers fielded the most gastronomic of Scottish half back lines – Rice, Currie and Sage – no doubt adding spice to the Rovers team!

HAMISH McALPINE

DARIUSZ DZIEKANOWSKI

ANDREI KANCHELSKIS

Some playing careers simply refused to conform to their surname's suggestion. A Livingston has yet to appear for the new town team; Morton have never had an eponymous player, and the Tynecastle faithful have yet to see one of the Harty's in maroon. (Jered) Stirling plays for Albion Rovers, and not the other, more appropriate Albion while (Willie) Kilmarnock played for Motherwell.

However, whilst many football supporters enjoy a bet on the fixed odds coupon every Saturday, Dundee United's signing of Mika–Matti (better known as Mixu) Paatelainen in 1987 provided a humorous extension to the terminology used by pundits!

Television and radio commentators have over the years of course, had to endure the perils of trying to correctly pronounce the names of foreign players where Scotland have played on the International stage and our club sides have played in the various European club competitions.

However, the 1990's started to see an influx of foreign nationals playing in our domestic game and whilst it is usually players and managers that experience sleepless nights on the eve of a match, no doubt some of our well known commentators also endured a similar fate when contemplating pronouncing the following list of players: Ilian Kiriakov, Tzanko Tzvetanov, Dariusz Dziekanowski, Dariusz Wdowczyk, Lubomir Moravcik, Dariusz Adamczuk, Piotr Czachowski, Miodrag Krivokapic, Milos Drizic, Olafur Gottskalksson, Dragoje Lekovic, Oleg Kuznetsov, Andrei Kanchelskis, Zurab Khizanishvili, Attili Sekerlioglu, Davide Xausa and, probably one of the longest surnames in the history of Scottish football, Alexei Mikhailitchenko. Thankfully it was not a prerequisite to have the sur–name of a player on the back of a jersey at the time when he played for Rangers!

Names, like hair colour, shape and size, are easy game for the terracing wags, and it was ever thus. A match at Shawfield in the late 1960's saw Harry Hood despatch a screamer past the Dunfermline goalkeeper. "What do you call that 'keeper?" said one Bully Wee fan to his companion. "Bent Martin" was the reply. "Bent?" said the enquirer. "He'd have to be ****** crooked to stoap that wan !"

JOHN LITSTER
(Editor, Programme Monthly & Football Collectable Magazine www.pmfc.co.uk)

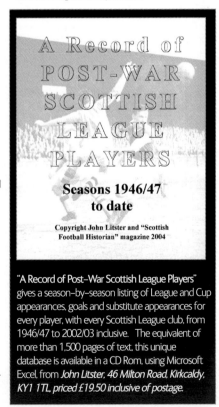

A Record of POST-WAR SCOTTISH LEAGUE PLAYERS

Seasons 1946/47 to date

Copyright John Litster and "Scottish Football Historian" magazine 2004

"A Record of Post-War Scottish League Players" gives a season–by–season listing of League and Cup appearances, goals and substitute appearances for every player, with every Scottish League club, from 1946/47 to 2002/03 inclusive. The equivalent of more than 1,500 pages of text, this unique database is available in a CD Rom, using Microsoft Excel, from *John Litster, 46 Milton Road, Kirkcaldy, KY1 1TL, priced £19.50 inclusive of postage.*

We must
Bridge
The Gap

Editorial by Tony Higgins
(Senior Organiser, The Scottish
Professional Footballer's Association)

When David Thomson called me to request an article for
The Scottish Football Review, I couldn't believe it was 25
years since I first featured on the front cover of the very
first edition. Andy Ritchie, Alex McLeish Colin Jackson, Paul
Hegarty, Ronnie Glavin and Peter McCloy to name but a
few, all there prominent in this excellent publication.

As age has taken its toll on me, the "beautiful game" has
also had a few makeovers and crises to deal with, particularly in the last few years following the Bosman decision.

I can never understand why clubs acted in the way they did
after the Bosman Judgement. At the end of the day, each
club has an allocation of monies to pay for players' costs be
it on wages and transfers etc., but for whatever reason,
Bosman changed their reasoning and all fiscal sensibility
disappeared and clubs paid way beyond what they
could afford.

Of course, we at The Scottish Professional Footballers'
Association want players to make as good a living as pos-
sible and ensure they have some financial security for the
future, but not at any cost. Football is a sport and a business, they are not mutually exclusive but the relationship
between income and expenditure has been lost resulting
in many clubs in Scotland and indeed, throughout Europe,
facing administration and, in some instances, liquidation.
What is particularly galling is this comes at a time when the
game in the last few years has never received so much
money from commercial and television deals yet paradox-
ically, has never faced such a financial crisis.

I recall prior to Bosman lobbying the Football Authorities in
Scotland and indeed, in other parts of Europe, requesting
the adoption of the French system as a compromise to
the potential transfer issue being decided by a court.
Basically in France until the age of 23, players were still

subject to a transfer fee, but after 23 when their contract expired they were free agents. Most clubs and players knew by that age if they were going to make the grade at the highest level which allowed clubs some return for their investment, but allowed players over 23 to exploit their talent financially for the rest of their careers. Unfortunately, our message was in vain, but interestingly the system introduced by FIFA in 2001 is reminiscent of that original French system although compensation payments are greatly reduced. The only positive development to emerge from the financial crisis is the return of many clubs to the belief in developing their own young players as being the way forward for Scottish football. During my time with Hibernian in the 1970's, I played against players like Kenny Dalglish, Jimmy Johnstone and Danny McGrain of Celtic,

Derek Johnstone, Davie Cooper and Sandy Jardine of Rangers, Joe Harper, Tommy Craig, Arthur Graham of Aberdeen, Paul Sturrock, David Narey, Paul Hegarty of Dundee United, all class acts and many of them world class.

The common factor in the aforementioned is that all these players were developed by their own clubs. I would require 20,000 words in this publication to explain my view of where it all went wrong but the climate of the post Bosman era until now created a negative attitude towards clubs rearing their own talent.

Proper resources have to be allocated to develop young players and the development of these clubs will depend largely on what they do over the next few years. The game requires a period of financial stability with clubs resisting the temptation to spend money before they get it. The structure in football of course, does not only relate to youth development but to the development of football as a whole. The SPFA believes that Scottish football cannot afford to have two separate bodies running the professional clubs at senior level. We feel that from the SPL and the SFL, a new body has to emerge again. One body running the professional game in Scotland (call it the Scottish National League for instance) rationalised with more resources going into more clubs. For whatever reason, the current system has not delivered what it set out to do and football should be brave enough to admit that the new structure has failed and therefore, we should look to create a new structure. However, I am not optimistic that the individuals concerned at the various clubs are prepared to compromise on the way forward. The last time I contributed an article for the Review in

season 1998/99, I made the following observation:

" The future success of the new Scottish Premier League will not only rely on the quality of player playing for clubs currently playing in that set-up but will also depend on the quality of the clubs that will come in from the First Division in the future. Promotion and relegation are vital and essential elements of football, providing excitement for fans for all clubs as well as acting as an incentive for players of clubs wishing to gain status to the top level. One of the great strengths of the Premiership in England is that many clubs in the Nationwide First Division have the ability and financial base to go into the top League and compete at that level. This ensures that standards are not only set at the top level but are also being continually pushed up from below."

Unfortunately however, the financial consequences of rel-egation from the SPL concerns most clubs and that is why I feel it is so important that by creating a new body with greater financial stability and revenue sharing between the top two divisions in particular, we should ensure better competition.

"Gie us a break,
can you no see
some of us are
trying to sleep
oot here."

Good football and real competition is the key to ensuring that fans will attend football matches in the future. The Old Firm have always dominated Scottish football and will continue to do so, but the gap between them and the rest is getting bigger and bigger. Until recently, a number of other clubs successfully challenged Celtic and Rangers and from time to time would win the League Championship thereby creating good competition and stimulating spectator interest.

Indeed, a number of clubs would also win the League Cup and Scottish Cup competitions on a regular basis. However, the domination of the Old Firm in recent times now means that fans of many of our other top clubs are not attending in such vast numbers because they do not think they have any chance of winning, and the Old Firm fans are not excited by the prospect of playing other clubs outside their Glasgow neighbours because they see little evidence of real competition. That is why they flock in such numbers to see European teams.

Uncertainty of the outcome is what keeps football alive; predictability in any sport creates boredom.

The great players I mentioned earlier in the article, will they ever return to Scottish football? Let's hope so, although I doubt in such vast numbers. I remember late in my career playing for Morton against Aberdeen when Alex Ferguson was manager. Always a tense affair, we won a corner which was taken by the inimitable Andy Ritchie. As he ambled over, a small section of the Aberdeen fans near the corner area gave him dogs abuse. Big Andy gave a laconic look and said to them "Gie us a break, can you no see some of us are trying to sleep oot here.".

Scottish Football, (to use footballer's parlance) has had a bit of a nightmare in the last few years; Brave men with courage and ideas are required to move things forward. Any out there?

On the road with the
TARTAN ARMY

It's 6.00 a.m. in the morning, but it could be 3.00 a.m. No-one is really sure, but there is no doubt about a couple of other factors central to our mood – it's very cold, and we've just had one of the worst nights' sleep in memory. There isn't a lot of the Tartan Army's much-trumpeted bonhomie and goodwill going round when there are a dozen strangers getting territorial over ten square feet of carpeted floor space in the cashpoint lobby of a Bordeaux bank.

The year is 1998, and Scotland have a game later that day against Norway, their second match of the World Cup Finals. A 2–1 defeat against Brazil in the opening match has failed to dampen spirits, and as we are about to find out, there's hardly a soul left in Scotland who has any real interest in football. Everyone's here in Bordeaux, which is why these not-so-happy campers have failed to find a bed within a 30-mile radius of the city. None of us are short of funds; the bloke next to me is a doctor, and if spending a few hours as a down-and-out is good enough for him, it's the way ahead for me too.

Those of us who have ended up in the bank lobby are, to an extent, the lucky ones. Countless others of no fixed abode have tried to muscle in on a bit of the action as they wandered the streets, only to find they are encouraged to "try elsewhere".

But pity the poor swine who has laid himself down nearest the doors. The slightest twitch from him activates a sensor and throws open the electric doors, allowing another blast of the cold night air which sends us diving deeper into our sleeping bags. Or should I say, those of us lucky to have sleeping bags. The rest just resort to hurling a series of alarming threats towards the offender. Curiously, none of the customers of this popular French bank feel the need to make a withdrawal.

By 7.00 a.m., we begin to disperse, dusting ourselves down and heading for the nearest cafe. It occurs to me that there must be more stylish ways of starting your 30th birthday. But if a one-night stand as a vagrant meant that I was in Bordeaux to see Scotland, that was good enough for me.

Following the Scotland team drives supporters to extraordinary lengths just to see a game of football. My own hardship in France was nothing compared to the hundreds who have made considerable personal sacrifice over a lifetime to give the team their backing at Hampden and abroad. If results permit, it can be a richly rewarding experience. Right now, the annihilation in the second leg of the European Championship Play-Off in Amsterdam and our dreadful start to the 2006 World Cup qualifying campaign has diminished enthusiasm within the ranks but hopefully, it won't be too long before the Tartan Army has the opportunity to attend future World Cup and European Championship Finals.

It's difficult to put military terminology aside when talking about the Tartan Army, yet it's the kind of problem over political correctness our national media would love to have if it means that Scotland are represented in Germany. Scots love their football team, and they love to be part of the big

event. A World Cup without Scotland is still hard for the nation to get its head round, with generations reared on a cycle of five consecutive qualifications from 1974 to 1990. This season marks the 30th anniversary of the 1974 World Cup in Germany, an occasion when central Europe was introduced to the phenomenon of a hairy and growling mass of tartan humanity. For 50 years, Scotland had enjoyed a huge support when the national team played at Wembley, and 1974 marked the opportunity – brought about by improved and affordable travel opportunities – to venture further afield. Although not widely known as the Tartan Army at this point, this is where it all started.

The advent of colour television meant that many fans hired a set for a month and watched the tournament unfold in the comfort of their own homes, itself a sense of adventure. Those who travelled took a step into the unknown. Dave Alexander, still a Tartan Army regular, was one of the Scotland fans who made the trip to Germany, an experience which saw him become hooked.

"A busload of us travelled with an organisation called the Friendship Travel Club," recalls Dave. "The guy who ran it was a diamond cutter to trade, but turned to doing those kind of trips as a hobby. I enjoyed it so much that I went to the Finals in Argentina in 1978 and Mexico in 1986, but I was so disillusioned after Mexico that I had a ten-year break which coincided with getting married and having kids. Now my son and I go abroad at every opportunity. We went to the World Cup in 1998, but on our second night my son got an ulcer and we spent two weeks in a French hospital instead. But we've made up for it since then – we've been to San Marino, Croatia, Czech Republic, Faroe Islands, Belgium and Holland, and now it's Moldova."

After Germany, hysteria was at an all-time high when Scotland qualified for Argentina 1978. The apocryphal story about fans chartering a submarine –a few did enquire about the price – did not materialise into a get-there-at-all-costs stampede, and it is estimated that only 600 Scotland supporters travelled to what was then a dark and mysterious land. Four years later in the far more tempting venue of Spain, there were 25,000 Scots exposing their pasty skins to the sunshine, but the next hoolie was to be in Mexico, when distance and doubt again combined – along with cost – to keep numbers down.

Italia '90 saw the Scots in heaven again – a return to Europe, sunshine, and affordable drink. A heady combination. Geoff Clark of Dundee travelled with four friends across central Europe in a 13-year-old converted Ford Transit with a top speed of 50mph.

"Beating Sweden in Genoa was one of the greatest feelings as a Scotland fan, until we got back to the camper van," says Geoff. "It had been ransacked by gypsies, who stole just about everything – except my psychedelic sleeping bag, which I still have to this day. No one of sound mind would have stolen that. The van was a wreck but it was worth the

discomfort because it was the only way we could afford to go to the World Cup. We kept seeing Germany fans in their great big modern mobile homes, and they were fascinated by our van. They must have thought it was something from the Flintstones, because they kept asking to see the engine."

Two years later, there was the bonus of reaching the European Championship Finals for the first time. Just a few weeks before the start of the tournament, The Scottish Football Association responded to the lack of interest in tickets by placing a newspaper advert in an attempt to shift them. The four or five thousand who took no notice of grim warnings over the £4 cost of a pint were rewarded with one of the most memorable trips on record. Along with four friends, I ate nothing but bread and cheese for ten days, slept by the riverside using Edinburgh District Council bin bags as groundsheets, and stayed for an hour after the Germany and CIS matches to cheer our gallant nearly-men. On this occasion – and not many since – they deserved it.

version of Purple Heather were reminded just how good life can be on the road. Of course, the Tartan Army does not just exist abroad. It can be seen at Hampden, although usually in far more reserved mood. The atmosphere of glory nights against the Czechs in 1973 and 1977, Spain in 1985 and France in 1989 may never be the same again, but the euphoria is there waiting to be tapped at every opportunity, as witnessed in last season's victory against the Dutch.

But it is on trips abroad with Scotland that the reputation of the Tartan Army is founded. It's almost impossible not to enjoy yourself on the journey of anticipation that leads you to a far-flung Scotland match, although to me the actual result is crucial. There are few sights more demeaning than a Scot singing "We're only here for the swally" after a 6-0 drubbing in the Netherlands, or "Two-nil, who gives a ****" on Wembley Way. Then there are the self-styled Tartan Army generals, who seem to believe in their own promotion and are quick to tell you about it. But being in the Tartan

Euro '96 was nowhere near as much fun. For a start, no one in England wanted us there. I began to wonder whether England wanted the tournament, or just the trophy thank you very much. It took place when I was living in London, and it's a time I'd rather forget, other than to say Gary McAllister would have changed my life had his penalty gone in, the aftermath hastening my return north of the border a year later. Walking out of Wembley as a winner just three years later was no consolation, considering we had, overall, lost again.

Scotland's exit from Euro '96 was agonising for all those at the narrow win over Switzerland at Villa Park, but possibly more so for actor Patrick Mower, who had travelled from London to Birmingham to support Scotland. He made the foolhardy journey by train, and if he had received the proverbial £1 for every time he was accosted on the return journey to Euston, he could have retired on the proceeds. Nevertheless, he retained a degree of privacy that would not have been achieved by Rod Stewart, an endearingly loyal Scotland fan, judging by the stampede towards the singer as he made his way to a bar in the main square of Amsterdam ahead of last season's match against the Dutch. Those who squeezed into the premises to hear Rod sing an impromptu

Army does not mean boasting perfect attendance, or holding a Scotland Travel Club card, or wearing a kilt, or singing Do-re-me. For me, it's about a huge collective expression of faith in both Scotland and in football, and a longing for the two to see eye-to-eye at long last. And if there are priceless memories and the experiences of a lifetime to be gathered on the way, then that's a welcome bonus. For many others, the Tartan Army is a way of life, with occupations arranged around fixtures rather than vice versa. It is an incredible level of commitment, and one which ensures that if Scotland arranged a friendly international away to Tristan da Cuna, the team would be guaranteed to run out to the strains of "We'll support you evermore" somewhere in the South Atlantic.

What always brings each section of the Tartan Army together, the die-hards and the blow-ins, is success. Let's hope that those cashpoint lobbies, wherever they are in the world, are waiting for us and are spacious and accommodating.

DONALD WALKER
(The Scotsman)

The changing face of programmes

The changing face of Scottish League football over the first 25 years of the "Scottish League Review" has not just been confined to the players and the stadia. Clubs' matchday programmes have also changed dramatically in the last two–and–a–half decades.

The first Scottish Football League Review in season 1980/81 featured League Champions Aberdeen, who had won the title by one point from Celtic. The Dons' match programme replicated that feat in the 1980/81 Scottish Programme of the Year Awards, the unlucky runners–up being Hamilton Academical.

By 1980, the Programme of the Year Awards were well established, having been first won by the estimable Accies in 1973/74. The awards were eagerly anticipated by editors and readers of the nation's matchday programmes, and while financial constraints have always been the major determining factor in the size, shape and quality of Scottish club programmes, it can be argued that the competitive element of the awards has inspired a few clubs to make that little bit more of an effort.

The changing face of programmes over the last twenty five years is exemplified by the commentary which accompanied the 1980/81 awards. "Without a doubt the major innovation this season is colour, with Aberdeen, Celtic, Hearts, Morton and Rangers all adopting a colour picture format for their covers. With the exception of Morton and to a lesser degree Hearts, the cover is changed for every match. To a lesser degree Ayr United, Clyde, Falkirk, Motherwell and Partick Thistle have brought a touch of colour to their cover, albeit without the use of photographs."

In season 2004/05, of course, full colour on every page is taken for granted in SPL programmes, and in the majority of Bell's First Division issues, but the slim volumes which cost 20p or 30p in season 1980/81 were some way removed from the thick, glossy (and of course expensive) programmes of today.

Hamilton Accies' innovative "Accies World", conceived and written by present day Partick Thistle Chief Executive Alan Dick, turned the tables on the slick, glossy and colourful Aberdeen programme the following season, but that 1981/82 triumph ended Accies' eight year spell at the pioneering frontier of Scottish programme production. The next 13 years saw the awards dominated by Premier Division clubs, belatedly aligning the quality of their programmes to their larger attendances.

The third phase in the awards came in season 1995/96, the first of current champions Clyde's nine–in–a–row domination of Scottish programmes. The "Clyde View" was always one of the better programmes in Scotland, and in season 1980/81, it finished a very commendable fourth, behind only the Dons, Accies and Motherwell. To the frustration of the award organisers, and the

despair of competing clubs, the Clyde programme somehow manages to improve, season after season, seeing off all challengers. The Bully Wee's narrow failure to win the First Division Championship last season has not dulled their enthusiasm or ambition for a top class matchday programme, which is even bigger and better in season 2004/05.

Many aspects of Scottish football are unrecognisable from twenty five years ago; the names of players and stadia, the transfer market and the media (no websites or satellite television in 1980). There are some things that never change, however. The loyalty of fans, much of it inherited down generations, pie and bovril and the matchday programme are enduring traditions of the game.

Their details may have changed (the pie is likely to be served in a tinfoil container, and the programme no longer contains a half–time scoreboard) but their continued existence binds the spectator to his or her footballing roots in an otherwise fast changing world.

Over the 25 years of The Scottish Football League Review, programmes have come in all shapes and sizes. It was noted in season 1980/81 that the more traditional A5 size, and occasional larger B4 page, had been joined by A4 sized programmes from Airdrie, Forfar Athletic and Hamilton. Other clubs have also dabbled with this size, along with square–shaped, landscape orientation (the staple on the shorter edge) and even pocket sized issues.

One major development has been universal production. Since programmes became a familiar part of the matchday scene after the Second World War, Scottish collectors have been frustrated by clubs not issuing at all in some seasons, intermittently in others (usually only for major cup ties) and rarely for midweek matches.

In season 1980/81, it was noted that, for the first time, every one of the 38 Scottish League clubs had issued, although Montrose and Clydebank confined their activities to a couple of programmes each. Nowadays, of course, fans expect a programme to be available at every match, wherein they may read the club news, identify the players of both sides, enjoy features on their favourites, and wallow in the nostalgia provided by historical articles.

A bit like The Scottish Football League Review, in fact. Like the Review, programmes have expanded in size and content, and improved in presentation, over the last 25 years – and promise to continue in that vein for years to come.

JOHN LITSTER
(Editor, Programme Monthly &
Football Collectable Magazine
www.pmfc.co.uk)

SCOTTISH PROGRAMME OF THE YEAR AWARDS 2003/04

SPL (2002/03)

1.	(1)	Aberdeen
2.	(2)	Dunfermline Athletic
3	(3=)	Hearts
4	(5)	Dundee
5.	(3=)	Partick Thistle
6.	(6)	Dundee United
7.	(11)	Hibernian
8.	(8)	Kilmarnock
9.	(7)	Celtic
10.	(9)	Livingston
11.	(10)	Rangers
12.	(12)	Motherwell

SFL FIRST DIVISION (2002/03)

1.	(1)	Clyde
2.	(2)	Falkirk
3.	(4)	St. Mirren
4.	(3)	St. Johnstone
5.	(5)	Ayr United
6.	(1 (SD))	Brechin City
7.	(6)	Queen of the South
8.	(6 (SD))	Raith Rovers
9.	(8)	Ross County
10.	(7)	Inverness Caledonian Thistle

SFL SECOND DIVISION (2002/03)

1.	(3 (TD))	Morton
2.	(10)	Hamilton Academical
3.	(5)	Airdrie United
4.	(4)	Dumbarton
5.	(2)	Stenhousemuir
6.	(3)	Forfar Athletic
7.	(6 (TD))	East Fife
8.	(7)	Berwick Rangers
9.	(9 (FD))	Alloa Athletic
10.	(10 (FD))	Arbroath

SFL THIRD DIVISION (2002/03)

1.	(1)	Queen's Park
2.	(2)	Montrose
3.	(4)	Stirling Albion
4.	(8 (SD))	Cowdenbeath
5.	(9)	Gretna
6.	(7)	Peterhead
7.	(9 (SD))	Stranraer
8.	(5)	Albion Rovers
9.	(8)	Elgin City
10.	(10)	East Stirlingshire

SCOTTISH PROGRAMMES OF THE YEAR – PREVIOUS WINNERS

1973/74	Ayr United	1974/75	Hamilton Academical
1975/76	Heart of Midlothian	1976/77	Motherwell
1977/78	Hamilton Academical	1978/79	Hamilton Academical
1979/80	Berwick Rangers	1980/81	Aberdeen
1981/82	Hamilton Academical	1982/83	Dundee
1983/84	Dundee United	1984/85	Aberdeen
1985/86	Celtic	1986/87	Rangers
1987/88	Rangers	1988/89	Rangers
1989/90	Aberdeen	1990/91	Celtic
1991/92	Aberdeen	1992/93	Rangers
1993/94	Rangers	1994/95	Rangers
1995/96	Clyde	1996/97	Clyde
1997/98	Clyde	1998/99	Clyde
1999/2000	Clyde	2000/01	Clyde
2001/02	Clyde	2002/03	Clyde
2003/04	Clyde		

PREMIER LEAGUE PROGRAMME OF THE YEAR

(as per Programmes of the Year, except for...)

1974/75	Motherwell (old Div.One)	1975/76	Heart of Midlothian
1976/77	Motherwell	1977/78	Rangers
1978/79	Morton	1979/80	Morton
1995/96	Kilmarnock	1996/97	Dundee United
1997/98	Dundee United	1998/99	Dundee United
1999/2000	Dundee United	2000/01	Dunfermline Athletic
2001/02	Aberdeen	2002/03	Aberdeen
2003/04	Aberdeen		

FIRST DIVISION PROGRAMME OF THE YEAR

1975/76	Hamilton Academical	1976/77	Hamilton Academical
1977/78	Hamilton Academical	1978/79	Hamilton Academical
1979/80	Berwick Rangers	1980/81	Hamilton Academical
1981/82	Hamilton Academical	1982/83	Queen's Park
1983/84	Hamilton Academical	1984/85	Clyde
1985/86	Clyde	1986/87	Clyde
1987/88	Hamilton & Clydebank	1988/89	Dunfermline Athletic
1989/90	Airdrieonians	1990/91	Dundee
1991/92	Partick Thistle	1992/93	Kilmarnock
1993/94	Dunfermline Athletic	1994/95	Dunfermline Athletic
1995/96	Dundee United	1996/97	Partick Thistle
1997/98	St. Mirren	1998/99	Hibernian
1999/2000	Dunfermline Athletic	2000/01	Clyde
2001/02	Clyde	2002/03	Clyde
2003/04	Clyde		

SECOND DIVISION PROGRAMME OF THE YEAR

1973/74	Hamilton Academical	1974/75	Hamilton Academical
1975/76	Berwick Rangers	1976/77	Albion Rovers
1977/78	Meadowbank Thistle	1978/79	Berwick Rangers
1979/80	Albion Rovers	1980/81	Clyde
1981/82	Clyde	1982/83	Stirling Albion
1983/84	Stirling Albion	1984/85	Stirling Albion
1985/86	Stirling Albion	1986/87	Raith Rovers
1987/88	Stirling Albion	1988/89	Stirling Albion
1989/90	Kilmarnock	1990/91	Stirling Albion
1991/92	Clyde	1992/93	Clyde
1993/94	Forfar Athletic	1994/95	Clyde
1995/96	Clyde	1996/97	Clyde
1997/98	Clyde	1998/99	Clyde
1999/2000	Clyde	2000/01	Partick Thistle
2001/02	Hamilton Academical	2002/03	Brechin City
2003/04	Morton		

THIRD DIVISION PROGRAMME OF THE YEAR

1994/95	Forfar Athletic	1995/96	Livingston
1996/97	Inverness C.T	1997/98	Montrose
1998/99	Queen's Park	1999/2000	Queen's Park
2000/01	Montrose	2001/02	Montrose
2002/03	Queen's Park	2003/04	Queen's Park

The Highland

Football League Directory of Clubs

BRORA RANGERS F.C.

Secretary:	Kevin MacKay
Manager:	Alan Munro
Club Address:	Dudgeon Park, Dudgeon Drive, Brora, KW9 6QN.
Ground Tel/Fax:	01408 621231
Sec Bus:	01408 623005 or 623018
Sec Home/Fax:	01408 621114
Sec Mobile:	07721 940938
E-Mail:	

brorarangersfc@highlandleague.com
Year of Formation: 1879

Capacity:	Total: 4,000
	250 Seated 3,750 Standing
Pitch Dimensions:	112 yds x 70 yds

Playing Kits:
1st Choice. Shirt: Red with White flash on sleeves
Shorts: Red Stockings: Red and White
2nd Choice. Shirt: White
Shorts: White
Stockings: White

BUCKIE THISTLE F.C.

Secretary:	Murray Duncan
Manager:	Kevin Will
Club Address:	Victoria Park, Midmar Street, Buckie, AB56 1BJ.
Ground Tel No:	01542 836468 (Matchdays Only)
Sec Bus:	01542 832170
Sec Bus Fax:	01542 832182
Sec Home:	01542 835660
Website:	www.buckiethistle.com
E-Mail:	

buckiethistlefc@highlandleague.com
Year of Formation: 1889

Capacity:	Total: 5,400
	400 Seated 5,000 Standing
Pitch Dimensions:	109 yds x 73 yds

Playing Kits:
1st Choice Shirt: Green & White Hoops,
Shorts: White with Green Trim, Stockings: White
2nd Choice Shirt: White. Shorts: Green
Stockings: White

CLACHNACUDDIN F.C. (1990) LTD.

Secretary:	Gilbert Skinner
Manager:	Robert Williamson
Club Address:	Grant Street Park, Wyvis Place, Inverness, IV3 6DR.
Ground Tel No:	01463 238825
E-Mail:	

clachnacuddinfc@highlandleague.com
Year of Formation: 1886

Capacity:	Total: 3,000
	154 Seated 2,846 Standing
Pitch Dimensions:	108 yds x 70 yds

Playing Kits:
1st Choice Shirt: White Shorts: Black
Stockings: White
2nd Choice Shirt: Yellow
Shorts: Yellow Stockings: Yellow

COVE RANGERS F.C.

Secretary:	Duncan Little
Manager:	John Sheran
Club Address:	Allan Park, Loirston Road, Cove, Aberdeen, AB12 3NR.
Ground Tel No:	01224 890433
Sec Bus:	01224 854990
Sec Home:	01224 896282
Sec Mobile:	07710 648154
Fax No:	01224 895199
E-Mail:	

coverangersfc@highlandleague.com
Year of Formation: 1922

Capacity:	Total: 2,300
	200 Seated 2,100 Standing
Pitch Dimensions:	104 yds x 65 yds

Playing Kits:
1st Choice Shirt: Blue & Yellow
Shorts: Blue Stockings: White
2nd Choice Shirt: Yellow & Blue
Shorts: Yellow Stockings: Yellow

DEVERONVALE F.C.

Secretary:	Stewart McPherson
Manager:	Gregg Carrol
Club Address:	Princess Royal Park, 56 Airlie Gardens, Banff, AB45 1HB.
Ground Tel No:	01261 818303
Sec Mobile:	07813 733617
Fax No:	01261 833646
Website:	www.deveronvale.co.uk
E-Mail:	

deveronvalefc@highlandleague.com
Year of Formation: 1938

Capacity:	Total: 2,600
	300 Seated 2,300 Standing
Pitch Dimensions:	109 yds x 78 yds

Playing Kits:
1st Choice Shirt: Red with White Trim
Shorts: White Stockings: Red
2nd Choice Shirt:
Sky Blue with White Trim
Shorts: White Stockings: White

FORRES MECHANICS F.C.

Secretary:	David Macdonald
Manager:	Alan Scott
Club Address:	Mosset Park, Lea Road, Forres, Moray, IV36 0AU.
Ground Tel/Fax No:	01309 675096
Sec Home:	01343 544294
Sec Mobile:	07779 782799
Sec Business:	01309 694012
E-Mail:	

forresmechanicsfc@highlandleague.com
Year of Formation: 1884

Capacity:	Total: 6,540,
	540 Seated 6,000 Standing
Pitch Dimensions:	106 yds x 69 yds

Playing Kits:
1st Choice Shirt: Chocolate and Gold Stripes
Shorts: Gold Stockings: Gold
2nd Choice Shirt: White
Shorts: White Stockings: White

FORT WILLIAM F.C.

Secretary:	James Campbell
Manager:	–
Club Address:	Claggan Park, Fort William
Sec Home/Fax:	01397 772298
Website:	www.fortwilliamfc.org.uk
E-Mail:	

fortwilliamfc@highlandleague.com
Year of Formation: 1984

Capacity:	Total: 4,600
	400 Seated 4,200 Standing
Pitch Dimensions:	102 yds x 80 yds

Playing Kits:
1st Choice Shirt: Gold
Shorts: Black Stockings: Gold
2nd Choice Shirt: Black with Blue Sleeves
Shorts: Blue Stockings: Blue

FRASERBURGH F.C.

Secretary:	Finlay M. Noble
Manager:	Charles Duncan
Club Address:	Bellslea Park, Seaforth Street, Fraserburgh, AB43 9BD.
Ground Tel No:	01346 518444
Fax No:	01346 516414
Sec Bus/Mobile:	07747 003806
Sec Home:	01346 513474
Website:	www.fraserburghfc.net
E-Mail:	

fraserburghfc@highlandleague.com
Year of Formation: 1910

Capacity:	Total: 4,500

THE SCOT-ADS HIGHLAND LEAGUE FINAL TABLE SEASON 2003/04

	P	W	D	L	F	A	Pts
Clachnacuddin	28	21	3	4	61	25	66
Buckie Thistle	28	18	7	3	56	32	61
Fraserburgh	28	18	5	5	81	36	59
Deveronvale	28	18	1	9	77	41	55
Keith	28	17	2	9	70	36	53
Huntly	28	16	5	7	73	47	53
Inverurie Loco Works	28	13	10	5	76	51	49
Forres Mechanics	28	13	4	11	63	49	43
Nairn County	28	9	5	14	40	60	32
Cove Rangers	28	7	6	15	46	61	27
Wick Academy	28	6	5	17	42	65	23
Brora Rangers	28	5	6	17	34	71	21
Lossiemouth	28	4	8	16	41	74	20
Rothes	28	2	9	17	19	62	15
Fort William	28	3	4	21	20	89	13

480 Seated 4,020 Standing
Pitch Dimensions: 106 yds x 66 yds
Playing Kits:
1st Choice Shirt: Black and White Stripes
Shorts: Black Stockings: Red
2nd Choice Shirt: Blue Tartan
Shorts: Blue Stockings: White

HUNTLY F.C.

Secretary: Peter Morrison
Manager: Billy Anderson
Club Address: Christie Park, East Park Street,
                    Huntly, AB54 8JE.
Ground Tel/Fax No: 01466 793548
Sec Bus: 01358 726649
Sec Home: 01466 793269
Sec Mobile: 07957 283127
Website: www.huntlyfc.co.uk
E-Mail:
huntlyfc@highlandleague.com
Year of Formation: 1928
Capacity: Total: 4,500
                    270 Seated 4,230 Standing
Pitch Dimensions: 105 yds x 72 yds
Playing Kits:
1st Choice Shirt: Black and Gold Stripes
Shorts: Black Stockings: Black with Gold Trim
2nd Choice Shirt: White
Shorts: White Stockings: White

INVERURIE LOCO WORKS F.C.

Secretary: Gordon Park
Manager: John Gardiner
Club Address: Harlaw Park, Harlaw Road,
                    Inverurie, AB51 4SG.
Ground Tel No: 01467 622168
Sec Bus: 01467 624500
Sec Home: 01467 621347
Sec Mobile: 07816 604434
Website:
www.eteamz.com/inverurielocoworks
E-Mail:
inverurielocoworksfc@highlandleague.com
Year of Formation: 1903
Capacity: Total: 1,925
                    125 Seated 1,800 Standing
Pitch Dimensions: 103 yds x 71 yds
Playing Kits:
1st Choice Shirt: Black & Red Vertical Stripes
Shorts: Black Stockings: Red
2nd Choice Shirt: Black &
White Vertical Stripes
Shorts: White Stockings: White with Black Trim

KEITH F.C.

Secretary: Alexander Stables
Manager: Martin Allan
Club Address: Kynoch Park, Balloch Road,
                    Keith, AB55 5EN.
Sec Bus/Fax: 01542 882629
Sec Home: 01542 887492
Sec Mobile: 07814 431760
Website: www.keith-fc.co.uk
E-Mail: keithfc@highlandleague.com
Year of Formation: 1919
Capacity: Total: 4,500
                    450 Seated 4,050 Standing
Pitch Dimensions: 110 yds x 75 yds
Playing Kits:
1st Choice Shirt: Maroon/Blue & White
Shorts: Maroon Stockings: Maroon/White
2nd Choice Shirt: White with Dark Blue Trim
Shorts: Dark Blue Stockings: White

LOSSIEMOUTH F.C.

Secretary: Alan McIntosh
Manager: Graham Tatters
Club Address: Grant Park, Kellas Avenue,
                    Lossiemouth, IV31 6JG.
Ground Tel No: 01343 813717
Sec Home: 01343 813328
Sec Bus/Mobile: 07890 749053
Fax No: 01343 815440/813717
E-Mail:
lossiemouthfc@highlandleague.com
Year of Formation: 1945
Capacity: Total: 3,500
                    250 Seated 3,250 Standing
Pitch Dimensions: 110 yds x 60 yds
Playing Kits:
1st Choice Shirt: Red
Shorts: Red Stockings: Red
2nd Choice Shirt: Yellow with Blue Trim
Shorts: Blue with Yellow Trim
Stockings: Blue with Yellow Trim

NAIRN COUNTY F.C.

Secretary: John McNeill
Manager: Les Fridge
Club Address: Station Park, Balblair Road,
                    Nairn, IV12 5LT.
Ground Tel No: 01667 454298
Sec Bus: 01463 792424
Sec Home/Fax: 01667 462510
E-Mail:
nairncountyfc@highlandleague.com
Year of Formation: 1914

Capacity: Total: 3,800
                    250 Seated 3,550 Standing
Pitch Dimensions: 110 yds x 62 yds
Playing Kits:
1st Choice Shirt: Gold
Shorts: Black or White Stockings: Black or White
2nd Choice Shirt: Red
Shorts: White or Black Stockings: Red or Black

ROTHES F.C.

Secretary: Neil McKenzie
Manager: Graham McBeath
Club Address: MacKessack Park, Station Street,
                    Rothes, Aberlour
Ground Tel No: 01340 831972
Sec Mobile: 07802 773695
Sec Home: 01340 831344
E-Mail: rothesfc@highlandleague.com
Year of Formation: 1938
Capacity: Total: 2,650
                    160 Seated 2,490 Standing
Pitch Dimensions: 108 yds x 74 yds
Playing Kits:
1st Choice Shirt: Tangerine with Black Trim
Shorts: Black
Stockings: Tangerine with Three Black Hoops

2nd Choice Shirt: Black with Tangerine Trim
Shorts: Tangerine
Stockings: Black with Three Tangerine Hoops

WICK ACADEMY F.C.

Secretary: Andrew Carter
Manager: Alistair Budge
Club Address: Harmsworth Park, South Road,
                    Wick, KW1 5NH.
Ground Tel/Fax No: 01955 602446
Sec Bus: 01847 803249
Sec Home: 01955 605313
Sec Mobile: 07776 175132
Website: www.wickacademy-fc.co.uk
E-Mail:
wickacademyfc@highlandleague.com
Year of Formation: 1893
Capacity: Total: 2,000
                    433 Seated 1,567 Standing
Pitch Dimensions: 106 yds x 76 yds
Playing Kits:
1st Choice Shirt: Black and White Stripes
Shorts: Black Stockings: Black with White Tops
2nd Choice Shirt: White with Red/Maroon Trim
Shorts: Red Stockings: Maroon with White Tops

ANNAN ATHLETIC F.C.
Secretary: Alan T. Irving
Manager: Sandy Ross
Club Address: Galabank, North Street, Annan, Dumfries & Galloway.
Ground Tel No: 01461 204108
Sec Bus: 01461 207218
Sec Home/ Fax No: 01461 203702
Website: www.annanathletic.2fs.com
E-Mail: ibroxx@aol.com
Year of Formation: 1942
Capacity: Total: 2,000 (All Standing)
Pitch Dimensions: 110 yds x 65 yds
Playing Kits: 1st Choice Shirt: Black and Gold Vertical Stripes Shorts: Black Stockings: Black with Gold Hoops 2nd Choice Shirt: Blue Shorts: Blue Stockings: Blue with White Hoops

CIVIL SERVICE STROLLERS F.C.
Secretary: Graeme Turnbull
Co Managers: Alex Fyvie/Gordon Wilson
Club Address: Civil Service Sports Ground, Marine Drive, Edinburgh.
Ground Tel No: 0131 332 1175 (Matchdays Only)
Sec Bus: 01698 804614
Sec Mobile: 07717 430730
Website: www.strollers.org.uk
E-Mail: ght1uk@yahoo.co.uk
Year of Formation: 1908
Capacity: Total: 500 (All Standing)
Pitch Dimensions: 110 yds x 75 yds
Playing Kits: 1st Choice Shirt: White Shorts: Navy Blue Stockings: Red 2nd Choice Shirt: Red Shorts: Navy Blue Stockings: Navy Blue

COLDSTREAM F.C.
Secretary: Robert Bell
Manager: Brian Lough
Club Address: Home Park, Coldstream, Berwickshire.
Ground Tel/Fax No: 01890 883085
Sec Home: 01890 883161
E-Mail: coldstreamfc@clara.co.uk
Year of Formation: 1895
Capacity: Total: 1,500 (All Standing)
Pitch Dimensions: 100 yds x 60 yds
Playing Kits: 1st Choice Shirt: Royal Blue Shorts: Blue/White Stockings: Royal Blue 2nd Choice Shirt: Red Shorts: Red Stockings: Red

CRAIGROYSTON F.C.
Secretary: Jim Sivewright
Manager: Alan Whyte
Club Address: St. Mark's Park, Warriston, Edinburgh
Sec Bus: 0131 346 5967
Sec Home: 0131 228 1803
Year of Formation: 1976
Capacity: Total: 1,000 (All Standing)
Pitch Dimensions: 106 yds x 76 yds
Playing Kits: 1st Choice Shirt: Yellow Shorts: Blue

Stockings: Yellow 2nd Choice Shirt: Royal Blue Shorts: Royal Blue Stockings: Royal Blue

DALBEATTIE STAR F.C.
Secretary: Robert Geddes
Manager: Brian Aitchison
Club Address: Islecroft Stadium, Dalbeattie.
Ground Tel No: 01556 611151
Sec Bus/Home: 01556 610563
Sec Mobile: 07860 549444
Fax No: 01556 611747
E-Mail: bob@solwaypressservices.wanadoo.co.uk
Year of Formation: 1905 (approx)
Capacity: Total: 4,000 (All Standing)
Pitch Dimensions: 110 yds x 70 yds
Playing Kits: 1st Choice Shirt: Red and Black Stripes Shorts: Black Stockings: Red 2nd Choice Shirt: Sky Blue and Maroon Shorts: Maroon Stockings: Maroon

EASTHOUSES LILY F.C.
Secretary: Robert Paul
Manager: David McQueenie
Club Address: Mayfield Park, Newbattle, Easthouses
Sec Home: 0131 663 9768
Year of Formation: 1969
Capacity: Total: 1,000 (All Standing)
Pitch Dimensions: 110 yds x 67 yds
Playing Kits: 1st Choice Shirt: Red Shorts: White Stockings: White 2nd Choice Shirt: Blue Shorts: Blue Stockings: Blue

EDINBURGH ATHLETIC F.C.
Secretary: Ms Moira Findlay
Manager: Eugene Taylor
Club Address: Civil Service Sports Ground, Marine Drive, Edinburgh.
Ground Tel No: 0131 332 1175
Sec Home: 0131 476 6730
Website: www.edinburghathletic.com
Year of Formation: 1968
Capacity: Total: 500 (All Standing)
Pitch Dimensions: 100 yds x 60 yds
Playing Kits: 1st Choice Shirt: Navy Blue Shorts: White Stockings: Navy Blue 2nd Choice Shirt: White Shorts: Blue Stockings: White

EDINBURGH CITY F.C.
Secretary: Grant Coffin
Manager: Tom Steven
Club Address: Meadowbank Stadium, London Road, Edinburgh, EH7 6AE.
Ground Tel No: 0131 661 5351
Sec Bus: 07740 443944
Sec Home: 0131 332 5506
Website: www.edinburghcityfc.com
E-Mail: grant@gcoffin.demon.co.uk
Year of Formation: 1928
Capacity: Total: 13,841 (All Seated)
Pitch Dimensions: 105 yds x 72 yds

Playing Kits: 1st Choice Shirt: White Shorts: Black Stockings: White 2nd Choice Shirt: Yellow Shorts: Black Stockings: Yellow

EDINBURGH UNIVERSITY ASSOCIATION F.C.
Secretary: Damian Wheeler
Manager: Douglas Samuel
Club Address: East Peffermill Playing Fields, Peffermill Road, Edinburgh.
Sec Bus: 07946 190070
Fax No: 0131 650 2371
Website: www.eusu.ed.ac.uk/clubs/euafc
E-Mail: euafc@ed.ac.uk
Year of Formation: 1878
Capacity: Total: 1,012 12 Seated 1,000 Standing
Pitch Dimensions: 115 yds x 66 yds
Playing Kits: 1st Choice Shirt: Green/Navy Blue Sleeves Shorts: Navy Blue Stockings: Navy Blue 2nd Choice Shirt: White with Claret Sleeves Shorts: Claret Stockings: Claret

EYEMOUTH UNITED F.C.
Secretary: Ian Thomson
Manager: Alec Flockhart
Club Address: Warner Park, Johns Road, Eyemouth
Sec Home: 01890 751301
Year of Formation: 1949
Capacity: Total: 1,000 (All Standing)
Pitch Dimensions: 102 yds x 65 yds
Playing Kits: 1st Choice Shirt: Maroon Shorts: Maroon Stockings: Maroon 2nd Choice Shirt: White Shorts: Maroon Stockings: Sky Blue

GALA FAIRYDEAN F.C.
Secretary: John Clayton
Manager: Alan McKenna
Club Address: Netherdale, Galashiels.
Ground Tel No: 01896 753554
Sec Home/Bus: 01896 753797
Sec Mobile: 07768 616397
Fax: 01896 754412
Website: www.galafairydean.com
E-Mail: john.clayton@sepa.org.uk
Year of Formation: 1907
Capacity: Total: 5,500, 495 Seated, 5,005 Standing
Pitch Dimensions: 110 yds x 72 yds
Playing Kits: 1st Choice Shirt: White/Black Band down Arms & Sides Shorts: Black Stockings: Black with White Top 2nd Choice Shirt: Sky Blue/Navy Blue Band down Arms & Sides Shorts: Navy Blue Stockings: Sky Blue/Navy Blue Stripe

HAWICK ROYAL ALBERT F.C.
Secretary: Douglas J. Purves
Manager: Murray Balloch
Club Address: Albert Park, Mansfield Road, Hawick.
Ground Tel No: 01450 374231
Sec Bus: 0131 537 9241
Sec Home: 01450 371261

PREMIER DIVISION

	P	W	D	L	F	A	Pts
Spartans	22	16	5	1	63	25	53
Edinburgh City	22	14	4	4	56	29	46
Threave Rovers	22	10	7	5	44	28	37
Annan Athletic	22	11	4	7	49	45	37
Gala Fairydean	22	9	4	9	34	38	31
Edinburgh University	22	8	6	8	32	30	30
Civil Service Strollers	22	9	2	11	43	38	29
Preston Athletic	22	8	4	10	34	36	28
Lothian Thistle	22	6	3	13	24	45	21
Whitehill Welfare	22	5	5	12	38	51	20
Vale of Leithen	22	4	7	11	35	56	19
Craigroyston	22	5	3	14	29	60	18

FIRST DIVISION

	P	W	D	L	F	A	Pts
Kelso United	22	15	3	4	52	29	48
Dalbeattie Star	22	14	4	4	76	35	46
Ormiston	22	14	4	4	49	27	46
Easthouses Lily	22	12	5	5	52	25	41
Heriot-Watt University	22	11	3	8	53	37	36
Peebles Rovers	22	10	6	6	53	44	36
Edinburgh Athletic	22	9	6	7	42	34	33
Selkirk	22	9	5	8	40	35	32
Coldstream	22	4	5	13	33	58	17
Hawick Royal Albert	22	4	4	14	24	61	16
Tollcross United	22	3	2	17	24	55	11
Eyemouth United	22	2	3	17	21	79	6

E-Mail: prvsjason@aol.com
Year of Formation: 1947
Capacity: Total: 2,000,
500 Seated, 1,500 Standing
Pitch Dimensions: 100 yds x 68 yds
Playing Kits: 1st Choice Shirt: Royal Blue with White and Red Stripe Shorts: Royal Blue Stockings: Red
2nd Choice Shirt: Red and Black
Shorts: Black Stockings: Black and Red Stripe

HERIOT-WATT UNIVERSITY F.C.

Secretary: Colin Matthews
Manager: Billy Henderson
Club Address: Heriot-Watt University Riccarton Campus, Riccarton, Edinburgh
Ground Tel No: 0131 451 3000
Sec Home: 07814 243126
Website: www.hwufc.org.uk
E-Mail: alimath01@yahoo.co.uk
Year of Formation: 1945
Capacity: Total: 1,000 (All Standing)
Pitch Dimensions: 115 yds x 75 yds
Playing Kits: 1st Choice Shirt: Yellow, Blue trim
Shorts: Blue Stockings: Yellow 2nd Choice Shirt: Blue
Shorts: Black Stockings: Blue

KELSO UNITED F.C.

Secretary: Andrew Torrance
Manager: Peter McNulty
Club Address: Woodside Park, Kelso.
Ground Tel No: 01573 223780
Sec Home: 01573 420432
Sec Bus: 01573 420760
E-Mail: andrew.torrance@btinternet.com
Year of Formation: 1924
Capacity: Total: 1,000 (All Standing)
Pitch Dimensions: 107 yds x 67 yds
Playing Kits: 1st Choice Shirt: Black and White Stripes
Shorts: Black Stockings: Black 2nd Choice Shirt:
Black/Red Stripe Shorts: Red Stockings: Red/Black

LOTHIAN THISTLE F.C.

Secretary: Tom Allison
Co Managers: Ricky Tulloch/Malcolm Tulloch
Club Address: Saughton Enclosure, Edinburgh.
Ground Tel No: 0131 444 0422 (Matchdays Only)
Sec Bus: 0131 333 1976
Sec Home: 0131 336 1751
Website: www.lothianthistlefc.co.uk
E-Mail: secretary@lothianthistlefc.co.uk
Year of Formation: 1969
Capacity: Total: 1,000 (All Standing)
Pitch Dimensions: 108 yds x 74 yds
Playing Kits: 1st Choice Shirt: White
Shorts: Black Stockings: Black/White 2nd Choice
Shirt: Red Shorts: Red Stockings: Red/White

ORMISTON F.C.

Secretary: John M. Greenhorn
Manager: Murray Cheyne

Club Address: Recreation Park, Ormiston.
Sec Bus: 0131 453 4411
Sec Home: 0131 538 0289
Sec Mobile: 07740 680904
E-Mail: john.greenhorn@blueyonder.co.uk
Year of Formation: 1884
Capacity: Total: 1,000 (All Standing)
Pitch Dimensions: 108 yds x 68 yds
Playing Kits: 1st Choice Shirt: Maroon Shorts: Maroon Stockings: Maroon 2nd Choice Shirt: White Shorts: White Stockings: White

PEEBLES ROVERS F.C.

Secretary: Gareth Smith
Manager: Robert Linton
Club Address: Whitestone Park, Peebles.
Sec Home: 01721 723532
Sec Bus: 0131 668 0333
Website: www.memberstripod.com/peeblesrovers
E-Mail: vandgsmith@hotmail.com
Year of Formation: 1893
Capacity: Total: 1,000
200 Seated, 800 Standing
Pitch Dimensions: 110 yds x 75 yds
Playing Kits: 1st Choice Shirt: Red/White Shorts: Red Stockings: Red 2nd Choice Shirt: Yellow/Black Stripe
Shorts: Black Stockings: Yellow/Black Hoops

PRESTON ATHLETIC F.C.

Secretary: Dr. Andrew Waddell
Manager: Stephen Myatt
Club Address: Pennypitt Park, Rope Walk, Prestonpans, East Lothian.
Ground Tel No: 01875 815221
Sec Bus: 0131 664 7838
Sec Home: 0131 664 3135
Sec Mobile: 07887 791505
Website: www.prestonathletic.com
E-Mail: preston@prestonathletic.co.uk
Year of Formation: 1945
Capacity: Total: 4,000
313 Seated 3,687 Standing
Pitch Dimensions: 110 yds x 70 yds
Playing Kits: 1st Choice Shirt: Blue Shorts: White
Stockings: Blue 2nd Choice Shirt: Red/Black facings
Shorts: Black Stockings: White/Black Tops

SELKIRK F.C.

Secretary: Mrs. Sheree Davison
Manager: Fraser Lothian
Club Address: Yarrow Park, Selkirk
Sec Home: 01750 21995
Sec Mobile: 07984 984572
Year of Formation: 1880
Capacity: Total: 1,000 (All Standing)
Pitch Dimensions: 108 yds x 70 yds
Playing Kits: 1st Choice Shirt: Blue and White Stripe
Shorts: White Stockings: Blue 2nd Choice Shirt:
Blue/Red Sleeve Shorts: Blue Stockings: White/Red Flash

SPARTANS F.C.

Secretary: James Murray
Co-Managers: Sam Lynch & Mike Lawson
Club Address: City Park, Ferry Road, Edinburgh.
Sec Bus/Fax: 0131 667 9923
Sec Home: 0131 668 2188
Sec Mobile: 07710 723563
Website: www.spartansfc.com
E-Mail: Jim.Murray@ICScotland.net
Year of Formation: 1951
Capacity: Total: 3,000 (All Standing)
Pitch Dimensions: 110 yds x 65 yds
Playing Kits: 1st Choice Shirt: White Shorts: Red Stockings: White
2nd Choice Shirt: Blue Shorts: Blue Stockings: Blue

TOLLCROSS UNITED F.C.

Secretary: Alistair Wilkie
Manager: Ronnie Dignan
Club Address: Fernieside Recreation Park, Fernieside Avenue, Edinburgh.
Sec Bus: 0131 467 5555
Sec Home: 0131 622 1148
Year of Formation: 1971
Capacity: Total: 1,000 (All Standing)
Pitch Dimensions: 115 yds x 72 yds
Playing Kits: 1st Choice Shirt: Red with White
Sleeves Shorts: White Stockings: White 2nd Choice
Shirt: White Shorts: White Stockings: Red

VALE OF LEITHEN F.C.

Secretary: Alex Currie
Co Managers: Jackie Diamond & Stuart Robertson
Club Address: Victoria Park, Innerleithen.
Sec Home: 01896 830708
Sec Mobile: 07952 809694
E-Mail: vale@leithen.wanadoo.co.uk
Year of Formation: 1891
Capacity: Total: 1,500 (All Standing)
Pitch Dimensions: 100 yds x 75 yds
Playing Kits: 1st Choice Shirt: White with Navy Blue
Band Shorts: Navy Blue Stockings: Navy Blue
2nd Choice Shirt: Red Shorts: Red Stockings: Red

WHITEHILL WELFARE F.C.

Secretary: Peter McGauley
Manager: John Clark
Club Address: Ferguson Park, Carnethie Street, Rosewell, Midlothian.
Ground Tel No: 0131 440 0115
Sec Home: 0131 440 3417
Website: www.whitehillwelfare.com
E-Mail: whitehillwelfare@supanet.com
Year of Formation: 1953
Capacity: Total: 4,000 (All Standing)
Pitch Dimensions: 110 yds x 66 yds
Playing Kits: 1st Choice Shirt: Claret Body with Sky
Blue Sleeves Shorts: White Stockings: White
2nd Choice Shirt: Sky Blue
Shorts: Claret Stockings: Sky Blue

The South of Scotland

Football League Directory of Clubs

ABBEY VALE F.C.

Secretary:	David Morton
Manager:	Robert Cameron
Club Address:	Maryfield Park, New Abbey
Fax No:	01387 256004
Sec Bus:	07762 230648
Sec Home:	01387 256004
Year of Formation:	1974

Playing Kits:
1st Choice
Shirt: Black and Gold
Shorts: Black
Stockings: Yellow
2nd Choice
Shirt: Red
Shorts: Black
Stockings: Black

ANNAN ATHLETIC F.C.

Secretary:	Alan T. Irving
Manager:	Sandy Ross
Club Address:	Galabank, North Street, Annan, Dumfries & Galloway.
Ground Tel No:	01461 204108
Sec Bus:	01461 207218
Sec Home/ Fax No:	01461 203702
Website:	www.annanathletic.2fs.com
E–Mail:	ibroxx@aol.com
Year of Formation:	1942
Capacity:	Total: 2,000 (All Standing)
Pitch Dimensions:	110 yds x 65 yds

Playing Kits:
1st Choice
Shirt: Black and Gold Vertical Stripes
Shorts: Black
Stockings: Black with Gold Hoops
2nd Choice
Shirt: Blue
Shorts: Blue
Stockings: Blue with White Hoops

CREETOWN F.C.

Secretary:	Andrew Ward
Manager:	James McCrossan
Club Address:	Castlecary Park, Creetown.
Sec Home:	01671 820251
Year of Formation:	1894
Pitch Dimensions:	110 yds x 66 yds

Playing Kits:
1st Choice
Shirt: Yellow & Black
Shorts: Yellow & Black
Stockings: Yellow & Black Hoops
2nd Choice
Shirt: Burgandy & White
Shorts: Burgandy
Stockings: Burgandy

CRICHTON F.C.

Secretary:	Kenny Cameron
Assistant Secretary:	Jane Brown
Manager:	James Thomson
Club Address:	Crichton Park, Dumfries
Sec Home:	01387 265930
Sec Bus:	01387 258462
Asst. Sec Home:	01387 255658
E–Mail:	kenny-ac.cameron@gbr.dupont.com
Year of Formation:	1970 (As Blackwood Dynamos)
Capacity:	Total: 2,500 (All Standing)
Pitch Dimensions:	106 yds x 67 yds

Playing Kits:
1st Choice Shirt: Blue & White
Shorts: Blue
Stockings: Blue
2nd Choice
Shirt: Red & White
Shorts: Black
Stockings: Red

DALBEATTIE STAR F.C.

Secretary:	Robert Geddes
Manager:	Brian Aitchison
Club Address:	Islecroft Stadium, Dalbeattie.
Ground Tel:	01556 611151
Sec Bus/Home:	01556 610563
Sec Mobile:	07860 549444
Fax No:	01556 611747
E–Mail: bob@solwaypressservices.wanadoo.co.uk	

Year of Formation:	1905 (approx)
Capacity:	Total: 4,000 (All Standing)
Pitch Dimensions:	110 yds x 70 yds

Playing Kits:
1st Choice
Shirt: Red and Black Stripes
Shorts: Black
Stockings: Red
2nd Choice
Shirt: Sky Blue and Maroon
Shorts: Maroon
Stockings: Maroon

DUMFRIES F.C.

Secretary:	Tommy Parker
Manager:	Colin Lennox
Club Address:	Norfolk Park, Dumfries.
Sec Home:	01387 263285
Sec Bus:	07710 679794
Website:	www.dumfriesfc.co.uk
E–Mail:	tparker3659@aol.com
Year of Formation:	2000
Capacity:	Total: 500 (Standing)
Pitch Dimensions:	105 yds x 63 yds

Playing Kits:
1st Choice
Shirt: Yellow & Navy Blue
Shorts: Navy Blue
Stockings: Navy Blue
2nd Choice
Shirt: Navy Blue & Yellow
Shorts: Navy Blue
Stockings: Navy Blue

FLEET STAR F.C.

Secretary:	Irvine Hannah
Manager:	Andrew Mellon
Club Address:	Garries Park, Gatehouse of Fleet
Sec Bus:	01671 403285
Sec Home:	01557 814829
Year of Formation:	1948
Capacity:	Total: 600 (All Standing)

SOUTH OF SCOTLAND LEAGUE FINAL TABLE SEASON 2003/04

	P	W	D	L	F	A	Pts
Stranraer Athletic	30	25	1	4	89	34	76
Queen of the South	30	24	3	3	100	23	75
Creetown	30	21	2	7	92	39	65
Stranraer	30	18	5	7	75	43	59
Annan Athletic	30	18	3	9	94	41	57
Dumfries	30	16	3	11	77	62	51
Girvan	30	15	3	12	70	59	48
St. Cuthbert Wanderers	30	10	10	10	64	53	40
Threave Rovers	30	11	6	13	55	69	39
Nithsdale Wanderers	30	11	4	15	77	84	37
Mid Annandale	30	10	5	15	49	61	35
Abbey Vale	30	8	4	18	67	88	28
Wigtown & Bladnoch	30	8	4	18	63	92	28
Dalbeattie Star	30	7	2	21	38	89	23
Newton Stewart	30	5	1	24	40	148	16
Crichton	30	5	0	25	59	124	15

Playing Kits:
1st Choice Shirt: Blue and White
Shorts: White
Stockings: Blue

MID ANNANDALE F.C.
Secretary: George Trudt
Manager: Sean Ross
Club Address: King Edward Park, Lockerbie
Sec Home No: 01576 202757
Sec Mobile: 07710 087783
Year of Formation: 1958
Pitch Dimensions: 116 yds x 66 yds
Playing Kits:
1st Choice
Shirt: Yellow with Black Trimming
Shorts: Black with Two White Side Panels
Stockings: Yellow with Two Black Hoops on Tops
2nd Choice
Shirt: Blue with Yellow Trimming
Shorts: Blue with Yellow Side Panels
Stockings: Blue

NEWTON STEWART F.C.
Secretary: John R. McNaught
Manager: Alan Groves
Club Address: Blairmount Park, Newton Stewart
Sec Bus: 01671 402499
Sec Home: 01671 403066
E-Mail: mc.holm.hol@talk21.com
Playing Kits:
1st Choice
Shirt: Black and White Vertical Stripes
Shorts: Black
Stockings: Black
2nd Choice
Shirt: Silver and Grey Vertical Stripes
Shorts: Black
Stockings: Black

NITHSDALE WANDERERS F.C.
Secretary: Sam MacFarlane
Sec Home: 01659 50546
Treasurer: William Watson

Treasurer's Home: 01659 58312
Club Address: Lorimer Park, Sanquhar
Coaches: Sam MacFarlane & George Bain
Playing Kits:
1st Choice
Shirt: Blue and White
Shorts: Blue
Stockings: Blue
2nd Choice
Shirt: Black and White
Shorts: White
Stockings: White

ST. CUTHBERT WANDERERS F.C.
Secretary: Steve Richard
Manager: David Clarke
Club Address: St. Mary's Park, Kirkcudbright.
Sec Bus/Home: 01577 331960
E-Mail: steve@tandsimmigration.co.uk
Year of Formation: 1879
Capacity: Total: 600
                     100 Seated 500 Standing
Pitch Dimensions: 100 yds x 56 yds
Playing Kits:
1st Choice
Shirt: Blue with White Hoops
Shorts: Blue
Stockings: White
2nd Choice
Shirt: Red and Black Hoops
Shorts: Black
Stockings: Black with Red Hoops

STRANRAER ATHLETIC F.C.
Secretary: Elizabeth Murdoch
Manager: Sandy Sutherland
Club Address: Stranraer Academy, Stranraer
Sec Home: 01776 705309
Sec Mobile: 07990 708244
Playing Kit:
Shirt: Blue and White
Shorts: Blue and White
Stockings: Blue and White

THREAVE ROVERS F.C.
Secretary: Ian Bendall
Manager: David McVitie
Club Address: Meadow Park, Castle Douglas,
                     Dumfries & Galloway.
Ground Tel No: 01556 504536
Sec Home Tel/Fax: 01556 650310
Sec Bus: 01556 503713
Website: www.threaveroversfc.co.uk
E-Mail: ianbendall@msn.com
Year of Formation: 1953
Capacity: Total: 5,000 (All Standing)
Pitch Dimensions: 110 yds x 74 yds
Playing Kits:
1st Choice
Shirt: Black and White
Shorts: Black
Stockings: Black
2nd Choice
Shirt: Red
Shorts: Red
Stockings: Red

WIGTOWN AND BLADNOCH F.C.
Secretary: Arlene Broll
Manager: Brian Balfour
Club Address: Trammondford Park,
                     Wigtown.
Ground Tel/Fax: 01988 402322
Sec Home: 01988 700677
Sec Mobile: 07766 658999
Year of Formation: 1880
Capacity: Total: 1,500 (All Standing)
Pitch Dimensions: 110 yds x 74 yds
Playing Kits:
1st Choice
Shirt: Red with White Trim
Shorts: Red/Pinstripe White
Stockings: Red/Pinstripe White
2nd Choice
Shirt: Blue and Yellow Trim
Shorts: Blue and Yellow Trim
Stockings: Blue and Yellow Trim

A look Back at
Scottish Football
Since Season 1980/81

Editorial by Rodger Baillie
(Chief Sportswriter, The Scottish Sun)

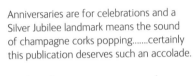

LIVINGSTON LIFT THE
CIS INSURANCE CUP IN SEASON 2004

RAITH ROVERS - WINNERS OF THE
COCA-COLA CUP IN SEASON 1994/95

Anniversaries are for celebrations and a Silver Jubilee landmark means the sound of champagne corks popping.......certainly this publication deserves such an accolade.

Not least from reporters as we seekers after truth were able to record accurate ages for players with for the first time, the revelation of the stars' birthdays. Whisper it quietly, but some ageing footballers had been known before 1980 to knock a few years off their age.

There has been much to admire from many players and many clubs in those 25 years since the fledgling Scottish Football League Review first hit the bookstands, price £2, to herald season 1980/81. Yet even the most optimistic fan has to feel a flicker of worry about Scotland's football future after the last years of that quarter of a century. As I stood outside grounds watching players thrown on the dole, I felt more like an industrial correspondent at the gates of a factory threatened with grim redundancies than a football writer.

Administration, a tag once unknown to most supporters – and sports journalists – became as common a football term as a penalty-kick and the scourge hit three Premier League clubs, Motherwell, Dundee and Livingston. In 2002, one team, Airdrieonians, even went out of

business – the first Scottish club to suffer such a fate since the fondly remembered Third Lanark in 1967.

Mercifully the romance of the sport can never be totally crushed and Airdrie United, who rose from the ashes of the once great Lanarkshire club, took their place – just as over those 25 years, Ross County, Peterhead, Elgin City, Inverness Caledonian Thistle and Gretna were added to the Scottish League football family.

The Inverness side crowned their exhilarating ten–year climb from the Third Division by gaining admission to The Scottish Premier League after captur–ing the First Division crown, although it involved a bitter off the field battle over disputed rules with Partick Thistle who finished bottom of the top twelve.

Livingston, who were in their old guise of Meadowbank Thistle when the Review was first published, just managed to stay alive last February then completed one of the most amazing episodes of this quarter century review by winning The CIS Insurance Cup – with a 2–0 victory against favourites Hibernian at Hampden – to collect the club's first major award. Typically in the mad, mad, mad world of football, the reward for their much admired manager Davie Hay was to be relieved of his job at the end of the season.

DUNDEE UNITED – PREMIER DIVISION CHAMPIONS IN SEASON 1982/83

Flick through the pages of that first issue of the series and such is the managerial mortality rate that only three of them active in 1980 are still plying their trade – one of them in England. Sir Alex Ferguson switched from Aberdeen to become world famous with Manchester United.

In Scotland, the daddy of them all is Alex Smith. Listed as Stirling Albion boss in 1980, the greatly respected Smith moved to St. Mirren then Aberdeen (guiding both to Scottish Cup success), on to Clyde and Dundee United before settling at Ross County.

When the Review was first published, Aberdeen were the reigning Premier Division Champions. They went on to lift two more titles under the magical touch of Ferguson, collect the Scottish Cup four times and the League Cup once. Apart from sporadic Cup success, his Pittodrie successors have tried in vain to come near the incredible silverware collection amassed by Fergie, with his stalwarts Alex McLeish and skipper Willie Miller at the heart of the defence and skilled attackers such as Gordon Strachan, Eric Black and Mark McGhee up front.

Only Hibs, with their legendary post-war "Famous Five" forward line,

earlier battled the Old Firm's League domination. Ferguson was the next to take them on successfully, and many judge that as great an achievement as his later victories in England with Manchester United.

Significantly in the twenty years since the Dons lifted the title in season 1984/85, no other club outside Celtic and Rangers has captured the Premier title – nor is such an upset likely again in the foreseeable future. The first half of the eighties were dominated by the New Firm, with Dundee United – under the effective dictatorship of Jim McLean – backing up Aberdeen's challenge to topple Rangers and Celtic.

The Tannadice side snatched their only League title on the last day of season 1982/83, won the League Cup twice but the Scottish Cup eluded them in five failures at Hampden. It was only when McLean moved upstairs to become chairman that Ivan Golac, one of a long list of men who succeeded him, guided United to victory against Rangers in the 1994 Final.

However, the aspirations of Aberdeen and Dundee United, and the rest of Scottish football, were shattered by the appointment of Graeme Souness as

Rangers' manager in 1986. It was to be the most significant step taken by either half of the Old Firm since Celtic made Jock Stein their boss twenty-one years earlier.

When the old MGM studios ruled Hollywood in the thirties and forties with a roster of the biggest film names in the business they boasted they had 'more stars than in the heavens'. Souness, too, believed in packing his side with box-office attractions and, a series of them delighted the Ibrox fans.

Terry Butcher, Chris Woods, Graham Roberts, Trevor Francis, Ray Wilkins, Mark Walters and Mark Hateley were just some of the names wooed to Ibrox. And with the backing of new owner David Murray, he smashed the sectarian barrier that had haunted Rangers for too long, when he signed former Celtic centre-forward Mo Johnston, who was a Catholic.

Another striker, peering shyly from the pages of that first Review, was introduced to the readers as 18-year-old St. Johnstone midfielder Alistair McCoist. He too played a significant part in the Light Blues history – becoming their most capped Scotland player and highest goalscorer.

KENNY DALGLISH RECEIVES HIS 100TH CAP
FROM FRANZ BECKENBAUER

TOMMY McLEAN CELEBRATES MOTHERWELL'S
1991 SCOTTISH CUP VICTORY

WALTER SMITH REFLECTS ON RANGERS
TREBLE SUCCESS IN SEASON 1992/93

Souness started as player-manager, the first such appointment by the Ibrox club. He sported a trade-mark moustache and his glare delivered with laser-beam intensity was directed at players who stepped out of line and pressmen alike. The fiery former Liverpool star, red-carded in his first League game for Rangers against Hibernian at Easter Road, was involved in controversy right to the end of his time at Ibrox. It ended with an almost laughable row over the state of the visitor's dressing room at McDiarmid Park with the feisty St. Johnstone tea-lady, Aggie Moffat.

But he laid the foundations of Rangers nine-in-a-row title run which matched Jock Stein's achievement of his great years at Parkhead. He was succeeded by his lieutenant, Walter Smith, who more than proved himself a worthy successor. Smith continued the big-money transfers and the winning ways, Danish star Brian Laudrup and Paul Gascoigne were two of the major names he attracted to Ibrox.

When Smith quit failing by the margin of only three points to make history with ten successive titles – he was replaced in 1998 by Rangers first foreign manager, Dick Advocaat. Again there was no let-up in the names that poured into Ibrox under the free-spending policy of the little general from Holland but perhaps his greatest legacy was the development of one of the few Scots in his line-up, teenager Barry Ferguson, into a mature midfielder.

Advocaat notched a treble in his first season, took the Cup and League double in the second – and then hit the buffers as a new name swept over the Old Firm horizon. Martin O'Neill was the man who delivered Celtic from the trauma of yet another season when they had won nothing.

It wasn't just the lack of silverware but the manner of their decline which depressed their support. Celtic under Billy McNeill were twice League winners, in the first two years of the fledgling Review. McNeill then had a dispute with the club who stupidly allowed him to leave for a spell in England, but he returned to win the League and Cup as a fitting climax to the Parkhead club's Centenary celebrations in 1988.

It took another ten years before Dutchman Wim Jansen, in his only season in charge, lifted the title to stop Rangers run of nine in a row. There was also a

new name at the top at Parkhead, Fergus McCann – the wee man with the bunnet – in a dramatic take-over sensationally ousted the families who had ruled the old board ever since the club's foundation.

Managers came and went with dizzying speed, before and after McCann. McNeill, twice, Davie Hay, Liam Brady, Lou Macari, Tommy Burns, Jansen, Dr. Jozef Venglos and then the dream ticket of legend Kenny Dalglish and John Barnes. But the dream became a nightmare as the inexperienced Barnes in his first managerial job struggled to make an impact. He was sacked after the sensational Cup defeat at Parkhead by Inverness Caley Thistle, and a few months later Dalglish himself quietly departed.

There was only room for one man who was going to run the team, and O'Neill demanded no interference. His success was immediate. New players were snapped up, Chris Sutton, Alan Thompson and Neil Lennon just three of many as the club romped to a treble victory. Next season there was a double and although a revitalised Rangers captured the treble in O'Neill's third season he picked up the double again in the following campaign.

The man who made the biggest contribution on the field was Henrik Larsson. The talismanic Swede, before and after a broken leg, made repeated and telling contributions to Celtic's goals total. Every club, whether it's at the wrong end of the Third Division or top of the Premier, eventually has to replace long-serving stars. But when Larsson's contract ended and he left Celtic to join Spanish giants Barcelona, many Hoops fans pondered how his famous number seven jersey could ever be filled.

Thankfully for the sake of competition in the top division, the two major Cup competitions produced pockets of resistance to the stranglehold the Old Firm put on the honours list. The League Cup, changing its name smoothly from Bell's to Skol to Coca-Cola to the current CIS Insurance Cup, produced one of the biggest shocks of the last century when First Division Raith Rovers stunned Celtic in the Final of the 1994/95 tourney at Ibrox. Jimmy Nicholl's men, skippered by Gordon Dalziel, took Tommy Burns side to extra-time and then won 6-5 in a penalty kick shoot-out.

HENRIK LARSSON'S DOUBLE STRIKE IN SEVILLE WASN'T ENOUGH TO WIN THE UEFA CUP IN 2003

The Scottish Cup, too, occasionally had different names on it apart from the Glasgow giants. Aberdeen in three consecutive seasons from 1982 to 1984 then again in 1986 and 1990. St. Mirren in 1987, Dundee United in 1994, Kilmarnock in 1997 and Hearts ending decades without an honour a year later.

As a veteran observer of watching over 40 consecutive Cup Finals, the most exciting of them all was served up by Motherwell and Dundee United in 1991– truly a family Final with Tommy McLean in charge of 'Well and big brother Jim, manager of United. It finished dramatically in extra-time with a 4-3 win for the Lanarkshire side.

The mercurial Alex Ferguson ensured Aberdeen's place in Scotland's Hall of Fame when they became the third Scottish team to lift a European trophy, beating the mighty Real Madrid in the Cup Winners' Cup Final in 1983. John Hewitt was the super sub who notched the winner on a rain-soaked Ullevi Stadium in Gothenburg to give the Dons a fantastic 2-1 win.

Sadly for Scottish football, the result stands out like a beacon, it was the only major victory in Europe in the last quarter century. There were near misses. Dundee United came so close in the 1987 UEFA Cup Final losing 2-1 on aggregate to Swedish opponents Gothenburg in a campaign which included a memorable win over the multi-millionaires of Barcelona. They also had the consolation of picking up UEFA's coveted Fair Play award for the behaviour of their fans in the two-legged Final.

Rangers nearly reached the European Cup Final in season 1992/93 and Celtic went one better ten years later, making the UEFA Cup Final against Porto in Seville. They were beaten only five minutes from the end of extra-time despite two goals by – who else? – Henrik Larsson. Take your pick of the number of Hoops fans who went to the Spanish city, anything from 30,000 to 70,000, but they turned it into a carnival and were also awarded accolades by soccer's top brass for their sporting behaviour.

Equally on the fan front, one of the phenomenan's of the past quarter century has been the 'Tartan Army', the supporters who travel with Scotland across the world and have added to their own and the nation's prestige.

Since the first Review, the Tartan Army have had much to cheer, and sadly much to despair about. Scotland qualified for the World Cup Finals in Spain in 1982, Mexico in 1986, Italy in 1990 and France in 1998 but since then, the results in major competitions have been on a decidedly downward curve.

The Scottish press were once dubbed 'fans with typewriters' (now we're supporters with lap-tops) and I've been so lucky to have had a press-box seat at the great moments for the international team over these 25 years such as Dave Narey's wonder goal against Brazil in the 1982 Finals, judged by Jimmy Hill in an ill-judged phrase as a 'toe-poke'.

A fine win against Sweden in Italy in 1990 to make up for the ignominy of defeat to unrated Costa Rica - one of the results seared on our souls- and the heart-warming display with the eyes of the whole world on our side in the opening game of the '98 World Cup. The Scots wowed the watching TV billions, when they walked over the Stade de France in Paris before the game dressed in kilts, and despite a 2-1 defeat, Brown's bravehearts were never over-

ALEX FERGUSON AND ARCHIE KNOX CELEBRATE ABERDEEN'S EUROPEAN CUP WINNERS' CUP T

whelmed by the skills of the defending holders of the tournament, Brazil.

The saddest moment in those 25 years was the death of Jock Stein in September, 1985, after the international manager collapsed from a heart attack in the dug-out at Ninian Park at the end of a 1-1 draw with Wales which pushed Scotland into a play-off with Australia, and eventually qualification for Mexico.

His passing stunned the nation and a collective grief settled over the country like a black cloud. One of the finest tributes was paid to him by Rangers fans, bitter rivals from his days as Celtic manager when he overlorded the Parkhead domination of their team. But at Clydebank the following Saturday as his death was marked by a minute's silence across Scotland at three o'clock – and observed at amateur games on public parks right through to League matches – the respect from the ranks of the Ibrox faithful was total. I mourn his loss

to this day! Scotland battled in vain for the right to stage, with Ireland, the European Championships in 2008 but earlier in 1989 we showed we could put on a show, when we hosted FIFA's Under-16 World Youth Cup, and Craig Brown's young men only lost to a Saudi Arabian side – with some suspiciously looking over-age teenagers – in a penalty shoot-out at Hampden.

Meanwhile, as the top division and the international side took their slice of the spotlight, the foot soldiers of the First, Second and Third Divisions battled on each week to provide competitive League football with honest endeavour, mixed with not a little skill, for fans the length and breadth of the country. They also competed for a successful new trophy, the League Challenge Cup.

Changes off the park often dominated events on the field. A new look Premier League was started in 1998, with a breakaway from the other clubs in the

SFL. SFA Chief Executive Jim Farry – who was Scottish League Secretary in 1980 – was controversially removed from office, the National Stadium at Hampden was rebuilt, and a host of clubs, Airdrieonians, Clyde, Dumbarton, East Fife, Falkirk, Hamilton Academical, St. Johnstone and Stirling Albion moved to new homes and, in the case of Clyde and Meadowbank Thistle, relocated to the new towns of Cumbernauld and Livingston respectively with Meadowbank changing its name to embrace the name of its new town of residence.

No one peering into a crystal ball a quarter of a century ago could possibly have predicted the path that Scottish football has taken since 1980.

So the long and winding road on the way to the golden jubilee of this publication – in season 2030/31 – is best left to Mystic Meg. Perhaps the toast to the next 25 years should simply be 'survival'.

Bank of Scotland Premierleague
Club Honours

ABERDEEN
League Champions:
Division I: 1954/55
Premier Division:
1979/80, 1983/84, 1984/85
League Cup Winners:
1955/56, 1976/77, 1985/86,
1989/90, 1995/96
Scottish Cup Winners: 1947, 1970,
1982, 1983, 1984, 1986, 1990
European Cup Winners' Cup:
1982/83
European Super Cup: 1983
Drybrough Cup Winners:
1970/71, 1980/81

CELTIC
League Champions:
Division I: 1892/93, 1893/94, 1895/96, 1897/98,
1904/05, 1905/06, 1906/07, 1907/08, 1908/09,
1909/10, 1913/14, 1914/15, 1915/16, 1916/17,
1918/19, 1921/22, 1925/26, 1935/36, 1937/38,
1953/54, 1965/66, 1966/67, 1967/68, 1968/69,
1969/70, 1970/71, 1971/72, 1972/73, 1973/74
Premier Division: 1976/77,
1978/79, 1980/81, 1981/82, 1985/86,
1987/88, 1997/98,
SPL: 2000/01, 2001/02, 2003/04
League Cup Winners:
1956/57, 1957/58, 1965/66, 1966/67,
1967/68, 1968/69, 1969/70, 1974/75,
1982/83, 1997/98, 1999/2000, 2000/01
Scottish Cup Winners:
1892, 1899, 1900, 1904, 1907, 1908,
1911, 1912, 1914, 1923, 1925, 1927,
1931, 1933, 1937, 1951, 1954, 1965,
1967, 1969, 1971, 1972, 1974, 1975,
1977, 1980, 1985, 1988, 1989, 1995,
2001, 2004
European Cup Winners: 1966/67
Runners-up: 1969/70
UEFA Cup Runners-up: 2002/03
Empire Exhibition Cup Winners: 1938
Coronation Cup Winners: 1953
Drybrough Cup Winners: 1974/75

DUNDEE
League Champions:
Division I: 1961/62
Division II: 1946/47
First Division:
1978/79, 1991/92, 1997/98

League Cup Winners:
1951/52, 1952/53, 1973/74
Scottish Cup Winners: 1910
B&Q Centenary Cup: 1990/91

DUNDEE UNITED
League Champions:
Division II: 1924/25, 1928/29
Premier Division: 1982/83
League Cup Winners:
1979/80, 1980/81
Scottish Cup Winners: 1993/94
UEFA Cup Runners-up: 1986/87

DUNFERMLINE ATHLETIC
League Champions:
Division II: 1925/26
First Division: 1988/89, 1995/96
Second Division: 1985/86
Scottish Cup Winners: 1961, 1968
Scottish Qualifying Cup: 1911/12

HEARTS
League Champions:
Division I: 1894/95, 1896/97,
1957/58, 1959/60
First Division: 1979/80
League Cup Winners: 1954/55,
1958/59, 1959/60, 1962/63
Scottish Cup Winners: 1891, 1896,
1901, 1906, 1956, 1998

HIBERNIAN
League Champions:
Division I: 1902/03, 1947/48,
1950/51, 1951/52
Division II: 1893/94, 1894/95, 1932/33
First Division: 1980/81, 1998/99
League Cup Winners: 1972/73, 1991/92
Scottish Cup Winners: 1887, 1902
Drybrough Cup Winners:
1972/73, 1973/74

INVERNESS CALEDONIAN THISTLE
League Champions:
First Division: 2003/04
Third Division: 1996/97
Bell's Cup Winners: 2003/04

KILMARNOCK
League Champions:
Division I: 1964/65

Division II: 1897/98, 1898/99
Scottish Cup Winners:
1920, 1929, 1997
Scottish Qualifying Cup Winners:
1896/97

LIVINGSTON
League Champions:
First Division: 2000/01
Second Division: 1986/87, 1998/99
Third Division: 1995/96
League Cup Winners: 2003/04

MOTHERWELL
League Champions:
Division I: 1931/32
First Division: 1981/82, 1984/85
Division II: 1953/54, 1968/69
League Cup Winners: 1950/51
Scottish Cup Winners: 1952, 1991

RANGERS
League Champions:
Division I: 1890/91 (shared), 1898/99,
1899/1900, 1900/01, 1901/02, 1910/11,
1911/12, 1912/13, 1917/18, 1919/20, 1920/21,
1922/23, 1923/24, 1924/25, 1926/27, 1927/28,
1928/29, 1929/30, 1930/31, 1932/33, 1933/34,
1934/35, 1936/37, 1938/39, 1946/47, 1948/49,
1949/50, 1952/53, 1955/56, 1956/57, 1958/59,
1960/61, 1962/63, 1963/64, 1974/75
Premier Division: 1975/76, 1977/78,
1986/87, 1988/89, 1989/90, 1990/91,
1991/92, 1992/93, 1993/94, 1994/95,
1995/96, 1996/97
SPL: 1998/99, 1999/2000, 2002/03
League Cup Winners:
1946/47, 1948/49, 1960/61, 1961/62,
1963/64, 1964/65, 1970/71, 1975/76,
1977/78, 1978/79, 1981/82, 1983/84,
1984/85, 1986/87, 1987/88, 1988/89,
1990/91, 1992/93, 1993/94, 1996/97,
1998/99, 2001/02, 2002/03
Scottish Cup Winners:
1894, 1897, 1898, 1903, 1928, 1930, 1932,
1934, 1935, 1936, 1948, 1949, 1950, 1953,
1960, 1962, 1963, 1964, 1966, 1973, 1976,
1978, 1979, 1981, 1992, 1993, 1996, 1999,
2000, 2002, 2003
European Cup Winners' Cup: 1971/72
Runners-up: 1960/61, 1966/67
Drybrough Cup Winners: 1979/80

The Bell's Scottish Football League
Club Honours

AIRDRIE UNITED
League Champions:
Second Division: 1975/76, 2003/04

CLYDE
League Champions:
Division II: 1904/05, 1951/52, 1956/57,
1961/62, 1972/73,
Second Division: 1977/78, 1981/82,
1992/93, 1999/2000
Scottish Cup Winners:
1939, 1955, 1958

FALKIRK
League Champions:
First Division: 1990/91, 1993/94, 2002/03
Division II: 1935/36, 1969/70, 1974/75

Second Division: 1979/80
Scottish Cup Winners:
1913, 1957
SFL Challenge Cup Winners: 1993/94
(known as B&Q Cup), 1997/98

HAMILTON ACADEMICAL
League Champions:
Division II: 1903/04
First Division: 1985/86, 1987/88
Third Division: 2000/01
B&Q Cup Winners: 1991/92, 1992/93
Scottish Cup Runners-up:
1910/11, 1934/35
Second Division Runners-up:
1952/53, 1964/65, 1996/97
Lanarkshire Cup Winners: 10 Times

ALLOA ATHLETIC
League Champions:
Division II:
1921/22
Third Division:
1997/98
Bell's Challenge Cup Winners:
1999/2000

ARBROATH
League Runners-up: Division II: 1934/35,
1958/59, 1967/68, 1971/72,
Second Division: 2000/01
Third Division: 1997/98

AYR UNITED
League Champions:
Division II: 1911/12, 1912/13, 1927/28,
1936/37, 1958/59, 1965/66
Second Division: 1987/88, 1996/97

BERWICK RANGERS
League Champions:
Second Division: 1978/79
Runners-up: 1993/94
Third Division Runners-up: 1999/2000

BRECHIN CITY
League Champions:
'C' Division: 1953/54

ALBION ROVERS
League Champions:
Division II:
1933/34
Second Division:
1988/89
Scottish Qualifying Cup:
1913/14

COWDENBEATH
League Champions:
Division II: 1913/14, 1914/15, 1938/39

EAST FIFE
League Champions:
Division II: 1947/48
League Cup Winners:
1947/48, 1949/50, 1953/54
Scottish Cup Winners:
1938

EAST STIRLINGSHIRE
League Champions:
Division II: 1931/32

First Division

Second Division

Third Division

PARTICK THISTLE
League Champions:
First Division: 1975/76, 2001/02
Runners–up: 1991/92
Division II: 1896/97,
1899/1900, 1970/71
Second Division: 2000/01
Runners–up: 1901/02
League Cup Winners: 1971/72
Runners–up: 1953/54,
1956/57, 1958/59
Scottish Cup Winners: 1921
Runners–up: 1930
Glasgow Cup Winners:
1935, 1951, 1952,
1954, 1960,
1981, 1989

QUEEN OF THE SOUTH
League Champions:
Division II: 1950/51
Second Division: 2001/02
Bell's Cup: 2002/03

RAITH ROVERS
League Champions:
First Division: 1992/93, 1994/95
Second Division: 2002/03
Division II: 1907/08, 1909/10 (shared)
1937/38, 1948/49
League Cup Winners: 1994/95

ROSS COUNTY
League Champions:
Third Division: 1998/99

ST. JOHNSTONE
League Champions:
First Division: 1982/83,
1989/90, 1996/97
Division II: 1923/24,
1959/60, 1962/63

ST. MIRREN
League Champions:
First Division: 1976/77, 1999/2000
Division II: 1967/68
Scottish Cup Winners:
1926, 1959, 1987
Victory Cup: 1919
Anglo Scottish Cup Winners:
1979/80
Summer Cup: 1943

Second Division:
1982/83, 1989/90
Third Division:
2001/02

DUMBARTON
League Champions:
Division I: 1890/91
(shared with Rangers), 1891/92
Division II:
1910/11, 1971/72
Second Division: 1991/92
Scottish Cup Winners:
1883

FORFAR ATHLETIC
League Champions:
'C' Division: 1948/49
Second Division: 1983/84
Third Division: 1994/95

MORTON
League Champions:
Division II: 1949/50, 1963/64, 1966/67
First Division: 1977/78, 1983/84, 1986/87
Second Division: 1994/95
Third Division: 2002/03
Scottish Cup Winners:
1922

STIRLING ALBION
League Champions:
League Champions:
Division II: 1952/53, 1957/58, 1960/61,
1964/65,
Second Division: 1976/77, 1990/91,
1995/96

STRANRAER
League Champions:
Second Division: 1993/94, 1997/98
Third Division: 2003/04
SFL Challenge Cup Winners:
1996/97

ELGIN CITY
**Season 2000/01 was the club's first
season in membership of S.F.L.**
The club's highest position to date was
6th position in Season 2001/02

GRETNA
**Season 2002/03 was the club's first
season in membership of S.F.L.**
The club's highest position to date
was 3rd position in season 2003/04.

MONTROSE
League Champions:
Second Division: 1984/85

PETERHEAD
**Season 2000/01 was the club's first
season in membership of S.F.L.**
The club's highest position to date was 4th position
in Seasons 2001/02, 2002/03 and 2003/04

QUEEN'S PARK
League Champions: Division II: 1922/23

'B' Division 1955/56
Second Division: 1980/81
Third Division: 1999/2000
Scottish Cup Winners:
1874, 1875, 1876, 1880, 1881, 1882,
1884, 1886, 1890, 1893
FA Cup: Runners–up: 1884, 1889
FA Charity Shield:
1899 (Shared with Aston Villa)

STENHOUSEMUIR
SFL Challenge Cup Winners: 1995/96

Scottish League Champions
Since 1890

CELTIC MANAGER MARTIN O'NEILL PARADES THE BANK OF SCOTLAND PREMIERLEAGUE TROPHY

INVERNESS MANAGER JOHN ROBERTSON CELEBRATES AS HIS SIDE CLINCH THE FIRST DIVISION CHAMPIONSHIP

SEASON	DIVISION ONE	POINTS
1890/91	Dumbarton/Rangers	29
1891/92	Dumbarton	37
1892/93	Celtic	29
1893/94	Celtic	29
1894/95	Heart of Midlothian	31
1895/96	Celtic	30
1896/97	Heart of Midlothian	28
1897/98	Celtic	33
1898/99	Rangers	36
1899–1900	Rangers	32
1900/01	Rangers	35
1901/02	Rangers	28
1902/03	Hibernian	37
1903/04	Third Lanark	43
1904/05	Celtic (after play-off)	41
1905/06	Celtic	49
1906/07	Celtic	55
1907/08	Celtic	55
1908/09	Celtic	51
1909/10	Celtic	54
1910/11	Rangers	52
1911/12	Rangers	51
1912/13	Rangers	53
1913/14	Celtic	65
1914/15	Celtic	65
1915/16	Celtic	67
1916/17	Celtic	64
1917/18	Rangers	56
1918/19	Celtic	58
1919/20	Rangers	71
1920/21	Rangers	76
1921/22	Celtic	67
1922/23	Rangers	55
1923/24	Rangers	59
1924/25	Rangers	60
1925/26	Celtic	58
1926/27	Rangers	56
1927/28	Rangers	60
1928/29	Rangers	67
1929/30	Rangers	60
1930/31	Rangers	60
1931/32	Motherwell	66
1932/33	Rangers	62
1933/34	Rangers	66
1934/35	Rangers	55
1935/36	Celtic	66
1936/37	Rangers	61
1937/38	Celtic	61
1938/39	Rangers	59

Seasons 1939/40 to 1945/46 – (No Competition)

SEASON	DIVISION ONE	POINTS
1946/47	Rangers	46
1947/48	Hibernian	48
1948/49	Rangers	46
1949/50	Rangers	50
1950/51	Hibernian	48
1951/52	Hibernian	45
1952/53	Rangers*	43
1953/54	Celtic	43
1954/55	Aberdeen	49
1955/56	Rangers	52
1956/57	Rangers	55
1957/58	Heart of Midlothian	62
1958/59	Rangers	50
1959/60	Heart of Midlothian	54
1960/61	Rangers	51
1961/62	Dundee	54
1962/63	Rangers	57
1963/64	Rangers	55
1964/65	Kilmarnock*	50
1965/66	Celtic	57
1966/67	Celtic	58
1967/68	Celtic	63
1968/69	Celtic	54
1969/70	Celtic	57
1970/71	Celtic	56
1971/72	Celtic	60
1972/73	Celtic	57
1973/74	Celtic	53
1974/75	Rangers	56

SEASON	DIVISION TWO	POINTS
1890/91	(No Competition)	
1891/92	(No Competition)	
1892/93	(No Competition)	
1893/94	Hibernian	29
1894/95	Hibernian	30
1895/96	Abercorn	27
1896/97	Partick Thistle	31
1897/98	Kilmarnock	29
1898/99	Kilmarnock	32
1899–1900	Partick Thistle	29
1900/01	St. Bernards	25
1901/02	Port Glasgow	32
1902/03	Airdrieonians	35
1903/04	Hamilton Academical	37
1904/05	Clyde	32
1905/06	Leith Athletic	34
1906/07	St. Bernards	32
1907/08	Raith Rovers	30
1908/09	Abercorn	31

SEASON	DIVISION TWO	POINTS
1909/10	Leith Athletic	33
1910/11	Dumbarton	31
1911/12	Ayr United	35
1912/13	Ayr United	34
1913/14	Cowdenbeath	31
1914/15	Cowdenbeath	37
1915/16	(No Competition)	
1916/17	(No Competition)	
1917/18	(No Competition)	
1918/19	(No Competition)	
1919/20	(No Competition)	
1920/21	(No Competition)	
1921/22	Alloa	60
1922/23	Queen's Park	57
1923/24	St. Johnstone	56
1924/25	Dundee United	50
1925/26	Dunfermline Athletic	59
1926/27	Bo'ness	56
1927/28	Ayr United	54
1928/29	Dundee United	51
1929/30	Leith Athletic*	57
1930/31	Third Lanark	61
1931/32	East Stirlingshire*	55
1932/33	Hibernian	54
1933/34	Albion Rovers	45
1934/35	Third Lanark	52
1935/36	Falkirk	59
1936/37	Ayr United	54
1937/38	Raith Rovers	59
1938/39	Cowdenbeath	60
Seasons 1939/40 to 1945/46 – (No Competition)		
1946/47	Dundee	45
1947/48	East Fife	53
1948/49	Raith Rovers*	42
1949/50	Morton	47
1950/51	Queen of the South*	45
1951/52	Clyde	44
1952/53	Stirling Albion	44
1953/54	Motherwell	45
1954/55	Airdrieonians	46
1955/56	Queen's Park	54
1956/57	Clyde	64
1957/58	Stirling Albion	55
1958/59	Ayr United	60
1959/60	St. Johnstone	53
1960/61	Stirling Albion	55
1961/62	Clyde	54
1962/63	St. Johnstone	55
1963/64	Morton	67
1964/65	Stirling Albion	59
1965/66	Ayr United	53
1966/67	Morton	69
1967/68	St. Mirren	62
1968/69	Motherwell	64
1969/70	Falkirk	56
1970/71	Partick Thistle	56
1971/72	Dumbarton¥	52
1972/73	Clyde	56
1973/74	Airdrieonians	60
1974/75	Falkirk	54

SEASON	PREMIER DIVISION	POINTS	FIRST DIVISION	POINTS	SECOND DIVISION	POINTS	THIRD DIVISION	POINTS
1975/76	Rangers	54	Partick Thistle	41	Clydebank¥	40	N/A	–
1976/77	Celtic	55	St. Mirren	62	Stirling Albion	55	N/A	–
1977/78	Rangers	55	Morton¥	58	Clyde¥	53	N/A	–
1978/79	Celtic	48	Dundee	55	Berwick Rangers	54	N/A	–
1979/80	Aberdeen	48	Heart of Midlothian	53	Falkirk	50	N/A	–
1980/81	Celtic	56	Hibernian	57	Queen's Park	50	N/A	–
1981/82	Celtic	55	Motherwell	61	Clyde	59	N/A	–
1982/83	Dundee United	56	St. Johnstone	55	Brechin City	55	N/A	–
1983/84	Aberdeen	57	Morton	54	Forfar Athletic	63	N/A	–
1984/85	Aberdeen	59	Motherwell	50	Montrose	53	N/A	–
1985/86•	Celtic¥	50	Hamilton Academical	56	Dunfermline Athletic	57	N/A	–
1986/87•	Rangers	69	Morton	57	Meadowbank Thistle	55	N/A	–
1987/88•	Celtic	72	Hamilton Academical	56	Ayr United	61	N/A	–
1988/89§	Rangers	56	Dunfermline Athletic	54	Albion Rovers	50	N/A	–
1989/90§	Rangers	51	St. Johnstone	58	Brechin City	49	N/A	–
1990/91§	Rangers	55	Falkirk	54	Stirling Albion	54	N/A	–
1991/92§	Rangers	72	Dundee	58	Dumbarton	52	N/A	–
1992/93	Rangers	73	Raith Rovers	65	Clyde	54	N/A	–
1993/94	Rangers	58	Falkirk	66	Stranraer	56	N/A	–
1994/95=	Rangers	69	Raith Rovers	69	Greenock Morton	64	Forfar Athletic	80
1995/96=	Rangers	87	Dunfermline Athletic	71	Stirling Albion	81	Livingston	72
1996/97=	Rangers	80	St. Johnstone	80	Ayr United	77	Inverness Caledonian Thistle	76
1997/98=	Celtic	74	Dundee	70	Stranraer	61	Alloa Athletic	76
	SCOTTISH PREMIER LEAGUE		S.F.L. FIRST DIVISION		S.F.L. SECOND DIVISION		S.F.L. THIRD DIVISION	
1998/99	Rangers<	77	Hibernian	89	Livingston	77	Ross County	77
1999/2000	Rangers<	90	St. Mirren>	76	Clyde>	65	Queen's Park>	69
2000/01	Celtic<	97	Livingston>	76	Partick Thistle>	75	¥Hamilton Academical>	76
2001/02	Celtic<	103	Partick Thistle>	66	Queen of the South>	67	Brechin City>	73
2002/03¥	Rangers<	97	Falkirk>	81	Raith Rovers>	59	Morton>	72
2003/04	Celtic<	98	Inverness Caledonian Thistle>	70	Airdrie United>	70	Stranraer>	79

* Champions on goal average.   § Competition known as B&Q League.   = Competition known as Bell's League Championship.
¥ Champions on goal difference.   > Competition known as Bell's Scottish Football League Championship.
• Competition known as Fine Fare League.   < Competition known as Bank of Scotland Premier League.

League Cup Final Results
Since 1946/47

SEASON 1946/47

5th April, 1947 at Hampden Park;
Attendance 82,584; Referee: Mr R. Calder (Rutherglen)

RANGERS 4　　　　　　　ABERDEEN 0
Gillick, Williamson,
Duncanson (2)

SEASON 1947/48

25th October, 1947 at Hampden Park;
Attendance 52,781; Referee: Mr P. Craigmyle (Aberdeen)

EAST FIFE 0　　　　　　FALKIRK 0
After Extra Time

REPLAY
1st November, 1947 at Hampden Park;
Attendance 30,664; Referee: Mr. P. Craigmyle (Aberdeen)

EAST FIFE 4　　　　　　FALKIRK 1
Duncan (3), Adams　　　Aikman

SEASON 1948/49

12th March, 1949 at Hampden Park; Attendance 53,359;
Referee: Mr W. G. Livingstone (Glasgow)

RANGERS 2　　　　　　RAITH ROVERS 0
Gillick, Paton

SEASON 1949/50

29th October, 1949 at Hampden Park;
Attendance 38,897; Referee: Mr W. Webb (Glasgow)

EAST FIFE 3　　　　　　DUNFERMLINE ATHLETIC 0
Fleming, Duncan, Morris

SEASON 1950/51

28th October, 1950 at Hampden Park;
Attendance 63,074; Referee: Mr J. A. Mowat (Glasgow)

MOTHERWELL 3　　　　HIBERNIAN 0
Kelly, Forrest, Watters

SEASON 1951/52

27th October, 1951 at Hampden Park;
Attendance 91,075; Referee: Mr J. A. Mowat (Glasgow)

DUNDEE 3　　　　　　　RANGERS 2
Flavell, Pattillo, Boyd　Findlay, Thornton

SEASON 1952/53

25th October, 1952 at Hampden Park;
Attendance 51,830; Referee: Mr J. A. Mowat (Glasgow)

DUNDEE 2　　　　　　　KILMARNOCK 0
Flavell (2)

SEASON 1953/54

24th October, 1953 at Hampden Park;
Attendance 88,529; Referee: Mr J. S. Cox (Rutherglen)

EAST FIFE 3　　　　　　PARTICK THISTLE 2
Gardiner, Fleming, Christie　Walker, McKenzie

SEASON 1954/55

23rd October, 1954 at Hampden Park;
Attendance 55,640; Referee: Mr J. A. Mowat (Glasgow)

HEART OF MIDLOTHIAN 4　MOTHERWELL 2
Bauld (3), Wardhaugh　　Redpath (pen), Bain

SEASON 1955/56

22nd October, 1955 at Hampden Park;
Attendance 44,103; Referee: Mr H. Phillips (Wishaw)

ABERDEEN 2　　　　　　ST. MIRREN 1
Mallan (og), Leggat　　Holmes

SEASON 1956/57

27th October, 1956 at Hampden Park;
Attendance 58,973; Referee: Mr J. A. Mowat (Glasgow)

CELTIC 0　　　　　　　PARTICK THISTLE 0

REPLAY
31st October, 1956 at Hampden Park;
Attendance 31,126; Referee: Mr J. A. Mowat (Glasgow)

CELTIC 3　　　　　　　PARTICK THISTLE 0
McPhail (2), Collins

SEASON 1957/58

19th October, 1957 at Hampden Park;
Attendance 82,293; Referee: Mr J. A. Mowat (Glasgow)

CELTIC 7　　　　　　　RANGERS 1
Mochan (2), McPhail (3),　Simpson
Wilson, Fernie (pen)

SEASON 1958/59

25th October, 1958 at Hampden Park;
Attendance 59,960; Referee: Mr R. H. Davidson (Airdrie)

HEART OF MIDLOTHIAN 5　PARTICK THISTLE 1
Murray (2), Bauld (2),　Smith
Hamilton

SEASON 1959/60

24th October, 1959 at Hampden Park;
Attendance 57,974; Referee: Mr R. H. Davidson (Airdrie)

HEART OF MIDLOTHIAN 2　THIRD LANARK 1
Hamilton, Young　　　　Gray

SEASON 1960/61

29th October, 1960 at Hampden Park;
Attendance 82,063; Referee: Mr T. Wharton (Glasgow)

RANGERS 2　　　　　　KILMARNOCK 0
Brand, Scott

SEASON 1961/62

28th October, 1961 at Hampden Park;
Attendance 88,635; Referee: Mr R. H. Davidson (Airdrie)

RANGERS 1　　　　　　HEART OF MIDLOTHIAN 1
Millar　　　　　　　　Cumming (pen)

REPLAY
18th December, 1961 at Hampden Park;
Attendance 47,552; Referee: Mr R. H. Davidson (Airdrie)

RANGERS 3　　　　　　HEART OF MIDLOTHIAN 1
Millar, Brand, McMillan　Davidson

SEASON 1962/63

27th October, 1962 at Hampden Park;
Attendance 51,280; Referee: Mr T. Wharton (Glasgow)

HEART OF MIDLOTHIAN 1　KILMARNOCK 0
Davidson

ACTION FROM THE 1971/72 LEAGUE CUP FINAL
FINAL – CELTIC'S JIM BROGAN (LEFT) IN ACTION
AGAINST PARTICK THISTLE'S DENNIS M°QUADE

1982/83 LEAGUE CUP FINAL
CELTIC CAPTAIN DANNY M°GRAIN WITH
THE LEAGUE CUP

SEASON 1963/64

26th October, 1963 at Hampden Park;
Attendance 105,907; Referee: Mr H. Phillips (Wishaw)

RANGERS 5   MORTON 0
Forrest (4), Willoughby

SEASON 1964/65

24th October, 1964 at Hampden Park;
Attendance 91,000; Referee: Mr H. Phillips (Wishaw)

RANGERS 2   CELTIC 1
Forrest (2)   Johnstone

SEASON 1965/66

23rd October, 1965 at Hampden Park;
Attendance 107,609; Referee: Mr H. Phillips (Wishaw)

CELTIC 2   RANGERS 1
Hughes (2 (2 pen))   Young (o.g.)

SEASON 1966/67

29th October, 1966 at Hampden Park;
Attendance 94,532; Referee: Mr T. Wharton (Glasgow)

CELTIC 1   RANGERS 0
Lennox

SEASON 1967/68

28th October, 1967 at Hampden Park;
Attendance 66,660; Referee: Mr R. H. Davidson (Airdrie)

CELTIC 5   DUNDEE 3
Chalmers (2), Hughes,   G. McLean (2), J. McLean
Wallace, Lennox

SEASON 1968/69

5th April, 1969 at Hampden Park;
Attendance 74,000; Referee: Mr W. M. M. Syme (Airdrie)

CELTIC 6   HIBERNIAN 2
Lennox (3), Wallace,   O'Rourke, Stevenson
Auld, Craig

SEASON 1969/70

25th October, 1969 at Hampden Park;
Attendance 73,067; Referee: Mr J. W. Paterson (Bothwell)

CELTIC 1   ST. JOHNSTONE 0
Auld

SEASON 1970/71

24th October, 1970 at Hampden Park;
Attendance 106,263; Referee: Mr T. Wharton (Glasgow)

RANGERS 1   CELTIC 0
Johnstone

SEASON 1971/72

23rd October, 1971 at Hampden Park;
Attendance 62,740; Referee: Mr W. J. Mullan (Dalkeith)

PARTICK THISTLE 4   CELTIC 1
Rae, Lawrie, McQuade, Bone   Dalglish

SEASON 1972/73

9th December, 1972 at Hampden Park;
Attendance 71,696; Referee: Mr A. MacKenzie (Larbert)

HIBERNIAN 2   CELTIC 1
Stanton, O'Rourke   Dalglish

SEASON 1973/74

15th December, 1973 at Hampden Park;
Attendance 27,974; Referee: Mr R. H. Davidson (Airdrie)

DUNDEE 1   CELTIC 0
Wallace

SEASON 1974/75

26th October, 1974 at Hampden Park;
Attendance 53,848;
Referee: Mr J. R. P. Gordon (Newport on Tay)

CELTIC 6   HIBERNIAN 3
Johnstone, Deans (3),   Harper (3)
Wilson, Murray

SEASON 1975/76

25th October, 1975 at Hampden Park;
Attendance 58,806; Referee: Mr W. Anderson (East Kilbride)

RANGERS 1   CELTIC 0
MacDonald

SEASON 1976/77

6th November, 1976 at Hampden Park;
Attendance 69,268; Referee: Mr J. W. Paterson (Bothwell)

ABERDEEN 2   CELTIC 1
Jarvie, Robb   Dalglish (pen.)
After extra-time – 1–1 After 90 Minutes

SEASON 1977/78

18th March, 1978 at Hampden Park;
Attendance 60,168; Referee: Mr D. F. T. Syme (Rutherglen)

RANGERS 2   CELTIC 1
Cooper, Smith   Edvaldsson
After extra-time – 1–1 After 90 Minutes

SEASON 1978/79

31st March, 1979 at Hampden Park;
Attendance 54,000; Referee: Mr I. M. D. Foote (Glasgow)

RANGERS 2   ABERDEEN 1
McMaster (o.g.), Jackson   Davidson

SEASON 1979/80 – BELL'S LEAGUE CUP

8th December, 1979 at Hampden Park;
Attendance 27,299; Referee: Mr B. R. McGinlay (Balfron)

DUNDEE UNITED 0   ABERDEEN 0
After extra-time

REPLAY

12th December, 1979 at Dens Park;
Attendance 28,984; Referee: Mr B. R. McGinlay (Balfron)

DUNDEE UNITED 3   ABERDEEN 0
Pettigrew (2), Sturrock

SEASON 1980/81 – BELL'S LEAGUE CUP

6th December, 1980 at Dens Park;
Attendance 24,466; Referee: Mr R. B. Valentine (Dundee)

DUNDEE UNITED 3   DUNDEE 0
Dodds, Sturrock (2)

SEASON 1981/82

28th November, 1981 at Hampden Park;
Attendance 53,795;
Referee: Mr E. H. Pringle (Edinburgh)

RANGERS 2   DUNDEE UNITED 1
Cooper, Redford   Milne

SEASON 1982/83

4th December, 1982 at Hampden Park;
Attendance 55,372; Referee: Mr K. J. Hope (Clarkston)

CELTIC 2   RANGERS 1
Nicholas, MacLeod   Bett

SEASON 1983/84

25th March, 1984 at Hampden Park;
Attendance 66,369; Referee: Mr R. B. Valentine (Dundee)

RANGERS 3   CELTIC 2
McCoist 3 (1 pen)   McClair, Reid (pen)
After extra-time – 2–2 After 90 Minutes

GASCOIGNE AND McCOIST CELEBRATE RANGERS COCA-COLA CUP VICTORY IN SEASON 1996/97

LIVINGSTON MIDFIELDER LEE MAKEL CELEBRATES WINNING THE CIS INSURANCE CUP IN SEASON 2003/04

SEASON 1984/85 – SKOL CUP

28th October, 1984 at Hampden Park;
Attendance 44,698; Referee: Mr B. R. McGinlay (Balfron)

RANGERS 1   DUNDEE UNITED 0
Ferguson

SEASON 1985/86 – SKOL CUP

27th October, 1985 at Hampden Park;
Attendance 40,065; Referee: Mr R. B. Valentine (Dundee)

ABERDEEN 3   HIBERNIAN 0
Black (2), Stark

SEASON 1986/87 – SKOL CUP

26th October, 1986 at Hampden Park;
Attendance 74,219; Referee: Mr D. F. T. Syme (Rutherglen)

RANGERS 2   CELTIC 1
Durrant, Cooper (pen)   McClair

SEASON 1987/88 – SKOL CUP

25th October, 1987 at Hampden Park;
Attendance 71,961; Referee: Mr R. B. Valentine (Dundee)

RANGERS 3   ABERDEEN 3
Cooper, Durrant, Fleck   Bett, Falconer, Hewitt
After extra–time – 3–3 After 90 Minutes
Rangers won 5–3 on Kicks from the Penalty Mark

SEASON 1988/89 – SKOL CUP

23rd October, 1988 at Hampden Park;
Attendance 72,122; Referee: Mr G. B. Smith (Edinburgh)

RANGERS 3   ABERDEEN 2
McCoist (2), I. Ferguson   Dodds (2)

SEASON 1989/90 – SKOL CUP

22nd October, 1989 at Hampden Park;
Attendance 61,190; Referee: Mr G. B. Smith (Edinburgh)

ABERDEEN 2   RANGERS 1
Mason (2)   Walters (pen)
After extra–time – 1–1 after 90 minutes

SEASON 1990/91 – SKOL CUP

28th October, 1990 at Hampden Park;
Attendance 62,817; Referee: Mr J. McCluskey (Stewarton)

RANGERS 2   CELTIC 1
Walters, Gough   Elliott
After extra–time – 1–1 After 90 minutes

SEASON 1991/92 – SKOL CUP

27th October, 1991 at Hampden Park;
Attendance 40,377; Referee: Mr B. R. McGinlay (Balfron)

HIBERNIAN 2   DUNFERMLINE ATHLETIC 0
McIntyre (pen), Wright

SEASON 1992/93 – SKOL CUP

25th October, 1992 at Hampden Park;
Attendance 45,298; Referee: Mr D. D. Hope (Erskine)

RANGERS 2   ABERDEEN 1
McCall, Smith (o.g.)   Shearer
After extra–time – 1–1 after 90 minutes

SEASON 1993/94

24th October, 1993 at Celtic Park;
Attendance 47,632; Referee: Mr J. McCluskey (Stewarton)

RANGERS 2   HIBERNIAN 1
Durrant, McCoist   McPherson (o.g.)

SEASON 1994/95 – COCA–COLA CUP

27th November, 1994 at Ibrox Stadium;
Attendance 45,384; Referee: Mr J. McCluskey (Stewarton)

RAITH ROVERS 2   CELTIC 2
S. Crawford, G. Dalziel   C. Nicholas, A. Walker
After extra–time – 2–2 after 90 minutes
Raith Rovers won 6–5 on Kicks from the Penalty Mark

SEASON 1995/96 – COCA–COLA CUP

26th November, 1995 at Hampden Park;
Attendance 33,099; Referee: Mr L.W. Mottram (Forth)

ABERDEEN 2   DUNDEE 0
D. Shearer, W. Dodds

SEASON 1996/97 – COCA–COLA CUP

24th November, 1996 at Celtic Park;
Attendance 48,559; Referee: Mr H. Dallas (Motherwell)

RANGERS 4   HEART OF MIDLOTHIAN 3
P. Gascoigne (2),A. McCoist (2)   D. Weir, S. Fulton,
     J. Robertson

SEASON1997/98 – COCA–COLA CUP

30th November, 1997 at Ibrox Stadium;
Attendance 49,305; Referee: Mr J. McCluskey (Stewarton)

CELTIC 3   DUNDEE UNITED 0
M. Rieper, H. Larsson, C. Burley

SEASON 1998/99

29th November, 1998 at Celtic Park;
Attendance 45,533; Referee: Mr H. Dallas (Motherwell)

RANGERS 2   ST. JOHNSTONE 1
S. Guivarc'h, J. Albertz   N. Dasovic

SEASON 1999/2000 – CIS INSURANCE CUP

19th March, 2000 at The National Stadium, Hampden Park
Attendance 50,073; Referee: Mr K. Clark (Paisley)

CELTIC 2   ABERDEEN 0
V. Riseth, T. Johnson

SEASON 2000/01 – CIS INSURANCE CUP

18th March, 2001 at The National Stadium, Hampden Park
Attendance 48,830; Referee: Mr H. Dallas (Motherwell)

CELTIC 3   KILMARNOCK 0
H. Larsson (3)

SEASON 2001/02 – CIS INSURANCE CUP

17th March, 2002 at The National Stadium, Hampden Park
Attendance 50,076; Referee: Mr H. Dallas (Motherwell)

RANGERS 4   AYR UNITED 0
T.A. Flo, B. Ferguson,
C. Caniggia (2)

SEASON 2002/03 – CIS INSURANCE CUP

16th March, 2003 at The National Stadium, Hampden Park
Attendance 50,034; Referee: Mr K. Clark (Paisley)

RANGERS 2   CELTIC 1
C. Caniggia,   H. Larsson
P. Lovenkrands

SEASON 2003/04 – CIS INSURANCE CUP

14th March, 2004 at The National Stadium, Hampden Par
Glasgow; Attendance 45,443
Referee: W. Young (Glasgow)

LIVINGSTON 2   HIBERNIAN 0
D. Lilley, J. McAllister

WINNERS AND APPEARANCES IN FINALS

	WINS	APPS*
RANGERS	23	29
CELTIC	12	25
ABERDEEN	5	12
HEART OF MIDLOTHIAN	4	6
DUNDEE	3	6
EAST FIFE	3	3
DUNDEE UNITED	2	5
HIBERNIAN	2	8
LIVINGSTON	1	1
MOTHERWELL	1	2
PARTICK THISTLE	1	4
RAITH ROVERS	1	2
KILMARNOCK	–	4
DUNFERMLINE ATHLETIC	–	2
ST. JOHNSTONE	–	2
AYR UNITED	–	1
FALKIRK	–	1
MORTON	–	1
ST. MIRREN	–	1
THIRD LANARK	–	1

* (Figures do not include replays)

Scottish Cup Final Results
Since 1873/74

SEASON 1873/74
21st March, 1874 at First Hampden; Attendance 2,500

QUEEN'S PARK 2   CLYDESDALE 0
W. McKinnon, Leckie

SEASON 1874/75
10th April, 1875 at First Hampden; Attendance 7,000

QUEEN'S PARK 3   RENTON 0
A. McKinnon, Highet,
W. McKinnon

SEASON 1875/76
11th March, 1876 at Hamilton Crescent;
Attendance 10,000

QUEEN'S PARK 1   THIRD LANARK 1
Highet   Drinnan

REPLAY
18th March, 1876 at Hamilton Crescent;
Attendance 6,000

QUEEN'S PARK 2   THIRD LANARK 0
Highet (2)

SEASON 1876/77
17th March, 1877 at Hamilton Crescent;
Attendance 12,000

VALE OF LEVEN 1   RANGERS 1
Paton   McDougall (o.g.)

REPLAY
7th April, 1877 at Hamilton Crescent;
Attendance 15,000

VALE OF LEVEN 1   RANGERS 1 (AET)
McDougall   Dunlop

SECOND REPLAY
13th April, 1877 at First Hampden; Attendance 8,000

VALE OF LEVEN 3   RANGERS 2
Watson (o.g.),   P. Campbell, W. McNeil
Baird, Paton

SEASON 1877/78
30th March, 1878 at First Hampden; Attendance 5,000

VALE OF LEVEN 1   THIRD LANARK 0
McDougall

SEASON 1878/79
19th April, 1879 at First Hampden; Attendance 6,000

VALE OF LEVEN 1   RANGERS 1
Ferguson   Struthers

VALE OF LEVEN WERE AWARDED CUP AFTER
RANGERS FAILED TO TURN UP FOR A REPLAY
ON 26TH APRIL, 1879.

SEASON 1879/80
21st February, 1880 at First Cathkin; Attendance 7,000

QUEEN'S PARK 3   THORNLIEBANK 0
Highet (2,) Kerr

SEASON 1880/81
26th March, 1881 at Kinning Park; Attendance 10,000

QUEEN'S PARK 2   DUMBARTON 1
McNeil, Kay   McAulay

AFTER A PROTEST BY DUMBARTON,
A REPLAY WAS ORDERED.

REPLAY
9th April, 1881 at Kinning Park; Attendance 10,000

QUEEN'S PARK 3   DUMBARTON 1
Smith (2), Kerr   Meikleham

SEASON 1881/82
18th March, 1882 at First Cathkin; Attendance 12,000

QUEEN'S PARK 2   DUMBARTON 2
Harrower (2)   Brown, Meikleham

REPLAY
1st April, 1882 at First Cathkin; Attendance 15,000

QUEEN'S PARK 4   DUMBARTON 1
Richmond, Kerr,   J. Miller
Harrower, Kay

SEASON 1882/83
31st March, 1883 at First Hampden; Attendance 15,000

DUMBARTON 2   VALE OF LEVEN 2
Paton, McArthur   Johnstone, McCrae

REPLAY
7th April, 1883 at First Hampden; Attendance 8,000

DUMBARTON 2   VALE OF LEVEN 1
Anderson, R. Brown   Friel

SEASON 1883/84
23rd February, 1884 at First Cathkin

VALE OF LEVEN   QUEEN'S PARK

VALE OF LEVEN FAILED TO TURN UP FOR THE
FINAL WITH QUEEN'S PARK AND IT WAS LATER
DECIDED TO AWARD THE CUP TO QUEEN'S PARK.

SEASON 1884/85
21st February, 1885 at Second Hampden;
Attendance 2,500

RENTON 0   VALE OF LEVEN 0

REPLAY
28th February, 1885 at Second Hampden;
Attendance 3,500

RENTON 3   VALE OF LEVEN 1
J. McCall, McIntyre (2)   Gillies

SEASON 1885/86
13th February, 1886 at First Cathkin; Attendance 7,000

QUEEN'S PARK 3   RENTON 1
Hamilton, Christie,   Kelso
Somerville

SEASON 1886/87
12th February, 1887 at Second Hampden;
Attendance 10,000

HIBERNIAN 2   DUMBARTON 1
Smith, Groves   Aitken

SEASON 1887/88
4th February, 1888 at Second Hampden;
Attendance 10,000

RENTON 6   CAMBUSLANG 1
D. Campbell,   H. Gourlay
McCallum, McNee,
McCall (2), J. Campbell

SEASON 1888/89
2nd February, 1889 at Second Hampden;
Attendance 17,000

THIRD LANARK 3   CELTIC 0
Oswald Jun. (2),
Hannah

A REPLAY WAS ORDERED AFTER PROTESTS
CONCERNING GROUND CONDITIONS.

REPLAY
9th February, 1889 at Second Hampden;
Attendance 16,000

THIRD LANARK 2   CELTIC 1
Marshall, Oswald Jun.   McCallum

SEASON 1889/90
15th February, 1890 at First Ibrox; Attendance 10,000

QUEEN'S PARK 1   VALE OF LEVEN 1
Hamilton   McLachlan

REPLAY
22nd February, 1890 at First Ibrox;
Attendance 14,000

QUEEN'S PARK 2   VALE OF LEVEN 1
Hamilton, Stewart   Bruce

SEASON 1890/91
7th February, 1891 at Second Hampden;
Attendance 14,000

HEART OF MIDLOTHIAN 1   DUMBARTON 0
Russell

SEASON 1891/92
12th March, 1892 at First Ibrox; Attendance 40,000

CELTIC 1   QUEEN'S PARK 0
Campbell

CROWD ENCROACHMENT OCCURRED AT THE ABOVE
GAME AND AS A RESULT THE GAME WAS CONSIDERED
A FRIENDLY.

REPLAY
9th April, 1892 at First Ibrox; Attendance 20,000

CELTIC 5   QUEEN'S PARK 1
Campbell (2),   Waddell
McMahon (2),
Sillars (o.g.)

SEASON 1892/93
25th February, 1893 at First Ibrox; Attendance 20,000

CELTIC 1   QUEEN'S PARK 0
Towie

A REPLAY WAS ORDERED BECAUSE OF GROUND
CONDITIONS AND THE ABOVE GAME WAS
CONSIDERED A FRIENDLY.

REPLAY
11th March, 1893 at First Ibrox; Attendance 15,000

QUEEN'S PARK 2   CELTIC 1
Sellar (2)   Blessington

SEASON 1893/94
17th February, 1894 at Second Hampden;
Attendance 15,000

RANGERS 3   CELTIC 1
H. McCreadie, Barker,   W. Maley
McPherson

SEASON 1894/95
20th April, 1895 at First Ibrox; Attendance 13,500

ST. BERNARD'S 2   RENTON 1
Clelland (2)   Duncan

SEASON 1895/96
14th March, 1896 at Logie Green; Attendance 16,034

HEART OF MIDLOTHIAN 3   HIBERNIAN 1
Baird, Walker, Michael   O'Neill

SEASON 1896/97
20th March, 1897 at Second Hampden;
Attendance 15,000

RANGERS 5   DUMBARTON 1
Miller (2), Hyslop,   W. Thomson
McPherson, A. Smith

SEASON 1897/98
26th March, 1898 at Second Hampden;
Attendance 14,000

RANGERS 2   KILMARNOCK 0
A. Smith, Hamilton

SEASON 1898/99
22nd April, 1899 at Second Hampden;
Attendance 25,000

CELTIC 2   RANGERS 0
McMahon, Hodge

SEASON 1899/1900
14th April, 1900 at Second Hampden;
Attendance 25,000

CELTIC 4   QUEEN'S PARK 3
McMahon,   Christie, W. Stewart,
Divers (2), Bell   Battles (o.g.)

SEASON 1900/01
6th April, 1901 at Ibrox; Attendance 15,000

HEART OF MIDLOTHIAN 4   CELTIC 3
Walker, Bell (2), Thomson   McOustra (2),
                        McMahon

SEASON 1901/02
26th April, 1902 at Celtic Park; Attendance 16,000

HIBERNIAN 1   CELTIC 0
McGeachan

SEASON 1902/03
11th April, 1903 at Celtic Park; Attendance 28,000

RANGERS 1   HEART OF MIDLOTHIAN 1
Stark   Walker

REPLAY
18th April, 1903 at Celtic Park; Attendance 16,000

RANGERS 0   HEART OF MIDLOTHIAN 0

SECOND REPLAY
25th April, 1903 at Celtic Park; Attendance 32,000

RANGERS 2   HEART OF MIDLOTHIAN 0
Mackie, Hamilton

SEASON 1903/04
16th April, 1904 at Hampden Park; Attendance 64,323

CELTIC 3   RANGERS 2
Quinn (3)   Speedie (2)

SEASON 1904/05
8th April, 1905 at Hampden Park; Attendance 55,000

THIRD LANARK 0   RANGERS 0

REPLAY
15th April, 1905 at Hampden Park; Attendance 40,000

THIRD LANARK 3   RANGERS 1
Wilson (2), Johnstone   Smith

SEASON 1905/06
28th April, 1906 at Ibrox; Attendance 30,000

HEART OF MIDLOTHIAN 1   THIRD LANARK 0
G. Wilson

SEASON 1906/07
20th April, 1907 at Hampden Park; Attendance 50,000

CELTIC 3   HEART OF MIDLOTHIAN 0
Orr (Pen), Somers (2)

SEASON 1907/08
18th April, 1908 at Hampden Park; Attendance 55,000

CELTIC 5   ST. MIRREN 1
Bennett (2), Hamilton,   Cunningham
Somers, Quinn

SEASON 1908/09
10th April, 1909 at Hampden Park; Attendance 70,000

CELTIC 2   RANGERS 2
Quinn, Munro   Gilchrist, Bennett

REPLAY
17th April, 1909 at Hampden Park; Attendance 60,000

CELTIC 1   RANGERS 1
Quinn   Gordon

CUP WITHHELD AFTER RIOT FOLLOWING REPLAY.

SEASON 1909/10
9th April, 1910 at Ibrox; Attendance 60,000

DUNDEE 2   CLYDE 2
Blair (o.g.), Langlands   Chalmers, Booth

REPLAY
16th April, 1910 at Ibrox; Attendance 20,000

DUNDEE 0   CLYDE 0 (A.E.T.)

SECOND REPLAY
20th April, 1910 at Ibrox; Attendance 24,000

DUNDEE 2   CLYDE 1
Bellamy, Hunter   Chalmers

SEASON 1910/11
8th April, 1911 at Ibrox; Attendance 45,000

CELTIC 0   HAMILTON ACADEMICAL 0

REPLAY
15th April, 1911 at Ibrox; Attendance 25,000

CELTIC 2   HAMILTON ACADEMICAL 0
Quinn, McAteer

SEASON 1911/12
6th April, 1912 at Ibrox; Attendance 45,000

CELTIC 2   CLYDE 0
McMenemy, Gallagher

SEASON 1912/13
12th April, 1913 at Celtic Park; Attendance 45,000

FALKIRK 2   RAITH ROVERS 0
Robertson, T. Logan

SEASON 1913/14
11th April, 1914 at Ibrox; Attendance 55,000

CELTIC 0   HIBERNIAN 0

REPLAY
16th April, 1914 at Ibrox; Attendance 36,000

CELTIC 4   HIBERNIAN 1
McColl (2),   Smith
Browning (2)

SEASONS 1914/15 TO 1918/19
NO COMPETITIONS DUE TO FIRST WORLD WAR

SEASON 1919/20
17th April, 1920 at Hampden Park; Attendance 95,000;
Referee: Mr W. Bell (Hamilton)

KILMARNOCK 3   ALBION ROVERS 2
Culley, Shortt, J. Smith   Watson, Hillhouse

SEASON 1920/21
16th April, 1921 at Celtic Park; Attendance 28,294;
Referee: Mr H. Humphreys (Greenock)

PARTICK THISTLE 1   RANGERS 0
Blair

SEASON 1921/22
15th April, 1922 at Hampden Park; Attendance 75,000
Referee: Mr T. Dougray (Bellshill)

MORTON 1   RANGERS 0
Gourlay

SEASON 1922/23
31th March, 1923 at Hampden Park;
Attendance 80,100; Referee: Mr T. Dougray (Bellshill)

CELTIC 1   HIBERNIAN 0
Cassidy

SEASON 1923/24
19th April, 1924 at Ibrox Stadium; Attendance 59,218;
Referee: Mr T. Dougray (Bellshill)

AIRDRIEONIANS 2   HIBERNIAN 0
Russell (2)

SEASON 1924/25
11th April, 1925 at Hampden Park;
Attendance 75,137; Referee: Mr T. Dougray (Bellshill)

CELTIC 2   DUNDEE 1
Gallacher, McGrory   McLean

SEASON 1925/26
10th April, 1926 at Hampden Park; Attendance 98,620
Referee: Mr P. Craigmyle (Aberdeen)

ST. MIRREN 2   CELTIC 0
McCrae, Howieson

SEASON 1926/27
16th April, 1927 at Hampden Park; Attendance 80,070
Referee: Mr T. Dougray (Bellshill)

CELTIC 3   EAST FIFE 1
Robertson (o.g.),   Wood
McLean, Connolly

SEASON 1927/28
14th April, 1928 at Hampden Park; Attendance 118,11-
Referee: Mr W. Bell (Motherwell)

RANGERS 4   CELTIC 0
Meiklejohn (pen),
Archibald (2), McPhail

SEASON 1928/29
6th April, 1929 at Hampden Park; Attendance 114,708
Referee: Mr T. Dougray (Bellshill)

KILMARNOCK 2   RANGERS 0
Aitken, Williamson

SEASON 1929/30
12th April, 1930 at Hampden Park; Attendance 107,47-
Referee: Mr W. Bell (Motherwell)

RANGERS 0   PARTICK THISTLE 0

REPLAY
16th April, 1930 at Hampden Park; Attendance 103,68-
Referee: Mr W. Bell (Motherwell)

RANGERS 2   PARTICK THISTLE 1
Marshall, Craig   Torbet

SEASON 1930/31
11th April, 1931 at Hampden Park; Attendance 104,80-
Referee: Mr P. Craigmyle (Aberdeen)

CELTIC 2   MOTHERWELL 2
McGrory, Craig (o.g.)   Stevenson, McMenemy

REPLAY
15th April, 1931 at Hampden Park; Attendance 98,579
Referee: Mr P. Craigmyle (Aberdeen)

CELTIC 4   MOTHERWELL 2
R. Thomson (2),   Murdoch, Stevenson
McGrory (2)

SEASON 1931/32
16th April, 1932 at Hampden Park; Attendance 111,98-
Referee: Mr P. Craigmyle (Aberdeen)

RANGERS 1   KILMARNOCK 1
McPhail   Maxwell

REPLAY
20th April, 1932 at Hampden Park; Attendance 110,69-
Referee: Mr P. Craigmyle (Aberdeen)

RANGERS 3   KILMARNOCK 0
Fleming, McPhail, English

SEASON 1932/33
15th April, 1933 at Hampden Park; Attendance 102,33-
Referee: Mr T. Dougray (Bellshill)

CELTIC 1   MOTHERWELL 0
McGrory

SEASON 1933/34
21st April, 1934 at Hampden Park; Attendance 113,430
Referee: Mr M. C. Hutton (Glasgow)

RANGERS 5   ST. MIRREN 0
Nicholson (2),
McPhail, Main, Smith

SEASON 1934/35
20th April, 1935 at Hampden Park; Attendance 87,286;
Referee: Mr H. Watson (Glasgow)

RANGERS 2   HAMILTON ACADEMICAL 1
Smith (2)   Harrison

SEASON 1935/36
18th April 1936 at Hampden Park; Attendance 88,859;
Referee: Mr J. M. Martin (Ladybank)

RANGERS 1   THIRD LANARK 0
McPhail

SEASON 1936/37
24th April, 1937 at Hampden Park; Attendance 147,365;
Referee: Mr M. C. Hutton (Glasgow)

CELTIC 2   ABERDEEN 1
Crum, Buchan   Armstrong

SEASON 1937/38
23rd April, 1938 at Hampden Park; Attendance 80,091;
Referee: Mr H. Watson (Glasgow)

EAST FIFE 1   KILMARNOCK 1
McLeod   McAvoy
REPLAY
27th April, 1938 at Hampden Park; Attendance 92,716;
Referee: Mr H. Watson (Glasgow)

EAST FIFE 4   KILMARNOCK 2
McKerrell (2),   Thomson (pen), McGrogan
McLeod, Miller
After extra–time

SEASON 1938/39
22nd April, 1939 at Hampden Park; Attendance 94,799;
Referee: Mr W. Webb (Glasgow)

CLYDE 4   MOTHERWELL 0
Wallace, Martin (2),
Noble

SEASONS 1939/40 TO 1945/46
NO COMPETITIONS DUE TO SECOND WORLD WAR

SEASON 1946/47
19th April, 1947 at Hampden Park; Attendance 82,140;
Referee: Mr R. Calder (Glasgow)

ABERDEEN 2   HIBERNIAN 1
Hamilton, Williams Cuthbertson

SEASON 1947/48
17th April, 1948 at Hampden Park; Attendance 129,176;
Referee: Mr J. M. Martin (Blairgowrie)

RANGERS 1   MORTON 1
Gillick   Whyte
After extra–time
REPLAY
21st April, 1948 at Hampden Park; Attendance 131,975;
Referee: Mr J. M. Martin (Blairgowrie)

RANGERS 1   MORTON 0
Williamson
After extra–time

SEASON 1948/49
23rd April, 1949 at Hampden Park; Attendance 108,435;
Referee: Mr R. G. Benzie (Irvine)

RANGERS 4   CLYDE 1
Young (2 (2 pens)), Galletly
Williamson, Duncanson

SEASON 1949/50
22nd April, 1950 at Hampden Park; Attendance 118,262
Referee: Mr J. A. Mowat (Burnside)

RANGERS 3   EAST FIFE 0
Findlay, Thornton (2)

SEASON 1950/51
21st April, 1951 at Hampden Park; Attendance 131,943
Referee: Mr J. A. Mowat (Burnside)

CELTIC 1   MOTHERWELL 0
McPhail

SEASON 1951/52
19th April, 1952 at Hampden Park; Attendance 136,304;
Referee: Mr J. A. Mowat (Burnside)

MOTHERWELL 4   DUNDEE 0
Watson, Redpath,
Humphries, Kelly

SEASON 1952/53
25th April, 1953 at Hampden Park; Attendance 129,861;
Referee: Mr J. A. Mowat (Burnside)

RANGERS 1   ABERDEEN 1
Prentice   Yorston

REPLAY
29th April, 1953 at Hampden Park; Attendance 112,619;
Referee: Mr J. A. Mowat (Burnside)

RANGERS 1   ABERDEEN 0
Simpson

SEASON 1953/54
24th April, 1954 at Hampden Park; Attendance 129,926;
Referee: Mr C. E. Faultless (Giffnock)

CELTIC 2   ABERDEEN 1
Young (o.g.), Fallon Buckley

SEASON 1954/55
23rd April, 1955 at Hampden Park; Attendance 106,111;
Referee: Mr C. E. Faultless (Giffnock)

CLYDE 1   CELTIC 1
Robertson   Walsh
REPLAY
27th April, 1955 at Hampden Park; Attendance 68,735;
Referee: Mr C. E. Faultless (Giffnock)

CLYDE 1   CELTIC 0
Ring

SEASON 1955/56
21st April, 1956 at Hampden Park; Attendance 133,399;
Referee: Mr R. H. Davidson (Airdrie)

HEART OF MIDLOTHIAN 3   CELTIC 1
Crawford (2), Conn   Haughney

SEASON 1956/57
20th April, 1957 at Hampden Park; Attendance 81,057;
Referee: Mr J. A. Mowat (Burnside)

FALKIRK 1   KILMARNOCK 1
Prentice (pen)   Curlett
REPLAY
24th April, 1957 at Hampden Park; Attendance 79,785;
Referee: Mr J. A. Mowat (Burnside)

FALKIRK 2   KILMARNOCK 1
Merchant, Moran   Curlett
After extra–time

SEASON 1957/58
26th April, 1958 at Hampden Park; Attendance 95,123;
Referee: Mr J. A. Mowat (Burnside)

CLYDE 1   HIBERNIAN 0
Coyle

SEASON 1958/59
25th April 1959 at Hampden Park; Attendance 108,951;
Referee: Mr J. A. Mowat (Burnside)

ST. MIRREN 3   ABERDEEN 1
Bryceland, Miller, Baker Baird

SEASON 1959/60
23rd April, 1960 at Hampden Park; Attendance 108,017;
Referee: Mr R. H. Davidson (Airdrie)

RANGERS 2   KILMARNOCK 0
Millar (2)

SEASON 1960/61
22nd April, 1961 at Hampden Park; Attendance 113,618;
Referee: Mr H. Phillips (Wishaw)

DUNFERMLINE ATHLETIC 0   CELTIC 0
REPLAY
26th April, 1961 at Hampden Park; Attendance 87,866;
Referee: Mr H. Phillips (Wishaw)

DUNFERMLINE ATHLETIC 2   CELTIC 0
Thomson, Dickson

SEASON 1961/62
21st April, 1962 at Hampden Park; Attendance 126,930;
Referee: Mr T. Wharton (Clarkston)

RANGERS 2   ST. MIRREN 0
Brand, Wilson

SEASON 1962/63
4th May, 1963 at Hampden Park; Attendance 129,527;
Referee: Mr T. Wharton (Clarkston)

RANGERS 1   CELTIC 1
Brand   Murdoch

REPLAY
15th May, 1963 at Hampden Park; Attendance 120,263;
Referee: Mr T. Wharton (Clarkston)

RANGERS 3   CELTIC 0
Brand (2), Wilson

SEASON 1963/64
25th April, 1964 at Hampden Park; Attendance 120,982;
Referee: Mr H. Phillips (Wishaw)

RANGERS 3   DUNDEE 1
Millar (2), Brand   Cameron

SEASON 1964/65
24th April, 1965 at Hampden Park; Attendance 108,800;
Referee: Mr H. Phillips (Wishaw)

CELTIC 3   DUNFERMLINE ATHLETIC 2
Auld (2), McNeill   Melrose, McLaughlin

SEASON 1965/66
23rd April, 1966 at Hampden Park; Attendance 126,559;
Referee: Mr T. Wharton (Clarkston)

RANGERS 0   CELTIC 0
REPLAY
27th April, 1966 at Hampden Park; Attendance 96,862;
Referee: Mr T. Wharton (Clarkston)

RANGERS 1   CELTIC 0
Johansen

SEASON 1966/67
29th April, 1967 at Hampden Park; Attendance 127,117;
Referee: Mr W. M. M. Syme (Glasgow)

CELTIC 2   ABERDEEN 0
Wallace (2)

SEASON 1967/68
27th April, 1968 at Hampden Park; Attendance 56,365;
Referee: Mr W. Anderson (East Kilbride)

DUNFERMLINE ATH. 3   HEART OF MIDLOTHIAN 1
Gardner (2), Lister (pen)   Lunn (o.g.)

SEASON 1968/69
26th April, 1969 at Hampden Park; Attendance 132,870;
Referee: Mr J. Callaghan (Glasgow)

CELTIC 4   RANGERS 0
McNeill, Lennox,
Connelly, Chalmers

SEASON 1969/70
11th April, 1970 at Hampden Park; Attendance 108,434;
Referee: Mr R. H. Davidson (Airdrie)

ABERDEEN 3   CELTIC 1
Harper (pen), McKay (2) Lennox

SEASON 1970/71
8th May, 1971 at Hampden Park; Attendance 120,092;
Referee: Mr T. Wharton (Glasgow)

CELTIC 1   RANGERS 1
Lennox   D. Johnstone

REPLAY
12th May, 1971 at Hampden Park; Attendance 103,332;
Referee: Mr T. Wharton (Glasgow)

CELTIC 2   RANGERS 1
Macari, Hood (pen) Callaghan (o.g.)

SEASON 1971/72
6th May, 1972 at Hampden Park; Attendance 106,102;
Referee: Mr A. MacKenzie (Larbert)

CELTIC 6   HIBERNIAN 1
McNeill, Deans (3), Gordon
Macari (2)

SEASON 1972/73
5th May, 1973 at Hampden Park; Attendance 122,714;
Referee: Mr J. R. P. Gordon (Newport–on–Tay)

RANGERS 3   CELTIC 2
Parlane, Conn, Forsyth Dalglish, Connelly (pen)

SEASON 1973/74
4th May, 1974 at Hampden Park; Attendance 75,959;
Referee: Mr W. S. Black (Glasgow)
CELTIC 3   DUNDEE UNITED 0
Hood, Murray, Deans

SEASON 1974/75
3rd May, 1975 at Hampden Park; Attendance 75,457;
Referee: Mr I. M. D. Foote (Glasgow)

CELTIC 3   AIRDRIEONIANS 1
Wilson (2),   McCann
McCluskey (pen)

SEASON 1975/76
1st May 1976 at Hampden Park; Attendance 85,354;
Referee: Mr R. H. Davidson (Airdrie)

RANGERS 3   HEART OF MIDLOTHIAN 1
Johnstone (2),   Shaw
MacDonald

SEASON 1976/77
7th May, 1977 at Hampden Park; Attendance 54,252;
Referee: Mr R. B. Valentine (Dundee)

CELTIC 1   RANGERS 0
Lynch (pen)

SEASON 1977/78
6th May, 1978 at Hampden Park; Attendance 61,563;
Referee: Mr B. R. McGinlay (Glasgow)

RANGERS 2   ABERDEEN 1
MacDonald, Johnstone   Ritchie

SEASON 1978/79
12th May, 1979 at Hampden Park; Attendance 50,610;
Referee: Mr B. R. McGinlay (Glasgow)

RANGERS 0   HIBERNIAN 0

REPLAY
16th May, 1979 at Hampden Park; Attendance 33,504;
Referee: Mr B. R. McGinlay (Glasgow)

RANGERS 0   HIBERNIAN 0
After extra–time

SECOND REPLAY
28th May, 1979 at Hampden Park; Attendance 30,602;
Referee: Mr I. M. D. Foote (Glasgow)

RANGERS 3   HIBERNIAN 2
Johnstone (2),   Higgins, MacLeod (pen)
Duncan (o.g.)
After extra–time – 2–2 After 90 Minutes

SEASON 1979/80
10th May, 1980 at Hampden Park; Attendance 70,303;
Referee: Mr G. B. Smith (Edinburgh)

CELTIC 1   RANGERS 0
McCluskey
After extra–time

SEASON 1980/81
9th May, 1981 at Hampden Park; Attendance 53,000;
Referee: Mr I. M. D. Foote (Glasgow)

RANGERS 0   DUNDEE UNITED 0
After extra–time
REPLAY
12th May, 1981 at Hampden Park; Attendance 43,099;
Referee: Mr I. M. D. Foote (Glasgow)

RANGERS 4   DUNDEE UNITED 1
Cooper, Russell,   Dodds
MacDonald (2)

SEASON 1981/82
22nd May, 1982 at Hampden Park; Attendance 53,788;
Referee: Mr B. R. McGinlay (Balfron)

ABERDEEN 4   RANGERS 1
McLeish, McGhee,   MacDonald
Strachan, Cooper
After extra–time – 1–1 after 90 minutes

SEASON 1982/83
21st May, 1983 at Hampden Park; Attendance 62,979;
Referee: Mr D. F. T. Syme (Rutherglen)

ABERDEEN 1   RANGERS 0
Black
After extra–time

SEASON 1983/84
19th May 1984 at Hampden Park; Attendance 58,900;
Referee: Mr R. B. Valentine (Dundee)

ABERDEEN 2   CELTIC 1
Black, McGhee   P. McStay
After extra–time – 1–1 after 90 minutes

SEASON 1984/85
18th May, 1985 at Hampden Park; Attendance 60,346;
Referee: Mr B. R. McGinlay (Balfron)

CELTIC 2   DUNDEE UNITED 1
Provan, McGarvey   Beedie

SEASON 1985/86
10th May, 1986 at Hampden Park; Attendance 62,841;
Referee: Mr H. Alexander (Irvine)

ABERDEEN 3   HEART OF MIDLOTHIAN 0
Hewitt (2), Stark

SEASON 1986/87
16th May, 1987 at Hampden Park; Attendance 51,782;
Referee: Mr K. J. Hope (Clarkston)

ST. MIRREN 1   DUNDEE UNITED 0
Ferguson
After extra–time

SEASON 1987/88
14th May, 1988 at Hampden Park; Attendance 74,000;
Referee: Mr G. B. Smith (Edinburgh)

CELTIC 2   DUNDEE UNITED 1
McAvennie (2)   Gallacher

SEASON 1988/89
20th May, 1989 at Hampden Park; Attendance 72,069;
Referee: Mr R. B. Valentine (Dundee)

CELTIC 1   RANGERS 0
Miller

SEASON 1989/90
12th May, 1990 at Hampden Park; Attendance 60,493;
Referee: Mr G. B. Smith (Edinburgh)

ABERDEEN 0   CELTIC 0
After extra–time. Aberdeen won 9–8 on Kicks from the
Penalty Mark

SEASON 1990/91
18th May, 1991 at Hampden Park; Attendance 57,319;
Referee: Mr D. F. T. Syme (Rutherglen)

MOTHERWELL 4   DUNDEE UNITED 3
Ferguson, O'Donnell,   Bowman, O'Neil, Jackson
Angus, Kirk
After extra–time – 3–3 after 90 minutes

SEASON 1991/92
9th May 1992 at Hampden Park; Attendance 44,045;
Referee: Mr D. D. Hope (Erskine)

RANGERS 2   AIRDRIEONIANS 1
Hateley, McCoist   Smith

SEASON 1992/93
29th May, 1993 at Celtic Park; Attendance 50,715;
Referee: Mr J. McCluskey (Stewarton)

RANGERS 2   ABERDEEN 1
Murray, Hateley   Richardson

SEASON 1993/94
21st May, 1994 at Hampden Park; Attendance 37,709;
Referee: Mr D. D. Hope (Erskine)

DUNDEE UNITED 1   RANGERS 0
Brewster

SEASON 1994/95
27th May, 1995 at Hampden Park; Attendance 38,672;
Referee: Mr L. W. Mottram (Forth)

CELTIC 1   AIRDRIEONIANS 0
Van Hooijdonk

SEASON 1995/96
18th May, 1996 at Hampden Park; Attendance 37,760;
Referee: Mr H. Dallas (Motherwell)

RANGERS 5   HEART OF MIDLOTHIAN 1
Laudrup (2), Durie (3)   Colquhoun

SEASON 1996/97
24th May, 1997 at Ibrox Stadium; Attendance 48,953;
Referee: Mr H. Dallas (Motherwell)

KILMARNOCK 1   FALKIRK 0
Wright

SEASON 1997/98
16th May, 1998 at Celtic Park; Attendance 48,946;
Referee: Mr W. Young (Clarkston)

HEART OF MIDLOTHIAN 2   RANGERS 1
Cameron, Adam   McCoist

SEASON 1998/99
29th May, 1999 at The National Stadium, Hampden Park;
Attendance 51,746; Referee: Mr H. Dallas (Motherwell)

RANGERS 1   CELTIC 0
Wallace

SEASON 1999/2000
27th May, 2000 at The National Stadium, Hampden Park;
Attendance 50,685; Referee: Mr J. McCluskey

RANGERS 4   ABERDEEN 0
Van Bronckhorst,
Vidmar, Dodds, Albertz

SEASON 2000/01
26th May, 2001 at The National Stadium, Hampden Park;
Attendance 51,284; Referee: Mr K. Clark

CELTIC 3   HIBERNIAN 0
McNamara, Larsson (2)

SEASON 2001/02
4th May, 2002 at The National Stadium, Hampden Park;
Attendance 51,138; Referee: Mr H. Dallas

RANGERS 3   CELTIC 2
Lovenkrands (2),   Hartson, Balde
Ferguson

SEASON 2002/03
31st May, 2003 at The National Stadium, Hampden Park;
Attendance 47,136; Referee: Mr K. Clark

RANGERS 1   DUNDEE 0
Amoruso

SEASON 2003/04
Saturday, 22nd May, 2004 at The National Stadium,
Hampden Park; Attendance 50,846
Referee: Stuart Dougal

CELTIC 3   DUNFERMLINE ATHLETIC 1
H. Larsson (2), S. Petrov   A. Skerla

League Challenge Cup Final
Results Since 1990/1991

INVERNESS CALEDONIAN THISTLE MANAGER
JOHN ROBERTSON WITH THE BELL'S CUP

DAVID BINGHAM AND STEVIE HISLOP
CELEBRATE CALEY THISTLE'S 2-0 VICTORY
OVER AIRDRIE UNITED

SEASON 1990/91
Sunday, 11th November, 1990 at Fir Park, Motherwell;
Attendance 11,506, Referee: K. J. Hope (Clarkston)

AYR UNITED 2   **DUNDEE 3**
(AET – 2-2 After 90 Minutes)
D. Smyth, I. McAllister   W. Dodds (3)

SEASON 1991/92
Sunday, 8th December, 1991 at Fir Park, Motherwell;
Attendance 9,663, Referee: L.W. Mottram (Forth)

HAMILTON 1   **AYR UNITED 0**
ACADEMICAL
C. Harris

SEASON 1992/93
Sunday, 13th December, 1992 at St. Mirren Park, Paisley;
Attendance 7,391, Referee: J.J. Timmons (Kilwinning)

MORTON 2   **HAMILTON 3**
                  ACADEMICAL
R. Alexander (2)   C. Hillcoat, G. Clark (2)

SEASON 1993/94
Sunday, 12th December, 1993 at Fir Park, Motherwell;
Attendance 13,763, Referee: D.D. Hope (Erskine)

FALKIRK 3   **ST. MIRREN 0**
C. Duffy, J. Hughes,
R. Cadette

SEASON 1994/95
Sunday, 6th November, 1994 at McDiarmid Park, Perth;
Attendance 8,844, Referee: H.F. Williamson (Renfrew)

DUNDEE 2   **AIRDRIEONIANS 3**
(AET – 2-2 After 90 Minutes)
G. Britton, G. Hay (o.g.)   P. Harvey, J. Boyle, Andrew
Smith

SEASON 1995/96
Sunday, 5th November, 1995 at McDiarmid Park, Perth;
Attendance 7,856, Referee: J. Rowbotham (Kirkcaldy)

STENHOUSEMUIR 0   DUNDEE UNITED 0
(A.E.T.) Stenhousemuir won 5-4 on Kicks from the
Penalty Mark

SEASON 1996/97
Sunday, 3rd November, 1996 at Broadwood Stadium,
Cumbernauld; Attendance 5,522,
Referee: K.W. Clark (Paisley)

STRANRAER 1   **ST. JOHNSTONE 0**
T. Sloan

SEASON 1997/98
Sunday, 2nd November, 1997 at Fir Park, Motherwell;
Attendance 9,735, Referee: R.T. Tait (East Kilbride)

FALKIRK 1   **QUEEN OF THE SOUTH 0**
D. Hagen

SEASON 1998/99
No Competition

SEASON 1999/2000
Sunday, 21st November, 1999 at Excelsior Stadium, Airdrie;
Attendance 4,043, Referee: Jim McCluskey

INVERNESS 4   **ALLOA ATHLETIC 4**
CALEDONIAN
THISTLE
(AET – 3-3 after 90 minutes)
P. Sheerin (3), B. Wilson   G. Clark, M. Cameron (2),
                              M. Wilson
Alloa Athletic won 5-4 on Kicks from the Penalty Mark.

SEASON 2000/01
Sunday, 19th November, 2000 at Broadwood Stadium, Cumbernauld;
Attendance 5,623 Referee: John Rowbotham

LIVINGSTON 2   **AIRDRIEONIANS 2**
(AET–2-2 After 90 Minutes)
J. Anderson, S. Crabbe   M. Prest, D. McGuire
Airdrieonians won 3-2 on Kicks from the Penalty Mark

SEASON 2001/02
Sunday, 14th October, 2001 at Broadwood Stadium, Cumbernauld;
Attendance 4,548 Referee: Michael McCurry

AIRDRIEONIANS 2   **ALLOA ATHLETIC 1**
O. Coyle, M. Roberts   G. Evans

SEASON 2002/03
Sunday, 20th October, 2002 at Broadwood Stadium,
Cumbernauld; Attendance 6,438 Referee: John Rowbotham

BRECHIN CITY 0   **QUEEN OF THE SOUTH 2**
                       J. O'Neil, D. Lyle

SEASON 2003/04
Sunday, 26th October, 2003 at McDiarmid Park, Perth;
Attendance 5,428 Referee: Willie Young

INVERNESS 2   **AIRDRIE UNITED 0**
CALEDONIAN
THISTLE
D. Bingham, S. Hislop

(In Season 1990/91 known as The B&Q Centenary Cup; In Seasons 1991/92 to 1994/95 known as The B&Q Cup; In Season 1995/96 to 1997/98 known as the League Challenge Cup; In Seasons 1999/2000 to 2001/02 known as Bell's Challenge Cup; In Season 2002/03 known as Bell's Cup)

Leading
Goalscorers
Per Divison 2003/04

HENRIK LARSSON – CELTIC

IAN HARTY – CLYDE

GARETH HUTCHISON – BERWICK RANGERS

MICHAEL MOORE – STRANRAER

Scottish Premier League

30	H. Larsson (Celtic)
20	I. Novo (Dundee)
19	C. Sutton (Celtic)
15	K. Boyd (Kilmarnock)
	J. Grady (Partick Thistle)
	D. Riordan (Hibernian)
13	S. Crawford (Dunfermline Athletic)
12	S. Arveladze (Rangers)
	M. De Vries (Hearts)
	D. Lilley (Livingston)

First Division

15	I. Harty (Clyde)
14	P. Ritchie (Inverness C.T)
13	D. Bingham (Inverness C.T)
	A. Burke (Queen of the South)
	J. Sutton (Raith Rovers)
12	P. Keogh (Clyde)
	S. O'Connor (Queen of the South)
11	M-M. Paatelainen (St. Johnstone)
	B. Wilson (Inverness C.T)
10	A. Smith (Clyde)
	D. Winters (Ross County)

Second Division

22	G. Hutchison (Berwick Rangers)
19	B. McPhee (Hamilton Academical)
18	P. Tosh (Forfar Athletic)
15	A. Williams (Morton)
14	B. Carrigan (Hamilton Academical)
	G. McCutcheon (Berwick Rangers)
	P. Weatherson (Morton)
13	R. Hamilton (Alloa Athletic)
12	O. Coyle (Airdrie United)
	A. Gow (Airdrie United)

Third Division

24	M. Moore (Stranraer)
21	S. McLean (Stirling Albion)
19	D. Graham (Stranraer)
18	M. Johnston (Peterhead)
	P. McManus (Albion Rovers)
17	M. Cameron (Gretna)
16	M. Bavidge (Peterhead)
15	A. Bone (Elgin City)
14	S. Michie (Montrose)
12	D. Shields (Cowdenbeath)